미국에서 가르치는  영문독해

미국에서 가르치는 Dr. Yang 영문독해

초판 1쇄 발행 | 2000년 11월 1일
초판 9쇄 발행 | 2008년 8월 16일

지은이 | 양규철
펴낸이 | 김태지
디자인 | 디자인 표현

펴낸곳 | 에디터
주소 | 서울시 마포구 공덕동 105-219 정화빌딩 3층
문의 | 02-753-2700, 2778
Fax | 02-753-2779
등록 | 1991년 6월 18일 제1-1220호

값 25,000원
ISBN 89-85145-46-0 03740

이 책의 한국어판 서작권은 에디터에 있습니다.
저작권법에 의해 한국 내에서 지적재산권의 보호를 받는 저작물이므로
본사의 서면 동의 없이는 어떠한 형태나 수단으로도 이 책의 내용을 이용하지 못합니다.

*잘못된 책은 구입하신 곳에서 바꾸어 드립니다.

Comprehensive Reading Skills

미국에서 가르치는 Dr. Yang 영문독해

양규철 박사 지음
필라델피아 템플대 교수

에디터

CONTENTS

프롤로그 · · · · 8
책머리에 · · · · 10

CHAPTER 1
읽기란 무엇인가 · 13
Overview of Reading

1. 독해 및 문자에 대한 개론 · · · · · 15
2. 문자/독해와 사회 · · · · · 17
3. 읽기란 무엇인가? · · · · · 18
4. 읽기 교육 · · · · · 19
5. 본 교재 학습에 대한 충고 · · · · · 24

CHAPTER 2
11가지 독해 기법 · 27
Specific Reading Skills

1. 속독 · · · · · 31
2. 글의 순서 찾기 · · · · · 39
3. 지시를 따라하기 · · · · · 51
4. 문맥 이용하기 · · · · · 71
5. 사실 및 정답 찾기 · · · · · 91
6. 주제와 요지 · · · · · 119
7. 주제문과 보충설명 · · · · · 139
8. 추론하기 · · · · · 157
9. 결론 끌어내기 · · · · · 175
10. 어조와 태도 · · · · · 199
11. 수사학상의 기법 · · · · · 231

CONTENTS

CHAPTER 3
내용 영역 독해 · 275
Reading Through Content Areas

1. 예술
- 1-1. 무용 · · · · · 279
- 1-2. 회화 · · · · · 287
- 1-3. 음악 · · · · · 297

2. 대중문화
- 2-1. 저명인사 · · · · · 307
- 2-2. 패션 · · · · · 319
- 2-3. 영화 · · · · · 331
- 2-4. 스포츠 · · · · · 349

3. 자연과학
- 3-1. 생물학 · · · · · 371
- 3-2. 화학 · · · · · 379
- 3-3. 컴퓨터 과학 · · · · · 391
- 3-4. 건강 · · · · · 401
- 3-5. 수학 · · · · · 411
- 3-6. 물리학 · · · · · 423

4. 사회과학
- 4-1. 실업 · · · · · 435
- 4-2. 지리 · · · · · 445
- 4-3. 정부 · · · · · 453
- 4-4. 세계사 · · · · · 459

CONTENTS

CHAPTER 4
언어 교과목을 통한 독해 · 469
Reading Through Language Arts

1. 문학

- 1-1. 연극 · · · · · 473
- 1-2. 픽션:소설 · · · · · 485
- 1-3. 시 · · · · · 495

2. 담화분석

- 2-1. 사회언어학적 함축 · · · · · 511
- 2-2. 협상 · · · · · 513
- 2-3. 개인간의 대화 · · · · · 517

3. 대중연설

- 3-1. 정보 전달형 연설 · · · · · 523
- 3-2. 설득형 연설 · · · · · 529
- 3-3. 특수한 경우를 위한 연설 : 사과문 · · · · · 535

CONTENTS

CHAPTER 5
일반지식을 통한 통한 독해 · 541
Reading Through General Knowledge For the Korean Scholastic Aptitude Test

ANSWER
해답편 · 643

프롤로그 ACKNOWLEDGEMENTS

이 책을 쓰기까지에는 지난 2년 여의 시간이 필요했다. 내가 이 책을 쓸 수 있었던 것은 많은 분들의 도움 덕택이다. 이곳 필라델피아, 펜실베이니아에서 이 책을 위한 자료수집, 질문준비 등으로 필자에게 많은 도움을 준 대학 및 고등학교 각 과목 동료교사들, 매우 협조적인 대학 및 대학원생들에게도 깊은 감사를 드린다.

특히, 헌신적으로 자료찾기와 온갖 자문에 발런티어로 응해 준 필라델피아 유니버시티 하이스쿨 동료교사들의 도움이 컸다. 필라델피아 유니버시티 하이스쿨은 내가 올해로 만 18년 동안 봉직해오고 있는 학교다. 정치, 경제, 사회 문화, 예술, 스포츠, 우주과학 등 내가 잘 모르는 분야에서 글들의 선택은 동료 선생님이 협조해 주었다.

또한, 이 영어학습서의 탄생을 위하여 중매역을 해주신 영문학 선배인 한국의 이혜란 전 숙명여대 교수님께 감사드린다.

영어학습서에 미국의 학생들이 학교에서 배우는 각 교과목들을 소재로 하자는 아이디어는 서울에서 직접 나를 만나러 온 에디터 출판사측이 내주었다. 오늘의 미국학생들이 배우는 교과서 내용을 간추려 생생한 미국영어의 진수를 맛보고, 미국의 여러가지 문화양식에 접할 수 있는 기회가 되도록 하자는 제안은 매우 중요하고 신선한 것이었다. 우리가 실사회생활에서 학구적으로 관련된 지식을 깊고 폭넓게 이해하고 구사하려면, "국어교과서"만 의존하는 게 아니고, 초·중·고·대학의 여러 교과목을 공부하여야 되듯이, 진정한 영어 공부도 이와 마찬가지이다. 또한 이러한 이론에 근거하여 미국 초·중·고에서 현재 실시하고 있는 외국인학생을 위한 영어프로그램(English as a second Language : ESL)도 20여년 전부터

Content area based ESL(여러 교과목을 중심으로 한 영어교육)을 실시하고 있다. 이 책이 가지는 중요한 뜻은 바로 여기에 있으며, 이처럼 여러 분야의 텍스트를 소재로 해서 영어학습서를 쓰다보니 내용이 훨씬 더 흥미롭고 다채로워졌다는 것을 느꼈다. 품은 많이 들었지만 아주 즐겁고 유익한 경험이었다.

나는 한국에서 고등학교 영어교사를 하다가 20대에 미국으로 건너와 학위를 받고 지금까지 고등학교와 대학에서 영어를 가르쳐 오고 있다. 한국을 떠나온 지가 30년 가까이 되다보니 한국에서 통용되는 말도 많이 바뀐 것을 보았다. 말은 흐르고 잘 바뀐다. 영어도 마찬가지다. 이런 부족한 점은 한국에 있을 때 고등학교 동료교사였던 곽은종 선생님이 적극적으로 도와 주셨으며, 고맙게도 이 책에 수록된 영문 번역은 물론, note, 그리고 쉬어가는 란 〈약수터〉를 써주셨다. 이 책에 수록된 모든 영문 본문 / 지문 및 문제는 필자인 내가 주로 하였으며, 어떠한 오류에 대하여서도 나의 책임임을 분명히 하고 싶다.

날마다 자정을 넘기며 책상머리에서 학습에 정열을 불태울 한국의 영어학습자들에게 이 책을 바친다. 그들은 나의 자랑스런 후배들이다. 나를 낳아주고 길러준 조국 한국을 위해 나는 지금까지 아무것도 내놓은 것이 없었다. 이 책이 밤을 지새우며 공부하는 영어학습자들에게 작은 선물이 되었으면 한다.

끝으로 본서의 출간을 가능하게 해주신 에디터 출판사 김석성 사장님께 깊은 감사를 드린다.

2000년 가을, 필라델피아 템플대학 연구실에서 양규철

책머리에 이 책이 가지는 차별적 가치

올해는 우리의 교육정책에 따라 영어교육이 시작된 지 반세기가 되는 해다. 이제는 세계화의 추세에 따라 우리의 영어교육도 국내무대를 벗어나 세계로 나아가야 한다. 그러나 현실은 여러가지 법적 제도나 사회경제적 제약으로 과거의 비능률에서 탈피하지 못하고 있다. 오히려 과거에 비하여 더 무원칙하여 학생들을 혼란스럽게 만들고 있다. 하루가 멀다하고 영어의 필요성은 절실해 지는데 무엇인가 돌파구를 찾아야 한다는 절박한 사명감에서 완전히 새로운 영어학습 교재를 만들어 스스로를 도와야 한다고 생각했다.

그러나 적당한 집필진을 찾기가 쉽지 않았다. 미래의 세계를 좀 더 넓은 곳에서 관찰하고 준비할 수 있는 식견과 경험을 가진 필자로는 국내학자 보다는 아무래도 영, 미국의 학자가 적임자라고 믿고 좋은 분을 물색하던 차에 운좋게도 양규철박사를 소개받게 되었다. 양박사는 필라델피아의 템플 대학에서 영어수사학을 강의하면서 고등학교 학생들에게는 영어독해를 가르치는 현직 교사다. 방학 때면 세계 여러 지역을 순회하며 특강을 하고, 교환 교수로 태국 등에서 몇 년씩 근무하며 유익한 경험을 쌓아 온 보기드문 열성파 학자다. 그외에도 그분의 조국사랑은 남다르다는 게 그를 아는 사람들의 증언이다. 이러한 자랑스런 해외동포를 초빙하게 된 것은 여간한 행운이 아니었다.

단순히 시험 준비만을 위한 일회용 참고서가 아니고 모든 학문분야와 사회 활동을 망라하는 통합적이고 종합적이어서 장서가치가 충분한 지식, 정보의 데이터 뱅크를 제작하려고 지혜를 모았다. 따라서 내용이 종전 참고서에 비하여 광범위하다. 지문의 시대적 분포도 고대에서 최근의 미 클린턴 대통령의 성추문에 대한 대국민 사과문까지 고루 배열했으며, 동서양의 사상 및 아시아적 가치를 비롯, 한국 관련 내용을 다수 제시하여 여타 서적과의 차별화를 시도했다. 결론적으로 이책에서 다루어지지 않은 독서기술, 언어기술, 수사법, 학문분야, 사회활동은 거의 없다고 자부하고 싶다.

원작이 영어로만 되어 있어 독자들에게 지나친 부담이 될까봐 별도의 해설과 번역을 실었다. 번역과 해설작업은 양규철박사의 추천에 의하여 그분이 가장 존경하는 35년 경력의 전직 영어교사 곽은종 선생님을 초빙했다. 이분도 현직 때는 물론 퇴직 후에도 영어교육의 생산성을 높이는 교수, 학습모형을 정립하기 위하여 각종 연구대회에 참석하는 등 쉬지 않고 정진하는 학구적 베테랑이다. 해설의 현장감을 살리고 미래지향적인 학습의 틀을 제시하기 위하여 어휘의 해설은 되도록 영어로, 생산성을 올리기 위하여 중요한 단어는 예문을 충실히 마련했고 심화학습을 돕는 참고사항을 추가로 제시했다. 가능한 대로 혼자의 힘으로 공부하는 습관을 들이도록 충분한 보충자료를 제시했다.

한편, 학습에 따른 지루함을 덜기 위해서, 교재 중간 중간에 마음의 양식이 될 〈약수터 : 영어 격언과 한문 격언의 만남〉을 삽입했다. 명실공히 교과 통합적이고 내용 종합적인 충실한 참고서를 출간하게 되어 앞으로의 영어교육 50년에 새로운 출발점이 되었으면 좋겠다.

이책을 다음과 같은 분들께 특히 권하고 싶다

1. 현직 영어교사를 포함한 영어 전공자
2. 고교생을 포함하여 대학 입학시험을 준비하는 수험생
3. TOEIC, TOEFL, TEPS 등을 포함하여 취업 및 유학을 준비하는 학생
4. 방송, 신문인을 포함하여 언제나 영어의 필요성을 절감하는 직장인
5. 예·체능을 포함하여 영어 관련 교양이 필요한 연예인
6. 가정 주부를 포함하여 자녀의 영어교육에 관심이 있는 학부모
7. 기타 퇴직하여 사회봉사를 원하는 사회인

도서출판 에디터

CHAPTER 1
제1장

읽기란 무엇인가
Overview of Reading

INTRODUCTION

본 인트로덕션(INTRODUCTION)에서는
첫째는 문자/독해와 사회생활 관계를 폭넓게 이해함을 목적으로 하고 있으며,
둘째는 영어공부의 필요성을 사회적인 측면에서 소개한다. 궁극적인 목적은 독자에게 영어공부에 대한
폭넓은 시야를 소개시켜서 훌륭한 영어습득자가 되는데 조금이라도 도움이 되었으면 하는 바람이다.

본란에서는 다음과 같이 서술하며, 독해에 대한 폭넓은 이해를 도모한다.

1. 독해 및 문자에 대한 개론
2. 문자/독해와 사회
3. 읽기란 무엇인가?
4. 읽기 교육
5. 본교재 학습에 대한 충고

읽기란 무엇인가

1. 독해 및 문자에 대한 개론

지구가 생긴 지 45억년, 그리고 오랜 시간이 흘러간 후 인간 최초의 시조라고 불리워지는 호모 에렉투스(Homo erectus)가 2백만년 전 석기시대(200만년~6000B.C.)에 살았고, 현대인간 즉 호모 사피엔스(Homo sapiens)가 약 20만년 전에 아프리카에서 중동, 유럽, 아시아로 이주하였다고 한다. 이주하고 생활하면서 사람들끼리의 의사소통은 어떻게 하였을까? 물론 대부분 원시적인 말에 의존하였고 처음 문자가 쓰여진 것이 발견된 것은 B.C. 3,500~3000에 수메르(Sumer)의 상형문자(pictographs)였으며 그후 다음과 같이 문자발달 및 사용과정을 요약해 볼 수 있다.

1. 이집트인들이 상형문자(Hieroglyphics)를 사용하기 시작했다 (3000B.C.).

2. 중국인들이 동물의 뼈와 구리판에 글자를 새겼다 (1500B.C.).

3. 시리아의 Ugriat 무역항에서 알파벳(Alphabet)이 사용되었다.
   이것이 최초의 완성된 알파벳이다 (1400B.C.).

4. 그리스인들이 모음을 가진 현대의 알파벳을 발전시켰다 (800B.C.).

1.

그리고 다음과 같은 역사적 사실로 인해 문자, 독해, 인쇄가 발달했다.

1. 로마인들은 제국의 국교로서 기독교를 받아들였다.
   이 무렵 크리스찬들은 성경, 찬송가 그리고 종교적 가르침을 위한 저술을 위하여 문자를 사용하기 시작했다 (313년).

2. 중국의 비밀기술이었던 제지방법은 이슬람의 도시들을 통해서 펴져나갔다 (751년경).

3. 구텐베르크가 인쇄술을 발명했다 (1445년).

4. 유럽에서 가장 먼저 인쇄된 책은 출판업자 Johannes Fust와 Pete Schoffer에 의해서였다 (1457년).

5. 타이프라이터(typewriter)는 사람들의 글쓰기 방식에 혁명적인 변화를 가져왔다 (1890년대 이후).

6. 인터넷은 언어와 문자가 통하는 가장 빠르고 가장 값싼 방법으로 발전되고 있다 (1990년대 이후).

앞으로 문자 및 독해가 어떠한 매개체에 의하여 더 넓고 빠르게 사용될 수 있을지는 모르겠으나 인터넷 문명이 발달할수록 우리 인간과 독해의 관계가 밀접하게 될 것임은 쉽게 예측할 수 있다.

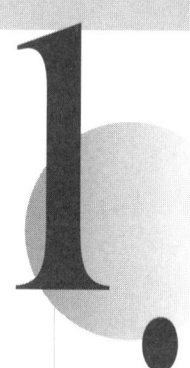

2. 문자/독해와 사회

우리가 알다시피 문자사용 이전을 선사시대, 그 이후를 역사시대라고 구분하는데 이는 그만큼 문자독해는 우리 역사문명과의 관계가 크다는 말이다. 문자의 독해능력을 갖게 된 인간은 지식의 전달, 축적, 보존, 이용, 발달을 통하여 만물의 영장으로서 자연을 개척, 이용할 수 있었으며 문화문명의 발달(종교, 사상, 학문, 기술, 철학 등)은 인간적인 삶을 영위하는 데 있어서 우리에게 준 혜택은 너무나 커 이루 다 말하기가 어렵다.

반면 문자 독해능력자로서 역사적으로 볼 때 우리 사회에 끼친 영향은 항상 고무적이었던 것만은 아니었다. 오늘처럼 교육기회가 넓게 보급되기 전에는 어떤 사회·국가에서 문자를 자유롭게 쓰고 독해할 수 있었던 인구가 과연 사회의 몇 퍼센트나 되었을까? 지배계급(왕족, 귀족, 관리, 승려)을 제외하고는 인구의 대부분인 피지배계급에 속한 사람은 문자 독해 능력 때문에 사회적으로 천대 및 착취를 당해야만 했고, 생존권의 불평등을 당하였음은 옛날이나 지금이나 별로 큰 차이가 없다고 생각된다. 독해를 매개체로 하는 교육, 그 교육의 힘이 가져다 주는 생존권 불평등의 사회적 현실은 우리가 더 이상 논함이 필요치 않을 것이다.

일반적으로 말할 때 어떤 사회에 문맹인구가 적을수록 그 사회는 높은 수준의 물질문화(정치, 경제, 산업, 기술, 학문, 사상)를 누리고, 개발한다고 할 수 있다. 1990년대

1.

초 기준으로 세계인구 40억 중 15세 이상자로 문맹자수는 10억명에 달한다고 한다. 선진국이라는 미국에서도, 인구 2억5천만명 중에서 성인 중의 5분의 1이 사실상 사회생활에 지장이 있는 무식자(functional illiterate)로서 일상생활에 필요한 글을 읽고 독해하는 능력이 부족하여 약병에 쓰인 처방, 이력서 쓰기, 읽기, 크레디트 카드 신청, 수입명세 작성 같은 것을 할 능력이 부족하다.

3. 읽기란 무엇인가?

읽기란 쓰여진 기호를 이해하는 정신적인 과정이다. 읽기는 여러가지 정보에 대한 열쇠다. 우리로 하여금 어떻게 이야기를 즐기며 다른 사람들이 믿는 것을 탐험하며 사물을 건설하고 규정하는가를 배우게 한다. 이렇게 독해, 즉 읽기는 우리의 사고방식과 생활에 혁명을 일으키는 힘을 가지고 있다.

읽기는 세가지로 구분된다. 하나는 취미, 학문연구, 그리고 조사이다. 취미중심인 읽기는 여러시간 책읽기를 통해서 즐거움을 느끼며, 연구를 위한 읽기는 텍스트에 아주 긴밀한 주의를 요한다. 조사를 위한 읽기는 그 내용의 일반적인 사상을 알아내기 위해서 많은 양의 텍스트를 포함한다. 이들 경우에 독자들은 먼저 주요 포인트를 이해하기 위하여 자료를 훑어보아야 할지도 모른다. 그런 후에 요점을 그린 각론을 찾아야 할 것이다.

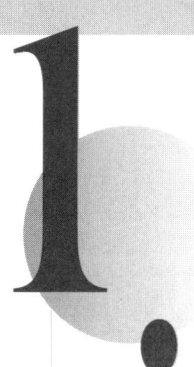

4. 읽기 교육

독해를 가르치는 방법은 아주 많아 이곳에 다 열거할 수 없으나, 초급독해자를 위한 교수방법 중 대표적인 것을 소개한다. 또 중급 독해자를 위한 독해 달성 목표를 간단히 소개한다.

초급독해란? 초등학교 1~3학년 정도를 말하며, The New England Primer가 1690년에 영국에서 미국으로 들어와 그후 오랫동안 초급독해를 위하여 사용되었다. 이 방법은 음성학(phonic knowledge)을 중심으로 시작하여 단계적으로 스펠링, 구문, 문장 읽기를 습득시키고, 짧은 이야기 및 우화 등을 가르쳤다. 이러한 방법은 다음과 같은 독해방법을 발달시키는 데 큰 영향을 끼쳤다.

a. 문자-소리 대응관계 (Letter-Sound correspondence)

이 방법은 알파벳 문자와 음성체계(sound system)의 관계를 중심으로 단어 및 문장 읽기를 가르친다 (예, A cat sat on a mat. 에서 발음 /æ/를 in cat, sat, mat에서 중복을 가능한 많이하여 /æ/ sound를 읽히고 cat, sat, mat과 같은 뜻을 익힌다. 전에 한국 초등학교 1학년 교과서에 "아가야, 아가야, 우리 아가야, 나 하고 놀자" 라는 문장이 생각나는데, 이 문장 구성은 "아" 소리음을 중심으로 "가", "나", "하", "자"를 반복해서 가르쳤음).

이 문자 · 소리 대응관계(Letter-Sound Correspondence)는 The New England

Primer에서 영향을 받았으며, 1960년대까지 미국 초등학교에서 많이 쓰여지다가 (Lippincott series는 대표적 예임), 그후 Language-Experience 와 Individualized approaches 등에 밀려나기 시작하였다.

b. Sight Words(Sight-Reading, Meaning-Emphasis라고도 함)

어린이들이 잘 사용하는 단어들을 그림을 곁들인 책이나 또는 그림을 칠판에 배열해 놓고 단어의 발음을 읽고 뜻을 간단히 설명한다. 그리고 교사는 단어 및 그림을 사용하여 어린이가 짧은 문장으로 말을 할 수 있도록 유도, 말한 것을 교사는 간략히 쓴다. 그리고 그 쓴 문장을 읽는 연습을 시킨다. 이 방법은 어린이의 독특한 환경에서 자라 온 자연적인 독서능력을 중요시하였으며, 문자·소리 대응관계(예, A cat sat on a mat.)에 너무나 인위적이고 어색한 문장구성을 반대하였다. 70년대 초에 조금 사용되었으나, 시간 및 경비가 많이 드는 탓인지 널리 쓰여지지는 않았다.

c. Language-experience approach

Sight Words 방법처럼 어린아이들이 흔히 쓰는 단어 및 언어표현을 사용하여 말하기, 쓰기, 읽기를 종합하여 독해를 가르치는 방법이며, 이는 어디까지나 어린이의 Verbal Repertoire in Language Experience에 중점을 두고 있다. 예를 들면 교사는 어린이가 한 이야기를 칠판에 간단히 쓰고 그 이야기를 전체 학생에게 크게 읽어준다. 그후 각 어린이는 얘기 읽는 법을 배우고 자기 얘기도 간단히 단문으로 써본다. 이 방법은 지난 60년대에 도입되어 지금도 말하기, 듣기, 읽기, 쓰기 능력을 높이기 위해 종종 사용되고 있다.

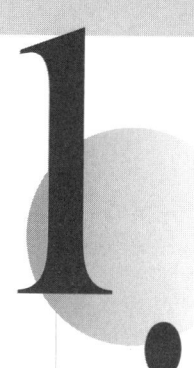

d. Basal Readers

주로 60년대 초부터 80년대 후반까지 미국의 초급 및 중급 독해를 위하여 가장 많이 쓰여졌던 방법으로(지금도 대단한 권위가 있음), 특징은 A Sequential Set of Books and Supplementary Materials(workbooks, teacher's manuals, exercises, tests 등)을 사용하여 제한되고 계획된 단어수(예, 1학년 과정을 마치면 생활에 쓰이는 단어 2,000개)를 이용, 완벽한 독해력을 달성하는데 목적을 두고 있다. 가르치는 방법을 다음과 같이 간단히 소개한다.

1. Word Cards를 이용하여 줄거리에 나오는 단어공부
2. 학생에게 단어 뜻 이해에 대한 반응조사
3. 단어를 phonic rule, structure, # of syllables, base/root words, affix, differences, prefix, suffix 등을 소개하면서 가르친다.
4. Review briefly the familiar word recognition techniques or system the pupils may employ with any unknown words that they will meet in the story.
5. Establish some experiential background when beginning a new unit or topic.
6. Review old vocabulary by word cards, blackboard presentations.

1.

e. Whole-language approach

80년대 초부터 눈을 끌기 시작한 이 방법은 읽기, 쓰기, 듣기, 말하기를 다 종합하여, 학생이 읽는 교과서의 해석이 맞고 틀림에 크게 신경쓰지 않고, 학생의 흥미 유발 및 reading process에 초점을 두고 있다. 독해는 학생이 교재를 이해하는 과정이며 그 과정을 교사는 종합적으로 잘 이끌어 나가는 게 중요하지, 교재이해의 옳고 그름을 따지는 게 중요치 않다는 말이다.

중급독해란?

중급독해란 초등학교 고학년 및 중학교(미국학교에서는 5~8학년까지) 독해 수준을 말하고, 중급독해를 위한 독해 방법은 remedial reading(본교재에 나오는 제2장 참조바람) 및 여러가지 보조 읽기자료(supplementary reading materials - Basal readers 포함)를 많이 쓰고 있다. 초급독해 학생은 독해력이 하루가 달라지게 진보됨을 보여 주지만, 중급 독해자는 교재를 대부분 소리 내서 읽지 않기 때문에 독해 능력을 측정하기가 힘드나, 다음과 같은 독해 목표를 두고 있다.

1. 자주 쓰지 않는 단어 및 긴 단어의 뜻을 알 수 있어야 한다.

2. 자기 학년에 맞는 어떤 책 1페이지 중에서 100단어 중 5단어 이상 모르는 단어가 있어서는 안된다.

3. 학년에 맞는 독해자료를 소리내어 읽지 않고 main ideas 및 supporting details을 알아야 함.

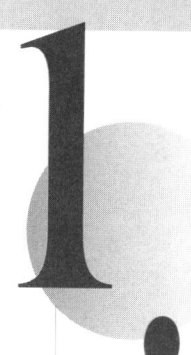

4. 독해를 통하여 new ideas를 충분히 알아야 한다.

5. 휴식과 즐거움을 위하여 독자적으로 독서할 수 있어야 한다.

6. 8학년 말에는 일간 및 주간신문, 잡지, 자기가 좋아하는 책, 기네스북 (The Guinness Book of World Records)과 같은 특별책을 읽을 수 있어야 한다.

고급독해란? 고급독해란 고등학생 및 대학생 정도 독해 수준을 말하며, 다음과 같은 독해 목표를 두고 있다.

1. ① 고등학교 1학년(9학년)은 대부분 일간신문 및 short stories, fictions, poems, drama 그리고 Reader's Digest를 basic reading skills을 응용하여 읽을 수 있어야 함.

② 고2 및 고3(10~11학년)은 고1(9학년) 수준을 포함하여, journals, academic papers, special magazines of interest, research publications 등을 advanced reading skill을 응용하여 읽을 수 있어야 함.

③ 고4(12학년)는 고1,2,3을 포함하여 더 어려운 신문(The New York Times), 잡지(Newsweek, Time) 및 문학작품을 읽을 수 있어야 됨.
단어는 어렵고 잘 쓰지 않는 단어, 추상적이고 전문 단어도 많이 알아야 되고, 문장은 long sentences and paragraphs을 포함한 중·복합문을 읽어야 됨.

2. College : Students should be able to read efficiently and with understanding text and other reading materials written at very high levels of linguistic complexity and on topics that may be exceedingly complex, technical, or abstract. These increasingly difficult materials require more advanced reading skills; students have to deal with more than one opinion/viewpoint. The assignments and examination questions require critical reading, the drawing of justifiable and logical conclusions and inferences, and the application of knowledge from reading.

5. 본교재 학습에 대한 충고

본교재 사용에 대한 suggestions을 말하고 싶다. "배움에는 왕도(王道)가 없다(There is no royal road to learning)." 라는 진리에 우선 따르고, 필자의 의견은 다음과 같다.

첫째, 학습에 대한 적극적 자세(positive attitude)를 갖고, "나도 할 수 있다."라는 자신감을 가져라. 인생의 갈림길은 고교때 적극적 또는 소극적 자세에 따라 결정된다고 필자는 믿고 있다. 어떤 일을 무서워하고 불평만 일삼는 학생은 자기에 대한 self-esteem이 약하여, 적극적 자세 소지자와는 인생의 갈림길이 다를 수밖에 없다. Attitude makes a big difference.

둘째, 독서는 하루아침에 이루어지는 게 아니니, 매일 매일 규칙적으로 1~2시간 이상 독서하는 습관을 기르길 바란다.

셋째, 본교재를 가능한 원문(영문)으로 읽고 즐기는 습관을 기르길 바란다. 원문과 번역은 비슷한 말이라도 표현방식에서 많은 차이가 있고 학습을 목적으로 한 독해는 특히 두뇌의 인식(cognition) 기능이 필요하여 (정확한 지식, 습득을 위하여), 2개

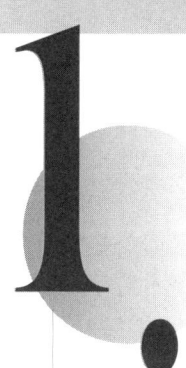

언어(영어 및 한국어 사용)로 교재를 이해할려고 하는 것 보다는, monolingual로 읽고 이해하는 게 immersion속에 쉽게 빠질 수 있고 교재를 넓고 깊이 이해하는데 효과적이다. 모르는 단어가 나올 때는, 단어는 문장의 문맥(context)에 따라 뜻이 달라지니 너무나 사전에 의존치 말고, 사전 찾기 전에 context에 맞게 단어의 뜻을 추측해 보는 것도 좋은일이다(사전은 영영사전을 이용하라고 권하고 싶다).

<u>넷째,</u> 독해순서는(어떤 지문에 대하여), 다음 순서로 하는게 가장 효과적이고 이곳에서도 독해시험때 학생들에게 권하는 점이다. 즉,

1. Subject matter (main idea, topic)를 찾고
   독자가 이글을 쓴 목적이 무엇인가를 알아낸다.
2. 단어의 뜻은 지문(passage)에 나오는 context에 따라 이해 할 것.
3. Passage에 나오는 ideas에 의거하여
   (주관적 사고방식 또는 주관적 경험의 지식을 피하고) 추리하라.
4. 저자의 tone이나 mood를 알아낸다.
5. 저자의 logical claims에서 conclusion을 찾아낸다.

필자는 다시한번 독지들에게 본교재의 〈The Subject Matter & Supporting Details〉를 철저히 복습하라고 강력히 권하면서, 제1장 Overview of Reading편을 마친다.

CHAPTER 2
제2장

11가지 독해 기법
SPECIFIC READING SKILLS

CHAPTER 2

This Chapter, "Specific Reading Skills" is designed to provide the readers with a variety of specific reading skills. As you know, reading is a set of keys for academic success. Without proper reading skills, there is very little you can achieve your academic and professional goals. This chapter is to help you achieve success, and provides you with specific reading skills such as (1) Speed-Reading; (2) Detecting the Sequences; (3) Following the Directions; (4) Using the Context; (5) Locating the Facts / Answers; (6) The Subject Matter and the Main Idea; (7) The Topic Sentence and the Supporting Details; (8) Making Inferences; (9) Drawing Conclusions; and, (10) Tone and Attitude; and, (11) Rhetorical Techniques.

To be specific, the section (1) Speed-Reading helps you improve your reading speed; (2) Detecting the Sequences for identifying specific facts/events based on chronological order; (3) Following the Directions for following specific instructions given; (4) Using the Context for judgmental skills in identifying the appropriate word or phrase based on the relationship between the meaning of the word and the language operation; (5) Locating the Facts/Answers for recalling factual information from the materials; (6) The Subject Matter and the Main Idea for recognizing key topic and point in a given passage; (7) The Topic Sentence and the Supporting Details for grasping the main idea of the passage, and for identifying a variety of details which support or explain the topic sentence; (8) Making Inferences for drawing a feasible interpretation, generalization, or conclusion without sufficient amount of information given; (9) Drawing Conclusions for reasonable or logical conclusion drawn from the generalizations or the details of the passage, which the writer has not explicitly mentioned; (10) Tone and Attitude for identifying the feeling or attitude of the writer towards the subject matter or the passage presented; and, (11) Rhetorical Techniques for identifying and interpreting a variety of communication techniques such as (a) the organization of the passage; and, (b) the ways or the styles of presenting proof, information, or persuasion (e.g. parallelism, repetition, antithesis).

Upon the completion of this chapter, the readers are expected to read materials rapidly, more effectively and accurately without bias or subjective interpretations. As mentioned previously, reading is a set of keys for success. Needless to say, poor reading is a problem, but it is not a hopeless one. Like other skills, the ability of reading depends on purposeful practice. Please keep in mind, "Practice makes perfect."

제2장 11가지 독해기법

제2장은 독자들에게 다양한 독해 기법을 구체적으로 제공하기 위하여 계획되었다. 아는 바와 같이 독해는 학문적인 성공을 위한 중요한 요소이다. 적절한 독해 기법을 모르면 학문적으로나 직업적으로 목표를 달성할 수 없다. 이 장은 여러분들의 성공을 위하여 다음과 같은 구체적인 독해 기법을 제공한다 :

1. 빨리 읽기 / 2. 글의 순서 찾기 / 3. 지시대로 따라 하기 / 4. 문맥을 이용하기 / 5. 사실·해답의 위치 찾기
6. 주제와 요지 파악 / 7. 주제문과 보조 사항 / 8. 추리하기 / 9. 결론 도출 / 10. 어조와 태도 / 11. 수사학상의 기법

구체적으로 말하면 제 **(1) Speed Reading**은 독서 속도를 늘리는 데 도움이 되고, **(2) Detecting the Sequence**는 글의 시간적 순서를 기초로 하여 사실이나 사건을 알아내는 데, **(3) Following the Directions**는 주어진 구체적인 지시대로 따라 하기에, **(4) Using the Context**는 어떤 단어의 뜻과 언어 운용사이의 관계에 입각하여 알맞은 단어나 어구를 식별하는 판단 기술을 기르는 데, **(5) Locating the Facts /Answers**는 자료로부터 사실적 정보를 생각해 내는 데, **(6) The Subject Matter and the Main Idea**는 주어진 글 안에서 주제나 요점을 알아내는 데, **(7) The Topic Sentence and the Supporting Details**는 글의 주제를 파악하고 주제를 지지하거나 설명하는 다양한 세부 사항들을 확인하는 데, **(8) Making Inferences**는 정보가 충분히 주어지지 않았어도 그럴듯한 해설, 일반화된 사실, 혹은 결론을 끌어 내는 데, **(9) Drawing Conclusions**는 저자가 명시적으로 밝히지 않았어도 일반화된 사실이나 글의 세부 사항으로부터 합리적이고 논리적인 결론을 도출하는 데, **(10) Tone and Attitude**는 주제나 주어진 글에 대한 저자의 감정이나 태도를 알아내는 데, **(11) Rhetorical Techniques**는 다양한 의사 소통의 기술들, 예를 들면 (a) 글의 구성 (b) 증거, 정보, 권유 등을 제시하는 다양한 방법이나 유형 (예 : 병렬구조, 반복, 대조, 삼단논법)을 알아내거나 해설하는 데 도움이 될 것이다.

이 장을 마치면 독자들은 자료를 편견이나 주관적 해석없이 빨리, 더 능률적이고 정확하게 읽을 수 있다. 앞에서도 말했듯이 독서란 성공의 열쇠다. 말할 필요도 없이 서투른 독서는 문제다. 그러나 희망이 없는 것은 아니다. 다른 기능들처럼 독서능력도 목표를 가지고 연습하느냐 않느냐에 달려 있다. '연습이 완벽을 이룬다.'는 격언을 유념하기 바란다.

Note

□ **specific** = detailed and exact : 상세한, 구체적인
- Be more specific about the project. (그 사업에 대하여 좀 더 구체적으로 말씀해 주시오)

□ **identify** : 신분을 말하다, 동일임을 증명하다
- Let me identify myself. (저를 소개하겠습니다.) • They identify the dictator with God. (독재자를 신과 동일시한다.)

□ **feasible** = practicable, possible, likely : 그럴듯한, 실행할 수 있는
- Your plan sounds feasible. (너의 계획은 그럴듯하게 들린다.)

2-1 SPEED READING

Speed-reading is to help improve your reading speed. It is determined in part by how many words you can grasp at a single glance. Slow readers tend to read every word in a sentence; whereas fast readers do so by a cluster of phrases.

Slow reader:

Being / able / to / read / by / phrases / instead / of / by / single / words / needs / practice. (The slow reader's eyes stop 13 times focusing on each word before moving on to the next).

Fast reader:

Being able to read by phrases / instead of by single words / needs practice. (The eyes of the fast reader stop 3 times, which saves a lot of time).

A few exercises are provided for you to improve your peripheral vision, rapid recognition of letters and words, and read by phrases without regression.

EXERCISE 1.

Focus your eyes on the center line and read down the column. Read as fast as you can but be sure to read each phrase correctly.

some	silk	thin	skin	hard	day
blue	book	short	story	cold	drink
green	grass	stand	still	faded	flowers
soft	towel	rich	robber	black	belt
fatal	fight	dig	out	tough	guy
blue	Hawaii	gray	hair	full	moon
semi	circle	long	hours	white	snow

2-1 속독

Speed reading은 여러분들이 지문을 빨리 읽을 수 있도록 돕기 위함이다. 속독은 부분적으로 한 번에 얼마나 많은 단어를 보고 파악하느냐로 결정된다. 속도가 느린 사람들은 문장 안의 모든 단어를 읽는 반면에 빨리 읽는 사람은 어구를 다발로 읽는다. 다음을 보자.

- **느린 사람** : Being / able / to / read / by / phrases / instead / of / by / single / words / needs / practice. (느리게 읽는 사람의 눈은 다음으로 넘어가기 전에 각 단어에 주의를 집중하며 13번 멈춘다.)
- **빠른 사람** : Being able to read by phrases / instead of by single words / needs practice. (빨리 읽는 사람의 눈은 세 번만 멈추고 많은 시간을 절약한다.)

Note
1. 주변 시각 (peripheral vision) : 한 단어를 중심으로 전 후를 함께 볼 수 있는 넓은 시각.
2. 한 단어씩 읽으면 주어, 술어의 관계가 모호하여 시제의 일치가 틀리기 쉽다. 위 예문의 주어는 words가 아니고 Being임으로 needs로 읽어야 한다.

다음에 몇 개의 연습 문제를 제공하여 주변시각을 넓혀 문자나 단어를 빨리 이해하고 읽은 것을 다시 보지 않고 어구 단위로 읽을 수 있도록 하였다.

눈의 초점을 중앙선에 맞추고 다음 어구를 아래로 읽자. 가능한 빨리 읽되 각각의 구를 정확하게 읽어야 한다.

EXERCISE 2.

Read the following as fast as you can with a careful attention to the rhythm and pronunciation.

Cats purr.
Lions roar.
Owls hoot.
Bears snore.
Crickets creak.
Mice squeak.
Sheep baa.
Monkeys chatter.
Cows moo.
Ducks quack.
Doves coo.
Pigs squeal.
Horses neigh.
Chickens cluck.
Flies hum.
Dogs growl.
Bats screech.
Coyotes howl.
Frogs croak.
Parrots squawk.
Bees buzz.

(Source: "I Speak, I Say, I Talk." Shapiro, Arnold (1985). <u>Silver Burdett English</u>)

EXERCISE 3.

This time the phrases are separated by spaces. Practice reading each phrase in a single glance, and make sure that your eyes move across the page with a smooth rhythm.

"Laughing time" by William J. Smith

It was laughing time,   and the tall giraffe   lifted his head,
and began to laugh   Ha! Ha! Ha! Ha!

And the chimpanzee   on the ginkgo tree   swung merrily down
with a Tee Hee Hee   Hee! Hee! Hee! Hee!

제2장 11가지 독해기법 **33** Comprehensive Reading Skills

다음을 리듬(강약)과 발음에 유의하며 가능한 한 빨리 읽어라.

Cats purr. 고양이는 그르렁 그르렁.
Lions roar. 사자는 어흥.
Owls hoot. 올빼미는 부엉.
Bears snore. 곰은 쿨쿨.
Crickets creak. 귀뚜라미는 찌르르.
Mice squeak. 쥐가 찍찍.
Sheep baa. 양이 매애.
Monkeys chatter. 원숭이가 재잘재잘.
Cows moo. 소가 음매.
Ducks quack. 오리가 꽥꽥.
Doves coo. 비둘기가 구구.

Pigs squeal. 돼지는 꽥꽥.
Horses neigh. 말은 힝힝.
Chickens cluck. 닭은 꼬끼오.
Flies hum. 파리는 윙윙.
Dogs growl. 개는 으르렁.
Bats screech. 박쥐는 끽끽.
Coyotes howl. 코요테는 으르릉.
Frogs croak. 개구리는 개골개골.
Parrots squawk. 앵무새는 거억거억.
Bees buzz. 벌은 윙윙.

Note
☐ 의성어 (Onomatopoeia) 연습 : 동물의 울음소리 등 사물의 소리를 귀에 들리는 대로 흉내내는 소리를 말하는데 그 소리는 문화마다 다르다.
☐ 의태어 (Mimesis)는 모양이나 태도를 묘사하는 표현이다.

이번에는 어구들을 여백으로 갈라 놓았다. 한눈에 각 어구를 읽는 연습을 하고 반드시 눈이 부드러운 리듬을 타고 가로로 움직이도록 하라.

"Laughing time" 웃기 시간 ⟨by William J. Smith⟩

웃기 시간이었다. 키 큰 기린은 고개를 들고 웃기 시작했다. 하!하!하!하!
은행나무의 침팬지도 즐겁게 그네 타고 내려오며 히!히!히!히!

"It's certainly not   against the law!"   croaked Justice Crow
with a loud guffaw: Haw! Haw! Haw! Haw!

The dancing bear   who could never say "No"   waltzed up and down
on the tip of his toe;   Ho! Ho! Ho! Ho!

The donkey   daintily took his paw,   and around they went:
Hee-Haw! Hee-Haw! Hee-Haw! Hee-Haw!

The moon had to smile as it started to climb;   All over the world
it was laughing time!   Ho! Ho! Ho! Ho!   Hee-Haw! Hee-Haw!
Hee! Hee! Hee! Hee!   Ha! Ha! Ha! Ha!

EXERCISE 4.

Again the phrases are separated by spaces. Practice reading each phrase in a single glance.

Oh say, can you see, by the dawn's early light
what so proudly we hailed
at the twilight's last gleaming?

Whose broad stripes and bright stars
Through the perilous fight
O'er the ramparts we watched,
Were so gallantly streaming?

And the rockets' red glare.
The bombs bursting in air.
Gave proof through the night
That our flag was still there.

Oh say, does that Star-Spangled Banner yet wave
O'er the land of the free and the home of the brave?

(Source : The U.S. National Anthem, March 3, 1931, by Act of Congress. Lyrics by Francis Scott Key in 1814)

Fort McHenry Flag 1812

재판관 까마귀도 "그거야 물론 위법이 아니지!" 하며 까악까악하며 큰소리로 너털웃음.
거절을 못하는 춤추는 곰도 위 아래 발 끝으로 왈츠를 추며 호!호! 호!호!
당나귀는 우아하게 앞발을 들고, 그들 모두 빙빙 돌며 히호! 히호! 히호! 히호!
달님도 떠오르며 어쩔 수 없이 웃기 시작했다. 온 세상이 웃기 시간이었다!
호!호!호!호! 히호! 히호! 히!히!히!히! 하!하!하!하!

다시 어구들을 여백으로 갈라 놓았다. 각 어구를 한 눈으로 읽는 연습을 하라.

성 조 기

아, 그대는 보는가 이른 새벽 빛에,
마지막 황혼 빛에 우리가 그토록 자랑스럽게 환호했던 것을?

위험한 전투 속에, 우리가 지키던 성벽 위로
그토록 늠름하게 나부끼던
그 넓은 줄무늬와 빛나는 별들이 보이는가?

붉은 로켓의 섬광과 공중에서 작렬하던 폭탄으로
우리는 확실하게 보여줬지
우리의 깃발이 그곳에 존재하고 있음을.

아, 말해보게, 그 성조기가
자유의 땅, 용감한 자들의 고향에 아직도 펄럭이고 있는가?

Note

- **say** : 미국영어 구어체에서 '여보게, 이봐.'
- **hail at = call out someone in greeting** : 환호하다, 소리쳐 부르다.
  - Because we missed the bus, I hailed at a taxi.
- **gleam = give out a bright light** : 빛나다.
  - The furniture gleamed after being polished. (닦은 후 가구들이 빛났다.)
- **gallantly = courageously, bravely** : 용감하게
- **give proof** : … 을 증명하다.
  - Can you give proof that you are Korean? (당신이 한국사람임을 증명할 수 있습니까?)

EXERCISE 5.

Read the following paragraphs aloud, and indicate word or phrase groupings by underlining the words that go together. The word or phrase groupings in the first sentences of the two paragraphs are underlined for you.

5.1. <u>The romantic world of Treasure Island, Robert Louis Stevenson's best known book, differed greatly from his real world.</u> Born in Scotland in 1850, Stevenson constantly fought against death during the 44 years of his life. The long hours of his childhood, spent mostly in bed, were brightened by his mother's story-telling. The understanding of what makes a good story was probably developed in him at an early age.

5.2. <u>Once upon a time, there was a miser who, hearing about the reputation of a greater miser</u> than himself, went to visit the other miser. He decided to take a gift to the other miser; it consisted of a bowl of water and a piece of paper cut in the form of a fish. The great miser was not at home, but his wife received the visitor. "Here is a fish and bowl as a humble present," said the visitor. The miser's wife thanked him and brought in an empty cup and asked him to have tea. He pretended to drink it, and then the miser's wife asked him to help himself to some cakes by drawing two circles in the air with her hand. Just then, the master miser came in and when he saw his wife drawing two circles, he shouted, "What extravagance! You are giving two cakes away! A semi-circle would do!"

(Source: Chinese folktale)

연습문제 5

다음을 소리 내어 읽고 단어나 숙어 그룹은 밑줄로 표시하라. 두 문단의 첫 문장에 있는 단어 또는 숙어 그룹은 밑줄로 표시해 두었다.

5._1. 로버트 루이스 스티븐슨의 대표작인 보물섬의 낭만적인 세계는 작가의 실제 세계와는 크게 달랐다. 1850년에 태어난 스티븐슨은 그의 44년 간 생애 동안 줄곧 죽음과 맞서 싸웠다. 그의 어머니가 들려주는 이야기는 대부분 병상에서 보낸 그의 어린 시절의 지루한 시간들을 즐겁게 해주었다. 무엇이 훌륭한 소설을 만드는가에 대한 이해는 어린 시절 그의 상상 속에서 발달했을 것이다.

5._2. 옛날 옛적에 어떤 구두쇠가 살았는데 그는 자기보다 더 지독한 구두쇠가 있다는 평판을 듣고 그를 만나러 갔다. 그는 그 구두쇠에게 선물을 하나 가지고 가야겠다고 결심을 했는데 그 선물은 물 한 사발과 물고기 모양으로 오린 종이 한 쪽이었다. 그 수전노는 집에 없었고 그의 아내가 손님을 맞이했다. "하찮은 선물이지만 물고기 한 마리를 사발에 넣어 가지고 왔습니다."

그 아내는 손님에게 경의를 표하고 나서 빈 컵을 가지고 들어 와서 차를 드시라고 권했다. 그가 마시는 체하자 그 아내는 손으로 공중에 두 개의 동그라미를 그리며 케익을 드시라고 권했다. 마침 그때 가장인 구두쇠가 들어오며 자기 아내가 동그라미를 두 개나 그리는 것을 보고 소리쳤다. "무슨 낭비야! 케익을 두 개나 주다니! 반 쪽이면 될 걸!" (중국 민화)

Note
- a fish and bowl : 물고기가 한 마리 들어 있는 사발
- a fish and a bowl : 물고기 한 마리와 사발하나

2-2 DETECTING THE SEQUENCES

"Detecting the sequences" is to identify specific facts/events based on chronological order. If facts happen in a story, they happen in time order. That is, some facts happen first or earlier, and others happen next or last.

Some clue words which help the readers detect the time sequences are provided as follows:

Initial stage : One, First, Once upon a time, At first, One day

Next stage : Two, Second, Then, Next, Afterward, After, Later

Final stage : Three, Third, Finally, At last, Lastly, Therefore, Consequently, Accordingly, In conclusion

Any stage : Now, Today, Soon, Often, Frequently, Then, Thus

The aforementioned clue words are not written in stone ; they are flexible or may be different depending on the context of the sentence / paragraph.

2-2 글의 순서찾기

글의 순서 찾기는 시간적 순서를 근거로 사건이나 사실을 알아내는 일이다. 어떤 이야기 안에서 사실들이 발생하면 그것들은 시간의 순서에 따라 일어난다. 바꿔 말하면 어떤 사실이 첫째로 혹은 더 빨리, 다른 것들은 다음에나 마지막에 일어난다.

독자들이 시간의 순서를 찾는데 도움이 될 몇 개의 실마리를 소개한다.

초기 단계 : One, First, Once upon a time, At first, One day
다음 단계 : Two, Second, Then, Next, Afterward, After, Later
최종 단계 : Three, Third, Finally, At last, Lastly, Therefore, Consequently, Accordingly, In conclusion
모든 단계 : Now, Today, Soon, Often, Frequently, Then, Thus

Note

□ 위에 언급한 실마리 단어들은 돌에 새겨진 (확고 부동한) 법칙은 아니고 융통성이 있고 문장이나 문단의 문맥에 따라 달라질 수 있다.

EXERCISE 1.

Read the following and see if you can follow the time sequences. Which sentence comes first, next, and last? Indicate the time sequences by numbering 1, 2, 3, 4 in the bracket provided below.

1.1 A cotton picker fills his bag.
He later takes it to be weighed and loaded on the truck.
Then he goes back to the fields to pick more cotton.

  ( ) The cotton is weighed.
  ( ) A cotton picker fills his bags
  ( ) Then he goes back to the field
  ( ) The cotton is loaded on a truck

1.2 Seeds travel in different ways.
The wind carries some seeds through the air.
The seeds land on the ground.
They rest all winter.
The next spring, the seeds begin to grow

  ( ) Seeds land on the ground
  ( ) Seeds begin to grow
  ( ) Wind carries seeds
  ( ) Seeds rest all winter

1.3 People have liked apples for many years.
There were not always apple trees in the New World.
People carried the trees to America about 400 years ago.
At first, people planted trees in the East.
Later, travelers carried them west.
Consequently, apples grow in most states.

  ( ) Later, travelers carried apple trees west.
  ( ) Consequently, apples grow in most states.
  ( ) At first, people planted the trees in the East.

다음을 읽고 글의 순서를 알 수 있나 알아보라. 어느 것이 첫째고 어느 것이 맨 끝에 오는가? 아래 주어진 괄호 안에 1, 2, 3, 4 번호를 붙여 표시하라.

1. 1. 목화 따는 이가 바구니를 채운다. 그리고 무게를 달고 트럭에 싣는다. 다음에 밭으로 되돌아 가서 더 많은 목화를 딴다.

   ( ) 목화의 무게를 단다
   ( ) 목화 따는 사람이 목화를 딴다.
   ( ) 그리고 나서 밭으로 다시 돌아간다.
   ( ) 목화가 트럭에 실린다.

1. 2. 씨앗들은 여행하는 방법이 다르다. 바람이 공중으로 운반해 준다. 씨앗들이 땅에 내려 앉는다. 겨울 내내 휴식한다. 그 다음 봄에 자라기 시작한다.

   ( ) 씨앗이 땅에 내려 앉는다
   ( ) 씨앗이 자라기 시작한다.
   ( ) 바람이 씨앗을 운반한다.
   ( ) 씨앗이 겨울 내내 휴식한다.

1. 3. 사람들은 오랫동안 사과를 좋아했다. 이 세상에서 사과가 언제나 있었던 것은 아니었다. 사람들이 약 400년 전에 사과나무를 아메리카로 옮겼다. 처음에 사람들은 사과나무를 동부지방에 심었다. 그 후에 여행 다니는 사람들이 서부로 옮겼다. 결과적으로 사과는 대부분의 주에서 자라고 있다.

   ( ) 후에 여행객들이 사과나무를 서부로 옮겼다.
   ( ) 결과적으로 사과는 대부분의 주에서 자라고 있다.
   ( ) 처음에는 사람들이 사과나무를 동부에 심었다.

EXERCISE 2.

Indicate the time sequences by numbering 1, 2, 3, ⋯

( ) Sneeze on a Monday, you sneeze for danger;
( ) Sneeze on a Tuesday, you will kiss a stranger;
( ) Sneeze on a Wednesday, you will sneeze for a letter;
( ) Sneeze on a Thursday, for something better;
( ) Sneeze on a Friday, you sneeze for sorrow;
( ) Sneeze on a Sunday, your safety's sake;
( ) Sneeze on a Saturday, your sweetheart tomorrow;
( ) For you will have trouble the whole of the week.

EXERCISE 3.

Read the following paragraphs, and indicate the time sequences in the brackets provided.

<u>3.1.</u> About 300 B.C. the strong and independent Greek states began to lose their power. Then the Roman Empire arose. It lasted for hundreds of years. After the downfall of the Empire, Europe entered a period of history called "The Dark Ages."

( ) "The Dark Ages." arrived.
( ) Roman Empire arose.
( ) Greek states began to lose power

<u>3.2.</u> Once upon a time in Korea, there lived a very poor young woodcutter. He lived alone in his tiny hut and longed for a wife. But he was sad, because he was too poor to get married. And also he was not handsome. So he cut wood and sold it in the market.

One day when he was out in the forest, a wounded doe suddenly came to him and asked, "Please help me! The hunter shot me already. If you don't help me, I cannot see and feed my little fawn waiting for me in the forest."

( ) "If you don't help me, I cannot see and feed my fawn," said the doe.

 시간의 순서를 1, 2, 3의 순으로 번호로서 나타내라.

( ) 월요일에 재채기를 하면 위험이 온다.
( ) 화요일에 재채기를 하면 낯선 사람과 키스한다.
( ) 수요일에 재채기를 하면 편지를 받게 된다.
( ) 목요일에 재채기를 하면 뭔가 좋은 일이 생긴다.
( ) 금요일에 재채기를 하면 슬픔이 찾아 온다.
( ) 일요일에 재채기를 하면 당신의 안전을 위해서다.
( ) 토요일에 재채기를 하면 내일 애인이 찾아 온다.
( ) 왜냐하면 일주일 내내 말썽거리가 생기기 때문이다.

 다음 문단들을 읽고 주어진 괄호 안에 시간의 순서를 나타내라.

3. 1. 기원전 300년 경에 강력한 독립국가 그리스는 국력을 잃기 시작했다. 그 후 로마제국이 일어났다. 로마는 수백년 간 지속됐다. 로마제국의 멸망 후에 유럽은 '암흑시대'라 불리는 역사의 한 시기에 접어들었다.

( ) 암흑시대가 도래했다.
( ) 로마제국이 일어났다.
( ) 그리스가 국력을 잃기 시작했다.

3. 2. 옛날 한국에 아주 가난한 젊은 나무꾼이 살고 있었다. 그는 작은 오두막에서 혼자 살면서 장가 들기를 몹시 바랐다. 그러나 너무 가난해서 장가갈 수 없는 것이 슬펐다. 또 그는 잘 생기지도 못했다. 그리하여 그는 나무를 베어 시장에 팔았다.

어느 날 그가 숲 속에 나왔을 때, 상처 입은 암사슴 한 마리가 그에게 다가와서 "제발 저를 살려 주세요! 저는 이미 사냥꾼의 총에 맞았어요. 만일 도와 주시지 않으면 숲 속에서 기다리고 있는 내 어린 새끼에게 젖을 줄 수가 없어요."라고 간청했다.

( ) The woodcutter lived by cutting and selling wood in the market.
( ) A wounded doe asked the woodcutter to help her.
( ) Once upon a time, there lived a woodcutter who was too poor to get married.

(Source: Adapted from a Korean folktale, "The Flying Fairy Wife")

3.3. In 1926 Margaret Mead, an American anthropologist, came to Samoa to study the existing cultural behaviors of the island. She feasted on native food as she talked with the daughter of a chief. She lived the life of a Samoan for nine months while always keeping careful notes. When she came to the United States, she published her first publication which described her life among the Samoan natives.

( ) When she returned to the U.S., she published her first book.
( ) She talked with Samoan people and ate their native food.
( ) She stayed in Samoa for nine months for her study.
( ) Mead came to Samoa in 1926 to study the islanders' culture.

3.4. The boy called out, "Wolf, Wolf," and the villagers came out to help him… Shortly after this, a wolf actually came, but this time the villagers thought the boy was deceiving them again and nobody came to help him. A liar will not be trusted, even when he speaks the truth.

(Source: Adapted from Aesop's Fable)

( ) The villagers came out to help the boy, but there was no wolf.
( ) But this time the villagers did not come.
( ) The boy called out, "Help me! The wolf is coming!"
( ) Soon a wolf actually came to attack the sheep.
( ) Once you are a liar, you cannot be trusted

3.5. A hare said to a tortoise, "You are stupid because you are so slow." The tortoise laughed, "We'll see about that," he said. "We can have a race." "Good!" said the hare, "I'll show you what real speed is."

They decided to race to the big forest which stood far away. The tortoise started right away at his steady speed, but the hare said boastfully,

(　) 만일 도와 주시지 않으면 새끼에게 젖을 줄 수가 없어요.
(　) 그 나무꾼은 나무를 베어 시장에 팔아 생활했다.
(　) 부상 당한 암사슴이 나무꾼더러 살려 달라고 애원했다.
(　) 옛날에 너무 가난하여 장가를 못 간 나무꾼이 살고 있었다.

3. 3. 1926년에 미국의 인류학자인 마가렛 미드가 섬에 남아 있는 문화적 행동을 조사하러 사모아 섬에 왔다. 그녀는 추장 딸과 대화하며 그곳의 토착 음식을 맛있게 먹고 지냈다. 그녀는 자세한 기록을 하면서 9개월 간 사모아 사람의 생활방식대로 살았다. 미국에 돌아와서 그녀는 사모아 원주민 사이에서의 생활을 서술한 최초의 책을 출판했다.

(　) 미국에 돌아와서 최초의 책을 출판했다.
(　) 그녀는 사모아인들과 대화하며 그들의 토착 음식을 먹었다.
(　) 그녀는 그 연구를 위해서 9개월 간 사모아에 살았다.
(　) 미드는 섬사람들의 문화를 연구하려 1926년에 사모아에 왔다.

3. 4. 그 소년은 "늑대가 왔어요. 늑대요."라고 소리쳤다. 그러자 마을 사람들이 그를 도우러 나왔다…. 잠시 후 정말로 늑대가 왔다. 그러나 마을 사람들은 그 소년이 또 자기들을 속이고 있다고 생각하고 아무도 도우러 오지 않았다. 거짓말쟁이는 비록 그가 진실을 말해도 신용하지 않는다.

(　) 마을 사람들이 그 소년을 도우러 왔지만 늑대는 없었다.
(　) 그러나 이번에는 마을 사람들이 오지 않았다.
(　) 그 소년은 소리 쳤다. "살려 주세요! 늑대가 왔어요!"
(　) 곧 정말로 늑대가 양 떼를 공격하러 왔다.
(　) 한 번 거짓말하면 남이 신용하지 않는다.

3. 5. 토끼가 거북이에게 말했다. "너는 그렇게 느리니 바보로구나." 거북이가 웃으며 말했다. "그거야 알아 보면 되지. 경주를 할 수도 있겠지." "좋아, 내가 빠르다는 게 무언지 보여 주겠다."라고 토끼가 말했다.

그들은 멀리 있는 큰 숲까지 달리기로 결정했다. "피곤하군, 그러니 잠시 자야겠다. 그래도 저 바보 거북이를 이기는 건 쉽지." 그는 기지개를 하고 잠이 들었다.

그러나 그는 날이 어둑해서야 잠에서 깼다. 그는 전력을 다해서 숲 근처까지 달렸다. 그러나 거북이가 그 곳에 이미 와 있는 것을 알고 깜짝 놀랐다.

"I feel tired, so I'll sleep for a little while. It'll still be easy to beat that stupid creature."

He stretched out, fell asleep, but woke up just as the daylight had started to fade. He raced to the edge of the forest as fast as he could go, but he was very surprised to find out that the tortoise was already there.

(Source: Adapted from Aesop's fable)

( ) "You are stupid for being slow."
( ) "I feel tired so I will sleep for a while."
( ) "How could you reach here already?"
( ) "I will keep going on without stopping."
( ) "We'll see about that when we have a race."

3.6. In the year 1260, two European traders, the Polos traveled to the distant and unknown land of China. They had many adventures there. Eleven years later in 1271, they made a second trip. But this time, the Polo brothers took along the son of one of them, a boy named Marco. The three Polos stayed in China about seventeen years. After their return to Italy, Marco had the story of his travels written down in book form. From this book, many Europeans became interested in the Far Eastern lands, and traders began to journey there.

( ) Book interested Europeans and traders.
( ) Polos traveled to China in 1260.
( ) Marco had his travel stories written down.
( ) Polos returned to Italy after seventeen years.
( ) Marco went on a second trip in 1271.

3.7. Jonathan Swift wrote Gulliver's Travels in 1726. Swift uses satire, a type of writing that ridicules certain customs, character traits, or situations in an attempt to cause change.

The plot of this fiction is that Lemuel Gulliver, a young English man, sets out into the world to find his own way. On these different sea voyages, he encounters strange beings with strange customs. On his first voyage, Gulliver finds himself in Lilliput where people are only six inches tall. On his second voyage, he is stranded in Brobdingno where the people are sixty feet tall.

( ) 너는 느리니까 바보야.
( ) 나른하니 잠시 자야겠다.
( ) 어떻게 벌써 여기 도착했니?
( ) 쉬지 않고 계속 가야겠다.
( ) 달리기를 하면 그건 알 수 있지.

3. 6. 1260년에 두 사람의 폴로집안 무역상들이 머나먼 미지의 땅 중국으로 길을 떠났다. 그들은 그 곳에서 많은 모험을 했다. 11년 후인 1271년에 그들은 두 번째 길을 떠났다. 이번에 두 폴로 형제는 그들 중 한 사람의 아들 마르코 폴로를 데리고 갔다. 세 사람의 폴로는 약 17년간 중국에 머물렀다. 이태리로 돌아 온 후, 마르코는 여행기를 책으로 출판했다. 이 책으로 말미암아 많은 유럽인들은 극동의 나라들에 관심을 갖기 시작했고 상인들이 그곳으로 여행을 떠났다.

( ) 책이 유럽인들과 상인들에게 흥미를 일으켰다.
( ) 폴로 집안 사람들은 1260년에 중국으로 여행했다.
( ) 마르코는 여행기를 책으로 출판했다.
( ) 폴로 집안 사람들은 17년 후에 이태리로 돌아 왔다.
( ) 마르코는 1271년에 두 번째 길을 떠났다.

Note
□ had the story of his travels written down는 두 가지 의미를 갖는다.
(1) 여행기를 완성했다는 완료의 의미와 (2) 다른 사람을 시켜 완성시켰다는 수동의 의미도 있다.

3. 7. 조나단 스위프트는 1726년에 걸리버 여행기를 썼다. 그는 변화를 유도하기 위한 시도로 어떤 풍습이나 성격 특성이나 상황을 조롱하는 글의 형태인 풍자를 사용한다.
이 소설의 구도는 아래와 같다. 영국인인 리뮤엘 걸리버가 자신의 길을 찾기 위하여 세계 속으로 길을 떠난다. 이 다양한 항해에서 그는 이상한 풍습을 가진 낯선 사람들과 만난다. 첫 번째 항해에서 키가 겨우 6인치인 Lilliput국에 오게 된다. 두 번째에는 사람들의 키가 6피트인 나라 Brobdingno에서 배가 좌초 당한다. 마지막으로 세 번째 항해에는 말이 통치하는 나라의 해안에 닿는다. 각기 다른 장소에서 그는 인간과 자신에 대하여 뭔가

Finally, on his third voyage, he is set ashore in a country ruled by horses. In each strange place, he learns something about humans and himself. When he returns home, he shuns others, thinking himself better than they are.

(　) Gulliver, after his sea voyages, thinks that he is better than those strange beings with strange customs.
(　) Gulliver acquires new knowledge and experience from each place he encounters.
(　) Gulliver faces a variety of strange people with different habits on his sea voyages.
(　) Gulliver travels to see the world by himself.
(　) Gulliver finds himself in three different places where tiny people, gigantic people, and horses live and control.

3.8. Rice is an important food of mankind. It is as much a part of everyday eating in some countries as bread is in America.

The growing of rice differs from the growing of many other foods. In Asian countries, rice is usually sown in seed beds. These beds are very wet. Actually, the seeds are sown in liquid mud. They are left to grow in this mud until the sprouts are two or three inches high. Then the rice plants are removed from the seed beds and are transplanted in what is called a rice paddy. They grow in water in the rice paddy until they reach a height of two to three feet. When the sprouts turn yellow, the rice farmer knows they are ripe. The field is then drained and the rice is cut with a sickle. It is then stacked in the field and left to dry. The next step is threshing rice. One method which has been used in China for many years is that of beating a handful of the sheaves of rice against an iron comb set in a frame. The grains of rice fall through the comb into a basket below.

(　) Rice is sown in beds of liquid mud.
(　) Sprouts grow in water until they are two to three feet high.
(　) Rice is cut with a sickle.
(　) Rice is stacked to dry.
(　) Sprouts are transplanted when they are two or three inches high.
(　) Rice is threshed by beating sheaves against iron comb.
(　) Rice field is drained.
(　) Rice starts to turn yellow when it is ripe.
(　) Grains of rice fall into basket.

를 배운다. 그는 집에 돌아온 후로 자신이 다른 사람들보다 우수하다고 생각하며 남들을 피한다.

(　) 걸리버는 항해 후 이상한 풍습을 가진 그 낯선 사람들보다 자기가 우수하다고 생각한다.
(　) 걸리버는 그가 마주치는 각각의 장소에서 새로운 지식과 경험을 얻는다.
(　) 걸리버는 그의 항해에서 풍속이 다른 다양한 사람들과 마주친다.
(　) 걸리버는 세상을 알기 위하여 홀로 여행을 떠난다.
(　) 걸리버는 소인들, 거인들, 말들이 살고 지배하는 다른 세 곳을 발견하게 된다.

3. 8. 쌀은 인류의 중요한 식량이다. 밥은 몇몇 나라에서 미국의 빵만큼 일상의 식품으로 큰 부분을 차지한다. 벼의 재배는 다른 많은 식량을 재배하는 것과 다르다.

　　아시아 국가에서 벼는 보통 못자리에 파종한다. 이 못자리에는 언제나 물이 있다. 실제로 볍씨는 진흙에 파종된다. 이들은 싹의 키가 2~3인치 될 때까지 이 진흙에서 자란다. 그 후 벼의 모는 못자리에서 옮겨져서 논이라고 부르는 곳에 옮겨 심어진다. 그것들은 키가 2~3피트 자랄 때까지 논의 물 속에서 자란다. 벼 잎이 누렇게 변하면 농부는 벼가 익었다는 것을 안다. 그러면 논에서 물을 빼고 낫으로 벼를 벤다. 그 후 논에 쌓아 마르도록 놓아둔다. 다음 단계는 벼의 탈곡이다. 중국에서 오랜 동안 쓰여져 온 탈곡 방법은 한 줌의 벼를 쥐고 어떤 틀의 고정된 빗살에 대고 때리는 것이다. 벼 낱알들이 빗을 통하여 밑에 있는 바구니에 떨어진다.

(　) 볍씨는 진흙 못자리에 파종된다.
(　) 싹들은 키가 2~3피트 될 때까지 물 속에서 자란다.
(　) 벼는 낫으로 벤다.
(　) 벼는 마르도록 쌓아 둔다..
(　) 모는 키가 2~3인치가 되면 이앙(옮겨심다)한다.
(　) 벼는 쇠빗에 대고 때려서 탈곡한다.
(　) 논의 물을 뺀다.
(　) 벼는 익으면 누렇게 변한다.
(　) 벼 알갱이는 바구니 속으로 떨어진다.

2-3 FOLLOWING THE DIRECTIONS

"Following the directions" is designed to help the readers develop reading skills in following directions. "Directions" refers to the specific instruction that tell us "how to do" something such as driving a car, cooking certain foods, playing certain games, etc. This proficiency in reading "how to do" is a must not only for academic success, but also for social requirements of our daily life activities.

EXERCISES.

Read the following directions from 1 to 8, and choose the best answer provided.

Direction 1: If you get lost in a deep forest while camping, what would you do? You should build signal fires. Find the clearest spot away from the tall trees which may prevent the smoke from rising. Build three fires spaced 10 feet from each other, since the smoke of one fire is not enough to attract attention. Once the signal fires are burning well, add dead wood, dried grass or leaves to make a dark and dense smoke. This type of smoke can be seen from a long distance.

1. Where should the signal fire be built?
   - (1) in the woods
   - (2) near the stream
   - (3) in a clearing
   - (4) in a deep cavern
   - (5) in a deep forest

2. The directions are prepared to teach "how to"
   - (1) save you
   - (2) cook
   - (3) help other members
   - (4) build signal fires
   - (5) put out fires

3. To get a dark and dense smoke, use _____.
   - (1) coal   (2) wood   (3) oil   (4) oak   (5) dried grass

4. How many fires should be built to attract attention?
   - (1) 1   (2) 2   (3) 3   (4) 4   (5) 5

5. How far apart should the signal fires be built from each other?
   - (1) 7 feet   (2) 10 feet   (3) 15 feet   (4) 20 feet   (5) 25 feet

2-3 지시를 따라하기

이 장은 독자들이 "지시를 따라하기"의 독해 기술을 개발하도록 도와 주기 위하여 마련됐다. "지시"란 자동차 운전, 음식 요리, 게임 등 "무언가 하는 방법"을 가르쳐 주는 구체적인 가르침을 가리킨다. 이 "방법" 읽기의 능숙은 학문적인 성공을 위해서 뿐 아니라 일상 활동의 사회적인 요구조건에 필수적인 것이다.

 다음 지시를 1에서 8까지 읽고 주어진 답 중에서 가장 좋은 것을 골라라.

지시 1.

만일 깊은 숲속에서 야영하다 길을 잃으면 어떻게 하겠는가? 신호용 불을 피워야 한다. 연기가 피어 오르는 것을 가릴지 모르는 나무로부터 멀리 떨어진 공지를 찾아야 한다. 서로 10피트 공간을 두고 세 개를 피워라. 왜냐하면 한 개의 불에서 나는 연기는 주의를 끌기에 충분하지 않기 때문이다. 일단 신호용 불이 잘 타면 마른 나무, 마른 풀이나 잎 등을 너 내워 섬고 신한 연기가 나도록 하라. 이런 형태의 연기는 먼 거리에서 눈에 잘 보인다.

Direction 2: More and more people are finding out that it is fun to prepare good things to eat. To do this well, you must know how to follow a recipe. Look over the one below, and follow the directions. Now we are making a Banana Split Pie.

Beat cream cheese with an electric mixer until smooth. Beat in milk and pudding mix until thick. Pour into prepared crust. Top with bananas and crusted pineapple. Spread whipped cream on top and refrigerate. Then, you can have 8 servings of Banana Split Pie.

Ingredients: 1 pack (8 oz.) cream cheese, softened
$3^{1}/_{3}$ cups milk
1 package (4 serving size) instant vanilla pudding mix
1 prepared graham cracker crust
3 or 4 bananas, sliced
1 can (15 oz.) crushed pineapple, drained
Whipped cream or frozen whipped topping

1. The prepared Banana Split Pie is for ___ people.
   (1) 5   (2) 6   (3) 7   (4) 8   (5) 9

2. How many bananas are needed in this recipe?
   (1) 1   (2) 2   (3) 3   (4) 4   (5) 3 - 4

3. How do you beat the cream cheese? Until it gets ___.
   (1) thick   (2) tough   (3) sticky   (4) smooth   (5) watery

4. With what do you beat the cream cheese?
   (1) electric mixer   (3) ice pick   (5) fork
   (2) microwave oven   (4) oven

5. The directions are for making _____.
   (1) North African Stew   (3) Banana Chips   (5) Banana Cream Pie
   (2) Banana Split Pie   (4) Potato Bud Cookies

Direction 3: Pizza.

Materials needed: 1 package ($13^{3}/_{4}$ oz.) hot-roll mix
1 cup warm water
1 tablespoon of vegetable oil
1/2 can (6 oz.) tomato paste
3 tablespoons of water
1/4 teaspoon, dried oregano, crushed

지시 2.

맛있는 음식을 만들어 먹는 재미를 발견하는 사람들이 점점 늘어나고 있다. 이 일을 잘 하려면 요리법을 따라할 줄 알아야 한다. 아래 요리법을 훑어 보고 지시를 따르하라. 지금 우리는 바나나 파이를 만들려고 한다.

크림치즈를 믹서로 응어리가 없어질 때까지 휘저어라. 우유와 푸딩재료에 넣고 진해질 때까지 휘저어라. 준비해 둔 파이 껍질 속에 부어라. 바나나와 크러스트를 입힌 파인애플을 위에 얹어라. 거품이 생긴 크림을 위에 바르고 냉장시켜라. 그러면 8인분의 바나나 파이를 만들 수 있다.

재료 : 묽게 한 크림치즈 1팩 (8온스)
우유 3 1/3컵
4인분 즉석 요리용 바닐라 푸딩 재료 1팩
준비된 통밀 크래커 크러스트 1
얇게 벤 3~4개의 바나나
으깨어 물기를 뺀 파인애플 1통조림 (15온스)
거품을 낸 크림이나 냉동시킨 거품 토핑

Note

□ **Banana Split Pie** : 바나나를 절반으로 잘라 아이스크림 볼이나 크림, 열매 등 고명을 곁들인 후식.
□ **cream cheese** : 흰색의 생치즈   □ **beat** : 휘저어 한데 섞다.   □ **graham** : 통밀
□ **cracker** : 비스켓   □ **crust** : 빵의 겉 껍질, 파이의 껍질
□ **topping** : 크림이나 케익의 위에 뿌리는 것   □ **whip** : 달걀, 크림을 거품이 나게하다.

지시 3. 피자

필요한 재료 : 핫롤 재료, 1봉지 (13 3/4온스)
온수, 1컵
식물성 기름, 큰 스푼으로 1
토마토 으깬 것, 1/2 통조림 (6온스)
물, 큰 스푼으로 3
말려 가루로 만든 오레가노, 차스푼으로 1/4

1/2 teaspoon of garlic powder
8 oz. shredded mozzarella cheese
4 oz. thinly sliced pepperoni
1/2 thinly sliced green pepper
1 small, thinly sliced onion
2 tablespoons of grated Parmesan cheese

   In a large bowl, sprinkle yeast (in hot-roll mix package) over 1 cup of warm water; stir until dissolved. Stir in packaged flour mixture until it is well blended and forms a ball of dough. Turn dough onto slightly floured surface. Knead dough about 5 minutes or until smooth. Let dough rest 5 minutes.
   Grease a 12 or 14-inch pizza pan. With floured rolling pin, roll dough on lightly floured surface into an 11-inch circle (13-inch circle for 14-inch pan). Transfer to pan. With greased hands, pat dough to rim of pan, forming 1/2-inch crust. Brush dough with oil.
   Preheat oven to 425 F. In small bowl, stir together tomato paste, 3 tablespoons water, oregano, and garlic until well blended. Pour sauce onto center of dough. Spread sauce evenly to edges of dough. Sprinkle sauce with mozzarella cheese.
   Arrange pepperoni, green pepper, and onion on top. Sprinkle with Parmesan cheese. Bake 25 to 30 minutes or until bubbly and edges are golden brown. Slice into 8 wedges.

1. Which of the following words does not give you a direction to do something?

   (1) Sprinkle   (2) Stir   (3) Preheat   (4) Transfer   (5) Bubbly

2. The recipe says to knead the dough. What does the word knead mean?

   (1) Stir until dissolved   (4) Press into mass with your hands
   (2) Spread evenly on pan   (5) Cut something into pieces
   (3) Roll flat with a rolling pin

3. If you want to make 3 pizzas, how much tomato paste would you need?
   _____ ounces.

   (1) 6   (2) 9   (3) 12   (4) 15   (5) 18

4. If you want to make 2 pizzas, how much dried oregano would you need?
   _____ teaspoon(s).

   (1) 1/2   (2) 1   (3) $1\frac{1}{2}$ (4) 2   (5) $2\frac{1}{2}$

5. Just before baking for 25-30 minutes, what should you put on the top of the dough?

   (1) Pepperoni, tomato paste, water   (4) Warm water, pepperoni, green pepper
   (2) Green pepper, yeast, onion   (5) Pepperoni, onion, green pepper
   (3) Mozzarella cheese, sauce, onion

마늘 가루, 차스푼으로 1/2
토막으로 자른 모자레라 치즈, 8온스
얇게 벤 페퍼로니, 4온스
얇게 벤 푸른 고추 반 쪽
얇게 벤 작은 양파 1개
강판에 간 파르메잔 치즈, 큰 스푼으로 2

　큰 사발에다 핫롤재료 봉지에 있는 이스트를 온수 1컵을 부으면서 뿌리고, 녹을 때까지 저어라. 봉지에 있는 혼합 밀가루를 붓고 잘 섞일 때까지 저어서 반죽 한 덩어리를 만들어라. 밀가루를 뿌린 판에 그 반죽을 굴려라. 그 반죽을 5분 혹은 말랑거릴 때까지 쳐대라. 5분 간 그대로 두어라.

　12~14인치 피자 냄비에 기름을 둘러라. 밀가루를 뿌린 밀대편으로, 약간 밀가루를 뿌린 표면위에서 반죽 덩어리를 11인치 원(냄비가 14인치면 13인치 원)까지 굴려 밀어라. 냄비로 옮겨라. 손에 기름을 바르고 반죽을 다독거려 냄비 가장자리까지 펴서 1/2인치 껍질로 만들어라. 솔로 반죽에 기름을 발라라.

　오븐을 화씨 425도까지 예열하라. 작은 그릇 안에 토마토 으깬 것, 큰 스푼 3개의 물, 오레가노, 그리고 마늘 가루를 잘 섞일 때까지 함께 저어라. 반죽 한가운데 소스를 부어라. 그 소스를 반죽 가장자리까지 발라라. 소스를 모자레라 치즈와 같이 뿌려라.

　위에 페퍼로니, 푸른 고추, 그리고 양파를 배열하라. 파르메잔 치즈를 뿌려라. 25~30분 간 혹은 거품이 일어나고 가장자리가 노란 갈색이 될 때까지 구워라. 8조각의 쐐기 모양으로 잘라라.

Note

- table spoon : 식탁용 큰 스푼
- oregano : 향신료
- mozzarella cheese : 신 맛이 나는 치즈
- Parmesan cheese : 수년 간 저장한 향이 진한 치즈, 스파게티나 소스 등에 양념으로 쓰임.
- pepperoni : 양념을 한 소고기, 돼지고기 소시지
- shred : 잘게 찢다
- rolling pin : 반죽을 늘리는 방망이
- grate : 강판에 갈다
- crush : 압착하다, 빻다

Direction 4: Do you know how to replace a flat tire? First, drive over to the side of the road. Take out the jack and spare tire from the trunk of your car. Remove the hubcap from the tire and loosen all the nuts of the tire that is flat. Place the jack under the side of the car nearest to the area of the flat tire and jack it up until the wheel spins freely. With the crowbar, remove all the nuts holding the tire in place. Remove the flat tire and place it in the trunk. Put the spare tire on the wheel and put the nuts on. Tighten the nuts by hand. Lower the jack to lower the car to the ground. Place the jack back in the trunk. With the car firmly on the ground, tighten all the nuts with the crowbar until you can't tighten them anymore. Drive the car to a garage to get the tire replaced or fix the flat.

1. What tool do you use to loosen and tighten the nuts?
   (1) jack   (2) screw driver   (3) hammer   (4) hubcap   (5) crowbar

2. What's the first thing you should do when you realize that you have a flat tire?
   (1) take off the hubcap
   (2) pull over to the side of the road
   (3) loosen the nuts
   (4) take out the spare tire
   (5) take out the jack

3. What's the last thing you should do when changing a flat?
   (1) tighten the nuts   (3) jack up the car   (5) loosen the nuts
   (2) jack down the car   (4) take off the hubcap

4. The main idea of these directions is _____.
   (1) How to put on a new tire
   (2) How to change a flat tire
   (3) How to operate a jack
   (4) How to loosen and tighten nuts
   (5) When to change a flat tire

5. What does the jack do?
   (1) loosen the nuts   (3) lower and raise the car   (5) recharge the battery
   (2) take off the hubcap (4) repairs the flat tire

Direction 5: Do you know how to put out a grease fire? If you are ever in a situation where you are cooking with grease or cooking oil, you have to be very careful of "grease fires." Grease fires are very dangerous because many people do not know the proper way to extinguish these fires. First, when the grease in your pan catches on fire, you must stay calm. The best thing to do is to put a lid on tightly so that you deprive the fire of oxygen and it will soon go out. But, if the pan does not have a lid, you should follow these steps. Never throw water on a grease fire! Doing this can seriously injure people because the water will splash the grease throughout the kitchen and even possibly on you. To put out a grease fire, you can throw baking soda or flour on it or even use a fire extinguisher. After being certain that the fire is out, remove the grease from the pan and dispose of it in a safe place.

지시 4.

빵꾸난 타이어를 갈아 끼우는 방법을 아는가? 첫째 차를 길가로 대라. 차 트렁크에서 잭과 타이어를 꺼내라. 타이어 덮개를 벗기고 빵꾸난 타이어의 6개 너트를 풀어라. 잭을 빵꾸 타이어 쪽 가까운 곳 밑에 놓고 바퀴가 자유롭게 돌 때까지 차를 올려라. 쇠지레로 타이어를 제 자리에 붙든 채 모든 너트를 빼라. 빵꾸난 타이어를 빼서 트렁크에 넣어라. 바퀴에 여분 타이어를 끼고 너트를 채워라. 손으로 너트를 죄어라. 잭을 내려 차를 땅에 닿게하라. 잭을 다시 트렁크에 넣어라. 차가 땅에 단단히 닿은 채 쇠지레로 더 이상 죌 수 없을 때까지 너트를 죄어라. 차를 몰고 차고에 가서 그 타이어를 넣어 두거나 빵꾸를 때워라.

note
- hubcap : 차바퀴 덮개, 휠 캡
- nut : 암나사 (opp. bolt)
- loosen : 풀다 (opp. tighten)
- crowbar : 쇠지레
- spin : 회전-자전
- garage : 차고, 정비소

지시 5.

기름에 붙은 불을 끄는 방법을 알고 있는가? 만일 앞으로 여러분이 수지나 식용유로 요리를 하게 된다면, "기름화재"를 대단히 조심해야 한다. 기름화재는 이 불을 끄는 적절한 방법을 모르는 사람들이 많기 때문에 대단히 위험하다. 첫째, 냄비의 기름에 불이 붙으면 침착해야 한다. 최선의 방법은 그 불에서 산소를 제거하기 위하여 뚜껑을 단단히 씌우는 것이다. 그러면 불은 곧 꺼진다. 그러나 만일 뚜껑이 없으면 다음과 같은 조치를 따라야

1. Which is the wrong way to put out a grease fire?

 (1) cover the pan with a lid   (4) throw water on the fire
 (2) throw baking soda on the fire (5) throw flour on the fire
 (3) use a fire extinguisher on the fire

2. What is the purpose of the directions?

 (1) To put out fires with water   (4) To avoid grease fires
 (2) To safely put out grease fires (5) To use baking soda on grease fires
 (3) To start a grease fire

3. Where do most grease fires take place?

 (1) in the woods   (3) in the kitchen   (5) in the bathroom
 (2) in the car   (4) in the garage

4. Grease fires are dangerous because they _____ .

 (1) pollute the environment   (4) spoil your meal
 (2) can injure people if put out improperly (5) draw children's attention
 (3) get too hot

5. Grease fires are similar to forest fires in that _____ .

 (1) both can be put out with water   (4) both need wood to burn
 (2) both start in kitchens   (5) both start while cooking
 (3) both can be put out with a smothering powder

Direction 6: Taking-off in an airplane.

 Before flying in an airplane, do necessary ground-checks: make sure the engines and instruments are working properly. If they are fine, strap yourself into your seat, taxi the plane to the beginning of the runway. Prepare for take-off. Stop the plane at the beginning of the runway by applying and holding down the brake ensuring that engines are at minimum revolutions. Slowly open the throttle to 100% and engines are at maximum. Then release the brake. While the plane is moving forward, line up the plane with the runway. As the plane reaches 60 knots, disengage the steering. At 60 knots, the plane is flying very close to the ground. Any sudden movement of the controls can cause the plane to crash. At 120 knots, pull back slowly on the yoke so the plane's nose starts to rise. After 5 to 10 seconds, raise the landing gear. Keep the nose up until you reach 1000 feet. At 900 feet, reduce the throttle to 80% and gently push the yoke forward so that you are flying horizontal.

1. When do you have to taxi the plane to the beginning of the runway?

 (1) after the ground-checks   (4) before strapping the seat belt
 (2) after the preparation for take-off (5) after the engines are at
 (3) before the preparation for take-off   maximum revolutions

한다. 절대로 기름불 위에 물을 뿌려서는 안 된다. 물을 뿌리면 사람이 중상을 입을 수도 있다. 왜냐하면 그 물이 부엌 전체에, 심지어 당신에게까지 기름을 튀게 할 수 있기 때문이다. 기름불을 끄려면 불에 중조(重曹), 또는 밀가루를 던지거나 소화기를 쓸 수 있다. 불이 진화된 것을 확인한 후 냄비에서 기름을 제거하여 안전한 곳에 버려라.

Note
- put out = extinguish : 불을 끄다
- baking soda : 중조, 중탄산나트륨
- smothering powder : 소화용 분말-산소차단으로 불을 끈다
- extinguisher : 소화기
- dispose of sth : 버리다, 처분하다.

지시 6. 비행기 이륙하기

비행기로 날기 전에 필요한 지상 점검을 하라. 엔진과 기기들이 제대로 작동하는지 확인하라. 이상이 없으면 조종석으로 들어가 벨트로 몸을 고정시키고 활주로가 시작되는 곳까지 비행기를 활주시켜라. 이륙 준비를 하라. 제동장치를 이용하여 엔진 출력이 최소 상태를 유지하도록 작동을 억제하라. 서서히 동력 조절 장치를 100%까지 열어라. 그러면 엔진 출력이 최고 상태가 된다. 그 다음 제동장치를 놓아라. 기체가 전방으로 움직이고 있는 동안 기체는 활주로와 평행이 되도록 하라 (활주로 정대). 비행기가 60노트에 이르면 방향을 조정하지 말라. 60노트에서 비행기는 지상에 접근하여 고속으로 달린다. 갑작스러운 조종 동작은 기체의 추락을 초래할 수 있다. 120노트에 이르면 기수가 올라 가도록 조종간을 서서히 당겨라. 5~10초 후 착륙장치를 올려라. 1000피트에 도달할 때까지 기수를 높인 상태에 유지하라. 900피트에서 동력 조절 장치를 80%까지 줄이고 조종간을 앞으로 밀어 좌우 앞으로 흔들리지 않는 비행을 하도록 하라.

2. When do you have to release the steering? When the plane reaches _____ .

   (1) 60 knots   (2) 100 knots   (3) 120 knots   (4) 900 feet   (5) 1000 feet

3. What can cause the plane to crash? Any sudden movement of the _____ .

   (1) brake   (2) regulating device   (3) steering   (4) rudder   (5) throttle

4. What do you do for the rising of the plane?

   (1) open the throttle   (3) disengage the steering   (5) raise the landing gear
   (2) apply the brake   (4) pull back on the yoke

5. At how many knots, do you think that the plane is off the ground?

   (1) 60 knots   (2) 70 knots   (3) 80 knots   (4) 100 knots   (5) 120 knots

Direction 7: Landing a plane.

First, relax. Check the engine gauges to make sure all the plane's instruments are functioning. When you are five miles from the airport, keep your left hand on the yoke (controls direction) and your right hand on the throttle (controls speed). Check your altimeter to make sure that you are at 3000 feet. Reduce your air speed to 175 knots by pulling back on the throttle. Pull back slightly on the yoke to bring the nose up. This will also reduce air speed. Check the panel for your rate of descent. You should be descending at around 750 feet per minute. At 2 - 3 miles from the airport, lower the flaps and the landing gear. When coming in to land, aim for the beginning of the runway. Adjust the throttle and yoke gently. Keep the nose up and maintain your speed at 150 knots. When the rear tires hit the runway, you have to use the rudder pedals to steer and brake.

1. How can you reduce air speed with the yoke? By _____ .

   (1) pushing it forward   (3) pushing it to the right   (5) touching it
   (2) pushing it to the left   (4) pulling it back

2. The altimeter is a gauge that checks _____.

   (1) speed   (2) direction   (3) height   (4) distance to the airport   (5) engine

3. Which is the correct sequence to land a plane?

   (1) relax, push the yoke forward, increase speed, step on the rudder pedals
   (2) pull back on the yoke, relax, increase throttle, point the nose down
   (3) relax, pull back on the yoke, reduce throttle, step on the rudder pedals
   (4) push up on the yoke, reduce throttle, step on the rudder pedals, relax
   (5) check altimeter, reduce throttle, relax, push the yoke forward

4. Just before reaching the airport, what steps should be taken?

   (1) push the yoke up   (4) say "Mayday, Mayday" through the radio

note
- ground-check : 지상 점검
- disengage the steering : 방향 조종을 그만두다
- minimum revolutions : 엔진 회전 최저 상태 (엔진 출력 최저 상태)
- throttle : 동력 조절 장치 (자동차의 엑셀레이터의 기능)
- taxi (v) 비행기를 taxiway에서 활주시키다
- yoke : 조종간

지시 7. 비행기 착륙하기

첫째, 긴장을 풀어라. 엔진 계기판을 점검하여 모든 기기들이 작동하는지 확인하라. 공항으로부터 5마일 떨어진 지점에서 왼손은 조종간 위에, 오른손은 동력 조절 장치 위에 고정시켜라. 고도계를 점검하여 고도 3,000피트인가를 확인하라. 동력 조절 장치를 뒤로 당겨 175노트까지 줄여라. 조종간을 약간 뒤로 당겨 기수를 높여라. 그러면 속도가 줄어든다. 강하비율 패널을 보고 점검하라. 분당 750피트로 강하해야 한다. 공항에서 2~3마일 떨어진 위치에서 보조익과 착륙장치를 내려라. 착륙하기 위하여 내려올 때는 활주로가 시작되는 곳을 겨냥해라. 동력 조절 장치와 조종간을 유연하게 조정해라. 기수는 높인 상태로 150노트 속도를 유지하라. 뒤 타이어가 착지할 때 방향타 페달을 이용하여 방향을 조절하고 제동을 시켜야 한다.

Airspeed Indicator

Altimeter

note
- engine gauges : 엔진 계기들
- rate of descent : 강하 비율
- altimeter : 고도계
- flaps : 보조익(항력 장치)

(2) step on the rudder pedals   (5) lower flaps and the landing gear
  (3) lower the nose

5. To make sure you are ready to land the plane, you should

   (1) aim at the beginning of the runway   (4) decrease the throttle
   (2) keep the nose pointed up   (5) all of the above
   (3) use the rudder pedals

Direction 8: When we make public speeches

In front of many people, we tend to be frightened or too nervous to begin work. It is a problem of anxiety, which can be substantially reduced by following the directions. Organize your ideas first. Lack of organization is one of the major causes of anxiety. Next, visualize yourself that you'll do a good job. Imagine yourself being introduced and delivering your presentation with enthusiasm, answering questions with confidence and leaving the room knowing that you did a good job. Breathe deeply when you feel your muscles tighten and feel nervous. In this case, inhale a number of times as a way of releasing tension. Move your body while delivering your speech. Speakers who stand in one spot without making any gestures experience tension. Establish eye contact with your audience, which helps you keep close with them. Try to make your speech appear as a one-on-one conversation.

1. The directions are to

   (1) make good speeches   (3) breathe deeply   (5) answer questions
   (2) deliver effectively   (4) reduce anxiety

2. To reduce the anxiety level, the directions offer _____ steps.

   (1) 4   (2) 5   (3) 6   (4) 7   (5) 8

3. The third step to reduce anxiety is

   (1) practicing speaking   (3) breathing deeply   (5) visualizing yourself
   (2) organizing ideas   (4) establishing eye contact

4. One of the benefits of establishing eye contact with the audience is that you

   (1) are less isolated from the audience   (4) can move your body
   (2) can deliver with enthusiasm   (5) can organize idea
   (3) can breathe deeply

5. Public speech is different from conversation in that it creates

   (1) practice   (3) organization   (5) eye contact
   (2) visualization   (4) anxiety

지시 8. 많은 사람 앞에서의 연설

　많은 사람들 앞에서 우리는 겁을 먹거나 너무 불안하여 연설을 시작하지 못하는 경향이 있다. 그것은 불안의 문제로서 다음 지시를 지키면 실질적으로 불안을 감소시킬 수 있다. 첫째, 생각하고 있는 것을 조직하라. 조직화하지 못하면, 주요한 불안 원인의 하나가 된다. 다음으로 네가 연설을 훌륭하게 할 수 있음을 마음에 그려라. 소개를 받고 열성적으로 설명을 하고 있는, 자신 있게 질문에 대답하고 연설을 잘 했다는 것을 알고 연설장을 떠나는 네 모습을 상상하라. 근육이 죄어들고 불안을 느낄 때는 심호흡을 하라. 이 때는 긴장을 몰아내는 한가지 방법으로 여러 차례 숨을 들여 마셔라. 연설 중에는 몸을 움직여라. 몸짓을 하지 않고 한 곳에 서 있는 연사는 긴장을 체험한다. 청중들과 눈을 맞추어라, 그러면 그들과 친근한 상태를 갖는데 도움이 된다. 네가 하는 말이 마치 1:1의 대화처럼 보이도록 노력해라.

Good speakers are audiencecentered. They work hard to find creative ways to evoke an enthusiastic response from their listeners. (Ulrike Welsch)

note

- eye contact : 눈과 눈과의 만남
- anxiety : 불안, 초조, 걱정
- substantially = virtually : 상당히, 실질적으로

Direction 9: How can you get a great lawn?

First, fertilize your lawn in late summer or early fall. If you do it earlier, you will get an intense surge of growth, but it makes the lawn less resistant to disease which kills grass quicker. Fertilize your lawn with the best fertilizer because they contain nitrogen which is released slowly, so you only have to fertilize your lawn once a year. Be sure that the fertilizer you purchase has the most nitrogen per pound. When fertilizing, use a spreader to evenly fertilize the lawn. Don't hand-toss the fertilizer or you'll get patches of dead grass. Water your lawn immediately after fertilizing so the pellets wash into the soil. Water your lawn in the morning until the ground is soaked. Water it once or twice a week. This forces the grass roots to go deeper into the soil to find water which in turn makes a healthier lawn. When mowing the lawn, only mow 1/3 of the grass, or you'll weaken the grass. If the grass clippings are short, leave them alone so they can decompose and release vital nutrients back into the soil.

1. What is the advantage of using nitrogen rich fertilizer?

    (1) you get a healthier lawn
    (2) you only have to fertilize once a year
    (3) the grass gets deeper roots
    (4) answers 1 & 2
    (5) answers 2 & 3

2. What causes dead patches of grass?

    (1) bugs and insects
    (2) too much nitrogen
    (3) disease of the grass
    (4) too much fertilizer
    (5) too much water

3. Which is the proper sequence for having a healthy lawn?

    (1) water lawn, mow lawn, fertilize lawn, water lawn
    (2) fertilize lawn, water lawn, mow lawn, water lawn
    (3) mow lawn, fertilize lawn, water lawn, fertilize lawn
    (4) fertilize lawn, mow lawn, water lawn, play on lawn
    (5) play on lawn, fertilize lawn, mow lawn, water lawn

4. Why do you think it is recommended to water the lawn in the morning?

    (1) the neighbors don't use up all the water
    (2) minimal time of evaporation
    (3) there are fewer insects
    (4) the water is cleaner
    (5) nitrogen is released more

5. Why should you use a spreader?

    (1) to save time
    (2) to release nitrogen more
    (3) to kill weeds
    (4) to spread the fertilizer evenly
    (5) for the grass roots to grow deeper

지시 9. 어떻게 하면 훌륭한 잔디를 가질 수 있는가?

첫째, 늦은 여름이나 초가을에 비료를 주어라. 만일 이보다 일찍 주면 잔디가 바람에 흔들릴 만큼 빨리 자랄 것이고, 그러면 잔디를 죽이는 병에 저항력이 약해질 것이다. 최상급의 비료를 주어라. 왜냐하면 그 비료 속에는 천천히 울어 나는 질소 성분을 포함하고 있기 때문이다. 그러므로 1년에 한번만 시비(施肥)해도 된다. 반드시 파운드당 가장 많은 질소 성분을 가진 비료를 사라. 시비할 때는 고루 시비하기 위해서 살포기를 사용하여라. 비료를 손으로 던지지 말아라. 그러면 군데군데 잔디가 죽을 것이다. 시비 직후에 작은 덩어리들이 흙 속으로 씻겨 들도록 물을 주어라. 아침에 땅이 푹신 젖을 때까지 물을 주어라. 1주일에 1~2번 물을 주어라. 그러면 잔디 뿌리가 부득이 땅 속 더 깊이 물기를 찾아 뻗게 된다. 그것이 더 건강한 잔디를 만들어 준다. 잔디를 깎을 때는 1/3의 길이만 깎아라. 그렇지 않으면 잔디가 약해진다. 깎여 나온 잔디가 짧으면 그것들만 따로 놔두어라. 그러면 분해되어 중요한 영양분을 흙 속으로 다시 되돌려 줄 것이다.

Note
- fertilize = enrich : 기름지게 하다, (알)수정하다
- fertilizer : 비료
- surge of growth : 솟구침, 급격하게 자라다 • a surge of anger : 솟구쳐 오르는 분노
- nitrogen : 질소
- spreader : 분무기, 살포기
- patch : 좁은 땅 • a patch of vegetable garden : 채소밭 한 떼기
- force the grass to go deeper : 꼼짝없이 더 깊이 뻗게하다
- in turn : 이번에는, 그러면
- weaken : 약화시키다 opp. strengthen
- decompose : 분해되다 (opp. compose)

지시 10. 퍼덕이는 새 접기

퍼덕이는 새는 많은 일본 학생들이 취미나 오락으로 만든다. 여러분도 다음 지시를 읽으면 만들 수 있다. 15~25cm의 정사각형 종이를 준비하고 그림으로 예시한 단계를 따라 하라.

- 1단계 : 산 접기 - 두 대각선을 접어라. 펴라.
- 2단계 : 골짜기 접기 - 수평으로 접고 수직으로 접어라. 펴라.
- 3단계 : 위 가장자리를 만들어진 주름을 따라 바닥 선까지 접어라.

Direction 10: "Flapping Bird" is made by many Japanese students as their hobbies or pastime. You can make it by reading the following directions. Prepare a 15 - 25 cm square paper and follow the steps as illustrated in the pictures.

(Source: Adapted from Jackson, Paul, "Classic Origami.")

Step 1
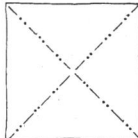
1 Mountain fold both diagonals. Unfold.

Step 2
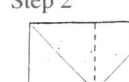
2 Valley fold horizontally and vertically. Unfold.

Step 3
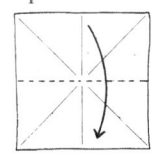
3 Fold the top edge down to the bottom along the existing crease.

Step 4
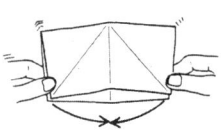
4 hold as shown. Swing your hands together ⋯

Step 5
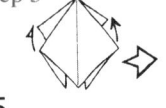
5 ⋯ to create this 3D star shape. If the pattern of mountains and valley is incorrect will not form, so check Steps 1-2.

Step 6
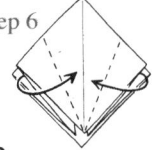
6 With the closed (neat) corner at the top, fold in the lower front edges to the centre crease ⋯

Step 7
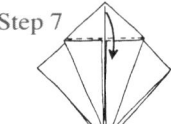
7 ⋯ like this. Fold down the top triangle.

Step 8
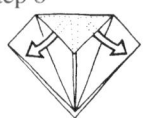
8 Pull out the side triangles.

Step 9
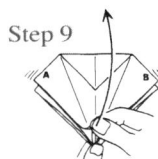
9 Take hold of just the top layer. Lift it upward⋯

Step 10
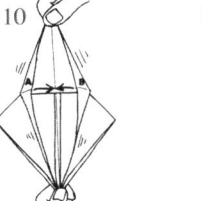
10 ⋯ swivelling it right up and over the top edge of the paper shape. A and B will move inwards.

Step 11
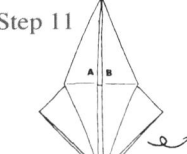
11 Flatten the diamond shape with strong creases. Turn over.

Step 12
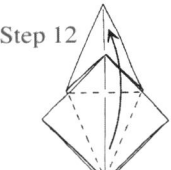
12 Repeat Steps 6 -11 on this side, to make another diamond shape to match the first. Note the loose triangle hidden between them.

Step 13
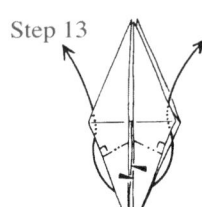
13 Reverse fold each of the lower points, so that each reverse starts a little below the centre of the diamond.

Step 14

14 Reverse the head.

Step 15
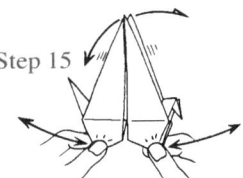
15 Hold as shown. To complete the Flapping Bird, move your hands gently apart and together, apart and together, and the wings will flap!

FLAPPING BIRD

Here is perhaps the greatest of all 'action models'. The bird shape is itself satisfying, but the wide, graceful arc made by the wings when flapped is dramatic and appealing. If you want to carry an origami design in your handbag or wallet to entertain people with, this must surely be the one. Use a 6-10inch (15-25cm) square of paper.

- 4단계 : 그림처럼 쥐고 두 손을 좌우로 움직여라. 입체모양을 만들기 위하여,

- 5단계 : 만일 산과 골짜기의 모양이 바르지 않으면 그 모양이 만들어 지지 않는다. 1~2단계를 점검하라.

- 6단계 : 막힌 (단정한) 모서리를 위로 한 채 아래 앞 가장자리들을 가운데 주름까지 안으로 접어라.

- 7단계 : 그림과 같이. 위 삼각형을 아래로 접어라.

- 8단계 : 옆에 있는 삼각형들을 밖으로 당겨라.

- 9단계 : 꼭지 접혀진 곳만 잡고 위로 들어 올려라.

- 10단계 : 그것을 회전시켜 곧장 위로 그리고 종이 꼭지점 위로 올려라. A와 B가 안쪽으로 접혀질 것이다.

- 11단계 : 다이아몬드 모양을 튼튼한 주름을 내며 펴라. 뒤로 돌려라.

- 12단계 : 이 쪽에서도 6~11단계를 되풀이하여 또 하나의 다이아몬드를 만들어라. 둘 사이에 숨겨진 느슨한 삼각형을 유념하라.

- 13단계 : 각각의 아래 꼭지를 뒤집어라. 각각의 밖으로 접는 시작이 다이아몬드 중심 약간 아래 쪽이 되게하라.

- 14단계 : 머리를 뒤집어라.

- 15단계 : 그림처럼 쥐어라. 퍼덕이는 새를 완성하기 위하여 양 손을 가만히 떼었다 붙였다, 붙였다 떼었다 하여라. 그러면 날개가 퍼덕일 것이다.

(— Paul Jackson의 "Classic Origami"에서 발췌 —)

퍼덕이는 새

'행동 모델' 중 가장 멋있는 것이 여기 있다. 새 모양 자체도 만족을 주지만 새가 퍼덕일 때 날개들이 만드는 넓고 우아한 활 모양은 극적이며 매력이 넘친다. 사람들을 즐겁게 해주기 위해 손가방이나 지갑속에 '오리가미(折紙)' 도안을 가지고 다니기를 원한다면, 이것이 바로 그런 도안임에 틀림없다. 6~11인치(15~25cm)의 정방형 종이를 사용하라.

1. The first step of making the Flapping Bird is

    (1) folding down the top triangle
    (2) pulling out the side triangle
    (3) folding paper diagonally from corner to corner
    (4) folding paper horizontally & vertically
    (5) folding the top edge down to the bottom

2. To make this 3 dimensional star shape, you should

    (1) swing your hands together   (4) pull out the side triangle
    (2) not form the pattern of valleys (5) fold down the top triangle
    (3) fold the top edge down

3. To create another diamond shape to match the first, you should repeat the steps

    (1) 1 - 2   (2) 6 - 11   (3) 7 - 9   (4) 10 - 12   (5) 13 - 15

4. To finish the Flapping Bird, you should

    (1) reverse the head
    (2) flatten the diamond shape
    (3) reverse each of the lower points
    (4) take hold of the top layer
    (5) move your hands gently apart and together

5. "Origami" is a traditional Japanese art of

    (1) cutting paper to form flowers or animal figures
    (2) folding paper to form only animal figures
    (3) folding paper to form flowers or animal figures
    (4) using paper to form just flowers
    (5) painting flowers or forming animal figures

Selected proverbs for the study of cross-cultural expressions

영어 격언과 한문 격언과의 만남 (1)

1. **It never rains but it pours.** 禍不單行, 福無雙至(화불단행, 복무쌍지)
   – 불행은 혼자 오지 않고, 복은 겹쳐오지 않는다.
   · Misfortunes never come singly / · Ill comes often on the back of worse.

2. **Hunger is the best sauce.** 飢者甘食(기자감식) – 시장이 반찬이다
   · A good appetite is a good sauce.

3. **Beggars cannot be choosers.** 飢者不擇食(기자불택식) – 배고픈 사람은 음식을 가리지 않는다.
   · Hunger finds no fault with cookery. / · All is good in famine. / · Nothing comes miss to a hungry man.

4. **Better be the head of a dog than the tail of a lion.** 寧爲鷄口 無爲牛後(영위계구 무위우후)
   – 소꼬리가 되느니 닭머리가 되어라. · Better be the first in a village than second at Rome.

5. **All is not gold that glitters.** 表裏不同, 口是心非(표리부동, 구시심비) – 겉과 속이 다르다.
   · Appearance is deceptive. / · The face is no index to the heart. / · A black hen lays a white egg.

6. **Fair face, foul heart.** 笑裏臟刀, 口蜜腹劍(소리장도, 구밀복검) – 웃음 속에 칼이 숨어 있다.
   · The bait hides the hook.

7. **Pretty face, poor fate.** 佳人薄命(가인박명) – 미인은 팔자가 세다.
   · Beauty and fortune are often bad friends. / · Grace will last, beauty will blast.
   · Beauties die young. / · The fairest flowers soonest fade. / · The fairest silk soonest stained.

8. **Man proposes, God disposes.** 謀事在人 成事在天(모사재인 성사재천)
   – 일을 꾸미는 것은 사람이지만, 성공은 하늘에 달렸다.

9. **Talk of the devil and it will appear.** 談虎虎至 談人人至(담호호지 담인인지)
   – 호랑이도 제 말하면 오듯이 사람도 제 말하면 온다. · Talk of angles and you'll hear their wings.

10. **Preserve the old, but know the new.** 溫故而知新(온고이지신) – 옛 것은 보존하고 새 것을 알라.

11. **When children stand quiet, they have done some ill.** 少年閑居爲不善(소년한거위불선)
    – 소년은 한가하면 못된 짓을 한다.

12. **Ever busy, ever bare** 食少事煩(식소사번) – 먹을 것은 적은데 일만 많다.

13. **Pride goes before a fail.** 驕者必滅(교자필멸) – 교만한 자는 반드시 망한다.

14. **No penny, no pardon.** 無錢有罪, 有錢無罪(무전유죄 유전무죄) – 돈 없으면 죄가 있고, 돈 있으면 무죄가 된다.

15. **Inscrutable are the ways of Heaven.** 塞翁之馬(새옹지마) – 사람의 일은 변화무쌍하여 알 수 없다.
    · God moves in a mysterious way. / · Afflictions are sent to us for good.
    · An evil may sometimes turn out a blessing in disguise.

16. **Where there's will, there's a way.** 有志者事竟成(유지자사경성 ; 竟 = at last)
    – 뜻이 있는 자는 반듯이 성공한다.

17. **After death, the doctor.** 死後藥方文(사후약방문 ; 方文 = prescription) – 사람이 죽은 뒤에야 약을 처방한다.

18. **The remedy is worse than the evil.** 矯角殺牛(교각살우 ; 矯 = correct) – 뿔 고치려다 소 죽인다.

19. **Penny wise, pound foolish.**
    小貪大失, 因小失大, 見小利大事不成(소탐대실, 인소실대, 견소리대사불성) – 작은 것을 탐하다 큰 것을 잃는다.

20. **What soberness conceals drunkenness reveals.** 醉中眞言(취중진언) – 취중에 진담 나온다.

2-4 USING THE CONTEXT

This section, "Using the Context" is designed to help the readers improve their judgmental skills in identifying the proper word or phrase based on the contextual interrelationship. The "contextual interrelationship" refers to the relations between the language operation (i.e. language patterns, word form and usage, acceptable grammatical rules) and the meaning of the word or phrase interpreted within the operation. In other words, the meaning of a certain word or phrase can vary according to the context of the language operation applied.

The other advantage of studying "Using the Context" is to help the readers develop precise thinking skills in terms of identifying and synthesizing the proper relationship between the meaning of the word/phrase and the language operation.

EXERCISE:

Read the following paragraph and choose the best word or phrase that properly fits in the context.

1. Mice are often found in a library. It seems that they like books, although they don't read (1)_____ .They like to eat the glue that (2)_____ the pages.

(1) (a) it	(b) them	(c) us	(d) you
(2) (a) holds	(b) cuts	(c) eats	(d) helps

2. Who sends "Thank you" notes? After a wedding, the (1)_____ and groom write the notes to everyone who (2)_____ a gift. Many people send short notes thanking their friends for birthday presents.

(1) (a) father	(b) mother	(c) sister	(d) bride
(2) (a) received	(b) accepted	(c) took	(d) sent

2-4 문맥 이용하기

　　이번 항 '문맥 이용하기'는 독자들이 문맥상의 상호관계에 입각하여 적절한 단어나 어구들을 선택하는 판단 기능을 향상시키고자 마련되었다. '문맥상의 상호관계'란 언어 사용(예 : 언어양식, 단어의 형태와 용법, 올바른 문법 규칙들)과 그 언어 사용 안에서 해석되는 단어나 어구의 의미와의 관계를 가리킨다. 바꾸어 말하면 어떤 단어나 어구의 의미는 이용되는 언어의 문맥에 따라 다양하게 변할 수 있다.

　　'문맥 이용하기'를 연구하는 또 다른 이점은 독자들이 단어나 어구의 의미와 언어 이용 사이의 적절한 관계를 확인 종합한다는 점에서 정확하게 사고하는 기술을 개발하도록 돕는 것이다.

다음 문단을 읽고 문맥상 가장 적합한 단어나 어구를 골라라.

1. 쥐들이 자주 도서관 안에서 눈에 띈다. 그들이 그것들을 읽지는 않지만 책을 좋아하는 것처럼 보인다. 그들은 책 페이지들을 접착하는 풀을 즐겨 먹는다

> **Note**
> ☐ glue : 접착제　• glue sniffing ; 본드 냄새 맡기　☐ hold : 쥐다　cf. fold : 접다

2. "감사편지"는 누가 보내는가? 결혼식 후 신부와 신랑은 선물을 준 모든 사람에게 그 쪽지를 써 보낸다. 친구들에게 생일 선물을 보내준 데 대하여 짧은 편지를 보낸다.

> **Note**
> ☐ receive : (가져 온 것을) 받다　　　cf. accept : (조건·제안) 호의적으로 받아 들이다
> • receive many wedding gifts　　　• accept one's proposal of marriage

3. Have you ever seen a whale crying? Whales often cry, because it is necessary for them to do so. By shedding (1)_____, the large oily tears wash the whale's (2)_____, and protect them from the salt.

(1) (a) sweat   (b) tears   (c) blood   (d) urine
(2) (a) eyes   (b) mouth   (c) ears   (d) stomach

4. Newspapers have a lot of advertisements in them. Two kinds of ads found in the newspaper are display ads and classified ads. A display ad tells us the stores where they have certain commodities for (1)_____; whereas, a classified ad helps some readers (2)_____ jobs.

(1) (a) purchase   (b) sale   (c) demonstration   (d) display
(2) (a) find   (b) offer   (c) read   (d) reject

5. It is easy to find pockets in men's clothes; whereas the women's clothes do not often include pockets. In other words, men wear their pockets while women (1)_____ theirs. Thus, they call them (2)_____.

(1) (a) take   (b) carry   (c) give   (d) cherish
(2) (a) sweethearts (b) husbands   (c) notebooks   (d) pocketbooks

6. Have you ever wondered where the term "as light as a feather" comes from? Hold a feather in your hand. Notice that it is so light that you hardly (1)_____ its weight. Now, toss it in the air. The feather (2)_____ as gently as a snowflake.

(1) (a) see   (b) calculate   (c) sense   (d) fly
(2) (a) glides (b) flies   (c) crashes   (d) melts

7. The earth's atmosphere contains a lot of dust particles. As such, any pictures of the stars and other celestial bodies are not always clear. Our best photos come from (1)_____ well above the (2)_____.

(1) (a) satellites   (b) boats   (c) planes   (d) rockets
(2) (a) clouds   (b) tree tops (c) atmosphere   (d) skyline

3. 고래가 우는 것을 본 적이 있는가? 고래는 자주 운다. 왜냐하면 그들은 그렇게 하는 것이 필요하기 때문이다. 눈물을 흘림으로써 기름기 있는 커다란 눈물이 고래의 눈을 씻어 주고 그것들을 소금으로부터 보호해 준다.

> **Note**
> ☐ **shed** : 흘리다, 버리다   • shed tears : 눈물을 흘리다

4. 신문 안에는 많은 광고들이 있다. 신문에서 눈에 띄는 두 종류의 광고는 디스플레이 광고와 항목별 구인, 구직 광고다. 디스플레이 광고는 구매를 위한 상품들이 있는 장소를 알려 준다. 그러나 항목별 광고는 독자들이 일자리를 찾는 것을 도와 준다.

> **Note**
> ☐ **display ads** : 디스플레이 광고   ☐ **classified ads** : 항목별 광고 – 구인, 구직 광고
> ☐ **whereas = but, although**   ☐ **purchase = buy - purchasing power** : 구매력

5. 남성 옷에서 주머니를 찾기는 쉽다. 그러나 여성 의류는 호주머니가 없는 때가 자주 있다. 바꾸어 말하면 남자들은 호주머니를 입고 다니지만 여자들은 호주머니를 들고 다닌다. 이리하여 여자들은 그것들을 핸드백이라고 부른다.

> **Note**
> ☐ **pocketbook** : 핸드백 (여성용)

6. '깃털처럼 가벼운'라는 표현이 어디서 왔는지 궁금했던 적이 있는가? 깃털 하나를 손에 쥐어 보라. 그것이 무게를 느끼지 못할 정도임을 주목하라. 자, 그것을 공중에 던져라. 그 깃털은 눈송이처럼 가볍게 날아간다.

> **Note**
> ☐ **직유 (Simile)** – like나 as를 써서 2가지 사물의 같은 점을 직접 비교하는 수사법
>   • (as) poor as a churchmouse   • Time flies like an arrow.
> ☐ **은유 (Metaphor)** – like나 as를 쓰지 않고 비유될 수 있는 다른 사물을 써서 간접 표현
>   • the rose in her cheeks   • All nature smiled.

7. 지구의 대기권은 많은 먼지 입자를 포함하고 있다. 그렇기 때문에 별들이나 다른 천체들의 사진이 항상 선명하지는 않다. 가장 훌륭한 사진은 대기권의 훨씬 위쪽 위성에서 보내 온다.

> **Note**
> ☐ **planet** : 혹성   ☐ **satellite** : 위성   ☐ **meteor** : 유성   ☐ **comet** : 혜성
> ☐ **as such** : 그 자체로서, 그런 이유로
> ☐ **celestial = heavenly** : 하늘의   • opp. terrestrial = earthly
>   • heavenly peace : 천국의 평화

8. If you are really adventurous, why don't you try eating a blowfish? However, you must be (1)_____ before cooking. The fish has a strong poison in its gland. Before cooking, remove all the internal (2)_____ completely without puncturing the poison gland. The best way, if you are not sure, is to get specific instructions from a certified chef.

(1) (a) dangerous   (b) aware   (c) careful   (d) sure
(2) (a) organs   (b) meat   (c) bones   (d) scales

9. On January 24, 1849, James Marshall (1)_____ gold in John Sutter's stream, Sacramento Valley, California. This news of gold did not keep long as a secret. (2)_____ it spread out quickly, and by September 1849, the news spread to the Midwest and the East.

(1) (a) lost   (b) invented   (c) discovered   (d) made
(2) (a) Instead   (b) Because   (c) Since   (d) While

10. Napoleon was born on August 15, 1769 in Ajaccio, on the island of Corsica. In 1779, at the age of 9, he (1)_____ a French military school at Brienne-le-Chateau, a town in France. He was an average student in most subjects, but he (2)_____ in mathematics.

(1) (a) went   (b) entered   (c) finished   (d) studied
(2) (a) interested   (b) studied   (c) excelled   (d) mastered

11. The Solar System includes nine known planets which are revolving around the sun and shining only because they (1)_____ the sun's light. Starting with the one nearest the sun and listing them in order of increasing distance (2)_____ the sun, they are Mercury, Venus, Earth, Mars, Jupiter, Saturn, Uranus, Neptune, and Pluto.

    They all revolve around the sun from west to east, as (3)_____ the earth. The farther from the sun they are, the (4)_____ they move in their orbits, and the longer it takes to complete one revolution about the sun.

(1) (a) take   (b) reflect   (c) color   (d) twist
(2) (a) to   (b) through   (c) in   (d) from
(3) (a) does   (b) do   (c) is   (d) revolves
(4) (a) faster   (b) slower   (c) stronger   (d) weaker

8. 만일 당신이 모험심이 있다면 복어를 먹어 보라. 그러나 요리하기 전에 조심해야 한다. 그 생선은 선(腺) 안에 강력한 독을 가지고 있다. 요리 전에 독 선을 터뜨리지 말고 내장을 모두 꺼내라. 자신이 없으면 공인 요리사에게서 구체적인 지시를 받는 것이 최선이다.

Note
- **blowfish** : 복어 등 몸을 부풀리는 고기
- **gland** : 선(腺, 샘) : 피에서 물질을 받아 여러 종류의 액을 만들어 내는 기관
  - sweat(lymphatic) gland – 한 선(임파선) • ductless gland (내분비선)

9. 1849년 1월 24일에 제임스 마셜은 캘리포니아 새크라멘토 계곡의 존 서터 개울에서 금을 발견했다. 이 금 발견 소식은 비밀로서 오래 가지 않고 대신 빠른 속도로 1849년 9월까지 중서부와 동부로 퍼져 나갔다.

Note
- **forty-niner** : 1849년 캘리포니아 지방의 황금러시 때 서부로 금광을 찾아 몰려든 광부들

10. 나폴레옹은 코르시카섬의 Ajaccio에서 1769년 8월 15일에 태어났다. 아홉 살이던 1779년에 프랑스의 작은 고을인 Brienne-le-Chateau에 있는 군사학교에 입학했다. 그는 대부분의 교과목에서 평균 정도의 학생이었지만 수학에서는 우수했다.

Note
- **average** : 평균의 • average monthly rainfall : 월 평균 강수량
  - strike an average : 평균을 내다 • above (below) average : 평균 이상(이하)
- **excel** : 를 능가하다. (be superior to) - He excelled all his classmates in math.

11. 태양계에는 태양의 주위를 공전하면서 단지 태양의 빛을 반사하기 때문에 빛나는 9개의 혹성들이 있다. 태양에서 가장 가까운 혹성으로부터 시작하여 태양으로부터 멀어지는 거리의 순서로 기록하면 수성, 금성, 지구, 화성, 목성, 토성, 천왕성, 해왕성 그리고 명왕성이 있다.

그들은 지구가 그렇듯이 모두 서에서 동으로 태양의 둘레를 회전한다. 그들이 태양으로부터 멀리 있을수록 그들은 궤도에서 느리게 움직이며 태양 둘레로 한 차례 공전을 끝내는 데는 그만큼 더 오래 걸린다.

Note
- **solar** : 태양의 • solar battery (태양 전지) • solar spot (태양 흑점)
  - solar (lunar) calendar (양(음)력) • solar heating system (태양 난방)
- **the more (less)…, the more (less)** : …하면 할수록 그만큼 더 (덜) …한다.
  - The more you have, the more you want. (가질수록 더 원한다.) • The less you eat, the better you feel. (적게 먹을 수록 기분은 더 좋다.) • The more in haste, the less speed. (바쁠 수록 속도는 줄여라.)
- **reflect** : 반사하다 • cf. **refract** : 굴절시키다   **revolution** : 공전 • cf. **rotation** : 자전

12. The source streams of the world's largest (1)_____, the Nile, are found in the heart of the African continent. These streams (2)_____ through Lake Victoria, one of the largest lakes in the world.
   Africa is the world's second largest (3)_____. It is a continent of (4)_____ diversity with almost every sort of physical feature, climate, and plant and animal life imaginable.

(1) (a) river   (b) pond   (c) lake   (d) stream
(2) (a) draw   (b) drive   (c) flow   (d) send
(3) (a) country   (b) land   (c) continent   (d) island
(4) (a) various   (b) diversified (c) enormous   (d) several

13. One spring a great rivalry (1)_____ among the beasts of the forest. The animals (2)_____ to have a contest about who had had the largest litter of young. They even elected a committee to run the contest.
   Some of the animals were forced to admit they had had only two offsprings. Others could boast that they had had a dozen. At (3)_____ the committee called on the lioness. "How many cubs did you give birth?" they asked. "One," said the lioness sternly. "But that (4)_____ is a lion."
(Theme : Quality is more important than quantity)

(1) (a) came   (b) developed (c) concealed (d) curtailed
(2) (a) terminated (b) delayed   (c) hesitated (d) decided
(3) (a) first   (b) last   (c) all   (d) most
(4) (a) kitten   (b) fawn   (c) puppy   (d) cub

14. What do you do when you are not President anymore? Well, if you are former President Jimmy Carter, you have a (1)_____ of work to do. Since (2)_____ the White House in 1981, Carter has volunteered for many different projects around the world. Why? "Because there are so many things wrong with the world," Carter says. "We often feel that we cannot do anything about them. But that isn't so. Your effort can make a (3)_____."

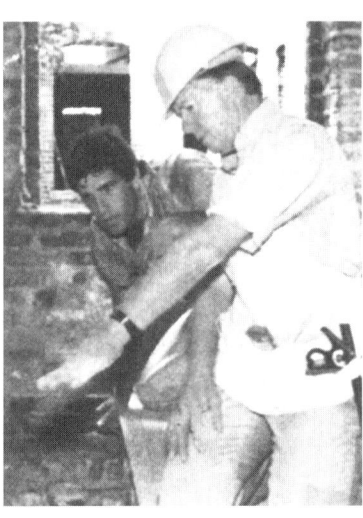

12. 세계에서 가장 긴 강인 나일강의 발원지들은 아프리카 대륙의 중심부에서 발견된다. 이들 흐름들은 세계에서 가장 커다란 호수 빅토리아호를 통과하여 흐른다.
　　아프리카는 세계에서 두 번째로 큰 대륙이다. 아프리카는 생각할 수 있는 거의 모든 종류의 자연적 특색, 기후, 그리고 동·식물의 수많은 다양성을 가진 대륙이다.

> **Note**
> □ 최상급, **every, all** + 명사에서 밑줄 친 부분을 강조하기 위하여 **-ible, -able**로 끝나는 형용사는 명사 뒤에 붙인다.
> • I tried every means possible.　• This is the best idea imaginable.
> • I employed all the means available. (이용할 수 있는 모든 수단을 동원했다.)

13. 어느 봄, 숲속 짐승들 사이에 대단한 경쟁이 일어났다. 동물들은 누가 가장 많은 새끼를 낳았나 선발대회를 갖기로 결정했다. 심지어 그들은 그 대회를 운영할 위원들까지 선발했다.
　　몇몇은 단지 두 마리만 낳았다고 인정하지 않을 수 없었다. 또 다른 동물들은 12마리를 낳았다고 자랑할 수 있었다. 마침내 위원들은 암사자를 찾아갔다. "사자님께서는 몇을 낳으셨습니까?" 그 사자는 엄숙하게, "한 마리지. 그러나 그 한 마리는 사자지." (주제 : 양보다는 질이 더 중요하다)

> **Note**
> □ **kitten** : 고양이 새끼　□ **fawn** : 사슴 새끼　□ **puppy** : 개 새끼　□ **cub** : 여우, 곰, 사자 새끼
> □ **litter** : 한 배 새끼　• a litter of puppies (pigs)
> □ **curtail** : 삭감하다, 줄이다 – cut short, reduce, limit
> • The government hopes to curtail the public spending. (공공부문의 지출을 줄이기를 …)
> □ **give birth to = bear** : 낳다. • Before the birth control policy came into effect, many women gave birth to as many as a dozen children. (가족계획 정책이 실효를 발휘하기 전에는 12명이나 되는 애기를 낳았다.)
> □ **terminate = come (bring) to an end** : (vi) 끝나다. (vt) 끝내다.
> □ **terminate a contract (conference)** : 계약(회의)을 끝내다.
> □ **terminate the employment with the company** : 고용을 끝내다.

14. 당신이 더 이상 대통령이 아닐 때 무슨 일을 하는가? 음, 만일 당신이 전 대통령 지미 카터라면 해야 할 일이 많다. 그가 1981년에 백악관을 떠난 후 전 세계에 걸쳐 다른 많은 일을 자원하여 하고 있다. 왜냐고요? "이 세상에는 잘못된 일이 하도 많기 때문이죠."라고 카터씨는 대답한다. "우리는 자주 그런 일에 대하여 무슨 일도 할 수 없을 것 같은 느낌이 들지만 그렇지 않습니다. 당신이 노력하면 달라지지요." 카터가 자원하는 계획 중 하나는 'Habitat for Humanity'라고 불리워 진다. 그 단체는 가난하고 집 없는 사람들을 위하여 집을 짓는다. 지금까지, 그들은 전 세계적으로 수백 채의 집을 지었다. 카터는 "나는 어려운

One program Carter volunteers for is called Habitat for Humanity. The group builds houses for the (4)_____ and the homeless. So far, they have built hundreds of houses all over the world. Carter enjoys pushing himself, "I get as much out of helping others as I put into it."

(1) (a) much   (b) lot   (c) many   (d) destiny
(2) (a) permitting (b) allowing   (c) resigning   (d) leaving
(3) (a) difference (b) separation   (c) discord   (d) disagreement
(4) (a) rich   (b) poor   (c) young   (d) old

15. Every profession or trade, every art, and every science (1)_____ its technical vocabulary. The function of the vocabulary is partly to designate things or processes which have no names in ordinary (2)_____, and partly to secure greater exactness in name. Such special terminologies or jargons are necessary in technical discussion of any kind. Being universally understood by the devotees of the (3)_____ science or arts, they have the precision of a mathematical formula. Besides, they save time, for it is much more (4)_____ to name a process than to describe it.

(1) (a) has   (b) have   (c) omits   (d) excludes
(2) (a) gesture   (b) language   (c) law   (d) linguistics
(3) (a) defined   (b) appropriate (c) particular   (d) precise
(4) (a) careful   (b) avaricious   (c) beneficent   (d) economical

16. Until 1860, the cross-country mail in the United States moved only by stagecoach or ship. It took at least 4 weeks for news to cross the continent. In that year, a company called R.M.W. bought 500 fast Indian (1)_____ and hired about 80 riders who (2)_____ the mail.
    The first Pony Express mail pouch left St. Joseph on April 3, 1860, and (3)_____ Sacramento in 10 days. However, the Pony Express lasted less than 2 years. In October, 1861, the Western Union Telegraph Company started telegraph service across the continent. (4)_____ could cross from coast to coast by wire. Soon the Pony Express became only as a distant (5)_____, and the R.M.W. lost $200,000.00.

(1) (a) hunters   (b) eagles   (c) ponies   (d) buffaloes
(2) (a) spend   (b) made   (c) shot   (d) carried
(3) (a) arrived   (b) reached   (c) went   (d) attacked
(4) (a) Newspapers (b) News   (c) Books   (d) Riders
(5) (a) memory   (b) dream   (c) nightmare   (d) gift

사람들을 돕는 일에 노력을 기울이는 만큼 얻는 것도 많지요."라고 즐거이 힘주어 말한다.

> **Note**
> ☐ volunteer = to offer one's services or help without payment : 자원하여 …하다.
>   • He volunteered to donate blood for the victim of leukemia. (백혈병 환자를 위하여 헌혈을 자원했다.)
> ☐ push oneself : 강력하게 추진하다. 힘주어 …하다.
>   • You must push yourself to reply the question. (싫어도 그 질의에 대답해야 한다.)
> ☐ so far = until now : 지금까지   • So far, so good. (아직까지는 괜찮다.)
> ☐ 'Habitat for Humanity' : '인간을 위한 주거마련 운동'

15. 모든 전문업, 혹은 일반 직업, 모든 예술, 모든 학문은 각기 전문 용어를 가지고 있다. 그런 어휘의 기능은 일부 일반 언어에는 명칭이 없는 사물이나 과정을 지칭하는 것이고, 일부는 명칭이 갖는 정확성을 보다 크게 확보하려는 것이다. 그러나 용어나 전문어는 모든 종류의 전문적 토의를 할 때 필요하다. 특정의 학문이나 예술에 전념하는 사람들이 전반적으로 이해할 때 그 용어들은 수학공식 같은 정확성을 갖는다. 그 외에도 전문 용어는 시간을 절약해 준다. 왜냐하면 어떤 과정을 설명하는 것보다 이름을 부르는 것이 훨씬 더 경제적이기 때문이다.

> **Note**
> ☐ jargon : 어느 특정 집단 사람들만 사용하는 언어
> ☐ Describe exactly what you did last night. (어제 밤에 한 일을 정확히 말씀하시오.)
> ☐ besides = in addition, also : 그 외에, 또   ☐ appropriate = correct and suitable : 적절한

16. 1860년까지 전국횡단 우편물은 단지 마차나 배에 의하여 운반되었다. 대륙을 횡단하여 소식이 전해지는 데는 최소한 4주가 걸렸다. 그 해에 R.M.W.라는 회사가 500마리의 빠른 인디언 조랑말을 타고 우편물을 전달할 80명의 기수(騎手)를 고용했다.

   최초의 속달 우편마차가 1860년 4월 3일에 세인트 조셉을 떠나 10일 후 세크라멘토에 도착했다. 그러나 그 조랑말 속달은 2년도 지속하지 못했다. 1861년 10월에 the Western Union Telegraph Company가 대륙 횡단 전보업무를 개시했다. 소식이 전보로 이쪽 해안에서 반대쪽 해안까지 갈 수 있었다. 곧 조랑말 속달은 먼 옛 추억이 되고 R.M.W는 20만 달러나 손해를 보았다.

> **Note**
> ☐ last = continue : 계속해서 …하다   • The Korean War lasted 3 years.
> ☐ in 시간 : … 후에   ☐ in a few days : 며칠 후   ☐ in (no) time : 세월가면(즉시)
> ☐ It took many a sleepless night for me to forget her. (내가 그녀를 잊는 데 잠 안 오는 여러 날 밤이 걸렸다.)

17. The Mayas were excellent painters. Many of the temples (1)_____ in the jungle have beautiful pictures (2)_____ on the walls. The Mayas painted with many different colors (3)_____ from plants and minerals. Their paintings show how they lived and what they wore.

 The Incas did not have written (4)_____. Instead, they tied knots in strings to tell the story of their people. The (5)_____ of the string was important. "Yellow" meant "good," "black" for "war," and "white" for "alpaca": a sheep-like animal raised for meat, milk, and fur.

(1) (a) invented   (b) created   (c) initiated   (d) discovered
(2) (a) made   (b) taken   (c) painted   (d) shot
(3) (a) squeezed   (b) made   (c) discovered   (d) drunk
(4) (a) records   (b) tools   (c) brushes   (d) pencils
(5) (a) light   (b) color   (c) shape   (d) weight

18. Who owns the largest American companies which (1)_____ cars, computers, and T.V. sets? They are owned by a large group of people called stockholders. A company needs money to build factories and to purchase machinery. To get this (2)_____, it (3)_____ shares of stock. The person who buys a share of stock becomes a part of the company and becomes a stockholder. A company can have thousands of stockholders. When a company makes money, each (4)_____ may receive a dividend check, which is his share of the (5)_____.

(1) (a) produce   (b) buy   (c) own   (d) consume
(2) (a) profit   (b) money   (c) product   (d) share
(3) (a) sells   (b) buys   (c) produces   (d) donates
(4) (a) company   (b) branch   (c) employee   (d) stockholder
(5) (a) wages   (b) profits   (c) interest   (d) income

19. William Penn (1644 - 1718) could have ruled Pennsylvania given to him by King Charles II of England (1)_____ he were a king. But he did not want to be a king. Being a member of a religious group called Quakers, he decided to (2)_____ his new colony according to Quaker beliefs. He made fair laws; (a) All men, poor or rich, could vote, (b) Members of all religious groups could have the same rights as the Quakers, (c) All children could have some kind of education, (d) Men

17. 마야족은 뛰어난 화가들이었다. 밀림에서 발견된 많은 여러 사원에는 벽에 그린 아름다운 벽화들이 있다. 마야인들은 식물이나 광물에서 얻은 여러가지 색깔로 그림을 그렸다. 그들의 벽화를 보고 그들의 삶의 방식과 의류를 알아 볼 수 있다.

　잉카족은 기록하지 않았지만 대신 그들끼리 의사전달하기 위해 끈으로 매듭을 지었다. 끈의 색깔은 중요했다. 노랑은 훌륭한 것, 검정은 전쟁, 고기와 젖과 모피를 얻으려고 길렀던, 양처럼 생긴 알파카는 흰색으로 나타냈다.

Note
- **the Mayas** : 마야족 – 6세기 경 중앙 아메리카의 인디언의 한 종족. 잉카족과 더불어 인디언 문화의 쌍벽을 이룸.
- **the Incas** : 잉카족 – 남미 페루지방을 점령했던 인디언의 한 종족
- **raise** : 들어 올리다. 재배, 사육하다, 양육하다, (돈을) 모으다.
  - Raise your hand high. (손을 높이 드시오.) • Raise fund for the jobless. (실업 기금을 모으다.)
- **squeeze = press together esp. from opposite sides** : 쥐어 짜다
  - squeeze juice from an orange / squeeze money from mother

18. 자동차, 컴퓨터, 그리고 TV 수상기를 생산하는 가장 큰 미국의 회사들을 소유하고 있는 사람들은 누군가? 그것들은 주주라고 불리는 사람들의 커다란 집단이다. 어떤 회사가 공장을 건설하고 기계를 구입하려면 돈이 필요하다. 이 돈을 마련하기 위하여 그 회사는 지분 주식을 판매한다. 주식을 산 사람은 그 회사의 일부가 되고 주주가 된다. 한 회사는 수천명의 주주를 가질 수 있다. 회사가 돈을 벌 때 각 주주는 배당금을 받는데 이는 그 이윤의 자기 몫이다.

Note
- **own = possess** : 소유하다, **admit** : 자인하다 • Who owns this puppy? (이 강아지 임자가 누구요?)
  - I had to admit I was wrong. (내가 틀렸다는 것을 인정하지 않을 수 없었다.)
- **divide** = 분할하다　　　**divisor** (제수)　　　**dividend** (피제수, 배당 몫)
- **consume = use up completely** : 소비하다, 낭비하다.
  - He consumed all his money on women and drink. (주색에 가산 탕진했다.)
- **stockholder = shareholder** : 주주　　　**stockbroker** : 주식 중개인

19. 윌리암 펜 (1644-1718)은 영국 왕 찰즈 2세가 하사한 펜실베이니아를 마치 왕처럼 통치할 수 있었을 것이다. 그러나 그는 왕이 되기를 원치 않았다. 퀘이커라고 불리는 종교단체의 일원이었기 때문에 그 새 식민지를 퀘이커 신조에 따라 다스리기로 마음 먹었다. 공정한 법을 제정했다. (a)누구나 부자든 가난하든 투표할 수 있고, (b)모든 종교단체의 회원들은 퀘이커교도와 같은 권리를 가질 수 있고, (c)모든 어린이들은 같은 종류의 교육을 받을 수 있고, (d)어떤 죄로 고발 당한 사람들은 배심원단 앞에서 공정한 재판 받기를 바랄 수 있었다.

accused of a crime would have a fair (3)_____ before a jury.

People in Europe listened with (4)_____ to these new ideas. Families from Germany, Sweden, Ireland, Scotland, and England came to America to the new colony. Soon, Pennsylvania's capital (5)_____ to be the largest city in the American colonies. The city was named Philadelphia, which is from a Greek word meaning "Brotherly Love."

(1) (a) like that   (b) as such   (c) as if   (d) such as
(2) (a) control   (b) govern   (c) free   (d) dominate
(3) (a) trial   (b) effort   (c) proof   (d) experiment
(4) (a) boredom   (b) shock   (c) speculation   (d) wonder
(5) (a) diminished   (b) spread   (c) vanished   (d) grew

20. Victor Hugo (1802-1885) opposed French ruler, Louis Napoleon for his dictatorship. As a result, he spent 20 years in exile. But the French regarded Hugo as a champion of democracy and of the common people. He wrote <u>The Hunchback of Notre Dame</u>, <u>Ninety-three</u>, and <u>Les Miserable</u> in which he used the actions of simple characters as a way of (1)_____ moral issues.

The plot of <u>The Hunchback of Notre Dame</u> is that the deformed orphan Quasimodo is abandoned on the steps of the Cathedral of Notre Dame in Paris. He is adopted and raised by a young priest there, Dom Claude Frollo. Quasimodo lives in the church, (2)_____ he rings the bells to signal services. He falls in love with a gypsy dancer, Esmeralda, convicted of murdering her lover, Captain Phoebus. Although being innocent, she is (3)_____ to hang. In a (4)_____ move, Quasimodo saves Esmeralda from hanging and gives her sanctuary in the church. But, Claude Frollo betrays her knowing that she will not love him. Consequently, she is hanged. Quasimodo kills Claude in (5)_____, and disappears. Later, his skeleton is found in the arms of his truly beloved Esmeralda.

(1) (a) explaining   (b) examining   (c) disclosing   (d) researching
(2) (a) where   (b) when   (c) how   (d) why
(3) (a) decided   (b) proclaimed   (c) sentenced   (d) spoken
(4) (a) timid   (b) halfhearted   (c) courageous   (d) coward
(5) (a) gratitude   (b) mercy   (c) retaliation   (d) fear

유럽인들은 이 새로운 착상을 듣고 놀라워 했다. 독일, 스웨덴, 아일랜드, 스코틀랜드, 그리고 잉글랜드에서 많은 가족들이 미국의 이 새 식민지로 왔다. 곧 펜실베이니아의 수도는 미국의 식민지들 중에서 가장 큰 도시가 되었다. 그 도시는 필라델피아로 명명되었는데 이는 '형제의 사랑'이라는 그리스어에서 온 것이다.

Note
- **could have ruled** : 가정법 과거 완료의 조건절 – If he had willed to 가 생략
- **according to** + 명사 • Spend according to your income.
- **according as** + 문장 • Spend according as you earn.
- **colony** : 식민지, 군락지, 집단지 • a colony of Japanese / artists / plants

20. 빅톨 위고는 프랑스의 통치자 나폴레옹을 독재한다는 이유로 반대했다. 그 결과 그는 망명하여 20년을 보냈다. 그러나 프랑스인들은 위고를 민주주의와 일반 사람들을 옹호하여 싸운 투사로서 간주했다. 그는 노트르담의 꼽추와 Ninety-three 그리고 레미제라블을 썼고 그 안에서 도덕문제를 고찰하는 방법으로 단순한 성격의 인물들을 등장시켰다.

　노트르담의 꼽추의 구도는 다음과 같다. 몸이 불구인 고아 콰지모도가 파리의 노트르담 성당 계단에 버려진다. 그는 젊은 신부 돔 클라우드 프롤로의 양자가 되어 양육된다. 그는 성당 안에 살면서 미사를 알리는 종을 친다. 그는 자기 애인 포에버스 대위를 살해한 죄목으로 유죄 판결을 받은 집시 무희 에스메랄다를 사랑하게 된다. 비록 결백했지만 그녀는 교수형 판결을 받는다. 콰지모도는 용감하게 그녀를 구하여 성당 안의 성역권에 숨겨 준다. 그러나 신부는 그녀가 자기를 사랑하지 않으리라는 것을 알고 그녀를 밀고한다. 그 결과 그녀는 교수형을 당한다. 콰지모도는 클라우드를 죽여 복수하고 사라진다. 후에 그의 뼈가 그가 진실로 사랑했던 죽은 에스메랄다의 품안에서 발견된다.

Note
- **exile** - unwanted absence from one's country esp. for political reasons : 귀양, 망명
  - He was sent into exile by the military regime. (군사정권에 의하여 망명당했다.)
- **oppose = object to-act against** : 반대하다　　• opposition party : 야당
  - We opposed building of the new road through the park. (공원을 관통하는 도로건설을 반대했다.)
- **adopt = take someone else's child into one's family** : 양자삼다
  - cf. adapt = change so as to make suitable : 적응시키다　• adapt oneself to : 적응하다
- **innocent = guiltless**　• He was innocent of the crime.
- **sentence = give a punishment to** : 언도하다.
  - He was sentenced to a fine of 5 million won. (그는 5백만원의 벌금형을 선고 받았다.)
- **retaliate = pay back with evil** : 복수하다　□ **sanctuary** : 교회 안의 지성소, 죄인 비호구역

21. How is the President of the United States addressed? Simply (1)_____ "Mr. President." One of the earliest congressional debates dealt with the title of the Chief Executive. A Senate committee recommended that the President (2)_____ addressed, "His Highness, the President of the United States of America, and protector of their liberties." But in the House, a debate on the (3)_____ was climaxed by James Madison's disclosure that the Constitution explicitly prescribed the Chief Magistrate's (4)_____ as "President of the United States of America." "Thus, it came about," writes Henry James Ford, "that the President of the U.S. is distinguished by (5)_____ no title." A governor is addressed as "Your Excellency," a judge as "Your Honor," but the Chief Executive of the Nation is simply, "Mr. President."

(1) (a) as   (b) to   (c) such   (d) for   (e) if
(2) (a) should be (b) be   (c) has to be (d) must be   (e) ought to be
(3) (a) area   (b) fact   (c) subject   (d) idea   (e) ideology
(4) (a) honor   (b) title   (c) job   (d) ownership   (e) domination
(5) (a) having   (b) doing   (c) being   (d) answering   (e) subtracting

22. The recorded history of Cambodia dates (1)_____ to the 1st century A.D., when it was known as Funan (100-500 A.D.). This was followed by the Angkor Period (500-1432) which displayed great accomplishments in culture, arts, and architecture. At its (2)_____, the empire extended from the Annamite Chain (now southern Vietnam) to the Gulf of Thailand.

The temples of Angkor were (3)_____ during the Angkor Period, which has been interpreted as the height of Cambodian domination in Southeast Asia. Angkor Wat one of the largest religious structures in the world, is one of the 7 (4)_____ of the world. A 2$\frac{1}{2}$ mile long moat surrounds the ornamented galleries with five lotus bud towers reaching 215 feet into the sky. Heavenly dancers (5)_____ "Asparas" are carved into walls and pillars. The Cambodians are very proud of these temples as their national treasure.

(1) (a) back   (b) forward   (c) on   (d) from   (e) forth
(2) (a) point   (b) decline   (c) summit   (d) peak   (e) ascension
(3) (a) erected   (b) demolished   (c) destroyed (d) reigned   (e) ruled
(4) (a) villas   (b) temples   (c) spots   (d) beliefs   (e) wonders
(5) (a) danced   (b) carved   (c) called   (d) smiled   (e) remembered

21. 미국 대통령은 어떤 호칭으로 불리나? 단지 "Mr. President"라고 불린다. 최초 국회 토의에서 행정 수반의 호칭을 다루었었다. 어느 상원 위원회는 '자유의 수호자이며 미합중국의 대통령 전하' 로 해야한다고 제안했다. 그러나 하원에서 James Madison의원이 헌법에 명백하게 행정 수반의 명칭을 '미합중국의 대통령' 으로 규정하고 있다고 밝힘으로써 그 안건의 논의는 절정에 달했다. Henry James Ford는 '이리하여 미국 대통령은 호칭을 안 가지는 특징을 갖게 됐다' 고 썼다. 주지사는 '각하' , 판사는 '각하' 라고 호칭되지만 국가의 행정 수반은 단지 'Mr. President' 라고 불린다.

Note
- **Your Majesty** : 폐하
- **Your Highness** : 전하
- **Your Holiness** : 성하
- **Your Excellency** : 각하
- **address = use a particular title or rank**
  - Don't address me as Your Majesty, but simply as 'Mr. President.'
  (날 각하라 부르지 말고 단지 대통령님이라 하시오.)
- **Congress** : 상, 하원 통칭
- **The House of the Senate** : 상원
- **The House of the Representative** : 하원
- **explicitly** : 명백하게 • opp. implicitly : 함축적으로

22. 캄보디아의 기록된 역사는 기원 1세기까지 거슬러 올라간다. 그때 그곳은 푸난으로 알려져 있었다. 이 나라 뒤에 문화, 예술 그리고 건축에서 위대한 업적을 발휘한 앙코르 시대가 뒤를 이었다. 전성기 때 그 제국은 지금의 남부 베트남인 Annamite Chain에서 타이만 까지 뻗어 있었다.

앙코르 사원들은 앙코르시대 동안에 세워졌고 이 시기를 캄보디아가 동남 아시아를 가장 강력하게 지배했던 때로 해석되고 있다. 세계에서 가장 커다란 종교 구조물의 하나인 앙코르와트는 세계 7대 불가사의 중의 하나다. 길이 2½마일의 해자(垓字)가 높이 215피트의 5개 연꽃 봉오리 팁으로 장식을 가진 맨 꼭내기 관람석을 에워싸고 있다. 아스파라스 라고 불리는 천상의 무희들이 벽과 기둥에 조각 되어 있다. 캄보디아인들은 이 사원들을 그들의 국보로서 매우 자랑스러워 한다.

Note
- **date back to = date from** : ~시대 부터 시작된다. • This custom dates back to the 14th century.
- **A is followed by B = B follows A** : A 뒤에 B가 따른다.
  - The war was followed by poverty and diseases. (전쟁 뒤에 가난과 질병이 따랐다.)
- **demolish = destroy, tear down** : 파괴, 타파하다.
  - They're going to demolish that Japanese building.
- **gallery** : 화랑, 맨 꼭대기 관람석, 하급 관람객, 테니스, 골프 고객

23. Because African languages, with only a few (1)_____, were not written, the Africans handed (2)_____ the record of a tribe's accomplishments orally. Oral history gradually became a very highly developed (3)_____ of expression. The legends, folklore, epic tales, and dynastic histories of every tribe were woven into stylized, musical recitations and were carried (4)_____ a region by tribal bards, musicians and singers and professional storytellers who wandered (5)_____ village to village.

(1) (a) rules   (b) regulations   (c) choices   (d) exceptions   (e) regularities
(2) (a) to   (b) down   (c) up   (d) over   (e) off
(3) (a) form   (b) condition   (c) deformity   (d) amorphism   (e) defacement
(4) (a) by   (b) throughout   (c) over   (d) into   (e) around
(5) (a) from   (b) to   (c) for   (d) by   (e) in

Some tribes, notably the Malinke of Mali, used drama as the (6)_____ for their tribal lore and regularly presented their plays both within their family circles and on a (7)____ organized basis for viewing. The singers and bards who recited the ancient legends were black Africa's official historians. Their position (8)_____ considerable training and skill, for their stories and chants were the record of their people's (9)_____ and demanded not only considerable musical ability but also (10)_____ memory and ability to teach all their learning to their chosen successors.

(Source: Clifford, L. Mary & Edward S. Ross (1971). The Creative African: Artists and Craftsmen.)

(6) (a) medium   (b) organ   (c) average   (d) project   (e) meditation
(7) (a) less   (b) little   (c) least   (d) much   (e) more
(8) (a) requested (b) required   (c) received   (d) regained   (e) retreated
(9) (a) past   (b) present   (c) future   (d) style   (e) time
(10) (a) limited   (b) outstanding (c) meager   (d) powerless (e) colorful

24. There was a time when the world was cold because there was no fire. The animals knew (1)_____ the fire was, but they couldn't get to it. They could see the smoke (2)_____ from the fire. It was at the bottom of a tree on an island. The animals wanted the fire, but they didn't know (3)_____ to get to it because of the water. They held a council to decide (4)_____ should try to go after it.

(1) (a) when   (b) how   (c) where   (d) why   (e) what
(2) (a) rise   (b) rising   (c) come   (d) climb (e) grow
(3) (a) how   (b) when   (c) where   (d) why   (e) what
(4) (a) how   (b) when   (c) where   (d) why   (e) who

First the Raven offered to go. He was so big and so strong (5)_____ the animals were sure he could get the fire. But Raven came back (6)_____ it. After that many animals tried to bring back the fire. They all failed. At (7)_____ Water Spider said that she would go. Water Spider could run on top of the water or

23. 아프리카 언어들은 몇 개의 예외를 빼고 문자로 쓰여지지 않았고, 그들 종족의 업적을 구두로 전했다. 역사를 구전으로 전하기는 점차 매우 발달된 표현 형식이 되었다. 전설, 민담, 서사적 이야기, 그리고 모든 왕조의 역사가 양식을 갖춘 음악적 낭송물로 짜여졌고, 전국을 마을에서 마을로 떠돌아다니는 종족의 음유시인, 음악가, 가수 그리고 전문적 이야기꾼에 의하여 한 지역에 전달되었다.

몇몇 종족들 특히 Mail의 Malinke족은 연극을 그들 종족의 민담을 알리는 매체로 사용하고 규칙적으로 그들 연극을 가족 집단이나 관람을 위해서 조직된 보다 큰 단위에게 제공했다.

고대 전설을 읊고 다니는 가수나 음유시인들은 흑인 아프리카의 공적인 역사가들이었다. 그들의 지위는 상당한 수련과 기능을 필요로 했다. 왜냐하면 그 이야기나 음송내용은 그들 국민의 과거기록 이고 상당한 음악적 재능뿐 아니라 그들의 학식을 선발된 후임자들에게 가르쳐 줄 뛰어난 기억력과 능력을 필요로 했기 때문이다.

Note
- epic : 서사시 • opp. lyric : 서정시 □oral = spoken, not written : 구두의
- recite : 암송하다 • recitation : 암송(문) • recital : 독주(창)회
- style = manner, fashion • What style of house do you want? □bard = minstrel : 음유시인
- tribe = a group of people of the same race, beliefs, language : 종족, 부족
- weave : (베를) 짜다, 구성하다 • He wove a play from a few facts in a history book.
- hand down : 후손에게 물려주다 • hand over : 소유권을 넘겨주다
- dynasty = a line of rulers of the same family : Yi dynasty : 이조
- notable : especial, noticeable : 특별한, 두드러진
- chant : 단순한 음조로 계속 소리 지르다 • The demonstrators chanted, "More job, more money."
- official : 공적인, 공인된 • official document (funds, record) : 공문서(공금,공식 기록)

24. 불이 없어서 세계가 추웠던 때가 있었다. 동물들은 불이 있는 곳은 알았지만 그 불이 있는 곳에 도달할 수 없었다. 그들 눈에는 불에서 피어 오르는 연기가 보였다. 그 불은 섬에 있는 어느 나무 밑동에 있었다. 동물들은 불이 필요했지만 물 때문에 그 불에 가까이 갈 수 있는 방법을 몰랐다. 그들은 누가 불을 가지러 가야할 것인가를 정하기 위하여 회의를 개최했다.

첫째로 갈까마귀가 가겠다고 자청했다. 그는 매우 크고 힘이 세서 동물들은 그가 불을 가져 오리라고 확신했다. 그러나 그는 가져오지 못했다. 그 후 많은 동물들이 불을 가져오려고 했으나 모두 실패했다. 마침내 수상거미가 가겠다고 말했다. 그녀는 물위를 달리거나 물밑으로 잠수할 수 있었다. 그녀는 섬에 도달했다. 그러나 어떻게 그 불을 가져

dive to the bottom. She could get to the island. But how could she bring back the fire?

(5) (a) such   (b) that   (c) too   (d) as   (e) if
(6) (a) but   (b) with   (c) without   (d) except   (e) not
(7) (a) most   (b) least   (c) last   (d) best   (e) worst

Water Spider spun a thread from her body. She wove it into a bowl (8)_____ she fastened to her back. Then she went to the island. She put one little coal of (9)_____ into the bowl and came back with it. Ever (10)_____, there has been fire. And the Water Spider has her bowl!

(Source: Told by the Cherokee Indians)

(8) (a) who   (b) which   (c) what   (d) when   (e) how
(9) (a) fire   (b) ash   (c) soot   (d) smoke   (e) flint
(10)(a) before   (b) ago   (c) since   (d) now   (e) then

25. The year? 1932! The place? Calcutta! Situation? The British did not know how to (1)_____ with the Indian protesters who refused to work in British factories or to pay their taxes. The British Governor-General (2)_____ Mr. Gandhi, and blurted out, "Mr. Gandhi, (3)_____ do you really want from us?"

(1) (a) deal   (b) solve   (c) distribute   (d) allot   (e) give
(2) (a) demanded   (b) called   (c) assisted   (d) asked   (e) presented
(3) (a) how   (b) which   (c) what   (d) where   (e) when

"We British have (4)_____ law, order, sanitation, and industry to your country. We have given you our best people and our finest ideas. All of this has been done at great personal (5)_____ to the British people. (6)___, you are not grateful. You refuse to (7)_____ with us."

(4) (a) produced   (b) brought   (c) purchased   (d) fixed   (e) imported
(5) (a) benefit   (b) merit   (c) favor   (d) cost   (e) attention
(6) (a) Because   (b) As   (c) Since   (d) Besides   (e) Yet
(7) (a) obstruct   (b) plot   (c) cooperate   (d) approve   (e) promote

The Governor-General had become red-faced. He pounded the desk, "(8)_____ a 100 years, we British, have done practically everything for you Indians!" Gandhi shook his head sadly. He (9)_____, "That, sir, is the supreme (10)_____ that you have committed against my people."

(Source: Adapted from "The Supreme Crime." Enjoying Global History (1996).)

(8) (a) During   (b) For   (c) Since   (d) As   (e) After
(9) (a) screamed   (b) yelled   (c) replied   (d) growled   (e) denounced
(10)(a) crime   (b) sin   (c) grace   (d) virtue   (e) benevolence

올 수 있겠는가?

수상거미는 몸에서 실을 뽑아 냈다. 그 실로 그릇을 짜서 등에 묶었다. 그 후 섬에 가서 불 붙은 석탄 하나를 그 그릇 속에 집어 넣어 가지고 돌아 왔다. 그 이후 불이 존재했고 수상거미는 그릇을 가지고 있는 것이다.

Note
- council = a group of people appointed or elected to make laws : 평의회
- call (hold) a meeting : 회의를 소집 (개최)하다.
- spin = to make thread by twisting cotton, wool : 실을 잣다
- Water Spider : 수상거미 – 수표면 바로 아래 종 모양의 집을 짓고 그 속에 지상에서 가져 간 공기를 물거품 모양으로 채워 둠
- crow : 까마귀   □ raven : 큰 (갈)까마귀   • cf. magpie : 까치

---

25. 때는? 1932년! 장소는? 캘커타! 상황은?

영국인들은 영국인 공장에서 일하기를 거부하고 세금 납부도 거부하는 인도인 반항자들을 어떻게 다루어야 할지 몰랐다. 영국 총독은 간디에게 전화를 걸어 불쑥 말을 꺼냈다. "간디 선생, 당신들이 진정으로 우리에게 바라는 것이 무엇이오?

우리 영국인들은 법과 질서, 위생시설 그리고 공업을 당신 나라에 가져다 주었소. 우리는 우리의 가장 유능한 사람들과 가장 훌륭한 아이디어를 당신들에게 제공해 왔소. 이 모든 것은 영국인의 개인적인 경비로 마련된 것이오. 그러나 당신들은 고마워하지 않소. 당신들은 우리와 협동하기를 거부하고 있소."

총독은 얼굴이 상기됐다. 그는 책상을 치면서 "100년 간 우리 영국인들은 당신들 인도인들을 위해서 실질적으로 모든 일을 다 했소!"

간디는 비탄스럽게 고개를 저었다. 그는 "그것이 당신들이 나의 국민에게 저지른 가장 커다란 죄악이오."라고 대꾸했다.

Note
- Governor - General : 식민지 총독
- blurt = say suddenly and without thinking : 불쑥 말하다
  • She blurted out that she would not marry him.
- commit = do something wrong, unlawful(저지르다) - commit crime, sin, an error : 저지르다
  • cf. make a mistake (blunder)
- sanitation = means for protecting public health esp. by removing and treatment of waste : 위생, 보건
- pound = strike or beat repeatedly   • My heart pounds with excitement.

2-5 LOCATING THE FACTS / ANSWERS

"Locating the facts / answers" is designed for the readers to develop skills in recalling factual information rather than opinionated ones from the target reading materials. Of course, recalling factual information does not come in an easy way; it needs a lot of practice with consistent reading habits.

To improve the skills in recalling factual information, the readers are advised to identify the main idea or topic supported by a variety of detailed facts. Then, the specific factual information supporting or describing the main idea/topic or the sub-idea in order will be better recalled.

EXERCISE:

Read the following paragraph or passage, and choose the best answer based on your memory. Do not re-read the passage, and choose the best answer as quickly as possible, which will help improve your memory span.

1. Birds are all around you. There are many kinds of birds in a city. There are many more birds in the country. Farm fields and the woods are good places for birds.
   Your own window or yard can be a good place for birds. But you have to ask them to come. You can ask them to come by putting out food and water.
   But don't think birds will come within two minutes after you put out food for the first time. You may have to wait a week. Then the birds will come, one following another.

(1) The places where you can see birds are

    (a) city and town   (c) city and country
    (b) country and village   (d) all around you where you are

(2) One of the good ways of loving or befriending birds is

    (a) shooting   (c) providing them with food and water
    (b) taking pictures   (d) ask them to come by whistling

(3) Birds will come to you if you

    (a) throw a party for them   (c) wait a week
    (b) put out food and wait   (d) ask them to come

2-5 사실 및 정답 찾기

"사실 및 정답 찾기"는 독자들이 읽으려 하는 글에서 이미 주장된 정보보다 사실적 정보를 기억하는 기술을 개발하는 데 있다. 물론 이 기능은 쉽게 얻어지는 것이 아니고 일관된 독서 습관으로 많이 연습하는 것을 필요로 한다.

사실적 정보를 기억하는 기능을 키우기 위해서 독자들은 상세한 사실들이 다양하게 뒷받침 하는 요지와 주제를 찾아내는 게 좋다. 그러면, 요지나 주제 혹은 부제를 순서대로 지지하거나 서술하는 구체적인 정보가 더 잘 기억될 것이다.

다음 문단이나 문절을 읽고 당신의 기억을 토대로 가장 좋은 답을 선택하라. 글을 다시 읽지 말고 가능한 빨리 골라라. 그러면 기억의 폭을 넓히는데 도움이 될 것이다.

Note

- **locate** = (1) find the position of : …의 위치를 알아내다
  - I located the nearest subway station as soon as I arrived.
  - (도착 즉시 가장 가까운 지하철역의 위치부터 알아냈다.)
  - (2) fix or set in a certain place : …에 위치시키다.
  - Our dormitory is located next to the library. (기숙사는 도서관 바로 옆에 있다.)
- **recall** = (1) remember : I can't recall what was said then.
  - (2) call or take back : 소환하다 • The ambassador to Russia was recalled.
  - (3) 상품의 리콜
- **opinionated** : 자기 의견이 옳다고 주장하는   **consistent** : 변함 없는, 일관된, 앞 뒤가 맞는
- **a variety of** = various   **in order** : …의 순서대로
  - Line up the boys in order of height. (키 순서로 줄 세워라.)
- **span** = a length of time • life span, memory span, eye span, the span of one's arm

2.　An incubator is a type of oven. The first incubator was heated with oil lamps and had to be looked after carefully. The danger was that they might get too warm or too cold.

　　Most incubators today are heated with electricity. It is easy to keep them at an even temperature. For chickens, the temperature is kept around 120 degrees Fahrenheit. The eggs are turned from time to time so that they are heated evenly all over. The air inside the incubator should be kept fresh and moist as well as warm.

　　A different kind of incubator is found in hospitals. These incubators are for babies who are abnormally tiny and weak when they are born. They are also for babies born prematurely. These babies must be kept warm as they were when they were still inside their mothers' bodies.

(1) The first incubator was heated by

　　(a) oil　　　　(b) oil lamp　　　　(c) gas　　　　(d) coal

(2) Incubators should maintain the temperature around 120 degrees Fahrenheit for hatching

　　(a) chickens　　(b) ostriches　　(c) hummingbirds　　(d) geese

(3) The incubators used in hospitals are for _____ babies.

　　(a) premature　　(c) sick　　(b) tiny and weak　　(d) tiny, weak, and premature

3.　The Industrial Revolution began in Great Britain. The new inventions helped many British people earn more money.

　　At first, the British tried to keep their inventions a secret. But they could not stop the Revolution from spreading to other parts of the world. Soon it spread to the rest of Europe and to the United States. Later, it spread to other parts of the world.

　　The Revolution changed the ways people all over the world lived and worked. Some changes made life better; whereas, others caused problems.

(1) The country where the Industrial Revolution started is

　　(a) England　　(b) France　　(c) U.S.A.　　(d) Germany

(2) The British could not stop the Revolution from

　　(a) secrecy　　(b) spending　　(c) expanding　　(d) covering

(3) The impact created by the Revolution on the people of the world was in the way of

　　(a) living and working anew　　　　(c) making life better
　　(b) standard of living for the better or worse　　(d) causing serious problems

4.　Many people think that the most typical American foods are steak, baked potato, hot dog, green salad, pizza, haogie, and hamburger. For drink, there are Coca Cola, Pepsi, and coffee; and for dessert, apple pie, carrot cake along with ice cream.

　　Americans often eat the aforementioned foods, and they enjoy these foods. Steak house restaurants and pizza parlors are very popular. During the warm summer season, many American families enjoy backyard barbecues while cooking steaks, hot dogs, chicken, and pork on charcoal or gas grills. But it is very difficult to name typical American foods.

　　The United States of America, the fourth largest country in the world, includes a

1. 새들은 우리 주변 어디나 있다. 도시에 여러 종류의 새들이 있다. 시골에는 더 많은 새들이 있다. 농경지나 숲은 새들이 살기에 좋은 장소들이다.

당신의 창문이나 뜰도 새들에겐 좋은 장소다. 그러나 새들을 오라고 요청해야 한다. 먹이나 물을 내주면 새들을 오게 할 수 있다.

그러나 당신이 처음으로 먹이를 내준 후 2분 이내에 새들이 오리라고 기대하지 말라. 일주일은 기다려야 한다. 그러면 새들이 차례로 올 것이다.

2. 인큐베이터는 솥의 한 가지 형태다. 최초의 인큐베이터는 기름 램프로 가열되었고 주의 깊게 돌봐야 했다. 너무 뜨거워지거나 너무 차거워질 위험이 있었다.

오늘날 대부분의 인큐베이터는 전기로 가열된다. 그것은 균등한 온도를 유지하기가 쉽기 때문이다. 병아리를 위해서는 화씨 120도를 유지한다. 달걀들은 전체가 균등하게 가열되도록 때때로 회전시킨다. 내부 공기는 따뜻해야 할 뿐 아니라 신선하고 습도를 유지해야 한다.

병원에는 다른 종류의 인큐베이터가 있다. 이는 태어날 때 비정상적으로 작거나 약한 영아를 위한 것이다. 또한 조산아를 위해서도 쓰인다. 이 영아들은 그들이 아직 엄마 뱃속에 있었던 때와 같은 온도를 유지해야 한다.

Note
- incubator = a machine for keeping eggs warm until they hatch : 부화기
- alive premature babies : 조산아 보육기
- even = level, regular : 고른, 규칙적인 • Her teeth were even and white.
- moist = slightly wet • moist eyes with tears
- hatch = break letting the young bird out : 부화하다, (n) 잠수함·비행기의 출입구 덮개

3. 산업혁명은 영국에서 시작되었다. 새로운 발명품들은 많은 영국인들이 돈을 버는 데 도움을 주었다.

처음에 영국인들은 그들의 발명품들을 비밀로 숨기려고 했다. 그러나 산업혁명이 세계의 다른 지역으로 퍼져 나가는 것을 막지 못했다. 얼마되지 않아 그것은 유럽의 다른 지역과 미국으로 퍼져 나갔고, 그 후 세계의 다른 지역으로 퍼져 나갔다.

이 혁명은 전 세계 사람들의 생활, 작업 방식을 변화 시켰다. 어떤 변화는 삶을 개선시켰지만 다른 것들은 문제를 야기시켰다.

variety of ethnic and cultural groups from almost every corner of the world. Like its people, American food comes from everywhere. Therefore, it is difficult to name typical American food. Typical American food is the one that came from another country.

(1) Typical American drinks are
    (a) steak, Coca Cola   (b) pizza, coffee   (c) apple pie, Pepsi   (d) soda and coffee

(2) In summer, American people cook meat outside on the
    (a) oven   (b) fireplace   (c) microwave oven   (d) gas/charcoal grills

(3) Typical American foods are those that came with the people from
    (a) Asia   (b) Europe   (c) their own motherlands   (d) Africa

5.   One of the American Indian tribes, the Osages, lived as hunters and gatherers. The men of this tribe hunted deer, turkey, skunk, and buffalo which provided them with food, clothing utensils and shelter. The women stayed home. Sometimes they gathered walnuts, pecans, acorns, and other nuts for food. They grew corn, squash, beans, pumpkins, and potatoes. Corn was their staple food, just as rice is the staple for Asians and wheat for Europeans.
    The Osages met the French, the first Europeans, in 1673. From then, their lives became different. They traded with the French, and received guns, metal utensils, tools, and alcoholic drinks. Later, they got horses through trade with the Europeans. In return, the Osages gave furs and slaves to the Europeans who sold furs in Europe, and slaves in the Caribbean.
    The Europeans found a land of wide open spaces. They kept pushing west without thinking about the rights of the Native Americans. The Osages were forced to move west many times over 200 years. They went to Missouri, to Arkansas, and to Kansas. They signed many peace or other treaties with the U.S. Government, which was not honored by the Government. By 1839, Native Americans were living on reservations set aside for them by the Government. In 1872, there were nearly 4,000 Osages living on the reservation in Oklahoma. There is still an Osage reservation in that state.

(1) One of the hunted animals that provided the Osages with the most meat and shelter was
    (a) deer   (b) buffalo   (c) skunk   (d) turkey

(2) One of the vegetables grown by the Osages was
    (a) corn   (b) pecan   (c) acorn   (d) walnut

(3) When the Osages first met the white people in 1673, they
    (a) traded   (b) fought   (c) received horses   (d) gave furs

(4) One of the commodities that the Osages got from the white people through trade was
    (a) whiskey   (b) slave   (c) fur   (d) corn

(5) Who did not honor the peace agreements?
    (a) Osages   (b) Native Americans   (c) French Government   (d) U.S. Government

(6) Which state should you go to visit the Osages now?
    (a) Missouri   (b) Kansas   (c) Oklahoma   (d) Arkansas

> **Note**
> □ **stop from** : 못하게 막다. • Nobody could stop him from gambling.
> □ **whereas = but, though** • She is slender, whereas her sister is fat.

4. 가장 전형적인 미국의 식품이 스테이크, 구운 감자, 핫도그, 녹색 샐러드, 피자, 샌드위치, 그리고 햄버거라고 생각하는 사람들이 많다. 음료는 코카콜라, 펩시, 커피가 있고 후식으로는 사과파이, 아이스크림과 함께 당근 케익이 있다.

  미국인들은 앞에 말한 식품을 자주 먹고 또 좋아한다. 스테이크점과 피자점들이 대단히 인기가 있다. 더운 여름날에는 뒤뜰에서 숯이나 가스 석쇠에 스테이크, 핫도그, 닭고기, 돼지고기를 요리하며 바베큐를 즐긴다. 그러나 전형적인 미국 식품의 명칭을 말하기는 어렵다. 넓이가 세계 제4대 국가인 미국은 세계의 거의 모든 지역에서 온 다양한 인종과 문화 집단을 포함하고 있다. 미국의 국민처럼 미국의 식품도 모든 지역에서 왔다.

  그러므로 전형적인 미국 음식의 이름을 말하기는 어렵다. 전형적인 음식은 바로 다른 나라에서 온 것이다.

> **Note**
> □ **hot dog** : 롤 빵에 구운 소시지를 넣어 만든 것   □ **barbecue** : 소, 돼지 바다가제 등의 야외 통 구이(틀)
> □ **grill** : 고기, 생선을 굽는 석쇠
> □ **name = say what the name of** : 이름을 말하다 • Can you name this plant?
> □ **give the name to** : 명명하다 • The new couple named their first baby John.
> □ **ethnic** : 인종의 • cf. ethic : 윤리의   □ **cultural and ethnic ties** : 문화적, 인종적 유대
> □ **haogie = submarine** : (미국 북부의) 샌드위치

5. 미국 인디언의 한 부족인 오세이지족은 수렵과 열매 채취로 살았다. 이 부족 사람들은 그들에게 먹을 것과 입을 것을 공급해 주는 사슴, 칠면조, 스컹크, 물소를 사냥했다. 여인들은 집에 있었다. 때때로 호두, 페칸, 상수리와 같은 식용 열매를 수집했다. 그들은 옥수수, 스쿼쉬, 콩, 호박과 감자를 재배했다. 쌀이 아시아인들에게, 밀이 유럽인들에게 주곡이듯이 옥수수는 그들의 주곡이었다.

오세이지족들은 1673년에 최초의 유럽인인 프랑스인들을 만났다. 그때부터 이들의 생활은 달라졌다. 그들은 프랑스인들과 교역하여 총과 도구, 금속 연장, 그리고 알콜 음료를 받아들였다. 후에 유럽인들과의 교역에서 말을 얻었다. 그 대가로 오세이지족은 유럽에서 모피를 팔고 카리브해에서 노예를 파는 유럽인들에게 모피와 노예를 제공했다.

6. The research laboratories of the automobile industry are continually experimenting with new ideas to improve our cars, and greater improvements are expected in the future. In 1925, the average life of a car was $6\frac{1}{2}$ years, and it had been driven less than 26,000 miles when it was junked. In contrast, cars junked today have had an average life of $11\frac{1}{2}$ years and have been driven an average of 110,000 miles. Credit for this great improvement can be given not only to manufacturers, but also to mechanics for better service and to drivers who have learned proper car maintenance.

With the increasing number of automobiles, it is easy to see why there are so many job opportunities in the automobile industry. In the service field, additional jobs open up each year for automobile mechanics and specialists, shop foremen, service managers, parts managers, and service station operators. With a background of automobile service and an interest in selling, the automobile dealers offer positions such as car salesman and sales manager. Automobile parts stores likewise require salesmen who had a background of service experience. Besides these, there are many jobs such as truck or bus drivers, car insurance adjusters, and technical instructors in which training in automobile service is an advantage. The job opportunities mentioned above are only a few of the many possibilities in the automobile industry and its related fields.

(1) In 1925, the average life of a car was

　　(a) $5\frac{1}{2}$ years　　(b) $6\frac{1}{2}$ years　　(c) $7\frac{1}{2}$ years　　(d) $8\frac{1}{2}$ years

(2) The average life of a car today is

　　(a) $9\frac{1}{2}$ years　　(b) $10\frac{1}{2}$ years　　(c) $11\frac{1}{2}$ years　　(d) $12\frac{1}{2}$ years

(3) Today's car improvements are due to the contribution from

　　(a) driver, mechanic, salesman　　(c) manufacturer, mechanic, driver
　　(b) mechanic, driver, specialist　　(d) manufacturer, driver, sales manager

(4) The person responsible for proper automobile maintenance of his own car is

　　(a) driver　　(b) salesman　　(c) mechanic　　(d) manufacturer

(5) The job related to the automobile service field is

　　(a) truck driver　　(b) bus driver　　(c) insurance adjuster　　(d) mechanic

(6) The job related to the automobile sales field is

　　(a) mechanic　　(b) manufacturer　　(c) service manager　　(d) sales manager

(7) If you want to learn how to drive a car, then you need

　　(a) mechanic　　(b) car salesman　　(c) technical instructor　　(d) manufacturer

(8) The job related to the automobile industry is

　　(a) insurance adjuster　　(b) seamstress　　(c) plumber　　(d) welder

유럽인들은 넓은 공지를 발견했다. 그들은 토착 원주민들의 권리는 생각하지 않고 계속 서쪽으로 밀고 나갔다. 오세이지족은 200년에 걸쳐서 여러 차례 서쪽으로 이동해야 했다. 그들은 미주리, 아칸소, 캔사스로 이동했다. 그들은 미국과 평화조약 등 다른 많은 조약을 체결했지만 정부는 이를 지키지 않았다. 1839년까지 아메리카 원주민들은 정부가 설정한 인디안 보호지구에서 살았다. 1872년에 오클라호마에서 사는 원주민들의 수는 거의 4,000명이었다. 지금 아직도 오클라호마에는 오세이지 보호 구역이 있다.

Note
- utensil = an object for use in a particular way : 도구
- kitchen utensils : 주방기구
- pecan : 북미 원산의 히커리 열매, 가루는 식용
- acorn : 도토리 등 깍지가 있는 열매
- squash : 호박류
- staple = something, esp. a food that forms the most important part : 주곡
- treaty = formal agreement : 조약
- sign a treaty : 조약을 체결하다
- honor : 지키다. 지불하다
- dishonored cheque : 부도수표
- reservation : 공공 보유지, 보호구
- military (school, Indian) reservation : 군사 (학교, 인디안) 보호구역

6. 자동차 산업의 연구 실험실은 차를 개량하기 위하여 계속 새로운 아이디어를 실험하고 있고 앞으로 커다란 개량이 기대되고 있다. 1925년에 차의 평균 수명은 6년 반이었고 주행거리 26,000마일이면 못쓰게 되었다. 대조적으로 오늘날의 차는 평균 수명이 11년 반이고 평균 110,000마일을 주행하고 있다. 이 개량의 공로는 자동차 제조인뿐 아니라 보다 낳은 서비스를 하는 기계공과 적절한 차 유지 관리를 해 온 운전자에게로 돌릴 수 있다.

차의 수가 증가함에 따라 자동차 업계에 왜 그토록 많은 일자리가 있는지 이해하기 쉽다. 서비스 분야에서 매년 자동차 기계공이나 전문가, 작업장 감독, 서비스 지배인, 부품 관리자, 주유소 기사 등의 일자리 기회가 열리고 있다. 자동차 서비스와 판매에 대한 관심을 배경으로, 자동차 판매상들은 자동차 판매원, 판매 과장 같은 지위를 제공하고 있다.

자동차 부품가게도 마찬가지로 서비스 경험을 가진 판매인들을 필요로 한다. 이외에도 트럭이나, 버스 운전 기사, 보험 사정인, 기술을 가르치는 교사같은 자동차 관련 업무에 훈련 경험이 있으면 유리한, 많은 일자리가 있다. 위에서 언급한 일자리들은 자동차 산업과 관련 분야에 있는 많은 기회들 중 단지 소수일 뿐이다.

7. Mikolaj Kopernik (1473-1543), the founder of modern astronomy is generally known by his Latin name, Copernicus. He completed mathematical and astronomical studies at Cracow University, and then studied law and medicine at Bologna, Ferrara, and Padua in Italy. Returning from Italy, he practiced medicine at Lidzbark and Frombork.

He spent the rest of his life at Frombork where he became absorbed in the observation of celestial bodies, using instruments he constructed. He discovered and proved the heliocentric system, upsetting the medieval notion that the earth was the center of the universe. His theory was expounded in his life's work, De revolutionibus orbium coelestium (The Revolutions of the Celestial Orbs), the first copy of which, printed at Nuremberg, he received on his deathbed on May 24, 1543. His theory claimed that the apparent motions can be interpreted very simply by supposing that the planets revolve around the sun, and that the earth itself is merely one of the planets.

Copernicus' discovery was truly revolutionary and up until the end of the 16th century was officially considered as "heretical." The Copernican concept was later corroborated by the German astronomer, Johannes Kepler (1571-1630) and formed the basis for the law of gravity, discovered by the English scientist, Issac Newton (1642-1727).

(Source: Poland (1971). Zieleniewicz, Andrzej. Center for Polish Studies and Culture)

(1) At Cracow University, Copernicus studied

    (a) medicine, law   (c) mathematics, law
    (b) mathematics, astronomy   (d) medicine, astronomy

(2) The cities where he practiced medicine are

    (a) Warsaw, Cracow   (c) Lidzbark, Frombork
    (b) Bologna, Ferrara   (d) Padua, Ferrara

(3) The city where he observed celestial bodies is

    (a) Cracow   (b) Ferrara   (c) Lidzbark   (d) Frombork

(4) His publication, The Revolutions of the Celestial Orbs, brought him

    (a) fame   (c) official recognition
    (b) a change of medieval claim   (d) rejection from both church and university

(5) "The planets revolve around the sun, and the earth is one of the planets" was claimed by him in

    (a) 1473   (b) 1543   (c) 1571   (d) 1630

(6) The scientist who first supported Copernicus' theory with assurance was

    (a) Kepler   (b) Newton   (c) Ptolemy   (d) Einstein

(7) Copernicus' theory was officially considered as "_____" until the end of the 16th century.

    (a) "scientific"   (b) "true"   (c) "inaccurate"   (d) "unacceptable and ungodly"

> **Note**
> ☐ research = advanced systematic study : 고급, 체계적인 연구
> ☐ experiment(vi) on : …에 관하여 실험하다
> ☐ experiment with : 관련된 연구   • experiment with medicine
> ☐ junk = become useless   ☐ junked : 폐차시켜 내버리다.
> ☐ credit : 영광, 공로   • This credit goes to my father. (이 영광을 아버님께 돌립니다.)

7. 현대 천문학의 아버지 Mikolaj Koperinik는 대개 그의 라틴어 이름인 코페르니쿠스로 알려져 있다. 그는 Cracow 대학에서 수학과 천문학 연구를 마치고 이탈리아의 볼로냐, 페라라, 파두아에서 법과 의학을 연구했다. 이탈리아에서 돌아온 후 Lidzbark와 Frombork에서 의사 개업을 했다.

그는 여생을 Frombork에서 그가 만든 기구로 천체를 관찰하는 데 몰두하며 보냈다. 그는 태양계를 발견, 증명하였고 지구가 우주의 중심이라는 중세의 생각을 뒤엎었다. 그의 학설은 뉘른베르크에서 인쇄되어 1543년 5월24일 그의 임종 때 주어진 생애의 역작 De revolutionibus orbium coelestium (천체의 회전)안에 설명되어 있다. 그의 학설은 외형적인 천체의 운동은 혹성들이 태양의 주위를 공전하며, 지구도 그 혹성들 중 하나일 뿐이라고 생각하면 아주 간단히 해석할 수 있다고 주장했다.

코페르니쿠스의 발견은 실로 혁명적이어서 16세기까지 공식적으로 이단으로 간주되었다. 코페르니쿠스 개념은 후에 독일 천문학자 케플러에 의하여 보강되었고 영국 과학자 아이작 뉴돈이 발견한 중력의 법칙에 대한 토대가 되었다.

> **Note**
> ☐ practice = do the work of a doctor or lawyer : 개업하다
>   • practice medicine (law) = practice as a doctor (lawyer)
> ☐ absorb = suck in : 흡수하다
> ☐ take up all the attention : 몰두시키다
>   • Use the cloth to absorb the spilled milk.   • He is being absorbed in gardening of wild plants.
> ☐ heliocentric : 태양중심의   • opp. geocentric (지구 중심의)
> ☐ upset = knock over : 화나게 하다, 교란시키다

8. Nelson Mandela was born in South Africa in 1918. His father being a tribal chief of an ethnic group, trained Nelson to be a tribal chief. But, Nelson chose to go to college to become a lawyer.

In 1944, Nelson joined the African National Congress (ANC), the largest Black group against the South African Government. He led protests against the Government, which led to his arrest in 1956. But he was found not guilty and was released. In 1960, the Government enacted the law which outlawed the ANC. Nelson led more protests against the Government, which led to his arrest in 1962. This time, however, was found guilty and was sent to prison for life.

Nelson as a symbol of the protest against the apartheid drew attentions from many people around the world. They consistently called for his release. More protests were held in South Africa, which led to the sociopolitical instability of that country. In 1989, the President of South Africa met with Nelson to work together for peace, which Nelson agreed. The Government allowed people to be members of the ANC, and Nelson was released from prison in 1990.

Nelson Mandela worked with the Government to create a new constitution. In 1994, both Blacks and Whites voted in the nation's first free election, and Nelson was elected president. He became the nation's first Black president. Nelson helped South Africa terminate apartheid and move toward democracy.

(Source: Adapted from World History and You. Bernstein, Vivian (1997).)

(1) Nelson Mandela's father was a
   (a) driver   (b) chief   (c) lawyer   (d) trainer

(2) Nelson went to the school of
   (a) law   (b) medicine   (c) engineering   (d) teaching

(3) Nelson became a member of the ANC in
   (a) 1944   (b) 1956   (c) 1960   (d) 1962

(4) The year when the Government outlawed the ANC was
   (a) 1944   (b) 1956   (c) 1960   (d) 1962

(5) The year Nelson was sentenced for life was
   (a) 1944   (b) 1956   (c) 1960   (d) 1962

(6) One of the reasons Nelson drew attention from many people was that he
   (a) was a symbol of justice against injustice   (c) worked with the Government
   (b) protested many times   (d) was released from prison

(7) Nelson and the President met together for
   (a) economic stability   (b) peace   (c) trade   (d) solving conflicts

(8) One of the important factors that created the sociopolitical instability in South Africa was
   (a) protest   (b) prejudice   (c) discrimination   (d) segregation

(9) The year that South Africa held a free election without racial discrimination was
   (a) 1989   (b) 1990   (c) 1994   (d) 1998

(10) Why should South Africa terminate apartheid? It is for
   (a) equal rights   (b) racial discrimination   (c) racial prejudice   (d) political harmony

□ **the notion that** 동격절을 이끄는 접속사.
  • No one can deny the fact that he is connected with the bribery scandal.
  (그가 뇌물 수수와 관련이 있다라는 사실은 부인할 수 없다.)
□ **expound** = explain - The priest expounded his religious ideas to us.
□ **celestial orbs** = heavenly bodies   □ **orb** = sphere, globe : 구
□ **apparent** (appear에서) : 표면상의   • apparent prosperity : 외형상의 호황
□ **heretical** : (heresy) : 이단, 이교) 이단적인
□ **corroborate** = support, strengthen : 증거에 의하여 보강하다
  • The witness corroborated the driver's statement.

8. 넬슨 만델라는 1918년에 남아공에서 태어났다. 그의 부친은 어느 부족의 족장이었기에 넬슨은 족장이 되기 위한 교육을 받았다. 그러나 넬슨은 변호사가 되려고 대학 진학을 선택했다.

1944년에 남아공 반정부 최대의 흑인 집단 아프리카 민족회의에 가담했다. 그는 정부에 반항하는 운동을 지휘했고 이로 말미암아 1956년 체포됐다. 그러나 그의 무죄가 밝혀져 풀려 났다. 1960년에 정부는 ANC를 불법화하는 법을 제정했다. 넬슨은 정부에 대한 반항 운동을 더 강력하게 했고 그 결과 그는 1962년에 체포되었다. 그러나 이번에는 유죄로 판명되어 종신형에 처해졌다.

넬슨은 apartheid(인종차별 정책)를 반대하는 항거의 상징으로서 전세계 많은 사람들의 주의를 끌었다. 그들은 한결같이 그의 석방을 요구했다. 남아프리카에서는 더 많은 반항 운동이 개최되었고 그 결과 그 나라의 사회 정치적 불안을 초래했다. 1989년에 남아공 대통령은 평화를 위한 공동 노력을 위하여 넬슨을 만났고 넬슨도 이에 동의했다. 정부는 국민들이 ANC에 가입하는 것을 허락했고 넬슨은 1990년에 석방되었다.

넬슨은 새 헌법을 제정하기 위하여 정부와 협력했다. 1994년에 흑백인들 둘 다 그 국가 최초의 자유선거에서 투표했고, 넬슨이 대통령으로 당선되었다. 그는 남아공 최초의 흑인 대통령이 되었다. 넬슨은 남아공의 인종차별 정책을 종식시키고 민주주의를 향하여 전진하도록 도왔다.

Note

□ **tribal chief** : 족장, 추장
□ **lead to** = cause, have as a result : 결과를 낳다.
  • Cigarettes smoking leads to lung diseases. (흡연은 허파 질환의 원인이 된다.)
□ **enact** = make or pass a law : 법률을 제정, 통과시키다.
□ **outlaw** = declare sth unlawful : 불법으로 선언하다. n. 무법자

9. A volcano is a break in the earth's crust. Deep below this crust, it is very hot to melt rock. The melted rock is called molten which is like a hot, thick liquid. This molten rock is called magma. But in some places, there are cracks in the solid rock. Magma is squeezed up these cracks to the earth's surface. Suddenly, the magma breaks through at a weak point in the crust and explodes. These eruptions and breaks in the earth's crust are called volcanoes.

One of the best ways to understand how magma erupts is to think about soda in a bottle. Soda contains gas in the liquid. As long as a top is on the bottle, the gas cannot escape. As long as the liquid is not shaken, you cannot see the gas. But if the bottle is shaken, bubbles form and rise to the surface of the liquid. The bottle top keeps the gas bubbles from exploding, or erupting, out of the bottle. If you open a bottle gently, the gas bubbles will rise slowly to the surface. If you shake a bottle before you open the top, bubbles will rise quickly. When you take off the bottle top, these bubbles will rush out of the bottle and bring liquid soda with them. The soda will explode all over you.

Hot magma works like the soda. Magma also has gas in it. And the gas forms bubbles when the magma moves. If magma moves quickly between the cracks in the rock under the earth's crust, the gas bubbles also move violently. As the magma moves toward a weak point in the earth's crust, the gas bubbles will burst through the crust. Magma will erupt through the crack also, just the way soda bursts out of the bottle. A volcano is born.

(1) Molten is
    (a) hot, thick liquid   (b) melted rock   (c) earth's crust   (d) solid rock

(2) Magma is
    (a) hot, thick liquid   (b) melted rock   (c) molten rock   (d) solid rock

(3) Volcanoes are the
    (a) eruptions of magma through the breaks of the weak crust
    (b) squeezed magma to the earth's surface
    (c) eruptions of molten through the mountains
    (d) eruptions of magma through the earth's surface

(4) If you shake a soda bottle violently before opening the top, bubbles will
    (a) form and rise   (b) form and rise quickly   (c) rush out of the bottle   (d) rise and explode

(5) If you leave a soda bottle alone, bubbles will
    (a) not form and rise   (b) form and rise   (c) form and rise quickly   (d) form but do not escape

(6) If you take off the bottle top without shaking, gas bubbles will
    (a) rise to the surface   (b) rise quickly   (c) rise quickly and explode   (d) spread all over you

(7) Hot magma works like soda because it has _____ in it.
    (a) heat   (b) gas   (c) electricity   (d) water

(8) By what are bubbles made when magma moves?
    (a) heat   (b) electricity   (c) crack   (d) gas

(9) When the magma moves toward a weak point of the earth's crust, it will
    (a) erupt   (b) explode   (c) burst out   (d) move violently

> □ apartheid = the separation of races in one country esp. of blacks and whites. : 흑백 차별정책, 특히 남아공
> □ draw(call) attention : 주의를 끌다.
>   • His suggestions drew no attention of those present. (그의 제안은 참석자 누구의 주의도 끌지 못했다.)
> □ be held = take place : 개최되다
> □ sociopolitical : 사회 정치적인   cf. geopolitical : 지정학적   □ instability : 불안
> □ social(political, economic) instability : 사회적(정치적, 경제적) 불안.
> □ constitution = the laws according to which a country is governed : 헌법, 골격
> □ terminate = bring to an end : 종식시키다

9. 화산이란 지각 부분의 파열이다. 이 표면 아래 깊은 곳은 바위를 녹일 만큼 뜨겁다. 녹은 바위를 몰튼이라 하는데 이는 뜨겁고 걸죽한 액체다. 이 용암은 마그마라 부른다. 그러나 몇 곳에는 단단한 바위 속에 균열이 있다. 마그마는 압착되어 지각의 파열 부분으로 밀고 올라 지각면에 다다른다. 갑자기 마그마는 지각의 약한 지점을 뚫고 나와 폭발한다. 이런 분출과 지각 파열을 화산이라 부른다.

마그마가 어떻게 분출하느냐를 이해하는 최선의 방법은 병 속에 있는 소다를 생각해 보는 것이다. 소다는 액체 상태에 가스를 내포하고 있다. 병 마개가 닫혀 있는 동안은 가스가 달아나지 못한다. 소다수가 흔들리지 않는 동안은 가스가 보이지 않는다. 그러나 병이 흔들리면 거품이 형성되고 액체 표면으로 올라 온다. 병 마개는 가스 거품이 병으로부터 분출하는 것을 막는다. 병을 얌전히 열면 가스 거품은 천천히 표면으로 올라 온다. 만일 병을 열기 전에 병을 흔들면 거품은 빨리 올라 온다. 마개를 열면 이 거품들은 소다수와 함께 병 밖으로 튀어 나와서 당신 몸 전체에 폭발할 것이다.

뜨거운 마그마는 소다와 같은 작용을 한다. 마그마도 내부에 가스를 가지고 있다. 마그마가 이동할 때 가스가 거품을 형성한다. 만일 지각 아래에 있는 바위의 균열 사이로 마그마가 빨리 이동하면 가스 거품도 맹렬하게 움직인다. 마그마가 지각의 약한 지점으로 움직일 때 가스 거품은 갈라진 틈으로 뿜어 나온다. 마치 소다가 병 밖으로 터져 나오듯이. 그래서 화산이 태어난다.

> **Note**
> □ crust = a hard outer covering as of earth, snow, bread : 지구나 눈, 빵의 표면에 굳어진 부분
> □ crack : 갈라진 부분, 실금 - a crack in a cup   □ erupt = explode and pour out fire : 분출하다
> □ bubble = a hollow ball of liquid : 거품   • cf. foam : 작은 bubble 이 모여 하얗게 엉긴 것
> □ liquid = a type of substance not solid or gas : 액체   □ solid : 고체   □ gas : 기체
>   • cf. liquefy - LP(N)G = (Liquefied Petroleum(Natural) Gas) : 액화 석유(천연)가스

10. Nit Noi's Notes: Thai Trivia

(1) According to Thailand's Department of Religious Affairs, there are approximately 19,000 temples in the nation, and 290,000 monks.

(2) Thailand's public schools have been told to provide locker space for students' books so they won't have to carry them from home to class everyday. It was discovered that the weight of the texts was hazardous to the pupils' health if it exceeded 2.2 pounds (1 kg) for kindergartner, 4.4 pounds for primary school child, and 6.6 pounds for secondary school student.

(3) There are 9.3 million vehicles in Thailand, the majority of them is in Bangkok, where 1,285 new cars, trucks, motorcycles, tuk-tuks, and other internal combustion engines hit the streets everyday.

(4) Bangkok has sunk 32 inches (80 cm) during the past 30 years due to groundwater pumping and construction; some areas are now below sea level.

(Source: <u>Sawasdee</u>, Vol. 25, No. 10, Oct. 1996. Thai Airways International)

(1) In 1996 it was estimated that there were about 19,000 temples and 290,000 monks in Thailand. The ratio of temples to monks is approximately

    (a) 1:10   (b) 1:15   (c) 1:20   (d) 1:25

(2) Thai students are risking their health because they have to carry their heavy

    (a) bags   (b) instructional materials   (c) school work   (d) textbooks

(3) The weight of the texts can jeopardize a high school student's health if it exceeds _____ pounds (lbs).

    (a) 2.2   (b) 4.4   (c) 6.6   (d) 8.6

(4) One of the ways of helping Thai students for their health mentioned in the above news is to

    (a) instruct them less at school   (c) let them exercise more
    (b) provide them with more food   (d) provide them with lockers

(5) The estimated number of vehicles in Thailand is

    (a) 8.3 million   (b) 9.3 million   (c) 10.3 million   (d) 11.3 million

(6) How many new vehicles are sold to be driven each day?

    (a) 1,185   (b) 1,285   (c) 1,385   (d) 1,485

(7) How many new vehicles are estimated to increase each week so as to make the Bangkok traffic more congested? Almost

    (a) 7,000   (b) 8,000   (c) 9,000   (d) 10,000

(8) Bangkok will sink to 64 inches after _____ years later if groundwater pumping and construction continue as they do now.

    (a) 30   (b) 40   (c) 50   (d) 60

10. Nit Noi's 메모 : 타이의 작은 통계

(1) 타일랜드의 종교국에 따르면 타일랜드 국내에는 대략 19,000개의 사원이 있고 승려 수는 290,000명이다.

(2) 타일랜드의 공립학교는 학생들이 책을 집에서 교실까지 매일 운반할 필요가 없도록 책 관물함 자리를 마련해 준다고 한다. 교재의 중량이 유치원생 한 사람 당 2.2파운드(1kg), 초등학생 4.4파운드, 중등학생 6.6파운드를 초과하면 학생 건강에 위험하다는 사실이 밝혀졌다.

(3) 타일랜드에는 9백 30만대의 차량이 있는데 이중 대부분은 방콕에 있고, 이곳에서는 매일 1,285대의 새로운 승용차, 트럭, 오토바이, 툭툭스, 그리고 다른 내연 기관들이 거리에 나온다.

(4) 방콕은 지난 30년간 지하수 품어 올리기와 건설 작업으로 32인치(80cm) 내려 앉았고 몇 지역은 해수면 아래에 있다.

Note

- **approximate** = almost correct but not exact
  - Approximately speaking, the victims in the plane crash were over 150.
    (대충 말하여 비행기 추락 사고 희생자 수는 150명 이상이었다.)
- **monk** = a member of a all-male religious group : 남자 탁발승
- **nun** = a member of a all-female religious group : 수녀
- **locker** = a small metalic closet for keeping the things : 관물함
- **won't have to** = will not need to : …할 필요 없을 것이다.
  - You won't have to worry about the layoff. (너는 해고에 대한 걱정을 할 필요가 없겠지.)
- **primary (secondary) school** : 초등 (중등)학교 • cf. grade school = primary school
- **hazardous** = dangerous   도덕적 해이 (moral hazard)
- **vehicle** = something in which or on which people or things are carried : 수레
- **R.V.** = Recreation Vehicle : 여가용 다인승차
- **majority** = the greater number or amount : 다수 • opp. minority
  - The majority of the voters voted for the economist governor. (경제학자 지사에게 투표한 사람이 다수였다.)
- The Koreans in America belong to a minority group. : 소수 민족
- **internal combustion engine** : 내연기관   **groundwater pumping** : 지하수 품어 올리기
- **jeopardize** = endanger : Excessive anxiety will jeopardize your mental health.
- **hit the street** = leave, set out on the road : 출발하다, 여행하다
- **hit the right path** : 옳은 길로 나서다

11. Aung San Suu Kyi (1945-) was born in Rangoon, Burma. Her father, Thakin Aung San, led the nation's fight for independence from Great Britain and Burma won her independence in 1948. But in 1962, military leaders toppled the government by force and seized power. Since then, the nation has been controlled by military rule, and the Burmese have had few rights and little freedom. In 1988, Aung San Suu Kyi helped form the National League for Democracy (NLD), the organization against the military government. She was put under house arrest, and was not allowed to leave her house.

In 1989, the government changed the official name of the country from Burma to Myanmar. In 1990, the government allowed NLD candidates to run in the election for congress. Aung San's group won most of the votes; however, the military government did not allow the new congress to assemble. Some congressmen elect were sent to prison instead. Aung San was held under house arrest for six years. During that period, she wrote a book titled <u>Freedom from Fear and Other Writings.</u> In 1991, she won the Nobel Peace Prize for the peaceful effort to change Myanmar's government.

In 1995, she was released by the government. Since her release, she has given a lot of speeches as a way of encouraging democracy and promoting human rights in Myanmar. The government has arrested thousands of people who support her, but she continues the struggle for sociopolitical changes in Myanmar.

(Source: Adapted from <u>World History and You.</u> Bernstein, Vivian(1997).)

(1) Burma got her independence from Great Britain in
    (a) 1945   (b) 1948   (c) 1962   (d) 1988

(2) The National League for Democracy was organized to support
    (a) military rule   (c) social crimes
    (b) human rights and freedoms   (d) Aung San's friends

(3) The military leaders overthrew the government and took power in
    (a) 1945   (b) 1948   (c) 1962   (d) 1988

(4) The year when Burma changed her name was in
    (a) 1948   (b) 1962   (c) 1988   (d) 1989

(5) Who won most of the votes in the election of 1990?
    (a) members of NLD   (c) retired generals
    (b) military leaders   (d) Aung San's relatives

(6) The Nobel Prize was given to her in the area of
    (a) literature   (b) economic science   (c) peace   (d) medicine

(7) Aung San was held under house arrest for six years and was released in 1995. Then, she must have been held under house arrest beginning in
    (a) 1988   (b) 1989   (c) 1990   (d) 1991

(8) Current sociopolitical situations in Myanmar must be
    (a) prosperous   (b) oppressed   (c) optimistic   (d) enhanced

11. 이웅산 수기는 버마 랭군시에서 태어났다. 그녀의 아버지 이웅산은 영국으로부터의 독립을 위한 투쟁을 지휘했고 버마는 1948년 독립을 쟁취했다. 그러나 1962년에 군부 지도자들이 정부를 무력으로 쓸어 뜨리고 권력을 잡았다. 그 이후 국가는 군정의 통제를 받았으며 버마인들은 권리도 자유도 별로 없었다. 1988년에 아웅산 수기는 군정에 반대하는 조직인 민주주의 민족 동맹을 결성하는데 도움을 주었다. 그녀는 가택 연금에 처해져 집을 떠나는 것이 금지당했다.

Aung San Suu Kyi

　1989년에 정부는 국가의 공식 명칭을 버마에서 미얀마로 바꾸었다. 1990년에 정부는 NLD후보들이 국회의원 선거에 출마할 수 있도록 허락했다. 아웅산의 그룹이 대부분 득표했다. 그러나 군사정부는 새 국회가 구성되는 것을 허락하지 않았다. 대신에 몇몇 국회의원 당선자들을 투옥했다. 아웅산은 6년간 가택 연금을 당했다. 그 기간 동안 그녀는 '공포로부터의 자유' 라는 책을 쓰고 다른 여러 저술을 했다. 1991년에 그녀는 미얀마의 정치를 변화시키기 위한 평화적인 노력을 한 공로로 노벨 평화상을 수상했다.

　1995년에 정부는 그녀를 석방했다. 석방 후 미얀마의 민주주의를 격려하고 인권을 증진시키기 위하여 많은 연설을 했다. 정부는 그녀를 지지하는 수천명을 체포했지만 그녀는 계속하여 미얀마의 사회정치적 변화를 위하여 투쟁하고 있다.

Note

- **topple** = make or become unsteady and fall down : 쓸어뜨리다.
  - The civilian government was toppled by the military coup d'état.
  (그 문민 정부가 군사 쿠데타에 의하여 무너졌다.)
- **seize** = take control of power by force : 완력으로 통제권을 빼앗다, 확보하다
- **house arrest** : 가택연금
  - He was held under house arrest during the presidential election. (대선 기간 중 가택연금 당했다.)
- **run** = to become a candidate for : 출마하다.
  - He's decided to run for the governor. (도지사 출마를 결심했다.)
- **assemble** = gather : 모으다(vt), 모이다(vi)　• If we can assemble in time, we can start quickly.
  - Do you know how to assemble the parts into a radio set?

12. The bottom of the ocean is divided into three distinct areas: the continental shelf, the continental slope, and the ocean floor. The continental shelf is a band of gradually sloping sea bottom surrounding all the continents. Sunlight penetrates most of it, and the bottom is covered with sand and soil washed from the land. Common species of saltwater fish are seen here.

The continental slope no matter how deep and far from the land drops off abruptly beyond the continental shelf. Since sunlight does not penetrate this deep slope, there is no plant life. Instead, the pressure, cold, and silence increase in this sea bottom covered with mud, rocks, and clay.

The ocean floor lies at the foot of the continental slope, and it is a true bottom of the ocean. This area, not fully explored, holds the mysteries of a strange and unknown world. These mysteries will be uncovered soon by oceanographers as well as other scientists.

(1) The ocean bottom can be classified into _____ areas.

    (a) 2   (b) 3   (c) 4   (d) 5

(2) The area where the sunlight penetrates and numerous kinds of ordinary saltwater fish inhabit is the

    (a) continental shelf   (b) ocean floor   (c) continental slope   (d) sand and mud floor

(3) The area as a true bottom of the ocean holds the mysteries of the unexplored world is the

    (a) continental shelf   (b) ocean floor   (c) continental slope   (d) deep abyss

(4) The cold area where plants do not survive due to the lack of sunlight is the

    (a) continental shelf   (b) ocean floor   (c) continental slope   (d) sand and mud floor

(5) The area which oceanographers and other scientists should explore more and disclose the mysteries of the earth science is the

    (a) continental shelf   (b) ocean floor   (c) continental slope   (d) deep abyss

13. You are invited to a short discovery tour through Germany, the vacation country. Between the North Sea and the Baltic coast, across rolling hills and wooded mountains to the Alps, there are many enticing travel destinations. Since reunification in 1990, Germany has become even more attractive as a vacation country. Now it encompasses the fascinating eastern regions and the east German cities with their historic buildings and art museums.

Starting in the north, the North Sea and the Baltic coastline with their numerous islands await your visit. The adjoining plains are covered by hills and lakes, and to the south are wooded highlands, traversed by great river valleys. Germany's southern border is defined by the mighty Alps.

The many cosmopolitan cities of Germany are cultural centers of the highest order. They welcome and invite you to enjoy their opera, concert performances, and their museums. They also invite you to shop, sample their culinary delicacies and discover the surrounding countryside on the many excursions offered.

Berlin, previously a divided city, presents itself again as the bustling metropolis in the heart of Europe. The infrastructure in the seven western states meets the highest

12. 해저는 별도의 세 영역으로 나뉘어 진다 : 대륙붕, 대륙사면 그리고 해저다. 대륙붕은 대륙을 에워싸고 있으면서 점차적으로 기울어져 가는 해저의 띠다. 대부분의 대륙붕에는 햇빛이 침투하며 바닥은 육지에서 씻겨 온 모래와 흙으로 덮여 있다. 흔히 눈에 띄는 종류의 바다 물고기가 보인다.

대륙사면은 깊고 육지로부터 멀어도 대륙붕 너머에서 갑자기 나타난다. 태양빛이 스며들지 않기 때문에 식물이 없다. 대신 진흙과 바위, 점토로 덮인 이곳에는 수압과 추위 그리고 적막이 더해 간다.

해저는 대륙사면의 맨 아래 쪽에 펼쳐 있는데, 이곳이 진정한 바다의 밑부분이다. 이 지역은 충분히 탐험되지 않아 이상하고 알려지지 않은 신비의 세계이다. 이 신비들은 해양학자들 뿐 아니라 다른 과학자들에 의해서도 벗겨질 것이다.

Note
- penetrate = enter through, cut into : 침투하다 • Rain has penetrated right through his coat.
- species = a group of plants and animals of the same kind : 동·식물의 종(種)
  • This is a rare species of fish. (희귀 어종이다.)
- abruptly = suddenly and unexpectedly : 갑자기, 불쑥
  • The train stopped abruptly making passengers fall down.
- abyss : 심연, 바닥이 없어 보이는 구렁텅이 • an abyss of sadness : 헤어날 수 없는 슬픔
- continental shelf : 대륙붕

13. 여러분을 휴양지 나라 독일에서의 단기간 탐험 관광으로 초대합니다. 북해와 발틱해안 사이로 울퉁불퉁한 구릉지와 숲이 우거진 산을 가로질러 알프스까지 매력적인 여행 목적지가 많습니다. 1990년 통일 이후, 독일은 훨씬 더 매력적인 관광지가 되었습니다. 지금의 관광은 매력적인 농부지역과 유서 깊은 건물과 미술 박물관이 있는 동독의 도시들을 일주합니다.

북쪽에서 출발하여 북해와 수많은 섬이 있는 발틱해안이 여러분의 방문을 기다리고 있습니다. 연접해 있는 평원은 언덕과 호수로 덮여 있고, 커다란 강의 계곡이 가로지르고, 남쪽으로는 숲이 울창한 고원 지대가 있습니다. 독일의 남부는 거대한 알프스로 경계를 이루고 있습니다.

많은 세계적인 독일의 도시들은 최상위의 문화 중심지들입니다. 여러분들이 오페라와 콘서트연주 그리고 박물관들을 즐기시도록 초대합니다. 또한 쇼핑도 하시고 진미의 요리도 맛보시며 제공되는 여러 차례 짧은 여행으로 주변 시골을 방문하시도록 초대합니다.

standards: restaurants, hotels, stores, and the transportation system have all earned a worldwide reputation for excellence. In the five new eastern federal states, the infrastructure is being modernized. Come to Germany! Everywhere there is so much to see and experience---you will return home with lasting memories.

(Source: Adapted from Today's Germany (1994), by German National Tourist Office)

(1) The above paragraph is written for
    (a) students   (b) engineers   (c) businessmen   (d) tourists

(2) The year in which Germany got reunified is
    (a) 1988   (b) 1989   (c) 1990   (d) 1991

(3) What do the east German cities offer to tourists since after 1990?
    (a) shops, art treasures   (c) museums, wooded mountains
    (b) historic buildings, art treasures   (d) rolling hills, the Alps

(4) Which part of Germany has many islands?
    (a) south   (b) north   (c) east   (d) west

(5) The Alps are in the _____ of Germany.
    (a) south   (b) north   (c) east   (d) west

(6) The wooded highlands are in the
    (a) south   (b) north   (c) east   (d) west

(7) The cultural centers of Germany are
    (a) villages   (b) towns   (c) cities   (d) states

(8) The one not mentioned as a city enjoyment is
    (a) museum   (b) fishing   (c) opera   (d) shopping

(9) The cities offer many excursions to tourists so that they can find out
    (a) castles   (b) museums   (c) surrounding countrysides   (d) lakes

(10) Berlin is located in the _____ of Europe.
    (a) center   (b) outskirts   (c) south   (d) north

(11) One of the excellent public facilities that earned a worldwide reputation is
    (a) transportation system   (c) communication system
    (b) mail system   (d) sewer system

(12) How many states were there all together in Germany before 1990?
    (a) 10   (b) 11   (c) 12   (d) 13

14. Postage stamps are one of the commonest objects in everyday life all over the world. Many people take them for granted without paying close attention to the stamps on mail,

예전에 분할되었던 베를린은 다시 유럽의 중심에서 활기 넘치는 대도시로서 모습을 보여 주고 있습니다. 서부 7개 주의 도시 기본시설은 최고의 수준입니다. 식당, 호텔, 상점과 교통체계는 모두 우수하여 세계적인 명성을 얻었습니다. 새로운 동부의 연방 주들도 도시 기반 시설을 현대화하고 있습니다. 독일에 오십시오. 어느 곳이나 구경하시고 체험하실 것들이 많이 있습니다. 영원히 잊지 못할 추억과 함께 귀국하실 것입니다.

> **Note**
> □ rolling = rising and falling in gentle slopes   □ enticing = tempting : 유혹적인
> □ destination : 목적지   • The parcel was sent to a wrong destination.
> □ encompass = surround   • The enemy encompassed the city.
> □ await = wait for   • Death awaits us all. (사람은 모두 죽는다.)
> □ excursion = a short journey : 소풍, 짧은 여행   □ infrastructure : 하부구조, 기본구조
> □ earn = get by effort
>   • Through incessant effort, he earned the fame as the best singer.
>   (부단한 노력으로 최고의 가수로서의 명예를 얻었다.)

<u>14.</u> 우표는 전 세계적으로 가장 흔한 사물 중의 하나다. 많은 사람들은 우편물에 부착된 우표에 세심한 주의를 기울이지 않고 당연한 것으로 생각하나, 반면에 봉투를 열기 전에 잠깐 멈추고 우표를 조사하는 사람들도 있다. 또한 우표의 연구와 수집에 몰두하는 소수의 집단이 있다. 이 집단의 범위는 초등학교 어린이에서부터 국가 원수까지 걸쳐 있다. 희귀한 우표를 소유하려는 열망으로, 부자들은 경매장에서 경쟁하며 지금은 가장 고가의 수제품으로 순위에 올랐지만, 그 옛날의 하잘것 없는 우표에 거액을 지불했다. 1970년에는 1856년에 발행된 하나 밖에 없는  One-Cent Black on Magenta of British Guiana를 사기 위해서 28만 달러가 지불되었다.

1860년대에 이 취미를 설명하기 위하여 George Herpin이 만들어 낸 이름인 우표수집이라는 단어는 인종, 피부색, 신념, 모든 사회 신분에 상관없이 매력을 준다. 장소와 시간을 구별하지 않

while others pause to examine the stamps before opening the envelope. Then, there is the minority group which is devoted to the study and collecting of stamps. This group ranges from school children to heads of state. In their eagerness to possess the rarest stamps, rich people have competed in the auction rooms and paid large sums that the humble postage stamp, now ranks as the most expensive man-made object. In 1970, $280,000 was paid for the unique **One Cent Black on Magenta of British Guiana** issued in 1856.

Philately, the name coined by Georges Herpin in the 1860s to describe the hobby, appeals to people of every race, color and creed in every walk of life. It is a hobby which does not discriminate space and time is now being used as a means toward world peace and better understanding between people.

Since the first adhesive stamps appeared in 1840, more than 200,000 different stamps have been issued by over 800 countries and postal administrations. Stamps can be used to raise money for governmental projects, to promote the image of the country, and to publicize all manner of persons, places, events, and even commercial products.

Fashions in philately have changed since the end of World War II. In the past, collectors would study their stamps according to the country of issue. Nowadays, thematic or topical classification is all the rage and collections are formed according to the subject of the design or the purpose of the issue. For this reason, religion, arts, sports, folklore, and zoology go together with the subjects depicted on the stamps.

(Source: Adapted from The Dictionary of Stamps in Color (1973). McKay, James)

(1) A philatelist is a person who collects

　　(a) old toys　　(b) stamps　　(c) mounted butterflies　　(d) old coins　　(e) old books

(2) Why do many people try to buy the rarest stamps? Because of the value of

　　(a) scarcity　　　　　　(c) investment　　　　(e) scarcity and investment
　　(b) beautiful design　　(d) education

(3) The people who collect stamps are

　　(a) politicians　(b) students　(c) from all walks of life　(d) housewives　(e) millionaires

(4) You can negotiate the price of a certain item at

　　(a) department store　(b) restaurant　(c) supermarket　(d) auction　(e) duty-free shop

(5) The **One Cent Black** stamp was from one of the _____ colonies.

　　(a) British　　(b) Spanish　　(c) French　　(d) Dutch　　(e) German

(6) The term, "philately," was first used by

　　(a) Einstein　　(b) Herpin　　(c) Edison　　(d) Columbus　　(e) Churchill

(7) The first adhesive stamps were issued in

　　(a) 1840　　(b) 1850　　(c) 1860　　(d) 1870　　(e) 1880

(8) Why are stamps issued?

　　(a) to go with mail　　(c) to be collected　　(e) to satisfy many public
　　(b) to raise money　　(d) to publicize people　　　interests and purposes

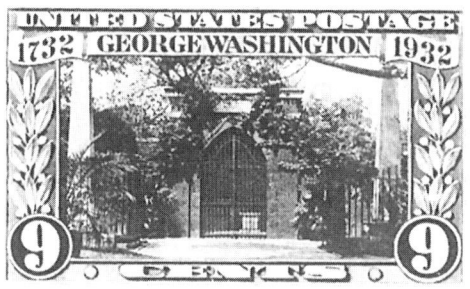

는 이 취미는 오늘날 세계평화와 사람들 사이에서 보다 낳은 이해를 위한 수단으로 쓰여지고 있다.

1840년에 접착 우표가 출현한 이후 20만 종류 이상의 다른 우표들이 800개 이상의 국가와 우편 기관에 의하여 발행되었다. 우표는 정부 사업을 위한 기금을 조성하기 위해서, 국가의 이미지를 증진시키기 위해서, 그리고 모든 사람들의 생활양식, 행사, 심지어 상품을 알리기 위해서 쓰여질 수 있다.

우표수집 방식도 2차 세계대전 이후 변했다. 과거에 수집가들은 발행 국가에 따라 연구하곤 했다. 오늘날은 주제나 제목에 따른 분류가 대유행이고, 도안의 주제나 발행 목적에 따라 수집된다. 이런 까닭으로 종교, 예술, 스포츠, 민담, 동물학 등이 우표에 표현되는 주제다.

Note

- auction : 경매
- rank = be put in a certain class : 서열이 … 이다 • He ranks among the upper 30% in his class.
- issue = give or distribute : 발행, 분배하다.
- philately = stamp collecting
- depict = describe
- creed = a system of beliefs : 신조, 신앙체계
- walk = social position : 사회적 신분
- adhesive tape : 반창고
- adhesive stamp : 접착성 우표
- all the rage : 대 유행이다 • Playing golf is all the rage.

15. 누군가를 사랑해 본 적이 있는가? 진실로 사랑하는 누군가와 결혼할 생각을 한 적이 있는가? 아마 그렇다고 대답할 것이다. 그렇다면 어떻게 결혼하고 싶은가? 단촐하게, 화려하게? 이 문제는 결혼할 준비가 되면 당신의 신부나 신랑과 대화를 해야 할 것이다. 일반적으로 우리는 몇 가지 정상적인 단계 - 미팅, 데이트, 사랑에 빠지기, 일이 잘되면 궁극적으로 결혼에 이를 약혼 - 가 필요하다. 이것이 오늘 우리 사회의 표준이 되는 결혼 절차다.

먼 옛날의 결혼 풍습은 어땠을까? 인류학자들은 문명의 발달을 3단계로 분류한다. : 수

(9) One of the purposes of issuing stamps is "to promote the image of the country." This "image promotion" will be good for

    (a) tourism   (c) religious education   (e) construction
    (b) trade war   (d) manufacturing industry

(10) The number of stamps issued since 1840 is estimated to be

    (a) 150,000   (b) 200,000   (c) 250,000   (d) 300,000   (e) 350,000

(11) Today people tend to collect stamps by the specific

    (a) country name   (c) year of issuance   (e) theme or category
    (b) stamp size   (d) stamp design

(12) Collecting stamps is a hobby which is less educational but more expensive than

    (a) reading   (b) skiing   (c) traveling   (d) golfing   (e) hunting

<u>15.</u>   Have you ever fallen in love with someone? Have you ever thought of marrying someone whom you really liked? Perhaps, you will say, "Yes." If so, how would you like to get wed? In a very simple or a luxurious way? Well, you have to talk about this matter with your bride or groom when you're ready to get married. Generally speaking, we need several normal steps such as meeting, dating, falling in love, engagement, which eventually leads up to marriage if it works out well. This is a standard marriage procedure in our society today.

    Well, how about the wedding custom long, long ago? Anthropologists classify the evolution of culture into three major periods: the hunting (600,000 - 10,000 years ago), the agricultural (10,000 - 5,000 years ago), and the civilization (5,000 years ago - present) periods. Several anthropologists speculate that there used to be a wedding custom called "marriage by capture" during the former two periods and even the large period of civilization before the concept of romance was developed during the 18th century. The custom of marriage by capture is quite different from the one we have now. Originally, it developed during the hunting period when the supply of food was extremely short, and women were scarce. The primitive men used to acquire them by warfare when they couldn't hunt enough animals for food and shelter, and get women for instinctive and other practical purposes. When a man needed a woman, he came with a group of other men armed with weapons such as clubs, sticks, spears and rocks. By force, he took the woman from her cave or hut as she screamed, kicked, and cried. The frustrated parents of the woman threw rocks or spears when the man took the woman with him. He hid out for a few days with the woman he took. Then the wedding was over.

    This wedding custom, marriage by capture, is still practiced by primitive tribes in remote parts of the world. But our current wedding custom owes its roots to the marriage by capture practiced a long time ago. For instance, the honeymoon custom is not completely free from the influence of a old one in which the groom hid out with his bride for a few days. The upset parents of the bride along with her relatives, and many people in the wedding ceremony throw flowers, confetti, rice or other grains, and soft objects to

렵기(600,000~10,000년 전), 농경기(10,000~5,000년 전) 그리고 문명기(5,000년 전~현재)다. 몇몇 인류학자들은 앞선 두 시기, 심지어 18세기 낭만이라는 개념이 발달하기 전인 문명기에도 '납치결혼'이라는 풍습이 있었다고 추측한다. 납치결혼 풍습은 지금 우리가 지니고 있는 풍습과는 판이하게 다르다. 원래 먹을 것이 태부족하고 여자가 희귀했던 수렵기에 발달했다. 원시인들은 먹이와 거처로 쓸 충분한 동물을 사냥하지 못하거나 본능적인 그리고 실용적인 용도로 이용할 여자를 얻지 못할 때는 전쟁으로 확보했다. 어떤 남자가 여자를 필요로 하면 몽둥이, 막대, 창, 돌 같은 무기로 무장한 다른 무리의 남자들과 함께 여자에게 왔다. 완력으로 여자의 동굴이나 오두막에서 비명을 지르고 발로 차고 울부짖는 여자를 데리고 갔다. 절망한 그 여자의 부모는 남자가 자기 딸을 데리고 갈 때 돌과 창을 던졌다. 그 남자는 자기가 데리고 온 여자와 며칠간 숨어 있었다. 그러면 결혼은 끝나 버린다.

　이 납치결혼 풍습은 세계의 벽지에 사는 원시 부족들에 의하여 지금도 시행되어 진다. 우리 현재의 결혼 풍습 뿌리는 옛날에 시행되었던 납치결혼의 덕이다. 예를 들면 신혼여행 풍속은 신랑이 신부와 함께 며칠간 숨었던 풍습의 영향으로부터 완전히 차유로울 수 없다. 속상한 신부의 부모는 친척들, 식장에 참석한 많은 사람들과 함께 꽃이며 색종이 조각이며 쌀, 다른 곡식과 부드러운 물체를 신혼부부에게 던진다. 수십 만년 전의 돌이나 창 대신. 실로 납치결혼은 이상하고 야만적으로 보이지만 그의 영향이 아직도 우리의 현대 결혼 풍습과 함께 살아 있다.

Note

- procedure = a set of actions necessary for doing something : 절차, 수속
- application (emigration) procedure : 지원(이민) 절차
- evolve = develop gradually : 진보(진화)하다 n. evolution
  - The Korean political system has evolved positively for the last 50 years.
- speculate : (사실의 확인 없이) 생각하다, 추측하다, 투기하다
  - We can only speculate what will become of this economy. (이 경제가 어떻게 될지 추측할 뿐이다.)
- scarce = not much or many, hard to find : 희소한
- odd = strange, unusual, queer : 이상한, 괴짜의

the newlyweds, instead of rocks and spears thrown a hundred thousand years ago. Indeed, marriage by capture seems to be odd and uncivilized, but its influences still live with our current wedding custom.

(1) Our current wedding custom is based on

    (a) contract (b) trade (c) dowry (d) negotiation (e) standard social procedures

(2) The hunting period starts _____ years ago.

    (a) 600,000   (b) 10,000   (c) 5,000   (d) 4,000   (e) 3,000

(3) The agricultural period ends _____ years ago.

    (a) 600,000   (b) 10,000   (c) 5,000   (d) 4,000   (e) 3,000

(4) The concept of romance developed during the _____ th century.

    (a) 16   (b) 17   (c) 18   (d) 19   (e) 20

(5) Marriage by capture was initiated during the _____ period.

    (a) hunting (b) agricultural (c) civilization (d) modern (e) contemporary

(6) Marriage by capture developed because there was a

    (a) surplus of women   (c) surplus of food   (e) surplus of manpower
    (b) scarcity of women   (d) scarcity of food

(7) Marriage by capture lingers today in the custom of the

    (a) funeral service   (c) baptism   (e) graduation ceremony
    (b) honeymoon   (d) coronation

(8) Marriage by capture seemed to be popular during the

    (a) hunting period   (c) agricultural period   (e) time before the 18th century
    (b) modern period   (d) civilization period

(9) Primitive man used to get their women by

    (a) fighting (b) capturing (c) negotiation (d) trade (e) contract

(10) In general, our current customs are largely _____ by our past customs.

    (a) postulated (b) demanded (c) influenced (d) activated (e) transacted

Selected proverbs for the study of cross-cultural expressions

영어 격언과 한문 격언과의 만남 (2)

1. It's good to learn by other men's cost.
他山之石, 前者之覆 後者之戒(타산지석, 전자지복 후자지계 ; 戒 =lesson)
- 남의 실수를 보고 배운다. · Let another's shipwreck be your seamark.

2. Prevention is better than cure. 人無遠慮 必有近憂(인무원려 필유근우 ; 憂 = anxiety)
- 앞날을 생각하지 않으면 반드시 가까운 걱정거리가 생긴다.
· He is wise who looks ahead. Forewarned is forearmed. / · One good forewit is worth two afterwits.

3. Content is more than a kingdom. 知足者富(지족자부) – 만족을 아는 자가 부자다.
· Happiness consists in contemtment.

4. Too much water drowns the miller. 過猶不及(과유불급 ; 猶 = no better than)
- 지나침이 못 미침만 못 한다. · Too much is no better than too little. You may go farther and fare worse.

5. Every miller draws water to his own mill. 我田引水(아전인수) – 자기 논에 물대기

6. You can't touch pitch without being defiled. 近墨者黑 近朱者赤(근묵자흑 근주자적)
- 먹을 가까이 하면 검어진다.

7. Don't make a mountain out of a molehill.
針小棒大, 少題大作, 泰山鳴動 鼠一匹(침소봉대, 소제대작, 태산명동 서일필) – 작은 일을 크게 불려서 말하다.

8. Muck and money go together.
水至淸無大魚 人至察無徒人(수지청무대어 인지찰무도인 ; 察 = watch)
- 물이 너무 맑으면 큰 고기가 없고, 사람이 너무 살피면 따르는 사람이 없다.

9. Small profits and quick returns. (=S.P.Q.R) 薄利多賣(박리다매) – 이익은 적으나 많이 팔다.

10. A man is known by the company he keeps. 交必擇友, 良禽擇木(교필택우 양금택목)
- 친구를 사귈 때는 가려서 하라. 좋은 새는 나무를 가려 앉는다.
· Better be alone than in bad company. As a man is, so is his company.

11. When in Rome, do as the Roman do. 入鄕循俗(입향순속)
- 어느 고장에 가면 그 고장의 풍속을 따르라. · One must howl with the wolves. Better bend than break.

12. Sweets are the mother of adversity 苦樂之母(고락지모) – 괴로움은 즐거움의 어머니다.

13. There's no smoke without fire. 突不煙不生燃,, 無風不起浪(돌불연불생연, 무풍불기랑)
- 불 안 땐 굴뚝에 연기 날까?
· No fire, no smoke. Out of nothing comes nothing. Where there's fire, there's smoke.

2-6 THE SUBJECT MATTER AND THE MAIN IDEA

This section, "The Subject Matter and the Main Idea," is designed for the readers to recognize the key *topic* and *point* implicitly or explicitly presented in a given passage. A passage includes the main idea as the head of our body, the sub-ideas as the bones, the supporting details as flesh, and the subject matter as the body. The subject matter refers to the specific topic of a passage. That is, what is the passage about? Is the passage about the tourism in Hawaii, or the watch industry in Switzerland? Whereas, the main idea refers to the specific key point of the writer. What is his or her key point? What point is he or she trying to make clear? Once the subject matter is identified, it is easy for the readers to recognize the main idea.

The passages used for this section are constructed with relatively short ones for the readers so that they can easily detect the target subject matter and the main idea with sharper focus and analysis. Also, the readers are advised to remember that the main idea is often stated in the first or last sentence. The subject matter can be drawn from the title of an article or a passage. (Note: In the EXERCISE provided in this section, the title of the passage is omitted to help the readers improve their detecting skills for the subject matter.) If they are not, the readers need more practice in recognizing them stated elsewhere. This reading skill in recognizing the main idea helps the readers grasp the point presented, and how the author's points were made clear. Then, the readers can enter the mood in which the writer is talking with them, which contributes the reading to be more enjoyable and informative.

2-6 주제와 요지

　이번 절 '주제와 요지'는 독자로 하여금 글 속에 명시적 혹은 암시적으로 제공된 주요한 화제와 요점을 인지하도록 계획되었다. 하나의 글은 우리 몸의 머리 같은 요지, 뼈와 같은 부제, 살과 같은 보조적 세부 사항, 그리고 몸과 같은 주제를 품고 있다. 주제는 어떤 글의 특수한 제목을 가리킨다. 바꾸어 말하면 그 글은 무엇에 관한 것인가? 그 글이 하와이 관광여행인가, 스위스의 시계공업인가?이다. 그러나 요지란 글 쓴 사람의 구체적인 요점이다. 작자의 요점이 무엇인가? 그는 어떤 점을 분명히 밝히려 하는가? 일단 주제가 밝혀지면 독자가 요지를 알아내기는 쉽다.

　이번 절을 위하여 쓰여지는 글들은 독자들에게 비교적 짧은 것들로 구성되었다. 보다 예리한 초점과 분석으로 목적하는 주제와 요지를 탐지하도록 하기 위해서다. 또한 요지는 자주 첫째 문장이나 끝 문장에 진술된다는 것을 잊지 말기를 충고한다. 주제는 기사나 글의 제목에서 도출할 수 있다. (주: 이 절에 마련된 연습문제는 독자들이 주제를 찾는 기술을 개선하는데 도움이 되도록 글의 제목을 생략했다.) 제목이 쓰여 있지 않으면 독자들은 어딘가 딴 곳에 진술된 주제들을 찾는데 더 많은 연습이 필요할 것이다. 요지를 알아내는 이 독서 기술은 독자들이 제시된 요점과 작가가 요점을 어떻게 밝히는가를 파악하는데 도움이 된다. 그러면 독자는 작가와 함께 대화하는 분위기 속에 들어갈 수 있고, 이는 또한 독서를 더 즐겁게 해주고 정보를 얻는데 더 유익한 것으로 만드는 일에 도움이 된다.

Note

□ **implicitly** = not plainly expressed : 묵시적으로, 함축적으로
　• opp. explicitly : 명백하게　• She trusted the doctor explicitly.
□ **refer to** = mention, speak about : 언급하다
　• He referred to the cause of the economic crises. (경제 위기의 원인에 대하여…)
□ **that is (to say)** = in other words : 바꾸어 말하면
□ **detect** = find out, notice : 탐지하다
　• He could detect the leaking spot in the roof. (지붕에서 새는 곳을 찾아냈다.)
□ **analysis** : 분석　• opp. synthesis : 종합
□ **contribute** = to help in bringing about something : 공헌, 이바지하다, 기부하다
　• Plenty of fresh air contributes to good health.

EXERCISE:

Read the following passage and choose the best answer provided.

1. The Springfield Country Club has always been a special place for Township residents. Over the years, residents have met at the Club to golf, swim, skate, or simply enjoy the company of family and friends.

(1) The subject matter is about

    (a) The Springfield Country Club   (c) the types of activities
    (b) Township residents   (d) how people meet at the Club

(2) The main idea is the

    (a) use of the Club   (c) role of the Club
    (b) benefits of the Township   (d) value of the Club

2. Drama has much in common with fiction. However, a play is different from a short story or novel. When the play is written, the playwright expects his work to be performed by actors on stage. A fiction writer expects his work to be read, instead of being performed.
    There are many types of plays such as comic or tragic, but all include certain features. Several aspects of playwrighting are setting, stage direction, dialogue, scenes, and events. Each aspect is an important part of playwrighting. Each helps actors to perform in the manner in which the writer intended.

(1) The subject matter is about

    (a) short story   (b) drama   (c) fiction   (d) playwrighting

(2) The main idea is

    (a) difference between drama and fiction   (c) how drama is written
    (b) types of drama   (d) many factors about drama

3. Fidel Castro overthrew the Bastista regime in 1958, and initiated ambitious social reforms, diversifying Cuba's economy and redistributing the land based on socialist economic ideology. Since then, almost a million Cubans have left Cuba, and came to the United States. At least half of them came to Miami, Florida, to start a new life there. Miami is not far from Cuba, and the climate there is not much different from that of Cuba. Thus, they began to settle

다음 글을 읽고 제공된 보기 중 가장 적당한 답을 골라라.

<u>1.</u> 스프링필드 컨츄리 클럽은 항상 주민들을 위한 특별한 장소였다. 수년 동안 주민들은 클럽에서 만나 골프, 수영, 스케이트 혹은 가족과 친구들의 모임을 즐겨왔다.

<u>2.</u> 연극과 소설은 공통점이 많다. 그러나 희곡은 단편이나 소설과는 다르다. 희곡을 쓸 때 희곡작가는 작품이 무대에서 배우에 의하여 공연되기를 기대한다. 소설가는 자기의 작품이 공연되는 대신 읽혀지기를 기대한다.

희곡에는 희·비극 등 여러 가지 형태가 있지만 모두 몇 가지 특색을 갖고 있다. 배경, 무대 감독, 대사, 장면, 사건들이다. 각각의 측면은 각본 제작에서 중요한 부분들이다. 각 부분은 배우들이 작가가 의도한 방식으로 연기하는 데 도움이 된다.

Note
- in common with = in shared possession : 공통적으로 가진
  - You and I have much in common in character. (너와 나는 성격상 공통점이 많다.)
- playwright = a writer of plays, dramatist : 극작가
- comic = funny, humorous   opp. tragic = unhappy, unfortunate

<u>3.</u> 피델 카스트로는 1958년에 바스티스타 정권을 타도하고 야심에 찬 사회개혁을 시작했다. 쿠바의 경제를 다양하게 변화시키며 사회주의 경제 이념에 입각하여 토지를 재분배했다. 그 이후 거의 수백만 명이 쿠바인들이 쿠바를 떠나 미국으로 왔다. 그들 중 최소한 반이 플로리다주 마이애미에 와서 새 생활을 시작했다. 마이애미는 쿠바에서 멀지 않고 기후도 쿠바의 기후와 별로 다르지 않았다. 이리하여 그들은 마이애미에 정착했고, '작은 하바나'라고 불리는 도시 일부를 개발했다. 이제 왜 쿠바인들이 '작은 하바나'에서 살고자 하는지 이해하기 쉽다. 그곳은 그들에게 고향을 생각나게 한다. 그들은 가능한 한 고향과 비슷한 것을 제공해 주는 환경에서 살기 원한다.

in Miami, developing a part of that city called "Little Havana." Now, it is not difficult to see why the Cubans want to live in Little Havana. It reminds them of home. They want to live in an environment which can provide them with as much closeness of home as possible.

(1) The subject matter is

    (a) socialist economy   (c) Castro's reforms   (e) Cubans in Miami
    (b) Little Havana   (d) Cuban's homesickness

(2) The main idea is

    (a) when Castro seized power   (d) why Cubans live in Little Havana
    (b) how Castro initiated reforms   (e) why Cubans were against Castro
    (c) why Cubans left Cuba

4. The role of an American President's wife is a difficult and demanding one. She as the First Lady must provide support and encouragement for her husband. Since her husband's job is one of the most burdensome in all the world, her help is crucially important. She must be a hostess at many official dinners and receptions. She must participate in many social activities outside the White House. When her husband is criticized, she must encourage him.

(1) The subject matter is the

    (a) job of an American President's wife
    (b) duty of an American President's wife
    (c) role of the First Lady of the U.S.
    (d) rights of an American President's wife
    (e) partnership of an American President's wife

(2) The main idea is a

    (a) variety of roles the First Lady has to do
    (b) variety of social activities imposed on the First Lady
    (c) way how the First Lady encourages her husband
    (d) importance of being the First Lady
    (e) reason why the First Lady provides support and encouragement

5. The theaters in ancient Greece were built largely for religious festivals. Therefore, the theater had to be large enough to hold the entire free male population of the city. Because of its great size, it would have been quite

Note
- overthrow = defeat, remove from official power : 전복시키다, 공직에서 몰아내다
  - They made a secret conspiracy to overthrow the inefficient regime.
    (그들은 무능한 그 정권을 타도하려고 비밀 음모를 꾸몄다.)
- regime = a particular type of government : 정권
  - The country was under the military regime. (그 국가는 군사 정권하에 있었다.)
- initiate = start working, originate : 처음으로 시작하다
  - Who initiated the vaccination in Korea? (한국에서 최초로 예방접종을 시작한 사람은 누구요?)
- diversify = vary, make various : 다양하게 바꾸다
- ideology = a set of ideas : 사상, 이념
  - Nowadays there is no longer conflict in ideology. (오늘날 더 이상의 사상 갈등은 없다.)

4. 미국 대통령 부인의 역할은 힘이 드는(만만치 않은) 역할이다. 그녀는 영부인으로서 남편을 위해서 후원과 용기를 주어야 한다. 그녀 남편의 업무는 세계에서 가장 부담스러운 것이기에 그녀의 도움은 결정적으로 중요하다. 그녀는 많은 만찬이나 피로연의 안주인이 되어야 한다. 그녀는 백악관 밖의 많은 사교적인 활동에 참석해야 한다. 자기 남편이 비판을 받을 때, 그녀는 남편에게 용기를 주어야 한다.

Note
- role = the part taken in an activity : 역할
  - Who is supposed to play the role of martyer? (누가 순교자의 역을 맡아야 할까?)
- demanding = needing a lot of effort or attention : 노력과 주의를 필요로 하는, 힘드는
  - Learning a foreign language is indeed a demanding job.
- burdensome = troublesome, hard to bear : 부담되는, 견디기 힘드는
  - It's burdensome to be one's superior. (남의 상사가 되는 것도 부담스러운 일이다.)
- crucially = critically, decisively : 결정적으로, 아주 중요하게
  - Speed is crucial to our business. (우리 사업에는 속도가 절대적으로 필요하다.)
- criticize = find fault with : 비난하다
  - Never criticize anyone in his absence. (안 듣는 곳에서 누구든 험담하지 말라.)

5. 고대 그리스의 극장들은 주로 종교적인 축제를 위하여 건축되었다. 따라서 극장은 그 도시에 사는 노예가 아닌 전체 남성인구를 수용할 만큼 커야 했었다. 그 크기 때문에 지붕이 있는 극장을 건축했더라면 굉장히 어려웠을 것이다. 결과적으로 희랍인들은 언덕 기슭에 터를 선택하여 야외극장을 지었다. 이 지붕 없는 극장들은 모든 사람들이 다 보고 들을 수 있도록 대개 그릇 모양으로 지어졌다.

difficult to build such a theater with a roof. Consequently, the Greeks often chose sites on sides of hills and built open-air theaters. These roofless buildings were generally built in the shape of a large bowl so that everybody would be able to see and hear.

But, the enormous size of the theater did not allow for the kind of naturalistic drama we have today. In ancient Greece, the distance between the back of the audience and the stage was so great that the actors could not speak as they do today. Therefore, the actors had to produce their words in a special way; their words were spoken in chorus or in a type of a song.

(1) The subject matter is about

    (a) religious festivals   (c) huge size of theaters   (e) ancient Greek actors
    (b) ancient Greek theater   (d) ancient Greek play

(2) The main idea is the

    (a) enormous size of the ancient Greek theater
    (b) reasons for building the theater so big
    (c) ways of building Greek theater
    (d) ways Greek actors performed
    (e) structure of the Greek theater in which actors performed

6.   Malaria was one of the world's greatest single cause of sickness. A team of doctors found that most babies in village after village in Papua New Guinea were infected by malaria. This hidden enemy had these village people in its power for hundreds of years. It was the number one killer, but the people could not do anything about it.

When the Aramco Oil Company came to this land, its doctors began to do something to help these people. The doctors knew that the mosquitoes served as the agent that spread the disease from the blood of infected animals or people.

(1) The subject matter is the

    (a) symptoms of malaria   (d) malaria in Papau New Guinean villages
    (b) spread of malaria   (e) death caused by malaria
    (c) conquest of malaria

(2) The main idea is how the Aramco Oil Company

    (a) spread malaria   (d) prevented malaria from spreading
    (b) helped the village people   (e) learned the causes of malaria
    (c) helped fight malaria

그러나 극장의 엄청난 크기는 오늘날 우리가 보는 사실주의적인 연극류는 고려하지 않았다. 고대 그리스에서는 관중 뒤에서 무대까지의 거리가 너무 멀어 배우들이 오늘날 처럼 대사를 말할 수 없었다. 그러므로 배우들은 특별한 방식으로 대사를 했는데 합창이나 노래의 형식으로 했다.

> **Note**
> □ **enough** : 명사 – Enough has been discussed. 토론은 충분했다. 토론은 그만.
> 　　　　　형용사 – We have enough money to buy a larger car.
> 　　　　　부사 – You're now old enough to know better. 철들 나이가 됐다.
> □ **It would have been difficult.** : 가정법 과거 완료의 주절 – 그게 어려웠을 것이다.
> 　(If they had tried to build one with a roof,) 가 생략됨.
> □ **allow for = take into consideration** : 고려, 참작하다.
> 　• Allowing for the train being late, we should be back by 10:30.

6. 말라리아는 세상에서 가장 무서운 질병의 원인 중 하나다. 한 의사 집단이 파푸아 뉴기니아에서 어린 아이들이 마을에서 마을로 말라리아에 전염되어 있는 것을 발견했다. 이 정체불명의 적이 수백년간 이 마을 사람들을 꼼짝 못하게 지배하고 있었다. 말라리아는 첫째가는 살인자였지만 사람들이 할 수 있는 일은 아무것도 없었다.

　어램코 석유회사가 이 땅에 왔을 때, 그 의사들은 이 사람들을 돕기 위하여 뭔가를 하기 시작했다. 의사들은 모기가 감염된 사람이나 동물의 피로부터 이 병을 퍼뜨리는 매개자임을 알았다.

> **Note**
> □ **infect = put disease into the body of** : 전염시키다. 병들게 하다.
> 　• Mosquitoes infect us with malaria.
> 　• Violence infects our society. (폭력은 우리 사회를 병들게 한다.)
> □ **agent = a person who acts for another** : 대리자, 청부인, 공작인
> 　• Rain and sun are the agents which help plants grow. (비와 태양은 식물을 자라도록 도와 주는 일을 하다.)
> 　• travel agent : 여행사 직원　　job agent : 직업 소개인

7. 전등은 1879년에 토머스 앨버 에디슨에 의하여 발명되었다. 뜨겁게 달구어진 철선이 빛을 발산한다는 것은 많은 사람들이 알고 있었다. 그러나 전구에 가장 좋은 철선은 무엇인가? 그 철선은 높은 저항력을 가지고 있어야 하고, 장시간 지속되어야 한다. 적합한 재

7. The electric light was invented by Thomas Alva Edison in 1879. Many people knew that a very hot wire gives off light. But what kind of wire is best for a light bulb? It must have a high resistance, give off a lot of light, and last a long time. In his search for the suitable material, Edison tried hundreds of different substances. The first successful electric lamp used a carbon filament. Filaments in light bulbs today are made of tungsten which has a high resistance and gives off a lot of light when it gets hot. But, the tungsten wire would quickly burn out if it were in the air. So the air is removed from inside the bulb, and nitrogen or argon is forced in.

(1) The subject matter is the

    (a) Thomas Edison
    (b) filaments in light bulb
    (c) electric light
    (d) tungsten in light bulb light bulb
    (e) Edison's search for the suitable material

(2) The main idea is

    (a) how Edison improved the quality of the light bulb
    (b) how the electric light was developed
    (c) what substances constitute the light bulb
    (d) why tungsten wire easily burns out
    (e) why nitrogen or argon is forced in

8. Lemmings, originated from a Scandinavian word, are small rodents. Like most rodents, lemmings have strong front teeth that grow continuously. They have a devastating effect on vegetation. They can destroy most of the plants in a wide area.

    Lemmings have strange behaviors which many people cannot answer. Every few days during the summer, they are seized by a mysterious instinct that causes them to leave their home. There are thousands and millions of them following one leader. All at once, they run together in a large group stopping for nothing and no one. They destroy every animal or plant on their way. They run toward the cliffs by the sea. When they reach them, they leap off the cliffs to the sea. Or they land in the water and swim out to sea until they drown. Not one of them ever returns, which is a mystery to many people.

(1) The subject matter is

    (a) rodents
    (b) death of lemming
    (c) lemming
    (d) lemming's mystery
    (e) lemming's behavior

료를 찾는 중에 에디슨은 수백가지 물체를 시험했다. 최초의 성공적인 전기램프에는 탄소 필라멘트를 사용했다. 오늘날의 전구 필라멘트는 높은 저항력을 가지고 있으며 뜨거워 졌을 때 많은 빛을 내는 텅스텐으로 만들어진다. 그러나 텅스텐 철사는 공기 중에서는 빨리 타 버린다. 그래서 전구 내부의 공기를 빼내고 질소나 아르곤을 주입한다.

> **Note**
> □ give off = send out, emit : 발산하다, 내뿜다
>   • By day the sun gives off light and heat for all the life on the earth.
>   (낮에는 태양이 지구상의 모든 생명을 위하여 빛과 열을 발산한다.)
> □ light bulb : 전구   □ screw (unscrew) the bulb : 전구를 끼우다 (빼다)
> □ resistance = opposition : 저항, 반대
>   • We as a free citizen should offer resistance against any kind of injustice.
>   (우리는 자유시민으로서 어떤 종류의 불의에도 저항 해야 한다.)
> □ filament = a thin thread : (전구내의) 얇은 실

8. 스칸디나비아 말에서 유래한 나그네쥐는 작은 설치류 동물이다. 대부분의 설치류처럼 나그네쥐도 계속 자라는 강한 앞이빨을 가지고 있다. 이들은 식물들에게 파멸적인 영향을 미친다. 그들은 넓은 지역에 있는 대부분의 식물을 파괴한다.

　나그네쥐들은 많은 사람들이 해명할 수 없는 이상한 행동을 한다. 그들은 여름 동안 3~4일 마다 그들을 집에서 떠나게 하는 신비한 본능에 사로잡힌다. 한 마리의 지도자를 수천, 수백만 마리가 따라간다. 갑자기 그들은 큰 무리를 지어 그 무엇 때문에도 그 누구 때문에도 멈추지 않고 달려간다. 도중에 있는 것이면 동물이든 식물이든 모두 없애버린다. 그들은 바닷가 벼랑을 향하여 달린다. 벼랑에 도착하면 벼랑에서 바다로 뛰어내린다. 더러는 물에 도착하여 익사할 때까지 헤엄쳐 나간다. 그들 중 돌아 오는 건 한 마리도 없다. 이 사실은 많은 사람들에게 수수께끼로 남아 있다.

> **Note**
> □ lemming : 북미산 나그네쥐
> □ rodent = a member of the family of small plant - eating animals with strong sharp
>   teeth = rats, mice rabbits (설치류)
> □ devastate = destroy completely : 황폐시키다
>   • The sudden heavy rainfall devastated most of the peaceful farming village.
>   (갑작스런 폭우가 평화로웠던 농촌 마을을 황폐시켜 버렸다.)
> □ instinct = natural force in people and animals that causes certain behavior : 본능

(2) The main idea is

    (a) lemming's behavior   (d) unknown answer
    (b) lemming's mystery   (e) lemming's strange behavior caused by its instinct
    (c) lemming's instinct

9.   In 1946, Akio Morita and Masaru Ibuka got $500 together and established an electronic equipment manufacturing company. Their first plant was a bombed-out department store. The company soon made its mark. SONY was first in Japan with all kinds of electrical equipment using transistors. The company began to expand overseas.

    From a handful of workers in 1946, SONY now employs more than 10,000. The employees working in a relaxed atmosphere are selected through a national competitive test. Once they are hired, they are given freedom to experiment, and are even offered lessons in American ways and manners. Morita and Ibuka often put on blue cotton work clothes and mingle with their employees.

(1) The subject matter is about the

(a) start of SONY   (d) expansion of SONY
(b) initial investment   (e) development & expansion of SONY
(c) products of SONY

(2) The main idea is

(a) the current personnel management of SONY
(b) how SONY developed so as to provide the best employee benefits
(c) how SONY developed so as to provide employee benefits
(d) how SONY developed so that the employees are given freedom to experiment
(e) how the SONY employees are selected

10.   Shoplifting is a big problem not only for honest shoppers, but also for most stores. Because of shoplifting, stores in the United States lose more than $2 billion per year.

    How can we stop shoplifting? Several cities are taking steps to discourage

9. 1946년 아끼오 모리따와 마사루 이부까는 함께 500달러를 마련하여 전자설비 제조회사를 설립했다. 그들의 최초 공장은 공습을 받아 부서진 백화점 건물이었다. 그 회사는 곧 이름을 떨쳤다. 트랜지스터를 사용하는 모든 종류의 전기설비에 관해서는 소니가 일본 내에서 처음이었다. 그 회사는 해외로 진출하기 시작했다.

   1946년에 소수의 직공으로 시작한 소니가 지금은 10,000명 이상의 종업원을 고용한다. 마음 편한 분위기 속에서 근무하는 종업원들은 전국적인 경쟁시험을 통하여 선발된다. 일단 채용되면 그들은 실험할 수 있는 자유가 주어지며 미국식의 교육도 받는다. 모리따와 이부까는 자주 파란 무명 작업복을 입고 종업원들과 섞여 일한다.

Note
- electronic : 전자의 • electric : 전기의 electronic engineering : 전자공학
- make one's mark = have an influence on : 영향력, 이름을 떨치다.
- expand = grow larger : 확장하다 • Iron expands when heated. (철은 가열하면 팽창한다.)

10. 좀도둑질은 정직한 손님들에게 뿐 아니라 대부분의 가게 주인에게도 커다란 문제다. 좀도둑 때문에 미국 내 가게들은 매년 20억 달러 이상을 손해 본다.

   어떻게 하면 좀도둑을 막을 수 있을까? 몇몇 도시에서는 좀도둑질을 단념시키기 위하여 몇 가지 조치를 취하고 있다. 예를 들면 미주리주 캔사스에서는 좀도둑 학교를 시작했다. 이 학교는 도둑질 현장에서 처음으로 붙잡힌 사람들을 위하여 존재한다. 감옥으로 가는 대신 이들은 좀도둑질을 그만둘 수 있는 방법을 가르치는 1일 학습에 출석한다. 이 반의 좀도둑들은 자신에게 대하여 몇 가지 사실들을 말하기로 되어 있다. 예를 들면 직업, 가족 및 교육배경, 좀도둑질하는 방법과 이유 등이다. 폭로된 몇 가지 사실은 놀랄 만하다. 그들 대부분은 그들이 가져 가는 상품을 돈 주고 살 수 있을 만큼 충분한 수입이 있는 규칙적인 직업을 갖고 있었다. 그 학습의 결과는 성공적이었다. 그 학습을 받은 최초의 400명 중 단지 한 사람만이 좀도둑질을 하다가 두번째로 붙들렸을 뿐이다.

Note
- commodity = an article of trade : 상품
- shoplifting = taking goods from a store without paying : 좀도둑질
- take steps = take actions : 조치를 취하다
  - We ought to take steps to sweep out the hooligans in the summer resorts.
  (피서지에서 불량배들을 소탕하기 위한 조치를 강구해야겠다.)
- discourage = try to prevent : 단념시키다. 용기를 꺾어 못하게하다.
  - His mother discouraged his son from joining the dancing group.
- reveal = allow it to be seen, make known : 폭로하다.
  - His stammering revealed that he stole the document.
  (그가 말을 더듬는 것이 그가 그 서류를 훔쳤다는 것을 나타냈다.)

shoplifting. For instance, a school for shoplifters has started in Kansas City, Missouri. The school is for people who have been caught shoplifting for the first time. Instead of going to jail, these people attend a one-day class on how to stop shoplifting. The shoplifters in this class are supposed to give some facts about them: their jobs, family and educational backgrounds, and reasons for and ways of shoplifting. Some of these revealed facts are surprising; most of them had regular jobs making enough money to pay for the commodity they took. The result of the class has been successful. Out of the first 400 people who took the class, only 1 was caught shoplifting a second time.

(Source: Adapted from G. & E. Spache (1982). Reading: Project Achievement C.)

(1) The subject matter is

    (a) a school for shoplifters   (d) ways of shoplifting
    (b) reasons for shoplifting   (e) shoplifting as a big problem
    (c) shoplifting

(2) The main idea is

    (a) a way for preventing shoplifting
    (b) a class for preventing shoplifting
    (c) why a school in Kansas City started
    (d) the amount of money stores lost per year
    (e) surprising facts about shoplifting

11. William Edward Burghardt Du Bois (1868 - 1967) was the leading spokesman for rights of the colored during the first half of the 20th century. He was also a well-known historian and teacher. He believed that the colored people should oppose discrimination anytime and anywhere they found it. In 1905, he founded the Niagara Movement, an organization started by the colored to fight discrimination. He also helped start the National Association for the Advancement of Colored People (NAACP), which came later.

    Throughout his long life, he worked for equal rights for the colored, but he was sad to see the slow progress of civil rights in the United States. In 1961, he left the United States to live in Africa. But the movement he had started carried on the fight.

(1) The subject matter is

    (a) W.E.B. Du Bois   (c) Du Bois' life in Africa   (e) civil rights
    (b) the life of Du Bois   (d) equal rights

제2장 11가지 독해기법 **131**

11. William Edward Burghardt Du Bois (1868-1976)는 20세기 초반에 유색인들(흑인)의 권리를 위한 선도적인 대변인이었다. 그는 또한 역사가와 교사로도 잘 알려져 있었다. 그는 인종차별을 발견하는 어느 때, 어느 곳에서든지 그 차별을 반대해야 한다고 믿었다. 1905년에 차별을 싸워 없애기 위하여 흑인들이 시작한 기구인 '나이아가라 운동'을 설립했다. 또한 그는 그 후에 생겨난 '흑인 발전 국민 연합'을 출발시키는 데에도 도움을 주었다.

그는 긴 생애를 통하여 흑인들의 동등한 권리를 위하여 일했으나 미국에서의 시민권 진행 속도가 느린 것에 마음이 아팠다. 1961년에 그는 미국을 떠나 아프리카에서 살았다. 그러나 그가 시작한 운동은 투쟁을 계속했다.

Note
- He's a leading figure in the opposition party. : 야당에서 주도적 인물
- spokesman = a person chosen to speak for a group officially : 대변인
- discriminate = treat a person or group as worse than others : 차별 대우하다
- found = set up, establish : 설립, 창립하다
  - He founded a hospital and a school in the town where he was born.
  (자기가 태어난 마을에 병원과 학교를 설립하다.)

12. 잉카제국은 11세기부터 16세기까지 번창했다. 잉카제국은 컬럼비아, 에콰도르, 페루, 볼리비아, 칠레 그리고 아르헨티나 등 여러 나라를 포함했었다. 잉카제국은 다른 종족들을 흡수함으로써 영토를 확장할 수 있었다.

신성한 태양의 도시 Cuzco는 Quechua어를 사용하는 잉카 제국의 중심지였다. 잉카 사회체계의 최상층부에는 왕이 있었고 국민들은 왕을 태양의 아들이라고 믿었다. 최하층부에는 토지를 경작하는 평민들이 있었다. 잉카의 법 아래서는 국가가 모든 국민들을 보살폈다. 왜냐하면 국민은 국가의 재산이었기 때문이다.

Note
- flourish = grow healthily, grow successfully : 번창하다. 무성하다
  - The firm has really flourished since the beginning of the IMF. (그 회사는 IMF가 시작된 이후로 번창했다.)
- territory = land ruled by one government : 영토
  - Some Japanese persistently claims that Dokdo is their territory.
  (몇몇 일본인들은 독도가 자기네 영토라고 끈질기게 주장한다.)
- swallow up = take in : 집어 삼키다.
  - Higher living costs have swallowed up the pay raise. (불어난 생활비가 봉급 인상분을 삼켜 버렸다.)

(2) The main idea is

    (a) the slow civil rights progress in the United States
    (b) Du Bois' struggle against discrimination
    (c) Du Bois' struggle for equal rights
    (d) Du Bois' activities for equal rights during his lifetime
    (e) Du Bois' support for NAACP and the Niagara Movement

12.   The Inca Empire flourished from the 11th to the 16th century. The empire included the countries of Colombia, Ecuador, Peru, Bolivia, Chile, and Argentina. The Incas were able to extend their territory by swallowing up other tribes.
    Cuzco, the Sacred City of the Sun, was the center of the empire with the Quechua language spoken by the Incas. At the top of the Inca social system was the King, who the people believed was the Son of the Sun. Everything including the animals, food, land, and people belonged to the King with absolute power. At the bottom of the system were the common people who worked the land. Under Inca law, the state took care of all the people because they are the property of the state.

(1) The subject matter is

    (a) Inca social system   (d) the Inca King
    (b) the Inca Empire   (e) the Inca domination over other tribes
    (c) Inca territory

(2) The main idea is

    (a) how the people worshipped their King
    (b) how the Inca Empire extended her territory
    (c) how the Inca Empire developed
    (d) how the Inca Empire developed, and how her social system worked
    (e) how the Inca social class worked

13.   Psychology is important because it tells us the little that is known about attention, association, memory, and interest. Without a knowledge of these, advertising people would have little idea of the best way to attract the attention of perspective buyers, or of the way to hold interest after it is secured. The aim of advertising people is to present the target commodity in such a way that pleasant association will be aroused. If the prospective buyer is pleased with the advertisement, he will be interested in the commodity; and when the need for it comes, he will remember that particular brand. The function of the

영어 격언과 한문 격언과의 만남 (3)

Selected proverbs for the study of cross-cultural expressions

1. **Familiarity breeds contempt.** 憐下食鼻, 頻來親疎也(연하식비, 빈래친소야)
   - 아이를 예뻐하면 코 묻은 밥 먹는다, 자주 오면 멀어진다.
     · Intimacy lessens fame. No man is a hero to his valet.
     · Respect is greater from a distance. No man fears what he has seen grow.

2. **Time flies like an arrow.** 光陰似箭(광음사전 ; 似 = like, 箭 = arrow) – 시간은 화살과 같다.

3. **The pitcher calls the kettle black.** 至愚責人明(지우책인명 ; 責 = blame)
   - 매우 어리석은 자가 현명한 사람을 나무란다.

4. **Haste makes waste. Hasty work, double work.** 欲速反拙, 欲速不達(욕속반졸, 욕속부달)
   - 빨리 하려면 오히려 일을 망친다, 서두르면 도달하지 못한다.
     · More haste, less speed. Good and quick seldom meet.

5. **A bird in the hand is worth two in the bush.**
   有粟不食, 無益於飢(유속불식, 무익어기 ; 粟 = millet)
   - 조가 있어도 먹지 않으면 시장함에 무익하다(부뚜막에 소금도 집어 넣어야 짜다).

6. **Let bygones be bygones.** 不念舊惡(불념구악) – 지난 일은 들추지 말라.

7. **All roads lead to Rome.** 殊途同歸(수도동귀) – 길은 달라도 같은 곳으로 돌아간다.

8. **Don't put the cart before the horse.** 本末顚倒, 主客顚倒(본말전도, 주객전도)
   - 주인과 손님의 위치가 바뀌다.

9. **Come empty, return empty.** 人生不帶來不帶去, 空手來空手去(인생부대래부대거, 공수래공수거)
   - 인생은 빈손으로 왔다 빈손으로 돌아간다.   · Shrouds have no pockets.

10. **Practice makes perfect.** 熟能生巧(숙능생교) – 열심히 익히면 재주가 생긴다.

11. **Great wisdom is often taken for foolishness.** 大智若愚(대지약우) – 많이 아는 사람은 마치 바보같다.

12. **Bystanders see more of the game.** 堂局者迷 傍觀者淸(당국자미 방관자청)
    - 당사자는 혼미하나 구경꾼이 더 잘 본다.   · Observers are wiser than the engaged.

13. **Give him an inch and he will take a mile.** 得寸進尺(득촌진척 ; 進 = advance)
    - 작은 것을 배워 큰 것을 깨친다.

14. **Heaven helps those who help themselves.** 自求者福, 天助自助者(자구자복, 천조자조자)
    - 스스로 찾는 자가 복이 있다, 하늘은 스스로 돕는 자를 돕는다.

advertisement is to attract attention, to create desire, to build confidence, and, finally, to stimulate action for purchase.

(1) The subject matter is

    (a) psychology   (c) attention getting   (e) building confidence
    (b) particular brand   (d) advertisement

(2) The main idea is how

    (a) to attract attention
    (b) psychology is used for advertisement
    (c) to stimulate action
    (d) to build confidence
    (e) to present the commodity with association

14. English is not an easy one to write and its grammar is monstrously difficult⋯. It's not only the grammar that makes English a difficult language to write. English has an enormous vocabulary⋯. How large you can see for yourselves by comparing a French dictionary of synonyms with Roget's Thesaurus. The French dictionary is a slim volume of 300 loosely printed pages; Roget is a volume of nearly 1000 pages printed in double columns⋯. English, as everybody knows, is an amalgam of several languages, and it is this amalgam that has made it more difficult for us to write prose⋯. None of us can expect never to make mistakes. The best we can hope is that we shall not make many.

(Source: William Somerset Maugham (1874-1965), English novelist and playwright)

(1) The subject matter is the English

    (a) language   (c) grammar   (e) prose
    (b) vocabulary   (d) dictionary

(2) The main idea is that English is difficult for us to write because of its

    (a) vocabulary and grammar   (d) enormous vocabulary
    (b) different aspects in prose   (e) amalgam of several languages
    (c) difficulty in grammar

15. Study is a good way to transform small-scale individuals into large-scale individuals. We are now moving from local citizenship to world citizenship. In our homes, our community, our everyday person-to-person contacts, we need to know. He who does not know, and does not know that he does not know, he is a

13. 심리학은 중요하다. 왜냐하면 주의, 연상, 기억, 흥미 등에 대하여 잘 모르는 것을 가르쳐 주기 때문이다. 이런 것들을 모르면 광고업계 종사자는 장래성 있는 고객의 주의를 끌거나 주의를 확보한 후 그것을 지속시키는 최선의 방법을 모를 것이다. 광고인의 목표는 유쾌한 연상이 일어날 수 있는 그런 방법으로 목표 상품을 소개하는 것이다. 만일 잠재 고객이 그 광고에 흡족하면 그 상품에 관심을 갖게 될 것이고, 그 상품이 필요할 때 그 특정 상표를 기억할 것이다. 광고의 기능은 주의를 끌고, 욕구를 창조하고, 신뢰를 쌓고, 마지막으로 구매활동을 자극하는 것이다.

> **Note**
> - psychology = the study or science of the mind : 심리학
> - association = the act of connecting things in mind : 연상하기
>   - We associate chrysanthemum with fall. (국화하면 가을이 연상된다.)
> - secure = get as a result of effort : 힘들여 확보하다. • He has secured himself a good job.
> - function = work : 기능 • The machine will not function well if you don't oil it.
> - confidence = full trust, belief in one's ability : 자신감, 신뢰

14. 영어는 쓰기(짓기)에 쉽지 않고 문법도 매우 어렵다. 영어를 쓰기 어렵게 만드는 것은 비단 문법만이 아니다. 영어에는 엄청나게 많은 어휘가 있다. 어휘가 얼마나 많은가는 프랑스어 동의어 사전과 Roget's Thesaurus를 비교해 보면 당신의 힘으로도 알 수 있다. 프랑스어 동의어 사전은 느슨하게 인쇄된 300페이지의 얇은 책인데 Roget는 2단으로 인쇄된 거의 1000페이지의 책이다. 모두 알다시피 영어는 서너개 언어의 혼합물이다. 그리고 이 혼합이 우리가 글 쓰는 것을 어렵게 만든다. 우리 중 그 누구도 실수를 한 번도 안 한다고 기대할 수 없다. 우리가 바라는 최선은 실수를 적게 하는 것이다.

> **Note**
> - a monstrous sum of money : 엄청나게 많은 돈
> - vocabulary = all the words known to a person : 어휘
>   - There is no word 'impossible' in my vocabulary. (내 사전에 불가능은 없다.)
> - synonym = a word with the same meaning • opp. antonym : 반의어
> - slim = attractively thin, not fat : 날씬한, (희망, 승산) 희박한
>   - Our chances of winning are slim. (이길 승산은 적다.)
> - amalgam : 혼합물

fool — shun him; he who does not know, and knows that he does not know, he is simple — teach him; he who knows that he does not know, he is asleep — wake him; he who knows, and knows that he knows, he is wise — follow him.

(Source: Anonymous)

(1) The subject matter is

    (a) small-scale individuals   (d) study
    (b) local citizenship   (e) world citizenship
    (c) large-scale individuals

(2) The main idea is

    (a) how to be a world citizen   (d) what we can be through studies
    (b) what makes a wise man   (e) what makes people different
    (c) how to be large-scale individuals

15. 공부란 소인을 대인으로 변형시키는 좋은 방법이다. 우리는 지금 지역시민에서 세계시민으로 옮아 가고 있다. 가정에서, 공동체 안에서, 일상적인 대인 접촉에, 우리는 지식이 있어야 한다. 무식하면서도 자기가 무식한 것도 모르는 사람은 바보다. 그를 피하라. 무식하지만 무식하다는 것을 아는 사람은 순박한 사람이다. 가르쳐라. 유식하며 자기가 유식한 줄 모르면 잠들어 있다. 깨워라. 유식하며 자기가 유식하다는 것을 알면 그는 현명하다. 그를 따르라.

Note

- **transform** = change completely in form, nature : 변형시키다
  - The device transforms heat into power. (그 장치는 열을 동력으로 전환시킨다.)
- **individual** = a single being : 개인
  - The rights of the individual are the most important in a free society.
  (개인의 권리는 자유사회에서는 가장 중요한 것이다.)
- **local** = of or in a certain place : 지역적인, 국부의
- **shun** = avoid, keep away from : 피하다
  - She was shunned from her classmates. (그녀는 급우들에게서 따돌림 당했다.)
- **contact** = the condition of touching : 접촉, 사귐
  - I broke contact with him, who proved a backbite.
  (나는 그와 접촉을 끊었다. 알고 보니 등뒤에서 남을 험담하는 사람이기에)

2-7 THE TOPIC SENTENCE AND THE SUPPORTING DETAILS

The <u>topic sentence</u> (the main idea of a paragraph) is what the passage is about. It should be broad enough to be supported or developed by supporting details through the remainder of the paragraph or passage. Therefore, the topic sentence summarizes the whole paragraph/passage, and makes a general statement. It is wider in its scope than the rest of the sentences in the paragraph/passage.

Sometimes there is no topic sentence in a paragraph. In that case, be sure to ask these questions to yourself: **(1) What is each sentence about?, (2) How do all the sentences relate to each other? and, (3) Think about the details of (1) and (2), and formulate the topic sentence (main idea) of the paragraph** (refer to the exercises 11 and 12 for more comprehensive practice and details).

The <u>supporting details</u> in the passage help explain or support the topic sentence. Several ways that the supporting details explain or support the topic sentence include the use of **(1) facts or statistics, (2) specific examples, (3) instance or anecdote; and, (4) comparisons or contrasts.**

An example is provided below for you:

Two kinds of goats are famous for their wool.
One is the Cashmere goat which is raised in Asia and India.
Its wool is called cashmere.
The other is the Angora goat which is raised in Texas.
Its wool is called mohair.

The topic sentence is *"Two kinds of goats are famous for their wool."*

The supporting details are given here as specific examples
(1) One is the Cashmere goat raised in Asia and India.
(2) Its wool is called cashmere.
(3) The other is the Angora goat which is raised in Texas.
(4) Its wool is called mohair.

2-7 주제문과 보충설명

주제문(한 문단의 요지)은 글이 무엇을 쓰려고 하는가다. 주제문은 그 자체를 제외한 남은 글이나 문단에서 보충설명에 의하여 보충되고 전개될 수 있을 만큼 폭 넓은 것이어야 한다. 그러므로 주제문은 전체의 글이나 문단을 요약하고 또한 전반적인 진술을 해야 한다. 주제문은 글이나 문단속의 나머지 문장보다 범위가 넓어야 한다.

문단 속에 주제문이 없는 경우도 때로 있다. 그럴 경우 스스로에게 다음과 같은 질문을 꼭 해야 한다. : (1) 각 문장은 무엇에 관한 것인가? (2) 모든 문장들은 상호 어떤 관계인가? (3) (1)과 (2)의 보충설명을 생각해 보고 문단의 주제문(요지)을 간략하게 표현하라 (종합적인 연습과 세부적인 사항에 대해 연습문제 11과 12를 참조하라).

글 속의 보충설명은 주제문을 설명하거나 보충하는 데 도움이 된다. 보충설명이 주제문을 설명 보충하는 방법에는 다음과 같은 것이 있다. (1) 사실이나 통계 (2) 구체적 보기들 (3) 사례나 일화 (4) 비교나 대조

아래에 보기를 제공한다. :   두 종류의 염소들이 털로 유명하다.
하나는 캐시미어 염소로 아시아나 인도에서 사육한다.
그의 털을 캐시미어라고 부른다.
다른 하나는 텍사스에서 사육되는 앙고라 염소다.
그의 털은 모헤아로 불린다.

주제문은 "Two kinds of goats are famous for their wool."이다.

구체적 보충자료를 제시하면   (1) One is the Cashmere goat raised in Asia and India.
(2) Its wool is called cashmere.
(3) The other is the Angora goat which is raised in Texas.
(4) Its wool is called mohair.

또 하나의 보기 :   나무는 가장 유용한 식물이다.
그들은 흙을 제자리에 있게 지켜 준다.
그들은 공기에 산소를 더해 준다.
그들은 목재를 공급한다.

Another example :

> Trees are the most useful plants.
> They help keep soil in place.
> They add oxygen to the air.
> They provide wood.
> Trees help keep soil from washing away.
> Farmers often plant trees to stop rain from washing soil away.
> Trees make oxygen.
> People and other animals need oxygen to live.
> Trees provide wood for people.
> Many people heat their houses with wood.

The topic sentence: *Trees are the most useful plants.*

The sub-topic sentences : *(1) They help keep soil in place.*
(2) They add oxygen to the air.
(3) They provide wood.

The supporting details :

(a) Trees help keep soil from washing away.
(b) Farmers often plant trees to stop rain from washing soil away.
   These are the supporting details for sub-topic sentence (1).

(c) Trees make oxygen.
(d) People and other animals need oxygen to live.
   These are the supporting details for sub-topic sentence (2).

(e) Trees provide wood for people.
(f) Many people heat their houses with wood.
   These are the supporting details for sub-topic sentence (3).

EXERCISE:

Identify the topic sentence from the following passage. Write the passage below, making the topic sentence in the first sentence, and complete the rest of the passage with other sentences as supporting details. The first word, phrase or some helping word of the topic sentence are provided for you.

1. George Neal, the 93-year-old recluse who died last Sunday, left more than $300,000 in cash to his four dogs. He also left them a stamp collection valued at

나무는 토양 유실을 막아 준다.
농부들은 토양 유실을 막기 위하여 자주 나무를 심는다.
나무는 산소를 만든다.
사람이나 다른 동물은 살기 위해서 산소가 필요하다.
나무는 인간에게 목재를 공급한다.
나무로 난방하는 사람들이 많다.

주제문 : Trees are the most useful plants.

부주제문 :
(1) They help keep soil in place.
(2) They add oxygen to the air
(3) They provide wood.

보충자료 :
(a) Trees help keep soil from washing away.
(b) Farmers often plant trees to stop rain from washing soil away.
(이것들은 부주제 (1)을 위한 보충자료다.)

(c) Trees make oxygen.
(d) People and other animals need oxygen to live.
(이것들은 부주제 (2)를 위한 보충자료다.)

(e) Trees provide wood for people
(f) Many people heat their houses with wood.
(이것들은 부주제 (3)을 위한 보충자료다.)

Note
- formulate = express in a short clear form : 공식화하다. 간단하게 표현하다.
- comprehensive = broad, including much : 종합적인
- statistics = collected numbers representing facts or measurements : 통계
- anecdote = a short interesting story about a particular person : 일화
- compare = examine to see if there is likeness or difference : 비교하다
  - cf. contrast = compare unlike things so that differences are made clear (대조)
- soil = the top covering of the earth : 흙   □ sub : under, below, slightly를 의미하는 접두사
- subtopic : 부제   □ submarine : 잠수함   □ subordinate : 하위의, 종속의
- subgroup : 소집단   □ subside : (반란, 해일) 가라 앉다

다음 글에서 주제문을 확인하라. 다음 글에서 주제문을 문두로 하여 쓰고 보충자료로서 다른 문장들과 함께 글의 나머지를 완성하라. 첫 단어, 첫 구절, 혹은 주제문을 도와 주는 몇 단어가 제시된다.

$10,000. Furthermore, he willed that his house on Sampson Street would become a home for lost dogs.

The topic sentence : <u>Recluse left fortune to dogs</u>.

Once the topic sentence is identified, now list three supporting details that support the topic sentence.

    1. Mr. Neal left… _____
    2. He also left a… _____
    3. He willed that… _____

<u>2.</u>   During the past seven years, Mr. Neal seldom left his house. He always kept the window shades closed. One neighbor, Cindy, says that she saw him only once when she came back from shopping. Neighbors describe Mr. Neal as an odd man.

The topic sentence : Neighbors describe…_____

The supporting details:

    1. _____
    2. _____
    3. _____

<u>3.</u>   In the setting, the playwright may include information about the time, place, and people in the scene. For example, if the play opens in a living room, the playwright may state the month, year, time of day, where the living room is, and if it is large or small, richly or poorly furnished. He may go on to describe the furniture. He may name the characters in the room and describe them.

The topic sentence : The playwright may include…_____

The supporting details:

    1. _____
    2. _____
    3. _____

1. 지난 일요일 사망한 93세의 은둔자 조지 닐은 현찰로 30만 달러 이상을 그의 네 마리 개에게 물려주었다. 또한 그는 1만 달러 값어치의 우표 수집품도 물려 주었다. 더욱이 샘슨가에 있는 그의 집도 집없는 개들에게 주겠다고 유언했다.

주제문 : 은둔자가 재산을 개에게 남겼다.

일단 주제문이 밝혀졌으면 주제문을 보충하는 세개의 세부 사항들을 써라.

1. Mr. Neal left …
2. He also left a …
3. He willed that …

Note
- □ recluse = a person who purposely lives alone away from the world : 은둔자, 속세를 버린 사람
  - cf. hermit : 종교적 목적으로 집을 떠난 은둔자
- □ will = leave possessions to be given after one's death : 유증(遺贈), 유언하다
  - My grandfather willed me these old paintings.

2. 지난 7년간 닐씨는 그의 집을 떠나지 않았다. 그는 항상 창문 차광막을 닫고 있었다. 이웃에 사는 신디는 쇼핑에서 돌아오는 그를 딱 한번 보았다고 말한다. 이웃 사람들은 그를 기인(奇人)이라고 표현한다.

3. 극작가는 배경에 연극 장면에서 나오는 시간, 장소, 그리고 인물에 대한 정보를 포함시킬 수 있다. 예를 들어 연극이 거실에서 시작된다면 년, 월, 일, 시와 거실의 위치, 거실의 크기, 가구가 화려하게 또는 초라하게 갖추어져 있는가를 서술할 수 있다. 그는 계속하여 가구에 대한 설명을 할 수도 있다. 거실 내에 있는 인물들의 이름을 알리고 그들을 묘사할 수도 있다.

Note
- □ setting = a set of surroundings, backgrounds : (연극) 배경
- □ furnish = put furniture, supply with furniture : 가구를 갖추다
  - The hotel is finished but not furnished yet. (완공됐으나 가구는 아직 갖추지 않았다.)
- □ character = a person in a play, book, etc : 등장 인물

4. In 1700, George Pierce acquired 402 acres from William Penn. Pierce's descendents established a working farm and, in 1798, began planting an arboretum that by 1850 was one of the finest in the nation. The farm was purchased in 1906 by Pierre S. DuPont (1870-1954) to preserve the trees, and from 1907 until 1954 he personally designed most of what is enjoyed today. Longwood Garden has matured into a magnificent horticultural showplace filled with countless opportunities for learning and enjoyment.

The topic sentence : Longwood Garden⋯_____

The supporting details:

1. _____
2. _____
3. _____

5. "⋯I do not believe that the Great Society is the ordered, changeless, and sterile battalion of the ants. It is the excitement of becoming ― always becoming, trying, probing, falling, resting, and trying again ― but always trying and always gaining. In each generation ― with toil and tears ― we have had to earn our heritage again⋯."

(Source: Inaugural Address of Lyndon B. Johnson, Jan. 20, 1965)

The topic sentence : I do not believe⋯_____

The supporting details:

1. _____
2. _____

6. People have treated others with unbelievable cruelty in the name of religion throughout history. They have often done so much without feelings of remorse or guilt. Muslims and Christians have fought "holy wars" against one another, which have been anything but holy. And within their own ranks, so-called Christians have persecuted other Christians. Like Saul of Tarsus before he became Christ's apostle to the Gentiles, they think they are doing God a service when actually they are persecuting Jesus (Acts 9:4).

4. 1700년에 조지 피어스는 윌리엄 펜으로부터 402에이커를 취득다. 피어스의 후손들은 작업 농장을 설립하고 1798년에 1850년까지로는 전국에서 가장 훌륭한 수목원을 창설했다. 그 농장을 1906년에 삐에르 듀퐁이 구입하여 그 나무들을 보전하고 1907년에서 1954년까지 오늘날 사람들이 즐기는 현재의 모습을 대부분 손수 고안했다. 롱우드 정원은 훌륭한 원예학 전시명소로 성장하여 학습과 즐거움을 위한 무한한 기회를 제공하고 있다.

> **Note**
> □ arboretum : 수목원, 식물원
> □ preserve = keep something alive, safe from destruction : 보호, 보전하다.
>   • It's our duty to preserve the nature for our descendant.
> □ mature = fully grown and developed - premature / immature : 조숙한 / 미숙한
>   • You are not a child. You must behave yourself in a mature way. (어른스럽게 처신해야지.)
> □ horticulture = the science of growing fruits, flowers and vegetables : 원예학

5. "나는 '위대한 사회' 란 질서 정연하고 변화가 없고 생식력이 없는 개미군단이라고는 믿지 않습니다. '위대한 사회' 는 뭔가가 되겠다는 - 항상 뭔가로 변화하고 노력하며 탐구하고, 실패하며, 휴식하고, 그리고 다시 노력하는 - 그러나 항상 노력하고 항상 성취하는 흥분입니다. 각 세대마다 땀과 눈물로 또 다시 우리의 유산을 이룩해야 합니다."

(원전 : 존슨 대통령의 취임사 – 1965년 1월 20일)

> **Note**
> □ sterile = unable to produce young, made free from germs : 불모의, 불임의, 무균질의
>   • sterile year / sterile culture : 흉년 / 무균배양   • opp. fertile
> □ heritage = something passed down over many years : 유산
>   • Much of our artistic heritage was plundered during the invasions.
>   (많은 우리의 예술적 유산들이 그 침략 때 약탈 당했다.)
> □ probe = search into : 철저한 조사, 탐색
>   • The prosecutory authorities swore that they'd probe the embezzlement scandal.
>   (검찰 당국은 그 횡령사건을 철저히 파헤치겠다고 맹세했다.)

6. 사람들은 전 역사를 통해서 종교라는 이름으로 다른 사람들을 믿을 수 없을 만큼 잔혹하게 다루어 왔다. 그들은 별로 죄책감이나 양심의 가책없이 그렇게 해왔다. 회교도들과 기독교인들은 서로를 적대시하여 '성스러운 전쟁' 을 했다. 그러나 그것은 결코 성스러운 것은 아니었다. 그리고 같은 병사들끼리도 소위 기독교 교인들이 다른 기독교 교인들을 박해했다. 예수의 제자가 되어 이교도들에게 가기 전의 타르수스의 사울처럼 그들은 실제

(Source: Adapted from "The Difference Jesus Makes." Our Daily Bread (1997). RBC Ministries, Grand Rapids, Michigan)

The topic sentence : People have··· _____

The supporting details:

1. _____
2. _____
3. _____
4. _____

7. The Roman Emperor Augustus ruled from 27 B.C. to A.D. 14. During this time, he attempted to improve the government within the Empire. One of his goals was to make the governments in the defeated territories more honest and reliable. That way, the people in the territories would have less reason to turn against his government. Augustus succeeded in his plan. Almost 200 years, the Roman Empire was peaceful, strong, and prosperous. This peaceful period was known as the Pax Romana, or Roman Peace.

The topic sentence is: The Pax Romana is a period of··· _____

The supporting details:

1. _____
2. _____
3. _____
4. _____

8. Do you know who started the International Red Cross? It is Henri Dunant, a rich Swiss banker. As a young man, Henri watched the Battle of Salferino between France and Austria. He had been concerned by the condition of the wounded left dying on the battlefield. Many years later, when he had become a rich banker, he organized the International Red Cross the purpose of which is to take care of all wounded, regardless of nationalities in time of war. Twenty two countries signed the Treaty of Geneva in 1864 to become members of the organization.

The topic sentence : Henri Dunant started··· _____

로 예수를 박해하면서도 하느님을 섬기고 있다고 생각하고 있었다.

Note
- remorse = sorrow for having done wrong : 후회, 가책
  - The jail breaker was filled with remorse after his mother's sudden death.
  (그 탈옥수는 어머니의 갑작스런 죽음 후 후회하는 마음이 가득했다.)
- anything but = not at all, far from : 결코 아닌 • The old bridge is anything but safe.
- so-called = improperly or falsely named : 소위, 이름이 잘 못 붙여진
  - They are so-called Christians who show no love to the poor.
- persecute = treat cruelly, cause to suffer : 박해하다
- Apostle = any of the 12 followers of Christ : 예수의 12제자
- Gentiles = heathens : 기독교에서 본 이교도
- Tarsus : 타르수스 – 터키 남부의 도시 : 성 바울의 출생지

7. 로마 황제 아우구스투스는 기원전 27년에서 기원 14년까지 로마를 통치했다. 이 기간에 로마 제국내의 정치를 개선하려고 시도했다. 그의 목표 중 하나는 정복한 영토내의 정부들을 더욱 정직하고 믿을 수 있게 만드는 것이었다. 그런 식으로 하면 영토내의 사람들이 그의 통치에 거역할 이유가 적어지리라는 것이었다. 그는 이 계획을 성공시켰다. 거의 200년간 로마 제국은 평화롭고 강력하게 번영했다. 이 평화기간이 '로마의 평화'로 알려졌다.

Note
- attempt = make an effort to do something : 시도하다
  - I attempted to speak but was told to be quiet. (발언하려고 시도 했으나 조용히 하라는 말을 들었다.)
- defeat = win a victory over, beat : 패퇴시키다
  - Our party defeated our opponents. (우리 당이 반대편을 물리쳤다.)
- Pax Romana = Roman Peace : 로마가 주는 평화 = 식민지적 평화

8. 여러분은 누가 국제 적십자를 창시했는지 아는가? 그것은 한 스위스의 부유한 은행원 앙리 뒤낭이다. 젊었을 때 앙리는 프랑스와 오스트리아 사이의 솔페리노전투를 보았다. 그는 전장에서 부상병들이 죽어가도록 방치되는 상황에 대해 관심을 갖게 되었다. 여러 해가 지난 후 그가 부유한 은행가가 되었을 때 전시에는 국적에 상관없이 부상병을 보살펴야 한다는 목적에서 국제 적십자를 조직했다. 22개 국가가 이 조직의 회원국이 되려고 1864년 제네바 조약에 서명했다.

The supporting details:

1. _____
2. _____
3. _____
4. _____

<u>9.</u>   The Aryans were the first of many groups of people to invade India. Parts of India were ruled by Persia by the early 500 B.C. Later, in 326 B.C., Alexander the Great reached the Indus River Valley with his Greek and Macedonian soldiers, but he died before he would take over India. The first empire ruled by Indian Kings was the Maurya founded in 32 B.C., extended about 2/3 of India, and lasted until 184 B.C.

The topic sentence : The first Indian Empire was··· _____

The supporting details:

1. _____
2. _____
3. _____

<u>10.</u>   Dozens of enterprising businessmen made American life richer, safer, and more comfortable. Gail Borden invented condensed milk, a healthy and safe product in a time of 1895 when fresh milk was often dangerous. Willis Carrier named his 1902 invention "air conditioning." Clarence Birdseye discovered frozen foods, and Aaron Montgomery Ward brought the department store to the most isolated farm through the innovation of the mail order catalog.

The topic sentence : Dozens of··· _____

The supporting details:

1. Gail··· _____
2. Willis··· _____
3. Clarence··· _____
4. Aaron··· _____

> **Note**
> □ regardless of = without regard to, irrespective of : …에 상관없이
>   • Every adult has a rights to regardless of sex, education or social position.
>   (모든 성인은 성별, 교육정도, 사회적 지위에 상관없이 한 표의 투표권을 가진다.)
> □ go on to = go on with … ing = continue
>   • They went on to talk (went on with talking) in spite of the teacher's warning.
>   (선생님이 경고했음에도 불구하고 계속 떠들었다.)
> □ nationality = membership in a particular nation : 국적
>   • What's your nationality? (국적을 말씀해 주시요)

9. 아리안족은 인도를 침략한 많은 부족들 중 첫번째였다. 인도의 여러 지방들이 일찍이 기원전 500년까지 페르시아의 통치를 받았다. 그 후 기원전 326년에 알렉산더 대왕이 그의 그리스와 마케도니아 병사들을 이끌고 인더스강 계곡에 도착했으나 인도를 접수하기 전에 죽었다. 인도의 왕이 통치한 최초의 제국은 기원전 32년에 세운 마우리아이고 이는 현재 인도 영토의 2/3까지 확장했으며 기원전 184년까지 계속되었다.

> **Note**
> □ take over = gain control over or responsibility : 접수하다. 인계맡다
>   • When the president is in trouble, the premier takes over his job.
>   (대통령 유고시에는 총리가 대통령 업무를 떠맡는다.)
> □ invade = to attack and spread into so as to take control of a country : 침략하다
>   • Korea has never invaded any land throughout his long history.

10. 수십 명의 기업가 정신이 왕성한 사업가들은 미국 생활을 더 부유하고, 더 안전하고, 더 편안하게 만들었다. 게일 보덴은 생우유가 자주 사람에게 위험했던 1895년에 건강에 좋고 안전한 제품인 농축우유를 발명했다. 윌리스 캐리어는 1902년의 자기 발명품을 '공기 닝빙 장치'라고 이름 붙였다. 글라렌스 버스아이는 냉동식품을워드, 아론 몽고메리 워드는 통신판매 목록을 혁신함으로써 벽지의 외딴 농장에 백화점을 도입했다.

> **Note**
> □ innovate = make new : 개혁하다
>   • They are trying to innovate the structure to survive the global competition.
>   (국제 경쟁에 살아 남기 위하여 구조를 개혁하려고 노력하고 있다.)
> □ condense = make more dense, more compact by compressing : 농축, 압축하다
>   • This chemical is condensed. Dilute it with ten times the water.(이 농약은 농축되어 있다. 10배의 물로 희석하라.)
>   • The government condensed the five-year plan into three years. (정부는 5개년 계획을 3년으로 압축했다.)
> □ mail order : 통신판매   □ catalog = a list of goods, names : 상품, 인명 목록
> □ enterprising : 모험심이 있는

11. The first type of volcano, the active one, always shows signs of volcanic action. The second type, the dormant volcano, is one that has not erupted yet, but it might someday. The third type, the extinct, is one that has not erupted in hundreds of years; it is dead.

(There is no topic sentence in the above paragraph.
You should summarize the main idea based on your logical reading skills.)

The topic sentence : There are _____ types of _____.

The supporting details:
        1. The first type⋯_____
        2. The second type⋯_____
        3. The third type⋯_____

12. The year 1968 will be remembered as the year in which Martin Luther King was killed. It will be remembered as the year Senator Robert Kennedy was killed. It will be remembered as a year of riots, wars, and strikes. It will be remembered as the year that three men saw the moon closely in Apollo 8, which no man has ever seen so closely before.

The topic sentence : The year 1968 will_____.

The supporting details :
        1. Martin Luther King⋯_____
        2. Senator Robert Kennedy⋯_____
        3. Riots, wars, and strikes⋯_____
        4. Three men⋯_____

13. Now, there are two different attitudes towards learning from others. One is the dogmatic attitude of transplanting everything, whether or not it is suited to our conditions. This is no good. The other attitude is to use our heads and learn those things which suit our conditions, that is, to absorb whatever experience is useful to us. That is the attitude we should adopt.

(Source: On the Correct Handling of Contradictions Among the People. (Feb. 27, 1957).
Quotations from Chairman Mao Tse-Tung, 1967)

The topic sentence : There are two⋯_____

The supporting details:
        1. One is⋯_____(as the sub-idea)
        2. This is⋯_____
        3. The other⋯_____(as the sub-idea)
        4. That is⋯_____

11. 화산의 제1유형인 활화산은 언제나 화산활동의 징조를 보여 준다. 제2유형인 휴화산은 아직 분출은 안 했지만 언젠가는 할 지도 모르는 것이다. 셋째 유형인 사화산은 수백년간 폭발하지 않은 것이다. 그것은 죽었다.

> **Note**
> □ volcano = a mountain with a large opening at the top through which lava, stream, gases, erupt : 화산
> □ active / dormant / extinct volcano : 활 / 휴 / 사화산
> □ erupt = explode and pour out fire : 폭발하고 불을 내뿜다. 감정을 분출하다
> • Violence erupted among the audiences after the soccer game.
> (축구 시합이 끝난 후 관중 사이에서 폭력 사태가 터졌다.)

12. 1968년은 마틴 루터 킹과 상원의원 로버트 케네디가 살해 당한 해로 기억될 것이다. 그 해는 폭동과 전쟁 그리고 파업의 해로 기억될 것이다. 그 해는 세 사람이 아폴로 8호에서 달을 면밀히, 그 전에는 그렇게 근접해서 본적이 없었던, 달을 관측한 해로 기억될 것이다.

> **Note**
> □ riot = a lot of violent action by a number of people : 다수에 의한 폭동
> • The army was called in to suppress the riots. (폭동을 진압하기 위하여 군이 투입되었다.)
> □ go on a strike : 파업하다

13. 자, 다른 사람들에게서 배우는 데는 두 가지 다른 태도가 있다. 하나는 그것이 우리 상황에 적합하건 않건 모든 것을 독단적으로 옮겨 심는 태도다. 이는 좋지 못하다. 다른 하나는 우리의 머리를 써서 우리 상황에 맞는 것들을 배우는 태도로, 바꾸어 말하면 우리에게 유용한 체험이면 무엇이나 흡수하는 것이다. 그것이 우리가 채택해야 할 태노인 것이다. (원전 : 국민 사이의 모순점을 바르게 조정하는 법 – 모택동 어록에서 인용)

> **Note**
> □ attitude = a way of feeling, thinking, behaving
> • What's your attitude toward this idea? (이 아이디어를 어떻게 생각하시나요?)
> □ dogma = a set of beliefs that people are expected to accept without question : 독단
> • It's harmful for a leader to be dogmatic in the matter of decision.
> (지도자가 결정을 내리는데 독단을 부리면 해롭다.)
> □ transplant = to move from one place and plant it in another place : 이식하다
> □ heart transplantation : 심장이식

14. Both President Lincoln and President Kennedy were attacked by an assassin on Friday, and each in the presence of his wife. Each man was shot in the head; in each instance, crowds of people watched the shooting. Lincoln's secretary, named Kennedy, had advised him not to go to the theater where the attack occurred. Kennedy's secretary, named Lincoln, had advised him not to go to Dallas where the attack occurred.

(Source: Building English Skills (1977))

The topic sentence : Both⋯_____

The supporting details :
          1. Each⋯_____
          2. Lincoln's⋯_____
          3. Kennedy's⋯_____

15. The spread of Islam was rapid for the following reasons. Muslims held that all believers were equal; therefore, they did not need priests or a church to practice their religion. They fought for one God, Allah, and to spread Islam.

    Muhammed died in A.D. 632, which was two years after he had taken over Mecca. By that time, his army had taken over most of Arabia. In the next 100 years, Islam spread from Arabia to all of the Middle East, Egypt, North Africa, and a part of Spain. It also spread to Persia, and parts of India.

The topic sentence : The spread of Islam⋯_____

The supporting details:
          1. Muslims⋯_____
          2. They⋯_____
          3. Muhammed⋯_____
          4. By⋯_____
          5. It⋯_____

16. At 17, Benjamin Franklin came to Philadelphia because it offered him opportunity. This noisy, bustling hub of colonial commerce was the largest English-speaking city in the New World. Ben took advantage of its promise and its hospitality. And the rest, as they say, is history.

    Philadelphia is steeped in the authentic and exciting history of America, and I encourage you to follow in Ben's footsteps. But, feel free to make up some steps of your own. Try our sports teams, an orchestra concert, a fine restaurant, a jazz club or a walk down South Street. Philadelphia offers everything and it offers it conveniently and safely. In fact, Philadelphia was recently named

14. 링컨 대통령도 케네디 대통령도 둘 다 금요일에 암살자의 공격을 받았고 또 각각 아내가 있는 자리에서 였다. 각각 머리에 총격을 당했고 많은 사람들이 총격을 지켜 보았다. 케네디라는 이름을 가진 링컨의 비서관이 그에게 습격이 일어났던 그 극장에 가지 말라고 충고했었다. 링컨이라는 이름의 케네디 비서관도 그에게 그 습격이 있었던 달라스에 가지 말라고 충고했었다.

> **Note**
> □ in the absence of = when one is not present : behind one's back : 없는 곳에서
> • Never find fault with anyone in his absence. (없는 사람 험담하지 말라.)
> □ assassin = a person who murders a ruler or politicians for political reason : 암살범
> □ in the presence of = close enough to be seen or heard : 보는 (듣는) 곳에서
> □ instance = case, event, example   □ for instance = for example
> • She is not reliable, for instance she stood me up last night.
> (그 여자는 믿을 수 없어. 예를 들면 어제 저녁에도 나를 바람 마쳤거든.)

15. 이슬람교의 전파는 다음과 같은 이유로 빨랐다. 모든 신자들은 평등하다고 믿었다. 그러기 때문에 그들의 종교의식을 수행할 승려나 교회당이 필요치 않았다. 그들은 유일신 알라를 위하여 싸웠고 이슬람교를 퍼뜨렸다.

모하메드는 기원 632년에 죽었는데 그가 메카를 차지한 2년 뒤였다. 그 때까지 그의 군대는 아라비아의 대부분을 점령했다. 그 다음 100년간 이슬람교는 아라비아로부터 중동의 전체, 이집트, 북 아프리카, 그리고 스페인의 일부, 페르시아, 인도의 몇 지역까지 퍼졌다.

16. 벤자민 프랭클린은 17세 때 필라델피아에 왔는데 그곳이 그에게 기회를 주었기 때문이었습니다. 이 소란하고 법석대는 식민지 상업 중심지는 신대륙에서 영어를 사용하는 최대의 도시였습니다. 벤은 이 도시가 가지는 장래성, 환대를 이용했습니다. 그리고 그 나머지는 흔히 말하듯이 역사입니다. 두말하면 잔소리지요.

필라델피아는 미국의 흥미 있고 진정한 역사 속에 흠뻑 젖어 있습니다. 나는 여러분들이 벤의 발자취를 따라가 보도록 권하렵니다. 그러니 마음 놓고 가보고 싶은 곳으로 가십시요. 우리의 스포츠팀, 관현악 연주회, 재즈클럽도 가 보시고, 혹은 사우스 스트리트를 따라 산책도 해보시지요. 필라델피아는 모든 것을, 또한 이를 편리하고 안전하게 제공합니다. 사실 필라델피아가 최근에 미국에서 가장 다정한 도시, 12개 대 도시 중 가장 안전한 도시, 최고의 식당 도시, 그리고 가장 정직한 도시로 명명되었습니다.

벤은 자랑스러울 것입니다. 우리 모두를 대표하여 내가 친히 여러분을 우정의 도시로 초대합니다. 여러분을 모셔서 반갑습니다.

필라델피아 시장 Edward G. Rendell

(원전 : 필라델피아를 즐기세요. 1998년 5월/6월호)

America's Friendliest City, the Safest of the 12 Largest Cities in America, the Best Restaurant City, and the Most Honest City.

Ben would be proud. On behalf of all of us, I would like to personally welcome you to the City of Brotherly Love. *We're glad you're here*.

                              Sincerely,

                              Edward G. Rendell,
                              Mayor of Philadelphia

(Source: <u>Enjoy Philadelphia</u>, May/June, 1998)

The topic sentence: *We're glad you're here* (Welcome to Philadelphia).

The supporting details:
        1. The first paragraph⋯_____
        2. The second paragraph⋯_____
        3. The third paragraph⋯_____

17. I recently asked some of my American friends what they thought a geisha was, and the comments I received were astonishing. For example, one friend said, "She is a woman who walks around in a hut." A second friend said, "A woman who massages men for money and it involves her in other physical activities." Finally, I got this comment from another friend, "She gives baths to men and walks on their backs." Well, needless to say, I was rather surprised and a little offended by their comments. I soon discovered that the majority of my American friends perceived the geisha with similar attitudes. One of them argued, "It's not my fault, because that is the way I have seen them on T.V." In many ways they are not mistaken because their misconceptions of the geisha are often resulted from American film producers and directors. In the movie, <u>The Barbarian and the Geisha</u>, the geisha is portrayed as a streetwalker.

    A geisha is neither a prostitute, streetwalker, or showgirl with a gimmick. She is a lovely Japanese woman who is a professional entertainer and hostess cultivated with exquisite manners and high-level of educational training.

The topic sentence : She is a lovely⋯_____
_____

The anecdotes used as supporting details :
        1. One friend said⋯_____
        2. Second friend said⋯_____
        3. Another friend said⋯_____
        4. One of them argued⋯_____
        5. In many ways⋯_____

Note

- □ bustle = make noise, hurry : 북적대다   □ hub = the center of activity : 활동 중심지
- □ take advantage of = make use of : 이용하다. 이용해 먹다
  - He took advantage of her innocence and sold the fake.(순진성을 이용하여 가짜를 팔았다.)
- □ hospitality : 인정, 환대
  - The Koreans are well known for their hospitality. (한국인들은 남을 대접하는 친절로 유명하다.)
- □ authentic = genuine, trustworthy : 진짜의, 원본의   • an authentic signature : 본인 친필 서명
- □ on behalf of = acting for someone : 대표(신)하여
  - The captain appealed to the referee on behalf of his team for fair judgment.
  (주장은 자기 팀을 대표하여 주심에게 공정한 심판을 호소했다.)
- □ feel free to : 마음 놓고 …하다   • Feel free to ask any questions.(마음 놓고 무슨 질문이든 하시오.)

17. 나는 최근에 미국 친구 몇 명에게 게이샤(geisha)에 대해서 어떻게 생각하느냐고 물었다. 그리고 내가 들은 설명은 놀랄 만한 것이었다. 예를 들면 한 친구는 "그 여자는 오두막 안에서 이리 저리 걷는 여자"라 했고 또 다른 친구는 "돈을 위해서 남자를 안마해 주는 여자인데 그 행위 속에는 다른 육체적인 행위도 포함된다"고 했다. 마지막으로 또 다른 친구에게서 다음의 논평을 들었다. "그녀는 남자들을 목욕시켜 주며 남자 등위를 걷기도 한다." 글쎄, 말할 필요도 없이 나는 그들의 논평에 놀랐고 약간 감정이 상했다. 나는 곧 대부분의 내 미국 친구들이 geisha를 비슷한 태도로 인식하고 있다는 것을 발견했다. 그들 중 한 사람과 논쟁했다. "그건 내 잘못이 아니야, 난 TV에서 그런 식으로 보았거든." 여러 면에서 그들이 틀린 것은 아니다. 왜냐하면 그들의 geisha에 대한 잘못된 인식은 미국영화의 제작자나 감독이 그런 결과를 낳았기 때문이다. "야만인과 geisha"라는 영화에서 geisha는 매춘녀로 그려졌었다.

geisha는 창녀도, 매춘녀도 아니고 속임수를 쓰는 유흥장의 저급 코러스걸도 아니다. 그녀는 교양 있고 섬세한 예절과 높은 수준의 교육수련을 받은 전문 연예인이며 호스티스인 아름다운 일본 여인이다.

Note

- □ geisha = a Japanese girl or woman who is trained to dance, sing and perform various arts to amuse men. : 일본기생(藝者)
- □ needless to say = of course : 말할 필요 없이, 물론
- □ misconception = understanding wrongly : 잘못된 인식
- □ prostitute = a person esp. woman who earns money by having a sex : 창녀
- □ gimmick : 주의를 끌려고 속임 장치
- □ cultivated = having or showing good education : 교양이 있는
- □ an exquisite taste / manners / piece of jewelry : 고상한 취미, 예절 / 정교한 보석

2-8 MAKING INFERENCES

This section, "Making inferences" is to help the readers develop interpretative and generalizing skills in drawing a probable conclusion without sufficient amount of information provided. In other words, the readers should see beyond the facts given. To do this, the readers should utilize gained knowledge and past experiences to get the information that is implied. A conclusion is a logical deduction drawn from the specific facts presented, whereas an inference is a probable conclusion drawn from less conclusive evidence.

Let's see the following example :

Mrs. Brown lives in a tiny one-room apartment in the ghetto area.
A social worker walks into the room, and he notices that there are no T.V. set, sofa, refrigerator in the room. The paint is peeling off the walls.

From the information given, you can infer her economic condition based on the following facts :

    (1) She lives in a tiny one-room apartment in the ghetto area.
    (2) There are no T.V. set, sofa, and refrigerator.
    (3) The paint is peeling off.

Thus, the inference is that <u>Mrs. Brown is poor</u>. But, please be reminded that the fact <u>Mrs. Brown is poor</u> is a probable conclusion rather than a logical deduction.

We can infer <u>the meaning of the word</u> based on (1) the main idea; (2) stated details; (3) cause and effect relationship; (4) implied comparison; and, (5) implied contrast. We can also infer <u>facts</u> based on the details or the contexts of the passage presented. The following exercise will help you develop more inference skills.

2-8 추론하기

이절 '추론하기'는 독자들로 하여금 제공된 충분한 양의 정보 없이도 그럴듯한 결론을 도출하는데 해석하고 일반화시키는 기능을 개발하도록 돕는 것이다. 바꾸어 말하면 독자들은 주어진 사실들, 그 이상을 보아야 한다. 이렇게 하려면 함축된 정보를 얻기 위하여 습득한 지식과 과거의 경험을 활용해야 한다. 결론이란 제시된 구체적 사실에서 끌어낸 논리적 연역이고 반면에 추론이란 덜 결정적인 증거에서 끌어낸 그럴듯한 결론이다.

다음 예를 들어보자.

브라운 여사는 빈민 거주지역의 단칸방 아파트에서 살고 있다.
어떤 사회 사업가가 방안에 들어와 방안에 TV수상기, 소파, 냉장고가 없음을 알아차린다.
벽에서 페인트가 벗겨지고 있다.

주어진 정보에서 다음 사실을 근거로 그녀의 경제적 형편을 추리할 수 있다.

(1) 그녀는 빈민 거주 지역내 작은 단칸 아파트에서 산다.
(2) TV 수상기, 소파 그리고 냉장고가 없다.
(3) 페인트가 벗겨지고 있다.

이리하여 추론은 브라운 여사는 가난하다는 사실이다. 그러나 브라운 여사가 가난하다는 사실은 논리적인 추론이라기보다는 있음직한 결론이라는 것을 기억하기 바란다.

우리는 모르는 단어의 의미를 다음의 근거로 추리할 수 있다. **(1) 요지 (2) 진술된 세부사실 (3) 인과관계 (4) 함축된 비교 (5) 함축된 대조.** 우리는 또한 사실들을 제시된 글의 세부사항이나 문맥을 토대로 하여 추리할 수 있다. 다음 연습문제는 더 많은 추론 기능을 개발하는데 도움이 될 것이다.

Note

- **interpretative = explanatory** : 설명해주는
- **generalize = to form a general principle** : 일반화하다, 보편적인 사실로 만들다
  - Is it fair to generalize from these two accidents and say that all young people are bad drivers?
    (이 두건의 사고로 젊은 사람들은 운전이 서툴다고 일반화하여 말하는 게 공정한가요?)
- **utilize = make good use of** : 이용하다 • Utilize your abilities in the suitable job.
- **imply = express indirectly, suggest** : 함축하다
- **logical = in accordance with the rules of logic** : 논리적인
- **deduction** : 연역법 : 보편적 원리에서 특수한 사실을 끌어내는 것 : 연역, 추리
  - cf. induction (귀납법 : 특수한 여러 사실에서 보편적 원리를 도출하는 방식)
- **ghetto area** : 빈민가, 흑인 밀집 지역   **cause and effect relationship** : 인과 관계
- **peeling = remove the outer covering** : 껍질을 벗기다 – peel a banana / an apple / a pear

EXERCISE

Choose the best answer on the basis of your inference.

INFERENCE BASED ON THE MAIN IDEA

1. When I went to the zoo, I wondered where the zoo keeps its many kinds of birds. I asked one of the zoo keepers, and he said, "You can go to the aviary." I went there without knowing the meaning of the aviary. It was really huge and there were hundreds of different kinds of colorful birds inside. The aviary looked like a jungle.

(1) The word, "aviary" must be the place where the _____ are kept.

- (a) peacocks
- (b) birds
- (c) reptiles
- (d) flamingoes
- (e) cranes

2. No one really knows the length of time that men have been on earth. It is estimated between one to four million years, depending on the definition of "men." However, archaeologists claim that the homo sapiens who were physically similar to modern men have existed about 50,000 years.

(1) The word, homo sapiens must be the

- (a) orangutans
- (b) gorillas
- (c) chimpanzees
- (d) first men
- (e) monkeys

INFERENCE BASED ON STATED DETAILS

3. It was a very hot summer day in New York City. The asphalt was slowly being cooked by the summer heat. Most of the neighbors were watching their televisions with their air conditioners on. Suddenly there was a power failure and the cool houses began to turn into hot and humid ones since the air conditioners were off. As people began to go outside to escape the stifling heat in their homes, they began to talk with each other. When one of the neighbors

연습문제
추론을 토대로 하여 최선의 답을 골라라.

요지를 토대로 한 추론

1. 동물원에 갔을 때 나는 동물원이 그 많은 종류의 새들을 어디에 넣어 놓는지 궁금했다. 동물원 관리인에게 물었더니 'aviary'에 가보라고 했다. 난 aviary의 뜻도 모르는 채 그 곳으로 갔다. 그곳은 거대했고 안에는 형형색색의 새들이 있었다. 그 aviary는 마치 밀림 같았다

> **Note**
> □ aviary : a large cage or enclosure for keeping birds in : 큰 새장이나 막아 놓은 곳
> □ reptile = a rough skinned creature whose blood changes according to the surrounding : 파충류 • Snakes and lizards are reptiles.(뱀과 도마뱀은 파충류다.)

2. 아무도 인간이 지구상에 살아온 시간의 길이를 모른다. 그 시간은 인간을 어떻게 정의하느냐에 따라서 1백만년에서 4백만년으로 추산된다. 그러나 고고학자들은 현대인과 유사한 인간은 약 5만년간 존재해 왔다고 주장한다.

> **Note**
> □ homosapiens : (분류학 상의) 인간 – 지능을 가진 생물로서의 인간 – homo = man, sapiens = wise
> □ homoerectus : 직립 인간   □ homoludens : 유희인
> □ estimate = calculate and form an opinion : 견적, 추산하다
>   • I asked the building company to estimate the cost of the repairs.(건물 수리비의 견적을 물었다.)
> □ archaeologist = a scientist who studies buried remains of an ancient times : 고고학자

진술된 세부사항을 근거로 한 추론

3. 뉴욕시의 그날은 몹시 더운 여름날이었다. 아스팔트는 여름의 열기로 서서히 달아오르고 있었다. 대부분의 이웃들은 에어컨을 켠 채 TV를 보고 있었다. 갑자기 정전이 되었고 서늘한 집들은 에어컨이 꺼져 덥고 눅눅해졌다. 사람들은 실내의 숨막힐듯한 더위를 피하기 위하여 밖으로 나가면서 서로 대화하기 시작했다. 어느 이웃사람이 음식을 가지고 나왔을 때 다른 사람들도 가지고 나왔다. 이렇게 하여 즉석 동네 잔치로 커졌다.

brought out some food, so did the other people. Thus, an impromptu block party developed.

(1) The word "impromptu" must be

    (a) planned   (d) elaborate
    (b) spontaneous   (e) unwanted
    (c) hosted

4. Today's young people seem to enjoy a lifestyle known as "Joie de vivre." That is, they want to earn a substantial amount of money in a short period of time. They love to go out for extravagant dinners, parties, and other social activities. And in romance and friendships, they prefer short term encounters.

(1) The word "Joie de vivre" must be

    (a) realistic   (d) practical
    (b) responsible   (e) enjoyment of life
    (c) pragmatic

INFERENCE BASED ON CAUSE AND EFFECT RELATIONSHIP

5. The sign beside the faucet in the restroom in Italy carries the warning, "Aqua no potable." The people who ignored the warning could become sick from drinking the water.

(1) "Aqua no potable" must mean

    (a) no smoking   (d) undrinkable water
    (b) no littering   (e) no washing
    (c) no eating

INFERENCE BASED ON IMPLIED COMPARISON

6. My seven years old niece, Lily, is an amalgam of the most desirable traits of all the members of her family. Lily has her father's sense of responsibility; her mother's tenderness and cheerfulness; her grandfather's intellectual pursuit and calmness; and, her grandmother's affection and sincerity.

> **Note**
> ☐ stifle = cause difficulty to breathe : 질식시키다 　 ☐ stifling : 숨막히는
> ☐ impromptu = without preparation, at once : 즉석에서, 준비없이
> ☐ impromptu verse : 즉흥시 　 ☐ impromptu dinner : 즉석 요리

4. 오늘의 젊은이들은 '삶의 기쁨'이라고 알려진 삶의 형태를 즐기는 것 같다. 즉 그들은 단기간에 상당히 큰 돈을 벌고 싶어한다. 호화스런 만찬, 파티 및 사교활동에 참여하기 위하여 외출하기를 좋아한다. 또한 애정이나 우정에 있어서도 단기간의 우연한 만남을 선호한다.

> **Note**
> ☐ joie de vivre = joy of living : 삶의 기쁨, 즐기는 삶
> ☐ substantial = of some size or value, noticeable : 상당한, 튼실한, 실속있는
> ☐ substantial income / meal / victory / amount of money :
> 　상당한 수입 / 실속있는 식사 / 사실상의 승리 / 상당한 액수의 돈
> ☐ extravagant = wasteful esp. of money 　 ☐ extravagant man : 돈을 헤프게 쓰는 사람

인과 관계를 기초로 한 추론

5. 이탈리아의 공중 화장실 수도꼭지 옆에 게시문은 "Aqua no potable"라는 경고의 의미를 갖고 있다. 그 경고를 무시한 사람들은 그 물을 마시고 병이 나기도 했다.

> **Note**
> ☐ warning : 경고, 해고 통보, 사전 주의 　• without warning (사전 경고 없이)
> 　• Let that be a warning for you. (미리 경고해 두겠네)
> ☐ aqua no potable : 음료부적 - aqua = water, potable = drinkable 　• cf. portable (휴대용)

함축된 비교를 근거로 한 추론

6. 나의 7세된 조카딸 릴리는 그녀의 모든 가족들의 가장 바람직한 특성들을 섞어 놓은 아이다. 그녀는 아버지의 책임감, 어머니의 다정함과 명랑함, 조부의 지적 연구심과 침착함, 그리고 조모의 사랑과 성실함을 가지고 있다.

(1) The "amalgam" must mean

    (a) separation   (d) particles

    (b) characters   (e) combination/mixture

    (c) operation

INFERENCE BASE ON IMPLIED CONTRAST

7. Most Americans would find it difficult to follow the ascetic lifestyle of traditional Buddhist or Taoist monks. Many modern inventions such as computers, VCR, dishwasher are considered necessities to the Americans, but to the monks, they are just luxuries which they do not depend on too much.

(1) The word "ascetic" must be

    (a) simple   (d) luxurious

    (b) complicated   (e) fanatic

    (c) comfortable

8. Read the following paragraph and decide whether each sentence provided below the paragraph is an Inference (I), a False statement (F), or a True statement (T). Check X on the appropriate box provided.

8.1. On Monday, Tom worked for a farmer. He was paid a half dollar, but he lost it. "You should have put it in your pocket," said his mother.

    On Tuesday, Tom worked for the farmer again. He was given milk as payment. Tom put the milk in his pocket. "You should have carried the jug on your head," said his mother.

    On Wednesday, Tom worked for the farmer again. He was given a donkey for pay.

	I	F	T
(1) He will carry the donkey on his head	(x)	( )	( )
(2) He will put the donkey in his pocket	( )	(x)	( )
(3) He will ride the donkey	( )	(x)	( )
(4) He was given a donkey for pay	( )	( )	(x)

8.2. Susan Guy gets up at 6:00 every morning, prepares some food for her children, and drives them to the day care center before she goes to work. At 6:00 p.m., she picks them up and drives home to cook dinner. After dinner, she reads and reviews some chapters in criminology, international law, and the Civil

> **Note**
> □ trait = particular quality, characteristic : 특질, 특성
>   • Generosity is her best trait. (너그러움이 그녀 최대의 특징이다.)
> □ pursuit of truth, beauty, happiness : 진리 탐구, 미의 추구, 행복의 추구
> □ sincerity = honesty, being true and real : 정직, 성실

함축된 대조에 근거한 추론

7. 대부분의 미국인들은 전통적인 불교 승려나 도교 신자들의 금욕적인 생활 형식을 따르기가 힘들다는 것을 알게 될 것이다. 많은 현대 발명품들, 예를 들면 컴퓨터, 비디오 녹화기, 접시 세척기 같은 것들은 미국인들에게 필수품으로 여겨지고 있지만 그 승려들에게 그것들은 그들이 별로 의존하지 않는 단지 사치품일 뿐이다.

> **Note**
> □ ascetic = of a person who does not allow himself or herself bodily pleasures esp. for religious reasons : 금욕주의자 - 자기 자신에게 육체적인 쾌락을 허용하지 않는 고행자
> □ Taoist : 도교신자 : 노자의 가르침을 신봉.   □ VCR = Video Cassette Recorder

8. 다음 문단을 읽고 다음 문단 아래 주어진 문장이 다음 어느 것인지 결정하라 : 아래 주어진 ( )에 X표시를 하라.
    (I) 추론   (F) 허위 진술   (T) 바른 진술.

8.1. 월요일에 톰은 농부의 일을 도왔다. 그는 50센트를 받았는데 분실했다. "그걸 호주머니에 넣었어야지."라고 어머니가 말씀하셨다.
  화요일에 그는 또다시 그 농부를 위해서 일했다. 대가로 우유를 받아 호주머니 속에 넣었다. "그 우유단지를 머리에 이고 날랐어야지."
  수요일에 또 그 농부를 도왔다. 그는 보수로 당나귀 한마리를 받았다.

> **Note**
> □ jug = a pot for liquids with a handle and a lip for pouring : 손잡이가 있고 따를 때 쓰이는 주둥이가 있는 항아리
> □ appropriate = correct, suitable : 적합한
>   • His bright clothes were not appoariate for the funeral. (그의 화려한 옷은 장례식에 적합하지 않았다.)

Proceeding Acts for her evening courses. She is attending the Law School of Yale University and she plans to take the bar examination next year.

	I	F	T
(1) Susan wants to be a lawyer	( )	( )	( )
(2) Susan has probably never been married	( )	( )	( )
(3) Susan is an irresponsible woman	( )	( )	( )
(4) Susan is probably a single parent	( )	( )	( )
(5) Susan's children are too young to go to school	( )	( )	( )

<u>8.3.</u> Until recently, people fantasized about the discovery of life on Mars or Venus. In the past, many people thought that there were some creatures alive on the moon. Now it has been discovered that only one planet in our solar system can support and develop life because this planet provides the necessary condition for life to develop.

	I	F	T
(1) Some people thought that there were some forms of life on Mars or Venus	( )	( )	( )
(2) In the solar system, there are no planets which offer proper conditions for life to develop	( )	( )	( )
(3) In the solar system, Earth is the only one planet that provides proper conditions for life to develop	( )	( )	( )
(4) In the solar system, there is only one planet that supports life	( )	( )	( )
(5) Besides the Earth in the solar system, there might be life on Jupiter or Neptune	( )	( )	( )

<u>8.4.</u> Whales are air-breathing mammals that live in the sea. Sometimes, when a whale gets near a beach or shallow water, it can get stuck there. Few people know why a whale gets stranded. Scientists have offered some possible answers; most stranded whales are ill, and, the sick ones need to stay near the surface to breathe easily. But most of them die shortly after being stranded.

(Source: Adapted from "Stranded Whales." G. & E. Spache (1984). Reading: Project Achievement D)

	I	F	T
(1) The way that the whales breathe is			
(a) through their mouth in the sea	( )	( )	( )
(b) through their nose and mouth in the sea	( )	( )	( )
(c) coming up to the sea surface	( )	( )	( )
(d) breathing only once every half and hour	( )	( )	( )
(e) through their gills	( )	( )	( )

8.2. 스잔 가이는 매일 아침 6시에 일어나, 자식들의 식사를 준비하고 출근하기 전에 차로 탁아소에 실어다 준다. 오후 6시면 그들을 집에 실어오고 저녁 식사를 준비한다. 저녁 후 야간 수업을 받기 위하여 형사학, 국제법, 민사 소송법 몇 장을 읽거나 복습한다. 그녀는 지금 예일 대학교 법학부에 다니고 있으며 내년에 변호사 시험을 볼 계획이다.

> **Note**
> □ day care center : 탁아소
> □ criminology : 형사학, 범죄학
> □ bar exam : 변호사 시험
> □ medical center : 중앙 의료원
> □ Civil Proceeding Acts : 민사 소송법
> □ Criminal Procedure Law : 형사 소송법

8.3. 최근까지 사람들은 화성이나 금성에서 생명체를 발견하는 것에 대해 환상을 가졌다. 과거에 많은 사람들은 달에 몇몇 살아있는 동물이 있다고 생각했다. 지금 태양계에는 생명체를 먹여 살리고 키울 수 있는 단 하나의 혹성만 존재한다는 사실이 발견되었다. 왜냐하면 이 혹성만이 생명체가 발육할 수 있는 조건을 공급하기 때문이다.

> **Note**
> □ fantasize = dream : 공상하다
> • She spends too much time in fantasizing about her married life that is to come.
> (그녀는 앞으로 다가올 결혼생활을 꿈꾸는 데 시간을 너무 많이 보낸다.)
> □ solar system = the sun together with the bodies going round it : 태양계
> • Mercury, Venus, Earth, Mars, Jupiter, Saturn, Uranus, Neptune, Pluto (수, 금, 지, 화, 목, 토, 천, 해, 명)

8.4. 고래는 물속에 사는 허파로 숨을 쉬는 포유류다. 때때로 고래가 해변이나 얕은 물에 접근하여 그곳에서 꼼짝 못하게 될 수 있다. 왜 고래가 오도가도 못하는(좌초 당하는)지 아는 사람은 드물다. 과학자들이 몇가지 해답을 제시했다. (1) 대부분의 좌초 당한 고래는 병들었다. (2) 아픈 고래들은 호흡을 쉽게 하려고 수면 근처에 머무른다. 그러나 그들 대부분은 좌초 즉후 죽는다.

> **Note**
> □ mammal = an animal of the type which is fed on mother's milk : 포유류
> □ stick to = refuse to leave : 달라붙다, 고집하다 • Stick to your original plan. (원안대로 하라.)
> □ be stranded = 좌초당하다, 오도가도 못하다
> • The wrecked sailors were stranded on the deserted island. (난파 선원들은 무인도에서 꼼짝 못했다.)

(2) Sometimes whales get stranded on a beach when they
   (a) look for mates ( ) ( ) ( )
   (b) look for food ( ) ( ) ( )
   (c) are very weak ( ) ( ) ( )
   (d) take care of their young ( ) ( ) ( )
   (e) swim into shallow water to breathe easily ( ) ( ) ( )

8.5. The Chiricahua Apache Chief Geronimo (1829-1909) and his warriors fought bitterly with the U.S. soldiers and settlers in the Southwest, mainly in Arizona. The Apaches could not beat them; instead they were driven back. Chief Geronimo gazed at the small cloud of dust traveling with his people to the south. The remainder of his small warrior band stood in silence, hunger, and fatigue. The group now numbered fourteen. In two days they would reach the relative security of the box canyon on the Rio Oro. Several years later, Geronimo was captured and imprisoned, which ended the large scale resistance of the American Indians.

	I	F	T
(1) Apache Geronimo and his warriors were traveling south	( )	( )	( )
(2) Eventually, Geronimo was captured	( )	( )	( )
(3) Geronimo and his warriors were being pursued by an enemy	( )	( )	( )
(4) After Geronimo's capture, there have not been any battles between the American Indians and the U.S. soldiers	( )	( )	( )
(5) Geronimo and his warriors reached the Rio Oro within two days	( )	( )	( )

8.6. A small group of people from northeastern Europe called Easterlings came to England to devise and develop a new system of coinage. They lived in towns well known for the accuracy of their coins. The coins they worked out for England were made of silver known as the Easterling coins. Later, the word Easterling was shortened to "sterling." Since the new coins were made of such fine quality, the word sterling gradually began to refer to all silver articles of very fine quality. Even today the term is used to refer to silver articles of a very high grade.

	I	F	T
The Easterlings were			
(a) primitive people	( )	( )	( )
(b) skilled and honest workmen	( )	( )	( )
(c) of English origin	( )	( )	( )

8.5. Chiricahua 아파치의 추장인 제로니모와 그의 투사들은 남서부, 주로 메인주에서 미국 병사들과 그리고 정착민들과 치열하게 싸웠다. 아파치들은 그들을 이길 수 없었고 오히려 뒤로 밀렸다. 추장은 그의 부족과 함께 남으로 이동하며 먼지 구름을 물끄러미 보았다. 남아있는 소수의 전투부대는 침묵과 기아와 피로 속에 서 있었다. 부족의 수는 14명이었다. 이틀후면 비교적 안전한 Rio Oro변의 협곡에 도착할 것이다. 몇년 후 제로니모는 체포되어 투옥 당했고, 이로써 아메리카 인디언의 대규모의 저항은 끝났다.

Note
- warrior = a soldier, experienced fighter : 투사
- bitterly = very extremely : 지독하게, 맹렬히 • I was bitterly frustrated. (철저히 좌절했었다.)
- gaze = look steadily for a long time : 주시하다
  • She sat gazing out of the window. (창밖을 물끄러미 내다보고 앉아 있었다.)
- fatigue = great tiredness : 피로

8.6. 이스터링즈라고 불리는 한 작은 무리의 사람들이 북동부 유럽에서 새로운 동전 주조제도를 개발하기 위하여 영국에 왔다. 그들은 동전의 정확성으로 잘 알려진, 마을들에 살았다. 그들이 영국을 위하여 연구해 낸 동전은 이스터링 동전으로 알려진, 은으로 만든 것이었다. 후에 이스터링은 줄여서 스터링이 되었다. 그 동전은 매우 훌륭한 품질로 만들어져 스터링이라는 단어는 점차 고품질의 은제품을 가리키기 시작했다. 오늘날도 그 용어는 아주 높은 등급의 은제품을 가리키는 데 쓰여진다.

Note
- devise = plan or invent, contrive : 고안하다
  • He devised a plan for winning the game. (게임을 이길 방안을 고안했다.)
- coinage : 동전 주조
- refer to = mention • He referred to the plan for studying abroad. (유학 계획에 대하여 언급했다.)
- term = a word or expression used in a particular activity : 용어, 술어
- a medical term : 의학 용어   • technical term : 전문 용어

8.7. 두뇌 크기의 점전적인 증가는 인류진화의 가장 괄목할 만한 특징 중의 하나다. 3~5백만년 전에 지구상에 존재했던 오스트랄로피테쿠스족은 현대인 두뇌 크기의 1/3이었다. 2백만년 전에 살았던 호모하빌리스족과 호모에렉투스(1백50만년에서 50만년전까지 살았음)는 시간이 흐름에 따라 더 커졌다. 호모네안데르탈인(50만년-3만5천년전)은 호모 하

(d) from northeastern Europe ( ) ( ) ( )
(e) of Spanish origin ( ) ( ) ( )

8.7. The gradual increase in brain size is one of the most notable characteristics of human evolution. Australopithecus who dwelt on earth about 3~5 million years ago had a brain about 1/3 the size of a modern human brain. The Homo habilis who existed on earth two million years ago, and the Homo erectus (existed from 1.5 million~500,000 years ago) got larger through time. The Homo neanderthalensis (500,000~35,000 years ago) had a brain larger than the Homo habilis and the Homo erectus, but smaller than that of Homo sapiens. Therefore, the hypothesis, "As their brains developed, so did their ability to make tools, use fire and hunt" seems to be true.

	I	F	T
(1) Australopithecus lived between 5~3 million years ago	( )	( )	( )
(2) The brain size of Neanderthal is smaller than that of Home erectus	( )	( )	( )
(3) The larger the brain size, the more functional abilities the brain generates	( )	( )	( )
(4) One of the most notable traits of human evolution can be detected from the gradual increase in brain size	( )	( )	( )
(5) The size of the brain and the gender difference are correlated; A man's brain size is larger than that of a woman	( )	( )	( )

8.8. John Locke (1632-1704) advocated common sense and practicality in opposing to absolutism. In his book, <u>Two Treaties in Government</u> (1690), he explicated that people have a natural right to life, liberty, and property. Rulers have a responsibility to protect those rights. People have the right to change a government that fails to do so.

	I	F	T
(1) Locke's ideas might have influenced the writers of U.S. Declaration of Independence, and French revolutionaries in 1790s	( )	( )	( )
(2) His ideas were probably not welcomed by the European monarchs who struggled to centralize their powers	( )	( )	( )
(3) His ideas opposed the divine right of Kings	( )	( )	( )
(4) His ideas did not impress the U.S. colonists	( )	( )	( )

빌리스나 호모 에렉투스보다 더 큰 두뇌를 가졌었지만 호모사피엔스의 뇌보다는 작았다. 그러므로 '그들의 뇌가 발달할수록 연장을 만들고, 불을 사용하고 사냥하는 능력이 발달했다' 는 가설은 사실인것 같다.

> **Note**
> - **Homo habilis** : 처음으로 도구를 만든 직립 원인
> - **Homo Neanderthalensis** : 구석기시대 유럽에 살았던 인류
> - **gradual** = happening slowly and by degrees : 점진적인
>   - There has been a gradual raise in wages. (임금이 점진적으로 인상됐다.)
> - **evolution** = the development of various types from simpler forms : 진화
> - **hypothesis** : 가정, 전제
>   - According to the government's hypothesis, the high cost of living is caused by increased wages.
>   (정부측 가설(증명되기 전의 주장)에 의하면 높은 생활비는 임금 인상 때문이란다.)

<u>8.8.</u> 존 로크는 절대론에 반대하여 상식과 실용성을 주장했다. 그의 저서 정부론(정부에 관한 두 논문)에서 인간은 생명, 자유, 그리고 재산에 대하여 천부적 권리를 갖는다고 밝혔다. 통치자에게는 이러한 권리를 보호할 책임이 있다. 국민은 그렇게 할 능력이 없는 정부를 바꿀 수 있다.

> **Note**
> - **John Locke(1632~1704)** : 영국의 경험주의 철학자, 심리학자, 교육자
> - **advocate** = speak in favor of, support : 옹호, 주장하다
>   - The opposition advocated the reduction in taxes. (야당은 세금을 낮추라고 주장했다.)
> - **common sense** = a practical good sense and judgement gained from experience rather than special knowledge from school and study : 경험에서 터득한 상식
>   - Although he's not very intelligent, he's got lots of common sense.
>   (그렇게 총명하지는 못해도 상식이 풍부하다.)
> - **absolutism** : 절대론 – 나라의 권력은 절대적인 것으로 개인은 복종해야 한다는 주장
> - **explicate** = explain, expound : 상세히 설명하다
>   - He explicated that duty precedes right for the common good.
>   (공동선을 위하여 의무가 권리를 선행해야 한다고 설파했다.)

<u>8.9.</u> 독일의 사회경제학 이론가인 칼 마르크스는 1848년에 엥겔스와 함께 '공산당 선언'이라는 소책자를 발간했다. 그 선언에서 경제는 역사의 원동력이라는 이론을 전개했다. 그는 역사의 전 과정은 가진 자와 가지지 못한 자간의 계급 투쟁이라고 주장했다. 가진 자들은 항상 생산 수단을 소유하고 사회와 부를 지배해 왔다. 산업화된 유럽에서 가진 자들은

(5) His ideas were probably welcomed by the   ( )   ( )   ( )
fundamental religious sect which was so certain
of its exclusive truth in interpreting the scripture
and its congregation

8.9. Karl Marx (1818-1883), German socioeconomic theorist, published a pamphlet, The <u>Communist Manifesto</u> with Engels in 1848. In the <u>Manifesto</u>, he theorized that economics was the driving force in history. The entire course of history, he argued, was "the history of class struggles" between the "haves" and "have-nots." The "haves" have always owned the means of production and thus controlled society and all its wealth. In industrialized Europe, the "haves" were the bourgeoisie or middle-class. The "have-nots" were the proletariat or working class.

	I	F	T
(1) His ideas might have influenced the Russian Revolution of 1917	( )	( )	( )
(2) His ideas was welcomed and adopted by all the leaders of the socialist countries during the early 20th century	( )	( )	( )
(3) Marx despised capitalism, because the system of capitalism was only for the few "haves."	( )	( )	( )
(4) Marx was symbolized as champion of the working class, and his prediction, "the working class will have their own days," came true	( )	( )	( )
(5) At first, his ideas had little impact; however, in time it grew to have worldwide effects. Later, revolutionaries around the world would adopt his ideas to their own ends.	( )	( )	( )

(Note: Refer to the attached article on Karl Marx and Friedrich Engels for additional information)

부르조아 즉 중산계급이었다. 가지지 못한 자들은 프롤레타리아 즉 노동자 계급이었다.

> **Note**
> ☐ driving force = motive power : 원동력 ☐ haves and have - nots : 가진자와 안가진자
> ☐ means of production : 생산 수단 ☐ a mile or 1609 meters : 1마일 즉 1609미터

그들의 운명과 공산당 선언

칼 마르크스(Marx, Karl Heinrich) : 1818년 독일 태생, '공산당 선언의 주된 작성자' 광범위한 연구, 파리로 이민, 과격한 정치 활동 몰두, 이민 1년만인 1844년 프랑스에서 추방당함. 벨기에 브뤼셀로 가서 역사 연구에 헌신. 런던에 본부를 둔 공산당 연맹 가입. 1847년 연맹 회의에서 평생 동지 프리드리히 엥겔스와 공산당 선언 작성 위임 받음. 여생을 정치연구와 저술에 종사. 잠시 뉴욕 데일리 트리뷴지 특파원. 1883년 런던에서 사망.

프리드리히 엥겔스(Engels, Friedrich) : 독일 태생, 1820년 부유한 방직업자의 아들로 태어남. 청년시절 경제, 사회개혁을 주장하는 사회주의자들의 모임에 참석, 급진적 정치를 위한 출판 원고 작성. 1844년 파리에서 마르크스와 해후. 두 사람 동일한 정치적 견해 공유 확인. 공산당 선언을 포함하여 많은 저술에서 동지가 됨(선언의 중심 작성자는 마르크스). 20년 가까이 가업에 종사하고 이익금으로 마르크스 후원. 마르크스 사후 독자적 저술. 1895년 런던에서 사망. 유산을 마르크스의 자손들에게 남김.

8.10. 1941년 12월 7일 이른 시간에 일본 전투기와 폭격기들이 미국 함대를 공격하여 19척의 배를 격파하고 지상 미군기들을 대파하고 2,400여명의 민간인을 죽였다. 그 다음날, 엄숙한 얼굴을 한 루즈벨트 대통령은 12월 7일을 '치욕 속에 살아야 할 날'이라고 국민에게 말했다. 일본의 기습공격 조금 뒤에 연합군은 힘 센 지원군을 얻었으니 그 일본의 기습공격이 미국을 전쟁 속으로 던져 넣었기 때문이었다.

　1930년대 후반부터 일본은 중국을 정복하려고 노력하여 왔었다. 비록 일본은 중국의 동쪽지방을 많이 점령했지만 중국인들은 여간해서 항복하지 않았다. 1939년에 유럽에서 전쟁이 터졌을 때 일본인들은 동남 아시아에 있는 유럽의 영지들을 차지할 기회로 생각했다. 이 지역의 풍부한 자원, 기름, 고무, 주석을 포함한 풍부한 자원들이 제국주의자 일본인 지도자들에게 막대한 가치가 될 것이었기 때문이다.

> **Note**
> ☐ reconnaissance plane : 정찰기
> ☐ smash = break into pieces violently : 박살내다. (정구, 배드민턴, 탁구) 강타
> ☐ 형용사-명사+ed ; 명사-명사+ed : …한, …을 가진
> • high-nosed : 콧대 높은 • long-haired : 장발의 • rough-skinned : 까칠한 피부의
> • hard-fisted : 인색한 • warm-hearted : 가슴이 따뜻한 • three-headed : 머리가 셋 달린
> • poker-faced : 무표정한 • iron-hearted : 무정한 • pigeon-hearted : 소심한
> ☐ infamy = disgrace : 치욕, 악명 ☐ surprise attack : 기습 • surprise party : 깜짝 파티
> ☐ grab = seize with a sudden rough movement : 갑자기 움켜 쥐다
> ☐ imperialist : 강대국이 약소국에 대하여 정치, 경제적 이익을 차지하는 자, 제국주의자

8.10. Early on December 7, 1941, Japanese fighters and bombers struck the American fleet, destroying 19 ships, smashing American airplanes on the ground, and killing more than 2,400 people. The next day, a grim-faced President Roosevelt told the nation that December 7 was "a date which will live in infamy." Soon after Japanese surprise attack, the Allies gained a vital boost because that attack pitched the United States into the war.

From the late 1930s, Japan had been trying to conquer China. Although Japan occupied much of eastern China, the Chinese would not surrender. When the war broke out in Europe in 1939, the Japanese saw a chance to grab European possessions in Southeast Asia. The rich resources of the region, including oil, rubber, and tin, would be of immense value for the imperialist Japanese leaders.

	I	F	T
(1) The sudden Japanese attack on December 7, 1941, must be the one on Pearl Harbor, Hawaii	( )	( )	( )
(2) "Japan occupied much of eastern China," which refers to Korea	( )	( )	( )
(3) President Roosevelt's phrase in his congress speech, "A date which will live in infamy" infers that he asked congress to declare war on Japan	( )	( )	( )
(4) "European possessions in Southeast Asia" refers to such countries as India, Pakistan, Ceylon, Thailand, and Singapore	( )	( )	( )
(5) "The Allies gained a vital boost" because the U.S. would declare war on Japan first, which eventually led to Germany and Italy	( )	( )	( )

Selected proverbs for the study of cross-cultural expressions

영어 격언과 한문 격언과의 만남 (4)

1 Beauty is potent, but money is omnipotent. 金錢無所不爲(금전무소불위) – 돈이면 안되는 일이 없다.
· Gold goes in at any gate except Heaven's. / · A golden key opens every door.
· A sliver key can open an iron lock. / · All things are obedient to money.
· Money makes the mare go. / · When money speaks, the world is silent.

2 None so blind as those who will not see.
心不在焉 視而不見 聽而不聞(심부재언 시이불견 청이불문)
– 마음이 없으면 보아도 보이지 않고 들어도 들리지 않는다. · None so deaf as those who will not hear.

3 Praise the sea, but keep on land. 不謀危險(불모위험) – 위험을 사서 하지 마라.

4 Afterwit is dear bought. 亡羊補牢(망양보뢰 ; 牢 = stable) – 소 잃고 외양간 고친다.
· It's too late to shut the stable door after the horse has bolted. / · Afterwit ever comes late.

5 A near neighbor is better than a far-dwelling kinsman. 遠親不如近隣(원친불여근린)
– 먼 친척이 가까운 이웃만 못하다.(이웃사촌)

6 The less you eat, the better you feel. 食淡精神爽(식담정신상) – 적게 먹으면 마음이 상쾌하다.

7 Be careful not to invite suspicion. 瓜田不納履 梨下不整冠(과전불납리 이하부정관)
– 오이 밭에서 신을 고쳐 신지 말고 배나무 아래서 갓을 고쳐 쓰지 마라. · Leave no room for scandal.

8 As you sow, so shall you reap. 自業自得, 種瓜得瓜, 種豆得豆(자업자득, 종과득과, 종두득두)
– 콩 심은데 콩 나고 팥 심은데 팥 난다. 씨는 뿌리는 것만큼 거둔다.

As you make your bed, so you must lie on it. 因果應報(인과응보) – 그 원인에 그 결과.
– 자기가 저지른 업보는 자기가 받는다. · As you bake, so shall you eat.

9 A bad workman always blames his tools. 能書不擇筆(능서불택필)
– 글씨 잘 쓰는 사람은 붓을 고르지 않는다(선무당이 장구 탓 한다).
· Idle folk lack no excuses. / · Everybody puts his fault on the times.

10 An eye for an eye, and a tooth for a tooth 同態復讐(동태복수) – 같은 식의 복수, 눈에는 눈 이에는 이.

11 Happiness lies in contentment. 知足者富(지족자부) – 만족을 아는 사람이 부자다.
· Enough is as good as a feast. / · Learn to be contented.

12 Know yourself. 知己心自閑(지기심자한) – 자신을 알면 저절로 마음이 한가롭다.
· Know what you're made up of. / · Know your place. / · Every man is best known to himself.

13 No man is indispensable. 代人不乏(대인불핍 ; 代 = substitute)
– 대신 못할 사람 없다.(그 사람 없어도 대신 할 사람이 있다.)

14 Silence seldom does harm. 不對心自閑(부대심자한) – 응대를 안하면 마음이 편하다.
· No reply is best. / · Quietness is a great pleasure.

15 Better say nothing than not to the purpose. 言不中理 不如不言(언부중리 불여불언)
– 이치에 맞지 않는 말이면 안하는 것만 못하다. · Speak fitly or be silent wisely.

2-9 DRAWING CONCLUSION

      This section, "Drawing conclusion" is designed to help the readers develop an important interpretive skill in arriving at overall understanding. To do this, the readers should know factual information presented first, then infer details or facts given, and finally put them all together logically for a valid conclusion. An example is provided for you.

    Beasts in the Serengeti Game Park of Tanzania respect Simba as their mighty King.
    When he roars, his humble subjects tremble in fear.
    When he runs, his majestic mane flows in the wind.
    When he strolls through his kingdom, he walks with his pride.
    Even the best hunter in the world probably could not harm the King with his best gun.

    The facts and inferences :

    (1) Beasts respect Simba ················· (Fact)
    (2) When he roars, animals tremble ················· (Fact)
    (3) When he runs, his mane flows ················· (Fact)
    (4) When he strolls, he walks with his pride ·········· (Fact)
    (5) Even the best hunter probabl ················· (Inference)

      Based on the facts, (1), (2), (3), (4), and inference, (5), your logic tells you that Simba is a lion. There are other references leading to conclusive inferences such as "roar," "King of the Beasts," "mane," "pride (group of lions)" as the word or phrase context, and "animals tremble in fear," "his mane flows in the wind," and, "he walks with his pride." These clear facts and inferences help you draw a logical conclusion about Simba; **<u>he is a lion</u>**.

2-9 결론 끌어내기

이번 절 '결론 끌어내기'는 독자들이 전체적인 이해에 도달하는 데 중요한 해석기능을 개발하도록 돕기 위하여 계획되었다. 이렇게 하기 위해서 독자들은 주어진 사실적인 정보를 먼저 알아야 하고, 다음으로 주어진 사실이나 세부사항을 추론하고, 마지막으로 타당한 결론을 위하여 이 모든 것들을 종합해야 한다. 예를 들어 보겠다.

> 탄자니아의 세란게티 동물 보호구역의 짐승들은 심바를 그들의 왕으로 존경한다.
> 그가 포효하면 그의 얌전한 신하들은 두려움에 떤다.
> 그가 달리면 그의 당당한 갈기가 바람에 나부낀다.
> 그가 그의 왕국을 거닐때면 그는 자기가 거느리는 사자 무리와 함께 걷는다.
> 이세상 아무리 유능한 사냥꾼도, 아무리 좋은 총으로도 그를 해칠 수 없을 것이다.

사실과 추론

(1) 짐승들은 그를 존경한다 ·· 사실
(2) 그가 포효하면 동물들이 떤다 ······································ 사실
(3) 그가 달리면 갈기가 나부낀다 ····································· 사실
(4) 자기 왕국을 산책할 때는 자기가 거느리는 사자무리와 함께 걷는다 ········ 사실
(5) 아무리 솜씨 좋은 사냥꾼도 아마 ·································· 추론

사실들 (1), (2), (3), (4)과 추론 (5)를 토대로 당신의 논리는 '심바'는 왕이다고 알려준다. 결정적인 추론을 이끌어주는 문맥어나 어구로써 다른 참조사항들, 예를 들면 "포효한다", "짐승들의 왕", "갈기", "그의 자랑(사자 무리)", 또한 "동물들이 두려워 떤다.", "그의 갈기가 바람에 나부낀다.", "그는 자기의 무리와 함께 걷는다." 이러한 분명한 사실들과 추론들이 심바에 대한 논리적인 결론을 도출하는 데 도움이 되는 것이다. ; 그는 사자.

Note

- interpretive = interpretative = explanatory : 설명적인
- overall = including everything : 총괄적인, 전체의
  - What's your overall impression about this program? (전체적인 인상은?)
- factual = based on facts - factual inference : 사실적 추리
- infer = reach an opinion after thinking about : 생각에 의하여 추리하다 • I infer from your letter that you do not wish to see us. (당신 편지를 보고 당신이 우리를 보고 싶어하지 않는다고 생각했소.)
- put together = combine : 결합, 조립하다 opp. take apart –분해(리)하다
- valid = having a strong base : 타당한 • The excuse that your kids were hungry is not a valid reason for your theft.(새끼들이 굶주려서 도둑질을 했다는 구실은 타당한 이유가 될 수 없다.)
- game park : 아프리카의 동물 보호구역   mane : (말, 사자의) 갈기
- stroll = walk slowly for pleasure : 산책하다   majestic : 당당한, 위엄있는
- pride = the most valuable person, things : 자랑거리(사람, 물건) ; (사자) 무리

EXERCISE.

Choose the best answer based on your logical conclusion.

1. A myth is an ancient story that attempts to explain some natural phenomena or the beliefs and customs of a particular group of people. Characters in myths are gods, heroes, and imaginary animals, and the events are mainly supernatural.

(1) Based on the information given, it can be concluded that one of the following is not considered as a myth.

   (a) the Titans and the 12 Great Olympians   (d) Romeo and Juliet
   (b) Cupid and Psyche   (e) the Korean Tangoon and Bear
   (c) the Roman Romulus

(2) Which of the following can be considered a myth?

   (a) MacBeth   (c) The Iliad   (e) The Arabian Nights
   (b) Merchant of Venice (d) Robin Hood

2. Would you like to visit Argentina, Australia, New Zealand, Brazil, or Chile some day? Then, please don't forget that these countries are in the Southern Hemisphere, far below the equator. In your country, perhaps you have Christmas in cold December, but such places like Buenos Aires, Argentina, the Christmas season comes in the middle of hot summer.

(1) Based on the information given, it can be concluded that the climate in your country and the one in the Southern Hemisphere is quite different. If you want to enjoy skiing in the southern part of Argentina, you are expected to leave your country during the month of _____.

   (a) May or June   (d) November or December
   (b) July or August   (e) January or February
   (c) September or October

(2) If you go to Buenos Aires in December, what types of clothing do you have to pack?

   (a) T-shirts/short pants   (c) Suit   (e) Parka
   (b) Overcoat   (d) Sweater

논리적 결론으로 가장 좋은 것을 골라라.

1. 신화는 어떤 자연적 현상이나 어느 특정 집단 사람들의 신앙이나 풍습을 설명하려고 시도하는 옛날 이야기다. 신화 속의 등장 인물은 신이나, 영웅들 그리고 상상적 동물이며 사건들은 주로 초자연적인 것들이다.

Note
- phenomenon = a factor or event in nature that is unusual and of scientific interest : 현상
  - Snow in Egypt is an almost unknown phenomenon. (눈은 이집트에서 보기드문 현상이다.)
- imaginary characters : 가공 인물
- imaginative = having imagination : 상상력이 풍부한
  - an imaginative writer : 상상력이 풍부한 작가
- imaginable = that can be imagined : 생각할 수 있는
  - every possibility imaginable : 머리로 생각할 수 있는 모든 가능성
- supernatural = not explained by natural laws : 초자연적인
  - supernatural power : 신통력
  - supernatural phenomena : 초자연적 현상들
- Romulus : (로마 전설)-로마의 건설자, 초대왕

2. 언젠가 아르헨티나, 오스트렐리아, 뉴질랜드, 브라질 혹은 칠레를 방문하고 싶은가? 그렇다면 이들 국가들은 적도 저 아래 남반구에 있다는 사실을 잊지 말라. 아마 당신 나라에서는 크리스마스가 추운 12월에 있을 것이다. 그러나 브에노스 아이레스, 아르헨티나 같은 곳에서는 크리스마스철이 더운 한여름에 있다.

Note
- hemisphere = half of a sphere, a half of the earth esp. the northern or southern hemisphere, a half above the equator : 반구
- semiautomatic : 반자동
- equator : 적도

3. It is estimated that 2/3 of our body is composed of liquid, and 1/3 is composed of bone and flesh. An average adult has about eight liters of blood which pass through the heart every two minutes when he is resting. When he works very hard, the heart can pump all eight liters of blood three times every minute.

(1) Blood passes through the heart _____ times more when an adult is working hard.

   (a) 3   (b) 4   (c) 5   (d) 6   (e) 7

(2) When we are working hard, blood circulates throughout our body _____ times faster than when we are resting.

   (a) 2   (b) 4   (c) 6   (d) 8   (e) 10

4. Do you know which insect has the greatest capacity to survive? It is the cockroach, which has been on earth for about 350 million years. One of the reasons for its long survival is that it is very speedy and easily avoids enemies. Also, there are not many predators who like to eat the cockroach because of its odor. Therefore, it is likely that this insect will outlive people on earth. After people are gone, this insect will still survive on earth.

(1) Based on the information given, it can be concluded that cockroaches will

   (a) attack people for food   (d) eat up all the stored food
   (b) pollute our tap water   (e) be used for the test of insecticides
   (c) be used as a source of food

(2) One of the reasons why the cockroach will outlive people on earth is

   (a) It is small   (d) It has better survival abilities than people
   (b) It is fast   (e) It has few predators
   (c) It eludes the enemies

5. Xian (pronounced "She Ahn"), situated in the center of the Shaanxi Plain, is a world-famous ancient capital city. Long ago, Xian was called ChangAn. For more than 1000 years Xian served as a capital city for ten dynasties: Zhou, Qin (pronounced "Chin"), Han, and Tang. Xian ranks the first among China's six major ancient capital cities in terms of earliness when it became a capital, the number of dynasties by which it was made the capital, the length of time lasting as well as the scale, thus being generally acknowledged as "the most renowned historical city."

3. 우리 몸의 2/3은 액체로, 1/3은 뼈와 살로 구성되어 있다고 추산한다. 보통 성인은 약 8리터의 피를 가지고 있고, 그 피는 휴식하고 있을 때 2분마다 심장을 통하여 지나간다. 그가 고되게 일을 할 때, 심장은 1분마다 3번씩 모두 8리터의 피를 펌프질한다.

Note
- be composed of = be made up of, be formed : …로 구성되어 있다.
  - Water is composed of hydrogen and oxygen. (물은 수소와 산소로 구성되어 있다.)
  - Man is composed of body and soul. (인간은 영과 육으로 만들어져 있다.)
- circulate = move or flow around the body along a closed path : 피, 돈, 신문 – 순환하다
  - Blood circulates around the body. (피는 온 몸을 순환한다.)
  - Bad circulation can cause tiredness. (피의 순환이 좋지 않으면 피로가 온다.)

4. 어느 곤충이 살아남기에 가장 적합한 능력을 가지고 있는지 아는가? 그것은 이 지구상에 3억 5천만년 동안 살아온 바퀴벌레다. 그것이 가장 오래 살아남는 이유 중 하나는 빠르고 쉽게 적을 피하기 때문이다. 또한 불쾌한 냄새 때문에 그를 잡아먹으려는 포식동물이 많지 않다. 그러므로 이 곤충은 지상에서 인간보다 오래 살 가능성이 있다. 인간이 사라진 후에도 이 곤충은 계속 살아남을 것이다.

Note
- insect : 곤충
- mammal : 포유류
- reptile : 파충류
- amphibia : 양서류
- capacity = ability, power : 능력, 용량
  - Understanding this poem is beyond my capacity. (이 시는 내 능력으로 이해할 수 없다.)
- survive = continue to live : 살아 남다
  - Nobody survived the plane crash. (그 비행기 추락 사고에서 살아 남은 사람은 아무도 없다.)
- cockroach : 바퀴벌레
- predator = predatory animals living by killing and eating other animals.
  - carnivorous animals (포식(捕食)동물, 육식 동물)
- herbivorous : 초식 동물
- omnivorous : 잡식 동물

5. 중국어로 '쉬안' 으로 발음되는 서안(西安)은 산쉬평원의 중심부에 위치하고 있으며 세계적으로 유명한 고대의 수도다. 옛날 Xian은 장안으로 불렸다. Xian은 1000여년간 10개 왕조, 주, 진, 한, 당의 수도였다. 쉬안은 수도가 되었던 시기가 일렀다는 점과 그곳을 수도로 정한 왕조들의 숫자, 규모뿐 아니라 지속된 시간의 관점에서 6대 고대 수도들 중에서 서열이 첫째다. 이런 이유로 세계에서 가장 유명한, 역사적인 도시로 인정받는다.

(1) The best city to visit for the studies of all Chinese historical literature and archaeological relics is

 (a) Shanghai   (c) Chungking   (e) Xian
 (b) Beijing   (d) GuangZhou (Canton)

(2) The best city to visit for the studies of modern Chinese literature and politics is

 (a) Shanghai   (c) Chungking   (e) Xian
 (b) Beijing   (d) GuangZhou

6. The Aryans who had lighter skin, and were taller than the Indus Valley people began to move to India about 1500 B.C. At that time, their social system had three classes: the ruler and his warriors, the priests, and the commoners. Eventually, a new four class system emerged, probably as a result of intermarriage between the Aryans and the Indus Valley people. In this system, priests or Brahmans were the most powerful and highest class. Next were warriors. Merchants and peasants were the third class. The servants were at the bottom.

(1) The class which supplied food, clothing, and other goods is

 (a) Priests   (c) Merchants and Peasants   (e) Brahmans
 (b) Warriors (d) Servants

(2) Considering the function of each class, the Aryan Social Classes must have been _____ each other

 (a) interdependent on (c) separated from (e) autonomous of
 (b) independent of   (d) exclusive from

7. You cannot solve a problem? Well, get down and investigate the present facts and its past history! When you have investigated the problem thoroughly, you will know how to solve it. Conclusions invariably come after investigation, and not before. Only a blockhead cudgels his brains on his own, or together with a group, to "find a solution" or "evolve an idea" without making any investigation. It must be stressed that this cannot possibly lead to any effective solution or any good idea.

(Source: Mao, Tse-Tung (May 1930). Oppose Book Worship, 1st pocket ed. p. 2.)

(1) Based on the information given, it can be concluded that a problem can be solved effectively after

 (a) a solution was found   (d) discussing with people
 (b) identifying causes   (e) identifying the current facts
 (c) a careful investigation of facts and causes

> **Note**
> ☐ **in terms of = with regard to** : …의 관점에서, …에 관하여
> • Many people see success in terms of money. (성공을 돈의 관점에서 보는 사람이 많다.)
> ☐ **acknowledge = accept or recognize** : 인정하다, 알고 고마워하다
> • When the results of the election were reported, the party acknowledged defeat.
> (선거 결과가 보도되었을 때 그 당은 패배를 자인했다.)
> ☐ **renowned = famous**
> • The young professor is renowned for his new theory. (그 젊은 교수는 새 학설로 유명하다.)
> ☐ **relics** : 유물, 유품

6. 인더스 계곡 사람들보다 피부가 희고 키가 큰 아리안족이 기원전 약 1500년에 인도로 이동했다. 그 당시 그들의 사회는 3계급 체계였다: 통치자와 그의 투사계급, 승려계급, 그리고 평민계급이었다. 결국 새로운 4계급 체계가 출현했다. 아마 아리안족과 인더스 계곡 사람의 서로 다른 종족간의 결혼 결과였을 것이다. 이 체제에서는 승려계급 즉 브라만이 가장 강력하고 가장 높은 계급이었다. 그 다음으로 투사들이었다. 상인과 농부들이 셋째 계급이었다. 최하층은 종들이었다.

> **Note**
> ☐ **Aryans** : 아리안 족   ☐ **Brahman** : 인도의 4 카스트 중에서 최고인 승려계급
> ☐ **emerge = come or appear out of somewhere** : 출현하다
> • The sun emerged from behind the clouds.
> ☐ **intermarriage** : 다른 종족, 계급간의 결혼   ☐ **autonomy = self-governing** : 자치
> ☐ **autonomous** : 자율적인   ☐ **interdependent** : 상호 의존하는

7. 어떤 문제를 해결할 수 없다고? 자, 차분하게 시작하여 현재의 사실과 지난 역사를 조사하라! 그 문제를 철저히 조사하면 해결 방법을 알게 된다. 결론이란 변함없이 조사하면 나타나지만 조사하지 않고는 나오지 않는다. 단지 돌대가리들만이 조사해 보지도 않고 자신의 머리를 짜내거나, 집단과 함께 결론을 찾거나, 아이디어를 발전시키려고 한다. 이러한 일은 도저히 효과적인 결론이나 어떤 좋은 착상을 낳지 못한다.

(원전:모택동– '서적 숭배를 배격하라')

(2) The author, Mao Tse-Tung, probably wished his readers, especially those who loved reading traditional Chinese books which did not offer practical guidelines, to be more _____ in solving a problem.

   (a) realistic   (c) romantic   (e) illusive
   (b) emotional   (d) idealistic

8. The Smithsonian Institution located in Washington, D.C., is a center to encourage scientific knowledge, to support the arts, and to promote education. This institution became to be founded at the bequest of James Smithson (1765 - 1829) who donated $500,000 to the United States government to increase and spread knowledge. In 1846 the Smithsonian Institution was officially founded. From its activities, a number of bureaus have been developed, including the Gallery of Arts, the National Museum of American History, the Museum of National History, the Freer Gallery of Oriental Arts, National Portrait Gallery, and more. Later additions include the John F. Kennedy Center for the Performing Arts and the Joseph H. Hirshhorn Museum and Sculpture Garden.

(1) Why do you think that James Smithson donated half a million dollars which was a large sum of money at that time? It was probably that there were a very few _____ in the U.S.

   (a) higher educational institutes   (d) cultural centers
   (b) theaters   (e) social services centers
   (c) churches

(2) To whom do you think the Smithsonian Institution is popular?

   (a) Politicians   (c) Engineers   (e) Tourists
   (b) Businessmen   (d) Lawyers

9. Every country has a variety of national symbols, which is usually represented on its flag. For example, the national symbol of Laos displayed on its flag shows a three-headed elephant with a white parasol over it and a five-step platform under it. The three-headed elephant signifies the three sixteenth century kingdoms of Laos; the parasol as a symbol of royalty; and the five-steps of the platform as the five commandments of the Laotian official

> **Note**
> □ **get down to** = begin to give serious attention to : 정신차려 착수하다.
>   • Instead of rambling about, just get down to the assignment. (서성대지 말고 바로 숙제를 시작하라.)
> □ **blockhead** = a stupid person
> □ **stress** = to give importance to=emphasize
>   • She stressed the need for careful spending.(주의 깊은 소비의 필요을 강조했다.)
> □ **cudgel(beat, rake) one's brain** : 머리를 짜내다
>   • They cudgeled their brains in vain to work out the math quiz.
>   (수학 문제의 정답을 내려고 머리를 썼지만 헛수고였다.)
> □ **effective** = producing the desired effect : 효과적인   • effective efforts
> □ **illusive** = illusory : 상상적인, 허황한   • an illusive hope : 허황된 희망

<u>8.</u> 워싱턴 D.C.에 있는 스미스소니언 협회는 과학지식을 보급하고, 예술을 후원하며, 교육을 촉진하는 중심지다. 이 협회는 지식을 증가시키고 전파하기 위하여 50만 달러를 미국정부에 기증한 제임스 스미스소니언의 유산으로 창립되었다. 1846년에 스미스소니언 협회가 정식으로 설립되었다. 그곳의 활동으로 말미암아 많은 부서들이 확장되었는데 미술품 전시장, 미국 역사의 국립 박물관, 국사 박물관, 동양 미술의 자유 화랑, 국립 초상화 화랑 등 그외 여러가지가 많다. 후에 추가된 것으로 공연예술을 위한 존 에프 케네디 센터와 Joseph H. Hirshhorn 박물관 그리고 조각공원이 여기에 포함된다.

> **Note**
> □ **bequest (v. bequeath)** = something given or passed down to others after death : 유산
>   • The university decided to build a cancer - center at the bequest of a benefactor.
>   (그 대학은 어느 독지가의 유산으로 암 센터를 건립하기로 결정했다.)
> □ **institution** = an organization which provides people with help, work, medical treatment such as schools or hospitals : 학교, 병원 같은 공공기관

<u>9.</u> 나라마다 다양한 국가의 상징물이 있다. 그리고 그것들은 대개 국기에 표현된다. 예를 들면 국기에 나타난 라오스의 국가 상징은 흰 파라솔 아래 머리가 셋 달린 코끼리와 그 아래에 있는 5개의 계단으로 된 연단이다. 3두 코끼리는 라오스의 16세기 3개 왕국을 의미하며 파라솔은 왕권의 상징이고 5계단으로 된 연단은 살생, 도둑질, 거짓말, 간음 그리고 술의 남용을 금지하는 라오스 공식 종교의 5계명을 의미한다.

religion that proscribe killing, stealing, lying, adultery, and abuse of alcohol.

(1) Based on the information given, what do you think the official religion of Laos?

    (a) Christianity   (c) Buddhism   (e) Islam
    (b) Taoism   (d) Confucianism

(2) Overall, it can be concluded that the Laotian flag represents three basic elements. They are

    (a) historical pride, royalty, religious life   (d) king, monk, people
    (b) royalty, religious life, courage   (e) elephant, platform, parasol
    (c) purity, diligency, courage

10. Many people think that they know about Napoleon. He was born on August 15, 1769 at Ajaccio, Corsica as the fourth child and second son of Carlo and Letizia Ramolino Bonaparte. His parents were members of noble Italian families; his father was an eloquent lawyer and mother was beautiful and strong-willed.

    In 1779, at the age of 9, Napoleon entered a French military school. In January 1785, at the age of 16, he received commission in the French Army as a 2nd Lt. of artillery, and was promoted to 1st Lt. in 1791, and to brigadier general in 1793. The important dates of his life are briefly summarized as follows:

Year	Fact
1796	Married Josephine de Beauharnais
1799	Seized power in France
1804	Crowned himself Emperor of France
1805	Crushed the allied armies at Austerlitz
1806	Defeated the Prussians at Jena and Auerstedt
1809	Defeated Austrians at Wagram
1810	Married Marie Louise of Austria
1812	Occupied Moscow
1814	Abdicated his throne
1814	Exiled and arrived on Elba
1815	Returned to get power in France
1815	Defeated in the Battle of Waterloo
1815	Exiled to St. Helena
1821	Died at Longwood, St. Helena, on May 5.

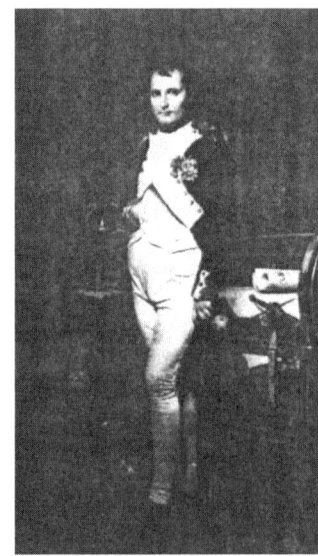

National Gallery of Art, Washington, D.C. Samuel H. Kress Collection

Napoleon I posed in his study for Jacques Louis David in 1812, above. David served as the court painter to the French emperor.

Note

- **a variety of = various** : 갖가지의
  - I took a day off for a variety of reasons. (갖가지 이유를 대고 하루 결근했다.)
- **five-step platform** : 5계단 연단 • **four-day tour** (3박 4일의 여행)
- **signify = mean, to be sign of** : 상징하다
  - What does the red headband signify? (빨간 머리띠는 무얼 상징하는가?)
- **royalty** : 왕의 신분, 특허권 사용료, 인세   cf. **loyalty** : 충성
- **commandment = any of the ten laws** : 10계명 중 하나
- **proscribe = forbid** : 금하다
  - The law proscribes selling cigarettes and alcoholic drinks to minors.
    (미성년자에게 담배와 술 판매는 법으로 금지되어 있다.)
- **abuse = put to wrong use, use badly** : 남, 오용
  - Some high officials are reported to have abused their authority for unfair gains.
    (일부 고위 공직자들이 부당한 이익을 위해서 직권을 남용했다고 보도되었다.)
- **Confucianism** : 유교   **Confucius** : 공자   **Mencius** : 맹자

---

10. 나폴레옹에 대하여 알고 있다고 생각하는 사람이 많다. 그는 1769년 8월 15일에 코르시카 아자치오에서 카르로와 레티지아 라몰리노 보나파르트의 사이에서 네번째, 아들로는 차남으로 태어났다. 양친은 이탈리아의 명문이고 아버지는 말이 유창한 변호사이고 어머니는 미모와 강한 의지의 소유자였다.

1779년 그의 나이 9세 때 프랑스 군사학교에 입학했다. 1785년 1월 16세 때 포병 소위로 육군에 임관되었고 1791년에 중위로, 1793년에 준장으로 진급했다. 그의 생애의 주요한 연대는 다음과 같이 요약될 수 있다.

연도	사실
1796	Josephine de Beauharnais와 결혼
1799	권력을 잡다
1804	황제 대관식
1805	Austerlitz에서 연합군 섬멸
1806	Jena와 Auerstedt에서 프러시아군 격퇴
1809	Wagram에서 오스트리아군 격퇴
1810	오스트리아의 Marie Lousie와 결혼
1812	모스코바 점령
1814	황제 퇴위
1814	엘바섬으로 유배
1815	프랑스로 귀환 재집권
1815	워털루 전투에서 패전
1815	세인트 헬레나 섬으로 유배
1821	5월 5일 세인트 헬레나 섬 롱우드에서 사망

Note

- **eloquent = able to express ideas and opinions well** : 웅변을 잘하는, 말이 유창한
  - Eyes are more eloquent than lips. (말보다 눈을 믿어라.)
- **commission = the act of giving special power, certain duties to a person or groups** : 임관, 훈령, 지령
- **2nd lieutenant** : 소위   **1st lieutenant** : 중위   **warrant officer** : 준위   **captain** : 대위
- **artillery** : 포, 포병대   **brigadier general** : 준장   **major general** : 소장   **general** : 대장
- **lieutenant general** : 중장   **abdicate = give up a position or right** : 물러나다
- **crush = press with great force to destroy** : 빻다, 부수다   cf. **crash** : 추락, 무너지다
  - This machine crushes wheat. (이 기계는 밀을 빻는다.)

(1) One of the major sociopolitical factors Napoleon could seize power as a soldier in 1799 was probably that he

   (a) was a general with political ambitions
   (b) was rich and ambitious
   (c) was intelligent and brave
   (d) married Josephine
   (e) took advantage of the social unrest caused by the French Revolution

(2) How many years do you think Napoleon enjoyed his life as a political leader?

   (a) 10 years   (b) 15 years   (c) 20 years   (d) 25 years   (e) 30 years

11. The Empress Wu Chao, formerly a harem official during Tang Tai-Tsung's (another name, Li Shih-Min) reign (627-650), was called to become empress after Tang Kao-Tsung had ascended to the throne. After the death of the imperial husband, she took control of the government from her sons, and became the first female ruler of China. The following is a dialogue between the Empress and her royal advisor, Lan.

"Good morning, Empress, there are many decisions to be made today." said Lan.
"What problems have you prepared for me?" asked the Empress.
"Majesty, the farmers are complaining about the great amount of labor they must give to the government each year."
"I understand their complaint, and I agree with them⋯. I decree that their forced-labor time should be cut in half. This order is to go into effect immediately."
"Thank you, Majesty," said Lan. "And now I bring you another complaint from your subjects. They say that the taxes they are forced to pay have created great burdens. They seek relief from these burdens."
"The finance minister tells me that the treasury is full. More money is coming into the treasury than we can use. You may cut taxes by one-third," replied the Empress.
"Your wishes will be carried out," bowed Lan.
"Lan, I have made another decision. I am not happy with the caliber of some of our government officials. I don't care what a man's family background and connections are. I want you to start using written examinations to test and pick the best of the best." Lan nodded.

(Source: Adapted from "An Empress Understands the People's Needs," Enjoying Global History (1996)).

(1) Based on the information given, the Empress Wu Chao must have been a

   (a) wise and capable ruler   (d) cruel and evil ruler
   (b) arrogant and ambitious ruler   (e) timid and humble ruler
   (c) greedy and proud ruler

(2) During her reign, the Tang society must have been

   (a) distressed (b) prosperous (c) corrupted (d) afflicted (e) inflicted

11. 당 태종(다른 이름 이시민)의 치세 때 궁녀관직에 있었던 Wu Chao(武照)는 당 고종이 왕위에 오른 뒤 왕비로 부름을 받았다. 황제 남편이 죽은 뒤 그는 아들들로부터 통치권을 차지하고 중국 최초의 여성 통치자가 되었다. 다음은 그 여황제와 왕의 자문관이었던 Lan과의 대화다.

"밤사이 편안하셨습니까? 폐하. 오늘 결정하실 일이 많이 있습니다."
"무슨 문제들을 준비해 왔는가?"
"폐하, 농부들이 매년 조정에 바쳐야하는 노역의 양이 많다고 불평을 하고 있습니다."
"그들의 불만을 알겠구나. 나도 그들과 같은 생각이다. 그들의 강제 노역을 반으로 줄이도록 포고한다. 이 명령은 즉시 시행되도록 하여라."
"성은이 망극하옵니다, 폐하. 백성들의 또다른 불만 사항을 아뢰겠습니다. 그들은 그들이 납부해야할 조세가 큰 부담이 된다고 합니다. 그들은 이 부담에서 벗어나기를 바라고 있습니다."
"재정 대신이 말하는데 국고가 충실하다는구나. 쓸 수 있는 것보다 더 많은 돈이 국고에 들어오고 있구나. 1/3로 감세 조치하여라."
"분부대로 거행하겠습니다."
"Lan아, 내가 한가지 더 결정을 했다. 난 몇몇 조정대신들의 능력에 대해서 마음이 언짢구나. 나는 어떤 인물의 가정 배경이나 인척들이 어떤가는 상관하지 않는다. 나는 네가 인물중의 인물을 선발하도록 필기시험 제도를 시작하기 원하노라." Lan은 머리를 끄덕였다.

Note
- **harem** : 회교의 여성 방   cf. Harlem : 뉴욕의 맨허턴 서부 흑인 거주지역
- **reign** = rule, sovereignty, dominance : 통치, 치세   cf. rein : 말 고삐, 권력
- **in the reign of King Sejong** : 세종대왕 치세 때
- **complaint** = an object of annoyance, pain, dissatisfaction : 불만사항
  - The residents made a list of complaints to report to the authorities concerned.
  - (주민들은 관계당국에 제출하기 위하여 시정사항을 표로 작성했다.)
- **decree** = order given by a ruler, official command : 포고령, 행정 명령
- **go into effect** : 시행되다, 효력을 발생하다
- **caliber** = the size of a bullet : 총알의 직경, 구경, 사람의 능력
  - a man of poor caliber (재능이 부족한 사람)

12. 인간은 빵만으로 살 수 없다. 인간은 살아남기 위해서 사랑을 필요로 한다. 왜냐하면 그의 생존에 사랑하는 사람과 사랑 받는 사람이 동시에 필요하기 때문이다. 사랑이 없는 삶은 결코 만족스런 삶이 될 수 없다. 사랑이란 행복을 열어주는 한 벌의 열쇠다. 사랑은 우리가 인간으로서 지상에 태어난 우리의 존재가치를 깨닫게 하는 것이기 때문이다.

12. Man cannot live on bread alone. Man needs love to survive; for his survival man needs someone to love and to be loved at the same time. Life without love can never be a contented one. Love is a set of keys leading to happiness, which helps us learn to appreciate our own existence as human beings born on this earth.

　　The pleasure of working in a healthy condition brings us happiness. Man finds happiness in doing his business; whereas woman in love⋯. To live in happiness, we need a strong belief in whatever domain it is: religion, ideology, thought, arts, or other discipline. Then, the belief serves as a strong supporting system during our life time⋯. To live within our means without too much avarice is wise. To know our means without complaint is a short cut leading to happiness. He who is not contented with his means drives happiness away. Happiness comes to those who do not have complaints, but it passes by those who have complaints. If you desire happiness, nurture your mind to develop an attitude of appreciation. Love, work, and faith contribute to our true happiness.

(Source: Adapted and translated from "A metaphor for happiness." Ahn, Byungwook (1998). <u>Literature for Sr. High School Students</u> (Advanced Level). pp. 307-312. Han Sehm Pub. Co. Seoul, Korea)

(1) Based on the information given, it can be concluded that happiness comes or goes depending on our _____.

　　(a) aptitude　　　(c) appreciation　　(e) love
　　(b) attitude　　　(d) faith

(2) What is the main idea of the passage, and why did the writer stress the value of happiness? It is probably that he wanted us to

　　(a) find happiness in love
　　(b) develop a sense of appreciation
　　(c) make our lives more meaningful through happiness
　　(d) develop our faith for happiness
　　(e) find true happiness by minimizing avarice and complaints

13. The following is a conversation between Madam Mathilde Loisel and Madam Jeanne Forestier adapted from <u>The Necklace</u>, Guy de Maupassant (1850-1893).

　"Good day, Jeanne." said Mathilde Loisel.
　Madam Forestier, astonished to be familiarly addressed by this plain good-wife, did not recognize her at all, and stammered, "But Madam, I do not know you. You must be mistaken." "No, I am Mathilde Loisel."
　Her friend uttered a cry, "Oh, my poor Mathilda! How you are changed!"
　"Yes, I have had days hard enough, since I have seen you, days wretched enough, and that because of you."
　"Of me! How so?"

건강한 상태에서 일하는 기쁨이 우리에게 행복을 가져다 준다. 남자는 일하는 가운데 행복을 찾고 여자는 사랑 안에서…. 행복하게 살려면 행복 안에 존재하는 모든 영역에 대하여 확실한 믿음이 있어야 한다. 종교, 이념, 사상, 예술 혹은 다른 교양 등. 그러면 그 믿음이 생애동안 우리를 강력하게 밑받침되어 도와준다. 자기 분수 안에서 지나친 욕심없이 산다는 건 현명하다. 불평하지 않고 분수를 안다는 건 행복으로 가는 지름길이다. 자기 형편에 만족하지 못하는 사람은 행복을 쫓아버린다. 행복은 불평이 없는 사람에게 찾아오지만 불평하는 사람은 지나쳐 가버린다. 만일 행복을 바란다면 감사하는 태도를 키우도록 마음을 길러라. 사랑과 일과 신앙은 우리의 참 행복에 이바지한다.

(원전 : 안병욱 지음 『행복을 위한 은유』 인용 번역)

Note

- □ contented = satisfied, happy
  - He seems to be contented with his lot.(자기 운명에 만족하고 사는 것 같다.)
- □ appreciate = understand and enjoy : 가치를 알고 감상, 감사하다
  - You can't appreciate poetry without a complete master of the language.
  (그 나라 언어를 완전히 모르면 시를 감상할 수 없다.)
- □ in whatever domain it is = any domain in which it is : 그것(행복)이 들어 있는 모든 영역
- □ discipline = training of mind and body : 훈련, 단련, 규율
- □ military / mental discipline : 군사훈련, 정신훈련
- □ means = money, income, wealth : 부, 재력, 수단, 분수   • a man of means : 수완가
- □ within / beyond one's means : 분수 안에서 / 빚지고
  - An end can't justify means.(아무리 목적이 좋아도 수단이 정당해야 한다.)
- □ avarice = a great eagerness and desire to get, seek wealth : 재산에 대한 탐욕
- □ shortcut = a quicker, more direct way : 첩경, 지름길
- □ nurture = give care and food : 양육하다
- □ nature and nurture : 천성과 교육   □ metaphor : 은유
- □ aptitude = natural ability or skill in learning : 적성
  - She showed early great aptitude for music. (어려서 음악성이 나타났다.)
- □ minimize = lessen to the smallest possible : 최소화하다
  - In this financial crisis, we ought to minimize the cost of living.
  (이런 금융 위기에는 생활비를 최소화해야 한다.)

13. 다음은 개작된 모파상의 소설 '목걸이'에서 로이젤 부인과 포레스티어 부인 사이의 대화다.

"안녕하십니까, Jeanne." Mathilda Loisel이 말했다.
  Forestier 부인은 별로 예쁘지 않은, 한 가정주부가 친숙하게 말을 걸어오는데 놀라 전혀 그녀를 알아보지 못하고, "그런데, 저는 아줌마를 모르겠는데요. 틀림없이 사람을 잘못 보셨어요."라

"Do you remember that diamond necklace which you lent to wear at the ministerial ball?"
"Yes. Well?"
"Well, I lost it."
"What do you mean? You brought it back."
"I brought you back another just like it. And for this we have been ten years paying. You can understand that it was not easy for us, we who had nothing. At last, it is finished, and I am very glad."

Madam Forestier had stopped.
"You say that you bought a diamond necklace to replace mine?"
"Yes, you never noticed it then! They were very alike."

And she smiled with joy which was proud and naive at once. Madam Forestier, strongly moved, took her two hands.
"Oh, my poor Mathilde! Why, my necklace was paste. It was worth at most 500 francs!"

(1) Based on the information given, it can be concluded that Jeanne could not recognize Mathilde. Probably it was because

    (a) Mathilde had lost a lot of weight
    (b) They had not seen each other since childhood
    (c) Mathilde had worn a colorful dress
    (d) Jeanne must have a bad memory
    (e) Mathilde did not look young and good as she did the last time they met

(2) Which of the following would be an appropriate title for the story?

    (a) "An Unforgettable Big Mistake"   (d) "Crime and Punishment"
    (b) "A Forgotten Debt"   (e) "An Unbroken Promise"
    (c) "Ten Years of Suffering"

14. The following is an article introducing The Observation Deck at The World Trade Center, New York City.

From over a quarter mile up in the sky, New York looks like paradise. The Observation Deck on the 107th floor of the World Trade Center towers above the rest of the city. And, weather permitting, you can go even higher to the open-air rooftop promenade, the highest outdoor observation platform on earth. Day or night, the view is breathtaking.

You can see to the horizon in all directions-the skyscrapers of midtown Manhattan, the famous New York neighborhoods, New Jersey, the Hudson and East Rivers, the magnificent bridges and the busy harbor. It is the most spectacular view in New York. While you are at the top, visit the New York Snack-New York's highest snack bar-and shop for a souvenir at the gift shop. Then browse along the lively History of Trade exhibit, which runs around the

고 더듬거리며 말했다. "어쩌나, 제가 Loisel부인인데요."

그녀의 친구가 비명을 질렀다. "오, 가엾은 Mathilda! 이렇게 변하다니!"

"예, 부인을 만났던 이후 힘들고 아주 비참한 나날을 보냈지요. 그리고 그건 부인 때문이었지요."

"나 때문이라니! 어떻게 그런 일이?"

"부인이 장관님댁 무도회 때 착용하라고 빌려주셨던 그 목걸이가 생각나십니까?"

"그래요. 그런데요?"

"응, 그걸 분실했었거든요."

"무슨 말씀이세요? 돌려 주셨잖아요."

"제가 그와 똑같을 것을 돌려드렸지요. 그리고 이 때문에 우리는 그 빚을 10년간 갚아왔지요. 아무것도 가진 게 없는 우리는 그게 쉽지 않았다는 것을 이해하시겠어요. 마침내 끝났어요. 저는 지금 몹시 기쁩니다."

Forestier부인은 걸음을 멈추었었다. "아주머니는 내 것을 반환하기 위하여 다이아몬드 목걸이를 가져왔다는 말인가요?"

"맞아요, 그때 전혀 눈치를 못채셨군요! 아주 비슷했지요." 그녀는 한편 자랑스럽고 한편 순진한 미소를 지었다. Forestier부인은 크게 감동하여 그녀의 두손을 잡았다.

"오, 가엾은 Mathilde! 저런, 내 목걸이는 가짜였어. 그건 기껏해야 500프랑짜리였어!"

> **Note**
> - **stammer = speak or say with pauses** : 더듬거리며 말하다
>   - The boy stammers when he is nervous. (불안하면 말을 더듬는다.)
> - **wretched = miserable** : 비참한
>   - The flood victims are living in wretched poverty. (수재민들이 비참한 빈곤 속에서 지내고 있다.)
> - **ball = dance party**
> - **naive = natural and innocent** : 꾸밈이 없고 순진한
> - **be moved = be touched** : 감동하다
>   - The child's suffering moved his father to tears. (자식의 고통하는 것을 보고 흥분하여 눈물이 났다.)
> - **paste** : 가짜 보석

14. 다음은 뉴욕시 세계 무역 센터에 있는 관측데크를 소개하는 기사이다.

1/4마일 이상의 상공에서 보면 뉴욕이 천국 같습니다. 세계무역센터의 17층에 자리한 관측데크는 뉴욕시 위에 높이 솟아 있습니다. 날씨가 허락하면 지상에서 가장 높은 야외 관측단인 노천 지붕산책로까지 더 높이 올라갈 수 있습니다. 밤이나 낮이나 경관은 숨이 막힐 지경입니다. 사방 팔방으로 지평선까지 보입니다-맨해튼 중심부의 마천루들, 그 유명한 뉴욕의 이웃들, 뉴저지, 허드슨강과 이스트강, 훌륭한 교량들과 북적대는 항구들이 눈에 들어옵니다. 꼭대기에 있는 동안 뉴욕에서 가장 높은 스낵바인 뉴욕 스낵바를 가보

inside walls of the Observation Deck. The exhibit, free with admission to the Deck, brings the birth and growth of commerce, barter and finance to life. The Observation Deck is open from 9:30 a.m. to 9:30 p.m. everyday; for information call: (212) 466 - 7377.

(1) What is the article for? It can be concluded that the article is for _____ purposes.

    (a) informative   (c) industrial   (e) academic
    (b) commercial   (d) entertaining

(2) Whom does the main idea of the article target?

    (a) businessmen   (c) tourists   (e) athletes
    (b) students   (d) politicians

15. The Greek pantheon developed as a fusion of the gods worshipped by immigrants and invaders in various parts of the Greek peninsula and the islands near it. By the time of the Homeric epics (about 7th century B.C.), Zeus and his dozens of wives, and divine and heroic offsprings were recognized and venerated throughout the Greek city-states. For example, Zeus was venerated as the chief god and rainmaker; Hera as queen of the gods and goddess of marriage; Athena, the wise virgin goddess of Athens and protectress of the arts; Hermes, the messenger; Aphrodite, the goddess of love; Artemis, the goddess of the hunt; and her brother Apollo, the divinely handsome god of youth, music and poetry.

    The Homeric pantheon was highly sophisticated. The gods were no longer aspects of nature or even personifications of them. They were anthropomorphic with human shape and attributes and were immortal creatures in charge of various divisions and functions of nature and human activity. Their behavior, fights, and love affairs were very human, and the Greek sculptors portrayed them as realistic human beings. Like some early cultures, the Greeks did not fear their gods.

(1) The sophisticated Homeric pantheon system shows that the gods with their specific functions fought, hated, loved, stole, revenged as we do. From the passage, what do you conclude that the system lacked?

    (a) relation between gods and men   (d) strong social content
    (b) the function of the gods   (e) strong ethical content
    (c) the divisions of the gods

시고 선물가게에서 기념품도 사십시요. 그런 다음 관측데크의 안쪽 벽을 삥 돌아 전개되는 생생한 무역 전시장을 천천히 둘러보며 구경하십시오. 데크까지의 입장권만 가지면 무료인 전시장은 상업, 물물교환, 금융의 탄생과 발전을 생생하게 보여줍니다. 관측데크는 매일 오전 9:30에서 오후 9:30까지 개방합니다.

자세한 정보를 알려면 (212)466-7377로 전화하십시오.

> **Note**
> □ promenade = a wide path beside a road along the coast in a town : 산책길
> □ breathtaking = very exciting : 손에 땀을 쥐게하는
> □ spectacular = grandly unusual, attracting notice : 볼만한, 대단한 구경거리의
>   • The events before the main opening were spectacular. (식전행사는 볼만했다.)
> □ browse : 띄엄 띄엄 읽다, 목적없이 뒤적이다.
> □ barter = exchange goods for other goods : 물물교환
>   • They bartered farm products for machinery. (농산품과 기계를 맞바꾸다.)

15. 희랍의 판테온은 이주민들이나 그리스 반도 및 근처 섬들의 여러 지역에 사는 침입자들이 숭배하던 신들의 연합신전으로 발달했다. 호머의 서사시 시대(기원전 약 7세기)까지는 제우스와 수십명의 그의 처들, 신격(神格)의 혹은 영웅적인 그의 후손들이 희랍 도시국가들 전체에서 인정받고 존경받았다. 예를 들어 제우스는 최고의 신이요, 비를 관장하는 신으로서, 헤라는 신들의 여왕이요, 결혼의 신으로서, 아테나는 아테네의 현명한 처녀신이고 예술을 보호하는 신으로서, 헤르메스는 사자(使者)로, 아프로디테는 사랑의 신으로, 아르테미스는 사냥의 신으로, 그리고 그의 남자형제인 아폴로는 젊음과 음악과 시의 대단한 미남 신으로 존경을 받았다.

호머의 판테온은 고도로 세속화되어 있었다. 신들은 더이상 자연의 모습(번개, 천둥, 폭풍 같은 위력을 발휘하는)이나 그런 면모를 의인화한 존재가 아니었다. 그들은 인간의 모습과 속성을 가진 의인화된 신이었고 자연과 인간 활동을 다양하게 분할하여 담당하는 불멸의 피조물이었다. 그들의 행위, 전투, 연애사건은 대단히 인간적이었고 희랍 조각가들은 사실적인 인간으로 표현했다. 옛 시대의 다른 문화권들처럼 그들은 신을 두려워하지 않았다.

(2) What do you think that the system might have influenced the educated classes? They

    (a) became more dogmatic about their religion
    (b) began to dislike their pantheon system
    (c) turned to Christianity for personal involvement
    (d) attempted to develop a monotheistic system
    (e) inquired more plausible speculations about the world and man

16. On August 6, 1945, an American plane dropped an atomic bomb on Hiroshima. The residents saw "a strong flash of light," and then, total destruction. More than 70,000 people were killed. In the months that followed, many more would die from radiation sickness, a deadly after-effect from exposure to radioactive materials.

    Truman warned the Japanese that they could expect "a rain of ruin from the air the like of which has never been seen on this earth," if they did not surrender. And on August 8, the Soviet Union declared war on Japan and invaded Manchuria. But, Japanese leaders did not respond. The next day, an American airplane dropped a second atomic bomb on Nagasaki killing more than 65,000 people. Some members of the Japanese cabinet wanted to fight on, while other leaders disagreed. Finally, on August 14, Emperor Hirohito intervened, forcing the government to surrender. On September 2, 1945, the formal peace treaty was signed on board the American battleship Missouri which was anchored in Tokyo Bay. The war had ended.

(1) Based on the facts presented, it can be concluded that dropping the two atomic bombs on Japan

    (a) brought peace and order in Japan
    (b) invited the Russians to declare war
    (c) brought a quick end to World War II
    (d) made Japanese leaders fight on
    (e) brought liberation for Korea only

(2) Dropping the atomic bombs on Japan unleashed terrifying destruction of people and properties. Was it really necessary to drop the mass-destruction bomb? After the war, many good citizens of the world have discussed the issue. Their discussion might have been in the fashion of

    (a) pro ("for")   (d) deadlock
    (b) con ("against")   (e) imposing religious doctrine
    (c) ongoing controversy

> **Note**
> ☐ pantheon : 그리스나 로마의 만신전(萬神殿) • pan(all)+theon(gods)
> ☐ epic = a long poem about the deeds of gods and great men : 서사시, 영웅시
> ☐ venerate = treat with great respect and honor = worship : 숭배, 경배하다
> ☐ sophisticated = having or showing signs of experience in social life : 세련된, 닳은
> ☐ anthropomorphic : 신의 의인화(擬人化)   ☐ fusion : 융합
> ☐ attribute(n.) = quality forming part of the nature of a person or thing : 속성
>   • Kindness is just one of his attributes. (그 사람 특성의 하나는 친절이다.)
> ☐ attribute (V.) something to : …을 누구의 덕으로 돌리다 • He attributed his success to his mother's sacrificial care.(자기의 성공을 어머니의 희생적인 보살핌의 덕으로 돌렸다.)
> ☐ plausible = seeming to be true : 그럴듯한
>   • Your explanation sounds plausible. (네 설명이 듣기에 그럴듯하다.)

16. 1945년 8월 6일 미군기 한대가 히로시마에 원자폭탄을 투하했다. 주민들은 "강렬한 빛의 번뜩임," 그 후 완전한 파괴를 보았다. 7만여명이 죽었다. 그후 몇개월이 지난후 더욱 많은 사람들이 방사능 질환 즉 방사능 물질에 노출됨으로써 치명적인 후유증에 죽어가게 되어 있었다.

　트루만은 일본인들에게 만일 항복하지 않으면 "지구상에서 비슷한 것도 본 적이 없었던 파멸의 비"를 만날지도 모를 것이라고 경고했다. 그리고 8월 8일 소련이 일본에 선전 포고하고 만주를 침략했다. 그러나 일본 지도자들은 응대하지 않았다. 다음 날 미군기 한대가 나가사키에 또 한발의 원자탄을 투하했고 65,000명 이상이 죽었다. 일본 내각의 몇 사람들은 계속 싸우기를 원했으나 다른 지도자들은 동의하지 않았다. 마침내 8월 14일에 히로히토 천황이 개입하여 정부에게 항복을 강요했다. 1945년 9월 22일, 정식으로 평화조약이 도쿄만에 정박 중인 미군함 미주리호 선상에서 체결되었다. 전쟁이 끝난 것이었다.

> **Note**
> ☐ radiate = to send out light or heat : 방사하다
>   • These vessels radiate harmful cancer-causing substance.(이 용기들은 유해한 발암물질을 방사한다.)
> ☐ after-effect : 후유증   ☐ side-effect : 부작용   ☐ ripple-effect : 파급 효과
> ☐ exposure : 노출, 무방비 • We nearly died of exposure on the cold mountain.(우리는 추운 산위에서 추위를 막아줄 것이 없어 거의 죽을 뻔했다.)
> ☐ cabinet = the most important department heads of government : 내각 각료
> ☐ intervene = interrupt to prevent a bad result : 개입하다, 말리다
>   • They were starting to fight, when their father intervened.
> ☐ ongoing = continuing : 계속적인
>   • The motion brought about much controversy. (그 동의안은 많은 논란을 불러 일으켰다.)
> ☐ deadlock = disagreement that can't be settled = standstill, stalemate : 교착상태
>   • The diplomatic negotiations came to a deadlock. (그 외교협상이 교착상태에 빠졌다.)

17. The purpose of living between animals and men is well contrasted; the former is to satisfy the present needs, and the latter to pursue and attain ideals. To attain the ideals, men have to pay a high price. The first price to pay is effort, and the second one is wisdom. Wisdom can be classified into two: intelligence and knowledge. Intelligence can be innate, whereas knowledge should be acquired.

How can we acquire knowledge? First, it can be acquired through direct experience (e.g. five senses), which provides us with very limited access to gaining unlimited amount of knowledge. Second, it can be acquired through learning at home, school, and in society, which provides us with relatively feasible access to gaining knowledge; however, it is still far from being enough for gaining knowledge. Third, it can be acquired through research and self-taught understanding, which provides us with relatively easy tools in gaining knowledge.

What are the tools? They are the books which offer a variety of ways leading to the acquisition of knowledge. The books are an accumulation of our own experiences, imaginations, inferences, hypotheses, theories, rules, and social and universal laws constructed for thousands of years based on our own efforts and actual experiences and experiments. Indeed, the books are the tools through which we can acquire and develop our knowledge, thus helping us attain our ideals. Needless to say, the books are a storage of knowledge and wisdom accumulated from the ancient time in the multidisciplinary areas such as social science, natural science, literature, arts, music, hobbies, recreations, and even the information related to our daily life.

(Source: Adapted and translated from "Reading and Life." Lee, Heeseung (1998). Korean Language (Advanced level). pp. 5-10. Ministry of Education, Seoul, Korea.)

(1) Based on the information advocated, it can be concluded that men differ from animals in the sense that men can

    (a) store accumulating knowledge through books and computers
    (b) read and write books and other materials
    (c) gain knowledge and wisdom
    (d) invent sophisticated tools and machines for practical purposes
    (e) utilize knowledge and wisdom gained from books for their ideals

(2) Why do you think the author stressed the value of reading books? It is probably to

    (a) acquire knowledge   (d) develop intelligence
    (b) attain our ideals   (e) develop our civilization and culture
    (c) acquire wisdom

17. 삶의 목적이 동물과 인간사이에는 잘 대조된다 ; 전자는 현재의 욕구를 만족시키는 것이고 후자는 이상을 추구하고 성취하려는 것이다. 이상 실현을 위해서 인간은 많은 대가를 지불해야 한다. 첫째 대가는 노력이고 둘째는 지혜다. 지혜는 두 가지로 분류될 수 있는데 지능과 지식이다. 지능은 선천적인데 반하여 지식은 습득해야 한다.

지식은 어떻게 습득할 수 있는가? 첫째, 직접체험(예를 들면 5관을 통해)을 통하여 얻을 수 있는데 이 방법은 무한한 양의 지식을 획득하는데 유한한 접근만 제공한다. 둘째, 가정, 학교 및 사회 안에서 학습을 통하여 얻어지는데 이 방법은 지식 획득에 비교적 실질적인 접근을 제공한다. 그러나 이것도 역시 지식을 얻기 위해서 결코 만족스럽지 못하다. 셋째, 지식은 연구와 스스로 깨친 이해를 통하여 획득되는데 이 방법이 지식을 얻는 비교적 쉬운 수단이다.

도구에는 어떤 것들이 있는가? 지식 획득에 이르는 다양한 길을 제공하는 책이 도구다. 책이란 수천년에 걸쳐 우리 자신의 노력과 사실적인 경험과 실험을 토대로 한 체험들, 상상, 추리, 가정, 이론, 규칙, 사회적 보편적 법칙의 축적이다. 실로 책은 우리가 지식을 얻고 발달시킬 수 있는, 그리하여 우리의 이상 실현을 돕는 도구다. 말할 것도 없이 책은 고대로부터 여러 전문분야에서, 예를 들면 사회학, 자연과학, 문학, 음악, 취미, 여가선용 심지어 일상 생활과 관련된 지식과 지혜의 저장고다.

(원전 : 이희승 지음 『독서와 생활』에서 인용 번역)

Note

□ **attain** = succeed in arriving at after efforts : 성취, 도달하다
  • She attained the position of the chief of a police station. (그녀는 경찰 서장 자리에 올랐다.)
□ **innate** = inborn, (of qualities) which someone was born with : 선천적인
  • Is the talent for music innate or acquired? (음악 재능은 선천적인가, 노력으로 얻어지는가?)
□ **access to** = means of entering, way in : …에 접근하다
  • Gaining access to the Blue House has become easier than before.(청와대는 전보다 쉽게 들어가 볼 수 있다.)
□ **feasible** = able to be done, possible : 가능한, 그럴듯한   □ **self-taught** : 독학한
□ **accumulate** = make or become greater in amount, size : 축적하다
  • He has been accumulating rare curios. (희귀한 골동품을 모으고 있다.)
□ **universal** : 보편적인   • universal gravitation : 만유인력

2-10 TONE AND ATTITUDE

This section is designed to help the readers develop a "comprehensive inference skill" in identifying the "tone" and "attitude" of the speaker or writer. The "tone" refers to a manner of speaking or writing that shows a certain mood or attitude on the part of the speaker or writer, consisting in choices of words, phrasings, or styles. The "attitude" refers to the manner of thinking, acting, or feeling that shows the speaker's or writer's disposition or opinion. What is the "comprehensive inference skill"? This skill is to infer the meaning of word, phrase or sentence based on not only linguistic but also nonlinguistic factors in order to identify the tone and attitude of the speaker or writer. Then, what are the "nonlinguistic factors"? They are the ones which powerfully condition the meanings of word, phrasing, or sentence without using linguistic codes.

To be more specific, we communicate for specific purposes with different manners of speech or writing depending on different setting (time, place, situation), and interpersonal relationship (age, sex, social status, relation between the participants). These nonlinguistic factors condition the meaning of linguistic ones: word, phrase, sentence. For example, the meaning of such an expression as "I love you" would be much different depending on setting ((1) When did he/she say, at 7:00 a.m. or p.m.? (2) When did he/she say, in a public or private place? (3) In what situation did he/she say? (4)Why and how did he/she say?). Also, the meaning of that expression, as we know, is different depending on interpersonal relationship ((1) How old are the participants? (2) What are the sexes of the participants? (3) What are their social status, teacher and student? (4) What is the relation between them, father and daughter?).

Likewise, the meaning of that expression is different depending on the manner of speaking and writing (e.g. "frozen, formal, consultative, casual, intimate," "very polite, polite, normal, less polite, very impolite," or "threatening, aggressive, sarcastic, pleasant, very pleasant."). Thus, the meaning of "I love you" expressed in a very threatening manner with an insulting mood, or done in a very sincere and polite manner with a pleasant mood, has quite different interpretations.

2-10 어조와 태도

　　이번 절은 독자들이 말하는 이나 글쓴이의 '어조'나 '태도'를 알아내어 '종합적인 추론 기능'을 기르도록 하기 위하여 마련됐다. '어조'란 말하는 이나 글쓴이 편에서 어떤 기분이나 태도를 보여주는 말씨 및 글쓰는 방식이며, 단어, 어구 및 문제를 여기에 일치시키는 것이다. '태도'란 말하는 이나 글쓴이의 기질 혹은 견해를 보여주는 사고, 행동 방식 혹은 감정상태를 가리킨다. '종합적인 추론기능'이란 무엇인가? 이것은 말하는 이나 글쓴이의 어조나 태도를 추리하기 위하여 언어적인 요소뿐 아니라 비언어적인 요소를 토대로 단어, 숙어, 또는 문장의 의미를 추리하는 기능이다. 그렇다면 비언어적 요소는 무엇인가? 그것들은 언어적 기호를 사용하지 않고 단어나 숙어 또는 문장의 의미를 강력하게 조절하는 것이다.

　　좀더 구체적으로 말하면 어떤 특수한 목적으로 의사를 교환할 때 각기 다른 배경(시간, 장소, 상황)과 대인관계(나이, 성별, 사회적 신분, 참석자 사이의 관계)에 따라 다른 방식의 말씨나 글을 사용한다. 이러한 비언어적 요소들이 언어적 요소들 즉 단어, 숙어, 문장의 의미를 조절한다. 예를 들어 다음과 같은 표현, '나는 당신을 사랑한다.'의 의미가 다음과 같은 배경에 따라 달라질 수 있다; (1) 언제 말했는가, 오전 7시인가, 오후 7시인가? (2) 어떤 경우에 말했는가, 공적인 장소인가, 사적인 장소인가? (3) 어떤 상황에서 말했는가? (4) 왜 그말을 했는가?) 또한 우리가 아는 바처럼 그 표현의 의미는 상대와의 관계에 따라 다르다. ((1) 참석자의 연령은? (2) 참석자의 성별은? (3) 그들의 사회적 신분은 무엇인가, 선생인가, 학생인가? (4) 두사람 사이의 관계는 무엇인가, 부녀간인가?)

　　마찬가지로 그 표현의 의미는 말하고 글을 쓰는 방식에 따라 다르다(예를 들면, '쌀쌀한, 형식을 중시하는, 상담적인, 무관심한, 친근한, 매우 예절바른, 예절바른, 보통의, 덜 공손한, 매우 무례한, 혹은 겁주는, 공격적인, 냉소적인, 유쾌한, 매우 유쾌한). 이런 이유로 모욕적인 기분에서 위협적으로, 혹은 진지하고 유쾌하게 표현된 "사랑합니다."의 의미는 아주 다른 해석이 가능하다. 지금까지 살펴본 바와 같이 '어조'란 어떤 기분이나 태도를 반영하는 한 형태의 방식이다. 그리고 그것은 '배경'이나 '대인관계'의 예에서 본 것처럼 어떤 표현의 의미를 바꿀 수 있다.

As we have seen, the "tone" is a type of manner reflecting certain mood or attitude, which can change the meaning of an utterance as shown in the examples of "setting" or "interpersonal relationship."

The "attitude" is also a manner reflecting the speaker's or writer's disposition or opinion. Unlike the "aptitude" which refers to someone's partially inherited particular ability, the "attitude" is formed through a variety of long learning experiences at home, school, and in society. In general, attitude is largely influenced by cultural and academic domains as well as the way how he/she grew up as individuals in that society. For example, if Mr. X is called by many as a racist, sexist, or anti-communist, then we can infer that he has an attitude against or for racism, sexism, or communism. This is an attitude which Mr. X has now, but that attitude has been formed through long learning experiences from his parents and siblings at home, teachers and classmates at school, and many diversified people and reading materials in his society. Then, how can we know the writer's disposition or opinion? Of course, it seems to be difficult, but it will not be difficult at all as long as we remember that there are linguistic and nonlinguistic factors which provide us with feasible solutions as we have seen. As nonlinguistic factors, we have to consider "setting" (i.e. In what situation? For what purposes?), "interpersonal relationship" (i.e. What is the writer's role to his readers?), and "manner" (i.e. How did the writer express his idea or opinion, aggressively or defensively?). As linguistic factors, we have to identify the subject matter and the main idea as previously shown in 2.6., Chapter 2. And find out, "What words, phrasings, or sentences did the writer use to express his disposition or opinion? What is his feeling, philosophy, value, or opinion as revealed in the text he presented?" Then, the identification of the writer's tone and attitude would be a lot simpler and easier. To provide the readers with more opportunities for the mastering of "the comprehensive inference skill," the following exercises are provided.

'태도' 또한 말하는 이나 글쓴이의 기질이나 생각을 반영하는 방식이다. 어떤 사람의 물려받은 특수한 능력을 가리키는 '적성' 과는 달리 '태도' 는 가정, 학교, 사회 안에서의 긴 학습 체험을 통해서 형성된다. 대체로 태도는 문화적, 학문적 영역에 의해서 뿐아니라 사회 속에서 그가 어떻게 성장했는가에 의하여 크게 영향을 받는다. 예를 들어 어떤 사람이 만일 많은 사람으로부터 인종차별주의자, 성차별주의자, 반공주의자 라고 불리면 우리는 그가 인종차별주의, 성차별주의 혹은 공산주의를 반대 혹은 찬성하는 태도를 가지고 있다고 추리할 수 있다. 이것이 지금 그의 태도다. 그러나 그 태도는 가정에서 양친, 형제, 학교에서 선생님들과 급우들, 사회에서 많은 다양한 사람들, 독서물로부터 오랫동안 배워 형성된 것이다. 그렇다면 우리는 어떻게 글쓴이의 기질이나 의견을 알 수 있는가? 물론 어려워 보인다. 그러나 우리가 보아온 그럴듯한 해결방법을 제공하는 언어적, 비언어적 요소를 기억하면 그리 어렵지 않을 것이다.

비언어적 요소로서 '배경' (어떤 상황? 무슨 목적?), 대인관계(작가는 독자에게 어떤 역할을 하나?) 그리고 방식(어떻게 글쓴이는 자기 의견을 표현했는가, 공격적인가, 방어적인가?) 등을 고려해야 한다. 언어적 요소로서는 앞서 제2장 2.6.에서 본바와 같이 주제와 요지를 확인해야 한다. 그리고 다음을 알아보라: 작가는 자기의 기질을 표현하기 위하여 무슨 단어, 표현법, 혹은 문장을 사용했나. 그가 제시한 본문속에 드러난 감정, 철학, 가치 혹은 의견은 무엇인가? 그러면 글쓴이의 어조나 태도를 확인하는 일은 훨씬 간단하고 쉬워질 것이다. 독자들에게 '종합적 추론 기능' 을 정복하는 더 많은 기회를 제공하기 위하여 다음 연습문제를 제공한다.

> **Note**
> - **on the part of** : …편에서
>   - No objection on the part of those present.(참석자 편에서는 이의 없소.)
> - **consist in = lie in, depend on** : …에 있다, 내재하다
>   - Happiness consists in contentment with one's lot.(행복은 자신의 분수에 만족하는 데 있다.)
> - **disposition = a general tendency of character, behavior** : 기질, 성품
>   - He has an optimistic disposition. (기질이 낙천적이다.)
> - **linguistic** : 언어학적   **informant = one who gives information** : 정보 제공자, 밀고자
> - **-wise = manner, position, direction**을 표시하는 접두사
>   - likewise : 같은 방법으로   · otherwise : 다른 방법으로   · clockwise : 시계방향으로
>   - lengthwise : 세로로   · counterclockwise : 시계 방향반대로
>   - endwise : 끝을 위로   · contrariwise : 반대로
> - **frozen** : 냉동된(분위기), 쌀쌀한   **consultative** : 상담하는
> - **aggressive = offensive** : 공격적인   **sarcastic** : 냉소적인

EXERCISE:

Read the following passage and choose the best answer provided.

1. I hate the communists.
   They killed my father, a college professor.
   They killed my mother, a high school teacher.
   They killed my older brother, a college student.
   And they killed many good people in Cambodia.
   I really hate the communists and the Khmer Rouge.

   (Source: Speech Sample collected in 1983)

Spring 1978. Scene from the Khmer Rouge massacre at Ha Tien.

Informant : Sokha Cheng, 18 years old, female student, junior.
Sokha was born in Cambodia, and escaped to the United States as a refugee when she was eleven.

Situation: After watching The Killing Fields, the class had a discussion about the movie for literary analysis: plot, character, theme. During the discussion, Sokha expressed her own experiences and opinion about the Khmer Rouge.

(1) The tone of the speaker as revealed in the passage is

    (a) sarcastic   (b) contented   (c) confused   (d) angry   (e) happy

(2) The attitude of the speaker toward the passage is the

    (a) hatred of communists   (d) enjoyment of freedom in America
    (b) hatred of Cambodian people   (e) disgust in American society
    (c) pessimism in politics

2. "What's the name, *boy*?" the policeman asked.
   "Dr. Poussaint. I'm a physician…"
   "What's your first name, *boy*?"
   "Alvin."

   (Source: Speech Sample by Susan Ervin-Tripp, 1969)

Setting : (1) Time: During the mid-1960s when the American society was in turmoil with the issue of racism and other internal problems.
          (2) Place: In the South where the White Supremacy was dominant.
          (3) Situation: A white policeman stopped a car driven by a black male, Dr. Poussaint.

다음 글을 읽고 주어진 가장 좋은 답을 골라라.

1. 나는 공산당을 미워한다.
   그들은 대학 교수인 내 아버지를 죽였다.
   그들은 고등학교 교사인 내 어머니를 죽였다.
   그들은 대학생인 내 오빠를 죽였다.
   그리고 그들은 캄보디아의 많은 선량한 사람들을 죽였다.
   나는 정말로 공산당과 크메르 루즈를 미워한다.

   제보자 : Sokha Cheng, 18세, 여학생, 고교11학년, 캄보디아 태생, 11세때 피난민으로서 미국으로 탈출

   상황 : '킬링 필드'를 보고 학급학생들이 문학적 분석 즉, 줄거리, 등장인물, 주제를 위해 그 영화에 대하여 토의를 했다. 토의 중 Sokha는 자신의 실제 체험과 크메르 루즈에 관한 자기 의견을 말했다.

   Note
   □ sarcastic : 냉소적인   □ confused : 혼란스런   □ hatred : 증오
   □ disgust : 메스꺼움   □ pessimism : 염세, 비관주의   opp. optimism : 낙천, 낙관주의

2. "어이, 이름이 무언가?" 경찰이 물었다.
   "Poussaint박사요. 내과 의사요."
   "어이, 이름이 뭐냐고?"
   "Alvin이요."

   배경 : (1) 시간 : 미국사회가 인종차별과 다른 국내문제의 현안으로 소란스러웠던 1960년대 중반
   (2) 장소 : 백인 우월주의가 우세하던 남부
   (3) 상황 : 백인 경찰이 흑인 남자 Dr. Poussaint가 운전하는 차를 세웠다.

Participants : (1) Policeman: male, about late 40s, officer.
(2) Driver: male, about mid 40s, medical doctor.

Comment : The policeman used "*boy*" as an insulting form of address to the black male, Dr. Poussaint. His answer, "I'm a physician" might have made the policeman upset, because to the policeman, the blacks were wrong to claim adult status or occupational rank. The policeman believed that the blacks should be called "*boys*."

(1) What do you think the tone of the policeman would be toward Dr. Poussaint?

    (a) insulting   (b) polite   (c) courteous   (d) demanding   (e) sincere

(2) It can be inferred that the tone of Dr. Poussaint toward the policeman would be

    (a) mildly aggressive   (c) cautiously defensive   (e) very informal
    (b) very polite   (d) extremely humorous

(3) The attitude of the policeman reveals that he can be a/an

    (a) racist   (b) sexist   (c) alcoholic   (d) misanthropist   (e) philanthropist

3. I'm nobody! Who are you?
Are you nobody too?
Then there's a pair of us - don't tell!
They'd banish us, you know.

How dreary to be somebody!
How public, like a frog
To tell your name the live-long day
To an admiring bog!

(Source: Emily Dickinson's (1830 - 1886) poem, "I'm Nobody! Who Are You?")

The Bettmann Archive
Emily Dickinson

Background : Emily was born in the lovely old college town of Amherst, studied briefly at the Mt. Holyoke Seminary, and then withdrew to a frame house behind a picket fence where she lived out the rest of her days like a New England nun, seeing only her family and close friends. Her life seemed to be a quiet and even a wasted one, but it was in fact a life brimming with inward excitement.

(1) The tone of the poem sounds

    (a) very urgent   (c) very arrogant   (e) strongly diffident
    (b) very demanding   (d) mildly cynical

참가자 : (1) 경찰관 : 남자, 약 40대 후반, 순경
(2) 운전자 : 남자, 약 40대 중반, 의사

해설 : 경찰관은 흑인 남자 Dr. Poussaint에게 모욕할 때 부르는 말 '어이(boy)'를 사용했다. "나 의사요"라는 그의 대답이 경찰관 속을 뒤집어 놓았을지도 모른다. 왜냐하면 경찰관은 흑인들이 어른 신분이나 직업상의 지위를 주장하는 건 잘못이라고 생각했기 때문이다. 그 경찰관은 흑인들을 '어이(boy)'라고 불러야 한다고 믿었다.

> **Note**
> □ **turmoil** = a state of confusion, excitement, and trouble : 소요, 소동
>   • The streets in front of the National Assembly were in great turmoil.
>   (의사당 앞 도로들이 큰 혼란 속에 쌓였었다.)
> □ **internal** = of or in the inside : 내부의, 국내의
>   • Internal bleeding (내출혈)   • internal combustion engine (내연기관)
> □ **cautiously** = with great care : 조심스럽게
>   • I opened toe door cautiously lest I wake the baby. (애기 깰까봐 조심히…)
> □ **misanthropist** : 인간을 싫어하는 사람   opp. philanthropist : 박애주의자

3. 난 아무것도 아니야! 넌 누구지?
역시 아무것도 아니라고?
그럼 우린 짝이로군, 그런데 말하면 안돼.
사람들이 우리를 몰아내거든. 그렇지?

뭔가 된다는 게 얼마나 따분할까!
숭배하는 대중을 향해
개구리처럼 이름을 하루종일 외쳐대는 것,
얼마나 남에게 알려지려나!

해설 : 에밀리는 Amherst의 아름답고 역사 깊은 대학촌에서 출생, 잠시 Mt. Holyoke 예과 대학에서 공부한 후 말뚝 울타리가 있는 목조건물로 물러나 그곳에서 가족과 가까운 친구들만 만나며 뉴잉글랜드의 수녀처럼 여생을 살았다. 그녀의 생애가 한적하고 심지어 황폐한 것처럼 보이지만 사실은 내적 흥분이 넘쳐나는 삶이었다.

(2) The attitude of the poet toward the glory of the world is

    (a) envy   (c) jealousy   (e) wonder
    (b) contempt   (d) excitement

4. Join Today! Save Hundreds This Year!

Your Membership includes thousands of locations via the Internet. Simply point and click to see updated listings of hotels, golf courses, theme parks, activities, condos, and much more!

Mail or fax this form to : PRIMECARD VISA 20 William Street Wellesley, MA 02181 FAX (781) 237-6163

    Name _____
    PRIMECARD VISA# _____
    Exp. Date _____ Phone _____
    Address _____
    Signature _____

Your Access Membership comes with a no-question-asked, 60-day money-back guarantee.

Situation: PRIMECARD wants you to apply for membership to promote their business.

(1) The tone of the writer seems to be

    (a) insincere   (c) bitter   (e) respectful
    (b) negative   (d) encouraging

(2) The writer's attitude is based on

    (a) persuasion   (c) entertainment   (e) matter-of-fact
    (b) information   (d) pleasure

5. If God gave me a chance to express my wish, without hesitation I would answer to Him, "The independence of Korea." "What is your next wish?" "It is the independence that I just expressed." "Then, what is your final wish?" I'd

> **Note**
> □ banish = send away esp. out of the country as a punishment : 귀양보내다
> □ bog : 수렁, 늪지 vt. 수렁에 빠뜨리다 • My car was bogged down. (차가 수렁에 빠졌다.)
> □ frame house : 목조가옥   □ picket fence : 말뚝 울타리
> □ Seminary : 종교단체가 운영하는 전문학교   □ cynical : 비꼬는
> □ arrogant : 건방떠는   □ diffident : 자신이 없는   opp. confident

4. 오늘 가입하세요. 금년에 수백 달러를 절약하세요.
　당신이 회원이 되시면 인터넷을 통하여 수천개의 지역을 이용할 수 있습니다. 단지 지목하시고 클릭하시면 호텔, 골프장, 테마파크, 활동, 콘도 그리고 훨씬 많은 곳의 최신 목록을 알 수 있습니다.
　이 서식을 우편이나 팩스를 이용하여 다음 주소로 보내시오.

```
Name _____ PRIMECARD VISA# _____
Exp. Date _____ Phone _____
Address _____
Signature _____
```

당신의 액세스 회원증은 신원조회 없는, 60일간 환불보증서와 함께 나옵니다.

　　상황 : 우리 회사는 회원간의 사업을 촉진시키기 위하여 여러분께서 회원이 되어 주시기를 바랍니다.

> **Note**
> □ via = by way of, by means of : 경유하여, …을 통해서
> • I sent a message to Mary by way of airmail.
> □ update = make more modern, up-to-date : 최신의 것으로 만들다
> □ directory = a book of list of names, facts, numbers arranged in alphabetical order

5. 만일 하느님이 나에게 소원을 말해보라는 기회를 주신다면 주저하지 않고 그분께 대답하겠어요, "조선의 독립입니다."

answer to Him with a more heightened voice, "The fully independent sovereignty of Korea!"

My fellow Koreans! This is the only wish that, I, Koo Kim, have! This being "independent" has been with me as my only wish, for which I have lived for 70 years, for which I live today, and for which I will live to see my wish come true.

(Source: Translated from "My Wish," a speech delivered by Kim Koo (1877 - 1949))

(1) The tone of the second paragraph is

   (a) cynical   (d) didactic
   (b) appealing   (e) humorous
   (c) apologetic

(2) It can be inferred that Kim, Koo's attitude toward the passage is based on his philosophical ideal of

   (a) theology   (c) astrology   (e) politics
   (b) economy   (d) science

6.   The primary goal of the U.S. Environmental Protection Agency (EPA) is to protect human health and the environment. One of the ways in which the EPA tries to achieve that goal is to educate the public on matters of local and national concern. Acid rain affects both the health of humans and our environment and is an issue with which the EPA is actively involved. The EPA provides information on research, regulation, and other issues associated with acid rain. Because acid rain is of national and international concern, many other government organizations are also responsible for working on this problem.

Situation : The U.S. EPA is disseminating its publications regarding acid rain as a way of educating the public and controlling air pollution: the cause of acid rain.

(1) The writer's style in this passage can be best described as

   (a) formal   (c) intimate   (e) casual
   (b) consultative (d) frozen

"그 다음 소원은 무엇이지요?"
"방금 말씀드렸던 조선의 독립입니다."
"그러시면 마지막 소원은 무엇인지요?"
나는 더 소리 높여 하느님께 대답하겠어요.
"조선의 완전한 독립 주권입니다."

친애하는 국민 여러분! 이것만이 나 김구가 가지고 있는 단하나 소원입니다. 독립되는 것이 나의 유일한 소원으로 나와 함께 해왔으며, 나는 이것을 위하여 70년을 살아왔고, 오늘을 살고 있으며, 앞으로도 이것을 위하여 살아 내 소원이 이루어지는 것을 볼 것이오.

Note

□ **without hesitation** : 주저없이, 망설이지 않고
  • Without a moment's hesitation, the rescue man jumped into the flood.
  (잠시도 머뭇거리지 않고 그 구조대원은 홍수 속으로 뛰어들었다.)
□ **sovereignty** : 주권, 통치권
□ **come ture = happen just as one wished, expected, dreamed** : 꿈, 기대가 실현되다
  • Sooner or later our wish for national unification will come true before us.
  (조만간 민족통일의 소망이 우리 앞에 실현될 것이다.)
□ **deliver = say, read aloud** : 말하다, 전달하다
  • The president delivered his New Year address effectively. (대통령은 신년사를 효과적으로 했다.)
□ **didactic = instructive** : 교훈적인
□ **apologetic = expressing sorrow for some fault** : 사죄하는   □ **theology** : 신학

6. 미국 환경보호청(EPA)의 일차적 목표는 인간의 건강과 환경을 보호하는 일이다. EPA가 그 목적을 달성하려는 한가지 방법은 지역적이면서 국가적인 관심사에 대하여 대중을 교육하는 일이다. 산성비는 인간의 건강과 우리 환경에 영향을 미치며 EPA가 적극적으로 관여하고 있는 현안이다. EPA는 산성비와 관련된 연구, 규제, 그리고 다른 현안 문제들에 관한 정보를 공급한다. 산성비는 국내 및 국제적 관심사이기 때문에 다른 많은 정부기관들도 이 문제 연구에 책임이 있다.

상황 : 미국 EPA는 대중교육과 산성비의 원인인 공기오염 억제의 한 방편으로 산성비에 관한 출판물을 배포하고 있다.

(2) The attitude of the writer toward the passage is

    (a) contemptuous   (c) cynical   (e) reasonable

    (b) paternal   (d) coercive

7.   Although the Japanese, like all other modern peoples, are the result of racial mixtures, they are essentially a Mongoloid people, clearly related to their neighbors on the continent in Korea and China. According to popular theories, the early Japanese came to their islands from the south by way of Formosa and the Rhykyu Islands, but archaeological evidence indicates clearly that most of the early Japanese came to Japan by way of Korea.

(Source: Quoted from Reishauer, Edwin (1964). Japan: Past and Present.)

Background : Dr. Reishauer, former professor of Far Eastern Language at Harvard University, then U.S. ambassador to Japan, and a well-known authority on the history of Japan, academically describes "The early Japanese" in his publication, Japan: Past and Present (1964).

(1) The tone of the writer toward the passage seems to be

    (a) convincing   (c) pedantic   (e) subjective

    (b) anecdotal   (d) personal

(2) The writer's attitude toward the passage seems to be based on his

    (a) personal experience   (d) work in Japan

    (b) academic research   (e) aptitude and attitude

    (c) travel experience

8. **Line 1** : John Lewis : ···but, just say that there is a God, what color is he? White or black?
    Line 2 : Larry : Well, if it is a God··· I wouldn' know what color, I couldn' say, -couldn' nobody say what color he is or really would be.
    Line 3 : JL : But now, jus' suppose there was a God -
    Line 4 : Larry : Unless'n they say···
    Line 5 : JL : No, I was jus' sayin' jus' suppose there is a God, would he be white or black?

> **Note**
> ☐ the primary cause of the IMF crisis : IMF 위기의 첫째 원인
> ☐ acid rain : 산성비
> ☐ affect=influence, cause some result or change : 영향을 미치다
> • Smoking affects health seriously. (흡연은 건강에 심각한 영향을 미친다.)
> ☐ disseminate=spread, scatter : 퍼뜨리다, 분배하다
> ☐ coercive : 강제적인, 고압적인
> ☐ paternal=fatherly : 아버지의   ☐ paternal love : 부성애
> • I'm still under paternal roof.(아직도 아버지에게 얹혀산다.)
> ☐ contemptuous : 멸시하는
> • They used to be contemptuous of the 3D jobs.

7. 다른 모든 현대 국민들처럼 일본인들도 인종 혼합의 결과지만 그들은 본질적으로 대륙의 중국과 한국(일본이 섬나라이기 때문에)에 사는 그들의 이웃들과 분명하게 관련된 몽고인종의 국민이다. 통설에 의하면 초기 일본인들은 남쪽에서 대만과 유구열도를 경유하여 그들 섬에 왔다고 하지만 고고학적 증거는 대부분의 초기 일본인들이 한국을 경유하여 일본에 온 것을 확실하게 지적하고 있다.

> 배경 : 전 하버드 대학 극동지역 언어교수였고 후에 주일 미대사였으며 일본역사의 권위자인 라이샤워교수는 그의 저서 '일본의 과거와 현재'에서 학문적으로 '초기 일본인'라고 표현하고 있다.

> **Note**
> ☐ racial mixture : 인종간의 혼합
> ☐ popular theory : 통설   ☐ established theory : 정설
> ☐ the Rhykyu Islands : 유구 열도 – 일본 규슈에서 대만에 이르는 50여개의 섬
> ☐ convincing : 설득력 있는

8. 1행 : 존 루이스 : 그러나, 단지 신이 있다고 하자. 그는 무슨 피부색일까, 백인, 흑인?
   2행 : 래리 : 글쎄, 그게 신이라면 무슨 색인지 모르겠는데… 모르겠어. 무슨 색인지, 무슨 색일지 누구도 모르겠지.
   3행 : 존 루이스 : 그러나, 단지 신이 있다고 가정하고…

Line 6 : Larry : ···He'd be white, man.
Line 7 : JL : Why?
Line 8 : Larry : Why? I'll tell you why. 'Cause the average whitey out here got everything, you dig? And the nigger ain't got shit, y'know?
Y' unnerstan'? So - um - for - in order for that to happen, you know it ain't a black God that's doin' that bullshit.

(Source: Speech Sample by William Labov (1972), in Language in the Inner City.)

Participants : (1) Larry, 15 years old, male, core and active member of Jets. Larry causes troubles in and out of school. He was put back from the 11th grade to the 9th grade, and has been threatened with further action by the school authorities.
(2) John Lewis, a white interviewer.

Situation : In a New York public school, John under the direction of William Labov, a leading sociolinguistics professor at the University of Pennsylvania, undertook an interview with a black student, Larry, to test whether the black English vernacular is logical/deficient or not. Labov claims that the black English is neither illogical nor deficient at all.

Comment : Line 8 can be rephrased in standard English as follows:

Line 8: Larry: Why? I'll tell you why. Because the average white person in this country has everything, do you understand? The black person doesn't have anything, you know? You understand? So - um - for - in order for that to happen, you know it isn't a black God that's doing that nonsense.

(1) What do you think that the tone of Larry in line 8 would be when he was being interviewed by John?

   (a) bitter   (c) flattering   (e) amusing
   (b) pleasant   (d) respectful

(2) The attitude of Larry toward the questions being asked seems to be

   (a) approving   (c) indifferent   (e) jaded
   (b) distasteful   (d) pedantic

4행 : 래리 : 사람들이 그러는데…

5행 : 존 루이스 : 아니야, 난 단지 신이 있다고 가정하면 무슨 색일까 말하는거야.

6행 : 래리 : 그는 백인이겠지.

7행 : 존 루이스 : 왜?

8행 : 래리 : 왜냐고? 이유를 말해줄까. 여기에 살고있는 흰둥이들은 모든 것을 다 가지고 있거든, 알겠니? 근데 깜둥이들은 아무것도 없어, 그렇지? 알겠어?
이처럼 하느님이 깜둥이라면 그런 바보짓을 하지 않겠지.

참가자 : (1) 래리. 15세, 남, Jets의 핵심이자 활동적인 회원. 래리는 학교 안, 밖에서 말썽을 일으킴. 11학년에서 9학년으로 유급.
그외 학교당국으로부터 그 이상의 조치를 위협당하고 있음.
(2) 존 루이스, 백인 면담자

상황 : 한 뉴욕의 공립학교에서 존은 U.Pen.대학의 지도적 사회언어학 교수인 윌리암 라보브 교수의 지도아래 흑인 토착어가 논리적인가 아닌가, 결함이 있는가 아닌가를 시험하기 위하여 흑인 학생 래리와의 인터뷰를 맡았다. 라보브 교수는 흑인영어가 비논리적이지도 않고 결함이 있는 것도 아니라고 주장한다.

주석 : 8행을 표준영어로 저자가 고쳐 썼음.

Note

□ Jus = just : 단어 끝에오는 파열음(/p,/t,/k/)은 파열되지 않는다. 소리 나는대로 적으면 must도 mus'로 can't도 can'까지만 들린다. 또한 because의 경우도 강세가 2음절에 오기 때문에 be는 안들리고 'cause로, enough도 'nough로 들린다. 따라서 강세가 2음절에 오는 단어는 평소 강세부분에 힘을 주는 습관을 들여야 한다.
□ unless'n = unless and : 의미없이 쓰이는 말이다. unless and until = until
□ whitey : (미 속어) 흰둥이   □ You dig? = You understand?
□ shit, bullshit : 우리 말에 '개 똥같은…', '얼어죽을…' 등의 비속어로 무의미어다.
□ core = central, most important part : 핵심적인
□ to the core : 씨까지, 철저히   • She's French to the core. (철저한 프랑스인)
□ vernacular = using the native spoken language : 토착어를 쓰는
□ pedantic : 학자인체하는   □ approving : 시인하는
□ distasteful : 싫은   □ jaded : 넌더리나는, 지겨운

9. Dear Friend,

It's a great day to start your vacation. The bright summer sky welcomes you and your family as you enjoy the beautiful outdoor scenery. However, one thing that spoils your wonderful travel experience is the inevitable need for food as we all have experienced. Why interrupt your travel to stop at fast food restaurants, spending nearly $20 to $30 just for one lousy meal?

Now, you don't have to do that anymore! With our newly crafted portable refrigerator : Arctic Kool, you can solve this problem and enjoy your travel more. Most importantly, you can enjoy healthy home-cooked meals stored in this Arctic Kool while saving time and money.

The Arctic Kool is a roomy yet lightweight portable refrigerator. The original price is $140, but through this special mail offer, you will receive a 40% discount. Please be advised that supplies are limited, and this offer is valid only for two weeks!

Sincerely,
Peter Kool, Sales Director

Situation : A company manufacturing portable refrigerators introduced its new product: The Arctic Kool to the prospective consumers, especially to those who love automotive travel. An advertising letter was prepared as shown above.

(1) What do you think the tone of the writer toward the passage would be?

(a) motivating
(b) courteous
(c) threatening
(d) factual
(e) informative

(2) The attitude of the writer toward the passage can be considered to persuade the letter receiver to

(a) take action
(b) be informed
(c) be entertained
(d) travel
(e) enjoy summer travel

10. Professor Park's remark on Study.

Background : Professor Park, former Dean of the College of Foreign Studies (now Hankook University of Foreign Studies) devoted most of his life to the teaching of English for Korean students. He was a self-taught scholar with a very high value on education.

9. 귀한 손님께

휴가를 떠날 아주 좋은 날입니다. 당신과 가족들이 야외 경치를 즐기실 때 찬란한 여름 하늘이 반겨줍니다. 그러나 멋있는 여행을 망치는 한 가지가 있는데 우리가 다 겪어 봤듯이 음식에 대한 불가피한 필요입니다. 왜 패스트 푸드점에서 여행길을 중단한 채 형편없는 한끼 식사를 위해서 20~30달러를 쓰십니까?

자, 더이상 그러실 필요가 없습니다. 우리가 새로 만든 이동 냉장고, Arctic Kool로 문제를 해결하고 여행을 더 즐기실 수 있습니다. 더욱 중요한 것은 Arctice Kool에 보관하여 건강에 좋은, 집에서 만든 식사를 시간과 돈을 절약하시며 즐기실 수 있다는 점입니다.

Arctic Kool은 공간이 넓으면서도 가벼운 휴대용 냉장고입니다. 가격은 140달러지만 이번 특별 통신판매를 통하여 40% 할인을 받으실 수 있습니다. 공급 물량이 한정되어 있음을 통지합니다. 이 판매는 2주일간만 유효합니다.

상황 : 이동용 냉장고를 제작하는 이 회사는 신제품을 소개합니다. 유망한 고객들, 특히 자동차 여행을 즐기는 사람들에게 Arctic Kool을.
광고 문안은 위에 보여준 바와 같습니다.

Note
- spoil = ruin, make useless : 해치다, 망치다
- inevitable = which isn't prevented from happening : 막을 수 없는, 불가피한
  - An argument was inevitable because they disliked each other so much.
    (그들은 하도 서로 싫어해서 시비가 불가피했다.)
- interrupt = break the flow of speech, something : 말을 가로 막다, 끼어 들다
  - Sorry to interrupt you, but I have an urgent business. (말씀 중에 죄송하지만 급한 용무가 있어서.)
- lousy = very bad, useless
  - What a lousy weather! (빌어 먹을 날씨가 왜 이러지!)
- roomy = with plenty space = spacious : 안이 널찍한   • a roomy car (안이 넓은 차)

10. 학문에 대한 박교수의 말씀

배경 : 전 외국어대(현재 한국 외국어 대학교) 학장이었던 박술음교수는 생애의 대부분을 한국학생들의 영어교육에 바쳤다. 그분은 교육의 가치를 중시하시고 독학하신 학자였다.

I hope the readers of this book are real students. "Study crosses the centuries as easily as it does national boundaries; it neighbors with greatness; it gets us through all weathers. The space available to the mind is of whatever dimensions you choose to make it. No life is long enough to exhaust the privileges and excitement of that fact." You must have seen bored card players, but have you ever come across a bored student?

(Source: Quoted from Park, Solemn's "Prefatory Note" (1962).
<u>In Reader's English : Passages from Modern Writers</u>. The Eulyoo Publishing Co, Seoul, Korea)

(1) The writer's style in this passage seems to be

   (a) coercive   (c) pleasant   (e) humorous
   (b) advising   (d) inventive

(2) The writer's attitude toward the "real students" in the passage is

   (a) sincere   (c) personal   (e) sanguine
   (b) factual   (d) detached

<u>11.</u> **Nehru speaks to mourning millions of a few hours after the murder of Gandhi. January 30, 1948.**

Situation : Gandhi, Mohandas (1869-1948), social reformer, and leader of Indian nationalism was shot down by a Hindu nationalist. Jawaharlal Nehru (1889-1964), the first Prime Minister of India made an eulogy for the sorrowing and speechless crowds massed to catch one last glimpse of Gandhi's face. It was at the place where he had fallen. In this crisis of paralyzing sorrow and fear, in the evening a few hours after the bullet was fired, Nehru spoke extemporaneously, using the radio to reach millions of his countrymen.

Mahatma Gandhi

   Friends and comrades, the light has gone out of our lives and there is darkness everywhere. I do not know what to tell you and how to say it. Our beloved leader, Bapu as we called him, the father of the nation, is no more. Perhaps I am wrong to say that. Nevertheless, we will not see him again as we

나는 이 책을 읽는 독자들이 진정한 학생이기를 바랍니다. "학문이란 국경을 초월하듯 수백년을 쉽게 초월합니다. 학문은 위대한 사상과 이웃하며, 모든 역경을 무릅쓰고 우리를 성취에 도달하게 합니다. 마음이 사용할 수 있는 공간은 여러분이 넓히려고 마음 먹는 만큼의 크기까지 넓힐 수 있습니다. 우리의 인생은 그 특권과 그 흥분을 다 쓸만큼 길지 못합니다." 여러분들은 카드놀이에 지쳐버린 사람은 보았어도 학문에 지쳐버린 사람은 만나지 못했을 겁니다.

Note
- □dean : 대학 학장   cf. president : 총장   □provost : 교무처장
- □devote = give wholly, completely : 헌신하다, 송두리째 바치다
  - The scientist devoted his time and money to discovering a cure of cancer.
  - (그 과학자는 암치료법을 발견하는데 시간과 돈을 바쳤다.)
- □dimension = measurement in all direction, size, extent : 크기, 차원
- □exhaust = use up, deal with completely, tire out : 고갈시키다, 피곤하게 하다
  - We've exhausted all the supplies. What are we supposed to do? (보급품이 다 떨어졌다. 어떻게하지?)
- □detached : 초연한   detached view (공정한 견해)
- □sanguine = hopeful, optimistic, cheerful : 낙관하는, 확신하는, 다혈질의
  - I'm sanguine of your quick recovery. (빠른 회복을 확신한다.)

<u>11. 1948년 1월 30일 간디가 살해된 수시간 후 네루는 애도하는 수백만에게 연설을 했다.</u>

배경 : 사회개혁가, 인도의 민족주의 지도자 간디는 어느 힌두 민족주의자에게 총격당해 쓰러졌다. 인도의 최초 국무총리 Jawaharlal 네루가 간디의 얼굴이라도 잠깐 보려고 모여든 슬픔에 찬 말을 잊은 군중에게 고인을 칭송하는 연설을 했다. 그곳은 그가 쓰러진 곳이었다. 이 모든 것을 마비시키는 슬픔과 공포의 위기에, 총탄이 발사된 수 시간 후의 저녁에, 네루는 수백만의 자기 동포에게 라디오를 통하여 즉석에서 연설을 했다.

친애하는 동포 여러분, 우리의 삶에서 빛은 사라졌고 모든 곳이 깜깜합니다. 나는 무슨 말을 어떻게 해야할지 모르겠습니다. 우리가 Bapu라고 불렀던 우리의 사랑하는 지도자, 이 민족의 아버지는 이 세상에 더 이상 계시지 않습니다. 어쩌면 그렇게 말씀드리는 것이 잘못된 것일지도 모르겠습니다. 그러나 우리가 지금까지 여러해 동안 보아왔던 모습으로

have seen him for these many years. We will not run to him for advice and seek solace from him, and that is a terrible blow, not to me only, but to millions and millions in this country, and it is a little difficult to soften the blow by any other advice that I or anyone else can give you.

The light has gone out, I said, and yet I was wrong. For the light that shone in this country was no ordinary light. The light that has illuminated this country for these many years will illuminate this country for many more years, and a thousand years later that light will still be seen in this country and the world will see it and it will give solace to innumerable hearts. For that light represented the living truth… the eternal truth, reminding us of the right path, drawing us from error, taking this ancient country to freedom….

Tomorrow should be a day of fasting and prayer for all of us…. And at the appointed time for cremation, that is, 4:00 p.m. tomorrow afternoon, people should go to the river or to the sea and offer prayers there. And while we pray the greatest prayer that we can offer is to take a pledge to dedicate ourselves to the truth and to the cause for which this great countryman of ours lived and for which he has died.

(Source: Adapted from "Nehru speaks to mourning millions of a few hours after the murder of Gandhi." In A Treasury of the World's Great Speeches (1954))

(1) The tone of Nehru in this passage can be best inferred as

(a) grievous & bitter
(b) grievous & angry
(c) grievous & inspiring
(d) didactic & sanguine
(e) impatient & sad

(2) Nehru made a eulogy for Gandhi with an attitude of

(a) respect & inspiration
(b) pitying & approving
(c) matter-of-fact
(d) dignity & integrity
(e) bitterness & hatred

그분을 다시는 뵐 수 없을 것입니다. 충고를 듣고 위로를 찾으러 그분께 달려갈 수 없을 것입니다. 그건 나에게 뿐아니라 이 나라 수억의 사람들에게 엄청난 충격입니다. 그리고 나나 다른 어느 누가 줄 수 있는 충고로도 이 충격을 누그러뜨리기는 어렵습니다.

 나는 빛이 꺼졌다고 말씀드렸는데 그 표현은 잘못이었습니다. 왜냐하면 그 빛은 보통 빛이 아니었습니다. 오랫동안 이 나라를 비추어 주었던 그 빛이 더욱 많은 시간 이 나라를 비춰 줄 것이기 때문입니다. 그리고 수 천년이 지난 후에도 그 빛은 여전히 이 나라를 비출 것이며 전세계가 그 빛을 볼 것이며 수많은 사람들의 가슴에 위로를 줄 것입니다. 왜냐하면 그 빛은 살아있는 진리, 영원한 진리, 우리에게 올바른 길을 깨우쳐 주고, 우리를 잘못에서 끌어내 주고, 이 역사 깊은 나라를 자유로 이끌어 갈 살아있는 진리이기 때문입니다.

 내일은 우리 모두 금식과 기도를 드릴 날로 정하겠습니다. 또한 정해진 화장시각 내일 오후 4시에 국민 모두 강과 바다로 가서 기도를 해야 합니다. 우리가 할 수 있는 가장 위대한 기도를 하는 동안 위대한 우리 국민이 지금까지 이룩하려고 살아왔고 그분이 이룩하려고 돌아가신 그 진리와 대의를 위하여 헌신할 것을 맹세하는 것입니다.

Note

□ **mourn** = feel sorrow, show grief for the death of someone : 애도하다
  • The world mourned the loss of the young leader of human rights.
  (세계 사람들은 인권을 위하여 선두에 섰던 그 젊은 지도자의 죽음을 애도했다.)
□ **reformer** : 개혁자   □ **nationalism** : 민족주의   □ **eulogy** : 사자에 대한 칭송의 말
□ **paralyze** = make body unable to move : 마비시키다
  • The power failure paralyzed the train service.(정전으로 열차 운행이 마비됐다.)
□ **extemporaneously** = spoken or done in haste, without time, preparation :
  즉시, 준비없이 즉흥적으로
□ **solace** = comfort in grief or anxiety : 슬픔, 걱정에 대한 위로
  • The war-bereaved widow finds solace in her children. (그 전쟁 미망인은 자녀에게서 위로를 받는다.)
□ **illuminate** = give light to : 조명하다   • The room was illuminated by candles.
□ **innumerable** = too many to be counted : 무수한
□ **eternal** = going on forever : 영원한   • eternal life (영생)
□ **fast** = eat no food for religious reasons : 단식하다
□ **cremation** = burning of the dead body : 화장   • crematorium : 화장터
□ **pledge** = a solemn provise : 서약, 맹세
□ **pity** = sensitiveness to sorrow, suffering : 동정, 연민의 정
  • Don't take pity on me. I'm Ok. (동정말게. 나 괜찮아.)
□ **impatient** = unable to wait, bear : 성미를 못견디는
  • The teacher is impatient with his slow - learners. (공부 못하는 아이에 대해 참지 못한다.)

12. Roosevelt Asks For a Declaration of War Against Japan.

Situation : On December 7, 1941, the Japanese forces launched a surprise attack on the United States Naval Base at Pearl Harbour. This surprise attack prompted President Franklin D. Roosevelt to address the U.S. Congress on December 8, 1941 so that a formal declaration of war could be made against the Japanese Empire.

Franklin D. Roosevelt

Pearl Harbor, Hawaii

To the Congress of the United States :

Yesterday, December 7, 1941 - a date that will live in infamy - the United States of America was suddenly and deliberately attacked by naval and air forces of the Empire of Japan···.

The attack yesterday on the Hawaiian islands has caused severe damage to American naval and military forces. Very many American lives have been lost. In addition, American ships have been reported torpedoed on the high seas between San Francisco and Honolulu.

Yesterday, the Japanese government also launched an attack against Malaya. Last night, Japanese forces attacked Hong Kong. Last night, Japanese forces attacked Guam. Last night, the Japanese forces attacked the Philippine Islands. Last night, the Japanese attacked Wake Island. This morning, the Japanese attacked Midway Island.

Japan has, therefore, undertaken a surprise offensive extending throughout the Pacific area. The facts of yesterday speak for themselves. The people of the United States have already formed their opinions and well understand the implications to the very life and safety of our nation.

As Commander in Chief of the Army and Navy, I have directed that all measures be taken for our defense···. Hostilities exist. There is no blinking at the fact that our people, our territory, and our interests are in grave danger. I ask that the Congress declare that since the unprovoked and dastardly attack by Japan on Sunday, December 7, a state of war has existed between the United States and the Japanese Empire.

(Source: Adapted from Franklin D. Roosevelt's "Pearl Harbour Speech" delivered on December 8, 1941 to the Congress of the United States)

(1) What do you think the tone of Roosevelt would be?

   (a) solemn   (b) sad (c) afraid   (d) happy   (e) frustrated

(2) What do you think the attitude of the speaker would be?

   (a) determined   (b) scared   (c) hopeful   (d) hopeless(e) worried

12. 루즈벨트는 일본에 대한 선전포고를 요청한다.

상황 : 1941년 12월 7일 일본군이 진주만에 있는 해군기지에 대한 기습공격을 개시했다. 이 기습공격이 프랭클린 루즈벨트 대통령으로 하여금 국회에 나가 일본제국에 대하여 공식적인 선전포고의 인준을 위한 연설을 하도록 촉구했다.

미합중국 국회에게 :

치욕 속에서 기억되어질 1941년 12월 7일 어제, 미합중국은 제국주의 일본의 해군과 육군의 기습적이고 고의적인 공격을 받았습니다.

하와이 군도에 대한 어제의 공격은 미 해군과 육군에 심각한 손해를 끼쳤습니다. 다수 미국인의 인명 손실이 있었습니다. 그외에도 미국 선박들이 샌프란시스코와 호놀룰루 사이의 공해상에서 어뢰의 공격을 받았다고 보고 되었습니다.

어제 일본 정부는 역시 말레이 반도에 대한 공격을 개시하였습니다. 어제밤 일본군은 홍콩을 공격했습니다. …괌을 공격했습니다. … 필리핀 군도를…, 웨이크섬을…, 오늘 아침에는 미드웨이 섬을 공격하였습니다.

즉, 일본은 태평양 전체까지 확대하는 기습 공세를 감행했습니다. 어제의 사실들은 자명합니다. 미국 국민들은 이미 자신들의 소신을 결정했으며 그 사실이 국가의 생명과 안전에 대하여 무엇을 암시하고 있는지 잘 이해하고 있습니다.

육·해군의 총사령관으로서 방위를 위하여 취할 수 있는 모든 조치를 취하도록 명령을 했습니다. 전투가 일어나고 있습니다. 우리 국민, 우리 영토, 우리의 이해문제가 중대한 위험에 빠져 있음을 무시할 수 없습니다. 나는 국회가 12월 7일 일요일의 일방적이고 야비한 공격 이후, 전쟁 상태가 미국과 일본제국 간에 존재해 왔음을 선포해주시기 바랍니다.

Note

- launch = set a new-built boat into water : 진수시키다
  - launch a rocket (로켓을 발사하다) • launch a business (사업을 착수하다)
- prompt = urge : 촉구, 재촉하다 Hunger prompted him to steal.
- deliberately = intentionally : 고의적으로 • It was not an accident; it was planned deliberately.
- in addition = as well as : 그밖에, 또 • In addition to visiting the zoo, we went to the museum.
- torpedo = long explosive shell driven along under the sea to destroy ships : 어뢰
- high seas = open seas : 공해 □ hostilities = acts of fighting in war : 전투행위
- implication = a suggestion not expressed plainly : 암시, 내포된 의미
  • What's the implication of his sudden resignation? (갑작스럽게 사표를 낸 속 뜻은?)

13. **Situation:** Nayan Chanda, Indochina Correspondent for the Far Eastern Economic Review, watched the final night of Saigon, as American helicopters evacuated the last remaining Americans and their Vietnamese associates from the U.S. Embassy. The capital city of South Vietnam fell on April 30, 1975.

Liberation day in Saigon, April 30, 1975. A Vietcong tank enters the palace grounds to hoist the NLF flag.

Darkness fell like fate on Saigon on April 29, 1975. By 06:30 P.M. a power outage blacked out the city, but that was almost a blessing, since it hid the shame of defeat. I stood on the terrace of the Hotel Caravelle under a light drizzle, watching Saigon's last night. Giant American helicopters hovered before swooping down on rooftops to remove remaining Americans and some of their Vietnamese associates to the safety of the United States Seventh Fleet lying offshore in the South China Sea. Moments later they zoomed up and their engines roared deafeningly, to melt into the darkened sky. Against the backdrop of a sky filled with glowing tracer bullets, the helicopters looked like giant fiery fireflies engaged in some gruesome dance over a dying city.

(Source: Adapted from "Introduction: The Exit" from Chanda, Nayan (1986). Brother Enemy.)

(1) What do you think the tone of the author would be?

   (a) ironic   (b) fearful   (c) worried   (d) gloomy   (e) cheerful

(2) What do you think the attitude of the author toward the passage would be?

   (a) defiant   (b) joyful   (c) hopeful   (d) fearless   (e) reminiscent

14. **Dr. Sun, Yat-Sen's Lecture, "The Three Principles of the People" (1924).**

Background : Dr. Sun (1866 - 1925), physician, advocator of nationalism, and one of the leading founding fathers of the Republic of China, spent most of his life to set China free not only from the political dominance of the Manchu Dynasty, but also from foreign exploitation. Dr. Sun died at the age of 59 in Peking after serving forty years for China's millions. This lecture, one in a 16 lecture series, "The Three Principles of the People" was delivered to the audience of his followers in 1924.

13. **상황** : Far Eastern Economic Review지 인도차이나 특파원인 Nayan Chanda는 미 헬기들이 마지막 남아있는 미국인들과 그들과 관련된 베트남인들을 미 대사관으로부터 후송시키고 있을 때인 사이공 최후의 밤을 지켜보았다.
남 베트남의 수도는 1975년 4월 30일에 함락되었다.

1975년 4월 29일 암흑이 죽음처럼 내렸다. 오후 4시 30분까지 정전상태가 도시를 암흑으로 만들었다. 그러나 그건 축복에 가까웠다. 왜냐하면 그 정전이 패배의 수치를 숨겨주었기 때문이다. 나는 안개비를 맞으며 사이공 최후의 밤을 지켜 보면서, Caravelle호텔의 테라스에 서 있었다. 거대한 미 헬기들이 붕붕거리며 지붕꼭대기에 내려와 남은 미국인과 몇몇 관련있는 베트남인들을 남지나해 해안에 정박중인 미 7함대의 안전지대까지 옮겼다. 잠시후 헬기들은 떠올랐고 엔진 소리에 귀가 막힐듯 하더니 어두운 하늘로 사라졌다. 번쩍이는 예광탄이 가득한 하늘을 배경으로, 헬기들은 죽어가는 도시 위에서 음산한 춤을 추는 거대한 불나비들 같아 보였다.

Note

- **evacuate** = take all the people away from : 소개(疏開)시키다, 후송하다
  - The village was evacuated because of the danger of the flood.
- **fate** = one's future, end, death-like fate : 최후의 죽음처럼
- **power outage** : 정전상태 • The power outage lasted for 30 minutes.
- **drizzle** = fine misty rain : 안개비
- **hover** = (of birds, helicopters) stay in one place : 공중 선회하다
- **swoop** = descend sharply an attack : (새가) 지상으로 덮치다
- **zoom** : 헬기가 급히 떠오르다, 무비 카메라가 피사체에 따라 급히 확대, 축소하다
- **deafeningly** : 귀청이 떨어질 듯이
- **backdrop** = background : 배경 • The events of the 1930's provided the backdrop of the movie.
- **tracer bullet** : 예광탄
- **gruesome** = connected with death : 으스스한, 음산함
- **defiant** = showing no fear, or respect : 도전적인, 반항적인

Gentlemen,

I have come here today to speak to you about the San Min Principles (The Three Principles of the People). They are the principles for our nation's salvation. Why do we say that the San Min Principles save our nation? Because they will elevate China to an equal position among the nations, in international affairs, in government, and in economic life, so that she can permanently exist in the world.

What is the principle of the San Min? I shall first begin the discussion of the principle of nationalism. There are five great forces which constitute the principle of nationalism : race, livelihood, language, religion, customs and habits. We must attribute the development to these five forces: blood kinship, common language, common livelihood, common religion, and common customs which are not products of military occupation, but of natural evolution.

Sun Yat-sen

What is the standing of our nation in the world? In comparison with other nations, we have the greatest population and the oldest culture. But the Chinese people have only family and clan groups ; there is no national spirit. We are the poorest and weakest state in the world, occupying the lowest position in international affairs ; *the rest of mankind is the carving knife and the serving dish, while we are the fish and the meat.* Our position now is extremely perilous. If we do not earnestly promote nationalism and weld together our four hundred millions into a strong nation, we will face tragedy: the loss of our country and the destruction of our race. To ward off this danger, we must espouse nationalism and employ the national spirit to save the country.

Imperialist nations wanted to control China's trade.

(Source: Adapted from "Sun, Yat-Sen takes up the Yellow man's burden" in A Treasury of the World's Great Speeches (1954))

(1) What do you think the tone of the speaker would be?

    (a) strongly emotional   (d) informative & persuasive
    (b) appealing & bitter   (e) dogmatic but logical
    (c) sarcastic & insincere

(2) It can be inferred that Dr. Sun's attitude toward the passage is based on

    (a) imperialism   (c) socialism   (e) fascism
    (b) nationalism   (d) colonialism

14. 손문 박사의 강의. '삼민주의'

상황 : 의사, 민족주의 주창자, 선도적인 중화민국 건국 아버지의 한 사람인 손문 박사는 중국을 만주 왕조의 정치적 지배에서 뿐만아니라 외국의 착취에서 해방시키기 위하여 생애의 대부분을 보냈다. 손박사는 북경에서 40년간 수많은 중국인을 위하여 봉사한 후 59세로 사망했다. 연속된 16회 강연 중의 하나인 이 강연 '삼민주의'는 1924년 그의 신봉자 청중에게 행하여 진 것이다.

여러분, 오늘 나는 여러분들에게 삼민주의에 대하여 말씀드리려고 이곳에 왔습니다. 이것들은 우리 민족의 구원을 위한 원칙들입니다. 왜 삼민주의가 우리 민족을 구한다고 말하느냐구요? 왜냐하면 그것들이 국제문제, 정치, 경제 생활에서 중국을 여러 국가들과 동등한 위치로 상승시켜 이 나라가 영원히 이 세계에 존재할 수 있도록 할 것이기 때문입니다.

삼민의 원칙이 무엇입니까? 첫째로 민족주의 원칙부터 토의를 시작하겠습니다. 민족주의를 구성하는 다섯가지 커다란 힘이 있습니다. 인종, 생계, 언어, 종교, 풍속과 습관입니다. 우리는 다음 다섯개의 힘에 맞추어 발달해야 합니다: 군사적 점령의 산물이 아니라 자연스러운 발전의 산물인 혈연적 친척, 공통어, 공통 생계, 공통 종교, 그리고 공통 풍속입니다.

세계에서 우리나라 위치는 어디일까요? 다른 나라들과 비교하여 최대의 인구와 가장 긴 문화를 가지고 있습니다. 그러나 중국인들은 가족과 씨족 집단일 뿐입니다. 국민정신이 없습니다. 국제 문제에서 최하위를 차지하는 가장 가난하고 가장 약한 나라입니다. 다른 사람들이 요리하는 칼이고 음식을 담아먹는 접시라면, 우리는 생선이고 고기입니다. 우리의 위치가 극도로 위험합니다. 만일 우리가 열심히 민족주의를 촉진시키지 않고 우리 4억 국민을 강력하게 단합시켜 강력한 한 국가로 만들지 않으면, 우리는 나라를 잃고 민족이 파괴당하는 비극을 겪게 됩니다. 이 위험을 막으려면 우리는 민족주의를 받아들이고 나라를 구하려는 민족의 혼을 동원해야 합니다.

Note

- **advocator** = a person who speaks for or support an idea : 주창자, 옹호자
  - He is a strong advocator of tax reforms.(그는 세제개혁을 강력하게 주창한다.)
- **exploitation** = the act of using unfairly force for one's profit : 착취
- **elevate** = make higher, better : 상승시키다
- **constitute** = make up, form • Seven days constitute a week.
- **standing** = rank, position in a system : 조직체 안에서의 순위
- **clan** = a group of families, tribe, clique : 종족, 씨족, 도당
- **espouse** = adopt : 채택하다
- **ward off** = protect oneself against : 방어하다

15. Douglas MacArthur defends his conduct of the war in Korea. April 19, 1951.

Background : General Douglas MacArthur (1882-1964), U.S. military leader who led successful invasion of the Philippines in 1944-1945, and accepted the Japanese surrender in 1945. After the surrender, he became Supreme Commander of the Allied forces in Japan, and, on South Korea's being invaded, Commander of the U.N. forces there. On April 11, 1951, he was relieved of both commands by Truman in a dispute over Far East policy.

MacArther, who loved the smell of tobacco

Situation : MacArthur, after being fired, immediately flew back to the U.S., and made a triumphant trip across the country. Most Americans welcomed him as a hero of World War II and Korean War. He accepted the invitation to speak before both Houses of Congress --- an unheard-of procedure in American history. On April 1951, he made a speech before the highest legislative bodies with millions present through television, and millions more listening in. His topic was not merely the conduct of a limited war in Korea, but world strategy. However, his speech immensely impressed the vast majority at that time with his posture, voice, and tempo. It was the provocative prologue to one of the most searching inquiries in American history, which made him a possible candidate for President.

Mr. President, Mr. Speaker and distinguished members of the Congress:

I stand on this rostrum with a sense of deep humility and great pride --- humility in the wake of those great architects of our history who have stood here before me, pride in the reflection that this home of legislative debate represents human liberty in the purest form yet devised···.

Once war is forced upon us, there is no other alternative than to apply every available means to bring it to a swift end. War's very objective is victory, not prolonged indecision. *In war, there is no substitute for victory*····.

The tragedy of Korea is further heightened by the fact that its military

15. 더글러스 맥아더 한국에서의 자신의 전쟁 수행을 변호하다. 1951년 4월 19일

배경 : 더글러스 맥아더, 1944~1945년의 필리핀 침공을 성공적으로 이끌고, 1945년에 일본의 항복을 받아낸 미 군사 지휘관. 일본 항복 후 일본 주둔 연합군의 최고 사령관, 남한이 침략당하자 주한 유엔군 사령관이 됐다. 1951년 4월 11일 극동 정책에 관한 분쟁으로 트루만에 의하여 두 사령관직에서 해임당했다.

상황 : 맥아더는 해임 후 즉시 본국에 돌아가 전국을 의기양양하게 여행했다. 대부분의 미국인들은 그를 세계 2차대전과 한국 전쟁의 영웅으로 환영했다. 그는 미 국회 양원 합동회의에서 연설을 해달라는 초청을 수락했다. 이는 미국 역사상 전례가 없는 조치였다.
1951년 4월 19일 TV로 수많은 사람들이 라디오를 통해서 귀를 기울이고 지켜보는 가운데 최고의 입법기관 앞에서 연설을 했다. 그의 주제는 한반도에서의 한정된 전쟁 수행뿐 아니라 세계 전략에 관한 것이었다. 그러나 그의 연설은 당시 그의 자세, 목소리, 속도 때문에 굉장히 많은 사람들에게 엄청난 감명을 주었다. 그의 연설은 미국 역사상 가장 엄중한 심리(審理)에 대한 도발적인 서막의 하나였다. 그리고 이것은 그를 유망한 대통령 후보로 만들어 주었다.

대통령 각하, 국회 의장님, 그리고 저명하신 국회의원 여러분 :

나는 이 연단에 깊은 겸허함과 자긍심으로 서있습니다. 겸허함은 나보다 앞서 이곳에 섰던 우리 역사를 세우신 저 위대한 분들이 지나가신 자리이기 때문이며, 자부심은 입법토의의 산실인 이곳은 지금까지 고안된 것 중 가장 순수한 형태로 인간의 자유를 대표하기 때문입니다.

일단 우리에게 전쟁이 강요되면 그것을 속히 끝내기 위해서 가능한 한 모든 수단을 사용하는 것 외에 다른 선택은 없습니다. 전쟁의 진정한 목적은 승리입니다. 오래 끄는 우유부단이 아닙니다. 전쟁에서 승리를 대신할 것은 없습니다.

한국전쟁의 비극은 군사행동이 한국의 영토 내에 국한되어 있다는 사실 때문에 훨씬 더 커지고 있습니다. 그 사실이 우리가 구해주려는 그 나라로 하여금 전폭적인 해군 및 공중폭격의 파괴적인 충격을 당하도록 운명지우고 있습니다. 반면에 적의 주요 시설들은 공격과 파괴로부터 완전하게 보호받고 있습니다. 세계의 모든 국가들 중에서 지금까지 유독 한국만이 공산주의에 대항하기 위하여 모든 것을 보험하고 있습니다. 한국인들의 용기와 불굴의 정신의 위대함은 말로 표현할 수 없습니다. 그들은 노예로 사느니보다 죽음을 무릅쓰기로 선택하였습니다. 그들이 나에게 마지막으로 한 말은 "태평양을 포기하지 마라"는 것이었습니다.

나는 52년간의 군인생활을 마감하려고 합니다. 내가 금세기가 시작되기도 전에 군에 입대했을 때, 그것은 내 모든 소년시절의 희망과 꿈을 달성하는 것이었습니다. 내가 웨스트 포인트 연병장에서 선서를 한 후 세계는 여러 번 바뀌었고 그 희망과 꿈은 사라진지 오래입니다만 아직도 나는 아주 자랑스럽게 표현하던 '노병은 죽지 않고 사라질 뿐이다' 라던 그 당시 가장 인

action is confined to its territorial limits. It condemns that nation, which it is our purpose to save, to suffer the devastating impact of full naval and air bombardment while the enemy's sanctuaries are fully protected from such attack and devastation. Of the nations of the world, Korea alone, up to now, is the sole one which has risked its all against communism. The magnificence of the courage and fortitude of the Korean people defies description. They have chosen to risk death rather than slavery. Their last words to me were: "Don't scuttle the Pacific."

    I am closing my fifty-two years of military service. When I joined the army, even before the turn of the century, it was the fulfillment of all of my boyish hopes and dreams. The world has turned over many times since I took the oath on the plain at West Point, and the hopes and dreams have long since vanished, but I still remember the refrain of one of the most popular barracks ballad of that day which proclaimed most proudly that *old soldiers never die; they just fade away*. And like the old soldier of that ballad, I now close my military career and just fade away, an old soldier who tried to do his duty as God gave him the light to see that duty. Good-bye.

(Source: Adapted from "Douglas MacArthur defends his conduct of the war in Korea."
In A Treasury of the World's Greatest Speeches (1954))

(1) The tone of MacArthur in this passage can be best described as

    (a) dramatic, powerful, didactic   (d) condemning, critical, bitter
    (b) proud, sarcastic, insincere   (e) arrogant, sarcastic, didactic
    (c) flattering, cynical, didactic

(2) MacArthur looks back at his military career with an attitude of

    (a) respect, regret, resolution   (d) disapproving, indulgence, glory
    (b) dignity, honor, integrity   (e) amusement, nostalgia, optimism
    (c) bitterness, indifference, glory

기이었던 한 군가의 후렴을 기억하고 있습니다. 나는 군가의 그 노병, 하느님이 그 의무를 깨닫도록 밝혀 주신대로 그 의무를 다 하려고 노력했던, 그 노병은 이제 군인생활을 끝내고 사라지려고 합니다. 안녕히 계십시오.

Note

- **relieve = take a duty from** : 해임시키다
  - He was relieved of his post as a top manager.(최고 경영자 자리에서 해임당했다.)
- **command = control** : 통수권, 지휘권, 언어의 자유로운 구사능력 • A sound command of English is prerequisite to this position.(이 자리에는 영어의 확실한 구사력이 필수 조건이다.)
- **triumphant = victorious, successful** : 의기양양한, 개선하는
- **a triumphant general** : 개선 장군   **a triumphant homecoming** : 금의 환향
- **not merely (only) A but (also) B = B as well as A** : A뿐아니라 B도 (B를 강조함)= A and B as well
- **strategy = the art of planning a war, a skillful planning** : 전략
- **General MacArther was a master of military strategy.** : 군사 전략의 대가
- **immense = very large** : 막대한, 광대한
  - An immense improvement has been made in brain operation. (뇌 수술에 엄청난 진보가 이루어졌다.)
- **posture = the general way of holding one's body** : 자세
  - Upright posture is natural only to man. (직립자세는 인간에게만 자연스럽다.)
- **provocative = causing argument, anger** : 도발적인, 자극적인
- **prologue = an introduction to a play** : 서막, 시작   **opp. epilogue** : 끝말
- **speaker** : 국회 의장   **floor leader** : 원내 총무
- **distinguished = celebrated, marked** : 저명한, 고귀한   **rostrum** : 연단, 강단
- **humility = being humble** : 겸손   **in the wake of** : …뒤를 따라
- **wake** : 배가 지나간 흰 거품의 길
  - Many diseases will spread in the wake of the war.(전쟁이 지난 후 많은 질병이 퍼질 것이다.)
- **alternative = an action in place of something else** . 내안, 차선 • The alternative to being taken prisoner was to die fighting. (싸우다 죽는 것만이 포로로 끌려가는 것에 대한 다른 선택이었다.)
- **substitute A for B = replace B with A** : B 대신 A를 쓰다
  - I substituted gas for oil in heating. (난방에 기름대신 가스로 대체했다.)
- **heighten** : 높아지다, 커지다   • As she waited, her excitement heightened.
- **condemn = give judgement on, sentence** : 형량을 선고하다
- **sanctuary** : 성소, 가장 중요한 곳
- **fortitude = firm and lasting courage in bearing trouble, pain** : 불굴의 정신
- **defy = resist, challenge openly** : 저항, 공개적으로 도전하다
  - The splendor of the landscape defies description.(그 대지의 황홀함은 언어로 표현할 수 없다.)
- **risk = take the chance of** : …을 운에 걸다, 모험을 무릅쓰고 하다
  - We must risk getting caught in the traffic congestion.(교통 체증에 걸릴 것을 각오해야 한다.)
- **scuttle = cut a ship's sides or bottom to sink it = abandon**, : 적에게 잡힐까봐 배에 구멍을 뚫어 침몰시키다, 버리다, 포기하다
- **vanish = disappear** : 사라지다   • Many types of animals have vanished from the earth.
- **fade = lose strength, color, freshness** : 시들다, 사라지다
- **nostalgia = fondness for something in the past** : 향수, 지난일에 대한 그리움
- **regret = be sorry about** : 유감으로 생각하다   • We regret to inform you that you owe the bank $1,000. (통고하기에 유감이지만 1,000달러를 은행에 납부하셔야 합니다.)

2-11 RHETORICAL TECHNIQUES

The final section of Chapter 2, "Rhetorical techniques" is designed to help the readers recognize a variety of paragraph patterns, word choices, and rhetorical significance. The skill of recognizing these rhetorical patterns is essential for the readers to improve not only speed reading, but also reading comprehension.

To be specific, "paragraph patterns" refer to the patterns of organization. In other words, where are the main idea and the topic sentence placed in a paragraph? And how did the writer choose to develop his paragraph? For these, five common paragraph patterns are included in this section so that the readers can intensively and extensively explore them. The common patterns are (1) Analysis; (2) Cause and Effect; (3) Comparison and Contrast; (4) Definition; and (5) Description. The readers, however, are advised to realize that there is often overlapping, and several patterns may be mixed within a single paragraph.

"Word choice" refers to the appropriate use or choice of right word in its context. If we know each word exactly, we are less likely to make errors called "diction error." Diction is the clarity with which someone speaks, writes, or sings. The diction error is often made when we are confused with words or idioms that look or sound similar. A list of commonly misused or confused words is provided for review. Diction can be divided into "formal, informal, and popular."

Finally, "rhetorical significance" refers to the use or arrangement of particular words, phrases, or sentences to gain a desired effect of the speaker or writer. In other words, what type of figure of speech did he use to enhance his desired effect? For example, did he use simile or metaphor? There is a variety of rhetorical devices employed in a particular situation for a particular purpose. In this sub-section of "rhetorical significance," we will deal with such devices as (1) figurative language (i.e. simile, metaphor, analogy), and (2) structural arrangement (i.e. antithesis, repetition, parallelism, inversion, and persuasion).

2-11 수사학상의 기법

　　제 2장 마지막 절인 '수사학상의 기법'은 독자로 하여금 다양한 문단 유형, 어휘 선택, 수사학상의 기법을 인식하도록 도와주려고 계획했다. 수사학상의 기법을 인식하는 기능은 빠른 독서뿐만아니라 독해력을 개선하는 데 필수적이다.

　구체적으로 말하면 문단유형은 구성의 유형을 가리킨다. 환언하면 요지와 주제문이 문단 안 어디에 위치하고 있느냐는 문제다. 그리고 글쓴이는 그의 문단을 어떻게 전개하기로 선택했느냐이다. 이 문제를 위해서 독자들이 심도있고 폭넓게 탐구할 수 있도록 5가지 문단 유형을 포함시켰다. 일반적인 유형들은 (1) 분석 (2) 인과관계 (3) 비교와 대조 (4) 정의 내리기 (5) 기술(記述)이다. 그러나 자주 중복이 있고 몇개의 유형들이 한 문단에 혼합되어 있음을 알려두는 바다.

　'어휘선택'은 문맥 속에서 적절한 단어를 선택 사용하는 것을 가리킨다. 만일 우리가 각 단어를 정확하게 알고 있으면 '어법의 오류'라는 오류를 일으킬 가능성이 적어진다. 어법이란 말하고 글을 쓰고 혹은 노래하는 데 있어서의 명확성이다. '어법의 오류'는 유사해보이는 단어나 숙어를 혼동할 때 일어난다. 흔히 오용되는 단어나 혼동되는 단어 목록을 연습용으로 제공한다. 어법은 형식적, 비형식적, 대중적인 것들로 나뉘어진다.

　마지막으로 '수사의 중요성'은 말하는 사람이나 글을 쓰는 사람이 소망하는 효과를 얻기 위하여 특정의 단어, 구 혹은 문장을 사용하거나 배치하는 것을 가리킨다. 바꾸어 말하면 바라는 효과를 높이기 위하여 어떠한 형태의 비유를 사용했는가다. 예를 들어 그가 직유를 썼느냐 은유를 썼느냐. 어느 특정의 목적을 위해서 어느 특정한 상황에서 동원하는 수사상의 장치는 다양히다. 다음의 '수사의 중요성'이라는 하부 절에서 (1) 비유직 언어 (예: 직유, 은유, 유추)와 (2) 구조상 배치 (대구법, 반복법, 병렬법, 도치법, 설득법) 같은 장치를 다루게 한다.

Note

- rhetoric = the art of speaking or writing so as to persuade people effectively : 효과적으로 설득시키기 위하여 사용하는 수사법
- explore = examine thoroughly in order to learn about : 탐구, 탐색하다 • Medical men are exploring every new possibility of AIDS treatment.(의료인들이 에이즈 치료법의 모든 가능성을 탐구하고 있다.)
- overlap = partly cover, involve duplication : 일부 겹치다, 중복되다 • History and politics overlap and should be studied together. (역사와 정치는 일부 중복됨으로 함께 연구해야 한다.)
- enhance = increase good things : 드높이다 • Reflection enhances the quality of life.

2.11.1. Paragraph Patterns

A paragraph is a group of closely related sentences dealing with a single topic, part of a larger subject perhaps, but still a self-contained topic by itself. Although a paragraph includes several ideas about topic, one idea is more important than the others. This is the main idea, and it is usually stated in the topic sentence. All the other sentences are related to the topic sentence as supporting details or explanations. The topic sentence is often, but not always, the first sentence of the paragraph. Where the topic sentence is placed depends on the type of pattern the writer chooses to develop his idea.

Five common paragraph patterns are provided for the readers to recognize. Recognizing each type of patterns (Analysis, Cause and Effect, Comparison and Contrast, Definition, Description) will help the readers follow the writer's presentation more accurately and quickly.

2.11.1.1 Analysis

In this type of paragraph pattern, a topic is analyzed. The topic is broken down into causes, effects, reasons, methods, purposes, or other categories that support the topic sentence. This topic sentence is often presented in the beginning of the paragraph, which is called "deductive" organization. If the main idea is presented at the end of the paragraph, then it is called "inductive" organization. We will see the following paragraphs paying a close attention to the patterns.

<u>Deductive organization:</u>
(a) Indians cultivated and developed many plants that are important in the world today. (b) Some of them are white potatoes, corn, beans, tobacco, and cotton. (c) Plants were also used for dyes, medicine, soap, clothes, and basket.

The topic sentence placed in the beginning of the paragraph is (a). And the sentences (b) and (c) support the topic sentence.

2.11.1. 문단 유형

　　문단이란 아마 더 큰 주제의 일부지만, 그 자체로 완전한 주제를 가지며 단일 주제를 취급하도록 밀접하게 관련된 문장들의 집합이다. 비록 문단은 주제에 관한 몇가지 생각들을 내포하고 있지만, 그 중 한가지 생각이 다른 것들보다 더 중요하다. 이것이 요지이며 일상적으로 주제문에 진술된다. 다른 모든 문장들은 보충하는 세부 사항으로, 설명용으로 주제문에 관련된다. 주제문은 언제나 그런 건 아니지만 문단의 첫째 문장이다. 주제문이 어디에 자리잡느냐는 글쓴 사람이 자기 생각을 전개시키기 위하여 선택하는 문형의 형태에 달려 있다.

　　다섯가지 흔히 쓰는 문단 유형을 독자들이 알아보도록 제공한다. 각 유형(**분석, 인과, 비교, 대조, 정의, 기술**)을 알면 작가의 설명을 정확하고 바르게 이해하는데 도움이 된다.

2.11.1.1. 분석

　　이 문단 유형에서 주제가 분석된다. 주제는 주제문을 보충하는 원인, 이유, 방법, 목적, 혹은 다른 부류로 세분화된다. 주제문이 자주 문단의 시작 부분에 소개되는데 이를 '연역적 구성' 이라 부른다. 만일 요지가 문단 끝에 오면 '귀납적 구성' 이라 부른다. 문형에 유의하면서 다음 문단을 살펴보자.

연역적인 구성

　　(a) 인도인들이 오늘날 중요한 식물을 경작하고 개발했다. (b) 그 중 몇가지는 감자, 옥수수, 콩, 담배, 목화다. (c) 식물들은 역시 염료, 약, 비누, 의복, 바구니로 쓰였다.
　　문단 시작하는 곳에 위치한 주제문은 (a)다. 문장 (b), (c)는 주제문을 보충한다.

귀납적인 구성

　　(a) 이태리어에서 우리는 'balcony, opera, umbrella' 같은 다양한 단어들을 얻는다. (b) 스페인어는 'cigar, ranch, mosquito'를 공급해 주었다. (c) 네덜란드어는 'golf, brandy, measles'를 주었다. (d) 아라비아어에서 'alcohol, zero, chemistry'를 빌렸다. (e) 페르샤어는 'chess, lemon, paradise'를 빌려주었다. (f) 일본어는 'kimono, sushi, origami'를 주었다. (g) 우리는 한국말에서 'taekwondo, kimchee, boolgogee'를 얻는다. (h) 영어는 여러 출처에서 빌린 언어라는 사실은 명백하다.
　　주제문은 문단 끝에 위치한 (h)이다. 다른 (a), (b), (c), (d), (e), (f), (g)는 (h)를 보충한다.

Inductive organization:

(a) From Italian, we get a variety of words such as balcony, opera, umbrella. (b) Spanish has provided us with cigar, ranch, mosquito. (c) Dutch has given us golf, brandy, measles. (d) From Arabic we have borrowed alcohol, zero, chemistry. (e) Persian has loaned us chess, lemon, paradise. (f) Japanese has given us kimono, sushi, origami. (g) We get taekwondo, kimchee, boolgogee from Korean. (h) It is clear that English is a language that has borrowed from many sources.

The topic sentence placed at the end of the paragraph is (h). The other sentences (a), (b), (c), (d), (e), (f), (g) support (h).

2.11.1.2. Cause and Effect

The cause-and-effect paragraph often begins with a clear, detailed examination of the effect that is the subject matter of the paragraph, and then each of the causes is discussed, usually in order of importance. However, the cause-and-effect is very complicated because both causes and effects are often multiple. And there are several causes and effects: primary and secondary.

(a) John was not doing well at school. (b) He was failing English, mathematics, and science. (c) He was often involved in fights with some of his classmates. (d) He received several negative letters from his teachers that he was not prepared for class at all, and his behavior should improve. (e) At the end of the spring semester, he received several letters from several colleges and universities that his admission was not accepted.

The causes are: (1) primary cause is (a).
                (2) secondary causes are (b), (c), (d).
The effect is (e).

> **Note**
> - **self-contained** : 자체로 완전한, (사람) 감정을 들어내지 않는, 남의 도움을 안 받는
> - **category = division, class** : 범주, 부류
>   - Translation also belongs to the category of literature.(번역도 문학 범주에 속한다.)
> - **deductive** : 연역적   □ **inductive** : 귀납적
> - **dye = chemical or vegetable substance to color things** : 염료
> - **ranch = very large farm esp. where sheep, cattle, or horses are produced** : 농원
> - **public and government loan** : 국 공채
>   - I asked them for the loan of 1,000 dollars.(1천 달러의 대부를 요구했다.)

2.11.1.2. 인과 관계

인과 관계의 문단은 문단의 주제인 결과에 대한 명백하고 자세한 조사로부터 시작하여 대개 중요한 순서로 각각의 원인들이 토의된다. 그러나 인과관계는 원인이나 결과가 여러가지이기 때문에 매우 복잡하다. 그래서 몇가지 원인과 결과가 있는데 1차적인 것과 2차적인 것들이 있다.

(a) 존은 학교에서 공부를 못했다. (b) 그는 영어, 수학, 과학에서 낙제했다. (c) 그는 자주 급우들과의 싸움에 관련되었다. (d) 그는 선생님들로부터 전혀 학과 예습을 않고 품행을 고쳐야 한다는 부정적인 편지를 몇 번 받았다. (e) 봄학기 말에 몇 대학들로부터 그의 입학이 허락되지 않았다는 편지를 받았다.

원인들은 (1) 1차적 원인은 (a)
　　　　(2) 2차적 원인들은 (b), (c), (d)
결과는 (c)

> **Note**
> - **in order of size/merit/importance** : 크기, 성적, 중요성의 차례로
> - **in alphabetical (chronological) order** : 알파벳 (연대)순으로
> - **complicated = made up of many parts = difficult to understand** : 복잡한
> - **secondary infection** : 2차 감염
> - **negative = saying or meaning 'no'** : 부정적 음성, (수)음수, 소극적
>   - A negative attitude toward the world goes nowhere.(부정적인 태도는 아무 일에도 성공 못한다.)
> - **semester = either of the two periods** : 2학기제의 학기   □ **term** : 3학기제의 학기
>   - I'm taking Spanish this semester.(이번 학기에는 스페인어를 선택해야겠다.)

2.11.1.3. Comparison and Contrast

This pattern is to show how it is similar to or different from between A and B. This type of paragraph usually states the main idea which shows similarities and differences between A and B, in the first sentence. Then the idea is developed in subsequent orders, often with examples.

(a) There are interesting similarities and differences between Bach and Handel. (b) They were both great musicians, were born in the same year, 1685, (c) in the same country, Germany, and (d) were blind in old age. (e) Yet, their lives were different, and their music was different.

(f) Bach labored in a quiet corner of Germany for his beloved music and his many children. (g) Handel never married and lived a life as full of adventure as a story-book: contests, duel, fame and fortune made, lost, and regained. (h) Bach was the last and greatest of the masters of the old polyphonic music which grew from the music of the church choir. (i) Handel was a composer of operas, and all his music was more in the new homophonic style, founded on the solo of the opera.

The main idea is (a), and the sentences which show similarities are (b), (c), (d). The sentences, (e), (f), (g), (h), (i) are the ones that illustrate the differences between Bach and Handel.

"Comparison" is to identify both similarities and differences between A and B, while "Contrast" is to show differences between them.

2.11.1.4. Definition

The purpose of "definition" is to define, explain, or clarify the meaning of a particular topic or term. Depending on the nature of definition, it may include

2.11.1.3. 비교와 대조

이 유형은 A와 B 사이가 어떻게 비슷하고 어떻게 다른가를 보여주는 것이다. 이 유형의 문단은 첫째 문장에 A와 B의 유사점과 상이점을 보여주는 요지를 진술한다. 그런 다음 그 뒤의 순서에서 예를 들어가며 생각을 전개한다.

(a) 바하와 헨델 사이에는 흥미있는 비슷한 점과 다른 점들이 있다. (b) 둘 다 위대한 음악가, 같은 해 1685년생이고 (c) 같은 나라 독일 태생이고 (d) 둘다 노년에 눈이 안보였고 (e) 그러나 그들의 생애와 음악은 달랐다. (f) 바하는 독일의 조용한 시골 외딴 곳에서 사랑하는 음악과 많은 자녀들을 위해 열심히 일했다. (g) 헨델은 결혼을 하지 않고 소설처럼 모험이 충만한 삶을 살았다. 시합, 결투, 명성과 돈을 벌었다 잃고 또 다시 복구했다. (h) 바하는 교회 성가로부터 발달한 다성음악의 가장 위대한 마지막 대가였다. (i) 헨델은 오페라 작곡가였고 모든 음악은 오페라 독창에 기반을 둔 새로운 단성음악이 더 많았다.

요지는 (a)이고 유사점을 말하는 문장들은 (b), (c), (d)이다. (e), (f), (g), (h), (i)는 바하와 헨델의 차이점을 예시하는 문장들이다.

> **Note**
> - 'comparison'은 A와 B 사이의 유사점과 차이점을 둘다 확인 (같은가, 다른가)하는 것이고 'contrast'은 둘 사이의 차이점을 밝히는 것이다.
> - duel = fight agreed between two persons usu. with swords and pistols : 합의 결투
> - contest = competition : 시합, 경연
> - a close contest : 호각의 경쟁
> - English oratorial contest : 영어 웅변 대회
> - beauty contest : 미인 선발대회
> - regain = get possession of again = win something back : 회복, 복구하다
> - choir = a group of people who sing together esp. during religious service : 성가대
> - poly = many, much-polygamy : 일부다처제
> - polysyllable : 다음절
> - polytheism : 다신교
> - homo = same-homosexual : 동성연애자
> - homogeneous : 동질적
> - homonym : 동음이의어, 동명이인
> - master of arts : 석사

2.11.1.4. 정의 내리기

'정의내리기' 의 목적은 특정의 주제나 용어의 의미를 한정, 설명, 확실히 하는 일이다. 성질에 따라 정의 속에는 분석, 비교, 대조, 혹은 주제나 용어에 초점을 맞춘 기술이 포함된다. 이러한 정의 유형은 주제나 용어를 어떤 범주안에 한정시켜 집어넣는 일부터 시작한다. 그리고나서 그 범주의 다른 구성요소(주제, 용어)에 대하여 분석, 기술, 비교, 대조로 사용될 수 있는 보충사항을 열거한다.

analysis, comparison and contrast, or description focused on the topic or term. This pattern of "definition" often begins by placing the topic or term being defined into a certain category, then it lists the details which can be used as analysis, description, or comparison and contrast to other members of that category.

The following example shows several features related to the pattern of definition.

Energy has many forms. The more familiar forms of energy are light, heat, sound, electricity, and nuclear energy. Energy is defined as ability to do work. By definition, work is done when a force is used to move something. When you lift something, you are doing work because you moved something. Merely holding the object, no matter how heavy it is, is not doing work because nothing is moved.

Topic : Energy
Category : Forms of energy are (1) light, (2) heat, (3) sound, (4) electricity, (5) nuclear energy.
Definition of energy : The ability to do work
Description : Work is done when a force is used to move something.
Comparison : When you lift something, you are doing work because you moved something. Merely holding the object is not doing work because nothing is moved.

2.11.1.5. Description

The pattern of "description" is one in which something is described often based on "sensory perception." The sensory perception refers to describing something based on our five senses: sight, hearing, smell, taste, and touching. In other words, the "description" may include a more specific description of a person or place, of a process or a step-by-step direction of how something is done.

The following paragraph describes a "sight of sunrise" constructed based on a visual description.

We were enjoying a gorgeous sunrise at the summit of Mt. Diamond. The East Sea was about to reveal herself out of darkness.

다음 예가 정의 내리기 유형과 관련된 몇가지 특색을 보여준다.

에너지에는 여러 형태가 있다. 좀더 친숙한 에너지의 형태들은 빛, 열, 소리, 전기, 그리고 원자 에너지가 있다. 에너지는 일을 할 수 있는 능력으로 정의될 수 있다. 정의에 의하면 일이란 어떤 힘이 뭔가를 움직일 때 한 것이다. 당신이 어떤 물건을 들어 올릴 때 무엇인가를 움직였기 때문에 일을 하는 것이다. 어떤 물체를, 그것이 아무리 무거워도, 단지 붙잡고만 있는 것은 움직여지는 것이 없기 때문에 일을 하는 것이 아니다.

주제 : 에너지
범주 : 에너지의 형태들은 (1) 빛, (2) 열, (3) 소리, (4) 전기, (5) 원자력
기술 : 일은 어떤 힘이 뭔가를 움직일 때 한 것이다.
비교 : 뭔가를 들어올릴 때 그것을 움직였기 때문에 일을 하는 것이다. 단지 붙잡고만 있는 것은 움직여지는 것이 없기 때문에 일을 하는 게 아니다.

> **Note**
> ☐ lift = raise to a higher level or position : 들어올리다
>   • I'm too rundown to lift a finger.(하도 지쳐서 손가락 하나 들 힘도 없다.)
> ☐ clarify = make clearer, more easily understood : 명확하게 하다, 정화하다
>   • Your detailed explanation has clarified the ambiguity.(자세한 설명을 들으니 애매했던 게 밝혀졌다.)
> ☐ feature = characteristic or striking part : 특색, 특징
>   • a geopolitical feature of Korean Peninsula (한반도의 지정학적 특색)

2.11.1.5. 기술하기

'기술유형'은 자주 '감각적 지각'을 기초로 어떤 사물을 기술하는 유형이다. 감각적 지각이란 5감(시각, 청각, 후각, 미각, 촉각)을 토대로 기술하는 것을 가리킨다. 다시 말하면 '기술'은 어떤 인물, 장소, 어떤 과정 혹은 어떤 일을 하는 단계적 지시 등을 내포할 수 있다. 다음 문단은 시각적 묘사를 토대로 구성한 '일출 광경'을 기술하고 있다.

우리는 금강산 정상에서 황홀한 일출을 즐기고 있었다. 동해가 막 암흑 속에서 모습을 드러내려 하고 있었다. 사방이 고산 준령이었고 봉우리들은 떠오르는 태양의 눈부신 빛을 막 띄어가고 있었다. 낮은 곳에는 아직 그렇게 빨리 햇빛이 닿지 않았다. 지켜보는 사이 온 하늘과 바다와 산비탈들이 점점 다채로운 색으로 물들어가고 있었다.

또하나의 예는 단계적 지시를 토대로 하는 독서 방법을 기술한다.

당신은 좀더 이해를 잘하며 독서하기를 바라는가? 첫째, 제목을 주의깊게 연구하라. 그러면 그 이야기나 주제가 무엇에 관한 것인가에 대하여 단서를 얻을 수 있다. 혹시 있으면 삽화를 조사하라. 그 아래 자막을 주의깊게 읽어라. 그러면 더 많은 단서를 얻는다. 그 다음 작은 제목을 찾아라. 이것 또한 다루어진 주안점을 가르쳐 줄 것이다. 읽는 것이 책이라면 장의 제목을 주의깊게 조사하라. 이제부터 읽을 준비를 하여라.

On every side were lofty mountains, the peaks just taking on a brilliant coloring from the emerging sun. Daylight did not so soon reach the lower places. As we watched, the whole sky and the sea, and the slopes of the mountains were gradually touched with a variety of colors.

Another example describes the method of reading based on a "step-by-step" direction.

Do you want to read with more understanding? First, study the title carefully. It will give you some clue as to what the story or article is about. Study the illustrations if there are any. Read the captions under them carefully. They will give you even more clues. Then look for small headlines. This will tell you what major points are covered. If your reading material is a book, study the chapter titles carefully. Now, be ready to begin reading.

EXERCISE :

Read each of the following paragraphs, and identify whether the main pattern of organization is structured based on (1) Analysis, (2) Cause and Effect, (3) Comparison and Contrast, (4) Definition, or (5) Description.

1. What is a magnetic field? A magnet can attract a magnetic substance at some distance from it. It can make a compass needle turn so that the North-pole of the needle faces the South- pole of the magnet. Thus you can see that the magnet exerts a magnetic force in the space around it. This space around the magnet is called its magnetic field.

What is the main pattern of organization?_____

2. English is clearly an international language. It is used by many educated people in virtually every country in the world. It is the language of diplomacy, the predominant language in which mail is written, the principle language of aviation and of mass media, the first language of nearly 350 million people, and the second or the foreign language of perhaps five times more.

The main pattern of organization is _____.

> **Note**
> - gorgeous = splendid, magnificent, terrific : 훌륭한, 멋있는
>   - gorgeous sunset : 황홀한 일몰
>   - The whole mountain was gorgeous with azaleas in full bloom.(온 산이 만개한 진달래로 눈부시게 황홀했다.)
> - be about to = on the point of · As I was about to say, you interrupted. (내가 막 말하려는데 네가 막았다.)
> - reveal = allow to be seen : 폭로하다, 누설하다
>   - Our experiment revealed that his report was not reliable.(실험 결과 그의 보고서는 믿을 수 없다는 것이 밝혀졌다.)
> - clue = hint = tip = a fact, idea that suggests a possible answer : 단서, 실마리
>   - Have any clues been found that can help the police? (경찰에 도움이 될만한 단서가 발견됐소?)
> - as to = with regard to · As to joining you, I haven't decided yet.(내가 참가하는 문제에 대하여 결심이 아직 서지 않았다.)
> - illustration = picture esp. in a book
>   - It's not a very good book, but I like the illustrations.(책은 썩 좋지는 않지만, 삽화는 마음에 든다.)
> - caption = words written above or below a picture to explain it : 자막
>   - I didn't undersatnd the drawing until I read the caption.(자막을 읽고 나서야 그 그림을 이해했다.)
> - headline = the heading printed in large letters above a story in a newspaper : 제목

다음의 각 문단을 읽고 주요한 구성유형이 (1)분석, (2)인과 (3)비교, 대조 (4)정의내리기 (5)기술 어느 것을 토대로 조직되었는지 확인하라.

1. 자장(磁場)이란 무엇인가? 자석은 약간 떨어진 곳에 있는 자성체를 끌어당긴다. 자석은 바늘의 북극이 자석의 남극을 향하도록 나침반 바늘을 돌게 만들 수 있다. 이런 방법으로 여러분은 자석이 주변 공간 안에서 자력을 발휘한다는 사실을 알 수 있다. 이 자석의 주변 공간을 자장이라 부른다.

> **Note**
> - exert one's influence(strength, pressure) on : 영향력(힘, 압력)을 …에게 행사하다
> - magnetic = having the properties of magnet : 자성을 가진
> - magnet = a piece of iron able to attract iron : 자석
> - exert = put forth. bring into use : 발휘, 행사하다
> - horseshoe(bar) magnet : 말굽(막대) 자석

2. 영어는 분명히 국제어다. 영어는 실제로 세계 모든 나라에서 교육을 받은 많은 사람들이 사용한다. 영어는 외교의 언어고 우편물에 압도적으로 많이 쓰이며 항공과 대중매체의 으뜸가는 언어이고 거의 3억 5천만의 제1의 언어이며 그 다섯배 이상 사람들의 제2의 언어 혹은 외국어다.

> **Note**
> - virtually = practically, being in fact : 사실은, 실제로는 · He is virtually dead.(실제로는 죽었다.)
> - virtual head of the business : 실세 사장 · virtual defeat (사실상의 패배)
> - diplomacy = the art and practice of estsablishing and continuing relations between nations : 외교
>   - This is a matter of diplomacy.(이것은 외교상의 문제다.)
> - predominant = prevailing, having more power or influence than others : 지배적인
>   - The predominant feature of his character is pride.(그분 성격상 두드러진 특징은 자만심이다.)
> - aviation = art and science of flying in the aircraft : 비행, 항공
>   - Aviation is man's long - cherished dream.(난다는 것은 인간의 오랜 꿈이다.)

3. Orchids are among the most prized and expensive flowers that we know. Collectors risk their lives to go into the swamps and jungles of South America and of countries in Southeast Asia. Some people cultivate a variety of orchids in greenhouses to bring high prices from lovers of the beautiful, fragrant flowers.

The main pattern of organization is _____.

4. A squirrel is on the lookout every minute, watching for enemies. When he nibbles a nut, he takes a small bite and then turns his head this way and that while he chews. He notices every rustle of the leaves. This habit of alert observation is necessary for the protection from his enemies.

What is the main pattern of organization?_____

5. The term "astrology" is different from "astronomy." Astrology is the belief that the sun, the moon, and other planets influence individual lives and societies as symbols of human growth and potential. Astronomy as a science of heavenly bodies, deals with phenomena the astronomers study from a distance observational. They observe and record the positions and appearance of celestial objects in order to interpret the nature, constitution, and behavior of the universe. The development of astrology is much longer than that of astronomy. The former was developed around B.C. 2000 by the ancient Chaldeans, Egyptians and Chinese, while the latter was crystalized about A.D. 150 in Ptolemy's Almagest in which the earth was regarded as a sphere fixed at the center of the universe.

The main pattern of organization is _____

3. 난은 우리가 아는 꽃 중에서 가장 소중하고 비싼 꽃의 하나다. 수집가들은 목숨을 걸고 남미나 동남 아시아의 늪이나 밀림 속에 들어간다. 어떤 사람들은 온실에서 다양한 난을 배양하여 아름답고 향기 높은 이 꽃의 애호가로부터 높은 가격을 받아낸다.

Note
- orchid : 난 · cf. flagrant = obviously wicked : 극악한
- fragrant : 향기로운 · The air in the morning garden was fresh and fragrant.

4. 다람쥐는 적이 오나 항상 감시한다. 그가 열매를 갉아 먹을 때 작게 물어뜯어 씹으면서 머리를 이리저리 돌린다. 나뭇잎의 모든 바스락거리는 소리도 주의한다. 이 긴장하는 감시는 적으로부터 보호하기 위해서 필요한 것이다.

Note
- lookout = the act of watching or searching for : 감시, 경계
  · She is on the lookout for a job.(일자리를 찾기 위하여 살피고 있다.)
- nibble = take tiny bits : 작은 조각을 떼다, 갉아 먹다. · Aren't you hungry? You're only nibbling (at) your food. (배고프지 않니? 음식을 조금씩만 깨지락거리고 있니?)
- rustle = make a slight sound : 바스락 거리다, 살랑거리다 · Her long silk skirt rustled when she walked.
- alert = watchful, quick to see and act : 방심하지 않은, 긴장하고 있는 · The residents were on the alert against the possible overflow of the river. (주민들은 일어날지도 모르는 강의 범람에 긴장하고 있었다.)

5. '점성술'이라는 용어는 '천문학'과 다르다. 점성술이란 인간의 성장과 가능성의 상징으로서 태양, 달, 다른 혹성들이 개인 및 사회생활에 영향을 미친다는 믿음이다. 천문학은 천체의 과학으로서 천문학자들이 원거리 관측소에서 연구하는 현상을 다룬다. 그들은 우주의 성질, 구성, 운행을 해석하기 위하여 천체들의 위치와 출현을 관찰 기록한다.
점성술의 발달은 천문학의 발달보다 훨씬 길다. 전자는 기원전 2,000년 무렵에 칼데아인, 이집트인, 중국인들에 의하여 발달되었지만 후자는 기원 150년 지구는 우주의 중심에 고정 되어 있는 구로 여겨져 있는 프톨레마이오스의 알마게스트라는 책에 구체화되어 있다.

Note
- astrology : 점성술 · astronomy (천문학)
- potential = possibility for developing or being developed : 성장 가능성
  · That must be an invention with a big sales potential.(많이 팔릴 가능성이 있는 신제품)
- celestial = of the sky, of heaven : 하늘의, 천상의 opp. terrestrial : 지상의
  · celestial bodies = heavenly bodies (천체) · celestial bliss (지복(至福))
- interpret = make clear meaning of : 해석, 해설, 통역하다
  · We interpreted her long silence as a refusal.(우리는 그녀가 오래 말이 없기에 거절한다고 해석했다.)
- the Chaldeans : 칼데아인, 바빌로니아 지배의 기초를 닦은 고대 셈족, 점성가
- crystalize = form into crystals : 결정체로 구체화하다.
  · His vague ideas crystalized into a definite plan.(막연한 생각이 확실한 안으로 구체화되었다.)
- Ptolemy : 프톨레마이오스 – B.C. 2세기 알렉산드리아의 수학자, 천문학자 : 천동설 주장

2.11.2. Word Choice

As previously mentioned in 2.2., "word choice" refers to the appropriate use of right word within its context. In other words, the choice of a word or phrase should be appropriate so as to fit a specific occasion and purpose for which writing or speech is intended. Most formal passages, for instance, avoid the use of a flowery word for the clarity and accuracy of the meaning of the word.

Likewise, words that are colloquial or illiterate do not find their acceptable places in formal passage. This sub-section looks at the word choice in terms of (1) style of diction: formal, informal, popular; and, (2) misused or confused words.

2.11.2.1. Formal Diction

Formal diction is usually found in writing related to a variety of academic disciplines both in social and natural sciences. Legal, technical, commercial, medical, documentary, and other records for practical purposes are written in a style of formal diction. Thus, the formal diction, as previously mentioned, avoid the use of colloquial, illiterate, and dialectal expressions which do not honor acceptable grammatical rules, and the meaning of which can vary.

The following expressions are not appropriate in formal diction.

Inappropriate	Appropriate	Inappropriate	Appropriate
(1) alright	all right	(7) I've had it!	I had enough!
(2) alot	a lot	(8) different than	different from
(3) get going	go	(9) guess so	think
(4) try and give	try to give	(10) a half an hour	half an hour
(5) use to	used to	(11) for sure	sure
(6) has got to go	has to go	(12) hold on	wait

2.11.2. 어휘 선택

앞의 2.2.에서 말한 바와 같이 '어휘 선택'은 문맥 안에서 옳은 단어를 적절하게 사용하는 것을 이른다. 즉 단어나 어구는 글과 말이 의도하는 구체적인 경우나 목적에 맞게 적절해야 한다. 예를 들어 대부분의 격식을 차린 글은 단어의 의미가 가지는 명확성이나 정확성을 위하여 미사 여구의 사용은 피하여야 한다.

마찬가지로 구어체나 교양없는 어휘는 격식있는 글에서는 들어설 자리가 없다. 다음 하부절에서는 (1) 어법의 형태: 격식을 차린, 격식을 차리지 않은, 대중적인 형태 (2) 잘못 쓰였거나 혼동하여 쓰여진 관점에서 어휘의 선택을 보여준다.

> **Note**
> - flowery = ornamented, fanciful : 화려한, 미사여구를 쓴, 멋부린
> - likewise = in the same, similar way : 비슷하게, 마찬가지로   opp. otherwise
>   • Watch him and do likewise.(그 사람 하는 것을 잘보고 똑같이 하시오.)
> - colloquial = (word, phrases, style) suitable for ordinary, informal or familiar conversation : (단어, 어구, 문체가) 구어체, 대화체의
> - illiterate = with little or no education, unable to read : 배우지 못한, 문자를 모르는
> - computer illiterate : 컴맹   • She is an illiterate.
> - in terms of = with regard to, by means of : …에 관하여, …를 수단으로
>   • Thoughts are expressed in terms of words.(생각은 말로 표현된다.)

2.11.2.1. 격식을 차린 어법

격식 어법은 사회과학이나 자연과학의 다양한 학문적 교육과 관련된 글에서 대개 발견된다. 법적, 공학적, 상업적, 의학적, 기록적인 그리고 다른 실질적인 목적의 기록들은 격식 어법의 문체로 쓰여진다. 이리하여 앞에서 언급한 것처럼 올바른 문법 규칙이나 의미가 달라질 수 있는 구어적인, 교양없는, 방언적 표현은 피한다.
다음 표현들은 격식 어법에서는 적절하지 못하다.

> **Note**
> - diction : 말투, 말씨, 어법   □ dialect : 방언   □ poetic diction : 시적 어법
> - discipline = training esp. of the mind, and character : 정신 단련, 교육, 훈육, 징계
> - school discipline : 학교 교육   □ military discipline : 군기   □ legal defense : 정당 방위
> - legal = in according with, authorized by law : 법적, 합법적인
> - take legal action against : 법적 조치를 취하다   □ disciplinary committe : 징계위원회
> - vary = change   • Prices vary according to supply and demand. (가격은 공급과 수요에 따라 변한다.)

2.11.2.2. Informal Diction

Informal diction is colloquial language: the language of everyday conversation. It includes contractions, slang, dialect, and provincialism (e.g. the word "hoagie" is used in the Philadelphia area; whereas "submarine" that means the same type of sandwich is used in the New York area).

Some expressions from colloquialism, dialect, and slang can be acceptable in informal diction. A list of common expressions of slang and colloquialism is provided for reference.

Slang :
(1) Take the air! - Go away!
(2) Put on air - To assume manners, refinement or prestige which one does not have.
(3) Bawl out - To scold someone angrily.
(4) The blues - Despondency, a sad, depressed mood.
(5) City slicker - A city dweller who can be a shrewd, worldly, or stylishly dressed one.
(6) Dust someone off - To hit someone.
(7) Rip off - To steal or to take advantage of in an unfair way.
(8) Keep an eye on someone - To constantly observe someone.
(9) Freak out - To lose control over one's conscious self due to the influence of hallucinogenic drugs or any sort of psychological shock.
(10) Go broke - To lose all one's money, especially by taking a chance.
(11) Hammertails - A formal or dress suit.
(12) Keep one's nose clean - To stay out of trouble, do only what one should do.
(13) Hit the road - To become a wander, to live an idle life, to leave, especially in a car.
(14) Hit the ceiling - To become violently angry, to go into a rage.
(15) Horn in - To come in without invitation or welcome.
(16) In the soup - In serious trouble, confusion or disorder.
(17) Take the rap - To receive punishment, to be accused and punished.
(18) Jazz up - To brighten up, add more noise, movement or color.
(19) Lay an egg - To fail to win the interest or favor of an audience.
(20) Rub out - To destroy completely, to kill, to eliminate.

Colloquialism :
(1) All wet - Mistaken, wrong.
(2) Ace in the hole - An important fact, plan, person, or thing held in reserve until needed.
(3) Put on the dog - To dress in one's fanciest clothes.
(4) Dry up - To shut up or stop talking.
(5) Dub - One who does something awkwardly.
(6) Dummy - A stupid person.
(7) Flare up - To become angry or enraged.
(8) Fly off the handle - To lose one's temper.
(9) Hang around - To loiter or linger.
(10) Horny - Carnal-minded, lusty, sexually obsessed.

2.11.2.2. 비격식 어법

비격식 어법은 구어체 언어다. 즉 일상 대화의 언어다. 그 속에는 축약, 속어, 방언, 그리고 사투리가 들어있다. 예를 들면 뉴욕에서 'submarine'이라고 사용되는 같은 형태의 샌드위치를 필라델피아에서는 'hoagie'라는 단어를 쓴다.

구어체, 방언, 속어에서 온 어떤 표현들이 비격식 어법에서는 받아들여진다. 흔한 속어와 구어체 표현 목록을 참고삼아 제공한다.

속어:

> **Note**
> - contraction = the shortened form of a word or words : 축약
> - 'Broke' is a slang for 'having no money'. broke = penniless : 무일푼인
> - provincialism : 지방색, 시골 사투리
>   • Provincialism is often taken for cliquism.(지방색이 가끔 붕당주의로 착각된다.)
> - bawl = shout, cry loudly : 고래고래 소리 지르다. • He bawled out a curse.(그는 큰소리로 욕설을 했다.)
> - the blues = condition of being sad, melancholy
>   • How come you are in the blues? (웬일로 기분이 우울하냐?)
> - despondency = loss of hope : 낙담, 의기 소침   □ city slicker : 도시출신, 세련된 사람, 야바위꾼
> - shrewd : 빈틈없는, 물정에 밝은 • He's shrewd in business. (사업에 꼼꼼하다)
> - dust off : 먼지 털다, 때리다   □ rip off : 껍질을 벗기다, 바가지 쓰다   □ keep an eye on : 감시하다
> - freak out : 환각제 사용으로 의식이 몽롱하다   □ go broke : (모험성 투자로) 빈털털이가 되다
> - hammertail : 야회복, 정장   □ keep one's nose clean : 끼어들지 않다   □ horn in : 간섭하다
> - hit the road : 다시 여행을 시작하다   □ hit the ceiling : 화를 머리끝까지 내다   □ jazz up : 흥을 돋우다
> - in the soup : 곤경에 빠져 꼼짝 못하다   □ take the rap : (남을 대신하여)심한 꾸람 듣다
> - lay an egg : (egg = bomb) : 인기를 끌지 못하다   □ rub out : 문질러 없애다, 완전히 없애버리다

colloquialism—구어체 표현

> **Note**
> (1) all wet : 완전히 빗나간   • You are all wet.(네 말은 완전히 틀렸다.)
> (2) ace in the hole : (포커) 엎어 놓은 패 – 비장의 술수
> (3) put on the dog : 고상한 티를 내다, 허세 부리다
> (4) dry up : 화제가 말라 버리다, 대사를 까먹다, 말 못하게 하다
> (5) dub : 솜씨 없는 사람
> (6) dummy : 바보, 멍청이
> (7) flare up : 확타오르다, 격분하다
> (8) fly off the handle : 자제심을 잃고 갑자기 화를 내다
> (9) hang around : 어슬렁거리다
> (10) horny : 관능적인, 호색적인

2.11.2.3. Popular Diction

As a boundary between formal and informal dictions, popular diction is the language of mass-media publications and of commercial persuasion. The primary purpose of using popular diction is to appeal to the average readers or to attract attention from average consumers.

Some common expressions used in this type of diction are provided for reference.

Topic of Newspaper Article :

(1) End for 'mom-and-pop' market. (Popular diction)
   Small family owned businesses are closing down. (Formal diction)

(2) He was once the top dog at the Pentagon. (P.d. = Popular diction)
   He was once the most important person at the Pentagon. (F.d. = Formal diction)

(3) Jay sticks his neck out. (P.d.)
   Jay is taking responsibility for his actions, whether he's credited or blamed. (F.d.)

(4) Park delivers in the clutches. (P.d.)
   In spite of stressful situations, Park succeeds. (F.d.)

(5) Some of the tasks will be hard to swallow. (P.d.)
   Some of the work is too difficult to do. (F.d.)

(6) They're keeping tabs on the President. (P.d.)
   They're watching the President very closely. (F.d.)

Commercial Persuasion/Advertisement :

(1) Now losing a butt or belly won't cost an arm or leg. (P.d.)
   It is inexpensive to lose your weight these days. (F.d.)

(2) Things are looking up. (P.d)
   Things are getting better. (F.d.)

(3) Setting the record straight. (P.d.)
   Clarify the story so there is no confusion or misunderstanding. (F.d.)

(4) Put some spice in your life. (P.d.)
   Add some excitement to your life. (F.d.)

(5) Help your child make the grade. (P.d.)
   Help your child succeed at school. (F.d.)

(6) Look what's in store for August. (P.d.)
   Look at what's happening in August. (F.d.)

2.11.2.3. 대중 어법

격식 어법과 비격식 어법의 경계선으로 대중 어법은 대중 매체 출판물과 상업상 설득의 언어다. 대중 어법 사용의 1차적인 목적은 일반 독자들에게 호소하고 일반 고객들의 관심을 끌려는 것이다.

이런 어법을 가진 문체의 흔한 표현을 참고로 제공한다.

> **Note**
> □ boundary = the limiting or dividing line between spaces, countries : 경계선
> • A river forms the boundary (line) between the two countries.(강이 국가간의 경계선을 이룬다.)
> □ persuasion = the act of causing others to do something : 설득, 권유
> • I obtained his consent by persuasion.(설득하여 그의 승락을 얻었다.)
> □ appeal = make a strong request for help, support, money, mercy, etc. : 호소하다
> • The government is appealing to the people to save dollars.
> (정부는 달러를 아껴쓰자고 국민들에게 호소하고 있다.)

신문기사 제목

  (1) mon-and-pop market - 부부만으로 경영하는 소매점
  (2) top dog - 격렬한 경쟁 후의 승리자 (투견에서) – 중요 인물
    opp. under dog - 아래 깔린 개 – 패자
  (3) stick one's neck out - 위험을 각오하다 – 목을 내밀다
  (4) in the clutches - 꽉 쥐어 있는, 위기 속에서
    deliver in the clutches : 위기에서 잘해내다.
  (5) swallow - 삼키다, 차지하다, 해내다
  (6) keep tabs on = keep under observation - 계속 감시하다

상업상의 설득/광고

  (1) butt or belly - 엉덩이와 아랫배(살이 많이 붙는 부위) - butt = buttocks
    don't cost an arm or leg - 손빌을 쓸 것 없다. – 경비가 안든다
  (2) look up - 위를 향하고 있다 : 좋아진다
  (3) set straight - 똑바로, 확실하게 표현하다
  (4) put spice in - 양념을 넣다 – 흥미를 돋구다
  (5) make the grade - 표준에 달한다, 성공하다
  (6) in store for - 대기하고 있는, 닥쳐 오고 있는
    I have a surprise in store for you. 너를 깜짝 놀라게 할 일이 있다.

2.11.2.4. Misused or Confused Words

Diction error is easily made when we are confused with words or expressions that look or sound similar. A list of commonly misused and confused words is provided, but you are not required to memorize them. Read each word carefully so that confusion will not arise in the future.

accept: (v) receive
except: (v) exclude
except: (prep) but, other than

affect: (v) influence
effect: (v) bring about
effect: (n) result

afflict: (v) cause suffering
inflict: (v) impose

allusion: (n) indirect reference
illusion: (n) false perception

detain: (v) confine
retain: (v) keep

hospitality: (n) kindness
hostility: (n) animosity

compare: (v) deal with differences & similarites
contrast: (v) deal with differences

complement: (v) complete
compliment: (v) praise

continual: (adj) frequently repeated
continuous: (adj) never ending

incredible: (adj) unbelievable
incredulous: (adj) unable to believe

principal: (adj) main
principle: (n) rule of conduct

a number of: (n) many *(plural)*
the number of: (n) amount, number *(singular)*

Main verb	Present tense	Past tense	Past participle	Present participle
lie (vi) *rest*	lie	lay	lain	lying
lie (vi) *tell untruth*	lie	lied	lied	lying
lay (vt) *place, put*	lay	laid	laid	laying
rise (vi) *go up*	rise	rose	risen	rising
raise (vt) *lift*	raise	raised	raised	raising
sit (vi) *be seated*	sit	sat	sat	sitting
set (vt) *put*	set	set	set	setting

("vi" refers to Intransitive Verb which does not require an Object. "vt" is the Transitive Verb which needs an Object.)

2.11.2.4. 잘못 쓰여지거나 혼동되는 단어

우리는 모양이나 소리가 비슷한 단어나 표현으로 혼동을 일으킬 때 어법 착오를 저지른다. 흔히 오용되거나 혼동되는 단어표를 제공한다. 그러나 그들을 암기할 것을 요구하지는 않는다. 앞으로 혼란을 일으키지 않도록 각 단어를 주의깊게 읽어라.

Note

- complement : 보완하다, 보어
- afflict : 괴롭히다
- incredible : 믿을 수 없는
- continual : 거듭하여 되풀이되는
- continual rain : 그쳤다 내렸다 계속하여 내리는 비
- allusion : 넌지시 비침, 암시
- detain : 감금, 억류하다
- principal : 주요한
- hospitality : 친절, 인정
- a number of : 수많은

- compliment : 찬사
- inflict : (타격, 상처를) 가하다
- incredulous : 안 믿는, 의심 많은
- continuous : 중단 없이 계속하는
- continuous rain : 쉬지 않고 내리는 비
- illusion : 망상
- retain : 보존하다
- principle : 원리
- hostility : 적개심
- the number of : …의 수

• A number of books are not returned. (많은 수의 책이 회수되지 않았다.)
• The number of books is rather small. (책의 권수가 얼마 안된다.)

2.11.3. 수사의 중요성

'수사의 중요성'은 2.11.에서 보았듯이 바라는 효과를 얻기 위하여, 그래서 기억에 남을 글이나 연설을 창조할 수 있도록 특정의 단어나 어구의 사용과 배열을 가리킨다. 기억에 남을 작품들(예를 들면 케네디 대통령의 1961년도 취임사나 마틴 루터 킹 목사의 1963년도 '나는 꿈이 있네'라는 연설)과 다른 수사상의 방법, 즉 비유적인 언어를 살펴보자.

이번 하부절들은 다음과 같이 나누어 진다.
(1) 비유적 언어 : 직유, 은유, 유추, (2) 구조상의 배열 : 대구(對句), 반복, 도치, 권유

2.11.3. Rhetorical Significance

"Rhetorical significance," as we have seen in 2.11., refers to the use or arrangement of particular words or phrases to gain a desired effect, which can create a memorable prose or speech. Some of the elements that create memorable pieces (e.g. John F. Kennedy's Inaugural Address in 1961, and Dr. Martin Luther King's speech, "I have a dream" in 1963), and other rhetorical devices: figurative languages, will be examined.

This sub-section is divided into (1) figurative language: simile, metaphor, analogy, and, (2) structural arrangement: antithesis, repetition, inversion, persuasion.

2.11.3.1. Figurative Language

Figurative language is used to create a tone that appeals to the readers and allows them to identify with the writer or speaker. Since such language builds an appealing tone with figures of speech for comparison and contrast between the writer and the readers, the figurative language plays an important role in helping the readers follow the writer's/speaker's meaning quickly and easily. The language used for comparison or contrast includes (1) simile, (2) metaphor, and, (3) analogy.

2.11.3.1.1. Simile

Simile is a figure of speech that makes explicit comparisons between two things by using the terms such as 'like, as, as if.' Writers/speakers often use simile to make their ideas more colorful.

Examples : (1) O, my love is <u>like</u> a red, red rose. (Burns)
(2) That man is as sly <u>as</u> a fox.
(3) The comb felt <u>as if</u> it was raking my skin off. (Malcolm X)

Common expressions of simile are provided for references.

(1) as black as coal
(2) as brave as a lion
(3) as cold as ice

(13) like an angry buffalo
(14) like an arrow
(15) like a black widow

> **Note**
> - prose = written language in its usual form (as different from poetry) : 산문
> - element = a substance that makes up all substances : 물질, 원소
>   - Hydrogen and oxygen are elements.(수소와 산소는 원소다.)
> - memorable = worth remembering, deserve to be rememberd : 기억할 가치가 있는, 중대한
>   - This poem is memorable for its influence on 'Independence Movement.'
>   - (이 시는 독립운동에 끼친 영향 때문에 기억될 것이다.)
> - Inaugural Address : (미국)대통령 취임사　　□ inaugural ceremony : 취임식
> - device = something invented or adapted to a special purpose : 장치, 고안품
> - rhetoric device : 수사 기법
> - figurative = used not in the literal sense but in an imaginative way : 비유적인
> - e.g.fiery : (직역의미) – 불같은 / (비유적) – 화를 잘 내는
> - analogy = process of reasoning between parallel cases : 유추
> - a forced analogy : 견강부회(牽强附會) = a far-fetched
> - antithesis : 대구법 – 뜻이 상반되는 어구를 대조시켜 주장을 강조하는 수사법

2.11.3.1 비유적 언어

비유적 언어는 독자가 작가나 연설가의 진술에 공감하는 '어조'를 창조한다. 이 언어들은 작가와 독자 사이에서 비교와 대조법을 이용, 직접 말하는 말하는 듯한 '어조'를 만들기 때문에, 독자가 작가나 연설가가 말하고자 하는 의미를 쉽고 빠르게 이해할 수 있도록 돕는다. 비교와 대조에 사용되는 언어는 (1)직유 (2)은유 (3)유추를 포괄한다.

2.11.3.1.1. 직유법

직유는 'like'나 'as', 'as if' 같은 용어를 써서 두가지 사이를 명백하게 비교하는 비유법이다. 글을 쓸때나 말을 할 때 자기의 생각을 좀더 다채롭게 하기 위하여 자주 직유를 사용한다.

　　보기 : (1) 아, 나의 사랑은 붉고 붉은 장미같구려.
　　　　 (2) 저 남자는 여우처럼 교활하다.
　　　　 (3) 그 빗은 마치 살갗을 갈퀴로 긁어내는 듯한 느낌이었다.

참고 삼아 흔한 직유 표현들을 제공한다.

(4) as fast as lightning
(5) as gentle as a lamb
(6) as irritating as fingernails on a chalkboard
(7) as nervous as a mouse nibbling on a cat's food
(8) as poor as a church mouse
(9) as strong as a bull
(10) as priceless as a 5-carat diamond
(11) as white as snow
(12) as wise as an owl

(16) like a blanket
(17) like a child
(18) like a wild dog
(19) like a new penny
(20) like soldiers on guard
(21) like snowflakes
(22) light like a feather
(23) like a frightened rabbit
(24) eat like a vulture

2.11.3.1.2. Metaphor

A metaphor is a figure of speech that makes implicit comparisons <u>without</u> using terms such as 'like, as, as if.' It is an imaginative way of describing something by referring to something else which has the qualities that the writer/speaker is trying to express.

Examples : (1) She was an **oak tree** standing straight. (She stood up straight.)

(2) She was a **mouse**. (She was shy and timid.)

(3) All the world is a **stage**. (The place we act as individuals under the control of "time, space, and situation.")

(4) Black women are called…" **the mule of the world**," because we have been handed the burden that everyone else refused to carry. ("The woman who are doing all the hard work")

The underlined words and phrases above include implicit comparisons of metaphor.

> **Note**
> ☐ as fast as lightning : 전광석화같은
> ☐ as irritating as fingernails on the chalkboard : 칠판에 긁히는 손톱소리처럼 거슬리는
> ☐ like a black widow : 독거미처럼 무시무시하게
> ☐ like a blanket : 담요로 덮듯이   ☐ a blanket of snow : 온통 덮인 눈
> ☐ like a vulture : 독수리처럼 게걸스럽게

2.11.3.1.2. 은유

은유는 like나 as, as if 같은 용어를 사용하지 않고 암시적인 비교를 하는 비유법이다. 은유는 글쓴이나 말하는이가 표현하려고 하는 특질을 가진 그것이 아닌 딴 것을 언급하는 방법으로 뭔가를 묘사하는 상상력을 발휘하는 방식이다.

보기 : (1) 그녀는 똑바로 서있는 한 그루 참나무였다.(그녀는 우뚝 서 있었다.)
　　　(2) 그녀는 생쥐였다.(그녀는 수줍어하며 겁이 많았다.)
　　　(3) 모든 세상은 하나의 무대다.
　　　　　(시간, 장소, 상황의 통제를 받으며 활동하는 장소)
　　　(4) 흑인 여자들은 "이 세상의 노새"라고 불린다. 왜냐하면 다른 사람들이 운반하기를 거부하는 짐이 우리에게 건네졌기 때문이다.
　　　　　(우리가 힘든 일을 다 한다.)

위의 밑줄친 단어나 어구는 은유가 가지는 암시적인 비유를 내포한다.

> **Note**
> ☐ implicit = implied thought not plainly expressed : 암시적인   opp. explicit : 명백한
> 　• an implicit consent (내락)   • implicit threat (무언의 협박)
> ☐ mule = animal that is the offspring of an ass and mare : 당나귀와 암말의 새끼

2.11.3.1.3. Analogy

An analogy is simply a comparison, though often detailed, between two things that are alike in some way. For examples, "day" is characterized by "light"; whereas "night" is by "darkness." This is **characteristic** analogy. An **antonym** analogy is "senior" to "junior" as "tall" to "short." **Parts** analogies are about the relationship between the "whole" and the "part" : "book" is to "library" as "painting" is to "art gallery." This reasoning comparison is often extended to several sentences or paragraphs in length as a way of clarifying a particular point.

Examples : (1) William Adams Brown compared life to a drinking glass. "Life is a glass given to us to fill; a busy life is filling it with as much as it can hold; a hurried life has had more poured into it than it can contain."

(Life and drinking glass are compared to each other based on characteristic analogy.)

(2) If the aircraft industry had developed as dramatically as the computer industry over the past two decades, a new jumbo jet passenger airplane would cost a few thousand dollars today, and it would encircle the globe in 30 minutes.

(The difference between the development of the aircraft and the computer industries is described based on a strong **contrasting** analogy.)

(3) "It is with narrow-souled people as with narrow-necked bottles; the less they have in it, the more noise they make in pouring it out." (Alexander Pope)

(The relation between narrow-souled people and narrow-necked bottles is compared based on characteristic analogy)

2.11.3.1.3. 유추

유추는 상세하게 표현될 때도 자주 있지만 단순하게 어떤 점에서 비슷한 두가지를 비교하는 것이다. 예를 들면 '낮'은 '빛'으로, '밤'은 '어두움'이 특징이다. 이것을 '특징적 유추'라 한다. '대조어 유추'는 '성인과 미성년', '키 큰과 키 작은' 등이다. '부분 유추'는 전체:부분, 책:도서관, 그림:화랑이다. 이러한 논리적 추리는 어떤 특별한 점을 명백히 밝히려는 한 방법으로 길이가 몇개의 문장, 문단들에게까지 확대된다.

보기 : (1) 윌리엄 아담스 브라운은 인생을 술잔에 비유했다. "인생이란 우리더러 채우라고 주어진 잔이다. 바쁜 삶이란 그 잔에 들어갈 만큼 채우는 것이고 서두르는 삶은 그 잔에 들어갈 수 없을 만큼 쏟아부운 것이다." (인생과 술잔은 특징적 유추를 근거로 비유된 것이다.)

(2) "만일 비행기 산업이 지난 20년간 컴퓨터 산업만큼 극적으로 발달했다면 새로운 점보여객기가 오늘날 수천 달러면 제작되고 30분이면 지구를 한바퀴 돌 것이다." (비행기와 컴퓨터 발달간의 차이가 대조 유추에 근거하여 묘사되어 있다.)

(3) "마음이 좁은 사람과 목이 좁은 병은 같다. 속에 든 것이 적을수록 쏟아낼 때 소리가 많이 난다." (마음 좁은 사람과 목이 좁은 병은 특징적 유추로 비유되고 있다.)

Note
- clarity = clearness : 명쾌함
- contain = have or hold within itself : 안에 포함하다
  - The atlas contains 40 maps including three of Great Britain.
  (그 지도책은 영국지도 석장을 포함하여 40장의 지도가 들어있다.)
- encircle = surround : 에워싸다
  - The police encircled the campus in search of the escaped mastermind of the walkout.
  (경찰이 피신한 파업 주동자 색출을 위하여 대학 구내를 포위했다.)

EXERCISES FOR REVIEW: SIMILE, ANALOGY, CONFUSED WORDS

1. <u>Simile Questions</u>: Choose the best answer provided.

(1) John is as strong as a _____.
    (a) pig   (b) sheep   (c) horse   (d) bull

(2) My dog named Rex is as gentle as a _____.
    (a) mouse   (b) lamb   (c) hamster   (d) rabbit

(3) The airplane soared gracefully like a _____.
    (a) hawk   (b) sparrow   (c) owl   (d) vulture

(4) Mr. Smith who has never been employed is as poor as a _____.
    (a) dog   (b) house cat   (c) wolf   (d) church mouse

(5) Bob is very hard working. People say he is as industrious as an _____.
    (a) owl   (b) ant   (c) anteater   (d) insect

(6) Okhee is a bookworm. She is as wise as a/an _____.
    (a) fox   (b) dragon   (c) owl   (d) mule

(7) My younger brother never listens to me and my parents. He is as stubborn as a/an _____.
    (a) tiger   (b) mule   (c) bull   (d) camel

(8) "Tom, it has been a long time since we last met. It's been over 10 years. Time flies like a/an _____."
    (a) bullet   (b) airplane   (c) arrow   (d) cannon ball

(9) Tall dark evergreens lined the country road like _____.
    (a) a pride of lions   (c) a pack of wild dogs
    (b) a herd of angry buffalo   (d) soldiers on guard

(10) White pear blossoms fell from the trees like _____.
    (a) snowflakes   (c) leaves
    (c) white, soft cotton   (d) white cotton candy

2. <u>Analogy Questions</u> : Choose the best answer provided.

(1) A "frame" is to a "picture" as a "_____" is to a "_____."
    (a) cup : saucer   (b) table : floor   (c) radio : sound   (d) cover : book

직유 · 유추문제 · 혼동되는 단어

1. 직유

(1) 존은 ___처럼 힘이 세다.

(2) 이름이 렉스인 우리 개는 ___처럼 순하다.

(3) 비행기가 ___처럼 우아하게 솟아 올랐다.

(4) 취직이 되어본 적이 없는 스미스씨는 ___처럼 가난하다.

(5) 봅은 열심히 일한다. 사람들은 그가 ___처럼 부지런하다고 한다.

(6) 옥희는 책벌레다. 그녀는 ___처럼 현명하다.

(7) 내 동생은 부모님 말씀도 내 말도 듣지 않는다. 그는 ___처럼 고집이 세다.

(8) "톰, 우리 만난지 오랜만이구나. 10년 넘었지. 세월은 ___처럼 빠르구나."

(9) 키 큰 집은 상록수들이 ___처럼 시골길에 줄지어 서 있다.

(10) 하얀 배꽃들이 ___처럼 나무에서 떨어졌다.

Note
- **hamster** : (유럽, 아시아산) 명주쥐
- **sparrow** : 참새 • cf. swallow : 제비
- **soar = rose far or fast** : 치솟다 • The price of commodities soared by 10%. (물가가 10% 올랐다.)
- **industrious = diligent, hard-working**
  - cf. industrial (산업, 공업의) • industrial alcohol (공업용 알콜)
  - industrial unrest (산업계의 불안) • industrial area (공단)
- **stubborn = obstinate, difficult to deal with** : 완고한, 다루기힘든
- **pride** : (사자) 무리
- **cannon ball** : 대포 알
- **white cotton candy** : 솜사탕

2. 유추문제

(1) 액자 : 그림 =   (2) 검 : 펜싱 =

(3) 사자 : 새끼 =   (4) 천 : 직물 =

(5) 슬픔 : 죽음 =   (6) 개 : 동물 =

(2) "Foil" is to "fence" as "_____" is to "_____."
   (a) pencil : pen   (b) candle : heat   (c) train : travel   (d) sleep : bed

(3) A "lion" is to a "cub" as a "_____" is to a "_____."
   (a) mother : aunt   (b) aunt : child   (c) mother : child   (d) father : grandfather

(4) "Cloth" is to "texture" as "_____" is to "_____."
   (a) wool : silk   (b) book : text   (c) wood : grain   (d) linen : flax

(5) "Sorrow" is to "death" as "_____" is to a "_____."
   (a) laugh : cry   (b) plum : peach   (c) fear : hate   (d) happiness : birth

(6) A "dog" is to an "animal" as a "_____" is to a "_____."
   (a) rose : soil   (b) tree : garden   (c) tool : carpenter   (d) tulip : flower

(7) "Food" is to "body" as "_____" is to "_____."
   (a) cow : grass   (b) less : greater   (c) cells : blood   (d) gasoline : engines

(8) A "lion" is to a "lamb" as "_____" is to "_____."
   (a) food : hunter   (b) puppy : dog   (c) brave : gentle   (d) principal : main

(9) A "horse" is to a "bridle" as a "_____" is to a "_____."
   (a) road : driver   (b) man : conscience   (c) fine : law   (d) lawyer : client

(10) A "brim" is to a "hat" as a "_____" is to a "_____."
   (a) bumper : car   (b) belt: waist   (c) skin : bone   (d) tail : cow

3. **Questions for Confused Words** : Choose the best answer provided.

(1) Countries may _____ large sums of money from the World Bank.
   (a) borrow   (b) lend   (c) let   (d) give

(2) _____ on his back, he studied the clouds.
   (a) Lying   (b) Laying   (c) Laiding   (d) Laining

(3) Thomas Jefferson's home _____ on a hill overlooking the Washington D.C. area.
   (a) sets   (b) locates   (c) sits   (d) situates

(4) Jane enjoys _____ there and making sardonic remarks about her stepfather.
   (a) lying   (b) laying   (c) setting   (d) raising

(5) To assure the safety of our school, the school authority should not _____ any visitors enter the building without prior permission.
   (a) live   (b) make   (c) keep   (d) let

(7) 음식 : 몸 = (8) 사자 : 새끼양 =
(9) 말 : 고삐 = (10) 테 : 모자 =

Note
- saucer : 컵받침
- fence : 펜싱하다
- texture : 직물
- foil : 펜싱연습용 칼
- cub : 사자, 곰, 이리 새끼
- flax : 아마류
- plum : 자두
- grain = small, hard seed of food plants : 곡식 알갱이
- cell = microscopic unit of living matter : 세포
- client = one who gets help or advice from a lawyer or any professional man
  : 고객, 피상담자(고소, 투자, 신변문제, 자녀교육, 성격…)
- bridle • Try to bridle your passions.(감정을 억제하라.)
- brim = edge of a cup, bowl, glass - full to the brim : 가득

3. 혼동되는 단어

(1) 국가들이 세계은행에서 거액을 _____.

(2) 등대고 _____ 채, 구름을 자세히 보았다.

(3) 토마스 제퍼슨의 집은 워싱턴 DC가 내려다 보이는 언덕에 _____ 다.

(4) 제인은 그곳에 _____ 채 자기 계부에 대하여 비꼬는 말을 하기 좋아한다.

(5) 우리 학교 안전을 확실히 하기 위하여 학교 당국은 사전 허락없이 방문객이 교내로 들어오는 것을 _____ 해선 안된다.

(6) 생활비가 지난 몇년사이 20% 이상 _____ 다.

(7) 다이아나비의 사망에 대한 _____ 서적들이 많은 외국어로 번역되었다.

(8) Sioux를 _____ 한 모든 아메리카 인디언들이 유럽 정착민들에게 패배했다.

(9) 어린 시절의 궁핍으로 인한 허약한 시력과 청력으로 _____ 지만 그녀는 출세하여 최고 봉급을 받는 경영인이 되었다.

(10) 히말라야 고지의 평균 고도는 20,000피트고, 에베레스트 산은 정상이 29,000피트 이상 _____ 있다.

(6) The cost of living has _____ over 20% in the past few years.
    (a) risen   (b) raised   (c) rose   (d) raising

(7) _____ of books about the death of Princess Diana have been translated into many foreign languages.
    (a) A number   (b) Much   (c) The number   (d) Many

(8) All of the American Indians _____ the Sioux were defeated by the European settlers.
    (a) include   (b) expect   (c) except   (d) exclude

(9) _____ with poor eyesight and hearing as a result of her indigent childhood, she rose to become the top-paid executive manager.
    (a) Inflicted   (b) Affected   (c) Afflicted   (d) Effected

(10) The average elevation of the Himalayas is 20,000 feet, and Mount Everest _____ to more than 29,000 feet at its apex.
    (a) raise   (b) rises   (c) roses   (d) arises

2.11.3.2. Structural Arrangement

"Structural arrangement" refers to rhetorical devices in which particular words, phrases, or sentences are structuarally arranged in order to give the speaker's/writer's ideas extra impact by creating a strong emotional effect. In this sub-section, a few common features and examples related to (a) antithesis; (b) parallelism; (c) inversion; (d) repetition; and, (e) persuasion, will be briefly examined.

2.11.3.2.1. Antithesis

An antithesis, usually in parallel structure, can contribute to memorable speech or writing by highlighting contrasting ideas in a balanced sentence. It provides a neatly tuned rhythm while giving extra impact to the ideas.

Examples : (1) Man proposes, God disposes.

(2) Love is an ideal thing, marriage is a real thing.

> **Note**
> □ prior = earlier in time, order, importance : …에 앞서
>   • The house was sold prior to the auction.(경매에 앞서 집이 팔렸다.)
> □ afflict = torment, distress : 괴롭히다. 들볶다
>   • She is afflicted with insomnia.(그 여자는 불면증에 시달린다.)
> □ indigent = very poor   □ elevation : 고지대, 고도   □ sardonic = scornful : 냉소적인
> □ apex = top or highest point - the apex of a triangle : 삼각형의 꼭지점
> □ inflict = impose : 고통, 충격을 가하다
>   • He inflicted a severe blow on the opponent.(그는 상대에게 강타를 가했다.)

2.11.3.2. 구조적 배열

'구조적 배열'은 강력한 감정의 효과를 일으킴으로써 말하는 사람이나 글을 쓰는 사람의 생각에 특별한 충격을 주기 위하여 특별한 단어나 어구, 또는 문장을 구조적으로 배열하는 수사상의 기법이다. 이번 하부 절에서는 (a) 대구법 (b) 병렬구조 (c) 도치 (d) 반복 (e) 권유와 관련된 몇 개의 흔히 쓰이는 특색과 보기들을 간략하게 살펴보겠다.

> **Note**
> □ extra = additional, beyond what is usual : 추가의, 임시의
>   • extra pay : (초과 수당)   • extra news : (호외)   • extra innings : (야구) 연장전
>   • Extra work demands extra pay.(초과 작업에는 초과 수당을 주어야 한다.)

2.11.3.2.1. 대구법

대구법은 대개 병렬 구조에서 대조를 이루는 생각들을 균형잡힌 문장에서 강조하여 오래 기억될 글이나 연설을 하는데 이바지할 수 있다. 생각에 특별한 충격을 주면서 단정하게 조화된 리듬을 제공한다.

　　보기 : (1) 계획은 인간이 하지만 성사는 신이 한다(謀事在於人 成事在於天).
　　　　　(2) 사랑은 이상이고 결혼은 현실이다.
　　　　　(3) 타인의 악을 믿는 것은 죄악이지만 그게 실수는 아니다(누구나 그러기 쉽다).
　　　　　(4) 두려움 때문에 협상하지 맙시다. 그리고 협상을 두려워하지도 맙시다.
　　　　　(5) 국가가 당신을 위하여 무엇을 할 수 있느냐고 묻지 말고 당신이 국가를 위하여
　　　　　　　무엇을 할 수 있나 물으시오.(권리보다 책임을 먼저 생각합시다.)
　　　　　　　(두 가지 생각들이 강한 느낌을 주면서 균형 잡힌 문장으로 훌륭하게 대조되어 있다.)

(3) It is a sin to believe evil of others, but it is not a mistake.
(H. L. Mencken)

(4) Let us never negotiate out of fear. But let us never fear to negotiate. (John F. Kennedy)

(5) Ask not what your country can do for you; ask what you can do for your country. (John F. Kennedy)

(The two ideas are well contrasted in a balanced sentence while giving extra impact to the ideas).

2.11.3.2.2. Parallelism

"Parallelism" is an arrangement in which two or more words, phrases, or sentences of equal importance are similarly expressed. This arrangement in parallel construction contributes clarity and smoothness to the speech or writing.

Examples : (1) <u>History became popular</u>, and <u>historians became alarmed</u>.
(Will Durant)

(2) <u>The love of liberty</u> is <u>the love of others</u>;
<u>the love of power</u> is <u>the love of ourselves</u>. (William Hezlitt)

(3) The battle, sir, is not <u>to the strong</u> alone;
it is <u>to the vigilant</u>, <u>the active</u>, <u>the brave</u>. (Patrick Henry)

(4) The math exam tested our knowledge of exponential functions, the quadratic <u>formula</u>, and linear <u>equations</u>.

(5) Let every nation know, whether it wishes us well or ill, that we shall
<u>pay any price</u>,
<u>bear any burden</u>,
<u>meet any hardship</u>,
<u>support any friend</u> or
<u>oppose any foe</u>,
to assure the survival and the success of liberty. (John F. Kennedy)

> **Note**
> □ highlight = emphasize = pick out as important part : 강조하다
>   • The TV news report highlighted the result of the local election.
>   (TV 뉴스 보도는 지방선거 결과를 중점 보도했다.)
> □ tuned = in tune : 조율된, 가락이 맞는 – stay tuned (TV나 라디오에서) 돌리지 말고 시청해 주세요.
>   • Will you tune in to the sports program? (스포츠 프로로 맞춰주시요.)
> □ dispose = place in good order or in suitable situation : 정리, 처리, 제거하다
>   • God disposes all things according to His will.(신은 모든 일을 당신의 뜻대로 처리하신다.)
> □ negotiate = discuss, confer in order to come to an agreement : 협상하다
>   • We've decided to negotiate with employers about our wage claims.
>   (임금 요구사항에 대하여 사측과 협상하기로 결정했다.)

2.11.3.2.2. 병렬 구조

'병렬구조'는 둘 이상의 동등한 중요성을 가진 단어, 어구, 문장을 비슷하게 배열하는 것을 지칭한다. 이 병렬구조의 배열은 글이나 말의 명확성과 부드러움에 이바지한다.

보기 : (1) 역사는 대중적인 것이 되었다. 그러자 역사가들은 겁을 먹었다.
(2) 자유를 사랑함은 남을 사랑하는 것이오, 권력을 사랑함은 자기를 사랑하는 것이다.
(3) 각하, 전투란 강자들만의 것이 아니고, 경계하고, 활동적이며 용감한 자들의 것입니다.
(4) 수학 시험은 우리가 가지고 있는 지수함수, 2차 방정식 그리고 1차 방정식의 지식을 측정했다.
(5) 모든 국가로 하여금 비록 우리에게 호의적이든 악의적이든, 생존과 자유의 승리를 확보하기 위하여 어떤 대가도 치룰 것이며, 어떤 부담도 감당할 것이며, 어떤 고난도 피하지 않고, 어떤 친구도 후원하고, 어떤 적도 대적할 것임을 알게 하시오.

> **Note**
> □ vigilant = watchful continually, on the lookout for dangers : 방심하지 않는
>   • A vigilant police force helps control crime.
>   (경계를 늦추지 않고 있는 경찰부대가 범죄를 억제하는 데 도움이 된다.)
> □ exponential : 지수의   □ function : 기능, (수학) 함수   □ quadratic : 정방형의, 2차 방정식의
> □ equation = statement of equality between two expressions by the sign : 방정식
> □ formula = statement of a rule, fact esp. in signs or numbers : 공식
>   • The chemical formula for water is H_2O.(물의 화학방정식은 H_2O이다.)
> □ linear = of or in lines : 선의, 1차의

2.11.3.2.3. Inversion

"Inversion" is a device of reversing the regular word order of a basic sentence in order to give a special emphasis. It can make for memorable writing by creating emphasis on a particular word or phrase.

Examples : (1) *Regular*: I may be hungry, but I am not desperate yet.
　　　　　　Inversion: Hungry I may be, but I am not desperate yet.

(2) *Regular*: He was ready to sacrifice his money if necessary.
　　Inversion: His money he was ready to sacrifice if necessary.

(3) *Regular*: Two dead birds plummeted out of the tree.
　　Inversion: Out of the tree plummeted two dead birds.

(4) *Regular*: He was not good-looking, not wealthy, but brilliant.
　　Inversion: Good-looking he was not; wealthy he was not; but brilliant he was.

2.11.3.2.4. Repetition

"Repetition" is a popular rhetorical device in which the same or similar sound or set of words is placed in the beginning or at the end of successive clauses or sentences. It unifies a sequence of ideas by stating the main idea more than once, and helps create a strong emotional effect.

Examples :
(1) <u>In a land of great wealth</u>, families must not live in hopeless poverty.
<u>In a land rich in harvest</u>, children just must not go hungry.
<u>In a land of healing miracles</u>, neighbors must not suffer and die unattended.
<u>In a great land of learning and scholars</u>, young people must be taught to read and write.
(Lyndon B. Johnson, Inaugural Address, January 20, 1965)

2.11.3.2.3. 도치

'도치'는 특별한 강조를 위하여 정상적인 기본 문장의 어순을 뒤집는 것이다. 도치는 어느 특정의 단어를 강조하여 오래 남을 글을 쓰는데 도움이 된다.

보기 : (1) 나는 배가 고프지만 심각하지는 않다.
(2) 그는 필요하면 돈을 바칠 각오가 되어 있었다.
(3) 두 마리의 죽은 새가 나무에서 수직으로 떨어졌다.
(4) 그 남자는 미남도 아니고, 부자도 아니었지만 영리했다.

Note
□ reverse = invert = change around proper order or positions : 뒤집다, 전환하다
 • Today he will reverse the usual order of the lesson and start with homework checking.
 (일상적인 수업 순서를 뒤집어 숙제 검사부터 할 것이다.)
□ desperate = extremely serious or dangerous : 절망적인, 극히 심각한
 • The state of the country is desperate.(그 나라의 상황이 절망적이다.)
□ plummet = fall steeply : 급강하다 • Share prices have plummeted.(주가가 곤두박질 했다.)
□ brilliant = very bright, causing admiration : 눈부신, 재기 넘치는

2.11.3.2.4. 반복

'반복'이란 계속되는 문장, 또는 절들의 앞이나 끝에 같거나 비슷한 소리, 단어들을 위치시키는 일반적인 수사장치다. 요지를 여러 번 말하여 연속되는 생각들을 하나로 통일, 강력한 감정적 효과를 낸다.

보기 : (1) 막대한 부의 나라에서 가정들이 절망적인 빈곤 속에 살아서는 안됩니다.
풍요로운 수확의 나라에서 어린이들이 굶주려서는 안됩니다.
기적적인 치료의 나라에서 이웃이 고통하며 보살피는 이 없이 죽어서는 안됩니다.
위대한 학문과 학자들의 나라에서 젊은이들이 읽고 쓰는 교육을 받아야 합니다.

(2) 흑인 문제 없습니다. / 남부 문제 없습니다. / 북부 문제 없습니다.
오직 미국의 문제가 있을 뿐입니다.

(3) 지금은 민주주의의 문제를 실현해야 할 시간입니다.
지금은 어둡고 황량한 골짜기에서 일어서야 할 시간입니다….
지금은 국민을 인종문제의 함정에서 안아 올려야 합니다….

(2) There is <u>no Negro problem</u>.
There is <u>no Southern problem</u>.
There is <u>no Northern problem</u>.
There is <u>only an American problem</u>.
(Lyndon B. Johnson, 1967)

(3) <u>Now is the time</u> to make real the problems of democracy.
<u>Now is the time</u> to rise from the dark and desolate valley….
<u>Now is the time</u> to lift our nation from the quicksand of racial injustice…. (Martin Luther King Jr. - 1963)

(4) <u>We shall fight</u> in France, <u>we shall fight</u> on the seas and oceans,
<u>we shall fight</u> with growing confidence….
<u>we shall defend</u> our islands,….
<u>we shall fight</u> on the beaches….
<u>we shall fight</u> in the fields and the streets.
(Winston Churchill - June 4, 1940)

2.11.3.2.5. Persuasion

"Persuasion" is aimed at influencing others by modifying their beliefs, values, or attitudes through communication. In other words, persuasion can be accomplished if someone's belief, value, or attitude is moved from "neutral" toward "positive." If it is moved from "neutral" toward "negative," then it is "dissuasion."

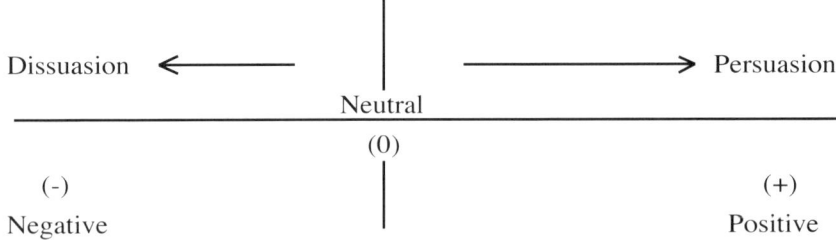

Persuasion can be done in a variety of ways, especially in the area of propaganda for commercial purposes. Several common rhetorical techniques often used as persuasion for commercial and other purposes are provided with examples. Please be advised to know that this type of commercial or political rhetorical skill is often presented on television and radio.

(4) 우리는 프랑스에서 싸워야 합니다, 우리는 바다에서 싸워야 합니다.
우리는 점점 자라나는 자신감을 가지고 싸워야 합니다…. 우리는 우리의 섬들을 지켜야 합니다….
우리는 해안에서 싸워야 합니다…. 우리는 들에서, 거리에서 싸워야 합니다.

Note
- **sequence** = succession, connected line of events : 연속, 순서
  - in historical sequence : 역사상의 순서로
  - in regular sequence : 질서 정연하게
- **heal** = cure • Time healed her broken heart.(세월이 가면서 실연의 아픔도 아물었다.)
- **miracle** = act or event which does not follow the known laws of nature : 기적
  - The doctors said that her recovery was a miracle.(그녀의 회복은 기적이라고…)
- **desolate** = sad, and lonely - She was desolate after the death of her husband.
- **make real** = realize (carry out) hope or purpose : 실현하다
  - She made real her intention of becoming an actress.(배우가 되려는 뜻을 이루었다.)
- **quicksand** : 유사(流砂):흘러 쌓인 모래 ; 밟으면 그 속에 빠짐;함정

2.11.3.2.5. 설득

'설득' 은 의사교환을 통해서 다른 사람들의 믿음, 가치관, 태도를 수정케 함으로써 타인들에게 영향을 주는 것을 목표로 한다. 바꾸어 말하면 누군가의 믿음이나, 가치관, 태도가 '중립' 에서 '긍정' 쪽으로 움직이면 설득이 이루어졌다고 말할 수 있다. 만일 '중립' 에서 '부정' 쪽으로 움직이면 '만류' 가 된다.

설득은 특히 상업 분야의 선전에서는 여러가지 방법으로 행하여 질 수 있다. 몇가지 상업상의 설득으로 자주 쓰이는 수사 기법을 보기와 함께 제공한다. 이런 유형의 상업적, 정치적인 수사기법이 텔레비전이나 라디오에 자주 등장함을 알아 두는 게 좋다.

Note
- **neutral** = without any feelings on either side of a question : 중립의
- **positive** = constructive, affirmative, practical : 긍정적, 건설적, 실질적
- **dissuasion** : 충고하여 만류하기
  - I couldn't dissuade her from marriage the entertainer.
  - (나는 그 여자가 그 연예인과 결혼하는 것을 만류할 수 없었다.)
- **propaganda** = spreading information, doctrine, ideas : 선전, 선동;정치, 사상)
  - The propaganda of a political party is planned to gain votes.(정당 선전의 목적은 득표를 위해서 계획된다.)

(A) **Bandwagon appeal** : A great movement is underway, so you had better join us or act now (i.e. buy). If not, you will be a fool.

Examples:

(1) "Everybody is going to buy that sneaker, so why don't you buy it?"

(2) "Nine out of ten doctors recommend Bayer Asprin as the best medicine for your headache."

(3) "Voters are flocking to candidate X by the millions, so you had better cast your vote the right way."

(B) **Flattery appeal** : Words or phrases are used to persuade listeners/readers to do something by suggesting that they are intelligent or thoughtful to agree with the writer.

Examples:

(1) "America, the land of equality, the land of opportunity, and the land of dreams, is for all."

(2) "We know you have the taste to recognize that an investment in our company will pay off in the future."

(C) **In-Crowd appeal** : A special kind of flattery invites readers to identify and associate with an admired group or agency.

Examples:

(1) "Only a highly educated and intelligent gentleman or lady like yourself is invited to join the most prestigious Beverly Hills Country Club."

(2) "Membership to the fraternal order of Alpha Omega Chi at Harvard University is open only to the college students who are on the honor roll and have strong recommendations from the brothers of the order."

(D) **Testimonial appeal** : A well-known person or authority in film, sports, or other area is shown using a particular brand of commercial item. People who like this highly publicized person may be influenced to buy the product.

(A) <u>홍보마차식 호소</u> : 대단한 운동이 일어나고 있다. 그러므로 지금 당장 가입하거나 활동(구입)하라. 그렇지 않으면 당신은 바보가 될 것이다.

    보기 : (1) "모두가 그 신발을 사려고 합니다. 물론 당신도 사셔야겠지요?"
           (2) "열 사람의 의사 중 아홉사람이 바이엘 아스피린은 최고의 두통약이라고 추천한다."
           (3) "유권자들이 수백만명씩 후보 'X'에게 몰려오고 있다. 그러므로 당신도 올바르게 투표하기를 권유한다."

(B) <u>아첨식 호소</u> : 청취자나 독자들에게 글쓴이와 같은 의견을 가지고 있다니 현명하다거나 생각이 깊은 사람이라고 말하여 어떤 일을 하도록 설득시키는데 쓰인다.

    보기 : (1) "평등의 나라, 기회의 나라, 꿈의 나라인 미국이 모든 이들을 기다리고 있다."
           (2) "우리 회사에 투자하면 앞으로 수지가 맞으리라는 것을 깨닫는 심미안이 당신에게 있음을 우리는 알고 있다."

(C) <u>무리에 끼워넣기식 호소</u> : 독자들을 존경받는 단체나 기관과 일치시켜 관계를 맺도록 하는 특별한 종류의 아첨.

    보기 : (1) "단지 당신과 같은 교육수준이 있고 총명한 신사나 숙녀만이 가장 권위 있는 비버리힐즈 컨트리 클럽에 초대됩니다."
           (2) "하버드대학의 우애조합인 알파와 오메가 카이의 회원자격은 우등생 명단에 올라있고 이 조합의 형제들로부터 든든한 추천을 받는 대학생에게만 열려 있습니다."

Note
- underway = under way = start to move forward : 진행중이다
  - Work on the new bridge is under way.(새 교량 공사가 진행중이다.)
- cast = make a vote : 투표하다 • She cast a vote against the motion.(그녀는 그 동의안에 부표를 던졌다.)
- flock = come, gather in great numbers : 떼지어 모이다 • Birds of a feather flock together.
- (in)the way : 제대로, 바르게
- candidate : 입후보자
- pay off = pay in full : 성공하다, 수지맞다 • The investment paid off handsomely.(그 투자가 성공적이었다.)

(D) <u>증거를 제시하는 호소</u> : 영화, 스포츠, 또는 다른 분야에서 유명인사나 권위자가 특정상표의 상품을 사용하는 것을 보여준다. 이 잘 알려진 인물을 좋아하는 사람들이 그 제품을 사도록 영향을 받게 된다.

Examples:

(1) "Michael Jordan became the best basketball player today by using Nike sneakers. If you want to play like Mike, then these sneakers are for you."

(2) "Collecting stamps is not only interesting but also instructive. President Franklin D. Roosevelt was a famous stamp collector. Why don't you start collecting stamps now? We have all kinds of unique and priceless stamps for you. Call or visit us."

(E) **Plain folks appeal** : It is often used by political candidates who attempt to seek public office by showing common ground between him and the audience. In other words, the candidate attempts to show that he is neither special nor different from them. He tries to convince voters that he belongs to the masses, understand their needs, and will satisfy their needs.

Examples:

(1) "I'm not different from you…, I'm just a *common man*." (Taewoo Noh, 1987)

(2) "You're all a bunch of hicks. That's right, Hicks! You're hicks and I'm a hick and us hicks are gonna run the state legislature."

"hick" means country bumpkin, or naive and inexperienced person from the rural area.

(3) "Let me say that my (military) service was *not a particularly unusual one*…."
I got a couple of letters of commendations, but I was just there when the bombs were falling, and then I returned."
(Richard Nixon's Checkers Speech, 1952)

(military) is added to make the meaning clear. The statements that "not a particularly unusual one…" "I was just there," and "then I returned." are sufficient enough to build common ground between Nixon and his audience who were "not unusual ones," "were just there," and "they returned from the war."

보기 : (1) "마이클 조던은 나이키 스니커를 사용하여 오늘날 최고의 농구 선수가 되었다. 만일 조던처럼 농구하고 싶다면 이 스니커를 사용하라."
(2) "우표 수집은 흥미있을 뿐만아니라 유익하다. 프랭클린 루즈벨트 대통령도 유명한 우표 수집가였다. 지금 우표 수집을 시작하라. 우리는 온갖 종류의 특이하고 값진 우표를 가지고 있다. 전화를 하거나 직접 찾아오라."

(E) <u>보통사람 호소</u> : 공직을 원하는 정치 입후보자가 자신과 청중들 사이에 공통되는 입장이 있음을 과시하는데 자주 쓰인다. 즉 후보자는 특별하지도 다르지도 않음을 보여 주려고 한다. 그는 유권자들에게 자기는 대중편이며 그들의 요구사항을 이해하고, 그 요구를 충족시킬 것을 납득시키려 한다.

보기 : (1) "이 사람 여러분들과 다르지 않습니다. 이 사람 단지 보통사람입니다."
(노태우, 1987)
(2) "여러분들은 시골 사람입니다. 맞아요, 촌사람이지요. 촌사람인 여러분과 촌사람인 나, 우리 촌사람들이 주의회를 책임지고 이끌게 됩니다.
(hick는 시골 얼간이, 시골 출신의 순박하고 경험이 없는 사람) (주:)
(3) 저의 군대복무는 특별히 다르지 않았습니다. 두어 통의 추천장을 받았습니다. 그러나 폭탄이 떨어지는 그곳에 있었습니다. 그 후 제대했습니다.

(주 : 의미를 선명하게 하려고 military를 첨가했다. "not a particularly unusual one… I was just there and then I returned"의 진술은 유별나지 않았던, 그곳에 바로 있었던, 전쟁에서 돌아온 청중들과 닉슨 사이에 공통지반을 구축하기에 충분했다.)

Note

□ **prestigious** : 권위있는, 유명한   □ N. **prestige** : 위신, 권위
  • The local lawmakers damaged the prestige of our country. (그 지방의회 의원들이 나라의 위신을 훼손시켰다.)
□ **fraternal** = brotherly : 형제같은, 우애의
  • fraternal love (우애)   • fraternal twins (이란성 쌍둥이)   • identical twins (일란성 쌍둥이)
□ **instructive** = giving or containing instruction : 교육적인, 배울 것이 많은
□ **seek** = look for, try to find : 구하다, 찾다   • Seek and you shall find.(구하라, 그러면 찾으리라.)
□ **hick** = 시골뜨기   □ **publicized** : 널리 알려진, 공표된   □ **state legislature** : 주 의회
□ **bumpkin** = awkward peron with unpolished manners esp. from the country : 촌사람
□ **naive** = natural and innocent : 순박한, 꾸밈없는
□ **rural** = in or of characteristic of countryside : 전원의, 농촌의
  • live in rural seclusion (촌에 틀어박혀 살다)
□ **commend** = praise, speak favorably of : 칭찬하다, 추천하다
  • His work ought to be highly commended. (그가 한 일은 칭찬받아 마땅하다.)

CHAPTER 3
제3장

내용 영역 독해
READING THROUGH CONTENT AREAS

CHAPTER 3

This Chapter, This chapter, "Reading Through Content Areas" is designed for the readers to develop comprehensive reading skills through content areas. The content area refers to the interrelated multidisciplinary academic areas such as music, film, space science, world history, etc. These content areas are categorized, for convenience, according to the following sections: 1. Arts; 2. Popular Culture; 3. Natural Science; and, 4. Social Science as displayed in The Table of Contents. In other words, music is categorized under the section of Arts; film under Popular Culture; biology under Natural Science; and, geography under Social Science.

The primary purposes of this chapter are, first, to provide the readers with opportunities to read a variety of passages related to the specific content area through reading in English. Never is it expected for the readers to fully understand all the subject matters of a specific content area, which is totally unrealistic. It is just designed to improve reading skills through a wide exposure to the content areas. Again, the focus is language study, since language is an essential tool through which we acquire knowledge and information. We study language and use it for practical purposes. This chapter is for that purpose: rich and direct exposure to the learning experience through the content areas with the use of the English language.

Second, this chapter as a supplementary practice for Chapter 2, will provide us with more comprehensive reading skills presented in the previous chapter. To meet this essential purpose, five questions to answer are provided at the end of each passage. These questions will be within the framework of the following categories:

1. (a) Subject matter, or Topic sentence
   (b) Main idea, or Supporting details
2. Locating the facts/answers
3. Using the context
4. (a) Making inferences
   (b) Tone and attitude, or Rhetorical techniques
5. Drawing conclusions

To be more specific, the questions to answer in Category 1 will always ask either Subject matter, Topic sentence, or Main idea, Supporting details depending on the content and length of the passage provided. The questions to answer in Category 2 will pertain to Locating facts/answers. Category 3 includes the questions related to Using the context, the questions to answer in Category 4 is in either Making inferences, Tone and attitude, or Rhetorical techniques. Finally, Category 5 includes only the questions related to Drawing conclusions.

Simply put, by repeated practices with questions within these categories, the readers can develop an active searching attitude and logical reading abilities when reading a variety of expository passages in content areas. Please read the following maxim:

"All I have read
Teaches me to believe
All I have not read." (Anonymous)

제3장은

이 장 "내용 영역 독해"는 독자들이 내용 영역을 통해서 종합적인 독서 기술을 키우도록 계획되었다. 내용 영역은 음악, 영화, 우주과학, 세계사 등 상호 관련된 여러 전문 분야의 학문적 영역을 가리키는 말이다. 이 영역들은 편의상 목차에 밝힌 대로 다음 절들에 따라 범주별로 분류하였다. 1.예술 2.대중문화 3.자연과학 4.사회과학. 바꾸어 말하면 음악은 예술의 절에, 영화는 대중문화, 생물학은 자연과학 그리고 지리학은 사회과학에 분류하였다.

이 장의 주요 목적은 첫째, 여러 내용을 독자들에게 소개함으로써 독서기술을 기르도록 구상하였으나 여러 분야의 모든 주제를 완전히 습득하고 이해함을 기대하지는 않는다. 그건 현실적으로 불가능하기 때문이다. 다시 말하건데 초점은 언어학습이다. 왜냐하면 언어란 우리가 지식과 정보를 얻는 필수적인 도구이기 때문이다. 우리는 실용적인 목적으로 언어를 공부하고 사용한다. 이 장의 목적은 바로 그것이다. 여러가지 내용영역을 영어로 읽어 학습할 기회를 풍부하게 직접적으로 경험시키는 것이다.

둘째, 제2장의 보충적 연습인 제3장은 앞장에서 소개된 좀 더 많은 종합적인 독서기술을 제공한다. 이 필수적인 목적을 충족시키기 위하여 각 글의 끝에 해결해야 할 5개의 문제를 제시한다. 그 질문들은 다음 범주의 테두리에 있다.

1. (a) 주제, 주제문 · (b) 요지, 보충자료 / 2. 사실, 정답의 위치 찾기 / 3. 문맥 이용하기
4. (a) 추론하기 · (b) 어조, 태도, 수사기법 / 5. 결론 도출

좀 더 구체적으로 말하면, 범주 1의 문제들은 항상 제시된 글의 내용과 길이에 따라 주제, 주제문이나 요지, 보충적 세부사항을 물을 것이다. 범주 2의 문제들은 사실, 정답의 위치 찾기에 관한 것이다. 범주 3에는 문맥 이용에 관련된 문제가 들어가고 범주 4의 문제는 추론하기나 어조, 태도 혹은 수사 기법에 들어간다. 마지막으로 범주 5에는 결론 도출에 관련된 문제만 넣는다. 간단하게 말하면 내용 영역 안에 있는 다양한 설명적 글을 읽을 때 여러 범주들의 문제를 반복 연습함으로써 독자들은 적극적인 탐구적 태도와 논리적 독서능력을 개발할 수 있다. 다음 경구를 읽어 보시라.

"내가 읽어 본 모든 것은 내가 읽어보지 못한 모든 것을 믿게 해 준다." (필자 불명)

Note

- □ interrelated = coming together in reciprocal relationship : 상호 관련된
- □ multidisciplinary : 여러 전문 분야의 • multicelluar (다세포의) • multilateral : (다각도의)
- □ multi- = many • multifold (여러겹의) □ categorize : 분류하다, 유별하다
- □ convenience = freedom from difficulty or worry : 편의, 편리
- □ display = place or spread out so that there's no difficulty in seeing : 전시하다, 진열하다
  - The flag is displayed on August 15.(8월 15일에는 국기가 게양된다.)
- □ totally = completely • I totally agree with you. (자네와 의견이 완전히 같네.)
- □ supplementary = an additional amount of something : 증보의, 보충적인
  - The hospital has a supplementary water supply if the main supply fails.
    (그 병원은 수도본관이 고장날 경우를 대비하여 추가 수도시설을 갖추었다.)
- □ pertain to = belong to, have a connection with : …에 관한, 연관된
- □ simply put : 간단히 말하자면 • If it is simply put
- □ expository = explanatory : expose의 형용사 파생어
- □ maxim = widely accepted rule of conduct or general truth : 행위규범, 금언
  - Waste not, want not. (낭비가 없으면 궁핍도 없다.)
- □ anonymous = without a name : 익명의
  - an anonymous letter (발신자 불명의 편지) • an anonymous benefactor (익명의 독지가)

3-1 ARTS

This section, "Arts" includes nine passages related to the target content areas: Dance, Music, and Painting, allocating 3 passages for each content area. Most passages deal with each content area as a universal art of performance across time and space within cultural context of a particular society, which will help us acquire an in-depth insight and broader understanding of the arts concerned.

3.1.1. Dance

Passage 1:

Dancing is an art of moving the body and its parts in rhythm, usually in time to music. People have a *natural* urge to express their feelings through rhythmic movement. Most children, for example, jump up and down when they are excited.

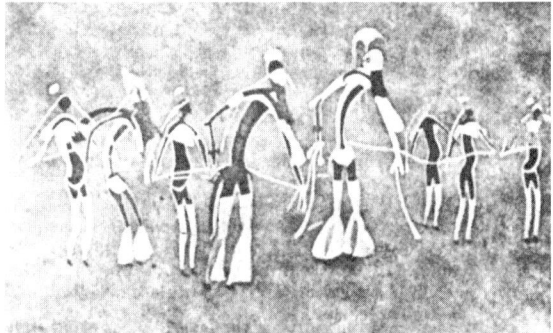

Prehistoric dancers are pictured in paintings up to 20,000 years old. Such paintings, found on rock surfaces, prove that dancing is one of the oldest forms of human expression.

Dancing is both an art and a form of recreation. As an art, a dance can tell a story, set a mood, or express an emotion. For example, some Asian dances consist of symbolic gestures that tell a story through body movements. As a form of recreation, dancing provides us with fun, relaxation, and companionship. On the American frontier, for example, square dances gave pioneer families a welcome chance to socialize. These days dancing at a party or other gatherings serves as a popular way for making new friends and for recreation.

3-1 예술

이 절 "예술"에는 목표내용 영역과 관련된 9개의 글이 들어 있다: 무용, 음악, 회화에 각각 3개의 내용영역이 할당되어있다. 대부분의 글들은 특정 사회의 문화맥락에서 볼 수 있는 예술형태를 초월하여 보편적인 표현예술의 내용 영역을 취급한다. 왜냐하면 그렇게 함으로써 관련된 예술에 대한 깊은 통찰과 보다 넓은 이해를 얻는 데 도움이 되기 때문이다.

> **Note**
> □ context = the words around a word, phrase used for helping to explain the meaning of the word or phrase : 전후관계, 문맥, 주변정황
>   • Don't quote my words out of context. (내 말뜻은 그렇게 아니요, 멋대로 해석하지 마시오.)
> □ universal = concerning all members of a group : 전반적인, 보편적인
>   • There was a universal agreement that you should be a chairman.
>   (당신이 회장이 되어야 한다는 게 전체의 합의사항이오.)
> □ in-depth : 심층의, 상세한
> □ insight : 직관, 통찰 – 외부의 도움없이 사물을 알 수 있는 능력   • have an insight to : 꿰뚫어 보다
> □ concerned = interested, taking part : 관련된   • authorities concerned : 관계당국
> □ allocate = set apart for somebody as a share, for some purpose : 할당, 분배하다
>   • That space has been allocated for building a public library. (저 곳은 공공도서관 건축 부지로 할당된 곳이다.)

3.1.1. 무용

지문 1

무용이란 대체로 박자에 맞추어 몸과 신체부위들을 리듬있게 움직이는 예술이다. 사람들은 율동적인 동작으로 감정을 표현하고 싶은 선천적인 충동을 가지고 있다. 대부분 어린이들이 흥분하면 위 아래로 뛰는 것이 그 한 예다.

무용은 예술이자 오락의 한가지 형태다. 예술로서 무용은 이야기를 하고 분위기를 조성하고 감정을 표출한다. 예를 들면 어떤 아시아 무용은 신체동작을 통하여 이야기를 하

There are two major types of dancing: theatrical and social. Theatrical dancing is performed for the entertainment of spectators, which includes ballet, modern dance, musical comedy dance, and tap dancing. Theatrical dances may take great personal satisfaction in creating something beautiful. In social dancing, the participants dance for their own pleasure. There are many types of social dances which require specific steps and rhythms.

All types of theatrical and social dancing involve movements, energy, rhythm, and design. Movement is the action of dancers when they use their bodies to create organized patterns. Energy provides the force needed to perform movement. Rhythm refers to the pattern of timing around which the dance movement is organized. Design is the visual pattern made by the movements of a dancer's body.

(1) A good title of the passage would be _____. (Subject matter)

    (a) Definition of dance   (d) Types of dance
    (b) History of dance   (e) Definition, types, components of dance
    (c) Function of dance

(2) The basic components of dancing are narrated in the _____ paragraph. (Locating the fact)

    (a) First   (b) Second   (c) Third   (d) Fourth   (e) None

(3) The word, *natural* in the first paragraph can be substituted as _____. (Word context)

    (a) Extrinsic   (b) Innate   (c) Objective   (d) True   (e) Essential

(4) The writer's purpose of writing this passage is for us to _____. (Making inferences)

    (a) Know the definition of dance
    (b) Love dance
    (c) Be informed of types & components of dance.
    (d) Know the function of dance
    (e) Be excellent dancers

(5) It can be concluded that dance as an artistic and recreational form has been performed since _____ times. (Drawing conclusions)

    (a) Prehistoric   (c) Medieval   (e) Contemporary
    (b) Ancient   (d) Modern

는 상징적인 몸짓으로 구성된다. 오락의 한 형태로서 무용은 우리에게 기쁨과 긴장해소 그리고 동료애를 부여한다. 예를 들어 스퀘어 댄스는 미국의 변경지방에서 개척자들에게 서로 사귈 수 있는 환영의 기회를 주었다. 오늘날 파티에서나 다른 모임에서 춤은 새친구를 사귀고 오락을 위한 대중적인 방법으로서 역할을 한다.

무용에는 두가지 주요한 형태가 있는데 무대무용과 사교무용이다. 무대무용은 관객들에게 여흥을 주기 위하여 공연되며 그 안에 발레, 현대무용, 뮤지컬과 탭댄스가 포함된다. 무대무용은 무언가 아름다운 것을 창조함으로써 대단한 만족을 갖는다. 사교춤은 참가자들이 자신들의 즐거움을 위하여 추는 것이다. 사교춤에는 특정의 스텝과 리듬을 필요로 하는 여러가지 형태가 있다.

모든 형태의 무대무용이나 사교무용에는 동작과 활력과 리듬과 구상이 들어있다. 동작은 조직적인 양식을 창조하기 위하여 신체를 사용할 때 무희들의 활동이다. 활력은 동작을 수행하는 데 필요한 힘을 준다. 리듬은 무용동작이 조직될 때 맞추는 양식을 가리킨다. 구상은 무희의 신체 동작이 만들어 내는 시각적인 양식이다.

Note

- □ (in) time (to) = the rate of speed of a piece of music : 음악의 박자(에 맞춰)
- □ duple (triple, quadruple) time : 2 (3, 4) 박자
  - Beat time and I will sing. (네가 박자를 맞추어라. 내가 노래하마.)
- □ in time : 박자가 맞는   □ out of time : 박자가 틀린
- □ companionship : 동료의식, 동료애
- □ frontier = a limit or border, the border between the settled and wild areas : 변경(邊境)
- □ frontier spirit : 개척정신
- □ square dance : 쌍쌍이 짝을 이루어 네모지게 추는 춤
- □ socialize = spend time with other people in a friendly way : 어울리다, 사회화하다
  - Kindergarten is a good institution to socialize the kids.
    (유치원은 어린아이들을 사회화하기에 좋은 기관이다.)
- □ component = any of the parts that make up a whole : 부품, 구성요소
- □ narrate = tell a story, describe an event in order : 순서에 맞게 이야기하다
  - Shall I narrate a strange experience of mine? (내가 겪었던 이상한 이야기 해줄까?)
- □ extrinsic = external, not a part of real character : 외래적인, 부대적인
  - opp. intrinsic = belonging naturally (본래적인)
- □ innate = in born = in one's nature, possessed from birth : 선천적인
- □ prehistoric = belonging to a time before recorded history : 선사시대의
- □ medieval : 중세의
- □ contemporary = modern, of the present : 현대의, 동시대의
  - contemporary literature (현대문학)
  - Goethe was contemporary with Beethoven. (괴테와 베토벤은 동시대 인물이었다.)

Passage 2 :

    There are many different types of dances in India. Some are folk dances and others require a great deal of training. One dance requires at least eight years of training before a person is allowed to perform it. This is the Kathakali which is danced only by men. They dressed in brightly colored costumes and wear heavy make-up. With the movements of their hands and bodies, and the expressions of their faces, these dancers act out interesting stories. A good Kathakali dancer is so skillful that if he pretends to throw an imaginary rock, the audience will duck.

    Another beautiful dance is the Bharata Natyam which is performed by women. They act out the words of a song with the movements of their bodies and the expressions on their faces. The *swishing* silk of their colorful costumes and the sound of the small bells tied around their ankles make the scene more impressive.

    In India, dancing has been an important form of worship in the Hindu religion for hundreds of years. Many dances tell stories of Hindu gods and heroes such as Rama and Sita, Krishna and Racha, Shiva and Parvati. These gods and goddesses are often portrayed in the dance forms, and the style may slightly vary according to the place of origin of the dance form. But, essentially all the traditional dance forms in India include the same purposes leading to the Supreme Lord, the Naayak.

(Source: Adapted from "Indian dances," by Addepalli, Swarnagowri, (1997), and India, (1988))

(1) The main idea of the passage is _____ . (Main idea)

    (a) Kathakali and Bharata Natyam
    (b) Indian dance
    (c) Two types of Indian dance
    (d) Different kinds of dance of India
    (e) Dancing as a form of worship in India

(2) The audience can interpret certain stories by the dancer's ____. (Locating the fact)

    (a) Story & song
    (b) Song & monologue
    (c) Movements of hands & bodies
    (d) Throwing a rock
    (e) Movements of hands, bodies, facial expressions

(3) The italicized *swishing* silk must mean _____ based on the context of the passage. (Word context)

    (a) Rustling   (b) Brilliant   (c) Colorful   (d) Soft   (e) Smooth

지문 2

인도에는 서로 다른 형태의 춤이 있다. 더러는 민속무용이고 더러는 많은 수련을 필요로 하는 것이다. 어떤 춤은 공연까지 하는데 최소 8년 간의 수련을 필요로 한다. 이 춤은 남자들만 추는 Kathakali춤이다. 그들은 화려한 색상의 옷을 입고 진한 화장을 한다. 손과 몸의 동작과 얼굴 표정으로 이 무용수들은 재미있는 이야기를 연기한다. 우수한 Kathakali무용수는 매우 기능이 뛰어나 만일 가짜 바위를 던지는 시늉을 하면 관객들이 몸을 숙여 피한다.

또 다른 아름다운 춤은 Bharata Natyam으로 여자들이 춘다. 그들은 노래가사를 몸의 동작과 얼굴 표정으로 실연한다. 다채로운 의상의 "휙휙"

Patson Travel, Chicago (WORLD BOOK photo)
Religious dance of India

하는 비단소리와 발목에 묶은 작은 종의 울림 소리는 장면을 더욱 인상적으로 만든다.

인도에서 무용은 수백년간 힌두교의 중요한 예배 형식이 되어 왔다. 많은 춤들은 힌두교의 신과 영웅들, 예를 들면 Rama, Sita, Krishna, Racha, Shiva, Parvati에 관한 이야기를 해준다. 이 신과 여신들의 모습은 춤 동작으로 표현되며 춤의 형태는 그 춤의 근원지에 따라 약간씩 다를 수 있다. 그러나 근본적으로 인도의 모든 전통 춤은 최고의 신인 Naayak을 숭배하는 똑같은 목적을 내포하고 있다.

Note

- **folk** = people of one race of nation sharing a particular kind of life : 사람들 : 같은 뿌리를 가진, 같은 문화를 가진 사람들의 총칭 • folk music (songs, art, medicine) : 민요, 민예, 민간요법
- **make-up** : 화장, 분장 □ **act out** = perform actions : 실연(實演)하다
- **duck** = move quickly down to avoid being seen or hit : 몸을 숙여 피하다
- **significant** = having importance : 의미심장한, 중요한 • Few things are more significant of a man's interests than the books on his shelves.(사람이 관심을 갖는 것 중에서 서가의 책보다 더 중요한 것은 없다.)
- **scandalous** = shameful = disgraceful = ignominious : 창피한, 파렴치한
- **detached** = impartial, not influenced by others : 초연한, 미련없는, 공정한 • It is not so easy to take a detached attitude in anything interested.(이해가 걸린 문제에서 초연한 태도를 견지하는 것은 그리 쉽지 않다.)
- **chronological** : 연대순의 • Put the events in the chronological order. (그 사건들을 연대순으로 배열하라.)
- **sentimental** = emotional : 감정적인, 감상적인, 정에 약한, 눈물이 헤픈
  • Don't approach the matter in sentimentalism. (감상적인 접근은 안됩니다.)
- **self-contradictory** : 자기 모순의, 자가당착의

(4) Based on the information given, it can be inferred that dance has been used for _____ purposes. (Making inferences)

    (a) Artistic   (c) Literary   (e) All of the above
    (b) Religious   (d) Entertaining

(5) It can be concluded that the dance is a/an _____ part of life. (Conclusion)

    (a) Integral   (c) Complicated   (e) Intellectual
    (b) Isolated   (d) Spiritual

Passage 3:

    Ballet, a theatrical dance requiring specific techniques, developed in the Italian and French courts during the 15th century. But the genuine ballet came into existence in France when Louis XIV founded the Academie Royale de Danse, the first ballet school, in 1661.

    During the 18th century, outstanding ballet performers emerged with advanced techniques. Leaps and aerial movements were used only by male dancers, because women's floor length skirts were too restrained. Marie-Anne de Cupis de Camargo who debuted in 1729, shortened her skirt to a *scandalous* ankle length and performed steps previously used by male dancers.

    Russia's prominence in ballet began in the late 19th century with the Frenchman, Marius Petipa's belief that dancing should be for its own sake, not for dramatic purposes. Petipa created *Raymonda*, *Don Quixote*, *The Sleeping Beauty*, and portions of *Swan Lake* with his assistant in St. Petersburg.

    Today there are many ballet companies around the world. Some of the prestigious ones are the Kirov Ballet which has followed the tradition of Leningrad; and now the center of Russian ballet is Moscow's Bolshoi Theater; the Royal Danish Ballet which used to perform romantic ballet, has now taken a more international avenue; England's Royal Ballet; New York City Ballet; and, The American Ballet Theater.

(1) The subject matter of the passage is _____. (Subject matter)

    (a) The origin of ballet   (d) Techniques of ballet
    (b) Function of ballet   (e) Major ballet companies
    (c) Development of ballet

(2) Significant development of ballet in terms of techniques and performance appeared during the _____ century. (Locating the fact)

    (a) 16th   (b) 17th   (c) 18th   (d) 19th   (e) 20th

지문 3:

특수한 기능을 요구하는 무대 무용 발레는 15세기 동안에 이탈리아와 프랑스 궁전에서 발달했다. 그러나 진짜 발레는 루이 14세가 1661년에 최초의 발레학교인 왕립 무용학교를 설립했을 때 프랑스에서 생겨났다.

18세기 중에 고급 기능을 가진 뛰어난 발레 공연자들이 나타났다. 도약과 공중동작은 남자 무용수들만 사용했다. 왜냐하면 여자들의 치마가 바닥에 닿아 너무 거추장스러웠기 때문이었다. 1729년에 데뷔한 매리앤 드 쿠피스 드 카마르고가 사람들이 쑥덕거릴만큼 발목까지 짧게 치마를 줄이고 이전에 남자들이 사용하던 스텝을 사용했다.

Two of the greatest starts of ballet today, Margot Fonteyn and Rudolf Nureyev, dance together in a scene from Swan Lake.

러시아가 발레에서 두각을 나타낸 것은 '무용은 연극적인 목적이 아니고 무용 자체를 위한 것이어야 한다' 는 프랑스인 마리우스 프티파의 신념과 함께 19세기 후반의 일이다. 프티파는 성 페테스부르그에서 그의 조수와 함께 라이몬다, 돈키호테, 잠자는 미녀, 백조의 호수 일부를 창작하였다. 오늘날은 전세계적으로 수많은 발레단이 있다. 그 중 권위있는 발레단은 레닌그라드 전통을 이어받은 키로프발레단, 오늘날 러시아 발레의 중심인 모스크바 볼쇼이 극장, 전에는 낭만적인 발레를 공연했으나 지금은 국제적인 대세를 따르는 덴마크 로얄 발레단, 영국 로얄 발레단, 뉴욕 발레단, 미국 발레 극장 등이 있다.

Note

□ **genuine = real** : 진짜의: • genuine leather (pearls, picture by Rubens) : 진짜 가죽(진주, 루벤스의 그림)
□ **come into existence (being) = come to exist** : 생겨나다
  • When and how did the earth come into existence? (지구는 언제 어떻게 생겼나요?)
□ **outstanding = attracting notices, better than others** : 뛰어난, 군계일학(群鷄一鶴)인
  • He was the most outstanding player in the final. (그는 결승전에서 가장 돋보였다.)
□ **leap = jump** : 뛰다 • Look before you leap. (돌다리도 두드려보고 건너라.)
□ **aerial** : 공중의 • aerial performance : (공중 곡예)
□ **restrain = hold back, keep under control** : 억제하다, 억누르다
  • If you can't restrain your anger, you'll be sorry for that some day.
    (화를 억제하지 못하면 언젠가 그 일로 후회하리라.)

(3) The opposite word of the italicized *scandalous* in the second paragraph can be _____. (Word context)

    (a) Infamous   (c) Shameful   (e) Ignominious
    (b) Disgraceful   (d) Respectful

(4) The writer illustrates the passage based on _____. (Rhetorical techniques)

    (a) Comparison & contrast   (d) Chronological order
    (b) Scientifically detached   (e) Sentimental mood
    (c) Self-contradictory

(5) Based on the information given, it can be concluded that the ballet has been performed by people for _____. (Drawing conclusions)

    (a) Entertainment   (d) Socialization
    (b) Personal satisfaction   (e) Ceremonial purposes
    (c) Theatrical purposes

3.1.2. Painting

Passage 1:

Painting is an art of using color plastically or dynamically. Its existence ranges from colored images in the earth colors on the walls of Paleolithic caves to the dribbling of paint by the New York School of *Action Painters*. The Paleolithic pigments, more than 20,000 years old, found in the Lascaux Cave of the southern part of France, are the oldest known. Painting in Western society began in Egypt and Crete with burial scenes and murals of everyday life. The Greeks and Romans made it pictorial with emphasis on shadow and space.

During the early 14th century, the two common media of painting, "tempera" and "fresco" became popular in Italy. Tempera is a method of painting with dry, powdered pigments mixed with a medium of water and some gelatinous substances such as gum arabic or a casein emulsion. It is an exceptionally permanent medium and its colors remain unchanged even after centuries. The other method for mural decorations was "fresco" in which pigment was applied to wet plaster.

The oil medium was developed before the 15th century in Holland, where the Van Dyck brothers were the first to make distinguished use of it. In the 19th century, additional media include "water color" and "pastel," both usually

> □ debut = first public appearance : 데뷔
>   • The singer made his debut at the campus song festival. (그 가수는 대학 가요제 때 데뷔했다.)
> □ step = a movement of feet in dancing : (춤) 스텝
> □ scandalous = shameful, offensive to feelings, disgraceful
>   • President Bill Clinton's scandalous sexual relationship with her would be a burden in his political career.(클린턴 대통령의 수치스런 성 추문은 그의 정치 생활에 부담이 될 것이다.)
> □ prominence = the state of being easily seen, distinguished, eminent : 탁월, 걸출
>   • He's one of the artists of prominence among his contemporaries.
>   (그는 동시대 사람들 중에서 뛰어난 화가다.)

3.1.2. 회화

지문 1

회화란 색채를 조형적으로 혹은 역동적으로 사용하는 예술이다. 회화의 존재는 구석기 시대의 벽에 흙빛으로 채색된 여러 모습으로부터 뉴욕 행동화가들의 물감 방울 떨어뜨리기에 이르기까지 범위가 넓다. 20,000여년 전에 프랑스 남부지방의 Lascaux 동굴에서 발견된 구석기 시대의 도료는 알려진 것 중에서 가장 오래된 것이다. 서양 사회에서의 회화는 이집트와 크레타 섬의 고대 무덤 주변과 일상 벽화로부터 시작되었다. 희랍인들과 로마인들은 음영과 공간을 강조함으로써 회화를 생생하게 만들었다.

14세기 중에 회화의 두가지 공통적인 수단인 "템페라"와 "프레스코"가 인기를 끌었다. 템페라는 물과 아라비아 수지 혹은 카페인 유

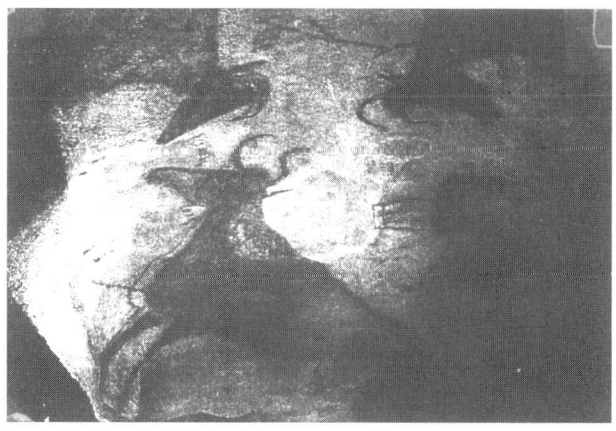

Lascaux Cave Paintins This dramatic view of an ancient hunt excites deep within a cave in lascaux, France. Religious beliefs probably inspired the Stone Age artists who created the scene by using paints made from crushed minerals and plants. The artists lighted their way by burning animal fats in stone dishes, and climbed wooden scaffolds to reach high walls and ceilings. **Art and Literature** What religious do you think this cave painting might have served?

considered part from the central traditions of painting since the greatest works in water color and pastel are those done by artists known for their excellence of their work in oil, such as Paul Cezanne and Edgar Degas.

    According to the 20th century concepts of painting, it was no longer considered essential that only brushes or other traditional tools be used in the application of color. Henry Matisse conveyed the radiance of color without paint, but by cutting out selected pieces of paper in the designs desired, and pasting the pieces to canvas. Any type of brush and tool, or "action" is acceptable today as long as the painter's purpose or feeling is artistically expressed with the use of color.

(1) What would be a proper subject matter for the passage? (Subject matter)

    (a) Painting as an eternal art
    (b) Painting as an expressive art
    (c) A development of painting
    (d) Painting as a social activity
    (e) A history of European painting

(2) The well-known painter who expressed his idea without using brush or paint, but by pasting pieces of papers on canvas is _____. (Identifying the answer)

    (a) Paul Cezanne
    (b) Edgar Degas
    (c) Van Dyck
    (d) Henry Matisse
    (e) Vincent Van Gogh

(3) In the first paragraph, based on the contextual clue the italicized *Action Painters* can refer to the painters who _____. (Word in contextual clue)

    (a) Are actively involved in painting
    (b) Paint under the influence of alcohol
    (c) Paint under the influence of drugs
    (d) Paint some objects in action
    (e) Paint by pouring paints

(4) The writer's presentation for the paragraph patterns is based on _____. (Rhetorical techniques)

    (a) Analysis
    (b) Description
    (c) Comparison & contrast
    (d) Analogy
    (e) Definition

(5) Based on the information given and your logic, it can be concluded that the initial development of painting is _____. (Drawing conclusion)

    (a) As old as writing system
    (b) As old as our history
    (c) As old as our pre-history
    (d) Older than music
    (e) Older than dancing

제 같은 미디엄을 건조 분말안료와 혼합하여 사용하는 회화의 방법이다. 템페라는 특히 영구불변하는 제작 기법이고 수세기가 지나도 색채가 변하지 않는다. 다른 하나의 벽화 방법은 프레스코기법으로 안료를 젖은 석고에 발라서 쓴다.

   기름용액은 15세기 이전에 홀란드에서 개발되었고 반 다이크형제가 그 용액을 가장 우수하게 사용한 첫 번째 사람들이다. 19세기에 추가된 제작 재료에 그림물감, 파스텔이 있다. 그 둘은 회화의 주된 전통기법으로부터 갈라져 나온 것으로 여겨졌다. 왜냐하면 수채화나 파스텔화의 최고 걸작으로 알려진 작품들은 유화를 잘 그렸던 폴 세잔이나 드가 같은 화가들의 작품들이다.

   20세기 회화의 개념에 따르면 색을 응용하는데 붓이나 다른 전통적 도구만을 꼭 사용해야한다고 더 이상 생각하지 않았다. 마티스는 도료를 사용하지 않고 대신 필요한 도안에 맞게 종이를 선택하여 오린 다음, 캔버스에 붙여 색의 광휘를 전달했다. 오늘날, 어떤 형태의 붓이나 도구 혹은 "행동"은 화가가 추구하는 목적이나 감정에 적합하게 색채를 사용, 예술적으로 표현만 하면 환영 받는다.

Note

- **plastically** : 조형적으로(회화, 조각, 제도)
- **plastic art** : 조형미술
- **plastic surgery** : 성형외과
- **plastic mind** : 유연한 마음
- **dynamical = full of activity, energetic** : 동적인, 역동적인
  - He who lives dynamically is said to live a true life.
  - (역동적으로 사는 사람을 제대로 산다고 말할 수 있다.)
- **range = reach from one end to another** : 범위가 …부터 …까지다
  - The age of the participants range from 12 to 82.
  - (참가자의 연령 분포는 12세에서 72세까지 걸쳐 있다.)
- **paleolithic** : 구석기 시대의 • cf. **neolithic** : 신석기 시대의
- **dribble = flow drop by drop** : 물방울이 뚝뚝 떨어지다, (축구) 짧고 빠르게 공을 차고 나가다, 드리블
  - Babies often dribble on their bibs. (애기들은 턱받이에 침을 흘린다.)
- **action painter** : 행동화가, 물감을 뿌리거나 하는 전위화가
- **pigment = coloring material** : 안료, 도료, 물감
- **mural** : 벽의 • **mural painting** : 벽화
- **scaffold** : 발 디딤판, 교수대
- **tempera** : 도료를 아교풀 같은 교질에 섞어 만든 재료
- **fresco** : 갓 회칠한 벽면에 수채를 그리는 벽화법
- **gum arabic** : 아라비아 고무나무에서 채취하는 수지
- **pastel** : 파스텔 – 광택을 없앤 부드러운 색조

Passage 2:

Paul Gauguin (1848-1903) is remembered as a well-known French painter who sought exotic environments in Tahiti, and frequently combined the people and objects in his paintings in novel ways, evoking in the process a mysterious personal world. The following is a letter (March, 1892) from Gauguin to his wife, Mette Sophie Gad who lived in Copenhagen, Denmark.

"For I am an artist and you're right ; you are not mad. I am a great artist and I know it. It is because I am sure that I have endured sufferings. To do what I have done in any other circumstances would make me out as a ruffian, which I am no doubt for many people. Anyhow, what does it matter?··· You told me that I am wrong to remain far away from the artistic center. No, I am right. I have known for a long time what I am doing, and why I do it. My artistic center is in my brain and not elsewhere, and I am strong because I am never sidetracked by others, and do what is in me.

Beethoven was blind and deaf, he was isolated from everything, so his works are redolent of the artistic living in a world of his own. You see what has happened to Pissarro, owing to his always wanting to be in the vanguard, abreast of everything ; he has lost every atom of personality, and his whole work lacks unity. He has always followed the movement from Courbet and Millet up to those petty *chemical persons* who pile up little dots.

No, I have an aim and I am always pursuing it, building up materials. There are transformations every year, it is true, but they always follow each other in the same direction. I alone am logical. Consequently, I find very few who follow me for long···"

(Source: Prather Marla, et. al. (1987). Gauguin: A Retrospective)

(1) What would be a suitable title of the letter? (Subject matter)

    (a) To my beloved wife
    (b) Difference between me and other artists
    (c) My works in Tahiti
    (d) My wonderful life in Tahiti
    (e) Wish you were here with me, honey

(2) Gauguin claimed that he was a great artist based on the following reasons. (Locating the fact)

    (a) Sufferings, talent, single goal
    (b) Isolation, single goal, creativity
    (c) Sufferings, single goal, creativity
    (d) Personality, creativity, talent
    (e) Excitement, personality, single goal

지문 2

폴 고갱은 타이티 섬에서 이국적인 환경을 그렸고, 그림 속에서 새로운 방법으로 인간과 사물을 결합시켜, 신비한 개인 세계를 표현한 유명한 프랑스 화가로 기억되고 있다. 다음은 고갱이 덴마크 코펜하겐에서 살았던 자기 아내 소피에게 보낸 편지다.

Paul Gauguin, a self-portrait dated 1889. (National Gallery of Art, Washington, D.C., Chester Dale Collection, 1962)

"나는 화가이기 때문이지만, 당신은 정상이요. 당신은 미친 게 아니요. 나는 위대한 화가요. 그건 내가 알지요. 나는 그것을 확신하기 때문에 수많은 고통을 견뎌왔소. 만일 지금껏 내가 해온 작업을 다른 환경 속에서 한다면 나는 난폭자가 될 것이오. 하긴 지금 많은 사람들이 나를 그렇게 보고 있는 것은 확실하지만, 하여간 그게 무슨 문제가 되겠소. 당신은 내가 예술의 중심에서 이탈하여 있는 게 잘못이라 말했지만 그렇지 않소. 내가 옳소. 내가 무엇을 하고 있으며 왜 그러는지는 내가 옛날부터 알고 있소. 내 예술의 중심은 딴 데 있는 게 아니고 내 머리 안에 있소. 나는 강하오, 왜냐하면 다른 사람들 때문에 길에서 빗나간 적이 한 번도 없고 내 안에 있는 것을 하기 때문이오.

베토벤은 눈이 안보이고 귀도 안들렸고 모든 것에서 소외되어 있었소. 그래서 그의 작품들은 그 자신 세계의 향기를 내는 것이오. 피사로에게 있었던 일을 당신도 알지요. 그는 언제나 선두에 서서 모든 것에서 멀어지지 않으려고 원했기 때문에 자기 개성의 알갱이까지 다 잃어버렸소. 그래서 그의 모든 작품은 통일성이 없어요. 그는 언제나 쿠베르와 밀레로부터 작은 점이나 모으는(화가가 못되는) 하찮은 화학적 인간들(개성도 없는, 인간이 아닌)이 펼치는 모든 운동까지 따라했소.

안됩니다. 나는 목표가 있어요. 그리고 항상 그것을 추구하며 자료를 쌓아가고 있소. 해마다 변형이 있지요. 그건 맞는 말이요. 그러나 그들은 똑같은 방향으로 서로 따라가지요. 나만 혼자 논리적이지요. 따라서 나를 모방하는 자는 별로 없소, 오랫동안…"

(3) The italicized *chemical persons* in the second paragraph refers to _____.
(Phrase in contextual clue)

   (a) Chemist
   (b) Persons working in chemical companies
   (c) Person who produce colors using chemical compounds
   (d) Unskilled painters
   (e) Professional painters

(4) Based on the information given, it can be inferred that the tone of Gauguin toward his wife seems to be _____. (Making inferences)

   (a) Pedantic   (c) Humorous   (e) Respectful
   (b) Sarcastic   (d) Critical

(5) Based on the information given it can be concluded that Gauguin probably might have _____. (Drawing conclusions)

   (a) Admitted his mistakes   (d) Pursued his goal
   (b) Changed his goal   (e) Made many friends in Tahiti
   (c) Returned to his wife

Passage 3:

Painting, as an art of expressing emotions, ideals, or belief system with the use of color, has created a variety of genre and forms. One of the forms is landscape painting the development and composition of which between China and the West are interesting.

The full maturity of Chinese landscape painting developed during the Tang Dynasty under the influence of a scholar and poet, Wang Wei (699-759). He expressed personal response to nature with brush and ink largely on the basis of Taoist view. The Taoist philosophy stressed a high value on the meaning of life by respecting the law of nature. Under this tradition, the artists were supposed to be at peace with nature, free from the shackles of society and from the temptation of gold, and whose spirit should be deeply immersed in mountains and rivers, and other manifestations of nature. This tradition in landscape painting continued through several dynasties (i.e. Tang, Sung, Yuan, Ming), and the Sung Dynasty (960-1279) saw its peak.

In composition, the painters achieved the effects of the landscape scene through the mastery of line and silhouette rather than the rendering of light and shadow. In other words, they painted the beauty of nature from different angles and views to enhance the effects of landscape scenes, which could more

> **Note**
>
> □ **exotic** = strange and unusual : 이국적인, 색다른
>   - exotic flower : 외래종인 꽃
>   - exotic idea : 외래사상
> □ **novel** = new, not like anything previously : 참신한, 기발한
>   - That's a novel suggestion.(참신한 제안이구나.)
> □ **evoke** = call out : 속에 들어있는 것을 불러내다.
>   - evoke admiration(surprise, a smile) : 찬탄을 (놀라움을, 미소를) 끌어내다
> □ **ruffian** = a violent, cruel man : 악한, 무법자
> □ **isolate** = separate, keep apart from others : 소외시키다
>   - When a person has an infectious disease, he must be isolated. (전염병을 앓고 있으면 격리시켜야 한다.)
> □ **redolent** = fragrant : 향기로운, 생각나게 하는
> □ **vanguard** = the soldiers marching at the front of an army : 선봉대, 첨병
> □ **keep abreast of** = on a level, keep pace with : 뒤떨어지지 않다
>   - She reads news magazines to keep abreast of the times. (시대에 뒤떨어지지 않으려고 시사지를 본다.)

지문 3

색채를 사용하여 감정, 이상 혹은 신념체계를 표현하는 예술인 회화는 다양한 장르와 형식을 창조해 왔다. 그 형식들 중 하나가 중국과 서양 사이에서 회화의 발달과 구성이 흥미로운 풍경화다.

중국 풍경화가 완전한 원숙기에 들어선 것은 당나라 때로서 학자이면서 시인이었던 Wang Wei(王維)의 영향 때문이었다. 그는 자연에 대한 개인의 느낌을 주로 도교적 견해를 바탕으로 붓과 먹으로 표현했다. 도교철학은 자연의 법칙을 존중하는 삶 속에서 높은 이상을 추구했다. 이 전통 속에서 예술인들은 자연과 더불어 평화로워야 하며, 사회의 속박과 재물의 속박으로부터 해방되어야 하며, 그들의 정신은 산과 강 그리고 다른 자연 현상에 깊이 몰입해야 했다. 풍경화의 이런 전통은 여러 왕조(당, 송, 원, 명)동안 계속되었고 송조 때가 전성기였다.

구성에 있어서 화가들은 명암의 표현보다 선과 실루엣을 완성하여 풍경의 효과를 나타냈다. 다시 말하면 풍경의 효과를 높이기 위하여 자연의 미를 다른 각도와 다른 시각에서 그렸다. 그리고 그것은 자연

A mountain landscape. In ancient times, Chinese artists often painted scenes from nature, such as mountains and streams.

intensify the *magnitude* of nature. Consequently, human figures were often diminished so as not to intrude on the orderly magnitude of nature. The magnitude of nature was stressed while human figures were just dependent parts of nature. It is because human beings can find the true meaning of their lives not through the shackles of society, but through the deep dependency of nature.

On the other hand, although paintings from the Greek era contained landscape backgrounds, landscape paintings as an independent art in the West developed around the 15th century in limited extent. For example, the Flemish painter, Quentin Metsy's *The Virgin Enthroned with Child* (1520), displays a confined scene of landscape: a window view. A more advanced stage can be seen in Gerald David's *Rest on the Flight into Egypt* (1498) in which the virgin is integrated into the landscape. Under this religious tradition, the landscape painting was used as background for religious subject matter. But after the Reformations when the use of religious subjects were restricted, landscape became a genre in its own right. During the 17th century, the ideal landscape was perfected in the serene pastoral scenes as shown by the works of Claude Lorrain. During the 19th century, landscape paintings displayed naturalistic views of Constable, and the visionary panorama of J.M.W. Turner. In the late 19th century, under the fashion of impressionism, landscape served as a source for realistic and abstract painters for the 20th century.

In composition, landscape often depicts the appearance, power, and atmospheric effects found in nature. For example, the American painter, Fitz Hugh Lane stressed the effects of light and space on a clear, calm morning on the New England sea coast in *Owl's Head*, symbolizing the importance of the sea coast to the ownership. Unlike the Chinese one, the landscape in the West often served as an dependent property to the owner, or as an equal interdependent agent between human beings and nature. Under this tradition, man is not subject to nature, but it is an equal and independent partnership to nature.

(1) One of the supporting details which does not support the influence of the Taoist view as in "Chinese landscape painting developed largely under the influence of the Taoist view" is that men should _____. (Supporting details)

   (a) Live within proper social rules
   (b) Be peace with nature
   (c) Depend on nature
   (d) Follow the law of nature
   (e) Be immersed in the manifestations of nature

(2) In composition, one of the contrasting factors between the Chinese and the Western landscape painting in terms of "human figures vs. nature" is _____. (Locating the fact)

의 광대함을 더욱 강화할 수 있었다. 따라서 인간의 모습은 질서정연한 자연의 장엄함에 끼어들지 못하도록 자주 축소되었다. 인간의 모습이 단지 자연에 의지하는 부분일 때 자연의 장엄함은 강조되었다. 그 이유는 인간은 그들 삶의 진정한 의미를 사회의 속박에서가 아니고 자연에 깊이 의존함으로써 찾을 수 있기 때문이다.

THE VIRGIN ENTHRONED WITH CHILD by Quentin Metsys.
GEMALDEGALERIE, STAATLICHE MUSEEN, BERLIN-PREUSSISCHER KULTURBESIN

반면에, 그리스시대부터 그림 속에 산수배경이 들어 있었지만 서양에서 독립된 예술로서의 풍경화는 한정된 범위안에서 15세기 무렵에 발달했다. 예를 들면 프랑드르의 화가 쿠엔틴 메시의 The Virgin Enthroned with Child는 국한된 풍경 즉 창문의 광경을 보여준다. 좀더 진보된 단계가 제랄드 다비드의 Rest on the Flight into Egypt에서 눈에 띄는데 그 작품에서 그 처녀는 풍경과 조화를 이루고 있다. 이 종교적인 전통 속에서 풍경화는 종교적 주제를 위한 배경으로 사용되었다. 그러나 종교적 주제의 사용에 풍경화를 제약하던 것이 종교개혁 이후 풍경화는 당연히 하나의 장르가 되었다. 17세기 중에 클라우드 로랭의 작품들에 의하여 보여지듯 청정한 목가적 장면에서 이상적인 풍경화가 완성되었다. 19세기 중에 풍경화는 컨스터블의 자연주의적 관점, 터너의 환영적인 파노라마를 보여준다. 19세기 말에 인상주의 화풍아래서 풍경은 20세기를 위한 사실주의파와 추상파 회기들의 발원지로시 역할을 했다.

구성에서 풍경은 자연안에서 발견되는 외관, 힘, 분위기적 효과를 묘사한다. 예를 들어 미국 화가 피즈 휴 레인은 Owl's Head라는 작품속의 고요한 아침 뉴잉글랜드 해안에서 빛과 공간의 효과를 강조하였고 그 해안이 소유주에게 가지는 중요성을 상징적으로 나타냈다. 중국의 풍경화와는 달리 서양에서는 풍경이 그 소유주에게 종속되는 재산이거나 인간과 자연 사이의 상호의존적인 평등한 대상으로 역할을 했다. 이 전통에서 인간은 자연의 지배를 받는 것이 아니고 평등하고 독립된 동반자 관계다.

(a) Dependent vs. independent
(b) Peaceful vs. turbulent
(c) Humble vs. aggressive
(d) Harmonious vs. distracting
(e) Logical vs. illogical

(3) Another suitable word for *magnitude* of nature in the third paragraph can be _____. (Word context)

(a) Fragment
(b) Grandeur
(c) Speck
(d) Insignificance
(e) Paucity

(4) The author's style of presenting the passage is mainly based on the paragraphs of _____. (Rhetorical techniques)

(a) Analogy
(b) Description
(c) Analysis
(d) Definition
(e) Contrast

(5) Based on the implication of the passage, it can be concluded that the differences in painting between them is probably the result of the following hypothesis. (Drawing conclusions)

(a) "Culture & man are separate"
(b) "Man conditions culture"
(c) "Culture conditions man"
(d) "Man conquers nature"
(e) "Nature conquers man"

3.1.3. Music

Passage 1:

Music, like language, seems to be one of the original possessions of mankind. For its origin, scholars have had to search the dark times of prehistory, but still no one can explain its origin with clear evidences; it is still cloudy.

Since the 18th century, however, many hypotheses have been formulated as an attempt to answer the origin of music. Charles Darwin (1809-1882), English naturalist, claimed that music developed as a mode of courtship. This hypothesis does not *hold water* in the sense that the primitive people alive today very rarely sing for love. Karl Bucker, German social philosopher in his publication <u>Work and Rhythm</u> (1896) claimed that music must have originated among the craftsmen because the song could ease the heavy burden of the craftsmen's hard labor. This hypothesis has been seriously challenged because the "work songs" are a relatively rare phenomenon. Herbert Spencer (1820-1903), English philosopher, believed that music originated from the imitation of language. This hypothesis is

> **Note**
>
> ▫ **genre** = category, kind(esp. literary form e.g. poetry, drama, the novel.) : 장르
> ▫ **on the basis of** = on the foundation, standard of = based on : …을 토대로
> • On the basis of what these indicate, we can make a profit next year.
>   (이것들이 지시하는 것을 토대로 하면 내년에는 이윤을 낼 수 있겠다.)
> ▫ **shackle** = fetters, a band fastening around the wrist or ankle : 수쇄, 족쇄, 구속
> • the shackles of convention (인습이라는 속박)
> • It took quite a long time of struggle to knock off the shackles of social classes.
>   (사회계급이라는 족쇄를 떨쳐버리는 데에는 오랜기간의 투쟁이 필요했다.)
> ▫ **immerse** = put under the surface of water, involve deeply : 물에 담그다, 열중시키다
> • They are immersed in books during the vacation. (휴가 중 책에 몰두하고 있다.)
> ▫ **manifest** = show clearly : 현시하다, 발현하다, 명백히 보여주다
> • It is a manifestation of God's will. (그건 신의 뜻의 발로다.)
> ▫ **silhouette** = the shadow : 실루엣, 그림자, 영상
> ▫ **render** = translate, describe, depict : 표현, 묘사하다
> • A good actor renders a character to the life. (명배우는 인물을 실물같이 연기하다.)
> ▫ **enhance** = intensify, magnify, add to the value, price : 늘리다, 높이다, 강화하다
> • A little wild flower may enhance our life quality.
>   (보잘 것 없는 한송이 야생화가 우리 삶의 질을 높일 수 있다.)
> ▫ **diminish** = lessen, make or become less : 감소시키다, 줄이다
> • The Japanese Yen has diminished its value for the past few months.
>   (일본 엔화의 가치가 수개월간 떨어졌다.)
> ▫ **era** = period in history starting from an event : 기원 • Christian era (서력 기원)
> ▫ **enthrone** : 왕위에 앉히다
> ▫ **confine** = hold within limits = restrict : 감금시키다, 국한하다
> • Please confine your remarks to the subject we're debating. (말씀을 주제에 국한시켜…)
> ▫ **integrate** = combine into a whole : 통합하다

3.1.3. 음악

지문 1

음악은 언어와 마찬가지로 인류가 최초에 가졌던 것 중의 하나로 보인다. 음악의 근원에 대하여 학자들은 역사 이전의 암흑 시대를 탐색해 왔지만 그것의 근원을 명료하게 증거를 가지고 설명할 수 있는 사람은 아직 아무도 없다. 음악의 근원은 분명하지 않다.

그러나 18세기 이후 음악의 근원에 대한 대답을 찾으려는 시도로서 많은 가설들이 형성되어 왔다. 영국의 박물학자인 찰스 다윈은 음악은 구애의 한가지 양식으로 발달했다고 주장했다. 이 가설은 오늘날 살아있는 원시 민족들이 사랑을 얻기 위하여 노래를 부르는

plausible but there have been many people who have a rich language intonation with insignificant level of musical riches. Finally, Geza Revesz (1946) attempted to prove that the "unarticulated call" could be the common origin of both language and music. But he did not provide clear evidences for it. None of these hypotheses is quite convincing in terms of providing explanation and presenting evidences regarding the origin of music.

    The question of the origin of music may be closely associated with the question of language. However, it will probably never be possible to clear up the question definitely as to whether it was song or instrumental music that came first. It may be possible that the development of music differed from different people in different communities. All these questions need more intensive and extensive studies for a satisfactory answer.

(1) A proper title for the passage is _____. (Subject matter)

    (a) Music & language   (d) Origin of music
    (b) Development of music   (e) Hypotheses of music
    (c) History of music

(2) Whose hypothesis do you think offers the broadest perspective regarding the origin of music? (Locating the fact)

    (a) Charles Darwin   (d) Geza Revesz
    (b) Karl Bucker   (e) None of them
    (c) Herbert Spencer

(3) The italicized phrase, "*hold water*" in the second paragraph means that "it should be _____." (Phrase in contextual clue)

    (a) Wrong   (c) Offensive   (e) Probable
    (b) Agreeable   (d) Defensive

(4) The writer presented the passage based on the paragraph pattern of _____. (Rhetorical techniques)

    (a) Deductive analysis   (d) Analogy
    (b) Definition   (e) Inductive analysis
    (c) Contrast and comparison

(5) Based on the hypotheses presented, it can be concluded that the writer of the passage disagrees the least with _____'s hypothesis. (Drawing conclusions)

    (a) Charles Darwin   (d) Geza Revesz
    (b) Karl Bucker   (e) All of them
    (c) Herbert Spencer

일은 거의 없다는 의미에서 허점이 많다. 독일의 사회철학자인 칼 벅커는 그의 저서『노동과 리듬 (Work and Rhythm)』에서 음악은 틀림없이 장인들 사이에서 시작되었다고 주장했다. 왜냐하면 노래는 장인들의 중노동을 완화시킬 수 있었기 때문이란다. 이 가설도 심각하게 도전을 받았다. 왜냐하면 "노동요"는 비교적 드물기 때문이다. 영국의 철학자인 허버트 스펜서는 음악은 언어의 모방에서 기원했다고 믿었다. 이 가정은 그럴듯해 보이지만 음악적인 재능은 보잘 것 없는데 풍부한 언어 억양을 가진 사람들이 많다. 마지막으로 게자 레베스는 "불명확하게 외치는 소리"가 언어와 음악의 공통적인 기원임을 증명하려고 시도했으나 그것을 지지할 분명한 증거를 제시하지 못했다. 지금까지 어느 가설도 음악의 기원에 대하여 설명이나 증거를 제시해야한다는 관점에서 설득력이 없다.

   음악의 기원에 대한 의문은 언어에 대한 의문과 밀접하게 연관되어 있다. 그러나 먼저 생겨난 것이 노래인가 기악인가에 대하여 명확하게 의문을 씻어버리기는 십중 팔구 영원히 불가능할 것이다. 음악의 발달은 공동체마다 그곳에 사는 사람들마다 다르다는 것은 가능할 수 있다. 이 모든 의문들의 만족스런 해답을 찾기 위해서는 좀더 집중적이고 광범위한 연구가 필요하다.

Note

- evidence = proof, anything that gives reason for believing something : 증거
- cloudy = not clear. not transparent : 흐릿한, 불분명한
- courtship = 구혼, 구애 (courting)
- hypothesis = idea, suggestion put forward as a starting point for reasoning or explanation : 가설
- formulate = express clearly and exactly : 공식으로 나타내다
    - It's rather long. Let me formulate it in codes and numbers.
      (약간 길어 부호와 숫자로 공식화 해보겠습니다.)
- hold water = be exactly right : 물샐틈 없다, 완벽하다
    - His theory holds water. (그 사람의 이론은 물샐 틈 없이 완벽하다.)
- ease = make less severe : 완화시키다
    - I gave him some medicine to ease his pain. (약간의 진통제를 주었다.)
- imitate = copy the behavior, appearance, speech : 모방하다
    - His imitation of the president's speech is almost perfect. (대통령의 연설을 거의 완벽하게 흉내낸다.)
- plausible = seeming to be true or reasonable : 참말같은, 그럴듯한
    - a plausible excuse (그럴듯한 변명)
- intonation = the rise and fall of the pitch of the voice in speaking : 말의 억양
- unarticulate : 발음이 똑똑하지 못한, 분절이 없는
- regarding = with regard to : …에 관하여
- be associated with = be connected (joined) with : …과 연관(연상)되어 있다.
    - What do you associate with chrysanthemum? (국화하면 무엇이 생각나니?)

Passage 2 :

Anyone who loves classical music has heard of Johann Sebastian Bach (1685-1750), and George Frederick Handel (1685-1759). Both were born in Germany in the same year, were blind in old ages, and are often called the great "twins of music." But it is very interesting to know that their lives were different, their music was different, and they never met.

Bach, a great contributor of Baroque counterpoint, started his career as a virtuous organist and produced a lot of cantatas and organ music. During twenty seven years (1723-1750) as Cantor of Leipzig's St. Thomas Church, he composed over 300 cantatas including *St. Mattew Passion* and the *B Minor Mass*. He wrote a lot of music for teaching purposes including inventions and others, which, when mastered, could provide the performer with solid base for proceeding to more complex problems. However, Bach could not attract appeal from his listeners because his music was structured based on "inward-directed and didactic" instead of "outward-projecting and theatrical." But the growth of this reputation can be attributed to the last few generations of care in editing, teaching, and performing of his masterpieces by dedicated musicians, and the general rise of concert music. Bach is recognized by musicians as one of the greatest composers in the history of Western music.

Handel, unlike Bach, was already an accomplished composer when he journeyed to Italy in 1706. There he composed operas and oratorios. For *the liberetti of the oratories*, he often looked to the Scripture, and for his famous oratorio, Messiah (1741) he used a libretto assembled by one of his friends from the Scripture. The "Messiah" was a great success in London. All the nobility was present, even the royalty. During the "Hallelujah Chorus," the King, in his enthusiasm, rose to his feet, so the whole audience rose, and ever since that time it has been the custom for audiences to stand during the singing of the "Hallelujah Chorus." Simply put, Handel's music was more dramatically structured, and less dense in meticulous details and less ornate than that of Bach. His music being structured based on clarity of techniques, sense of occasion and dramatic timing, attracted an immediate appeal from his listeners. After his death, his life of choral writing dominated England and American church music for more than 150 years.

(1) An acceptable title for the passage would be _____. (Subject matter)

    (a) A comparison between Bach and Handel
    (b) A contrast between Bach and Handel
    (c) An analogy between Bach and Handel
    (d) A comparative study between Bach and Handel
    (e) A history of Bach and Handel

(2) Handel's music gave more immediate appeal and effect on the listeners than that of Bach. These factors could attribute to such results as _____. (Locating the fact)

지문 2

고전 음악을 사랑하는 사람이라면 누구나 요한 제바스티안 바흐와 프레드릭 헨델에 대하여 들어본 적이 있다. 두 사람 다 같은 해 독일에서 태어났고, 둘 다 노년기에 눈이 안보였고, 위대한 "음악의 쌍둥이"로 불린다. 그러나 그들의 생애가 달랐고, 음악이 달랐고, 둘이 생전에 한번도 만난적이 없다는 것을 알면 흥미롭다.

바로크 대위법의 위대한 공헌자인 바흐는 덕망이 높은 오르간 연주자로 음악 인생을 시작했고 많은 칸타타와 오르간을 위한 음악을 작곡했다. 20년 간의 라이프찌히 성 토마스 성당의 성가대 지휘자로서 '마태 수난곡'과 미사곡을 비롯하여 300여 곡의 칸타타를 작곡했다. 그는 환상적 즉흥곡들과 다른 곡들을 포함하여 많은 교습곡을 썼으며 이

JOHANN SEBASTIAN BACH, who summed up the music of the Boroque Era in his compositions, composed suites and concertos for orchestra, over 200 cantatas, large choral works, and chamber music. In his time his fame rested mainly on his gifts as an organist and on his keyboard compositions : the great organ fugues, the Well-Tempered Clavier, and the inventions (Two-part Invention No. 9 is shown in his handwriting).

들을 완전히 끝냈을 때는 연주자가 더욱 복잡하고 어려운 곡으로 발전하는 확고한 기반을 마련해 주었다. 그러나 바흐는 그의 청취자들로부터 매력은 끌지 못했다. 왜냐하면 그의 음악은 밖으로 분출하는 무대를 위한다기보다 내부지향적이며 교육적이었기 때문이었다. 그가 점점 명성을 얻게된 것은 지난 몇 세대의 헌신적인 음악인들이 그의 걸작품들을 편집하고 가르치고 연주하는 데 주의깊은 배려를 했고, 연주음악의 전반적인 평가상승의 탓으로 돌릴 수 있을 것이다. 바흐는 음악가들에 의하여 서양음악의 역사에서 가장 위대한 작곡가 중의 한사람으로 인정받고 있다.

헨델은 바흐와는 달리 1706년 이탈리아에 여행했을 때 이미 완성된 작곡가였다. 그곳에서 그는 오페라와 오라토리오를 작곡했다. 교회음악을 작곡하기 위하여 자주 성서에 의지했고 그의 유명한 오라토리오 메시아를 위하여 자기 친구가 싱서에서 모은 구절들을 가사로 사용했다. 메시아는 런던에서 크게 성공했다. 모든 귀족과 왕족까지 참석했다. '할렐루야 코러스' 중에 왕은 열정에 들떠 일어섰고 따라서 전체 청중들도 일어섰다. 그때 이후 '할렐루야 코러스'를 부르는 동안에는 청중들이 일어나는 것이 습관이 되었다.

GEORGE FREDERICK HANDEL German-born composer, achieved fame in England. In a period dominated by Italian musicians, Handel wrote popular operas in Italian, as well as instrumental works. Later, he composed oratorios in English, including his masterpiece The Messiah, which was given a commemorative performance in Westminster Abbey.

간단히 말하면 헨델의 음악은 바흐의 음악에 비하여 더 극적으로 구성되어 있고 세부적인 부분에서는 치밀도가 낮고 장식이 적었다. 그의 음악은 명료한 테크닉과 축제적 느

(a) Techniques, situation, timing
(b) Prestige, situation, timing
(c) Scripture, prestige, situation
(d) Scripture, techniques, timing
(e) Situation, prestige, Scripture

(3) The italicized *libretti of the oratorios* in the third paragraph refers to the _____. (Phrase in contextual clue)

(a) Words & songs for church
(b) Songs for religious purposes
(c) Songs for funeral service
(d) Songs for wedding ceremony
(e) Songs for coronation

(4) When Handel attempted to compose Messiah, he used the sources for libretti from the Scripture. The Scripture might have been _____. (Making inferences)

(a) The Old Testament
(b) The New Testament
(c) The Analects of Confucius
(d) The Doctrine of the Koran
(e) The Buddhist Scriptures

(5) The writer's position toward Bach and Handel can be concluded to be _____. (Conclusion)

(a) Critical
(b) Sarcastic
(c) Bitter
(d) Factual but amusing
(e) Adulatory

Passage 3 :

Marian Anderson (1897-1993) was born in Philadelphia and grew up in its "Negro quarter" in a single rented room with her parents and two sisters, but she overcame racial and economic boundaries to become a highly acclaimed contralto. Despite her *sporadic* musical education, Marian's unique sound and extraordinary range of voice continued to impress listeners by the time she became sixteen. Her neighbors collected money for her to study under Guisepe Boghetti, a well-known voice mentor. In 1925, she entered the talent auditions for the Lewisohn Stadium Concert of the City College of New York and won first place over 360 other competitors with her rendition of "*O mio Fernando*" from Donizetti's opera, *La Favorita*.

Racism prevented Marian from advancing her career in the United States. She went to Europe where the walls of segregation were not so difficult to overcome. She made her London debut in 1930 and won accolades from Toscanini. In 1933, she made her formal New York debut at Town Hall. Marian was scheduled to sing at Constitution Hall in Washington, D.C. in 1939. The hall owned by the Daughters of the American Revolution was not available for an Afro-American performer. Mrs. Eleanor Roosevelt resigned her membership in protest of the fact that colored people were not allowed to perform in the hall. The concert was instead held on Easter Sunday, April 9 on the steps of the Lincoln

낌과 극적인 박자를 기초로 구성되었기 때문에 청중으로부터 직접적인 매력을 얻었다. 그의 사후, 합창곡 작곡에서 그는 살아남아 150년 이상 영국과 미국의 교회음악을 지배했다.

> **Note**
>
> □ **oratorio** : 종교음악의 일종   □ **libretto** : 가극 가사   □ **cantata** : 서정적 성악곡
> □ **cantor** : 성가대 합창 지휘자   □ **counterpoint** : 대위법, 화성법
> □ **assemble = gather, collect** : 모으(이)다
>   • A large crowd assembled to hear his sermon on the Mount.
>   (많은 군중이 그의 산상수훈을 들으려고 모여들었다.)
> □ **enthusiasm = strong feeling of admiration or interest** : 열광, 열광적 찬미
>   I feel no enthusiasm to school life. (학교생활에 열의를 못가진다.)
> □ **dense = not easily seen through, crowded together in large numbers** : 빽빽한, 짙은
>   • dense fog : 짙은 안개   • dense forest : 밀림   • dense population : 조밀한 인구
> □ **meticulous = giving or showing attention to detail** : 지나치게 세심한, 꼼꼼한
> □ **ornate = richly ornamented, full of flowery language** : 화려하게 장식된, 미려체
> □ **inward - directed** : 내부 지향의   • opp. outward - projecting (외부로 튀어나가는)
> □ **didactic = instructive, meant to teach** : 교훈적인   • didactic poetry (교훈시)
> □ **attribute… to** : 의 탓으로 돌리다
>   • He attributes his good health to moderate exercise. (그는 자기의 건강은 적당한 운동 덕택이란다.)
> □ **adulatory** : 추종하는, 아첨하는

지문 3.

마리안 앤더슨은 필라델피아에서 태어났고 흑인 지역의 단칸 셋방에서 부모와 두 누이들과 함께 자랐다. 그러나 그녀는 인종적, 경제적 한계를 극복하여 대단한 환호를 받는 콘트랄토가 되었다. 산발적인 음악 교육에도 불구하고 마리안의 독특한 음성과 뛰어난 음역 때문에 그녀가 16세가 될 무렵까지 청중들에게 계속하여 감명을 주었다. 그녀의 이웃사람들이 그녀가 유명한 성악 개인 교사 주세페 보게티의 지도아래 공부하도록 성금을 거두었다. 1925년에 뉴욕 시립대학의 Lewisohn Stadium콘서트에 출연할 탤런트 오디션에 도니제티의 오페라 파보리타의 O mio Fernando를 자신의 해석으로 노래 불러 360여명의 경쟁자들을 물리치고 최고상을 차지했다.

인종차별은 그녀가 미국에서 음악인생을 발전시키는 것을 방해했다. 그녀는 인종차별이 그리 심하지 않

Memorial before a throng of 75,000. After she sang America, the words of "*O mio Fernando*" filled the Washington area.

In 1955, a major wall of segregation fell in the operatic world. Marian became the first Afro-American to sing at the Metropolitan Opera in New York. She sang the role of Ulrica in Verdi's *Un Ballo in Maschera*. In her musical way, she embodied the words, "*We Shall Overcome!*" as a gift to all world citizens. In 1961, she returned to Washington D.C. to sing the national anthem at President John F. Kennedy's inauguration. Two years later, she encountered President Kennedy again when he bestowed upon her the Presidential Medal of Freedom.

Marian spent her retirement on a 155-acre farm in Danbury, Connecticut until she moved in with her nephew, James DePriest, in 1992. She died there on April 8, 1993 at the age of 96.

(1) A suitable title of the passage would be _____. (Subject matter)

   (a) How Marian lived
   (b) Marian's professional career
   (c) Marian's fight for equal rights
   (d) The first Afro-American to sing at the Metropolitan Opera
   (e) Marian Anderson: a life in song

(2) Which factor contributed the most to Marian to become an acclaimed contralto? It is her _____. (Locating the fact)

   (a) Consistent effort   (d) Friendship with Mrs. Roosevelt
   (b) Parents   (e) Unique sound & special range of voice
   (c) Neighbors

(3) The italicized word, *sporadic*, in the first paragraph must mean _____. (Word in context)

   (a) Infrequent   (b) Clustered   (c) Continual   (d) Concentrated   (e) Intensive

(4) It can be inferred that Marian's songs must have contributed to downing the barrier of _____. (Making inferences)

   (a) Nationalism   (c) Racism   (e) Communism
   (b) Fascism   (d) Imperialism

(5) It can be concluded that Marian's songs served as a step toward reaching the _____. (Drawing conclusions)

   (a) World peace
   (b) Social order in the U.S.
   (c) Society where equal rights are protected
   (d) Classless society
   (e) Society where the freedom of religion is guaranteed

은 유럽으로 갔다. 1930년에 런던에서 데뷔했고 토스카니니로부터 표창을 받았으며, 1933년 뉴욕 타운 홀에서 공식적으로 데뷔했다. 그녀는 1939년에 워싱턴 D.C.의 Constitution Hall에서 노래하기로 일정이 잡혀 있었다. The Daughters of the American Revolution의 소유인 그 홀은 아프리카계 미국인 연예인에게는 사용이 허락되지 않았다. 에리너 루즈벨트 대통령 부인은 유색인이 그 홀에서 공연이 허락되지 않는다는 사실에 항의하여 회원신분에서 사임했다. 그 대신 그 연주회는 링컨 기념관 계단에서 75,000명의 대중 앞에서 4월 9일 부활절에 개최되었다. 그녀가 America를 부르고 난 뒤 O mio Fernando라는 가사가 워싱턴 지역을 꽉 채웠다.

1955년 인종차별의 커다란 장벽은 오페라계에서 무너졌다. 마리안은 뉴욕의 메트로폴리탄 오페라에서 노래를 부른 최초의 아프리카계 미국인이 되었다. 그녀는 베르디의 '가면속의 아리아'에서 울리카 역을 노래했다. 그녀는 음악 인생에서, "우리는 승리하리라"라는 오페라곡처럼 세계시민 앞에서 그 의미를 구현했다. 1961년에 워싱턴 D.C.에 돌아와 케네디 대통령의 취임식에서 국가를 불렀다. 2년 후 케네디 대통령을 다시 만났을 때 그는 그녀에게 자유의 대통령 메달을 수여했다.

마리안은 은퇴생활을 코네티컷 주 댄버리에 있는 155에이커의 농장에서 보내다 1992년 조카 제임스 집에 이사하여 함께 살았다. 그녀는 1993년 4월 8일 96세의 나이로 그곳에서 세상을 떠났다.

Note

- □ overcome = fight successfully against, defeat : 극복하다
  - The most tenacious enemy to overcome is yourself. (극복해야할 가장 끈질긴 적은 바로 자신이다.)
- □ quarter = a part of a town, often one where a certain type of person lives : 지역
- □ the residential quarter : 주거지구   □ the manufacturing quarter : 공장지구
- □ acclaim = welcome with shouts of approval, applaud loudly : 갈채, 환호하다
  - The newspapers acclaimed her as the queen of the world golf.
    (신문들은 그녀를 세계 골프의 여왕으로 갈채를 보냈다.)
- □ contralto : 소프라노와 앨토 중간의 여성 최저음
- □ sporadic = occurring only occasionally : 산발적인, 간헐적인
  - sporadic raids : 산발적인 공격   • sporadic firing : 간헐적인 사격
- □ unique = having no like, being the only one of its sort : 특유의, 하나밖에 없는
  - Be unique rather than the best. (최고가 되지 말고 독특하여라.)
- □ mentor = a wise and trusted adviser
- □ audition : 음악가, 배우 등의 성량, 연기 심사
- □ rendition = translation, interpretation : 해설, 해석
  - His rendition of the piece was excellent. (그의 작품 해석력은 뛰어났다.)
- □ segregation = putting apart from the rest, isolate : 격리, 차별
- □ accolade : 기사 수여식 – 영예, 표창
  - The awards are considered the finest accolade a scientist can win.
    (그 상은 과학자가 받을 수 있는 최고의 영예다.)
- □ embody = give form to ideas, feelings : 구체화하다
  - They tried to embody their ideal. (이상을 구체화하려고 노력했다.)
- □ bestow = give as an offering : 거저주다, 하사하다
  - I sincerely thank you for the favors you've bestowed on me. (베풀어 주신 호의에 감사드립니다.)

3-2 POPULAR CULTURE

"Popular culture" is too broad to be defined; yet we can narrow its scope for a definition as "a variety of popular social performances including arts, habits, behaviors, and concepts of a given people in a given period for the people at large, as popular music." Students whether they are at college or at high school, as a certain group of given people in a given period, have and share their own interest, behaviors, concepts, and attitudes built based on "popular culture" with their peers. This sharing of interest, concepts, and arts related to the popular culture is inseparable from the students, since they are also "culture conditioned social beings" as we are.

This section, "Popular culture" includes twelve passages related to the sub-sections: (1) Celebrity; (2) Fashion; (3) Film; and, (4) Sports, allocating three passages for each sub-section. Most passages are constructed to be highly instructive, memorable, and entertaining.

3.2.1. Celebrity

Passage 1 :

Situation : On May 15, 1998, Frank Sinatra, a legend of popular music and film actor, passed away peacefully at the age of 82. Many people around the world have expressed their sincere condolences and remarks for him. Some remarks are provided below.

Frank Sinatra (1915-1998): A man to be remembered in many ways.

"Frank Sinatra was a true original. He had the patent, the original blueprint on singing the popular songs, a man who would have thousands of imitators but who, himself, would never be influenced by a single, solitary person." (Mel Torme, Singer)

"Frank Sinatra is an American musical treasure. He has been the voice of popular music for more than half a century, and his recorded legacy is in a cornerstone of American culture." (Thomas D. Mottola, President of Sony

3.2 대중문화

"대중문화"란 너무 광범위하여 정의하기 불가능하다. 그러나 정의를 위해서 "대중 음악처럼, 특정기간에 특정인이 갖고 있는 기술, 습관, 행동, 생각들을 내포하는 대중, 사회적인 공연행위의 다양성"으로 그 범위를 좁힐 수 있다. 학생들은 그들이 대학생이건 고등학생이건, 주어진 시대의 한 집단으로서 동료들과 함께 "대중문화" 위에 이룩된 자기 자신들의 흥미, 생각, 예술을 공유한다. 이것은 학생들과 불가분의 관계에 있는데, 학생들 역시 "문화에 의하여 조건화된 사회적 존재"이기 때문이다.

이번 절 "대중문화"는 다음의 작은 절, (1)유명인사, (2)유행, (3)영화, (4)스포츠 등에 세개씩 지문을 배당하여 12개의 글로 구성됐다. 대부분의 글들은 매우 교육적이며 기억할 만한 가치가 있고 흥미있다.

> **Note**
> □ peer = equal in rank, merit or quality : 동류, 동배, 같은 수준의 사람들
>   • It will not be easy to find his peer. (그를 상대할 만한 사람 찾기 쉽지 않을 것이다.)
> □ inseparable = that can't be separated : 불가분의

3.2.1. 저명인사

지문 1

장면 : 1998년 5월 15일, 팝 음악의 전설적 인물이자 영화배우인 프랭크 시나트라는 82세의 나이로 평화롭게 눈을 감았다. 전세계의 많은 사람들이 심심한 조의와 그를 기리는 논평을 냈다. 그중 몇 편을 아래 싣는다.

A Sinatra tribute
was put together Friday night in Ernest Foundas' Queen Village apartment.

Music Entertainment)

"I think every American would have to smile and say he really did do it his way." (President Clinton)

"There were certainly his talent, his charisma, and his voice-- which set the rhythm for, accompanied and made a whole era dream. But there was his warm and enthusiastic personality." (Jacques Chirac, President of France)

"Our father and grandfather was a man of dreams, man of passion, strength, loyalty and gentleness. His lessons and love were *the only constant* in an ever-changing world. He is and always will be the center of our universe. We offer our condolences to you as you offer yours to us." (Sinatra's children Nancy, Frank, and Tina, and grandchildren A.J., Amanda and Michael in a joint statement)

(Source: Adapted and quoted from The Philadelphia Inquirer, May 17, 1998)

(1) A proper title for the remarks expressed by several people would be _____. (Subject matter)

    (a) Frank Sinatra's life
    (b) Frank, the voice of popular music
    (c) Frank, a man of dreams, passion, strength
    (d) A remembrance of Frank Sinatra
    (e) Frank's contribution to music & film

(2) Who remarked Frank's ingenuity and uniqueness of his singing as his merit? (Locating the fact)

    (a) Thomas D. Mottola   (c) Frank's children   (e) President Chirac
    (b) Mel Torme   (d) President Clinton

(3) The italicized phrase, *the only constant* in the last paragraph, can be substituted as _____. (Phrase in the contextual clue)

    (a) "Never changed"   (d) "Never unpredictable"
    (b) "Never stabilized"   (e) "Never capricious"
    (c) "Never always there"

(4) The tone of President Clinton toward the public at the time of Frank Sinatra's death seems to be _____. (Tone & attitude)

    (a) Grievious (b) Inspiring (c) Didactic (d) Bitter (e) Solemn

(5) Based on the remarks given and other contemporary sociocultural factors, it can be concluded that the sorrow of Frank's death was shared the most by an age group of _____. (Drawing conclusions)

    (a) Teens (b) Twenties (c) Thirties (d) Forties (e) Over fifty

프랭크 시나트라(1915~1998) : 여러가지로 기억될 사람.

"진정으로 독창적이었다. 팝송을 부르는데 특허권과 창조적 청사진을 가진 사람. 수천명의 사람들이 그를 모방하려 했지만 자신은 단 한사람의 영향도 받지 않으려던 사람이었다."

"미국이 낳은 음악 재산이다. 그는 반세기 넘게 대중음악의 소리가 되어 왔으며, 그가 남긴 음악적 유산은 미국문화의 주춧돌이다."

"미국인은 누구나 그가 삶을 진정 자기 방식대로 살았다고 웃으며 말하지 않을 수 없을 것이다."

"그에게는 분명히 한시대 전체의 꿈을 만들고, 리듬을 붙이고, 반주를 하는 재능과 카리스마와 목소리가 있었다. 그러나 또한 그의 따뜻하고 열정적인 인간미가 있었다."

Sinatra and Ava Gardner's 1951 wedding was in Philadelphia's West Mount Airy section

"우리 아버지와 할아버지는 꿈과 정열과 힘과 성실성, 그리고 온화함을 가진 분이었습니다. 그분의 교훈과 사랑은 항상 변하는 세상속에서 유일하게 변치않는 것이었습니다. 그분은 지금도, 앞으로도, 언제나 우리 세계의 중심에 계실 거예요. 여러분들이 우리에게 조의를 보내주신 것처럼 우리도 여러분에게 위로를 드립니다."

Note

- **celebrity** = fame, renown : 명성, 명사 • a man of celebrity (저명인사)
- **legend** = a famous person in a particular area of activity : 신화적 인물
- **pass away** (of a person) = die : 돌아가시다(죽다의 완곡 어법)
  • She passed away in her sleep. (주무시다 돌아가셨다.)
- **condolence** = an expression of sympathy for someone who has experienced great sorrow, misfortune (조위, 애도의 말)
  • Please accept my condolences on your mother's death. (어머님의 별세에 조의를 표합니다.)
- **legacy** = money received by a person under the will of end at the death : 유산
- **cornerstone** : 주춧돌   □ **charisma** : 신에게 부여받은 재능, 권위, 신복

Passage 2 :

John Fitzgerald Kennedy (1917 - 1963): The Man Who Lives Long With Us

The place : Dallas, Texas. The date : November 22, 1963. A parade was winding through the streets of Dallas, and Kennedy rode in an open car. A shot rang out, the President was hit, and rushed to a hospital. People all over the United States waited by their radios and televisions with serious concerns. But, the news from them made the waiting people unbelievable, disappointed, and grievous.

After beating Richard Nixon in the 1960 election, John Kennedy was sworn in as the 35th President on January 20, 1961. In his inaugural speech, he asked Americans to help him solve the country's problems, *"Ask not what your country can do for you. Ask what you can do for your country."*

Kennedy's presidency was less than three years, but his achievements during that short period were unforgettable. His major achievements included (1) Asking Congress for a strong *Civil Rights for equal opportunities*; (2) Starting the Peace Corps. for people in developing countries; (3) Setting a goal of landing an American on the moon before 1970; (4) Fighting for medical care for the aged and all; and, (5) Signing a nuclear test ban treaty with the U.S.S.R. and other countries.

(1) A proper title for the above passage would be . (Subject matter)

   (a) The assassination of J.F.K.   (d) J.F.K. defeated Nixon
   (b) J.F.K.'s achievements   (e) J.F.K.'s life
   (c) A remembrance of J.F.K.

   J.F.K. is the abbreviation of John F. Kennedy

(2) America's major social problems during the J.F.K. administration are _____. (Locating the facts)

   (a) Nuclear test & treaty
   (b) Civil Rights & medical care
   (c) The Peace Corps. & foreign aids
   (d) Conflicts with U.S.S.R. & Cuba
   (e) Landing on the moon & space race with U.S.S.R.

지문 2

John F. Kennedy(1917~1963) : 우리와 함께 오래 살아있는 사람

Inauguration Day

장소는 텍사스주 달라스. 때는 63년11월22일. 하나의 행렬이 달라스 거리 사이를 구불 구불 나아가고 있었고 케네디는 무개차에 타고 있었다. 한 방의 총소리가 울려 퍼졌고 케네디가 총격 당했다. 그리고 급히 병원으로 실려갔다. 모든 미국인들은 라디오와 텔레비전 가까이에서 깊은 우려를 하며 방송을 기다렸다. 그러나 라디오나 TV에서 들려 온 뉴스는 기다리던 사람들의 귀를 의심하게 했고, 실망시켰고, 슬픔에 빠뜨렸다.

1960년 선거에서 닉슨을 이긴 후 1961년 1월 20일 35대 대통령으로 취임했다. 그는 취임사에서 국민들에게 국가의 문제들을 해결하는 데 도와줄 것을 부탁했다.

"나라가 당신을 위해서 무엇을 할 수 있는가를 묻지 말고 당신이 나라를 위해서 무엇을 할 수 있는지 물어보시오."

케네디의 대통령직 수행은 3년이 못됐지만 그 짧은 기간 중 그의 업적들은 잊을 수 없는 것이다. 주요한 그의 업적에는 (1)의회에 평등한 기회를 보장하는 강력한 공민권 요청 (2)개발도상국가들의 국민을 위한 평화봉사단의 발족 (3)1970년 이전 달에 미국인을 착륙시키려는 목표 설정 (4)노인과 빈민들의 의료를 위한 투쟁 (5)소련 및 다른 국가들과 핵실험 방지 조약 체결.

Note

- **grievous = sorrowful, doleful** : 비탄에 빠진
  - The plane crash resulted in a grievous loss of lives.
    (그 비행기 추락은 처참한 인명 손실을 낳았다.)
- **presidency = the office of president** : 대통령직
  - Roosebelt was elected 4 times to the presidency of the U.S
- **achievement = something finished or gained through skill and hard work** : 성취, 업적
  - A man's value ought to be judged not by his appearance but by his achievements.
    (한 사람의 가치는 그의 외모가 아니라 그의 성취로 판단되어야 한다.)
- **Civil Rights** : 시민권 : 인종, 피부색, 성별에 상관없이 모든 시민들에게 평등한 권리
- **nuclear** : 핵의, 원자력의
  - nuclear reactor (원자로)   • nuclear power station (핵발전소)   • nuclear fusion (핵융합)
- **ban = forbid by law** : 금지
  - There's ban on smoking in this building.(건물내 흡연금지)
- **treaty = a formal agreement** : 조약
  - NATO(The North Atlantic Treaty Organization)

(3) The italicized phrase, "*Civil Rights for equal opportunities*" in the last paragraph refers to the regulation that all Americans should have the equal rights _____. (Phrase meaning in context)

   (a) To vote
   (b) To get social rights regardless of race & sex
   (c) To go to school
   (d) To choose their jobs
   (e) To pursue their happiness regardless of social classes

(4) Rhetorical techniques, and Tone & attitude

(A) "The place? Dallas, Texas. The date? November 22, 1963" is a way of arranging words for _____.

   (a) Informative purpose   (d) Heightened tone for attention getting
   (b) Getting accurate facts   (e) Making a eulogy
   (c) Persuasive purpose

(B) The tone of the first paragraph is _____.

   (a) Excitement & anger   (c) Shock & wonder   (e) Hope & relief
   (b) Shock & despair   (d) Thrill & suspense

(C) The italicized, "*Ask not what your country can do for you Ask what you can do for your country*" is a/an

   (a) Parallelism   (c) Bandwagon appeal   (e) False dichotomy
   (b) Repetition   (d) Antithesis

(5) Based on the facts given in the passage, what do you conclude the most important factors that contributed J.F.K. to be unforgettable? (Conclusion)

   (a) His untimely death & the Peace Corps.
   (b) A nuclear test ban & medical care
   (c) Medical care & Civil Rights
   (d) Civil Rights & landing on the moon
   (e) His achievements & untimely death

Selected proverbs for the study of cross-cultural expressions

영어 격언과 한문 격언과의 만남 (5)

1. Pudding rather than praise.
   The belly carries the legs. 食後金剛山(식후금강산) – 금강산도 식후경이다.
   · The army marches on its stomachs.

2. The pupil will outshine his teachers.
   靑出於藍 靑於藍, 氷水爲之 寒於水(청출어람 청어람, 빙수위지 한어수)
   – 쪽에서 나온 푸른 물감이 쪽보다 더 푸르고, 물이 얼음이 되지만 물보다 더 차다.

3. One must be a servant before one can be a master.
   登高自卑(등고자비) ; 自 = from, 卑 = humble) – 높은 곳에 오르려면 낮은 곳에서 시작한다.

4. True gold does not fear fire. 眞金不怕火(진금불파화 ; 怕 = fear) – 진짜 금은 불을 두려워 하지 않는다.

5. The early bird gets the worms. 健足先登(첩족선등 ; 健 = agile) – 발 빠른 자가 먼저 오른다.

6. Do your utmost. Make every effort. 竭盡所能(갈진소능) – 최선을 다하여라.

7. Those who know much talk little. 知者不言 言者不知(지자불언 언자부지)
   – 지자는 말이 없고 말 하는 자는 아는 게 없다.

8. A drop in the bucket. 九牛一毛(구우일모) – 많은 것 가운데 아주 적은 것.

9. There is not enough to feed all. 粥小僧多(죽소승다 ; 粥 = porridge) – 죽은 적은데 중은 많다.

10. The latecomer gets to the top. 後來居上(후래거상) – 뒤에 온 사가 윗 자리에 앉는다.

11. Teaching of others teaches the teacher. 敎學相張(교학상장) – 가르치는 것이 배움을 키운다.

12. A tiny fish pollutes the whole streams of water. 一魚濁水(일어탁수) – 미꾸라지 한마리가 물을 흐린다.

13. Few words to the wise suffice. 聞一知十(문일지십) – 하나를 들으면 열을 깨친다.
    · A word to a wise man is enough.

14. A good medicine tastes bitter. 良藥苦於口 忠言逆於耳(양약고어구 충언역어이)
    – 좋은 약은 입에 쓰고 좋은 말은 귀에 거슬린다.

15. Virtue disarms opposition. 仁者無敵(인자무적) – 어진 사람은 적이 없다.
    · The benevolent know no enemy.

16. A man of virtue never worries. 仁者不憂(인자불우) – 어진 사람은 걱정이 없다.

Passage 3 :

Arnold Schwarzenegger (July 30, 1947 -), A man who got his dreams the right way.

Arnold Schwarzenegger is one of the most popular movie stars, and many people all over the world know his face. His multimillion dollar salaries are the highest ever paid to an actor, and his movies are the biggest, most expensive, special-effects action vehicles ever produced. Not only does Arnold have a successful acting career, but also he is a great businessman. He owns a multimillion dollar business in real estate and fitness enterprises. He has authored several best selling books, and produced several top selling fitness videos. Arnold has become a man who can change everything he wants into gold just by his touch.

At the same time, Arnold enjoys his social activities. He, as Chairman of the President's Council for Physical Fitness, develops strategies to get America's youths into shape. His marriage to Maria Shriver Kennedy, a well-known national news correspondent at the National Broadcasting Company (N.B.C.), enhanced his social position. Indeed, he has achieved his long desired dreams in America.

But, Arnold has paid a very high price for reaching his dreams. He was born to a poor family in Graz, Austria, with his father as a policeman and his mother a housewife. They could not afford enough food and clothes for their children. The family being poor, Arnold could not go to secondary school. He found another way to succeed in life. It was bodybuilding he thought of. At the age of 15, he began exercises for bodybuilding with a strong determination. As a result, his determination paid off; he won the Mr. Europe Jr. and Mr. Universe titles. For these successes, he spent from 6 to 8 hours per day for bodybuilding; to him the exercises for bodybuilding meant his total life. For inspiration, he put a picture of former Mr. Universe, Reg Park, on his wall. He had a clear vision of the importance of bodybuilding, and he spent several hours everyday for running, exercising, and lifting weights in the gym, sculpting his body as an artist does with clay. At last, the long years of dedication paid off as he started to get local recognition, and soon he became known throughout Europe as one of the rising young bodybuilding stars.

After winning the distinction in Europe, he came to the United States in 1968 at the invitation of muscle entrepreneur, Joe Weider. In America, he continued his dominance in bodybuilding by winning Mr. Universe five times, and Mr. Olympia seven times. But he understood the limitation of a bodybuilder, and he thought of achieving his success from a different angle. It was the movie industry for which he had to market himself through his physical attributes. He went on to star as a leading muscle bound hero in films as shown in, *Conan the*

지문 3

아놀드 슈왈츠네거 – 자기에게 어울리는 방법으로 꿈을 이룩한 사람

아놀드 슈왈츠네거는 가장 인기있는 영화 스타중의 한사람이며 세계적으로 그의 얼굴을 모르는 사람은 하나도 없다. 그가 받는 수백만 달러의 출연료는 어느 배우도 지금까지 받아본 적이 없는 최고 액수이며, 그의 영화는 지금까지 제작된 것들 중에 가장 규모가 크고 가장 비싸며, 빨리 번 돈을 실어다 주는 특수효과를 가진 차량이다. 아놀드는 성공적인 연기인생을 살 뿐아니라 위대한 사  업가다. 그는 부동산과 건강사업에서 수백만 달러의 사업을 한다. 서너 개의 베스트셀러 책을 집필했고 최고의 판매고를 가진 건강비디오를 제작했다. 아놀드는 그가 원하는 대로 손만 대면 모든 것을 황금으로 바꿀 수 있는 사람이 되었다.

동시에 그는 사회활동을 즐겨한다. 그는 President's Council of Physical Fitness의 의장으로서 미국의 젊은이들을 건강한 몸으로 만들 전략을 개발한다. NBC의 유명한 국내 뉴스특파원인 마리아 쉬리버 케네디와의 결혼은 그의 사회적 지위를 높여주었다.

실로 그는 미국에서 그의 오랜 꿈을 성취했다.

그러나 그가 꿈에 도달하는데는 비싼 대가를 지불해 왔다. 오스트리아 그래즈에서 경찰관인 아버지와 가정주부인 어머니를 가진 가난한 가정에서 태어났다. 부모는 자녀에게 충분한 음식과 의복을 대줄 여유가 없었다. 가정이 가난했기에 아놀드는 중등학교에 다니지 못했다. 그는 출세할 다른 길을 찾았다. 그가 생각한 것은 보디 빌딩이었다. 15세 때 굳은 결심으로 몸만들기를 위한 운동을 시작했다. 결과적으로 그 결심은 성공했다. 그는 미스터 유럽 주니어와 미스터 유니버스 타이틀을 땄다. 이 성공을 위해서 보디빌딩을 위한 운동으로 하루 6~8시간을 소비했다. 그에게

Arnold: first row, 2nd from left

Barbarian, *Conan the Destroyer*, and the blockbuster thrillers, *The Terminator*, *Total Recall*, *Terminator 2*: *Judgment Day*.

As we have seen, Arnold has achieved his dreams using bodybuilding as his first step, film acting, his multimillion dollar business and his social enhancement as the next steps. All have contributed to achieving his American dreams. But, we should not forget his long years of pain and hard work pursued with *relentless* determination before we think of his success.

(1) The main idea of the passage would be _____. (Main idea)

    (a) How Arnold got his dreams
    (b) How Arnold acted in films
    (c) How Arnold became an actor
    (d) How Arnold became a businessman
    (e) How Arnold enjoys his social life

(2) How many times did Arnold earn the title of Mr. Universe? (Locating the fact)

    (a) 3   (b) 4   (c) 5   (d) 6   (e) 7

(3) The italicized *relentless* in the last paragraph means _____. (Word in context)

    (a) Flexible   (d) Lenient
    (b) Rigorous   (e) Merciful
    (c) Compassionate

(4) At the age of 21, Arnold came to America from Europe. It can be inferred that he must have had language difficulty or adjustment especially in terms of _____. (Making inferences)

    (a) Grammatical rule   (d) Semantics
    (b) Morphological rule   (e) Rhetoric
    (c) Pronunciation

(5) Based on the information given, it can be concluded that the story of Arnold is very similar to one of the following proverbs. (Conclusion)

    (a) Old foxes want no tutors
    (b) No pain, no gain
    (c) A golden key opens every lock
    (d) A useless life is an early death
    (e) Life is in labor

보디빌딩을 위한 운동은 그의 생활 전체였다. 내적 자극을 얻기 위해서 전 미스터 유니버스 레그 펄의 사진을 벽에 붙였다. 그는 보디빌딩의 앞날에 대한 전망을 확실하게 가지고 있었으며 매일 서너시간씩 달리기, 운동, 체육관에서 중량운동으로, 마치 화가가 찰흙으로 물체를 조각하듯 몸을 조각했다. 마침내 오랜 세월의 전념은 그가 지역에서 인정을 얻음에 따라 대가를 지불해 주었고 곧 떠오르는 젊은 보디빌딩 스타로서 유럽 전역에 알려졌다.

유럽에서 명성을 얻은 후 1968년에 보디빌더 사업가인 조 웨이더의 초청으로 미국에 왔다. 미국에서 미스터 유니버스를 5차례, 미스터 올림피아 7차례를 차지하며 우위를 유지했다. 그러나 보디빌더의 한계점을 이해하고 다른 각도에서 성공을 이룩할 생각을 했다. 그는 '터미네이터' 등 다음과 같은 영화들에서 보여주듯이 근육으로 뭉쳐진 중요한 스타로 발전했다.

지금까지 우리가 본 바와 같이 아놀드는 첫단계로 보디빌딩을 이용하고 다음 단계로 수백만 달러의 사업과 사회적 신분상승으로 꿈을 이루었다. 모든 것이 그의 아메리칸 드림을 성취하는 데 기여했다. 그러나 우리는 그의 성공을 생각하기 전에 가차없는 결심으로 추구했던 긴 세월의 고통과 힘든 노력을 잊어서는 안된다.

Note

□ **real estate** = immovable estate consisting of land, building : 부동산 • personal estate (동산)
□ **fitness** = the state of being physically fit, good health : 건강, 쾌적함
□ **strategy** = the art of planning operation in war : 전략
□ **get someone into shape** : 건강한 몸으로 만들다   □ **news correspondent** : 뉴스 특파원
□ **pay off** = pay the whole of a debt, to be successful : 빚을 청산하다, 수지맞다, 성공하다
  • Our plan certainly paid off. (우리계획이 분명히 성공했다.)
□ **inspiration** = an urge to produce good and beautiful things : 영감, 내적 고취
  • Many poets and artists have drawn their inspiration from nature.
    (많은 시인, 예술가들이 자연에서 영감을 얻는다.)
□ **recognition** : 인정, 치하, 감사
  • Please accept this gift in recognition of all your help. (모든 도움에 대한 감사의 표시로 이 선물을 드립니다.)
□ **distinction** = the quality of being superior, excellent : 탁월, 비범
  • He is a columnist of distinction. (뛰어난 특약 기고자다.)
□ **attributes** = quality looked upon as naturally or necessarily belonging to : 본래의 속성
  • Politeness is an attribute of a gentleman. (예절은 신사의 속성이다.)
□ **entrepreneur** = a person who owns and runs a business : 사업가
□ **blockbuster** : 대중을 겨냥해서 만든 대작영화   □ **terminator** : 끝내주는 사람, 해결사
□ **relentless** = without pity : 무자비한, 잔혹한, 가차없는
  • He was relentless about himself. (자기 자신에게 가혹했다. 용서하지 않았다.)
□ **morphology** : (언어학)형태론, 어형론
□ **Old foxes want no tutors.** : 늙은 여우는 모르는 게 없다.
□ **A golden key opens every lock.** : 황금열쇠는 모든 자물쇠를 연다(돈이면 안되는 일이 없다).
□ **A useless life is an early death.** : 쓸모없는 인생은 요절과 같다.
□ **Life is in labor.** : 삶은 힘써 일하는데 있다.   □ **No pains, no gains** : 수고없이 소득 없다.

3.2.2. Fashion

Passage 1 :

Clothing is a general term for a variety of coverings designed to protect or adorn the human body. It may be made of woven materials or man-made fiber of animal skin or fur or even a type of paper known as "bark-cloth." To be specific, "clothing" is distinguished from "fashion," or "vogue," which signifies the prevailing mode or customary style of clothing. In present concept, "clothing" *connotes* the durable and substantial; "fashion," the novel and transitory. For example, a mother buys winter clothing for her children, and it is clear that in this context she would regard style as a secondary consideration. Her primary concern centers, rather than on fashion, on such matters as warmth of fabric, wearing qualities, ease of upkeep, and, most probably, a reasonable cost, all of which are attributes relevant to the purchase of winter clothing.

On the other hand, fashion reflects the events, surroundings, and customs of its era. It is influenced by laws, arts, culture, and personalities. For examples, laws and regulations have had their effect on fashion as seen in early New England laws that restricted women from wearing more costly clothes than their husbands could afford. Events in the arts have influenced the effect on fashion as exemplified in the tremendously successful musical comedy "My Fair Lady (1956)," based on George Bernard Shaw's Pygmalion, which inspired feminine adaptations of 1914-1918 costumes. Culture has powerfully conditioned fashion. The splendor of the Renaissance brought the magnificence of the merchant princes in their silks, satins, velvets, and jewels. In the fabulous, extravagant courts of Louis XIV, XV, and XVI of France, headdresses soared and skirts ballooned. Personalities have had great impact on fashion ever since the days when sumptuary laws differentiating nobles, farmers, and tradesmen were eliminated and when it became possible for all classes of society to dress more or less alike. In 1960-61, the "Jackie Kennedy look," a tribute to the beauty and style of the young wife of President Kennedy, spread so far and fast within weeks after the election that every fashion sketch in the newspapers looked like her.

The Gibson Girl, a truly "American look" in fashion, freed women from confining clothes by shirtwaists and flared skirts.

Generally speaking, changes in fashion occur

3.2.2. 패션

지문 1:

의복이란 인체를 보호하거나 장식하기 위하여 고안된 여러 종류의 감싸는 것을 총칭하는 용어다. 그것은 직조물이나 혹은 사람이 짐승 가죽이나 모피로 만든 섬유, 혹은 수피(樹皮)천으로 알려진 한 형태의 종이로 만들어 질 수 있다. 구체적으로 말하면 의복은 널리 유행하는 양식이나 풍속적 의복 형태를 의미하는 패션 또는 유행과는 구별된다.

현대적 개념에서 "의복"은 오래가고 실질적 가치가 있는 것을 의미하고, "패션"은 새롭고 일시적인 것을 말한다. 예를 들면 어떤 어머니가 자식들을 위해서 겨울 옷을 산다면 스타일은 2차적인 고려사항으로 간주할 것이다. 패션보다는 섬유의 따뜻함, 착용상의 성질, 보관상의 용이함, 그리고 십중 팔구 적당한 가격에 그녀의 1차적인 관심이 모아질 것이다. 이 모든 것들이 겨울 옷을 사는 일과 관련된 속성들이다.

반대로 패션은 행사, 주변의 일들, 그리고 그 시대의 풍습을 반영한다. 그것은 법, 예술, 문화 그리고 인품의 영향을 받는다. 예를 들어 법과 규제는 옛날 아내가 남편이 입을 수 있는 옷보다 비싼 옷을 입는 것을 규제했던 뉴 잉글랜드 법에서 볼 수 있듯이 복식양식에 영향을 끼쳤다. 예술적 행사들도 크게 성공했던 뮤지컬 코메니 'My Fair Lady'(버나드 쇼의 Pygmalion (여성 의상의 시대 적응 영감을 주었음)을 토대로 만든)에서 볼 수 있듯이 의상에 영향을 끼쳤다. 문화도 의상에 강력한 조건으로 작용했다. 르네상스의 영화는 돈 많은 상인들의 당당함을 비단, 공단, 우단 그리고 보석으로 나타내게 했다. 아주 멋지고 사치스런 프랑스 루이 14, 15, 16세의 궁전에서는 머리장식이 높이 솟아 있었고 치마는 부풀어 있었다. 귀족, 농부, 상인들을 차별하던 사치 단속법이 철폐되고 사회의 모든 계층이 거의 차별없이 옷을 입을 수 있게 된 이후로 유명신사들도 패션에 큰 자극을 주었다. 1960~1961년에, 케네디 대통령의 젊은 아내에 대한 미모와 옷맵시에 대한 찬사로서, '잭키 케네디 패션'이 선거 후 수주일 내에 매우 멀리 빠르게 전파되어 신문의 모든 패션 스케치는 그녀를 닮았었다.

slowly; at the height of the popularity of one silhouette or color, there are often faint indications of another. Editors, stylists, designers, and fabric manufacturers are trained to follow and gauge these faint indications and they can forecast the coming mode. But there will always be surprises, particularly if women accept a new fashion swiftly, or discard it with equal speed. Professionals are often accused of accelerating fashion change to create new business, but this simply is not practical. No fashion succeeds until women are ready to accept it.

(Source: Contributed by Elizabeth Ambrose Madeira)

(1) A proper title for the passage would be _____. (Subject matter)

    (a) Fashion & clothing   (d) Fashion & culture
    (b) Fashion & personalities   (e) Fashion & women
    (c) Fashion & Jackie Kennedy look

(2) Based on the information presented, the factors that condition fashion are _____. (Locating the facts)

    (a) Laws, regulations, culture, personalities
    (b) Laws, arts, culture, personalities
    (c) Louis XIV, cost, arts, personalities
    (d) Cost, culture, arts, clothing
    (e) Regulations, arts, culture, style

(3) The opposite of the italicized word *connotes* in the first paragraph can be _____. (Word in context)

    (a) Implies   (b) Infers   (c) Denotes   (d) Explicates   (e) Expresses

(4) The organization of the pattern in the passage is largely structured based on _____. (Rhetorical techniques)

    (a) Analysis   (d) Defintion
    (b) Cause-and-effect   (e) Description
    (c) Comparison & contrast

(5) As we have seen, fashion has been conditioned by a variety of sociocultural and personal factors. And more importantly, "no fashion succeeds until women are ready to accept it." Based on the information given, what age and gender group do you conclude is the most sensitive to fashion? (Conclusion)

    (a) Male teens & twenties   (d) Female thirties & forties
    (b) Female teens & twenties   (e) Female fifties & sixties
    (c) Male thirties & forties

일반적으로 말해서 의상의 변화는 느리게 일어난다. 한가지 실루엣이나 색채가 최정상의 인기에 올라 있을 때 또 다른 징후가 희미하게 존재한다. 편집자들, 스타일리스트, 디자이너, 옷감 제조업자들은 이들 희미한 징후를 좇아서 그 정도를 파악하고 다가올 유행을 예고할 수 있다. 그렇지만 특히 여인들이 새 패션을 신속하게 받아들이고 지난 것을 같은 속도로 버릴 경우 항상 놀라움이 있게 될 것이다. 패션 전문가들이 새로운 장사를 위해서 변화 속도를 가속화시킨다고 비난당하기도 하지만 이것이 실제적인 것은 아니다. 어떤 패션도 여인들이 받아들일 준비가 안되어 있으면 성공할 수 없다.

Note

□ **adorn = add beauty = decorate** : 장식하다
- He adorned his stories with lies. (그는 거짓말로 이야기를 재미있게 했다.)

□ **vogue = the fashion or custom at a certain time** : 유행
- out of vogue : 유행이 지난 • Long hair is no longer in vogue. (장발은 이미 한물 갔다.)

□ **prevail = gain victory** : 우세하다
- Justice has prevailed and the guilty man has been punished. (정의가 이겨서 그 죄인은 처벌 당했다.)

□ **connote = include, suggest, add to the fundamental meaning** : 내포하다, 암시하다
- The word home usually connotes comforts and security. (가정이라는 단어는 평안과 안전을 내포한다.)

□ **durable = long = lasting** : 지속적인, (옷)질긴
- We must make a durable peace. (항구적인 평화를 이룩해야 한다.)

□ **transitory = transient = passing = lasting only a short time** : 일시적인, 덧없는
- Happiness is in essence transitory. (행복이란 본질상 스치고 지나가는 것이다.)

□ **upkeep = maintenance** : 유지(비)
- We cannot afford the upkeep of a large house. (큰 집의 유지비를 감당할 수 없다.)

□ **exemplify = illustrate by example** : 예를 들어 설명하다
- The recent oil price increases exemplify the difficulties which the automobile industry is facing. (유가인상은 자동차 업계가 직면하고 있는 어려움을 예시하는 거다.)

□ **feminine = having the qualities of woman = suitable for woman** : 여성의, 여성스런
- She has a very feminine appearance. (모습이 여성스럽다.)   opp. masculine

□ **fabulous = unbelievable** : 우화같은, 엄청난
- The kidnapper demanded a fabulous sum of ransom. (유괴범은 엄청난 몸값을 요구했다.)

□ **extravagant = wasteful = lavish** : 낭비하는, 사치스런
- Before the IMF situation, it seems that most Korean people were extravagant. (IMF사태 이전에 한국인들은 씀씀이가 헤펐다.)

□ **soar = rise far and fast** : 치솟다
- Consumers' prices have sored as much as by 20%. (소비자 물가가 20%나 올랐다.)

□ **eliminate = get rid of, remove** : 제거하다
- The government swore that they would eliminate all the social evils. (정부는 모든 사회악을 철폐하겠다고 맹세했다.)

□ **tribute** : 감사, 경의
- The Memorial Day is a tribute to our dead soldiers. (현충일은 전몰장병에게 바치는 우리의 경의다.)

□ **discard = get rid of as useless** : 쓸모 없다고 버리다
- Don't discard your old wife married in penury. (조강지처 불하당-糟糠之妻不下堂)

Passage 2 : **Proper dress for proper situations**

"The clothes make the man" is a well-known proverb, but "the clothes" in the proverb does not necessarily refer to "expensive" or "extravagant" ones. Rather, it means "proper dress for proper situations."

Since we are social beings, it is almost impossible for us to enjoy a single social activity without wearing clothes. Whether we like it or not, our social norms require us to attire ourselves with specific types of clothes for specific situations. Knowing this type of social rules related to dressing or dress code is essential for our social interactions either at school or at work.

A list of tips for proper dress for specific occasions is provided.

(A) The interview:

(a) Wear a dark, conservative, solid colored suit.
(b) Wear well shined, unscuffed shoes.
(c) Avoid flamboyant styles, colors, and prints.

(B.1) The workplace for men:

(a) Wear whatever the company deems appropriate.
   (Follow the company's dress code)
(b) Wearing a suit is appropriate for upper management and executives.
(c) Avoid wearing ripped jeans, T-shirts, baseball caps, and sunglasses.
(d) Avoid wearing sneakers unless required or accepted as the norm.

(B.2) The workplace for ladies:

(a) Wear whatever the company deems appropriate.
   (Follow the company's dress code)
(b) Dress for your position.
(c) Avoid excessive make-up and accessories.
(d) Avoid mini-skirts, high heels, long or bright nails, low-cut or tight tops.

(C) The school for junior and senior high school students:

(Santa Barbara School Districts in California, prescribe the following regulations related to the dress code. This is an example of an American school dress code.)

(a) Clothes must properly conceal undergarments at all times. See-through,

지문 2 : 적절한 상황에 적절한 복장

"의복이 날개다"는 잘 알려진 속담이다. 그러나 이 속담 속의 옷은 반드시 비싸거나 사치스러운 옷은 아니다. 오히려 그것은 "적절한 상황에 적절한 옷"을 의미한다.

우리는 사회적 존재이기 때문에 단 한가지의 활동도 옷을 벗고 즐길 수는 없다. 좋든 싫든 사회적 규범은 특수한 상황에 특수한 옷입기를 요구한다. 복장 법도와 관계된 사회적 규칙을 안다는 것은 학교나 직장에서의 상호활동에 필수적이다.

> **Note**
>
> ☐ **not necessarily** : 반드시 …는 아니다(부분부정)
>   • Food that looks good does not necessarily taste good. (보기좋은 음식이 꼭 맛이 있는 것은 아니다.)
> ☐ **norm = standard of proper behavior** : 올바른 행동을 위한 규범
>   • We live in a society where there are norms to be observed. (우리는 지켜야 할 규범이 있는 사회안에서 산다.)
> ☐ **attire = dress, clothes** : 옷, 옷을 입히다
>   • They attended the party in Sunday clothes. (정장을 하고 참석했다.)
> ☐ **substantially = virtually** : 상당히, 많이   ☐ **dress code** : 복장 법도
> ☐ **essential = necessary** : 꼭 필요한, 필수적인   • We can live without clothes but food and drink are essential life. (옷을 안 입고는 살 수 있지만 먹을 음식과 물은 생명에 필수다.)

특수한 경우에 맞는 복장에 대한 충고 목록표를 제시한다.

(A) 면접
1. 진하고, 온건하고, 고른 색깔의 옷을 입어라.
2. 잘 닦은, 질질 끌리지 않는 신을 신어라.
3. 현란한 모양, 색깔, 무늬는 피하라.

(B.1) 남자들 직장
1. 회사측이 적당하다고 생각하는 옷을 입어라 (그 회사의 복장 법도를 따라라).
2. 위 아래 정장을 하는 것이 관리자나 경영 간부에게 적절하다.
3. 찢어진 진이나, 티셔츠, 야구모자, 선글라스는 피하라.
4. 받아들여지기 거북하거나 규범에 맞지 않으면 스니커는 신지 마라.

(B.2) 여자들 직장
1. (B.1)-1참조 (회사의 복장 규범을 따라라.)
2. 지위에 맞게 입어라.
3. 과도한 화장이나 액세서리는 피하라.
4. 미니 스커트, 하이힐, 길고 색채가 선명한 손톱, 너무깊게 패인 또는 달라붙는 상의는 피하라.

fishnet fabrics, halter tops, spaghetti straps, off-the-shoulder, low-cut tops, bare midriffs and skirts, shorts shorter than mid-thigh are prohibited.

(b) Clothing which is unduly revealing or attire which *detracts* in any way from the educational mission of the school's instructional program is unacceptable.

(c) The wearing of clothing which represents any group, gang, organization, or philosophy which advocates violence or disruption is unacceptable.

(D) The church:

(a) Men wear conservative suits.
(b) Women wear proper dresses for church services.
(c) Children wear their Sunday clothes.

(E) The wedding ceremony:

(a) Men wear formal suits.
(b) Women wear dresses in any color except white.
(c) The bride wears a white or ivory gown.
(d) The groom wears a tuxedo.

(F) The funeral service:

(a) Men wear black or dark suits with dark ties.
(b) Women wear black or dark dresses.
(c) Children dress the same as adults.

(1) The main idea of the passage would be _____. (Main idea)

(a) Dressing is important for seeking employment
(b) Dressing is the first step to socioeconomic success
(c) Dressing for proper situations is a must for social life
(d) Dressing is more important to women than to men
(e) Dressing is a means for popularity

(2) Which type of clothing does not violate the dress code of the Santa Barbara School Districts? (Locating the facts)

(a) Halter tops   (c) Spaghetti straps   (e) Midriff tops
(b) Low-cut tops   (d) Jeans

(3) The italicized word, *detracts* in Part (C), section (b) means _____ (Word in context)

(a) Focuses   (b) Encourages   (c) Diverts   (d) Highlights   (e) Attracts

(C) 중고등학교 학생

(캘리포니아 산타바바라 학교는 복장 법도와 관련된 아래 규제조항을 제정하고 있다. 이는 미국 학교의 복장 법도 중 한가지 예다.)

1. 언제나 복장은 내의가 적절히 감추어지도록 해야한다. 속이 보이는 옷, 어망같은 옷감, 팔과 등이 들어나 보이는 상의, 나선형 어깨 띠, 어깨가 드러나는 웃옷, 가슴까지 파진 상의, 몸통 중앙이 보이는 상의와 치마, 넙적다리 중간보다 짧은 드레스는 금한다.
2. 과도하게 노출시키는 옷이나 어떤 식으로든 학교의 교육 프로그램에서 이탈하는 복장은 인정되지 않는다.
3. 어떤 단체, 집단, 조직, 또는 폭력이나 파괴를 옹호하는 철학을 나타내는 복장 착용은 허락되지 않는다.

(D) 교회

1. 남자들은 온건한 정장을 입는다.
2. 여자는 예배에 적절한 옷을 입는다.
3. 어린이들은 나들이 옷을 입는다.

(E) 결혼식

1. 남자들은 격식차린 옷을 입는다.
2. 여자들은 흰색을 제외한 어느 색의 옷이든 입는다.
3. 신부는 흰색 또는 아이보리 겉옷을 입는다.
4. 신랑은 턱시도를 입는다.

(F) 장례식

1. 남자는 검거나 어두운 색의 정장과 검은 넥타이를 맨다.
2. 여자는 검거나 어두운 색의 옷을 입는다.
3. 어린이들은 검거나 어두운 색의 옷을 입는다.

(4) Based on the information given, it can be inferred that American public high school students, even though they live in the "Land of the Free," _____. (Making inferences)

  (a) Wear whatever they want
  (b) Wear school uniforms
  (c) Follow their school's dress code
  (d) Follow the current fashion trend
  (e) Attempt to dress for popularity

(5) Based on the information given, it can be concluded that 'Proper dress for proper situations' can _____. (Drawing conclusions)

  (a) Enhance academic life   (d) Enhance popularity
  (b) Enhance social success   (e) Improve self-esteem
  (c) Improve economic status

Passage 3 : **The following is a question-answer between students and a teacher of fashion.**

S means student, T is teacher, Q question, and A answer

S (Q1): Who are the top ready-to-wear designers in New York now, 1998?
T (A1): My personal list would include Calvin Klein, Donna Karan, Ralph Lauren, and Geoffrey Beene. All of them except Beene, are found in shops throughout the world. Beene is the most inventive designer working anywhere, but his clothes are so expensive that they are not well represented outside of the United States except for men's shirts and sweaters he designs for Van Heusen.

S (Q2): What are the newest trends?
T (A2): All over the world, the trend is to more casual clothes like sweaters and skirts for all occasions including evening. Some are calling this the Americanization of fashion because sportswear has been this country's major contribution to fashion since World War II. In the last fashion shows, lengths have dipped for the first time in years anywhere from below-the-knee to ankle length. Surprisingly, young people favor them while older women think they make them look too mature.

S (Q3): What is the big trendsetter?
T (A3): American sportswear, that is what even in Paris. Among the

Note

- **tip** = a helpful piece of advice to do something, information : 조언, 귀띔
  - If you take my tip, you will make a lot of money. (내가 귀띔 해주는 소리를 들으면 한 몫 잡을 것이네.)
- **conservative** = opposed to great or sudden change : 보수적인, 온건한   • opp. progressive
  - Old people are usually more conservative than young people.
- **unscuffed(shoes)** : 질질 끌리지 않는 (신발)   □ **top** : 투 피스의 윗도리
- **flamboyant** = showy, gay and bold : 화려한, 현란한, 야한
  - She likes to wear flamboyant yellow blouse. (화려한 노란 브라우스)
- **deem** = consider, have the opinion, regard : 간주하다
  - Do you deem the plan sensible. (자네는 그 계획이 무리가 없다고 생각하는가?)
- **rip** = tear or cut quickly : 찢다, 째다   • She ripped open the letter.
- **prescribe** : (법,규정)을 제정하다, (약)처방하다
  - What punishment does the traffic regulations prescribe for drunken driving?
  - (교통 법규에 음주운전의 처벌을 어떻게 규정하고 있는가?)
- **undergarment** = **underwear** = **underclothes** : 내의   □ **halter** : 팔, 등이 드러나는 여성용 스포츠 복

지문 3 : 다음은 학생들과 패션 선생과의 문답이다.

문 1 : 1998년 뉴욕에서 최고의 기성복 디자이너는 누구입니까?

답 1 : 나 개인적으로는 캘빈 클라인, 도나 카렌, 랄프 로렌, 제프리 빈을 꼽고 싶다. 빈을 제외한 모두의 작품은 전세계 시장에서 발견된다. 빈은 작품을 하는 사람들 중 가장 창의적인 디자이너이지만 그의 옷들은 너무 비싸서, 그가 반 해센을 위해서 디자인해주는 남자용 셔츠나 스웨터를 제외하고 미국 밖에서는 잘 나타나지 않는다.

문 2 : 최신 경향은 무엇입니까?

답 2 : 전 세계적인 경향은 야회를 비롯한 모든 행사에 스웨터나 스커트같이 더욱 캐주얼한 옷을 입는 것이다. 어떤 사람들은 이것을 패션의 미국화라고 부르는데 그 까닭은 운동복이 세계 제2차 대전이후 미국 패션에 주된 역할을 해왔기 때문이다. 지난 번 패션쇼에서 치마길이가 수년 내 최초로 무릎 아래서 발목까지 내려갔다. 놀랍게도 젊은 사람들이 긴 치마를 선호하는 반면에 나이 든 여성들은 너무 노숙하게 보인다고 생각한다.

문 3 : 그 경향을 선도하는 것은 무엇입니까?

American designers who have taken over French collections are Marc Jacob's at Louis Vuitton, Michael Kors at Celine, and Albert Elbaz at Guy Laroche. All of them have been successful.

S (Q4): What are the best color combinations?

T (A4): This is not written anywhere. You have to trust your eye. But gray is a big favorite, from silvery to dark. Designers like to combine different shades of gray in the same outfit, or use a contrasting shade like pink or blue to add interest.

S (Q5): How can I get the classic look of Jacqueline Kennedy on a college student's budget? I am 5' 4" and size 2 to 4.

T (A5): You are in luck. A typical component of the Kennedy look is widely available. That's the slim dress, sleeveless or with short sleeves, and matching jacket. It can be in linen or cotton, which would be appropriate for Houston where you live. Stay away from frills, pumps or plain sandals, and a good leather bag is good choice for this classical look.

S (Q6): Are the miniskirts still in fashion?

T (A6): After a very long run on the forefront of fashion, the miniskirts have retreated in favor of longer lengths. That alone gives a new look to clothes. Veteran fashion observers who have long been devoted to short miniskirts now agree that they have *lost their edge*. It is time for something else.

S (Q7): What are the best clothes for the new season?

T (A7): There will be some wild and woolly styles out there, but just ignore them. The best clothes for the new season are easy to wear and comfortable. That's what fashion is all about today. Clothes do not have to be frightening.

S (Q8): How much does a fashion designer make per year, and what does it take to be a great success?

T (A8): At the top of the heap are designers like Calvin Klein whose business draws in about $4 billion a year. Whatever profits are made go to him and his partner, Barry Schwartz, because it is not a public corporation. Starting salaries can be $50,000 per year, which is not a bad paying field. What you need to get ahead is business acumen, a nice personality and some great ideas.

(Source: Contributed by Bernadine Morris, 1998)

답 3 : 미국의 스포츠 웨어지, 그건 파리에서도 마찬가지지. 프랑스 작품을 이어 받은 미국 디자이너 중에는 루이 뷔통의 마크 제이콥스, 셀린의 마이쿨 코스, 기 라로쉬의 알버트 엘바즈 등이 있다. 그들 모두 성공했지.

문 4 : 가장 좋은 색의 배합은 무엇입니까?
답 4 : 이 문제는 고정되어 있는 건 아니다. 너희들의 눈으로 보아 결정하라. 그러나 회색, 즉 은색에서(옅은)진한 회색까지에 관심이 많다. 디자이너들은 같은 의상에 여러 회색을 배합하며, 혹은 흥미를 돋우기 위하여 분홍과 파랑처럼 대조되는 색상을 사용한다.

"The look of Jacueline Kennedy" :
A vision of glamour, youth, elegance, and political power.

문 5 : 어떻게 하면 대학생의 예산으로 재클린 케네디의 고전적 용모를 낼 수 있겠습니까? 저는 5피트 4인치이며 2~4 사이즈입니다.
답 5 : 너는 운이 좋구나. 케네디 패션의 전형적인 옷은 널리 살 수 있다. 그건 상의 자켓과 어울리는 소매가 없거나 짧은 소매의 날씬한 드레스다. 그 드레스는 린넨이나 면이면 되겠다. 왜냐하면 그 재질이 네가 사는 휴스턴에 적합하거든. 주름장식이나 펌프스나 평범한 샌들은 피하여라. 거기에 양질의 가죽 백이면 고전적 패션으로 좋은 선택이다.

문 6 : 미니스커트가 아직도 유행인가요?
답 6 : 패션의 선두를 오래 차지한 후, 미니스커트는 긴 치마를 위해서 물러갔다. 그것만으로도 패션에 새로운 변화를 준다. 패션 전문가들은 짧은 미니스커트가 한풀 꺾였다는데 동의한다. 지금은 뭔가 다른 것이 나타날 때다.

AFTERNOON DRESS of pink silk organza and shantung overlaid with self-fabric organza cut-out flowers. Spring/Summer Collection 1964. The metropolitan Museum of Art Gift of Mrs. charles B. Wrightsman, 1967 (CI 67.53.6abc)

"The most important thing today is awareness. Woman are more conscious of themselves as individuals than of their clothes. Conscious of their lives, of their bodies. Everything in life is more natural. Woman now know themselves better psycologically and physically." Yves Saint Laurent, 1972

문 7 : 새로운 계절에 제일 좋은 옷은 무엇입니까?
답 7 : 약간 야성적이고 모직 스타일이 나올 거야. 그

(1) A proper title of the dialogue would be _____. (Subject matter)

    (a) Top fashion designers
    (b) Newest fashion trend
    (c) Salaries of the fashion designers
    (d) The best clothes for the new season
    (e) Facts about fashion

(2) One of the non-American fashion designers is _____. (Locating the fact)

    (a) Calvin Klein   (c) Ralph Lauren   (e) Michael Kors
    (b) Donna Karan   (d) Louis Vuitton

(3) The italicized phrase, *lost their edge* in T (A6) can be substituted for _____. (Phrase in context)

    (a) Lost their appeal
    (b) Lost their money
    (c) Lost their manufacturers
    (d) Lost their agents
    (e) Lost their sponsors

(4) The tone of the teacher seems to be _____. (Tone & attitude)

    (a) Cynical & pedantic
    (b) Informative & confident
    (c) Persuasive & informative
    (d) Sarcastic but informative
    (e) Dogmatic but persuasive

(5) Based on the information given, it can be concluded that a successful fashion designer needs _____. (Drawing conclusions)

    (a) Patience, personality, speed
    (b) Efficiency, management, personality
    (c) Creativity, personality, persistence
    (d) Efficiency, speed, accuracy
    (e) Accuracy, creativity, management

3.2.3. Film

Passage 1 :

On December 28, 1895, Antoine Lumiere offered the first public exhibition of film with very short and simple events in Paris. Today the physical structure of film and the method in which it produces an illusion of motion, "living picture" or "motion picture," are fundamentally the same as those employed by Antoine.

Basic elements of film include (1) space and light; (2) sound; and, (3) tempo, accent, and rhythm. They do more than simply carry a story; they shape it, modify its

러나 그것들을 무시하라. 제일 좋은 옷은 입기에 쉽고 편안한 옷이다. 그게 오늘날 모든 패션의 관심거리다. 옷이 우리를 겁 줄 필요는 없지.

문 8 : 패션 디자이너는 일년에 얼마나 벌고 성공하는데 필요한 것은 무엇인가요?

답 8 : 많은 톱 디자이너에는 1년에 약 40억 달러를 벌어 들이는 캘빈 클라인같은 디자이너도 있다. 벌어들이는 모든 이익은 그와 동업자, 배리 슈와르츠에게 돌아간다. 왜냐하면 그의 사업체는 공적인 회사가 아니기 때문이다. 초봉은 연 5만달러가 가능한데 이는 수입이 적은 분야가 아니다. 성공하기 위하여 필요한 것은 사업적인 통찰과 훌륭한 인성과 약간의 아이디어다.

Note

- **ready-to-wear = ready-made** : 기성복의
- **dip = go below** : 아래로 기울다, 침하하다
  - The sun dipped below the horizon. (태양이 수평선 아래로 졌다.)
- **outfit = all the clothing or articles needed for a purpose** : 장비, 복장
  - a bride's outfit : 신부 혼수   • ski outfit : 스키 용품
- **edge = advantage** : 강점, 우세   • You have the edge on me. (네가 나보다 낫다.)
- **corporation** : 기업, 회사   • cf. cooperation : 협동
- **acumen = sharpness, accuracy, ability to understand clearly** : 통찰력, 안목
- **trendsetter = a person who starts a style which others follow** : 유행, 선도인
- **frill = ornamental edge on a dress** : 주름 장식
- **pumps** : 끈이나 걸쇠가 없는 구두   □ **retreat = go back, withdraw** : 후퇴, 철수하다
- **veteran = one who has had much or long experience** : 고참

3.2.3. 영화

지문 1 :

1895년 12월 28일 안톤 루미에르는 파리에서 아주 짧고 단순한 사건을 다룬 최초의 공공 영화 상영을 했다. 오늘날 동작의 착시현상인 '살아있는 사진' 혹은 '활동사진'을 제작하는 영화의 물

The Arrival of a Train.
Antoine Lumière. France, 1895.

content, and determine its meaning. Specifically, light and space serve as vehicles through which the film maker expresses his ideas. The "words" represented in light (e.g. black and white), and in space (i.e. shape, size, position, direction, proportion), mold, shape, and build the raw materials into expressive structures, translating form into meaning. Sound conveys specific meanings. Depending on the degree, whether heightened or lessened, sound conveys its meaning in a similar manner as light and space. Tempo, accent, and rhythm all involve relationships in time. For the film maker, time is not simply the interval in which a particular action takes place, but a *malleable* element to be shaped into patterns; it can be shortened or extended, retarded or accelerated.

    Film as an art of patterned space and light resembles the other visual arts such as painting, drawing, sculpture, and architecture. However, except for kinetic paintings or sculptures, film stands alone in terms of its incorporation of motion and its consequent immersion of time.

(Source: Adapted from Johnson, F. Lincoln (1974). Film: Space, Time, Light, and Sound.)

(1) The main idea of the last paragraph is that film as an art is _____. (Main idea)

    (a) Unique and different from other visual arts
    (b) Better than any other visual arts
    (c) Stronger than paintings and drawings
    (d) Similar to other visual arts
    (e) The same as kinetic paintings and sculptures

(2) Film is often called a "living picture" or "motion picture." It is because of its effect of _____. (Locating the facts)

    (a) Space and light   (c) Film structure   (e) Incorporation of motion
    (b) Sound of tempo   (d) An illusion of movement

(3) The italicized word, *malleable,* in the second paragraph can be substituted for _____. (Word in context)

    (a) Solid   (b) Flexible   (c) Fixed   (d) Malicious   (e) Powerful

(4) The underlined, except for kinetic paintings or sculptures, film stands alone, in the last paragraph refers to the author's key point that film _____. (Rhetorical techniques)

    (a) Is superior to sculpture and architecture
    (b) Is as comparable to other visual arts
    (c) Surpasses other visual arts in terms of motion and immersion
    (d) Is the best visual arts
    (e) Is the most powerful art

리적 구조나 방법은 기본적으로 안톤이 동원했던 것들과 같다.

영화의 기본적인 요소들 속에는 (1)공간과 빛 (2)음향 (3)속도, 강약, 리듬이 들어있다.

Worker Leaving the Lumière Factory. Antoine Lumière. France.1895.

이 요소들은 단지 이야기를 전달하는 것 이상의 일을 한다. 이야기를 형체화하고 내용을 수정하며 의미를 결정한다. 구체적으로 말하면 빛과 공간은 영화 제작자가 자기 생각을 표현하는 수단으로써 일을 한다. 빛이 대표하는 언어들(예 : 흑과 백)과 공간이 대표하는 언어들(형체, 크기, 위치, 방향, 비율)은 형체를 의미로 해석하게 하면서, 원자재를 표현 구조로 만든다. 음향은 특수한 의미를 전달한다. 높이거나 낮추는 정도에 따라 음향은 빛과 공간과 같은 방식으로 의미를 전달한다. 속도, 강약, 그리고 리듬은 모두 시간과 관련을 갖는다. 영화제작자에게는 시간이 단지 어떤 특수한 사건이 발생하는 간격만은 아니고 어떤 양식을 만들 수 있는 신축성을 가진 요소다. 시간은 단축할 수도, 연장할 수도 , 늦출 수도 있고 가속을 붙일 수도 있다.

모양을 갖춘 시간과 공간의 예술인 영화는 시각예술인 채색화, 선화, 조각의 건축과 유사하다. 그러나 동적인 그림과 조각을 제외하고 동작의 결합과 연속적인 시간 속의 몰입이라는 면에서 영화가 유일하다.

Feeding Baby. Antoine Lumière. France,1895.

Note

- □ exhibition = public show of objects, act of showing : 전시, 전람
- □ event = an important happening : 사건, 행사
  - What are the 10 most important events of this year? (금년 10대 사선은?)
- □ illusion = something seen wrong, the seeing of something that does not really exist : 환각, 환상
- □ optical illusion : 착시
  - I have no illusion about him - I know he is a liar. (그 남자에 대한 환상은 안가지고 있다. 그는 사기꾼이다.)
- □ mold : 거푸집, 녹여 만들다.
  - His character has been molded more by his experience than by his education.
    (그의 성격은 교육에 의해서 보다 체험에 의해서 형성되었다.)

(5) The development of film is much shorter than those of other visual arts (painting, drawing, sculpture, architecture), but film is predicted to grow faster with more powerful impact on us. This conclusion is based on its _____. (Conclusion)

    (a) Incorporation of motion & time immersion
    (b) Incorporation of time & millions of color
    (c) Exploration of the physical structure of film.
    (d) Basic elements of film
    (e) Composition of patterned space & light

Passage 2 :

SIDNEY POITIER (1927-). A star who overcame major hurdles: Poverty and language barrier.

    Sidney Poitier is one of the finest actors of our time. For him, the way up to being a star took many years of hard work.
    He was born in 1927, and grew up in the British West Indies as the youngest of eight children. At 12, he worked as a waterboy to laborers; at 13, he dropped out of school, and worked at a variety of menial jobs; and at 18, he came to New York with $1.50 in his pocket. He worked at a restaurant as a dish washer, and used to sleep in a pay toilet in a bus station to save money.

    One morning, he saw a newspaper ad, "Actors wanted. The American Negro Theater." He went to the theater and he tried out for a part in a play which people laughed at him. It was because of his Caribbean accent. But, it gave him a strong determination to improve his accent. That day, he bought a radio and began to listen to it, especially the American standard pronunciation as well as nonstandard one from the announcers. He studied the ways that both white and black people spoke and consistently practiced imitating variations of their speech every night for more than two years. As a result of his hard work in pronunciation, he could command those speech variations without too much difficulty.
    Now he could join the American Negro Theater and made his debut in the 1946 all-Negro production of "Lysistrata." Beginning in the 1950s, he rapidly became Hollywood's number one black actor, and by the '60s, he established himself as a popular screen star with *charismatic* personal appeal and the ability to tackle an ever-widening range of roles. On April 14, 1963, he won an Oscar for Best Actor of that year for his role in "Lilies of the Field."

```
□ malleable : 두드려서 펼 수 있는, 유연한
□ retard = check, delay, hinder : 방해하다. 늦추다    • a retarded child (지진아)
□ kinetic : 움직이는, 움직이는 예술의    opp. static (정적인)
□ malicious : 악의에 찬    □ flexible : 유연한, 쉽게 휘어지는
□ incorporation : 합체, 결합(영화는 정지된 동작들의 결합, 시각적 환각을 이용하는 예술)
```

지문 2 : 시드니 포이티어. 가난과 언어의 큰 장애를 뛰어 넘은 스타

시드니 포이티어는 우리 시대 가장 훌륭한 배우 중의 한사람이다. 그가 스타의 위치까지 가기에 여러 해 동안의 힘든 노력이 필요했다.

ABOVE Sidney Poitier and Dorothy Dandridge in Porgy and Bess, 1959

8형제의 막내로 1927년에 영령 서인도제도에서 태어났다. 12세 때 노동자들에게 물 심부름을 했고, 13세 때 학교를 그만두고 여러가지 천한 일에 종사했고, 18세에 호주머니에 1달러 50센트만 가지고 뉴욕에 왔다. 식당에서 접시닦이로 일하고 잠은 돈을 아끼기 위하여 버스 정류장 유료변소에서 자곤했다.

어느날 아침 신문에서 "배우모집함-미국흑인극장"라는 광고를 보았다. 그는 그 극장에 가서 한 연극의 배역을 해보았으나 카리브지방의 억양 때문에 웃음거리가 되었다. 그러나 그것은 그가 억양을 개선해야겠다는 강력한 결심을 하게 했다. 그날부터 그는 라디오를 사서 열심히 듣고, 특히 아나운서들로부터 비표준 발음뿐만아니라 표준 발음을 경청하기 시작했다. 그는 백인과 흑인들의 말씨를 연구했고 2년 이상 밤낮으로 그들 말씨의 변형들

Best Actor : Sidney Poitier as Homer Smith (left, with Lilia Skala) in Lilies of the Field (United Artists;directed by Ralph Nelson).

을 꾸준히 모방하는 연습을 했다. 발음에 대한 고된 노력의 결과 그다지 어렵지 않게 이들 말씨의 여러 변형들을 구사할 수 있었다.

이제 그는 미국 흑인 극장에 참여할 수 있었고 1946년에 여자의 평화 (Lysistrata)라는 모두 흑인만 참여하

(1) A proper topic sentence of the passage would be _____. (Topic sentence)

    (a) A man who became a successful star
    (b) Sidney Poitier became a star by overcoming obstacles
    (c) Sidney won an Oscar for Best Actor in 1963
    (d) Sidney overcame poverty & language barrier
    (e) Sidney worked hard to improve his pronunciation

(2.1.) The Oscar award is given to the actor/actress whose performance is acknowledged. It is given _____. (Locating the facts)

    (a) annually   (c) monthly   (e) once every 5 years
    (b) biannually   (d) weekly

(2.2.) Sidney starred in a variety of films such as "For Love of Ivy," "Guess Who's Coming to Dinner?," "A Raising in the Sun," "Lilies of the Field," "To Sir, With Love," and "In the Heat of the Night." Which film do you think helped him the most to become a well known star?

    (a) "For Love of Ivy"   (d) "Lilies of the Field"
    (b) "To Sir, With Love"   (e) "Guess Who's Coming to Dinner?"
    (c) "In the Heat of the Night"

(2.3.) One of the most difficult hurdles that Sidney tackled to become a star was ____.

    (a) He responded to the newspaper ad
    (b) He improved his pronunciation
    (c) He dropped out of school
    (d) He slept in a pay toilet to save money
    (e) He joined the American Negro Theater

(3) The italicized word, *charismatic* in the last paragraph can be substituted for _____. (Word in context)

    (a) Aggressive   (c) Intimidating   (e) Challenging
    (b) Inspiring   (d) Compassionate

(4) The passage is constructed based on a style of _____. (Rhetorical techniques)

    (a) Autobiography (b) Biography (c) Fiction (d) Journal (e) Drama

(5) A suitable theme of the passage is _____. (Conclusion)

    (a) Strike the iron before it gets cold.   (d) Slow & steady wins the race.
    (b) Every rule has an exception.   (e) Every dog has its own day.
    (c) There are no free rides in the world.

는 작품에 데뷔했다. 1950년대에 시작하여 빠른 속도로 헐리웃 최고의 흑인 배우가 되었다. 그리고 1960년대 무렵까지는 카리스마적인 개인 매력과 계속 폭넓은 배역을 맞받아 해낼 수 있는 능력을 가진 인기 영화 배우로 자리잡았다. 1963년 4월 14일 '들에 핀 백합' (Lilies of the Field)에서 맡은 역으로 그 해의 오스카 남우 주연상을 받았다.

Note

- □ overcome = fight successfully against, defeat : 싸워 이기다, 물리치다
  - So many difficulties for us to overcome are in store for us.
    (우리가 극복해야할 난관이 우리에게 닥쳐오고 있다.)
- □ hurdle = a difficulty which is to be conquered : 장애, 곤란
  - Envy is a hurdle to friendship.(시기는 우정을 가로막는 장애다.)
- □ substantially = virtually : 상당히, 많이
- □ drop out = withdraw from school : 학교를 자퇴하다.
- □ wanted ad = an advertisement that someone is wanted for a job : 구인광고
- □ try out for = make an effort to get or win, compete for : 한번 도전해 보다
  - He tried out for the play, but he couldn't make it. (그 연극에 나가 보았으나 성공 못했다.)
- □ consistently : 일관되게
- □ command : 언어를 자유자재로 구사하다
- □ tackle = deal with, attack : 맞붙어 싸우다
  - He tackled the thief fearlessly (그는 겁없이 도적을 잡고 싸웠다.)

Passage 3 : A Review of Titanic (1997)

This movie has gained exceptional popularity not only in the United States, but also worldwide for its dramatic effects of setting drawn from actual events, and the fictional story in which human conflicts are portrayed. By reviewing this film based on historical events and literary genre, we can widen our scope of appreciating film as a form of literature.

Historical Background:

Titanic was manufactured by the British White Star Line Company in 1911. The specifications of this finished huge luxury liner are: (a) Gross tonnage of 46,238; (b) Length, 883 feet; (c) Beam (width of a ship at its widest part), 93 feet; (d) Draught (the depth to which the vessel is immersed), 34 feet; (e) Displacement, 66,000 tons of water; (f) Total horse power, 51,000 h.p.; (g) Total passengers & crew, 3547; and, (h) Life boats, 20. The ship was so strong and huge that people called her as "The Unsinkable" or "The Ship of Dreams."

Titanic set off on its maiden voyage, carrying more than 2,222 passengers, from the docks of Southampton, England, in early April, 1912. Unfortunately, the voyage turned out to be the last one for many passengers, crew, and herself, when she struck an iceberg about 153 km south of the Grand Banks of Newfoundland while heading for New York. On April 14, 1912, she was swallowed by the sea in less than 3 hours, and even though there was enough room for half of the passengers in the lifeboats, the people panicked and loaded the boats themselves. They filled the boats much less than full because they worried about being crowded. As a result, out of the 2,222 passengers, 1,513 persons perished in the freezing ocean water.

Titanic is now at the bottom of the sea, but the dreadful occurrences of April 14, 1912 still live on the memories of the survivors and the loved ones of those perished. One of the survivors, Ms Eva Hart said, "The sound of people drowning is something I cannot describe to you and neither can anyone else. It is the most dreadful sound and then there is dreadful silence that follows it." Mr. Charles Lighttoller, the survived 2nd Officer, describes, "Slowly she reared up on end until at last she was absolutely perpendicular. Then quite quietly but quicker and quicker, she seemed to slide away… and disappear." These are the tragedies, and this is a disaster known as "Titanic."

Based on these historical facts, James Cameron and his associates used these events as dramatic settings for the movie industry. The movie released in

지문 3 : 영화비평 '타이타닉' (1997)

이 영화는 실제의 사건에서 끌어 온 배경과, 인간의 갈등이 묘사된 소설적인 이야기의 극적 효과로 미국에서 뿐 아니라 전 세계적으로 보기드문 인기를 얻었다. 역사상의 사건과 문학적인 장르에 근거들 둔 이 영화를 되돌아 봄으로써, 우리는 문학의 한 형식으로서 영화를 감상하는 폭을 확대할 수 있다.

역사적 배경 : 타이타닉호는 영국의 선박회사 '화이트 스타 라인'에 의하여 1911년에 제작되었다. 완성된 이 초호화 여객선의 세부사항은 다음과 같다.

1) **총톤수** : 46,238 2) **길이** : 883피트 3) **가로들보**(가장 넓은 곳의 폭) : 93피트 4) **흘수**(배가 물속에 잠기는 깊이) : 34피트 5) **배수량** : 물 66,000톤 6) **총마력** : 51,000마력 7) **승객, 승무원 총수** : 3547명 8) **구명정** : 20척. 그 배는 하도 크고 튼튼해서 사람들은 '가라앉을 수 없는 배'라거나 '꿈의 배'라고 불렀다.

타이타닉호는 2222여명의 승객을 싣고 영국 사우샘프턴부두를 1912년 4월초에 처녀 항해했다. 불운하게도, 그 항해는 많은 승객들과 승무원, 그리고 배 자체에게 최후의 항해가 되고 말았다. 뉴욕으로 가는 도중 뉴펀들랜드의 그랜드 뱅크 남방 153km 지점에서 빙산과 부딪히고 만 것이다. 1912년 4월 14일, 3시간도 못되어 바다가 그 배를 삼켰고, 비록 구명정에 승객의 반이 탈 수 있는 충분한 공간이 있었음에도, 사람들은 겁에 질려 배에 올랐다. 그들은 배가 너무 꼭 차지나 않을까 하는 걱정 때문에 탈 수 있는 총원보다 훨씬 적게 탔다. 그 결과, 2,222명의 승객 중에서 1,513명이 얼어붙는 듯한 바닷물 속에서 죽었다.

Captain- Edward J Smith (in front row, 3rd from left)
Chief Officer- Henry F Wilde
First Officer- William M Murdoch
Second Officer- Charles Herbert LIghtoller (survived)
Third Officer- Herbert John Pitman (survived)
Fourth Officer- Joseph Groves Boxhall (survived)

타이타닉호는 지금 바다 밑바닥에 있지만 1912년 4월 14일의 그 끔찍한 사건들은 아직도 생존자들과 사망자들이 사랑했던 사람들의 기억속에 살아있다. 생존자의 한사람인 에바하트 부인은 다음과 같이 말했다. "물속에

the United States as of December 17, 1997, became so successful that it broke all previous box office records. Besides, the movie won Golden Globe Awards for (a) Best Motion Picture (Drama); (b) James Cameron as Best Director; (c) James Horner as Best Original Score; (d) James Horner as Best Original Song; and, the movie was nominated as Best Picture of 1997 for the Oscar Award. Major features and cast are as follows:

Director : James Cameron.
Producers: James Cameron & Jon Landau.

Cast: Leonardo DiCaprio as Jack Dawson, a poor young artist;
Kate Winslet as Rose DeWitt Bukater, a young woman;
Billy Zane as Cal Hockly, a *socialite*, fiancé of Rose;
Frances Fisher as Ruth DeWitt Bukater, Rose's mother;
Gloria Stuart as elderly Rose;
Bill Paxton as Brock Lovett, treasure hunter

Features: Running Time: 3 hours 14 minutes
U.S. Distributor: Paramount Pictures

The story of the movie as the plot begins in the present on the Atlantic Ocean, 2.5 miles above the wreckage of the Titanic. Brock Lovett (Bill Paxton), treasure hunter, attempts to retrieve the "Heart of the Ocean," a 56 karat diamond which was rumored to have sunk along with the Titanic. Elderly Rose (Gloria Stuart), 100 years old is helicoptered to his boat because she was the woman wearing the diamond pendant. This old lady, young Rose at that time, flashing back, starts telling the events related to the sinking of the Titanic in 1912.

Rose is a young woman who is engaged to an heir of a large fortune, Cal Hockly (Billy Zane) whom she does not love, but she has to marry him to relieve her family's financial crisis. This forced marriage makes Rose so miserable that she tries to commit suicide by leaping off the Titanic into the ocean. At that moment, a young man, Jack (Leonardo DiCaprio) approaches the scene and saves her life, which initiates their romantic relationship. Rose begins to like Jack for his unlimited potential human quality, a man, unlike Cal, without social prejudice and power, but with the nature of loving human beings as they are.

On the night of April 14, 1912 when the Titanic hits an iceberg, the dramatic scenes of sinking demonstrate a variety of human instincts: the love and sacrifice between Rose and Jack; the selfishness, arrogance, dark side of Cal; the effort of keeping order by the crew members to the panicky and uncontrollable

서 허우적거리던 사람들의 소리는 말로 표현할 수 없어요. 누구도 못해요. 가장 무서운 장면이었고 그 뒤에는 끔찍한 침묵이 있었지요." 생존한 2등 기관사 찰스 라이톨러는 다음처럼 묘사한다.

"그 배는 서서히 기울어지다가 마침내 완전히 수직으로 곤두섰지요. 그 후 아주 조용히 그러나 점점 빠르게 옆으로 미끄러지는 듯하더니 사라졌어요." 이것은 엄청난 비극이며, 이것이 바로 '타이타닉'으로 알려진 재난이다.

이런 역사적 사실에 근거하여 제임스 카메런과 동료들은 이 사건들을 영화 산업에 대한 극의 배경으로 사용했다. 1997년 12월 17일자로 미국에서 개봉된 이 영화는 매우 성공하여 이전의 흥행 기록을 깨뜨렸다. 그외에도 그 영화는 다음 부문의 골든 글러브 상을 탔다.

1)최우수 작품상 2)감독상, 제임스 카메런 3)편곡상, 제임스 아너 4)주제가상, 제임스 아너, 그리고 1997년 오스카상 최우수 작품상 후보로 지명되었다.

주요한 특색과 배역은 다음과 같다.

감독 : James Cameron

제작 : James Cameron과 Jon Landau

배역 : 가난한 젊은 화가 Jack Dawson-Leanard DiCaprio / 젊은 여자 Rose DeWitt Bukater-Kate Winslet / 사교계의 명사, Rose의 약혼자 Cal Hockly-Billy Zane / Rose의 어머니 Ruth DeWitt Bukater-Frances Fisher / Rose의 늙은 역-Gloria Stuart / 보물수집가 Brock Lovett-Bill Paxton

특색 : 상영시간 3시간 14분 / 미국측 배급회사 : Paramount Pictures사

영화의 줄거리는 구도상 현재 시점에서 대서양 타이타닉호의 난파지점 2.5마일 위쪽에서 시작된다. 보물 수집가인 브록 러벳이 타이타닉호와 함께 가라앉았다고 소문이 나 있는 56캐럿 다이아몬드인 '대양의 심장'을 회수하려고 시도한다. 나이가 100세인 늙은 로즈가 헬리콥터를 타고 그 남자의 배에 실려 온다. 그 다이아몬드 펜던트를 차고 있던 여자가 바로 그녀였기 때문이다. 이 노인, 그 당시 젊은 로즈, 갑자기 과거를 회상하고 1912년 타이타닉의 침몰과 관련된 이야기를 시작한다.

passengers; some people play music almost to the end in spite of the impending crisis; and, the inefficient Captain meets his end with dignity in his office. But, all these chaotic tragedies slowly perish with the ship. The male protagonist, Jack, saves Rose on a piece of wreckage by paying with his life, which is symbolized as pure love and sacrifice, whereas Cal Hockly saves his life and finds himself elsewhere. Back to the present, Brock retrieves a safe which is suspected to hold the diamond, but when the safe is opened, there is only a drawing of Rose wearing the diamond drawn by Jack.

The symbolic features of the movie provide us interesting lesson as a *parable*, or a metaphor. The ship herself as a miniature of our society represents a variety of human beings from different social classes. The first class passengers, for example, as members of high social class represent their "glory, privilege, and power" as the bright side, and "arrogance, prejudice, and corruption" as the dark side. The third class passengers as members of low class society have their own privilege and disadvantages as Jack. The ship, Titanic, symbolizing our society has both sides; she enjoyed her brief but glorious and proud life when she was celebrated as "The Ship of Dreams," "The Unsinkable," and "The World's Most Luxurious Ship Ever Built." However, she has to admit her dark sides: excessive arrogance, and pride of her, and carelessness and inefficiency of her crew members, which eventually led her dramatic death in the Atlantic Ocean. Titanic as any society (e.g. the Roman Empire, the British Empire) enjoys her glory and prosperity once, but later declines or falls due to arrogance, inefficiency, and corruption.

Likewise, major protagonists, Jack, Rose, and Cal represent a variety of human behaviors from different attitude and morality. To them, life is meant to be both invaluable and inalienable to the same extent. However, when Titanic is about to sink with chaos and dramatic tragedies, the reactions of these protagonists display different aspects. The young and penniless Jack gives his life to his beloved Rose without expecting anything from her in return; the rich socialite, Cal attempts to save his life by bribing one of the officers, but he saves his life somehow, and finds himself somewhere; the young woman, Rose, becomes to understand the existing social realities shown to her: socioeconomic power vs. humanity generated by true love. These symbolic behaviors and conflicts demonstrated by the major protagonists are nicely illustrated based on excellent dramatic setting (i.e. the ship as a miniature of society), situations (i.e. conflicts between/among Jack, Cal, Rose; the time of sinking and the time Jack saves Rose), and attitude and morality (i.e. love, courage, sacrifice vs. opportunism, arrogance, corruption). Simply put, it is clear that Cameron and his

로즈는 많은 재산의 상속자인 칼 허클리와 약혼중이나 그를 사랑하지 않으면서도 그녀 가정의 재정적 위기에서 벗어나기 위해 그와 결혼하지 않을 수 없다. 이 강요된 결혼은 그녀를 어찌나 불행하게 했는지 그녀는 타이타닉호에서 바다속으로 뛰어내려 자살을 시도한다. 그 순간 청년 잭이 그 현장에 다가와서 그녀의 생명을 구해주고, 이 일로 그들 사이에는 애정이 싹트기 시작한다. 로즈는 잭이 칼과는 달리 무한한 인간적 특질의 가능성을 가진 사람, 사회적 편견도 권력도 없지만, 인간 그 자체를 사랑하는 본성으로 그를 좋아하게 된다.

1912년 4월 14일 밤 타이타닉호가 빙산을 들이 받았을 때 침몰의 극적인 순간들은 다양한 인간 본능을 드러내 보인다. 로즈와 잭 사이의 사랑과 희생, 칼의 어두운 면인 이기심과 교만, 공포에 질린 통제 불능의 승객들에 대해 질서를 유지하려는 승무원들의 노력, 임박한 위기에도 불구하고 거의 끝까지 음악을 연주하는 몇몇 사람들, 그리고 선장실에서 품위있게 최후를 맞이하는 무능한 선장. 그러나 이 모든 대혼란의 비극은 천천히 배와 함께 사라진다. 남자주인공 잭은 생명을 바쳐 난파선 조각 위로 로즈를 구한다. 이는 순수한 사랑과 희생을 상징한다. 반면에 칼은 생명을 건지고 딴 곳에서 모습을 보인다. 다시 현재로 돌아와서 브록은 그 다이아가 들어 있다고 생각되는 금고를 회수한다. 그러나 금고가 열렸을 때, 거기에는 단지 잭이 그린 로즈가 다이어를 걸고 있는 그림 한 장이 있을 뿐이다.

이 영화의 상징적 특색은 하나의 우화 즉 은유로써 흥미있는 교훈을 준다. 우리 사회의 축소판인 그 배 자체는 다른 계층에서 온 다양한 인간들을 대표한다. 예를 들어 특실 승객들은 상류계층의 구성원으로서 밝은 면으로는 영광과 특권과 권력을 대표하고 어두운 면으로는 오만과 편견 그리고 부패를 나타낸다. 하층계급의 구성원인 3등칸 승객들은 잭처럼 자기들 나름의 특권과 또 불리한 입장 두가지를 다 가진다. 우리 사회를 상징하는 배 타이타닉호도 두가지를 다 갖고 있다. '꿈의 선박' '침몰불가' '역사상 최고의 호화선'으로 축하를 받을 때 짧지만 영광되고 자랑스런 삶을 살았다. 그러나 그 배의 어두운 측면도 인정해야 한다. 지나친 오만, 배에 대한 자만, 승무원들의 부주의와 무능, 그것이 결국 대서양에서 그 배를 극적인 죽음으로 안내했다. 타이타닉은 다른 어떤 사회처럼(예 : 로마제국, 대영제국), 한 때는 영광과 번영을 구가하지만 후에 오만과 비능률과 부패 때문에 기울어 망한다.

associates contribute to the success of this movie by powerfully depicting symbolic features in terms of (a) setting, (b) characters, and (c) morality. Cameron as the writer and director of the movie is correct in his claim, "For Titanic is not just a cautionary tale- a myth, a parable, or metaphor for the ills of mankind. It is also a story of faith, courage, sacrifice, and, above all else, love (1997)."

The dramatic symbolic features in setting, character, story, and morality provide us interesting themes. The theme can vary depending on individual perception of interpreting the movie, but one thing is clear that the movie intensifies our fundamental inquiries about our life. What is the meaning of life? How can we make our life meaningful? Is it through financial or political power, health or education, opportunism or sacrifice, glory or faith, hatred or love? How should our attitude or relationships with others be maintained and developed, in isolation or in interdependency? The choice is yours. All these fundamental questions can be reexamined through this film, Titanic, as a form of literature.

(1) The main idea of the passage is _____. (Main idea)

    (a) How Titanic became successful
    (b) How film makers made Titanic
    (c) What does Titanic symbolize?
    (d) How conflicts & love are portrayed
    (e) How Titanic was produced & became successful

(2.1.) How many passengers survived the Titanic disaster? (Locating the facts: 2.1.-2.5.)

    (a) 689   (b) 699   (c) 709   (d) 719   (e) 729

(2.2.) Who are the major protagonists?

    (a) Jack, Rose, Ruth   (d) Elderly Rose, Jack, Brock Lovett
    (b) Jack, Rose, Cal   (e) Ruth, Cal, Brock Lovett
    (c) Jack, Cal, Ruth

(2.3.) Who acted as a major antagonist in the movie?

    (a) Jack   (b) Ruth   (c) Rose   (d) Cal   (e) Brock

(2.4.) Why did Titanic hit the iceberg? It was because _____.

    (a) The weather was stormy   (d) The ship had mechanical problems
    (b) The ship was overloaded   (e) The crew did not expect to see an iceberg
    (c) The Captain & crew were careless

마찬가지로 주요 주인공 잭, 로즈, 칼은 각기 다른 태도와 도덕성에 기반한 다양한 인간 행위를 대표한다. 그들에게 삶은 같은 정도로 귀중하며 소홀히 할 수 없는 것으로 의미가 잡혀있다. 그러나 타이타닉이 혼란과 극적 비극을 안고 침몰하려 할 때, 주인공들의 반응은 다른 면모를 보여준다. 젊고 돈이 없는 잭은 아무런 대가도 생각하지 않고 사랑하는 로즈에게 생명을 바친다. 돈 많은 사교계의 명사 칼은 기관사 한명을 매수하여 자기 생명을 구하려 한다. 그러나 어쨌든 그는 목숨은 구하며, 어딘가에서 자신의 모습을 발견한다. 젊은 여인 로즈는 그녀에게 보여진 사회 현실을 깨닫게 된다. 사회경제적 힘과 진정한 사랑으로 살아나는 인간애. 주인공들에 의하여 나타나는 상징적 행위와 갈등이 뛰어난 극적인 배경(사회의 축소판으로서의 배), 상황(둘, 혹은 세사람 사이의 갈등, 배의 침몰시간, 잭이 로즈를 구하는 시간), 그리고 태도와 도덕성(사랑, 용기, 희생 :기회주의, 오만, 부패)을 기초로 훌륭하게 증명된다. 간단히 말하면 카메런과 그의 동료들이 (a)배경 (b)인물 (c)도덕성을 통하여 강력하게 상징적 특징들을 표현함으로써 이 영화의 성공에 공헌한 것은 확실하다. 카메런이 이 영화의 작가이자 감독으로서 다음과 같이 주장한 것은 옳다. "타이타닉은 단순히 경고성 이야기 — 신화, 우화, 혹은 인간의 악에 대한 은유같은 것만은 아니다. 그것 또한 신념과 용기, 희생 그리고 더욱 값진 사랑의 이야기다." (1997)

German artist Willer Stoewer rendered the sinking for the news media in 1912.

배경, 인물, 이야기, 그리고 도덕성의 커다란 상징적 특색은 우리에게 흥미있는 주제를 제공한다. 그 주제는 그 영화에 대한 개별적인 이해와 해석에 따라 다르겠지만 한가지 분명한 것은 그 영화는 인간의 삶에 대한 근본적인 탐구를 강화한다는 점이다. 삶의 의미는 무엇인가? 어떻게 하면 삶을 의미있게 만들까? 그게 경제력이나 정치권력, 건강이나 교육, 기회주의나 희생, 영광이나 신념, 혹은 미움이나 사랑을 통해서 이뤄질까? 다른 사람들에 대한 우리의 태도나 관계는 어떻게 유지 발전되어야 하는가? 고립속에선가, 상호의

"My goal in making this film was to show not only the dramatic death of this infamous ship, but her brief and glorious life as well. To capture the beauty, exuberance, optimism and hope of Titanic, her passengers and crew and, in the process of baring the dark side of humanity underlying this tragedy, celebrate the limltless potential of the human spirit. For Titanic is not just a cautionary tale - a myth, a parable, a metaphor for the ills of mankind. It is also a faith, courage, sacrifice and, above all else, love."

Writer / director James Cameron, 1997

(2.5.) Which film company was responsible for the production of Titanic?

    (a) MGM   (c) Universal Studios   (e) Warner Bros.
    (b) 20th Century Fox   (d) Paramount

(3.1.) A proper synonym of the italicized word, *socialite* at the top, under Cast, is _____. (Word in context: 3.1.- 3.2.)

    (a) Blue collar worker   (c) Technician   (e) Elite
    (b) Proletariat   (d) Engineer

(3.2.) The italicized word, *parable* at the first paragraph of page 342 can be substituted for _____.

    (a) Folktale   (b) Legend   (c) Fable   (d) Allegory   (e) Myth

(4.1.) It can be inferred that the parables can be found the most in books such as _____. (Making inferences: 4.1.- 4.3.)

    (a) Bibles   (c) Science fiction   (e) Textbooks
    (b) Encyclopedia   (d) Bedtime stories

(4.2.) It can be inferred that one of the major causes of death to the most people left in the ocean was _____.

    (a) Exhaustion   (c) Heart attack   (e) Inability to swim
    (b) Hypothermia   (d) Shark attack

(4.3.) The cost of producing Titanic must have been _____.

    (a) Over $1 million   (c) Over $10 million   (e) Over $200 million
    (b) Over $5 million   (d) Over $25 million

(5.1.) Based on the information given, it can be concluded that the success of Titanic is largely due to the dramatic effect in utilizing _____. (Conclusion: 5.1.-5.2.)

    (a) Characters   (c) Setting based on actual facts   (e) Theme
    (b) Plot   (d) Mystery of the Titanic

(5.2.) What do you conclude is a proper theme of the movie?

    (a) Love is unconditional
    (b) A socialite makes a big difference
    (c) Birds of a feather flock together
    (d) Live life one day at a time
    (e) Life offers many opportunities; the choice is yours

존에선가? 선택은 당신이 한다. 이런 모든 근본적인 문제들이 문학의 한 형태로서 이 영화 타이타닉을 통하여 다시 고찰될 수 있다.

Note

- **plot** = plan, outline of a story esp.novel : 구도, 구상, 음모
  - The plot thickens. (줄거리가 얽히고 설키는 구나.)
- **exceptional** = unusual oft. in a good sense : 보기 드문
  - All her children are intelligent, but the youngest boy is really exceptional.
  (자식들이 다 머리가 좋은데 특히 막내가 보통이 아니다.)
- **conflict** = disagreement, quarrel : 갈등, 투쟁
  - The two political parties have been in conflict over the government system.
  (두 정당은 정부 체제에 관하여 갈등을 일으키고 있다.)
- **specifications** = any of the parts of a detailed plan or set of descriptions : 세부사항, 제원, 명세서
  - According to the radio specifications, the wire should go into this hole.
  (라디오 조립설명서에 의하면 이 선이 이 구멍으로 끼워야 한다.)
- **gross** = total - Gross Domestic Product : 국내 총 생산량   • gross proceeds : 총매출액
- **beam** : 크고 긴 들보재(목재, 철강재, 석재 포함)   □**H-beam** : H자 형태의 빔
- **draught** : 흘수(吃水):배의 밑이 물에 잠기는 깊이
- **displacement tonnage** : 배수량 – 물에 배가 뜰때 그 무게로 인하여 밀려나가는 물의 양
- **wreckage** = the broken parts of a destroyed thing : 난파선의 표류물, 파편, 난파
- **retrieve** = regain, find and bring back : 회수하다, 되찾다,(컴)정보 검색하다
  - I ran back to retrieve the bag I had misplaced in the department store.
  (백화점에 잊고 놓고 온 가방을 찾으러 다시 뛰어갔다.)
- **flash back** = to return suddenly : 갑자기 지난 생각이 떠오르다
  - My mind flashed back to last Christmas. (갑자기 지난 크리스마스 생각이 났다.)
- **initiate** = start working : 시작, 창시하다
  - The company will initiate the new agreement on vacation and sick days.
  (회사는 휴가와 병가에 대한 협약을 실시할 것이다.)
- **demonstrate** = show clearly : 시범을 보이다, 확실히 보여주다
  - Let me demonstrate how this machine works. (이 기계 작동법을 시범해서 보여드리겠습니다.)
- **instinct** = the natural force in people, animals : 본능
  - Some animals hunt by instinct. (몇몇 동물들은 본능적으로 사냥한다.)
- **arrogance** = pride, self - importance in a rude way : 무례한 자존심, 오만
- **impending** : 닥쳐오는, 긴박한
  - I'm worried about the impending exams. (닥쳐오는 시험때문에 걱정이다.)
- **protagonist** = chief character in a play or story : 주인공, 주역
- **parable** = short simple story which teaches a moral or religious lesson : 우화, 비유담
- **iceberg** : 빙산   □**head for** = move toward : …로 향하여 가다
- **panic(k)** = feel pain : 무서워하다   • The crowd panicked at the sound of the guns.
- **load** = put load : 짐을 싣다. 무리하게 싣다. 필름을 넣다. 총을 장전하다.
  - Is this camera loaded? (필름 들었니?)
- **perish** = die, completely destroyed   • Almost a hundred people perished at the hotel fire.
- **rear up** = rise upright on the back legs : 뒤쪽(뒷 발)으로 일어서다
  - The horse reared up and threw me off. (말이 뒷발로 일어서서 내게 떨어졌다)
- **on end** = upright : 직립으로   □**perpendicular** : 수직의
- **release** : 영화 개봉하다

3.2.4. Sports

Passage 1 : **The Summer Olympic Games**

The Summer Olympic Games are the world's most important international athletic event. The Games are held every four years in different cities selected by the members of the International Olympic Committee (I.O.C.). Athletes from almost every country in the world compete in a wide variety of sports in the Games. The development of these important athletic events trace back to the ancient times.

According to tradition, the games were first celebrated in 776 B.C. at Olympia, Greece, and were held at four-year intervals thereafter. Following the subjugation of Greece by the Roman Empire, the games declined and were abolished in A.D. 393 by the Emperor Theodosius I, who was probably opposed to the pagan rites associated with the games.

Baron Pierre de Coubertin (1863-1937) of France, believing that a restoration would be beneficial for the youth of the world, brought together an international group in Paris in 1894. He proposed his idea, "The most important thing in the Olympic Games is not to win, but to take part in, just as the most important thing in life is not the triumph, but the struggle. The essential thing is not to have conquered, but to have fought well." His suggestion was enthusiastically greeted by the group, and later it was adopted as the Olympic Creed at Antwerp, Belgium, in 1920. He actively helped form the I.O.C., which has governed the Games ever since. The first modern Games were held in 1896 under the royal patronage of the King of Greece in Athens, with 13 countries and 311 athletes taking part in the competition. Subsequent games were held in various cities of the world at four-year intervals, except for lapses during World War I and II. The Games were previously limited to only amateur athletes, but beginning with soccer in 1984, professionals were permitted to compete in several events. The Olympics has steadily grown to draw huge interest from almost every country in the world. The *Centennial* Games, held in Atlanta in 1996, were the largest in Olympic history, with 11,000 athletes from 197 countries competing, and more than 2 million people attending the events.

A brief profile of events in the modern Summer Olympic Games is listed in a chronological order.

3.2.4. 스포츠

지문 1 : 하계 올림픽 경기

하계 올림픽 경기는 세계에서 가장 중요한 체육 행사 중의 하나다. 이 경기는 국제 올림픽 위원회의 위원들이 선정한 다른 도시들에서 4년마다 개최된다. 세계의 거의 모든 국가의 체육인들이 올림픽 경기에서 다양한 스포츠를 겨룬다. 이 중요한 체육행사의 발달은 고대로 거슬러 올라간다.

Early Greek Olympic boxers, depicted on an Attic vase dating from the 6th century B.C.

구전(口傳)에 의하면 최초의 경기는 기원전 776년에 그리스의 올림피아에서 거행되었고 그 후 4년마다 거행되었다. 그리스가 로마에 정복당한 후 그 경기는 쇠퇴하여 기원 393년에 테어도시어스 황제에 의하여 폐지되었다. 그런데 그 황제는 아마 그 경기와 연관된 이교도의 의식(儀式)에 반대했던 것같다.

Pierre de Coubertin(1863-1937), founder of the modern Olympic Games. Credit IOC Archives.

프랑스의 삐에르 쿠베르텡 남작은 (올림픽 경기의)복구가 세계의 젊은이들을 위해서 유익하다고 믿고 1894년에 파리에서 국제적인 모임을 결성했다. 그는 다음과 같은 제안을 했다.

"경기에서 가장 중요한 것은 이기는 게 아니고 참가하는 것입니다. 마치 인생에서 가장 중요한 것이 승리가 아니고 노력이듯이 본질적인 것은 정복했느냐가 아니고 잘 싸웠느냐는 것입니다." 이 제안은 그 모임의 열광적인 환영을 받았고 후에 1920년 벨기에의 앤트워프에서 올림픽 강령으로 채택되었다. 그는 적극적으로 국제 올림픽 위원회의 결성을 도왔고 그 위원회가 그 후 계속하여 경기를 운영해 왔다. 최초의 현대 올림픽은 아테네에서 그리스 왕실의 후원으로 13개국 311명의 선수들이 경기에 참석한 가운데 1896년 개최되었다. 후속 경기들은 세계 1,2차대전 중의 휴식기를 제외하고 4년 간격으로 세계의 다양한 도시에서 개최되었다. 전에는 경기가 아마추어 선수들에게만 국한되었으나 1984년 축구를 시작

Long jump medalists Jesse (U.S.), Luz Long (Germany) and Naoto Tajima (Japan) at the 1936 Summer Games in Berlin, the last held until after World War II.

Running barefooted, Ethiopia's Abebe Bikila won the marathon in 1960.

Year	City	Country	Features
1896	Athens	Greece	9 games, the athletes were all males.
1900	Paris	France	Women took part in the competition for the first time.
1904	St. Louis	U.S.A.	The smallest number of competition in modern Olympic history
1908	London	England	A foul had been ruled during the championship race. A British runner, W. Halswelle won the gold medal in the 400 meter race without competitors.
1912	Stockholm	Sweden	The most successful since the renewal of the modern Olympic Games and helped the Games by restoring their prestige.
1916	Canceled due to World War I		
1920	Antwerp	Belgium	The Olympic Oath was introduced. Germany, Austria, Bulgaria, Hungary, Turkey- enemies of Belgium, were not invited to participate.
1924	Paris	France	Johnny Weismuller, who would later become world-famous Tarzan in the movies, won the 100-m and 400-m individual free style swimming events.
1928	Amsterdam	Holland	Women participate in track and field for he first time.
1932	Los Angeles	U.S.A.	Athletes were quartered in an "Olympic Village" that was specially constructed.
1936	Berlin	Germany	The torch relay was held for the first time in the modern games. Athletes took turns carrying the flame from Greece to Grunewald Stadium. Sohn, Keejung won the marathon.
1940 Canceled due to World War II			
1944 Canceled due to World War II			
1948	London	England	59 countries were represented by 4468 athletes.
1952	Helsinki	Finland	The Soviet Union entered Olympic competition for the first time. Emil & Dona Zatopek of Czechoslovakia became stars in track competition and in the javelin.
1956	Melbourne	Australia	Political controversies: Holland, Switzerland, Spain withdrew because of the Soviet invasion of Hungary; Egypt and Lebanon withdrew because of the Suez Canal conflict between Egypt and Israel. Mainland China did not participate because of the presence of Taiwan.

Sprinters in the first round of the women's 100-meter dash at the 1996 Centennial Summer Games.

In 1976 14-year-old Nadia Comaneci (Romania) captured three gold medals in women's gymnastics. She was to win two additional gold medals, in 1980.

으로 프로선수들도 몇 종목에서 시합이 허락되었다. 올림픽은 세계 거의 모든 국가의 지대한 관심을 끌만큼 계속 성장했다. 1996년 애틀란타에서 개최된 100주년 경기는 197개국에서 11,000명의 선수가 시합을 벌이고 2백만명 이상이 행사에 참여한 올림픽 역사상 최대의 것이었다.

현대 올림픽 종목에 대한 간단한 소개를 연대 순으로 기록한다.

Note

□ **trace back** = follow the course, line, history : 자취를 거슬러 올라가다
  • I traced my family back to the earlier period of Koryo Dynasty.
    (가문의 역사를 고려 초기까지 거슬러 올라갔다.)
□ **subjugate** = conquer and take power over, enslave : 정복하다, 복종시키다
□ **abolish** = put an end to, do away with : 폐지, 철폐하다
  • There are many bad customs and laws that ought to be abolished. (철폐해야할 많은 악습과 법들이 있다.)
□ **pagan** : 이교도   □ **creed** = a system of beliefs or principles : 신조, 교리, 강령
□ **rite** = a form of behavior with a fixed pattern usu. for religious purpose : 의식(儀式)
□ **restoration** : 복구, 회복, 복원   □ **patronage** = the support given by a patron : 후원, 보호
□ **centennial** = the day or year exactly 100years after a particular event : 100주년
□ **profile** = a short description : 간략한 소개   □ **in chronological order** : 연대 순으로
□ **oath** = a solemn promise, vow : 맹세, 서약   □ **torch** : 봉화, 성화
□ **quarter** = find lodgings for troops, place troops in lodging : 숙영시키다, 숙박시키다
□ **relay** = sent out by relay, take turns in keeping an activity going continuously : 계주하다, 중계방송하다 • A relay is the race in which each member of each team runs part of the distance. (릴레이는 각각의 선수가 전체 거리의 부분을 달리는 경주다.)
□ **javelin** : 투창   □ **sprinter** : 단거리 선수
□ **boycott** = refuse to do business, attend or take part in : 거부하다, 불매운동을 하다
  • They're boycotting the store because the poeple who work there aren't allowed to join a union.
    (사람들이 그 가게에서 일하기를 거부하고 있다. 왜냐하면 노조가입이 허락되지 않기 때문이다.)
□ **reverse** = change to the opposite : 역으로 하다, 파기하다
□ **mar** = spoil : 망쳐 놓다 • What a little makes a mar! (얼마나 하찮은 것이 인생을 망치는 건가!)
□ **intrude** : 밀고 들어오다, 강요하다 • Don't intrude your opinion on me! (네 생각을 나에게 강요하지 마라!)
□ **retaliation** = paying back evil with evil : 복수
  • If we raise import duties on their goods, they may retaliate against us.
    (만일 우리가 수입관세를 인상하면 그들도 우리에게 보복 할지도 모른다.)
□ **ban** : 금지하다   □ **Nuclear Test Ban Treaty** : 핵실험 금지 조약
  • The play was banned by the censor. (그 연극은 검열관에 의하여 금지 당했다.)

Year	City	Country	Notes
1960	Rome	Italy	U.S. sprinter Wilma Rudolph won three gold medals; Cassius Clay (later known as Muhammed Ali) won the light heavyweight boxing gold medal; Ethiopia's Abeba Bikila won the marathon running barefooted.
1964	Tokyo	Japan	Bikila defended his marathon title with shoes on this time.
1968	Mexico City	Mexico	The I.O.C. voted to readmit South Africa to the Olympic family, but a proposed boycott by 40 countries caused the ruling body to reverse its decision.
1972	Munich	Germany	Palestinian terrorists broke into the athlete's village and killed 2 Israeli athletes, 9 Israeli hostages taken at the village died later in an airport shoot-out, along with 5 of the terrorists and a German policeman.
1976	Montreal	Canada	Nadia Comaneci, a 14 year-old Romanian gymnast, stole the hearts of onlookers with a spectacular performance that included 7 perfect scores and earned her 3 gold medals.
1980	Moscow	U.S.S.R.	The Games were marred when about 50 countries joined the U.S. in boycotting the Games in protest against the 1979 Soviet invasion of Afghanistan.
1984	Los Angeles	U.S.A.	Politics once again intruded when the U.S.S.R. led a 15 nation boycott of the games as a retaliation for the U.S. boycott of 1980.
1988	Seoul	Korea	U.S. & Soviet athletes met in competition for the first time in 12 years.
1992	Barcelona	Spain	Baseball was introduced as an event. South Africa, banned since 1960 for racial policies, competed for the first time.
1996	Atlanta	U.S.A.	The Centennial Games after the modern Olympic Games were held in 1896. A record participation of 197 nations and 11,000 athletes. Thuywane, the first black South African man, won a gold medal in the marathon.

(1) A suitable title of the passage would be _____. (Subject matter)

    (a) Development of the Olympic Games   (d) Description of the Olympic Games
    (b) Origin of the Olympic Games   (e) Analysis of the Olympic Games
    (c) Definition of the Olympic Games

(2.1) The athlete who won gold medals twice in the marathon _____.
    (Locating the facts: 2.1.-2.3.)

영어 격언과 한문 격언과의 만남 (6)

Selected proverbs for the study of cross-cultural expressions

1. **Nobody is born without his own bread.**
   天不生無祿之人 地不張無名之草(천불생무록지인 지부장무명지초)
   – 하늘은 녹없는 인간을 내지않고 땅은 이름없는 풀을 키우지 않는다.

2. **Too many cooks spoil the broth.** 作舍道傍 三年不成(작사도방 삼년불성 ; 作 = build)
   – 길가에 짓는 집은 삼년이 걸려도 완성되지 않는다.

3. **A friend in need is not to be forgotten.** 貧賤之交不可忘(빈천지교불가망)
   – 어려울 때 사귄 친구는 잊혀지지 않는다.

4. **A leopard cannot change its spots.** 江山易改 本性難移(강산이개 본성난이)
   – 강산은 쉽게 바뀌어도 본성은 고치기 어렵다.

5. **One should not wash one's dirty linen in public.** 家醜不可外場(가추불가외장)
   – 집안의 불결한 것을 밖으로 들추는 일은 옳지 못하다.

6. **A pie in the sky.** 畵中之餠, 見而不食(화중지병 견이불식) – 그림의 떡

7. **Rome was not built in a day.** 大器晩成(대기만성) – 큰 그릇은 늦게 이루어진다.
   · Better late ripe and bear than early blossom and blast.

8. **He who goes to law over a hen will have to be content with an egg.**
   必也使無訟(필야사무송 ; 使＝make) – 절대로 소송은 하지 마라.

9. **A gem is not polished without rubbing, nor man perfected without learning.**
   玉不琢不成器 人不學不知道(옥불탁불성기 인불학부지도)
   – 옥은 다듬어야 그릇이 되고 사람은 배우지 않으면 길을 모른다.

10. **Forgive others everything, yourself nothing.**
    責人之心責己 恕己之心恕人(책인지심책기 서기지심서인)
    – 남을 나무라듯 자신을 나무라고 나를 용서하듯이 남을 용서하라.

11. **The greatest hero is he who can overcome himself.** 自勝者强(자승자강)
    – 자기를 이기는 자가 강자다.

12. **Necessity will teach a man to be wise.** 窮卽通(궁즉통) – 궁하면 통한다.
    · Necessity is the mother of invention.

13. **Love your neighbors as yourself.** 愛人若愛其身(애인약애기신) – 자신을 사랑하듯 남을 사랑하라.

14. **A heavy purse makes a light heart.** 有恒産有恒心(유항산유항심)
    – 일정한 재산이 있어야 마음이 떳떳하다.
    · An empty sack can't stand upright.

(a) Sohn, Keejung (c) Emil Zatopek (e) Abeba Bikila
(b) W. Halswelle (d) Wilma Rudolph

(2.2) The place where Muhammed Ali won an Olympic gold medal in boxing _____.

(a) Helsinki (b) Melbourne (c) Rome (d) Tokyo (e) Mexico City

(2.3) The Olympic Games were often used for political purposes. The case in which the Soviet Union was accused for invading Afghanistan was at _____.

(a) Munich (b) Montreal (c) Moscow (d) Tokyo (e) Seoul

(3) The italicized word, *Centennial* in the last paragraph can be substituted for _____. (Word in context)

(a) 10th (b) 50th (c) 100th (d) 150th (e) 200th

(4) Based on the information given, it can be inferred that the Olympic Games have not developed consistently and smoothly since the Roman era. It is probably because of _____ factors. (Making inferences)

(a) Economic   (c) Commercial   (e) Military
(b) Political   (d) Environmental

(5) Based on the facts presented, the Games have often been used for political purposes, which is against the idea of Baron Pierre de Coubertin. What do you conclude is one of the major reasons for these happenings? (Conclusion)

(a) The Games are as important as bread
(b) Honor is more important than politics
(c) Nationalism is as important as honor
(d) Principle is more important than reality
(e) Reality is more important than principle

Selected proverbs for the study of cross-cultural expressions

영어 격언과 한문 격언과의 만남 (7)

1. **Little strokes fell great oaks.** 十伐之木(십벌지목) – 열 번 찍어 안 넘어가는 나무 없다.
   · An oak is not felled at one stroke.

2. **Patience is the best buckler against affronts.** 忍一時之憤 免百日憂(인일시지분 면백일우)
   – 한 때의 울분은 참으면 백일의 근심을 면한다. · Patience is the key of joy, but hate is the key of sorrow.

3. **Money breeds (begets) money.** 富益富貧益貧(부익부빈익빈) – 돈이 돈을 번다.

4. **Constant dripping water wears away stone.** 滴水磨石(적수마석 ; 滴 = a drop of water)
   – 물방울이 돌을 닳게 한다.
   · Feather by feather the goose is plucked. / · Grain by grain a hen fills her belly.
   · Step by step the ladder is ascended. / · Step by step goes a long way.

5. **Poverty is an enemy to good manners.** 衣食足而知禮節(의식족이지예절)
   – 입을 것, 먹을 것이 풍족해야 예절도 알 수 있다. · Well-fed, well-bred.

6. **Poverty is the mother of all arts.** 飢寒發道心(기한발도심) – 춥고 배고파야 도를 닦으려는 마음이 생긴다.

7. **There's many a slip between the cup and the lip.** 好事多魔(호사다마) – 좋은 일에는 마가 낀다.
   · Lights are usually followed by shadows.

8. **Good news goes on crutches.** 好事不出門(호사불출문) – 좋은 일은 소문이 잘 나지 않는다.

9. **Bad news travels fast.** 惡事千里(악사천리) – 나쁜 일은 천리간다. (나쁜 소문은 빨리 퍼진다.)
   · Ill news runs space. / · Ill news never comes too late.

10. **It's good fishing in troubled waters.** 漁夫之利(어부지리) – 노력하지 않고 얻어지는 불로소득
    · Two dogs strive for a bone, and a third runs away with it.
    · Divide and rule. (분열시키고 싸우는 틈을 타서 지배하면 힘이 안든다.)

11. **What's done can't be undone.** 旣往不咎(기왕불구 ; 咎 = blame) – 지난 일은 탓하지 마라.
    Things past can't be recalled. 旣往之不諫(기왕지불간 ; 諫 = remonstrate)
    · It's no use crying over spilt milk. / · Repentance comes too late. / · Sorrow will pay no debt.

12. **Jack of all trades, master of none.** 博而不精(박이부정) – 많이 알면 정교하지 못하다.
    A dozen trades, thirteen miseries. 巧者卒之奴(교자졸지노) – 재주 많은 사람은 남의 종노릇 한다.
    · A man of trades begs his bread on Sunday.

13. **Two of a trade seldom agree.** 同業者不相合(동업자불상합) – 동업자는 서로 어울리지 못한다.
    · One potter envies another.

14. **Soldiers fight and kings are heroes.** 一將功成萬骨膏(일장공성만골고 ; 膏 = oil)
    – 한 명의 장수가 공을 이루는데 수 많은 사람이 희생된다. · The blood of the soldiers makes the glory of the general.

15. **Strike while the iron is hot.** 勿失好機(물실호기) – 좋은 기회를 놓치지 마라.
    · Make hay while the sun shines. / · Opportunity seldom knocks twice.
    · Hoist the sail when the wind is fair. / · The mill can't grind with the water past.
    · Gather roses while you may.

Passage 2 :

Jesse Owens (1913-1980): The First Black Goodwill Ambassador

Jesse Owens was born in Alabama to Henry and Emma Alexander Owens, sharecroppers, as their seventh child. Jesse's sensational athletic career began while he was in high school in Ohio. During these years, he won all the major track events, broke a variety of state, national, and world records. By the time he reached his senior year, many colleges and universities sought to recruit him, but he chose Ohio State University even though the university was not able to give him a track scholarship. During college, Jesse supported himself and his young wife, Ruth, with a variety of jobs such as a night elevator operator, waiter, gas pumper, library worker, and a page at the Ohio Statehouse, all between his collegiate studies and competitions. Jesse was named the captain of Ohio State's track team, the first Negro to hold such a position on any Ohio State athletic team. He had a brilliant collegiate career leading his team to several national track and field titles.

But, Jesse's proudest moment occurred during his collegiate career when he represented the United States in the 1936 Summer Olympic Games in Berlin, Germany. During the Games, he won four gold medals in track and field events. His greatest accomplishment was to prove that individual excellence, regardless of race or national origin, distinguishes one man from another, thus discrediting Adolf Hitler's political propaganda that the white man, especially the Aryan, was superior to the other races. Jesse won the gold medal in the 100 meter dash (set Olympic record), 200 meter dash (Olympic record), broad jump (Olympic record), 400 meter relay (Olympic and World record).

After the Olympics, Jesse returned to the United States to a hero's welcome. He could have earned a vast amount of money if he turned professional. But he decided to finish his college education at Ohio State University. After his education, he moved to Chicago, and he devoted himself as a board member to underprivileged youths. He served for five and a half years as the Sports Specialist of the State of Illinois Youths Commission. In 1955, he accepted commission from the State Department as America's Ambassador of Sports, and he toured India, Singapore, Malaysia, and the Philippines, meeting with government and sports officials and, as always, talking to underprivileged young people. In 1956, he was named the personal representative of President Eisenhower to the Olympic Games in Australia, and visited schools and youth clubs over there. Jesse traveled widely as an inspiring speaker who provided the underprivileged youths with courage throughout the world, so that they could have clear goals and dreams to strive for. For his accomplishments and inspiration, he was awarded numerous medals and honors from a variety of

지문 2 : 제시 오웬스-최초의 흑인 친선 대사

제시 오웬스는 소작농인 헨리와 에마 알렉산더 오웬스 사이의 7남으로 알라바마에서 태어났다. 세상을 놀래 준 육상인으로서 제시의 인생은 오하이오주 고교시절에 시작되었다. 이 고교 시절에 모든 주요한 트랙경기에서 우승했고 미국내의 각 주, 국내 그리고 세계 기록을 차례로 깨뜨렸다. 고교 졸업반이었을 때 많은 대학들이 그를 선발하려 했지만 그는 오하이오 주립대학을 선택했다. 비록 그 대학은 그에게 육상 장학금을 줄 수 없었지만, 대학시절에 그는 여러가지 일자리, 예를 들면 야간 엘리베이터 기사, 웨이터, 주유소 주유공, 오하이오주 주청 급사 등, 대학 공부와 육상시합을 하면서 스스로 돈을 벌어 자신과 식구들을 부양했다. 제시는 오하이오주 육상 팀의 주장에 임명되었는데, 오하이오주 육상 팀에서 흑인이 그런 자리를 맡기는 그가 처음이었다. 그는 자기 팀을 서너 개의 전국 트랙과 필드경기 선수권을 차지하도록 이끄는 눈부신 대학 경력을 쌓았다.

그러나 제시의 가장 자랑스러운 순간은 1936년 독일 베를린 하계 올림픽에서 그가 미국을 대표했던 대학 선수시절 중에 일어났다. 그 올림픽 기간중에 그는 트랙과 필드에서 4개의 금메달을 땄다. 그

의 가장 위대한 업적은 인종이나 민족적 근원에 상관없이 개인의 우수성이 한 인간을 다른 인간과 구별짓는다는 것을 증명한 일로서 백인 특히 아리안 족이 다른 인종보다 우수하다는 아돌프 히틀러의 정치적 선전을 불신하게 만든 것이었다. 제시는 100미터 경주(올림픽 기록), 200미터 경주(올림픽 기록), 넓이뛰기(올림픽 기록), 400미터 계주(올림픽 세계기록)에서 금메달을 땄다.

올림픽 후 미국에 돌아와 영웅적인 환영을 받았다. 그

people and organizations including Presidents Ford and Carter, and posthumously from President Bush to Jesse's wife, Ruth.

    Jesse Owens passed away on March 31, 1980, and President Carter made the following tribute for him, "Perhaps no athlete better symbolized the human struggle against tyranny, poverty and racial *bigotry*. His personal triumphs as a world-class athlete and record-holder were the *prelude* to a career devoted to helping others. His work with young athletes, as an unofficial ambassador overseas, and a spokesman for freedom are a rich legacy to his fellow Americans."

(1.1) The topic sentence of the second paragraph is _____. (Topic sentence)

    (a) When Jesse represented the U.S…
    (b) Jesse's proudest moment occurred…
    (c) During his collegiate career…
    (d) During the Games, he won…
    (e) His greatest accomplishment was…

(1.2) The supporting details of the second paragraph are _____. (Supporting details)

    (a) Jesse's moment occurred…, When he represented…, & The white man was superior…
    (b) He won 4 gold medals… Individual excellence…, & When he represented…
    (c) His greatest accomplishment…, Discrediting Hitler's…, & He won 4 gold medals…
    (d) He won 4 gold medals…, The white man was superior…, & During the Games…
    (e) During the Games… His accomplishment…, & He won 4 gold medals…

(2) Instead of wealth and glory, Jesse dedicated his life to inspiring underprivileged youths while rejecting racism and dogmatism. Who gave such a remark for Jesse? (Locating the facts)

    (a) Bush   (b) Eisenhower   (c) Ford   (d) Carter   (e) Hitler

(3.1) The italicized word, *bigotry* in the last paragraph can be substituted for _____. (Word in context)

    (a) Plot   (b) Affection   (c) Totality   (d) Prejudice   (e) Tolerance

(3.2) The antonym of the italicized word, *prelude* in the last paragraph is _____.

    (a) Preface   (c) Epilogue   (e) Key point
    (b) Introduction   (d) Surface

는 프로로 전향하면 엄청난 액수의 돈을 벌 수도 있었다. 그러나 그는 오하이오 주립대에서 대학 교육을 마치기로 결정했다. 교육을 마친 후 그는 시카고로 이사했고 한 위원회의 위원으로서 혜택받지 못한 젊은 이들을 위해서 헌신했다. 그는 5년 반 동안 일리노이주 청년위원회 스포츠 전문가로서 봉사했다.

　1955년에 국무성으로부터 스포츠 미국 친선 대사로서의 임무를 받아들여 인도, 싱가포르, 말레이지아 그리고 필리핀을 여행하며 정부나 스포츠 관리들을 만나고 언제나 불우한 젊은이들과 대화했다. 1956년에 오스트레일리아 올림픽에 아이젠하워 대통령의 비공식 대표로서 지명을 받아 그곳의 학교와 클럽들을 방문했다. 제시는 전세계 불우한 젊은이들에게 용기를 주어 목표로 삼아 노력할 명백한 꿈을 갖도록 혼을 일깨우는 연사로서 널리 여행했다. 그의 업적과 꿈을 심어주는 일로 포드 대통령, 카터 대통령, 사후에는 부시대통령이 그의 아내 루스에게 수여한 상을 포함하여 수많은 메달과 훈장을 받았다.

　제시 오웬스는 1980년 3월 31일 타계했고 카터 대통령은 그를 위해 다음과 같은 찬사를 보냈다. "아마 어느 체육인도 제시 오웬스처럼 전제(專制-인종적)와 빈곤 그리고 인종적 편협을 타파하기 위한 인간의 투쟁을 더 잘 상징적으로 보여준 사람은 없을 것입니다. 세계 일류 체육인으로서, 기록 보유자로서 그의 개인적인 승리는 남을 돕는데 헌신한 한 생애로 가기 위한 서곡입니다. 외국에 대한 비공식적 대사로서, 자유를 위한 대변자로서 그가 젊은 체육인들과 함께한 일은 그의 동료 미국인들에게 풍성한 유산입니다."

Note

- □ **goodwill** = friendly feeling, favor : 선의, 친선　• goodwill visit (친선 방문)
  - policy of goodwill in international relations (국제 관계의 친선 정책)　• goodwill envoy (친선사절)
- □ **sharecropper** = a tenant farmer who pays a share of his crop as rent to the owner of the land : 소작인, 노예제도 폐지 이후 미 남부에서 생긴 물납(物納)소작인
- □ **track events** : 트랙 종목　　　　□ **field events** : 필드 종목
  - Which event did you enter for? (어떤 종목에 참가했니?)
- □ **recruit** = find a new member : 신규 모집하다, 신규 채용하다
  - This year few firms will recruit the college graduates. (금년 대졸자 신규 채용 회사가 거의 없다.)
- □ **page** = a boy servant usu. in uniform in a hotel or club : 사환, 급사, 사동,
  (v)이름을 불러 찾게 하다
  - I'd like you to page a boy by the name of Inho. (인호라는 사내아이 좀 찾아주시오.)

(4) The underlined sentence, "individual excellence, regardless of race or national origin, distinguishes one man from another" can be a similar _____ with the Dr. Martin Luther King's remark in "I Have A Dream" (1963), "…they (my four children) will not be judged by the color of their skin but by the content of their character." (Rhetorical techniques)

   (a) Connotation   (d) Denotation
   (b) Juxtaposition   (e) Cliché
   (c) Justification

(5) Based on the information given, it can be concluded that Jesse Owens will live long with us. One of the reasons for this factor is his _____. (Conclusion)

   (a) Preference for wealth
   (b) Glory seeking
   (c) Inspiration for equal human rights & dignity as well as athletic excellence
   (d) Dedication to desegregation
   (e) Accomplishment in Berlin & inspiring speeches

Passage 3 : World Cup Soccer

Soccer is one of the most popular sports, and the game attracts huge crowds throughout the world. The game is both so *fanatic* and popular that even some tragic riots take place elsewhere. In Lima, the Olympic qualifying match between Argentina and Peru cost 309 lives, and caused 1000 fans injured in 1964. The 1970 World Cup qualifying match between Honduras and El Salvador sparked a border war between them, and the European Cup Final match between England and Italy in 1985, cost 38 lives and 200 people injured.

The origin of this game can be found in every corner of the world. A ball game was played in China, Japan, Egypt, and Assyria in ancient times. Modern soccer was born in 1863 when the London Football Association issued its first set of rules, and the game became to be introduced to many countries around the world by sailors, missionaries, and settlers. On May 26, 1928, the World Cup was launched by five European countries (Italy, Netherlands, Spain, Hungary, and Sweden) and Uruguay that wanted to hold the tournament. Jules Rimet, President of the Federation International of Football Association (FIFA), played a key role in helping form the World Cup claiming, "Soccer could *reinforce* the ideals of a permanent and real peace (1926)." On May 18, 1929 at the congress of Barcelona, Uruguay was proclaimed host of the 1st World Cup because of her record in the Olympic tournaments and of Rimet's efforts of making soccer as an universal sport. The following list shows the World Cup competitions from 1930 to 1998.

- **discredit** = cause the truth, value, or credit of sth or sb to seem doubtful : 불신하게 만들다, 가치를 떨어뜨리다
  - Such foolish behavior will discredit you. (그런 바보짓 하면 위신이 떨어진다.)
- **propaganda** = spreading of information, doctrines, ideas with the public : 선전
  - propaganda by government departments for public health, better driving (공중위생, 운전개선을 위한 정부의 홍보)
- **the dash** = short race : 단거리 질주
- **the 100(200)meters dash** : 100(200)미터 달리기
- **board** = group of persons controlling a business of a government department : 위원회, 평의회, (정부)부, 국, 청 성(table에서 유래)
  - School board (학교위원회)   • the Board of Education (교육위원회)
  - a board of directors (중역회)   • a board of health (보건국)
- **an inspiring sight** : 고무적인 장면
- **strive for** = struggle hard to get or conquer : 분투, 노력하다
  - She strove for recognition as an artist. (화가로서 인정받으려고 안간 힘을 썼다.)
- **tyranny** = cruel or unjust use of power : 전제, 전횡,   • cf. tyrant : 전제군주, 폭군
- **bigotry** = strong hold on to an opinion or belief in defiance of reason or argument : 편협, 아집, 광신   • racial bigotry (인종차별을 옹호하는 아집)
- **prelude** = introduction : 전주, 서곡   □ **interlude** : 간주   □ **postlude** : 후주곡
- **legacy** = money etc, that passes to somebody on the death of the owner : 유산
- **reject** = put aside, throw away as not good enough : 거절하다, 거부하다
  - She rejected my suggestions.
- **dogma** = an important belief that people are expected to accept without reasoning : 독단   • dogmatic (독단적인)   • dogmatism (독단론, 교조주의)   • church dogmatism (교회의 독선)
  - political dogmatism (정치적 독단)

지문 3 : 월드컵 축구

축구는 가장 인기있는 스포츠 중의 하나고 축구경기가 있는 곳엔 수많은 군중이 모인다. 축구시합은 너무 인기있고 열광적이어서 시합장 수가 아닌 딴 곳에서 비극적인 폭동이 발생한다. 1964년 리마, 아르헨티나와 페루사이의 올림픽 본선 진출 결정전에서 309명이 죽고, 1000명이 부상했다. 1970년 온두라스와 엘살바도르간의

The first rules of football were laid down in Rugby. The teams were composed of 15 to 60 players. In 1870, the Football Association fixed the number of players belonging to each team at 11.

Year	Championship Match	Location
1930	Uruguay 4, Argentina 2	Montevideo, Uruguay
1934	Italy 2, Czechoslovakia 1	Rome
1938	Italy 4, Hungary 2	Paris
1950	Uruguay 2, Brazil 1	Rio de Janeiro
1954	West Germany 3, Hungary 2	Bern, Switzerland
1958	Brazil 5, Sweden 2	Stockholm
1962	Brazil 3, Czechoslovakia 1	Santiago, Chile
1966	England 4, West Germany 2	London
1970	Brazil 4, Italy 1	Mexico City
1974	West Germany 2, Netherlands 1	Munich
1978	Argentina 3, Netherlands 1	Buenos Aires
1982	Italy 3, West Germany 1	Madrid
1986	Argentina 3, West Germany 2	Mexico City
1990	West Germany 1, Argentina 0	Rome
1994	Brazil 0, Italy 0 Brazil won the World Cup by a penalty kick (3:2) during extended time	Buffalo, USA
1998	France 3, Brazil 0	Paris

Also, a list of the top 15 ranking countries from 1930 to 1994 is provided. See the list on page 365.

 P = played ; W = won ; D = drew ; L = lost ; GF = goals for ; GA = goals allowed ; Pts = points

As we have seen in the list, Brazil is ranked as the highest team from 1930 to 1994. One of the reasons can be probably due to the contributions of Pele who

월드컵 본선진출 결승전은 국경 전쟁의 도화선이 되었고, 1985년의 영국과 이탈리아의 유럽컵 결승전에서는 38명이 죽고 200명이 부상당했다.

축구 시합의 기원은 세계 어느곳에서나 찾을 수 있다. 중국, 일본, 이집트, 앗시리아에서는 일종의 구기시합이 있었다. 현대축구는 1863년 런던 축구 협회가 최초로 경기규칙을 발표했을 때 탄생했으며 그 시합은 선원들, 선교사들 그리고 정착민들에 의하여 전세계 여러나라로 소개되었다. 1928년 5월 26일에 월드컵이 5개 유럽 국가들(이탈리아, 네덜란드, 스페인, 헝가리, 스웨덴)과 시합을 하고자 하는 우루과이에 의하여 시작되었다. FIFA 총재인 Jules Rimet는 월드컵이 개최되도록 하는데 중요한 역할을 했다. "축구는 영원하고 진실된 평화의 이념을 지켜준다(1926)." 라고 그는 호소하였다. 1929년 5월 18일 바르셀로나 회의에서, 우루과이는 Jules Rimet가 축구를 세계적인 스포츠로 만드는 데 노력한 공로와 우루과이의 올림픽 축구 게임 성적 때문에 제1회 월드컵 주최국으로 선정됐다. 다음표는 1930년에서 1998년까지의 월드컵 시합을 보여준다. 표에서 보여주는 바와 같이 브라질이 1930년에서 1994년까지 최고의 팀으로 서열이 정해졌다. 그 이유 중의 하나는 브라질 팀이 1958년, 1962년, 1970년 3차례 월드컵에서 우승하도록 힘이 됐던 펠레의 업적 때문이라고 할 수 있을 것이다. 1940년에 태어난 펠레의 본명은 Edson Arantes do Nascimento다. 그의 축구 재능은 전 브라질 월드컵 선수에 의하여 발견되었다.

1956년 펠레가 15세 때 브라질 프로 축구 클럽인 Santo Futebol Clube에서 경기했고 그 때 그의 뛰어난 기술들이 드러났다. 1958년 스톡홀름에서, 1962년 산티아고에서, 1966년 런던에서, 그리고 1970년 멕시코에서 월드컵을 위해 출전했다.

펠레는 14번의 월드컵 시합에서 12득점했고 선수로서 3차례 월드컵 우승권을 딴 유일한 선수다. 또한 1,363회 프로시합에서 1,280 득점을 했다. 그런 이유로 사람들은 그를 축구 황제라고 부른다.

helped the Brazilian team win the World Cup three times in 1958, 1962, and 1970. Pele's real name is Edson Arantes do Nascimento who was born on October 23, 1940. His soccer skills were discovered by a former Brazilian World Cup player. At the age of 15, in 1956 Pele played for the Santo Futebol Clube, a professional Brazilian soccer club in which his excellent skills were demonstrated. In 1958, he played for the World Cup at Stockholm; Santiago, 1962; London, 1966; and Mexico City, 1970.

    Pele scored 12 goals in 14 World Cup matches, and he's the only person to have won 3 World Cup titles as a player. He also scored 1,280 goals in 1,363 professional games, for which people called him, "Emperor of Soccer."

(1) A suitable title of this passage would be _____. (Subject matter)

    (a) World Cup Soccer   (c) FIFA   (e) The origin of soccer
    (b) Jules Rimet   (d) Pele

(2.1) Who devoted himself in founding the World Cup Soccer? (Locating the facts)

    (a) Edson Arantes do Nascimento   (c) Rimet   (e) Jesse Owens
    (b) Pele   (d) Coubertin

(2.2) What was the score of the 1994 World Cup and who won?

    (a) 3 to 2 - Brazil   (c) 3 to 0 - Italy   (e) 0 to 0 - no winner
    (b) 3 to 0 - Brazil   (d) 3 to 2 - Italy

(2.3) From 1930 to 1994, Argentina played ___ World Cup matches and won ___ of them.

    (a) 12   26   (c) 32   26   (e) 52   26
    (b) 22   26   (d) 42   26

(2.4) What is the first city to have hosted the first World Cup tournament?

    (a) Mexico City   (c) Rome   (e) Paris
    (b) Buffalo   (d) Montevideo

(2.5) From 1930 to 1994, Poland drew (tied) in how many matches?

    (a) 4   (b) 5   (c) 6   (d) 7   (e) 13

(3.1) A synonym for the italicized word, *fanatic* in the first paragraph can be substituted for _____. (Word in context)

    (a) famous   (c) infamous   (e) mellow
    (b) notorious   (d) enthusiastic

Rank	Flag	Country	P	W	D	L	GF	GA	Pts
1		Brazil	73	49	13	11	159	68	111
2		Germany	73	42	16	15	154	97	100
3		Italy	61	35	14	12	97	59	84
4		Argentina	52	26	9	17	90	65	61
5		England	41	18	12	11	55	38	48
6		Spain	37	15	9	13	53	38	48
7		Russia	34	16	6	12	60	40	38
8		Uruguay	37	15	8	14	61	52	38
9		Sweden	38	15	8	15	66	60	38
10		Yugoslavia	33	14	7	12	55	42	35
11		France	34	15	5	14	71	56	35
12		Hungary	32	15	3	14	51	52	33
13		Poland	25	13	5	7	39	29	31
14		Netherlands	25	11	6	8	43	29	28
15		Czechoslovakia	30	11	5	14	44	45	27

Note

□ **fanatic = fanatical = excessively enthusiastic** : 열광적인, 광적인
  • Most early teenage girls are fanatical about their music idols.
  (대부분의 10대 초반 소녀들은 그들의 음악 우상에 대하여 광적이다.)

□ **riot = violent outburst of lawlessness by the people in a district** : 폭동
  • The police had hard time in putting down the riot by force.
  (경찰은 그 폭동을 강제로 진압하는 데 애를 먹었다.)

(3.2) An antonym for the italicized word, *reinforce* in the second paragraph can be _____.

   (a) Strengthen   (c) Support   (e) Weaken
   (b) Terminate   (d) Buttress

(4) Some World Cup matches have created violent riots between the fans, resulting in injuries and even fatalities. One of the major reasons for this is probably that the fans are _____. (Making inferences)

   (a) Greedy   (d) Cruel
   (b) Fanatic   (e) Nasty
   (c) Murderous

(5) It is a known fact that World Cup Soccer is more popular than the soccer event in the Olympics. One of the major reasons for this can be concluded that it is probably more _____. (Conclusion)

   (a) Focused and nationalistic   (d) Diversified and extravagant
   (b) Appealing and professional   (e) Political and psychological
   (c) Affluent and attractive

Note

- **spark** = be the immediate cause of : 도화선이 되다, 촉발하다
  - His statement sparked off a quarrel between them. (그 말로 언쟁이 일어났다.)
- **issue** = publish, send out; important point : 발행하다, 중요한 문제
  - The real issue is not the pay but the collective dismissal. (문제의 핵심은 보수가 아니라 집단 해고다.)
- **launch** = set a newly - built boat(spacecraft)into the water, (sky) cause an activity to begin : 진수시키다, 발사하다, 시작하다
  - They persisted that they had launched a satellite, but the NASA maintained that they could find no trace of it. (그들은 위성을 발사했다고 우겼지만 미 항공우주국은 그 흔적을 못찾았다고 주장했다.)
- **tournament** = series of contests of skill between a number of players : 승자 진출식 경기
- **reinforce** = increase the size, make stronger by adding or supplying more : 강화하다
  - She reinforced the coat by sewing pieces of leather on the elbows.
  (팔꿈치에 가죽 조각을 덧대어 코트를 튼튼하게 했다.)
- **proclaim** = make known publicly, declare officially : 포고하다, 선포하다
  - In 1993, truce was proclaimed. (휴전이 선포됐다.)
- **host** = act as a host at a party, friendly meeting : 주최하다
  - In 2002, Korea and Japan are supposed to jointly host the World Cup Soccer.
  (2002년에 한국과 일본이 합동으로 월드컵 축구를 개최하기로 되어 있다.)
- **draw** = a result with neither side winning : 무승부
  - The game ended in a draw.
- **be due to** = because of, caused by
  - The recent floods were due to the reckless deforestation to build golf courses.
  (최근의 홍수는 골프장 건설을 위한 무분별한 삼림 벌채 때문이었다.)
- **contribution** = help in bring about, playing a share in : 공로, 기부
  - Do you consider contributions to the church funds a duty or pleasure?
  (교회기금을 위한 기부를 의무로 보나 기쁜일로 보나?)
- **demonstrate** = slow clearly by giving example : 실연, 시범하다
  - How would you demonstarte that the earth is round?
  (지구가 둥글다는 것을 어떻게 증명해 보이려나?)
- **mellow (of fruit)** = soft and sweet in taste : 익은, 말랑말랑한
- **buttress** = a support for a wall : 벽을 받치는 부벽, 버팀벽
  - Buttressed by its past profits, the company stayed in business through difficult period.
  (과거의 이익을 버팀목으로 그 난관에도 사업을 유지했다.)
- **fatalities** = violent, accidental deaths : 사상자
  - It was a bad crash, but surprisingly there were few fatalities.
  (끔찍한 추락 사고였는데도 사상자가 별로 없었다.)
- **affluent** = having plenty of money : 부유한
  - He was born and brought up in an affluent circumstance. (부유한 환경에서 태어나 자랐다.)

3-3 NATURAL SCIENCE

This section, "Natural science" includes 18 passages related to the target content areas: Biology, Chemistry, Computer science, Health, Mathematics, and Physics. These content areas as common curricula in the field of natural science for general senior high schools are being taught by a number of American school districts across the country.

Natural science refers to a cumulative body of systemized knowledge gained by observation, experiment, and reasoning, the result of which should be "explainable, controllable, and predictable." If any result of natural, social, or mental phenomenon cannot be explained, controlled, and predicted, then the target subject matter is beyond the boundary of natural science. Let's take "dream" for an example. Sometimes we dream while we sleep. Can we "explain" why and how we dream? Can we "control" our dreams, so that we have the same or different dream on a certain night? Can we "predict" our dreams, so that we can tell in advance that a certain dream in a certain night will be a nightmare or a pleasant one? These are quite improbable in terms of explanation, control, and prediction, thus the subject, "dream" is not yet within the boundary of natural science.

The field of natural science is still in its initial stage. It is not fully explored and developed yet, although the cumulative body of knowledge gained by observation, experiment, and reasoning is thousand years old. With us and around us, we have much more social, natural, mental and physical phenomena and events which are unexplainable, uncontrollable, and unpredictable than those that can be. We encourage your contributions toward the advancement of this field.

3-3 자연 과학

이 절의 '자연 과학'에는 대상으로 하는 내용영역과 관련된 다음의 18개 지문이 포함되어 있다 : 생물, 화학, 컴퓨터 과학, 건강, 수학, 물리 등이다. 이 내용 영역은 대부분 고등학교의 자연 과학 공통과정으로 미국 전역의 수많은 학교에서 가르쳐 지고 있다.

자연 과학이란 관찰, 실험 그리고 논리적 추론에 의하여 얻어진 체계화된 지식의 누적된 덩어리를 가리키며, 이 결과는 '설명이 가능하고, 통제할 수 있고, 예측할 수 있는 것'이어야 한다. 자연 과학이나 사회 과학 또는 정신 현상의 결과가 설명할 수 없고, 통제할 수 없으며, 예측할 수 없으면, 그 목표 주제는 자연 과학의 경계를 벗어난다. 꿈을 예로 들어보자. 때때로 우리는 자면서 꿈을 꾼다. 우리가 왜, 어떻게 꿈을 꾸는지 설명할 수 있는가? 우리가 어느 밤에 같은 혹은 다른 꿈을 꾸도록 꿈을 통제할 수 있는가? 우리가 사전에 어떤 밤의 꿈은 악몽이거나 즐거운 꿈일거라고 알 수 있도록 예측할 수 있는가? 이러한 것들은 설명, 통제, 예측이라는 관점에서 전혀 가능성이 없다. 그러므로 꿈은 아직 자연과학의 경계선 안에 들지 못한다.

자연 과학의 분야는 아직도 초기 단계에 있다. 비록 관찰과 실험, 논리적 추론에 의하여 얻어진 지식의 누적체가 수천년이 되었어도 충분히 탐구되고 발달되지는 않았다. 우리와 우리 주변에는 설명, 통제, 예측 가능한 것들보다 불가능한 것들이 훨씬 많다. 우리는 여러분들이 이 분야의 발달을 위해서 공헌해 주기를 격려하는 바다.

> **Note**
> □ natural science : 자연과학　　□ botany : 식물학　　□ social science : 사회과학
> □ psychology : 심리학　　□ chemistry : 화학　　□ physics : 물리학
> □ applied science : 응용과학　　□ engineering : 공학　　□ zoology : 동물학
> □ systematized = arranged according to a system : 체계화한, 계통화한
> □ cumulative = increasing steadily in number by one addition after another : 누적하는
> □ mental = of or in the mind : 정신의, 마음의　　• mental hygiene (정신 위생)
> 　• mental deficiency (정신 박약)　• mental test (지능검사)　• mental age (정신 연령)
> □ phenomenon = thing that appears to or perceived by the senses : 현상
> □ in advance = before in time　• Please pay the rent in advance. (집세는 선불해 주시오.)
> □ nightmare = a terrible dream : 악몽
> □ improbable = not likely to happen or to be true : 있을 수 없는, 사실일 수 없는
> 　• It's improbable that she survived the bad accident.

3.3.1. Biology

Passage 1 : An Introduction to Biology

Biology as a branch of the natural sciences deals with organisms, or living things: their structure, function, development, evolution, and their relation to each other and to the environment. Biology as an academic discipline is inseparable to other disciplines because no biological discipline is exclusive of others.

Foundations of biology go back to the beginning of recorded history. For example, the pollination of date palms can be found in the Code of Hammurabi, a Babylonian document prepared in 1800 B.C.. Biology as a general science did not develop until the 19th century. It was Karl Friedrich Burdach (1776-1847), a German scientist who coined the term, biology. But the formation of a variety of studies and theories such as the germ theory of disease, the cell theory, the in-depth studies of plant and animal functions, and physiology developed during the late 19th century contributed biology to be an academic discipline in natural science.

Today, the study of biology has tremendously expanded to more specialized fields of academic discipline. Major fields include the study of (1) Cell; (2) Molecular; (3) Chemistry; (4) Genetics; (5) Development; (6) Evolution; (7) Ecology; (8) Geography; (9) Systematics; (10) Physiology; (11) Neurology; (12) Immunology; (13) Ethology; and, (14) Structure. These areas have been studied and developed as interdependent fields of biology.

(1) The main idea of the passage is _____. (Main idea)

   (a) What is biology for?   (d) What is biology from?
   (b) What is biology toward?   (e) What is biology with?
   (c) What is biology about?

(2) Biology as an academic discipline developed during the _____ th century. (Locating the facts)

   (a) 16   (b) 17   (c) 18   (d) 19   (e) 20

(3.1.) The study of compounds and chemical reactions involved in life process is _____. (3.1.-3.5. Words in context)

   (a) Structural biology   (c) Molecular biology   (e) Systematics
   (b) Cell biology   (d) Biochemistry

(3.2.) The study of progressive changes throughout the life cycle of an organism is _____.

   (a) Genetics   (c) Physiology   (e) Developmental biology
   (b) Biochemistry (d) Ethology

3.3.1. 생물학

지문 1 : 생물학 개론

생물학은 자연과학의 한 분야로서 유기체, 즉 생물을 취급한다. 그들의 구조, 기능, 발달, 진화 그리고 그들 상호간 및 환경과의 관계를 다룬다. 한 학과로서의 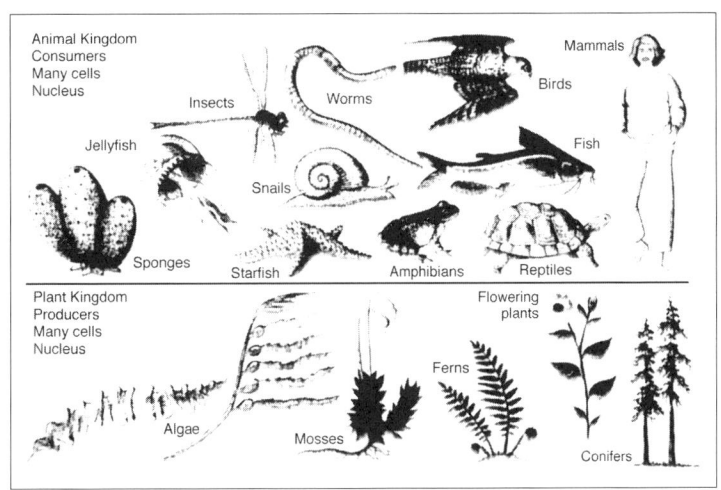 생물학은 관련 분야의 어떤 학과도 배제할 수 없기 때문에 다른 교과와 불가분의 관계를 갖는다.

생물학의 토대는 기록역사의 초기시대로 거슬러 올라간다. 예를 들면 대추야자의 수분(受粉)에 관한 기록이 기원전 1,800년에 작성된 바빌로니안의 문서인 함무라비 법전에서 발견된다. 일반 과학으로서의 생물학은 19세기가 되어서야 발달한다. 생물학이라는 술어를 처음으로 만든 사람은 독일 과학자인 Karl Friedrich Burdach였다. 그러나 다양한 연구나 학설, 예를 들면 19세기 후반에 발달한 질병의 세균설, 세포설, 동식물의 기능에 관한 상세한 연구, 그리고 생리학 등의 형성이 생물학이 자연과학 속에서 하나의 학문으로 자리잡는 데 이바지했다.

오늘날 생물학 연구는 학문의 특수한 분야로 엄청나게 팽창하였다.

주요한 분야에는 다음의 연구가 포함된다 : (1) 세포 (2) 분자생물학 (3) 화학 (4) 유전학 (5) 발달학 (6) 진화학 (7) 생태학 (8) 지리학 (9) 계통학 (10) 생리학 (11) 신경학 (12) 면역학 (13) 동물 행동학 (14) 구조학.

이런 분야들은 생물학의 상호의존적 분야로서 연구되고 발달되어 왔다.

(3.3.) The study of investigating organisms interacting in their environment is _____.

    (a) Biochemistry   (c) Ecology   (e) Neurobiology
    (b) Physiology   (d) Biogeography

(3.4.) The study of cellular function is _____.

    (a) Cell biology   (c) Evolutionary biology   (e) Immunology
    (b) Neurobiology   (d) Developmental biology

(3.5.) The study of proteins and nucleic acids is _____.

    (a) Molecular biology   (c) Structural biology   (e) Systematics
    (b) Cell biology   (d) Ethology

(4) The tone of the passage is _____. (Tone & attitude)

    (a) Matter-of-fact   (c) Approval   (e) Persuasion
    (b) Self-righteousness   (d) Criticism

(5) Based on the information given, it can be concluded that biology will be developed more _____ with other fields. (Conclusion)

    (a) Dependently   (c) Interdependently   (e) Inconclusively
    (b) Independently   (d) Exclusively

Passage 2 : Blood Types

Blood is a thick fluid that circulates throughout our body, supplying nutrients and oxygen to cells while removing waste from them. Blood is made up of plasma, red and white blood cells, and platelets. Plasma as a yellow liquid serves as a medium through which the blood is circulated. Red cells provide oxygen to other cells throughout the body. White cells protect our immune system by attacking foreign matters such as bacteria and viruses. Platelets as plate-like cells cause bleeding to clot/stop.

Among the three cells: white and red cells and platelets, and plasma, the protein in plasma and in the red blood cells determine the blood types such as A, B, AB, and O. In red cells, there are proteins called antigens. The antigens stimulate the formation of another protein and are classified as Antigen A and Antigen B.

Antibodies as another protein in plasma are chemicals that help destroy the foreign matters. The antibodies are classified as Alpha and Beta. The relation of these four factors: Antigen A & B, and Alpha and Beta, play key roles in determining the blood types. (see the chart on page 375.)

As we see from the chart, blood type is identified when Antigens A and B are absent while Antibodies Alpha and Beta are present. For example, Type O is identified when antigens A and B are absent while Antibodies Alpha and Beta are present. Type A is identified when Antigen A is present while Antigen B is

Note

- **biology = bio(life) + logy(study)** : 생물학
  - biorhythm (생체리듬)   • biochemistry (생화학)   • biography (전기)
- **deal with = treat, behave towards** : 취급하다, 다루다
  - How would you deal with an armed burglar? (무장 강도가 오면 어떻게 다루겠니?)
- **organism = living being with parts which work together** : 기관을 가진 유기체
- **evolution = process of opening out or developing** : 진화
  - In politics, England had preferred evolution(= gradual development) to revolution (= sudden or violent change). (정치에서 영국은 혁명(급진적 변화)보다 진화(점진적 발달)를 선호했었다.)
- **exclusive of = not including** : 배제하는
  - The ship had a crew of 57 exclusive of officers. (그 배에는 장교들을 제외하고 승무원이 57명이었다.)
- **pollination** : 식물의 가루받이(受粉)   □ **date palm** : 대추야자
- **germ = a very small living thing which causes illness** : 세균, 병원균
  - germ warfare (세균전)   • germ carrier (보균자)
- **cell = a very small division of living matter with one center of activity** : 세포
- **in depth** : 면밀한, 상세한   □ **genetics** : 유전학   □ **systematics** : 계통학, 분류학
- **immunology** : 면역학   □ **ethology** : 동물행동학   □ **physiology** : 생리학
- **molecular = molecule** : (분자의 형용사) 분자의
  - molecular formula (분자식)   • molecular weight (분자량)
- **ecology = scientific study of the pattern of the natural relations of plants, animals and people to each other and to their surroundings** : 생태학
- **interdependent** : 상호 의존적인   • Farmers are interdependent in their life style.

지문 2 : 혈액형

피는 세포들에게 영양분과 산소를 공급하며, 또한 그들의 노폐물을 제거하고 우리 몸을 구석구석 순환하는 진한 액체다. 피는 혈장, 적·백혈구 그리고 혈소판으로 구성되어 있다. 혈장은 노란 액체로서 피가 순환하도록 하는 매개물로서 일을 한다. 적혈구는 온몸의 다른 세포들에게 산소를 공급한다. 백혈구는 박테리아나 바이러스 같은 이물질을 공격함으로써 우리의 면역체계를 보호한다. 혈소판은 접시모양의 세포로 출혈을 응고시켜 멈추게 한다.

세 종류의 세포들(백혈구, 적혈구, 혈소판)과 적혈구 속에 있는 단백질인 혈장이 A, B, AB, O형 같은 혈액형을 결정한다. 적혈구내에는 항원이라는 단백질이 있다. 항원은 다른 단백질의 형성을 자극하고 항원 A와 항원 B로 분류된다.

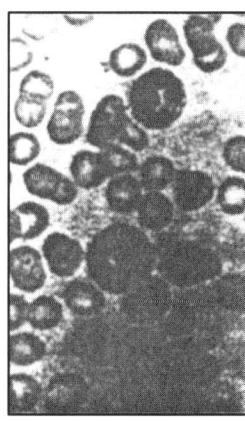

A microphotograph of the blood. The pale-stained cells, with their flexible, concave shape, are red cells. White cells are fewer than red cells and include neutrophills, lymphocytes, and monocytes.

absent, and Antibody Alpha is absent while Antibody Beta is present. Types B and AB follow the rules in the chart.

　　Based on the rule applied in the chart, it is estimated that of all people, 45% are Type O, 40% are Type A, 10% Type B, and 5% Type AB. In case of an emergency such as accidents, operations it is imperative that the person be given the correct blood type. If not, serious *complications* can arise.

Note (Blood types are also determined by the genetic inheritance, but that subject is not dealt with due to the limitation of space.)

(1) The main idea of the passage is _____. (Main idea)

    (a) How blood types are determined?   (d) How important are blood types?
    (b) What are the four factors?   (e) Why do we need blood types?
    (c) What are blood types?

(2.1.) The cells which cause bleeding to clot/stop are _____. (2.1.-2.3. Locating the facts)

    (a) Red blood cells   (c) Antigens   (e) Plasma
    (b) Platelets   (d) White blood cells

(2.2.) The protein in plasma that helps destroy foreign matters is _____.

    (a) Antigens   (c) White blood cells   (e) Platelets
    (b) Plasma   (d) Antibodies

(2.3.) The blood type is identified when Antigens A and B are absent while Antibodies Alpha and Beta are present.

    (a) Type O (b) Type B (c) Type AB (d) Type A (e) None of the above

(3) The italicized word, *complications* in the last paragraph can be substituted for _____. (Word in context)

    (a) Problems (b) Obstacles (c) Traps (d) Hurdles (e) Difficulties

(4) The passage is structured based on the paragraph pattern of _____. (Rhetorical techniques)

    (a) Description   (c) Comparison and contrast   (e) Cause and effect
    (b) Analysis   (d) Definition

(5) It can be concluded that the identification of blood type is most useful for _____. (Conclusion)

    (a) Personal identification (b) Population census (e) Medical care
    (d) Medical records   (c) Crime prevention

항체는 혈장내의 다른 단백질로서 이물질을 파괴하는 것을 도와주는 화학 물질이다. 항체는 알파와 베타로 분류된다. 이들 네가지 요소들, 항원 A, B와 항체 알파와 베타의 관계가 혈액형을 결정하는데 중요한 역할을 한다.(혈액형 표)

차트에서 보는 바와 같이 혈액형은 항체 α와 β는 존재하는데 항원 A, B가 없을 때 확인된다. 예를 들면 O형은 항원 A, B는 없고 항체 알파와 베타가 있을 때 나타난다. A형은 항원 A는 있고 B는 없으며 항체 알파는 없고 베타가 있을 때 확인된다. B형과 AB형은 차트에 표시된 규칙을 따른다.

TABLE OF BLOOD GROUPS

International Nomenclature	Antigens is Red Blood Cells		Antibodies in Blood Serum		Serum Agglutinates Cells of:
	A	B	α(anti-A)	β(anti-B)	
GROUP O	absent	absent	present	present	A, B, AB
GROUP A	present	absent	absent	present	B, AB
GROUP B	absent	present	present	absent	A, AB
GROUP AB	present	present	absent	absent	no group

차트에 적용한 규칙을 근거로 할 때, 모든 사람들의 45%는 O형이고, 40%는 A형이며, B형이 10%, AB형이 5%다. 사고나 수술 같은 응급시에는 그 사람에게 맞는 혈액형을 수혈해야 함은 필수다. 그렇지 않으면 심각한 합병증이 발생할 수 있다.

(주:혈액형은 유전적으로 물려받아 결정되기도 한다. 그 문제는 지면 관계상 취급하지 않는다.)

Note
- remove = get rid of : 없애다 • remove doubt, fear : 의심(두려움)을 제거하다
  • What do you advise for removing ink stains from clothes?
  (옷에서 잉크 얼룩을 제거하는데 무엇이 좋을까요?)
- waste = wasting or being wasted : 폐기물, 노폐물 • What a waste of energy! (이거야 정력 낭비군!)
- plasma : 혈장 □ blood cell(= corpuscle) : 혈구 □ platelet : 혈소판
- immune = unable to be harmed because of special powers in oneself : 면역된
  • Protective inoculation makes a man immune to diseases. (예방주사는 질병에 대하여 면역을 갖게 한다.)
- AIDS = Acquired Immune Deficiency Syndrome : 후천성 면역 결핍증
- clot : 응고시키다(피) □ protein : 단백질 □ carbohydrate : 탄수화물
- fat : 지방 □ fiber : 섬유질 □ antigen : 항원
- antibody : 항체 □ nomenclature : 학명, 분류학적 명칭
- serum : 혈청 □ complication : 합병증 □ agglutinate : 응집하다
- imperative = not to be disobeyed : 어겨서는 안되는, 꼭 필요한
  • It's imperative that you (should) rest a week. (반드시 1주일 요양이 필요합니다.)

Passage 3 : Cells

In 1665, Robert Hooke, an English scientist, looked at thin slices of cork under a microscope. He saw a lot of empty spaces, which he called cells. During the 19th century, scientists with the improvement of the microscope began to see the cells more clearly. In 1831, Robert Brown, an English botanist, discovered the central part of the cell, the nucleus. A few years later, German biologists, Matthew Schleiden and Theodor Schwann, did experiments to see what kinds of living things had cells. Later biologists concluded that cells reproduced to form new cells. Their experiments and studies led to the cell theory acceptable today.

(1) All living things are made of one or more cells.
(2) Cells are the basic units of structure and function in living things.
(3) All cells come from other cells.

Cells have a variety of parts and functions. As major parts of animal cell, there are (1) Nucleus; (2) Endoplasmic reticulum; (3) Mitochondria; (4) Golgi complex; (5) Microbodies; (6) Centrioles; and, (7) Ribosomes. The function of the nucleus is to control all the cell activities. Endoplasmic reticulum connects the nuclear membrane with the cell *membrane*, and its function is to move materials in the cell. Mitochondria as "powerhouses of the cell" produces energy when food is broken down. Golgi complex collects, packages, and distributes molecules that are synthesized at one location within the cell to another place. Microbodies carry enzymes. Centrioles help with cell reproduction. In cell reproduction, a single cell becomes two cells, and each cell must receive a set of chromosomes. Ribosomes are cell parts where proteins are made.

As major parts of plant cell, there are Cell wall; Vacuoles; Chloroplasts; Nucleus; Mitochondria; Golgi complex; and Ribosomes. Cell wall gives a plant support and shape while allowing oxygen, water, and minerals to enter the cell. Vacuoles store food, water, and minerals until the cell is ready to use them. Chloroplasts trap energy from the sun. The plant uses this energy to make food. The other cell parts, Nucleus, Mitochondria, Golgi complex, and Ribosomes have similar functions found in the animal cells.

(1) A proper title of the passage is _____. (Subject matter)

   (a) Parts of the cell   (c) Development of cell   (e) Facts about the cell
   (b) Functions of cell   (d) Basic units of cell

(2.1.) The basic units of structure and function in living things are _____.
   (2.1.-2.5. Locating the facts)

   (a) Nuclei   (b) Cells   (c) Microbodies   (d) Centrioles   (e) Ribosomes

지문 3: 세포

1665년에 영국 과학자 로버트 후크는 현미경으로 코르크의 얇은 조각을 관찰했다. 그의 눈에 많은 빈 공간이 보였다. 그는 이것을 세포라고 명명했다. 19세기 중에 과학자들은 개량된 현미경으로 세포들을 더 명확하게 보기 시작했다. 1831년 영국 식물학자인 로버트 브라운은 세포의 중심부, 즉 핵을 발견했다. 수년 후 독일 생물학자 매튜 슐라이덴과 테오도르 슈반은 어떤 종류의 생물들이 세포를 가지고 있나 알아보려고 실험을 했다. 후에 생물학자들은 세포가 번식하여 새로운 세포가 만들어진다고 결론을 내렸다. 그들의 실험과 연구가 오늘날 다음의 세포설을 인정받도록 했다.

(1) 모든 생물체는 하나 또는 그 이상의 세포로 구성되어 있다.
(2) 세포는 조직체의 기본 단위이며 생물체 내에서 작용한다.
(3) 모든 세포는 다른 세포로부터 만들어진다.

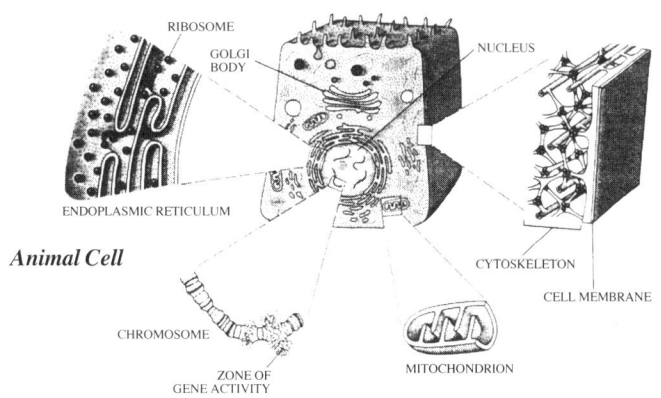

세포는 다양한 부분과 기능을 가지고 있다. 동물세포의 주요한 부분은 다음과 같다 : (1) 핵 (2) 소포체 (3) 미토콘드리아(絲危粒體) (4) 골지체 (5) 미소체 (6) 중심립 (7) 리보솜.

핵의 기능은 모든 세포 활동을 통제한다. 소포체는 핵의 세포막을 세포막들과 연결하며, 그것이 하는 일은 세포내의 물질을 이동시킨다. 미토콘드리아는 세포의 발전소로서 음식물이 분해될 때 에너지를 생산한다. 골지체는 세포 내의 한곳에서 합성되는 분자들을 수집하고 포장하여 다른 곳으로 분배한다. 미소체는 효소를 나른다. 중심립은 세포 분열을 돕는다. 세포가 분열할 때는 1개의 세포가 2개가 되며 각각의 세포는 일련의 염색체를 받아야 한다. 리보솜은 단백질이 만들어지는 세포의 부분이다.

식물세포의 주요 부분은 세포막, 액포, 엽록체, 핵, 미토콘드리아, 골지체, 그리고 리보솜이 있다. 세포막은 세포 안에 산소, 물, 광물질을 받아들이면서 식물을 부양하며 형태를

(2.2.) The cell part that controls the cell activities is _____.

    (a) Nucleus (b) Mitochondrion (c) Centriole (d) Ribosome (e) Vacuole

(2.3.) The plant cell parts that trap energy from the sun are _____.

    (a) Cell walls   (c) Centrioles   (e) Endoplasmic reticulum
    (b) Vacuoles   (d) Chloroplasts

(2.4.) The cell parts that are not found in animal cells are _____.

    (a) Golgi complex   (c) Mitochondria   (e) Centrioles
    (b) Chloroplasts   (d) Ribosomes

(2.5.) The cell parts that are involved with cell reproduction are _____.

    (a) Chloroplasts   (c) Mitochondria   (e) Centrioles
    (b) Golgi complex   (d) Vacuoles

(3) The italicized word, *membrane* in the second paragraph refers to _____. (Word in context)

    (a) Thin piece of skin   (c) Thick wall   (e) Delicate cell core
    (b) Thick liquidity   (d) Thick solidity

(4) The passage is structured based on the paragraph pattern of _____. (Rhetorical technique)

    (a) Description & definition   (d) Cause & effect
    (b) Analysis & description   (e) Description & analysis
    (c) Comparison & contrast

(5) Based on the information given, it can be concluded that the study of cell is as _____ as the study of the alphabet in Indo-European languages. (Conclusion)

    (a) Easy (b) Interesting (c) Attractive (d) Secondary (e) Primary

3.3.2. Chemistry

Passage 1 : Chemistry .

    Chemistry is the science dealing with matter, its chemical and physical properties, and changes that matter undergoes, and the energy changes that accompany these processes. Matter, after all, includes everything that is tangible, from our bodies and the stuff of our everyday lives to the grandest objects in the universe. Chemistry thus touches almost every aspect of our lives, our culture, and our environment. Its scope encompasses the air we breathe, the food we eat,

제공한다. 액포는 세포가 이들을 사용할 준비가 될 때까지 양분, 물, 광물질을 저장한다. 엽록체는 태양으로부터 오는 에너지를 붙잡는데 식물은 이 에너지로 양분을 만든다. 다른 부분들 - 핵, 미토콘드리아, 골지체, 리보솜은 동물세포에서와 비슷한 기능을 갖고 있다.

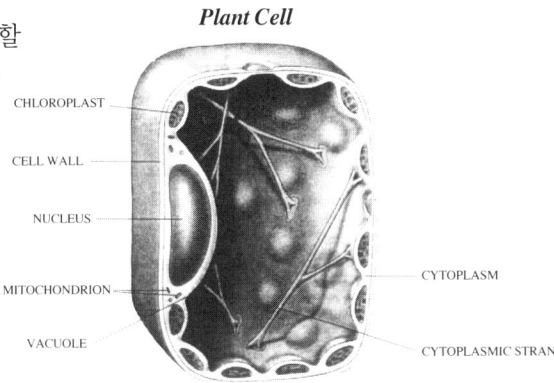

Note
- □ slice : thin wide flat piece cut off something : 얇게 썬 조각
  - Slices of cold beef between slices of bread make good sandwiches.
  - (소고기 냉육 조각을 빵조각 사이에 끼우면 훌륭한 샌드위치가 된다.)
- □ acceptable : good enough to receive, regard something correct : 옳다고 받아들이는
  - "Who do you want?" is ungrammatical, yet it is generally acceptable.
- □ membrane : 세포의 막
- □ cell wall : 세포막(벽)
- □ endoplasmic reticulum : 소포체
- □ centriole : 중심립
- □ mitochondrion(복수 : ···ria) = 미토콘드리아 = chondriosome : 콘디리오솜:세포내의 絲粒體
- □ golgi complex = golgi apparatus : 골지체 • Camillo Golgi (이탈리아의 내과의, 해부학자)
- □ microbody : 중심립 = peroxisome : 과산화 수소를 생성 분해하는 효소를 함유한 과립
- □ ribosome : 리보솜 : 단백질과 리보핵산으로 이루어지는 소립자
- □ chromosome : 염색체
- □ vacuole : 液胞, 空胞:세포내에서 주위의 원형질과 명확히 구분되고 수용액이 찬 공간
- □ enzyme : 효소
- □ chloroplast : 엽록체(chloro = green)

3.3.2. 화학

지문 1 : 화학

화학은 물질을 다루는 과학으로서 물질의 화학적, 물리적 특성과 그 물질이 겪는 변화, 이런 과정에 수반되는 에너지 변화를 다룬다. 물질이란 결국 우리가 만질 수 있는 모든 것-우리의 신체와 일상생활의 모든 재료들로부터 우주안에 있는 광대한 물체까지를 내포한다. 그러므로 화학은 우리 생활의 모든 면, 우리의 문화, 우리의 환경을 취급한다. 화학의 범위는 우리가 호흡하는 공기, 먹는 음식, 마시는 음료, 교통과 연료보급품, 우리 주거 그리고 동료 인간을 포함한다.

the fluid we drink, our clothing, our transportation and fuel supplies, our dwellings, and our fellow creatures. (see the chart on page 381.)

As we have seen, the scope of chemistry is very broad. To make the study of chemistry easier, chemical knowledge is arranged in separate systems or branches. Six major branches include (1) Analytical chemistry (the study of the separation, identification, and composition of matter); (2) Organic chemistry (the chemistry of carbon based compounds); (3) Inorganic chemistry (the study of matters other than those classified as organic); (4) Physical chemistry (the study of the physical characteristics of matters and the mechanisms of their reactions); (5) Biochemistry (the study of matters and processes that occur in living things); and (6) Nuclear chemistry (the study of subatomic particles and nuclear reactions). Each of these branches is further divided into more specialized areas.

(1) The topic of the passage is "The _____ of chemistry." (Subject matter)

    (a) Development (c) Careers   (e) Definition & organization
    (b) Definition   (d) Development & definition

(2) The scope of chemistry is so broad that it touches almost every aspect of our lives, culture, and environment. It is because chemistry is interested in studying _____ that is clear enough to be seen, felt, or noticed. (Locating the facts)

    (a) Property   (b) Change   (c) Process   (d) Energy   (e) Matter

(3.1) The study of the chemical processes that happen in plants, animals, or organs in our body is _____. (3.1 - 3.2. Words in context)

    (a) Analytical chemistry   (d) Nuclear chemistry
    (b) Organic chemistry   (e) Inorganic chemistry
    (c) Biochemistry

(3.2) The study of compounds of carbon in combination with hydrogen and other nonmetals is _____.

    (a) Organic chemistry   (c) Nuclear chemistry   (e) Analytical chemistry
    (b) Inorganic chemistry (d) Biochemistry

(4) The passage is structured based on the paragraph pattern of _____. (Rhetorical techniques)

    (a) Definition   (c) Analysis   (e) Comparison & contrast
    (b) Description (d) Cause and effect

(5) It can be concluded that the career opportunities in the fields of chemistry will be more _____. (Conclusion)

    (a) Diversified & developed   (d) Limited & intensified
    (b) Specialized & diversified   (e) Aggressive & challenging
    (c) Focused & intensified

(아래 그림 설명 : 모든 물질은 혼합물, 화합물, 원소 3개의 전반적인 집단으로 구분된다. 용액은 동질적인 혼합물이다.)

지금까지 살펴본 바와 같이 화학의 범위는 넓다. 화학의 연구를 좀더 쉽게 하기 위하여, 화학 지식은 별개의 체계나 분과로 나뉘어 있다. 6개의 주요 분과는 아래와 같다: (1) 분석 화학(물질의 분류, 정체 규명, 구성의 연구) (2) 유기 화학(탄소를 주성분으로 하는 화합물의 연구) (3) 무기 화학(유기물로 분류된 것들 이외의 물질 연구) (4) 물리 화학(물질의 물리적 특성과 그 반응 기제에 대한 연구) (5) 생화학(생물체 내에서 일어나는 물질의 특성과 그 과정의 연구) (6) 핵물리학(소립자와 핵반응의 연구). 이들 분과는 좀더 특수화된 분야로 나누어진다.

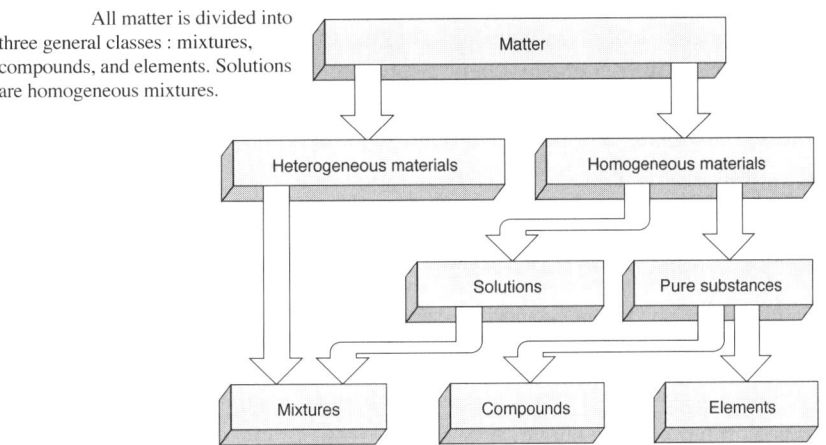

All matter is divided into three general classes : mixtures, compounds, and elements. Solutions are homogeneous mixtures.

Note

□ **property** = quality, power, or effect that belongs naturally to something : 특성
- Many plants have medicinal properties. (약의 특성을 가진 식물이 많다.)

□ **undergo** = experience esp. suffering or difficulty : 경험하다
- She's undergoing treatment at the hospital. (치료를 받고 있다.)

□ **tangible** = that can be felt by touch, clear and definite : 만져 알 수 있는, 확실한

□ **tangible asset** : 유형 재산　• opp. intangible asset : 무형의 재산　• tangible evidence (확실한 증거)

□ **encompass** = surround, contain : 싸다, 포함하다
- My plan encompasses every possibility. (내 계획에는 모든 가능성이 다 들어 있다.)

□ **homogeneous** : 동종, 동질의　**opp. heterogeneous** : 이질적인
- Korea has a homogeneous population.(한국은 동종의 인구를 가지고 있다.)

□ **analytical chemistry** : 분석 화학　• analytical geometry (해석 기하)

□ **subatomic** = smaller than an atom : 소립자, 원자 구성요소

□ **particle** = very small bit, smallest possible quantity : 입자
- In the polluted air, there are numerous particles of dust. (오염된 공기 속에는 무수한 먼지 알갱이가 있다.)

Passage 2 : **Periodic Table**

The periodic table is a chart in which chemical elements are arranged according to their atomic numbers and physical properties. It is laid out based on the periodic law of the Russian chemist, Dmitri Mendeleev (1834-1907) who published a table of elements in 1869. He published it based on both the properties of the elements and the order of their atomic weights.

The elements are arranged in horizontal rows in atomic-weight order so that elements having similar chemical properties are in the same vertical column. Mendeleev realized that all the elements were probably not yet discovered, and he studied the properties of the known elements and then left gaps in his table. He predicted that new elements would be discovered to fill these gaps. The periodic table has made it possible to predict undiscovered elements and their properties to fill in gaps that existed.

The modern table was revised during the mid 20th century, and its last major reconfigurations were done by Glenn Seaborg (1951 Noble Prize winner in chemistry). The table divides the elements into seven horizontal *period/series*, and vertical *group/family* numbered I through VII with various subgroups.
(see the chart on page 381.)

The attached table shows groups IA through VIIA. These groups are the "standard" elements that carry the specified number of electrons of that group (e.g. Li (Lithium) can only carry 1 electron). Groups IB through VIIB are called transition elements, meaning that the elements are capable of carrying a different number of electrons (e.g. Fe (Iron) can carry 2 electrons, or sometimes 3 electrons depending on the interaction).

The atomic weight for each group is given beneath its chemical symbol, and its atomic number appears above. A horizontal row of blocks on the table is called a period/series, whereas a vertical column is called a group/family.

To read the table, for example, H (Hydrogen), atomic number 1, is placed at the top of the table by itself because of its many unique properties. It is in the first column at the left of the table because its atom has one in electron in its highest energy level. Helium (He), atomic number 2 is at the top of the extreme right-hand column. Helium is classified as an *inert* gas because it cannot hold anymore electrons. Therefore, it does not react with other elements.

The second period consists of 8 elements: (1) Lithium, an active metal, whose atoms have 1 electron in the second energy level; (2) Beryllium, a less-active metal than lithium, whose atoms have 2 electrons in the same second energy level; (3) Boron, with some nonmetallic properties, includes 3 electrons in the same level; (4) Carbon, classified as a nonmetal, includes 4 electrons in the same level; (5) Nitrogen, nonmetallic, 5 electrons in the same level; (6) Oxygen, a colorless gas having strong nonmetallic properties, includes 6 electrons in the same level; (7) Fluorine, a pale yellow gas with very strong nonmetallic properties, includes 7 electrons in the same level; and, (8) Neon, a colorless inert gas, includes 8 electrons in the same level. The elements of Period 2 range from an active metallic element, Li, through two metalloids, Be and B, to an nonmetallic element, F. The last

지문 2: 원소 주기율표

주기율표란 화학 원소들을 원자 번호와 물리적 특성에 따라 배열한 도표다. 그것은 1869년에 원소표를 발표한 러시아 화학자 드미트리 멘델레예프의 주기법칙을 기초로 하여 배열되었다. 그는 이 표를 원소들의 특성과 원자량의 순서 두 가지를 토대로 하여 발표하였다.

Dmitri Mendeleev

원소들은 원자량 순서로 수평 배열하였고 비슷한 화학적 특성을 가진 원소들은 수직 세로 행에 있도록 했다. 멘델레예프는 아마 모든 원소들이 전부 발견되지는 않았음을 알고 알려진 원소들의 특성을 연구하고 자기가 만든 표에 공백들을 남겨 놓았다. 그는 이 공백을 메울 새로운 원소가 발견되리라고 예측했다. 원소 주기율표는 이 공백을 채울 미발견 원소와 그들의 특성을 예측하는 일을 가능하게 했다.

현대의 주기율표는 20세기에 수정되었고 최후의 주요한 재배열은 글렌 시보그(1951년 노벨화학상 수상자)에 의하여 이루어졌다. 그 표에서 원소들은 7개의 수평 열과 Ⅰ에서 Ⅶ

element in the second period, Ne, is inert. This variation in properties from metallic through metalloidal to nonmetallic is accompanied by an increase in the number of second energy level electrons from IA to VIIA.

(1) The main idea of the passage is _____. (Subject matter)

    (a) What is the table for?   (d) What is the table toward?
    (b) What is the table about?   (e) How is the table read?
    (c) What is the table from?

(2.1) The atomic number and the atomic weight of "sodium (Na)" are _____ and _____. (2.1 - 2.4. Locating the facts)

    (a) 11 & 22.98977   (c) 19 & 39.0983   (e) 3 & 6.941
    (b) 3 & 22.98977   (d) 12 & 24.305

(2.2) The atomic number and the atomic weight of "magnesium" are ____ & ____. It is _____ with _____ electron(s) in the third energy level.

    (a) 11; 22.98977; metallic; 1   (d) 20; 40.08; metallic; 2
    (b) 12; 24.305; metallic; 2   (e) 12; 24.305; nonmetallic; 2
    (c) 19; 39.0983; metallic; 2

(2.3) The chemical symbol of "chlorine" is _____ with the atomic number and the atomic weight as _____ and _____. It is _____.

    (a) Ar; 18; 39.948; metallic   (d) Cl; 17; 35.453; metallic
    (b) S; 16; 32.06; nonmetallic   (e) Ar; 18; 39.948; nonmetallic
    (c) Cl; 17; 35.453; nonmetallic

(2.4) The periodic table is useful for the _____ of identifying _____ chemical elements and properties to fill in gaps that existed.

    (a) Arrangement; undiscovered   (d) Prediction; undiscovered
    (b) Classification; undiscovered   (e) Formulation; undiscovered
    (c) Organization; undiscovered

(3) The italicized word, *inert* in the third paragraph refers to _____. (Word in context)

    (a) Reactive   (c) Interacting   (e) Unreactive
    (b) Active   (d) Moving

(4) The writer's attitude toward the passage is _____. (Tone & attitude)

    (a) Factual (b) Humorous (c) Approving (d) Sarcastic (e) Informal

(5) Based on the given facts related to the periodic chart, it can be concluded that the most difficult thing among the following is to determine the _____. (Conclusion)

    (a) Chemical symbol   (c) Atomic weight   (e) Total number of electrons
    (b) Atomic number   (d) Energy level

까지 번호가 매겨진 다양한 소집단을 가진 수직 행으로 나누어진다.

(주) : 첨부된 표는 IA집단에서 VIIA까지의 원소군을 보여준다. 이 원소군은 그 군의 지정된 수의 전자를 가지고 있는 표준 원소들이다 (예. 리튬은 단 1개의 전자를 갖고 있다). 원자군 IB에서 VIIB는 전이원소라고 불리며 그 원소들은 상호작용에 따라 다른 수의 전자를 가질 수 있음을 의미한다(예. 철은 2개의 전자, 혹은 3개의 전자를 갖기도 한다).

각각의 원자군의 원자량이 그 화학기호 밑에 주어졌고 그의 원자 번호는 위에 있다. 표 구획의 수평 가로열은 '주기'라 부르고 수직 세로행은 '족'이라 부른다.

이 표를 읽어보자. 예를 들어, 원자번호 1인 수소는 혼자 표의 상단에 위치하고 있다. 왜냐하면 수소가 가진 여러가지 특이한 특성들 때문이다. 수소는 표의 왼쪽 첫째 세로행에 있다. 왜냐하면 수소원자는 에너지 수준이 최고일 때 1개의 전자를 가지기 때문이다. 원자번호 2인 헬륨은 맨우측 세로행 상단에 있다. 헬륨은 비활성 기체로 분류된다. 왜냐하면 더 많은 전자를 가질 수 없기 때문이다. 그러므로 헬륨은 다른 원소들과 상호작용을 하지 않는다.

제2주기에는 8개의 원소로 구성되는데 아래와 같다. (1) 활성금속인 리튬, 원자는 제2에너지 수준에서 전자 하나를 갖는다. (2) 베릴륨, 리튬보다 낮은 활성금속으로 같은 수준의 2개 전자 (3) 붕소, 비금속성 특성을 띠고 같은 수준의 3개 전자, (4) 탄소, 비금속으로 분류, 같은 수준의 4개 전자, (5) 질소, 비금속, 같은 수준의 5개 전자 (6) 산소, 강한 비금속 특성을 가진 무색의 기체, 같은 수준의 6개 전자, (7) 붕소, 매우 강한 비금속 특성을 가진 옅은 황색 기체, 같은 수준의 7개 전자, (8) 네온, 무색의 비활성 기체, 같은 수준의 8개 전자. 제 2주기의 원소들은 활성금속 원소 리튬으로부터 2개의 반금속 원소 베릴륨과 붕소, 비금속 원소인 철까지 걸쳐 있다. 제2주기의 마지막 원소인 네온은 비활성이다. 이 특성상의 다양함(금속성에서 반금속을 지나 비금속에 이르는)은 제2에너지 수준의 전자 수가 IA에서 VIIA까지 증가함에 따라 생긴다.

Note
- lay out = spread out or arrange thing : 펼쳐 놓다, 진열하다, 지면배정
  - I laid out the fishing outfits before packing. (낚시도구를 짐싸기 전에 펼쳐 놓았다.)
- atomic weight : 원자량:산소원자 한개의 질량을 16으로 정하고 이에 비교하여 각 원소의 원자 한개의 질량을 나타낸 수
- reconfiguration : 원자배열을 다시함
- electron : 전자
- proton : 양성자
- molecule : 분자
- atom : 원자
- interaction : 상호작용
- inert : 비활성인
- inertia : 관성, 타성
- metalic : 금속성인
- metalloid : 반금속성의
- nonmetalic : 비금속의

Passage 3 : Artificial Radioactivity

Radioactivity is the spontaneous breakdown of an unstable atomic nucleus with the release of particles and rays. A very radioactive element called radium contained in uranium ores was discovered by Pierre and Marie Curie in 1898. Radioactive nuclides and their compounds have several unusual properties: (1) they affect the light-sensitive *emulsion* on a photographic film; (2) they produce an electric charge in the surrounding air; (3) they produce fluorescence with certain other compounds; (4) their relations have special physiological effects; and, (5) they undergo radioactive decay. The radiation given off by radioactive nuclides consists of three different kinds of particles and rays: (1) alpha particles, which are helium nuclei; (2) beta particles, which are electrons; and, (3) gamma rays, which are high energy X rays.

In 1934, Madame Curie's daughter Irene (1897-1956) and her husband Frederic Joliot (1900-1958) discovered that stable atoms can be made radioactive by artificial means. This occurs when the atoms are bombarded with deutrons or neutrons. Radioactive isotopes of all the elements have been prepared. For example, radioactive $^{60}_{27}Co$ can be produced from natural nonradioactive $^{59}_{27}Co$ by slow-neutron bombardment. The nuclear equation is

$$^{59}_{27}Co + ^{1}_{0}n \rightarrow ^{60}_{27}Co$$

Radioactivity from $^{60}_{27}Co$ consists of beta particles and gamma rays. To be specific, $^{59}_{27}Co$ is called Cobalt-59. The 27 is the atomic number which is the number of protons in the atom. The 59 is the mass number. Mass number represents the sum of protons and neutrons. From $^{59}_{27}Co$ we can determine that cobalt has 27 protons and 32 neutrons. 27+32=59. $^{1}_{0}n$ is a neutron. This symbol means that there are 0 protons and only 1 neutron. $^{60}_{27}Co$ is Cobalt-60 which is an isotope of Cobalt-59. An isotope is different forms of the same atom with the same atomic number but different atomic masses. $^{60}_{27}Co$ means that it has an atomic number of 27 (number of protons) and an atomic mass of 60 (sum of protons and neutrons); 27 protons, 33 neutrons. To determine these numbers is a matter of simple addition. We can assume that the arrow is equivalent to an equal symbol. 59+1=60 and 27+0=27.

Radioactive phosphorus, radioactive cobalt, and some other radioactive nuclides are used to treat certain forms of cancer. Radioactive drugs are used for diagnostic and testing purposes on blood and tissue samples. The gamma radiation from $^{60}_{27}Co$ can be used to preserve food. It also kills bacteria that spoil food and insects that infest food. Many radioactive nuclides are used for a

지문 3: 인공 방사능

　　방사능은 입자나 광선을 방사하면서 불안정한 원자핵이 자발적으로 파괴되는 현상이다. 우라늄 속에 들어있는 라듐이라는 방사성이 매우 강한 원소가 1898년에 피에르와 마리 퀴리에 의하여 발견되었다. 방사성 핵종과 그의 화합물은 몇가지 보기 드문 아래와 같은 특성을 가지고 있다 : (1) 그것들은 사진 필름의 감광성(感光性) 유탁액(乳濁液)에 영향을 끼친다. (2) 주변 공기 속에 전하(電荷)를 발생시킨다. (3) 어떤 다른 화합물과 함께 형광을 일으킨다. (4) 그것들의 관계는 특수한 생리적 효능을 가진다. (5) 그것들은 방사성 붕괴를 한다. 핵종에서 발산되는 방사물에는 다음과 같은 세 가지 다른 종류의 입자와 광선으로 구성된다. (1) 헬륨 핵종인 알파 입자 (2) 전자인 베타 입자 (3) 고 에너지 X선인 감마선.

　　1934년에 퀴리 부인의 딸인 아이린과 그의 남편 프레드릭 졸리어트는 안정된 원자는 인공적인 방법에 따라 방사성 상태로 될 수 있다는 것을 발견했다. 이런 일은 원자를 중양자나 중성자로 충격을 가할 때 일어난다. 모든 원소의 방사능 동위 원소는 만들어 질 수 있다. 예를 들면 방사성 60Co은 천연 59Co에서 저속 중성자 충격으로 생산될 수 있다. 핵 방정식은

$$59Co + 1n \rightarrow 60Co.$$

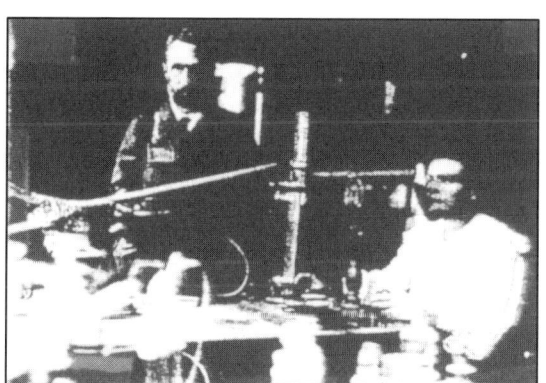

Pierre and Marie Curie at work

Marie Curie

　　코발트 60에서 나오는 방사능은 베타 미립자와 감마선으로 구성되어 있다. 구체적으로 말하면 59Co는 코발트 59라 부른다. 코발트의 원자번호는 27로서 원자 속의 양성자 수이다. 59는 질량수이다. 질량수란 양성자와 중성자의 합계를 나타낸다. 59에서 우리는 60Co는 27개의 양성자와 32개의 중성자를 가지고 있다고 결정한다. 27+32=59이고, 1n은 중성자를 가리킨다. 이 기호는 양성자수가 0이며 단 하나의 중성자가 있음을 의미

variety of purposes: the efficiency of fertilizers, the flow of fluids through pipelines, the cleaning ability of detergents, and the movement of sand along sea coasts. Many new radioactive nuclides are made by slow-neutron bombardment in the nuclear reactors throughout the world.

(1.1.) The topic of the first paragraph is _____. (1.1.-1.2. Subject matter)

    (a) A definition of radioactivity   (d) Discovery of Pierre & Marie Curie
    (b) Property of radioactivity   (e) Definition of radiation
    (c) Facts about radioactivity

(1.2.) The topic of the last paragraph is the _____ of artificial radioactivity.

    (a) Use   (b) Cause   (c) Effect   (d) Product   (e) Development

(2) The radiation generated by radioactive nuclides turns out to be _____.
(Locating the facts)

    (a) α, β, γ particles   (d) Cobalt, β, uranium
    (b) α, β, γ rays   (e) Phosphorus, cobalt, neutron
    (c) Helium nuclei, electron, high energy X ray

Note

(α = alpha, β = beta, γ = gamma)

(3) The italicized word, *emulsion* in the first paragraph refers to _____.
(Word in context)

    (a) Solidity   (b) Coating   (c) Gas   (d) Liquid   (e) Metal

(4) The writer feels that the mathematical explanation of the Nuclear Equation in the second paragraph is _____. (Tone & attitude)

    (a) Expected   (d) Interesting
    (b) Fascinating   (e) Hardly understood
    (c) Easily understood

(5) Based on the information given, the study of artificial radioactivity will be explored more for _____ purposes. (Conclusion)

    (a) Military   (d) Industrial
    (b) Medical   (e) All of the following
    (c) Agricultural

한다. 60Co는 코발트 59의 동위 원소인 코발트 60이다. 동위 원소란 같은 원자 번호를 갖고 있지만 원자량이 다른 동일한 원자의 다른 형태다. 60Co는 원자번호 27(양성자 수)과 원자량 60 (양성자와 중성자의 합계)을 가지고 있음을 의미한다. 이 수를 결정하는 것은 단순 가산으로 27+33이다. 화살표는 등호라고 생각할 수 있다. 59+1=60 27+0=27.

방사성 인, 방사성 코발트, 그리고 몇몇 다른 방사성 핵종들은 암의 어떤 형태를 치료하는데 쓰인다. 방사성 약품들이 진찰과 혈액과 조직 표본 검사를 위하여 쓰여진다. 코발트 60에서 나오는 감마 방사선은 식품 저장에 쓰일 수 있고 식품을 상하게 하는 박테리아와 식품에 달라붙는 곤충을 죽일 수 있다. 많은 방사성 핵종들이 다양한 목적으로 사용되는데, 비료의 효율을 높이고, 송수(유)관 속의 액체 흐름을 원활히 하며, 세제의 세척력을 높이고, 모래가 해안선을 따라 이동하는 것을 돕는 일 등이다. 많은 새로운 방사성 핵종들이 전세계적으로 원자로 안에서의 저속 중성자 충격으로 만들어진다.

Note

- **spontaneous** = happening from natural impulse : 자발적인, 충동적인
  - Nothing he says is spontaneous. He thinks carefully before he speaks.
    (그 사람 말은 무의식적인 것은 하나도 없다. 그는 말하기 전에 세심하게 생각한다.)
  - spontaneous generation (자연 발생)   • spontaneous combustion (자연 발화)
- **breakdown** = a sudden failure in operation : 고장, 파열, 절연
  - They reported a breakdown of talks between labor and employers.
    (노사간의 대화가 단절되었다는 보도다.)
  - nervous breakdown (신경 쇠약)
- **unstable** : (화합물이) 분해되기 쉬운, 불안전한
- **release** = set free, allow to come out : 석방하다, 투하하다
  - release a bomb (폭탄 투하)
  - release a man from a prison(promise) (감옥(공약)으로부터 자유롭게 하다)
- **ore** = rock, earth, mineral from which metal can be mined or extracted : 광석
- **nuclide** : 핵종(核種):원자핵을 양성자와 중성자의 수에 의하여 구별한 것
- **emulsion** : 유상액(乳狀液), 유탁액, 감광유체
- **fluorescence** : 형광(螢光)   • fluorescent lamp (형광등)
- **decay** = go bad, lose power : 썩다, 쇠약해지다, 방사물질이 붕괴하다
- **decayed tooth** : 충치   • What caused the Roman Empire to decay? (왜 로마제국은 기울었나?)
- **deutron** : 중양자:양성자와 중성자로 구성된 입자   □ **neutron** : 중성자:電荷가 없음
- **isotope** : 동위원소   □ **phosphorus** : 인
- **fertilizer** : 비료   □ **tissue** : 조직   □ **mass number** : 질량번호
- **detergent** : 세제   • natural (synthetic) detergent (천연(합성) 세제)
- **infest** = (of rats, insects) be in large numbers : 모여들다, 집적거리다
  - This is a shark - infested waters. (상어가 자주 나타나는 해역이다.)

3.3.3. Computer Science

Passage 1 : **The Computer**

The computer is so pervasive today that we can see it almost in any places. Indeed, the computer has become a necessity for our daily life. How did it come into being, and how is it used in conjunction with other disciplines? These questions will be briefly provided in the following charts, A and B.

Chart A

Name	Place developed	Person/Company	Date	Features
Abacus	Asia & Russia	Unknown	Ancient times	Simple computation
Babbage	England	Charles Babbage	1833	Computations for math & astronomical tables
Hollerith System	U.S.	Herman Hollerith	1890	*Automated* the census of 1890
Zuse	Germany	Konrad Zuse	1930s	Machine having an arithmetic unit, memory, & a control
Sibitz	U.S.	George Sibitz	1940	1st computer system to feature self-checking & unattended operation
Aiken	U.S.	Howard Aiken	1943	1st large-scale automatic digital computer
Atanasoff-Berry Computer	U.S.	Atanasoff & Berry	1940s	1st all-electronic binary computer
ENIAC	U.S.	Presper Eckert & associates	1945	1st all-electronic, general-purpose computer
Whirlwind	U.S.	Jay Forrester	1949	Developed a magnetic-core memory that increased the speed of the machine & decreased the maintenance time needed
Integrated Circuits	U.S.	Jack Kilbey	1958	World's 1st integrated circuit
PDP	U.S.	Ken Olson	1959	1st commercial minicomputer
Altair 8800	U.S.	MITS (small electronics firm)	1974	!st widely used personal computer sold as a kit
Apple	U.S.	Stephen Wozniak & Steven Jobs	1976-present	Computer of choice for nonprofessionals
IBM PC	U.S.	IBM Corporation	1981-present	Became the industry standard

Chart B

Discipline	Relations
Biology	Analogies between computing and nature of molecular biology (e.g. mechanisms of cell growth & reproduction).
Mathematics	For solving math logic, theorems, algorithms for solving equations and other classes of problems in math.
Management	For developing and extending management models and systems so that industrial organizations can compete in markets.
Economics	For modeling economic systems so as to forecast national and international economic conditions.
Engineering	To store a representation of a structure, perform simulations on it, show still and animated pictures on it, and even drive a manufacturing process.

3.3.3. 컴퓨터 과학

지문 1 : 컴퓨터

오늘날 컴퓨터는 널리 보급되어 어느 곳에서나 눈에 띈다. 실로 컴퓨터는 우리 일상의 필수품이 되어버렸다. 어떻게 컴퓨터가 나타났으며 다른 학문들과 어떻게 연관되어 쓰여지는가? 이러한 의문들은 간단하게 아래 표 A와 B에서 답을 제공한다.

This elaborate device, built in 1833, is part of an uncompleted calculating machine designed by Charles Babbage, an English mathematician. Known as a difference engine, it was designed for performing the long computations involved in preparing mathematical and astronomical tables.

표 A

명칭	개발된 장소	개발자 / 회사	시대	특징
Abacus	Asia & Russia	Unknown	고대	단순 계산
Babbage	England	Charles Babbage	1833	수학, 천문 표제작을 위한 계산
Hollerith System	U.S.	Herman Hollerith	1890	1890년의 인구조사를 자동화했음
Zuse	Germany	Konrad Zuse	1930년대	계산 단위, 기억, 조절을 가진 기계
Sibitz	U.S.	George Sibitz	1940	자동 점검과 무인 작동을 특징으로 하는 최초의 컴퓨터 체계
Aiken	U.S.	Howard Aiken	1943	최초의 대규모 디지털 컴퓨터
Atanasoff-Berry Computer	U.S.	Atanasoff & Berry	1940년대	최초의 전체 전자식 계수형 컴퓨터
ENIAC	U.S.	Presper Eckert & associates	1945	최초의 전체 전자식 일반용도의 컴퓨터
Whirlwind	U.S.	Jay Forrester	1949	기계의 속도를 늘려주고 조작시간을 단축시키는 자석식 핵심 기억장치 개발.
Integrated Circuits	U.S.	Jack Kilbey	1958	세계 최초의 통합 회로
PDP	U.S.	Ken Olson	1959	최초의 상업용 미니 컴퓨터
Altair 8800	U.S.	MITS (small electronics firm)	1974	최초로 널리 쓰이는 개인용 컴퓨터가 한 세트로 판매
Apple	U.S.	Stephen Wozniak & Steven Jobs	1976-현재	비전문인을 위한 최상품 컴퓨터
IBM PC	U.S.	IBM Corporation	1981-현재	컴퓨터 산업의 표준이 됨

Physical science	To have formations of atomic particles from quarks, calculations of chemical properties of materials, exploration of space, global climate modeling.
Library science	Libraries will change from storage places for books to be electronic data centers that grant wide-range access to readers.
Linguistics	Recognition of speech patterns in natural language and machine translation.

(1) The main idea of the passage and the charts is _____. (Subject matter)

    (a) How computer is developed & utilized   (d) Where computer is developed & used
    (b) Why computer is used & developed   (e) What computer is & how it is used
    (c) When computer is developed & used

(2.1) When computer is utilized for translation and for recognition of speech pattern, then it is related to the discipline of _____. (2.1.-2.5. Locating the facts)

    (a) Biology   (b) Economics   (c) Engineering   (d) Philosophy   (e) Linguistics

(2.2) When computer is utilized in developing a variety of models for business success, then it is related to the discipline of _____.

    (a) Engineering   (b) Biology   (c) Linguistics   (d) Management   (e) Mathematics

(2.3) When computer is utilized for launching rockets into space, then it is related to the discipline of _____.

    (a) Physical science   (b) Management   (c) Mathematics   (e) Library science   (d) Biology

(2.4) When we are able to read the information we want through the electronic data of computer at home, then the computer is related to the discipline of _____.

    (a) Management   (b) Library science   (c) Linguistics   (d) Engineering   (e) Biology

(2.5) The first all-electronic computer for general purposes is _____.

    (a) PDP   (b) Babbage   (c) Zuse   (d) Sibitz   (e) ENIAC

(3) The italicized word, *automated* in Chart A, refers to _____. (Word in context)

    (a) Operated automatically   (c) Operated reversely   (e) Operated manually
    (b) Operated simultaneously   (d) Operated at once

(4) The Charts A & B are condensed versions of the facts given. It can be justified that one of the major reasons for this condensation is to _____ the detailed facts. (Rhetorical techniques)

    (a) Epitomize   (b) Emphasize   (c) Expand   (d) Stress   (e) Highlight

(5) Based on the facts given, it can be concluded that the _____ of computer will be more demanded for more specialized areas. (Conclusions)

    (a) Durability   (b) Utilization   (c) Consumption   (d) Cost   (e) Marketability

표 B

학문	관련분야
생물	연산과 분자생물학 특성 사이의 유사성 (예 : 세포의 성장과 번식의 구조)
수학	수학 논리, 정의, 방정식 풀이와 다른 종류의 수학 문제 풀이를 도움.
경영	경영의 모형과 체계를 개발하고 확장하여 산업체들이 시장에서 경쟁할 수 있게 함
경제학	국가, 국제적 경제 상황을 예측하기 위하여 경제 체계의 모형 작성
공학	구조의 표현을 저장하고, 그 위에 시뮬레이션하고, 스틸사진 및 동영상을 보여주고, 제조 공정을 실행하기도 한다.
자연과학	쿼크로 원자입자를 형성하며, 물질의 화학적인 특성을 계산하고 대기권 밖을 탐구하여 지구의 기후모형도 제작한다.
도서관학	도서관이 책을 저장하는 장소에서 독자들에게 광범히, 접근하는 전자 데이터 센터로 바뀔 것이다.
어학	자연언어에 있는 문형을 인식하여 자동번역.

Note

- **pervasive = widespread** : 널리 보급된(pervade의 형용사)
  - A spirit of uneasiness about the future economy is pervaded the whole country. (앞날의 경제에 대한 불안감이 전국에 퍼져 있다.)
- **come into being (existence) = begin to exist** : (없던 것이) 생겨나다
  - We do not know when this world came into being. (이 세계가 언제 생겨났는지 모른다.)
- **in conjunction with = together with** : …과 함께
  - The fleet operated in conjuction with the Navy. (그 함대는 해군과 함께 작전을 했다.)
- **abacus** : 주산   **computation = calculation** : 계산
- **census** : 인구 조사
- **table = list, orderly arrangement of facts** : 표, 목록
  - conversion table (환산표) • multiplication table (구구표) • a table of contents (목차)
- **arithmetic** : 산수, 단순계산법
  - decimal arithmetic (십진법) • mental arithmetic (암산)
- **digital computer = one that performs by representing quantities as digits (binary or decimal)** : 정보의 양을 수(2진수, 10진수)로 대리 표현하는 컴퓨터
- **binary** : 둘로 이루어지는   **binary scale** : 2진법
- **integrated = combined into a whole**
  - He is a man of integrated personality. (그는 전인적 인성을 가진 사람이다.)
- **circuit = closed path for an electric current** : 회로
  - CCTV : Closed Circuit Television = a TV that has a closed circuit by which the current from the camera to the screen has its path along wires all the way instead of being transmitted through the air. : 폐쇄회로 TV
- **theorem** : (수학) 정리   **algorithm** : 특성의 연산 방식, 알고리즘

Passage 2 : Basic Structure of the Personal Computer

The personal computer's basic structure consists of three parts: (1) central processing unit (CPU); (2) memory; and, (3) input-output (I/O) devices. These three components communicate with each other via a common set of wires or connections called a "bus." This common set of connections is analogous to a real bus because it forms a pathway for the flow of information among the devices. Informational inputs travel on the bus to their specific destinations and are then modified to become informational outputs which reenter the bus and continue their travel. It should be noted that the bus is not classified as a basic structure of the personal computer since it is only a pathway for informational flow between the basic components.

To be specific, first, the CPU which is also called the "microprocessor" or the "processor" of the computer is analogous to the brain in living organisms. It performs arithmetic and logical operations when instructions stored in memory are *retrieved* and executed one at a time until the termination of the program.

Second, memory has two types, primary and secondary in the personal computer. But, before we explore them, we should note that memory can have two meanings. The first is the storage capacity of the computer, whether primary or secondary. The other is the actual data and/or set of instructions that is stored, and later read and processed by the CPU. Primary memory, often called random-access memory (RAM), refers to the portion of memory that is directly accessible by the CPU. As such, instructions and/or data can be processed and operated upon by the CPU very quickly. Secondary memory on the other hand, refers to memory that is too large to fit into primary memory, thus it must be stored externally, usually on a floppy disk or a hard disk. The access time for secondary memory is a magnitude larger than that of primary memory, since the CPU must access the respective drive. Information from floppy or hard disk, cannot be immediately accessed by the CPU. The required data must first be located and then transferred to primary memory piecewise. As a particular section is called, it will be located and then loaded into the RAM. Another critical difference between primary and secondary memory is the storability of data. Primary memory is only temporarily storable, while secondary memory can be saved on disks. Data in RAM can be saved permanently, but only in secondary memory. For example, in the event of a power failure, any information that was stored in RAM is lost. If any information was stored on disk, that saved information can be retrieved.

Finally, input-output (I/O) devices are those devices used to facilitate communication between the human user and the computer's processor. Two essential devices are the keyboard and the display screen or monitor. The keyboard is an input device used to communicate the desires of the user to the

지문 2 : PC의 기본 구조

퍼스널 컴퓨터의 기본구조는 다음 세 가지 부분으로 구성된다. (1) 중앙 정보처리 장치 (2) 기억 장치 (3) 입·출력 장치. 이들 세 부분들은 '버스'라고 불리워지는 공통 전선을 통하여 의사 소통한다. 이 공통 접속 세트는 진짜 버스와 비슷하다. 왜냐하면 장치들 사이에 정보의 흐름을 위한 통로를 형성

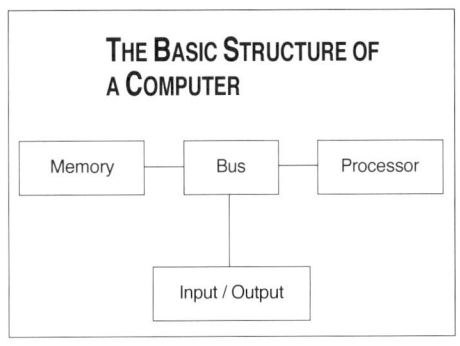

하기 때문이다. 입력 정보는 이 버스를 타고 특정의 목적지에 가서 변화되어 그 버스를 다시 타고 여행을 계속하는 출력 정보가 된다. 주목할 것은 이 버스는 기본장치로 분류되지 않는다. 왜냐하면 버스는 기본 부품 사이의 정보흐름을 위한 단지 통로이기 때문이다.

세부적으로 말하면 첫째, '마이크로프로세서'나 '프로세서'라고 불리우는 CPU는 유기체의 두뇌와 비슷하다. 그것은 기억장치 속에 저장된 지시가 불러져서 한 번에 하나씩 실행되어 프로그램이 끝날 때까지 산술적, 논리적 작동을 수행한다.

둘째, PC에는 두가지 형태의 기억 즉 1차적 기억과 2차적 기억이 있다. 그러나 그들을 탐색하기 전 기억에는 두가지 의미가 있음을 주목해야 한다. 첫째는 1, 2차를 막론하고 저장능력이다. 나머지 한가지는 저장되었다 후에 CPU에 의하여 판독되는 실제 데이터나 일련의 지시들이다. 자주 RAM(임의 액세스 기억 장치)으로 불리는 1차적 기억은 직접 CPU로 접근할 수 있는 기억의 부분을 가리킨다. 그러므로 지시나 정보는 CPU에 의하여 매우 빠르게 처리되고 작동될 수 있다. 반대로 2차적 기억은 1차적 기억에 맞추기에 너무 커서 외부에 보통 플로피 디스크나 하드 디스크에 저장되는 기억을 가리킨다. 2차적 기억에 접근하는 시간은 1차적 기억에 드는 시간보다 훨씬 더 걸린다. 왜냐하면 CPU가 각각의 길을 밟아야 하기 때문이다. 플로피나 하드 디스크의 정보는 즉시 CPU로 접근할 수 없다. 필요한 정보는 먼저 위치를 찾아서 구분적으로 1차적 기억으로 전환되어야 한다. 특정 부분을 부르면 위치가 확인되고 RAM속으로 실린다. 1, 2차적 기억의 또 다른 결정적 차이점은 정보의 저장 가능성이다. 1차적 기억은 단지 일시적으로만 저장되나 2차적 기억은 디스크에 저장된다. RAM의 정보도 영구히 저장되나 단지 2차적 기억으로서 가능하다. 예를 들어 정전이 되면 RAM속의 정보는 분실된다. 만일 어떤 정보가 디스크에 저장되면 그 저장된 정보는 다시 부를 수 있다.

마지막으로, 입·출력 장치는 사용하는 인간과 컴퓨터 프로세서 사이의 통신을 쉽게

computer. The display screen or monitor is an output device which enables the user to get a visual representation of the result or results derived by the processor. It is important to note that while other I/O devices exist which can facilitate the ease of data manipulation, whether for input or output, these said devices are not necessary for the day-to-day operation of the computer. A few such devices includes: the mouse, joystick, and printer.

On a side note, there is another I/O device, while not necessary for everyday operation, that is considered essential for certain uses. This device, the modulator-demodulator (best-known as modem) allows a computer to receive data from, or send data to another computer via the telephone lines.

(1) The topic of the passage is a brief _____ of the personal computer. (Subject matter)

    (a) Development   (c) Manufacture   (e) Commerce
    (b) Composition   (d) Outlet

(2.1) The part which performs arithmetic and logical operations is _____. (2.1 - 2.2. Locating the facts)

    (a) CPU   (c) Memory   (e) Keyboard
    (b) I/O devices   (d) Bus

(2.2) The component which stores information is _____.

    (a) CPU   (c) RAM   (e) Modem
    (b) I/O devices   (d) Bus

(3) The italicized word, *retrieved* in the second paragraph refers to _____. (Word in context)

    (a) Retained   (c) Released   (e) Retaliated
    (b) Recovered   (d) Registered

(4) The writer's style in the passage seems to be _____. (Tone and attitude)

    (a) Inventive   (c) Personal   (e) Factual
    (b) Critical   (d) Pedantic

(5) We can conclude from the passage that the people who _____ are most likely to claim that the modem is an essential I/O component of the computer. (Conclusion)

    (a) Manufacture computers   (d) Design web pages
    (b) Type reports   (e) Design computer graphics
    (c) Deal with numbers

하기 위하여 쓰여지는 장치들이다. 두 가지 필수적인 장치는 자판과 전시스크린 즉 모니터다. 자판은 사용자가 요구하는 것을 컴퓨터에게 전하는데 쓰이는 입력 장치다. 모니터는 사용자로 하여금 프로세서에 의하여 얻어낸 결과들을 시각적으로 보게 해준다. 정보 취급을 용이하게 해주는, 입력이든, 출력이든, 다른 입·출력 장치가 있지만 이들 장치는 일상적인 컴퓨터 가동에는 필요하지 않다는 것을 주목하는 게 중요하다. 몇가지 이런 장치중에는 마우스, 조이스틱, 프린터가 있다.

부연하면 일상적인 가동에는 불필요하나 어떤 용도에는 필수적인 것으로 여겨지는 입출력 장치가 있다. 모뎀으로 알려진 변, 복조 장치는 컴퓨터가 전화선으로 데이터를 받고 다른 컴퓨터로 보내는 일을 가능하게 한다.

note

□ **analogous to** = similar to, like, alike in some ways : 비슷한
- Your suggestion is analogous to the one that was made earlier. (자네 안은 지난번 것과 비슷하군.)

□ **input** = something put in the computer for procession : 입력 (정보)

□ **output** = something produced for use from a computer : 출력 정보

□ **retrieve** = regain, find and bring back : 다시 찾다, (정보)검색하다
- I'd like to retrieve my umbrella left in the car. (우산 찾으러…)

□ **execute** = carry out an order, plan, piece of work : 수행, 집행하다
- He asked his brother to excute his will. (동생에게 유언을 집행해달라고 부탁했다.)

□ **termination** = ending - termination of a contract : 계약 종료
- put a termination to = put an end to (끝내다)

□ **random** = made or done without any plan : 마구잡이의, 임의의
- a random guess (억측)   • a random sampling (무작위 표집)
- speak at random (닥치는 대로 말하다)
- RAM = Random Access Memory (랜덤 액세스 메모리(등속호출 기억장치))

□ **floppy disk** : 프로피 디스크-외부 기억용의 플라스틱제 자기 원반

□ **derive** = get, draw source or origin from : 끌어내다, 얻다
- We can derive great pleasure from books.

□ **manipulate** = handle with skill, manage or control craftly : 교묘하게 다루다, 조작하다
- You know how to manipulate the control of a computer, don't you?

□ **modulator** : 변조기   □ **demodulator** : 복조기   □ **modem** : 변복조장치

Passage 3 : The Computer Education in the United States

The computer education for the elementary and secondary school students began to start during the 1970s. A number of school districts across the country have continued to buy less powerful and less expensive computers, since schools need them in large numbers. As a result, a majority of students now use computers and computer software during the school year either to learn about the computer or as a tool for studying other subject areas.

Computers in elementary and secondary schools are used in two major contexts. The first one is "computer-education-instruction." In this context, children learn how to type on computer keyboards; how to use word processing programs; how to program computers in languages such as BASIC, PASCAL, LOGO; and, how to use other computer applications such as database programs and spreadsheets. One-half of computer use by secondary school students, and one-third of the use by elementary children is this type of context. The other major context is "computer-assisted instruction (CAI)" the programs of which are written for teaching individual students in school settings. The programs present students with a question and compare the student's answer with an explanation and another, similar problem. Studies of the effect of CAI on how well children learn basic skills have generally been supportive of CAI.

Some critics see computer education as merely the latest in a series of unsuccessful attempts to revolutionize education through the use of audio-visually oriented non-print media (e.g. film, TV, audio-recorder). However, supporters of the computer education claim that the computer is quite different from other audio-visual media that preceded it. They advocate that the essential interactive nature of using computers programmed helps children *provoke* decision making and manipulations of visual environment. Since each computer is operated by one student or by pairs of students, learning tasks can become more individualized, enabling each student to receive immediate feedback. Having students work collaboratively on computers leads to greater initiative and more *autonomous* learning. Computer proponents also argue that because computers are so pervasive in the American society, "computer literacy" is a worthy goal.

(Source: Adapted from Henry Jay Becker (1993). <u>Academic American Encyclopedia</u>, Vol. 5)

(1.1) The suitable topic of the second paragraph is _____. (1.1 - 1.2. Subject matter)

    (a) Computer education in the U.S.   (d) PASCAL, LOGOS, BASIC
    (b) Facts about "computer education"   (e) Facts about CAI
    (c) Two contexts in computer education

(1.2) The topic of the last paragraph is _____.

    (a) Computer literacy

지문 3 : 미국의 컴퓨터 교육

Using computers, students can conduct a simulated dissection of a frog.

초·중등학생을 위한 컴퓨터 교육은 1970년대에 시작되었다. 전국적으로 많은 학교들이 컴퓨터를 많이 필요했기 때문에 계속하여 성능이 약하고 값이 싼 컴퓨터를 샀다. 그 결과 대다수의 학생들이 학창시절 동안 컴퓨터를 배우고 또한 다른 분야의 교과목 학습을 위하여 컴퓨터와 컴퓨터 소프트웨어를 사용한다.

초·중등학교에서 컴퓨터는 두가지 주요한 상황에서 쓰인다. 첫째가 '컴퓨터-교육-지도(CAI)' 다. 이 상황에서 어린이들은 다음을 배운다. 컴퓨터 키보드에 타자하는 것, 워드프로세싱(서류, 문서작성)하는 법, Basic, Pascal, Logo어를 사용하여 컴퓨터 프로그램 짜는 법, 데이터 베이스나 스프레드 쉬트 같은 다른 컴퓨터 응용물을 사용하는 법. 중등학생 컴퓨터 사용의 반과 초등학생 컴퓨터 사용의 1/3은 이런 형태와 관련된다. 다른 주요한 사용상황은 컴퓨터의 도움을 받아 학생을 지도하는 것이며, 이를 위한 프로그램이 학교에서 개별 학생의 지도를 위하여 작성된다. 그 프로그램은 학생들에게 질문을 제시하고 학생의 해답과 해설, 또 다른 비슷한 문제와 비교한다. CAI(컴퓨터의 보조를 통한 교수)가 학생이 배워야 할 기본 기술을 얼마나 효과적으로 지도하는가에 대한 연구가 전반적으로 CAI의 밑받침이 되어왔다.

몇몇 비평가들은 컴퓨터 교육을 '시청각 지향의 비인쇄 매체를 통한 교육개혁'에 관련하여 가장 최근에 실패한 것이라고 본다. 그러나 컴퓨터 교육 지지자들은 컴퓨터는 그 이전의 시청각 매체들과 전혀 다르다고 주장한다. 그들은 프로그램화된 컴퓨터 사용의 쌍방향 특성이 학생의 의사결정과 시각적 환경을 조성하는데 도움이 된다고 옹호한다. 각각의 컴퓨터는 개별 학생이나 짝을 이룬 학생들이 조작하기 때문에 학습과제가 더욱 개별화되고 학생이 즉시 피드백을 받을 수 있도록 해준다. 학생들이 컴퓨터로 협동적인 작업을 하게 하면 학습을 더 창의적이고 더 자율적으로 하게 된다. 컴퓨터 찬성론자들은 컴퓨터가 미국 사회에 널리 보급되었기 때문에 '컴퓨터를 읽고 쓰는 능력'은 가치있는 목표라고 주장한다.

(b) Functions of computers in school
(c) "Pros & cons" for computer education
(d) Educational advantages of computer
(e) Differences between computer & audio visual media

(2.1) A type of programmed instruction for teaching individual students with a question and an explanation is _____. (2.1 - 2.2. Locating the facts)

(a) Computer literacy   (c) BASIC   (e) PASCAL
(b) CAI   (d) Computer-education-instruction

(2.2) A specific number of high schools that provides the students with computer education in the U.S. is _____.

(a) Over 30,000   (c) Over 50,000   (e) Unspecified
(b) Over 40,000   (d) Over 60,0000

(3.1) The italicized word, *provoke* in the last paragraph refers to _____. (3.1 - 3.2. Words in context)

(a) Incise   (b) Incite   (c) Indict   (d) Include   (e) Incline

(3.2) The antonym of the italicized word, *autonomous* in the last paragraph is _____.

(a) Dependent   (b) Independent   (c) Sufficient   (d) Substantial   (e) Interdependent

(4) The attitude of the writer toward the passage is _____. (Tone & attitude)

(a) Opinionated   (c) Prescriptive   (e) Contemptuous
(b) Descriptive   (d) Disapproving

(5) Based on the information given, it can be concluded that the computer education in the elementary and secondary schools in the U.S. will be _____. (Conclusion)

(a) Shrunk   (b) Excluded   (c) Expanded   (d) Minimized   (e) Discontinued

3.3.4. Health

Passage 1 : Hypertension: The Silent Killer

Millions of people ignore the signs of a dangerous condition, hypertension. Hypertension or high blood pressure affects more than 60 million people a year in the U.S. While often controllable, hypertension can lead to heart failure, stroke, kidney damage and more if not caught. There are usually no symptoms, and for this reason, it is known as "the silent killer."

A healthy blood pressure reading is around 120/80. The top number (systolic) measures blood pressure when the heart is pumping while the bottom

> **Note**
> □ **context** = circumstances in which an event occurs : 상황, 정황
> • The word means 'men in general' in this context. (그 단어가 이 문맥에서는 일반 사람을 의미한다.)
> □ **advocate** = speak in favor of, support : 옹호하다, 주장하다
> • Do you advocate holding all the students in the school till late at night?
> (학생들을 밤 늦게까지 학교에 붙들어 두는 것을 잘하는 일이라고 생각하십니까?)
> □ **provoke** = cause, arouse : 선동하다, 화나게 하다, 도발하다
> • The sudden change of policy provoked a violent riot on the part of laborers.
> (갑작스런 방침의 변경이 노동자 측의 격렬한 폭동을 선동했다.)
> □ **feedback** = advice, criticism etc. about how successful or useful something is : 피드백, 재투입, 송환, 반추
> • For a successful learning, immediate feedback of what one has learned is indispensable.
> (학습이 성공하려면 학습한 내용을 즉시 피드백 하는게 필수다.)
> □ **collaboratively** : 협동적으로, 합작으로

3.3.4. 건강

지문 1 : 고혈압-말없는 살인자

수많은 사람들이 위험한 상태인 고혈압의 징후를 무시한다. 하이퍼텐션 즉 고혈압은 1년에 미국에서 6천만명 이상의 사람들에게 영향을 미친다. 자주 억제될 수는 있긴 하지만 붙잡아 막지 않으면 심장마비, 뇌일혈, 신장손상, 그 외 더 많은 결과를 초래한다. 대체로 증상이 없기 때문에 '말없는 살인자' 라고 알려져 있다.

건강한 혈압수치는 120/80이다.

위의 수치(수축기 혈압)는 심장이 피를 품어낼 때를 측정하고 아래 수치(이완기 혈압)는 심장이 휴식할 때를 측정한다. Baylor의대의 심장 센터 전문가들에 의하면 만일 다음의 경우면 고혈압이 될 위험이 있다고 한다.

□ 과체중
□ 폐경기를 지났거나 65세 이상일 때
□ 집안내력에 고혈압이 있을 때
□ 피임약을 복용하고 있을 때
□ 그밖에 혈압을 높이는 요소들에는 흡연, 스트레스, 그리고 당뇨가 있다.

고혈압은 치료가 불가능하고 약 처방, 체중 감소, 염분 섭취의 줄이기, 운동, 알콜 사용

number (diastolic) measures pressure when the heart rests. According to experts at Baylor College of Medicine's DeBaky Heart Center, people are at risk for hypertension if they:

- Are overweight.
- Have been through menopause and/or are age 65 or older (women)
- Have a family history of hypertension
- Are taking birth control pills (women)
- Other factors that may play a role in elevating blood pressure are smoking, stress, and diabetes

There is no cure for hypertension, but it can often be controlled with medication, weight loss, reduction of salt intake, exercise, and limiting alcohol use. If you have any of the risk factors, see your physician. Mild hypertension may often respond to reduction of both weight and stress. For more serious cases, your doctor may recommend anti-hypertensive drugs that rid the body of excess fluids and salt. Others, called beta blockers, reduce the heart rate and the heart's output of blood. Still another class of drugs, called sympathetic nerve *inhibitors*, reduces blood pressure by affecting the nerves that *constrict* blood vessels. Your doctor may also recommend lifestyle changes that can help. Please give them serious consideration. They may save your life.

(Source: Contributed by Dr. James I. Phillips, 1998)

(1.1) The topic of the second paragraph is "The _____ of hypertension." (1.1 - 1.2. Subject matter)

   (a) Possible factors   (b) Cure   (c) Treatment   (d) Prevention   (e) Control

(1.2) The topic of the last paragraph is _____.

   (a) Treatments   (b) Factors   (c) Cure   (d) Control   (e) Symptoms

(2.1) One of the following factors that would not be considered for hypertension is _____. (2.1 - 2.2. Locating the facts)

   (a) Diabetes   (c) Smoking   (e) Consumption of vegetables
   (b) Overweight   (d) Stress

(2.2) What class of anti-hypertensive drugs reduces blood pressure by affecting nerves?

   (a) Sympathetic nerve inhibitors   (c) Antibiotics   (e) Tylenol
   (b) Beta blockers   (d) Medication for pain

(3.1) The italicized word, *inhibitors* in the last paragraph refers to _____. (3.1 - 3.2. Words in context)

   (a) Protection   (b) Prevention   (c) Prestige   (d) Preservation   (e) Production

의 제한 등으로 억제할 수 있는 경우가 많다. 만일 이런 위험 요소 중 하나라도 가지고 있으면 의사를 만나라. 가벼운 고혈압은 체중과 스트레스를 줄이면 효과가 있다. 심한 경우에는 의사가 체내의 과도한 분비물과 염분을 제거하는 항고혈압제를 권한다. 베타수용제 차단약이라고 부르는 다른 것들도 심장의 박동수와 혈액방출을 줄인다. 교감신경 차단제라 불리는 또 다른 부류의 약들도 혈관을 억제하는 신경에 영향을 미치게 하여 혈압을 내리게 한다. 의사들은 생활 방식을 바꾸기를 권한다. 그런 변화를 진지하게 생각해 보아라. 그것들이 당신의 생명을 구할 수도 있다.

WHAT IS BLOOD PRESSURE?

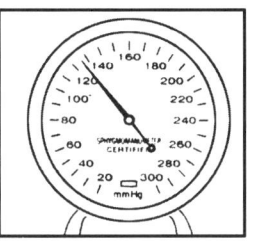 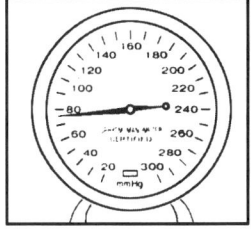

Systolic Reading   **Diastolic Reading**

What is Blood Pressure? Blood pressure is the pressure that flowing blood exerts on the arteries.

The heart contracts and relaxes, creating two levels of blood pressure. SYSTOLIC pressure is the highest level of blood pressure. It is the level of pressure when the heart contracts. DIASTOLIC pressure is the lowest level of blood pressure. It is the level of pressure when the heart relaxes.

Doctors measure blood pressure in terms of the height of a column of mercury. The numbers are measured in millimeters of mercury (written as mmHg). For example, if your blood pressure reading is 126/76 (read as 126 over 76), the systolic pressure is 126 mmHg, and the diastolic pressure is 76 mmHg.

High blood pressure, or hypertension, is a level of blood pressure consistently above normal. Most doctors consider a "normal" blood pressure reading for an adult to be approximately 120/80. Your doctor may consider other messurements to be normal for you.

Note

- **hypertension** : 고혈압, 과도한 긴장
- **stroke** = a sudden illness in part of the brain which can cause loss of movement in parts of the body : 뇌일혈
- **symptom** = an outward sign of an inward condition : 증세
- **syndrome** = symptoms : 증후군
  - Yellowness of the eyes is one of the symptoms of jaudice. (눈이 노랗게지는 것은 황달 증세다.)
- **systolic** : 심장 수축기의   **diastolic** : 심장 이완기의
- **risk** = danger   • Miners face a lot of risks in their daily lives. (광부는 일상 생활에서 많은 위험에 처해있다.)
- **menopause** = the time when a woman's periods stop : 폐경기
- **diabetes** : 당뇨병   **beta blocker** : 베타 수용제 차단약
- **sympathetic nerve** : 교감 신경   • parasympathetic nerve (부교감신경)
- **intake** = the amount of number allowed to enter or taken in : 흡수량, 섭취량
  - To shed extra weight, lessen the intake of calories. (체중을 줄이려면 칼로리 섭취를 줄여라.)
- **respond to** = get better, do the right things as a result of : 효과가 나다
  - The disease failed to respond to the drugs. (그 약이 그 병에 효과가(반응이) 없었다.)
- **antihypertensive** : 항고혈압제의   **blood vessel** : 혈관

(3.2) The antonym of the italicized word, *constrict* in the last paragraph is _____.

    (a) Dilate   (b) Dilute   (c) Diagnose   (d) Digest   (e) Diminish

(4) The attitude of the writer toward the passage is _____. (Tone and attitude)

    (a) Informative & pedantic   (d) Persuasive & Informative
    (b) Analytical but compassionate   (e) Self-righteous but inventive
    (c) Cynical but informal

(5) It can be concluded that the person with hypertension is advised to change his/her _____. (Conclusion)

    (a) Eating habits   (b) Medication   (c) Life style   (d) Doctor   (e) Sleep pattern

Passage 2 : HIV and Its Effect on the Immune System

    The immune system is a system within all vertebrates (animals with backbones) that are composed of two important types of cells: the B-cells and the T-cells. Without these cells, our immune system could not function. The B-cells are responsible for the production of antibodies, the T-cells are for assisting the B-cells produce antibodies, and for killing damaged cells such as virally-infected ones or foreign matter within the body. The B-cells require the aid of the T-cells to properly produce antibodies.

    Whenever foreign matter (e.g. bacteria, virus, other invaders) enters the host, the immune system is activated, with both the B-cells and T-cells responding to eliminate them from the body. The struggle between viruses and the immune system is ongoing. Our body responds to the invasion through the production of T-cells and B-cells to eliminate the foreign invaders. However, a particular virus, HIV (Human Immunodeficiency Virus), infects certain cells that defend against infection. HIV targets T-cells because these cells have a protein which the HIV finds to be very receptive. Unfortunately these cells are required to assist the B-cells in fighting disease. With the neutralization of the T-cells, the virus has an easier time in attacking the body without resistance from the body's natural defenders. HIV will infect T-cells and eventually kill them. As more T-cells are produced, the virus will multiply so it can spread and infect them as well. The result is a substantial loss of T-cells, and thus an ineffective immune system. This fight may continue for up to ten years when the body eventually *succumbs*. Consequently, the body is unable to defend itself against all other types of bacteria or viruses. This acquired condition of immunodeficiency is called AIDS (Acquired Immune Deficiency Syndrome). Those people infected do not die from AIDS, but rather from other opportunistic infections. AIDS only assists in death.

지문 2: 인간 면역 부전 바이러스와 면역체계에 대한 영향

　　면역체계는 B세포와 T세포라는 두 가지 중요한 형태의 세포로 구성된 척추동물 체내의 체계다. 이런 세포가 없으면 우리 면역체계는 기능을 발휘하지 못할 것이다. B-세포는 항체를 생산하는 역할을 하고, T-세포는 B-세포가 항체를 생산하는 일을 돕고, 체내의 바이러스에 전염된 세포나 이물질 같은 손상된 세포를 죽인다. B세포는 적절하게 항체를 생산하기 위하여 T-세포의 도움을 필요로 한다.

　　이물질(예 : 박테리아, 바이러스, 다른 침입자들)이 숙주의 몸에 들어올 때마다 B-세포와 T-세포가 몸에서 나오는 이물질을 제거하기 위하여 반응하는 가운데 면역체계가 활성화된다. 바이러스와 면역 체계 사이의 싸움이 계속된다. 우리 몸은 이질적인 침입자를 제거하기 위하여 T-세포와 B-세포를 생산하면서 이 침입에 반응하다. 그러나 특수한 바이러스인 HIV(인간 면역 부전 바이러스)는 공격에 대항하는 세포를 공격한다. HIV는 T-세포를 표적

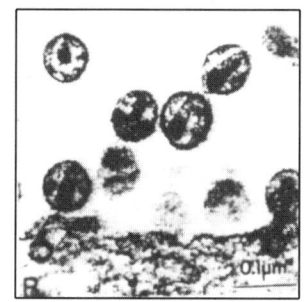
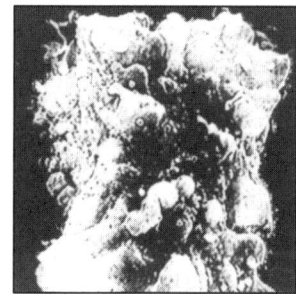

Cells infected with HIV　　Enlarged cells attacked by HIV

으로 한다. 왜냐하면 이 세포들은 HIV가 수용하기 좋은 단백질을 가지고 있기 때문이다. 불행히도 이 T-세포는 질병을 퇴치하는데 B-세포를 꼭 도와야 한다. T-세포를 중화시킴으로서 HIV 바이러스는 항체 자연 방어인자의 저항없이 항체를 쉽게 공격한다. HIV는 T-세포를 공격하고 결국 그들을 죽인다. 더 많은 T-세포가 생산될수록 바이러스는 기하급수적으로 불어나 퍼져서 역시 그들을 공격한다. 그 결과 T-세포가 크게 줄어들고 면역체계가 효력을 발휘하지 못한다. 이런 싸움은 그 항체가 결국 항복할 때까지 10년동안 계속되기도 한다. 결과적으로 몸은 다른 모든 형태의 박테리아나 바이러스를 상대로 자신을 방어할 수 없다. 이 후천성 면역 부전 상태를 AIDS(후천성 면역 결핍증)이라고 부른다. 전염된 사람은 AIDS로 죽는게 아니고 이 기회를 틈탄 다른 감염으로 죽는다. AIDS는 단지 죽는 일만 도와줄 뿐이다.

Rock Hudson(1925~1985)
A celebrity victimized by AIDS

Currently, there is no cure for AIDS, but after much research, we are able to learn more and more about this disease. First, what makes it difficult to fight AIDS is because there is no cure for most viruses. Chemical substances (e.g. medication, radiation) that are harmful to viruses, are also harmful to our healthy cells. Second, AIDS is like no other disease seen so far, because of its sophisticated replication process. The AIDS virus has the ability to multiply themselves and spread widely. The infected cells, once healthy cells, then become AIDS virus producing units. Finally, HIV also has an uncanny ability to mutate and develop a resistance to the medications used to combat it.

Some preventative measures that can be taken are; (1) Not sharing dirty intravenous needles; (2) Abstinence; and, (3) Careful screening of blood for transfusions. Today, although "cocktails" (a combination of several medications) are being used to treat AIDS, we are still a long way from a cure.

(1) The main idea of the second paragraph is _____. (Subject matter)

    (a) What the immune system is
    (b) How the immune system works
    (e) Why the immune system works
    (d) How HIV destroys the immune system
    (e) How the immune system defends against HIV

(2) _____ eventually will kill those people infected by HIV. (Locating the facts)

    (a) AIDS   (c) Chemical substances   (e) Other infectious diseases
    (b) Dirty intravenous needles   (d) B-cells & T-cells

(3) The italicized word, *succumbs* in the second paragraph can be replaced with _____. (Word in context)

    (a) Surrenders   (b) Succeeds   (c) Subjugates   (d) Supplements   (e) Sustains

(4) From the information given, it can be inferred that the group of people most likely at risk of contracting AIDS is _____ . (Making inferences)

    (a) Opium producer   (c) Marijuana user   (e) Cocaine user
    (b) Intravenous drug user   (d) Alcoholic

(5) There is a saying, "Sometimes the cure is as bad as the disease." It can be concluded that one of the major reasons why there are still incurable diseases to a certain extent such as cancer, diabetes, Alzheimer's besides AIDS is _____. (Conclusion)

    (a) No drug is strong enough to kill them
    (b) "There is no rule but has an exception"
    (c) "What is good for one is bad for another"
    (d) Healthy cells are too weak to resist
    (e) They attack only a small number of people

지금은 AIDS치료가 불가능하지만 연구를 많이 하면 이 병에 대하여 점점 많은 것을 알게 될 것이다. 첫째, AIDS퇴치를 어렵게 만드는 것은 대부분의 바이러스에 대한 치료 방법이 없기 때문이다. 바이러스에 해로운 화학물질들(예 : 약처방, 방사선)은 건강한 세포에도 유해하다. 둘째, AIDS는 그의 복잡한 복제(複製)과정 때문에 지금까지 발견된 다른 질병과 다르다는 점이다.

AIDS 바이러스는 스스로 급증하며 널리 퍼지는 능력이 있다. 한때 건강했던 세포가 병든 세포에 감염되면 AIDS 바이러스를 생산하는 단위가 된다. 마지막으로 HIV 역시 돌연변이하며, 자기를 퇴치하기 위하여 쓰였던 약처방에 대하여 저항력을 키우는 신비한 능력을 가지고 있다.

취할 수 있는 예방조치는 다음과 같다:
(1) 불결한 정맥주사 바늘을 같이 쓰지 말 것 (2) 금욕적 절제 (3) 수혈시 면밀한 검사
오늘날 비록 '칵테일(서너가지 약처방의 결합)'을 사용하여 치료하고 있지만 아직도 치료하기는 어렵다.

Note

- vertebrate = an animal(bird, fish etc.) which has a spine : 척추 동물
- virally : 바이러스에 의한 • virally infected (바이러스에 의하여 전염된)
- activate = make active, accelerate : 촉진하다, 가동시키다, 활성화시키다
  • This button activates the heating system. (이 버튼을 누르면 난방이 가동된다.)
- eliminate = remove, get rid of : 제거, 박멸하다
  • How could we eliminate these political type of evils out of this country?
  (이 나라에서 어떻게 하면 정치성 비리를 근절시킬 수 있을까?)
- ongoing = developing : 진행되고 있는
- HIV = Human Immunodeficiency Virus : 인간 면역 부전 바이러스
- receptive = quick or ready to receive suggestions, ideas : 잘 받아들이는
  • Any person with a receptive mind is already on the way to progress.
  (남의 의견을 잘 받아들이는 마음을 가진 사람은 이미 발전하고 있는 것이다.)
- neutralize = make neutral : 중립화하다, 중화시키다, 무효로하다
  • High taxes will neutralize increased wages. (세금이 오르면 봉급이 오르나 마나지.)
- multiply = increase by multiplication : 기하급수적으로 불어나다
  • When animals have more food, they generally multiply faster. (먹이가 풍부하면 동물은 급히 불어난다.)
- succumb to = yield to, give way to : 항복하다
  • She succumbed to his temptations after all. (결국 그의 유혹에 넘어갔다.)
- opportunism : 기회주의 • opportunist (기회주의자) • opportunistic (기회를 놓치지 않는)
- sophisticated = complex, having learnt the ways of the world : 닳아빠진, 순수를 잃은
- replication : 복사:암세포의 분열 재생   uncanny = weird, mysterious : 신비한
- mutate = alter, change : 변화시키다, 돌연변이시키다
  • Are mutations in plants caused by cosmic rays? (식물의 돌연변이는 우주線 때문인가?)
- intravenous : 정맥내의 • intravenous injection (정맥주사)
- abstinence : 금욕, 절제   transfusion : 수혈
- B - cell:bone - marrow - derived cell : 골수림프구   T-cell : 흉선 의존성 림프구

Passage 3 : Acupuncture

Acupuncture was first developed in China around 2696 B.C. and it was practiced during the reign of Huang Di (The Yellow Emperor, 3rd Great Emperor of China). The surviving document regarding the practice of acupuncture is found in <u>The Yellow Emperor's Classic of Internal Medicine</u> written around 2600s B.C. This practice has been widely used in China and the Far East Asian countries for many, many centuries.

In 1971, James Reston, reporter for the New York Times with Nixon's Chinese trip developed appendicitis. The Chinese proposed surgery for his *appendectomy* using acupuncture anesthesia. His post-operation pain after the appendectomy treatment was relieved by acupuncture at the Anti-imperialist Hospital in Beijing, which began to draw attention from the American audience. In 1987, the American Academy of Medical Acupuncture was formed as the first national physician and surgeon organization dedicated to the advancement of acupuncture within the U.S. In 1991, 13 states and the District of Columbia regulated the practice of acupuncture. In 1993, $500 million per year was spent by the U.S. public on acupuncture treatments. Many physicians in the U.S. began to receive training at University of California at Los Angeles in 1982, and to this day under Dr. Joseph Helms. These physicians learned traditional Chinese medicine, neuroanatomics, *auricular* and hand acupuncture. As a result, acupuncture treatment systems and microsystems are currently used throughout the country.

Our body has 361 points that can be acupunctured. For example, our hand has 27 points for the needle to pierce as a way of improving physical condition. As illustrated in the attached diagram(p. 409), the acupuncturing needle on point 1 can increase blood pressure; point 2 relieves lower back pain; point 3 relieves ankle pain; point 4 for chest discomfort; point 5 for eye problems; and, finally, point 27 for stomach pain. Is it fascinating? But never try to do this by yourself. See your certified oriental medical doctor near you.

(Source: Contributed by Dr. Gyengmo An, Summer 1997)

 Acupuncture as a high school curriculum is taught neither in the Far Eastern countries nor in the United States. However, the practice of acupuncture in the Far East is still so prevalent that it is worth being introduced here.

(1) The topic of the second paragraph is _____. (Subject matter)

   (a) History of acupuncture
   (b) Acceptance of acupuncture in the U.S.
   (c) Acupuncture training at UCLA
   (d) Reston's treatment by acupuncture
   (e) Foundation of the American Academy of Medical Acupuncture

지문 3: 침술

　침술은 기원전 2696년 무렵 중국에서 개발되어 중국의 황제(黃帝) 치세 중에 시행되었다. 침술 시행에 관한 남아있는 문서가 기원전 2600 무렵에 쓰여진 황제내경(黃帝內經)에서 발견된다. 이 요법은 중국과 극동 아시아 국가들에서 수세기 동안 시행되어 오고 있다.

　1971년에 뉴욕 타임스지 기자인 제임스 레스턴이 닉슨 대통령 중국 방문 취재 때 맹장염이 악화되었다. 중국인들이 침술 마취를 이용한 맹장 수술을 제안했다. 그의 맹장수술 치료 후의 통증은 북경 소재 반 제국주의자 병원에서 침술에 의하여 완화되었다. 그 치료법이 미국인들의 주의를 끌기 시작했다. 1987년에 미국침술의료학회가 미국내 침술 발전에 전념하는 최초의 국가적인 내, 외과 조직으로서 결성되었다. 1991년에 13개 주와 워싱턴D·C는 침술치료를 법으로 정하였다. 1993년에 미국 대중들이 연간 5억 달러를 침술 치료에 썼다. 미국의 많은 내과의사들이 1982년에 그리고 오늘까지 UCLA에서 Dr. Joseph Helms 밑에서 침술 교육을 받기 시작했다. 이들 내과의들은 전통중국 의술인 신경해부학, 심이(心耳), 수지침을 배웠다. 그 결과 침술 치료 체계가 전국적으로 사용되고 있다.

　우리 몸에는 361곳의 침을 놓을 자리가 있다. 예를 들면 우리 손에는 몸의 상태를 개선시키는 방법으로 침을 꽂을 27혈이 있다. 첨부된 도해에서 예시한 것처럼 1번 혈에 침을 놓으면 혈압을 높이고, 2번 혈은 허리 아랫부분 통증을 가라앉히고, 3번 혈은 발목 통증,

(1) Blood pressure elevating point
(2) Lower back and hips point
(3) Ankles point
(4) Chest point
(5) Eyes point
(6) Shoulder point
(7) Forehead point
(8) Top of the head point
(9) Migraine point
(10) Hiccup point
(11) Lowering fever point
(12) Perineum point
(13) Back of the head point
(14) Spine point
(15) Sciatic nerver point
(16) Throat point
(17) Neck point
(18) Diarrhea point
(19) Malaria point
(20) Tonsil point
(21) Cough point
(22) Indigestion point
(23) Vital point
(24) Toothache point
(25) Bedwetting point
(26) Calming point
(27) Stomach point

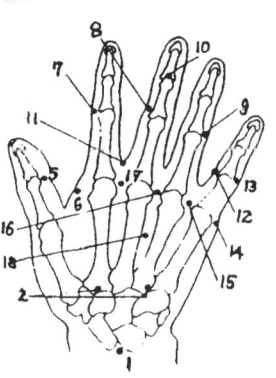

(2.1) Acupuncture was practiced in China around 2696 B.C. It is evidenced by the record of _____ (2.1 - 2.2. Locating the facts)

    (a) The Analects of Confucius
    (b) The Tao Te Ching of Lao Tzu
    (c) The Doctrine of the Mean
    (d) The Yellow Emperor's Classic of Internal Medicine
    (e) The Great Learning

(2.2) The year in which legislation regarding the practice of acupuncture was first passed within the U.S. is _____.

    (a) 1971   (b) 1982   (c) 1987   (d) 1990   (e) 1991

(3.1) The italicized word, *appendectomy* in the second paragraph refers to the _____ of the appendix by operation. (3.1 - 3.2. Words in context)

    (a) Removal (b) Application (c) Aid (d) Symptom (e) Adjustment

(3.2) The italicized word, *auricular* in the second paragraph refers to _____.

    (a) Eye   (b) Ear   (c) Neck   (d) Skin   (e) Nose

(4) It can be inferred that the area in which acupuncture initially developed would be the _____ parts of China where the inhabitants probably could not easily obtain plants and herbs for medicinal purposes. (Making inferences)

    (a) Eastern (b) Western (c) Northern (d) Southern (e) Central

(5) Based on the facts given, it can be concluded that the fundamental principle of the acupuncture treatment is based on the philosophy of _____. (Conclusion)

    (a) Taoism (b) Buddhism (c) Confucianism (d) Hinduism
    (e) "Yin-yang," a root & mixture of the traditional Chinese way of life

3.3.5. Mathematics

<u>Passage 1 :</u> **An Overview of the Development in Mathematics**

    Mathematics, the core academic discipline in the sciences, has developed as a logical reasoning applied to numbers, space, and quantity. The origin of mathematics dates back to prehistoric times, and the numbers were used as a tool for practical purposes.

    During the ancient times of Babylonia, China, and Egypt, mathematics was

4번 혈은 흉곽 고통, 5번 혈은 눈의 질환, 그리고 끝으로 27번 혈은 위통을 진정시킨다. 매력이 있지? 그러나 결코 혼자 시험하지는 말라. 주변에 면허가 있는 한의사를 찾아보아라.

> **Note**
> - acupuncture : 침술
> - appendicitis : 충수염, 맹장염
> - appendectomy (맹장수술)
> - an(a)esthesia : 마취법, 무감각증
> - post = after, following : …후
> - postscript (추신)
> - posthumous (사후의)
> - post-modernism
> - relieve = lessen or remove pain, distress : 통증을 덜다, 완화하다
>   - We were relieved to hear that you were safe. (무사하다는 소식에 마음 놓았다.)
> - regulate = control systematically, cause to obey a rule : 규제, 법으로 규정하다
> - neuroanatomics : 신경해부학
> - auricular : 심이(心耳)-마음으로 들음
> - certified : 면허가 있는, 공인된
> - prevalent = widespread : 널리 보급된, 유행하는
>   - Is malaria still prevalent in that country? (아직도 그 나라에는 말라리아가 유행하는가?)

3.3.5. 수학

지문 1 : 수학 발달의 개요

과학의 핵심 교과인 수학은 수와 공간 그리고 양에 응용되는 논리적 추론으로서 발달되어 왔다. 수학의 기원은 선사시대까지 거슬러 올라가고 수는 실용적 목적을 위한 도구로 쓰였다.

바빌로니아, 중국, 이집트의 고대에서 수학은 매년 나일강이나 황하의 범람으로부터 토지경계의 확정이나 건축의 공식같은 실용적인 문제를 해결하기 위한 도구로서 발달되어 왔다. 희랍사람들은 우주 자연은 수학적으로 설계되어 있고 수학을 통해서 그 모습을 꿰뚫어 볼 수 있다고 생각했다. 예를 들면 피타고라스 학파 사람들은 다르게 보이는 현상들이 동일한 수학적 특성을 나타낸다고 주장했고 직삼각형의 크기 사이의 관계를 계산하는데 $a^2+b^2=c^2$라는 공식을 끌어냈다. 플라톤은 수학적으로 설계된 이상적인 세계가 존재하며 우리가 감각기관을 통하여 인식하는 것은 그 이상세계의 불완전한 발현이라고 주장했다. 유클리드(B.C. 300)는 많은 고대 희랍인들의 개별적인 발견에 대해 체계적이고 연역적이며 광대한 설명으로, 논리적 구성을 기초로 한 공간과 수의 법칙들을 공리로 간주했다.

그리스 문명에 이어 인도, 아라비아도 수학에 지대한 공헌을 했다. 힌두족들은 부채는

developed as a tool for solving practical problems such as the annual flooding of the Nile and the Yellow River, establishment of land boundaries, and the formulas in construction. The Greeks thought that the universe/nature is mathematically designed, and through mathematics man can penetrate to that design. For examples, the Pythagoreans claimed that phenomena that appear different can exhibit identical mathematical properties, deriving a formula ($a^2 + b^2 = c^2$) in calculating the relationship between the size of a right triangle. Plato claimed that there is an ideal world that is designed mathematically, and what we perceive through our senses is an imperfect representation of the ideal world. Euclid (300 B.C.) postulated the laws of space and of figures in space in <u>Elements</u>, based on a logical organization in the form of systematic, deductive, and vast account of the separate discoveries of many classical Greeks.

   Following the Greek civilization, India and Arabia made important contributions to mathematics. The Hindus added to the logical *woes* of mathematics by introducing negative numbers to represent debts and positive numbers to represent assets. Their mathematicians originated the concept of zero, and developed the decimal system based on the number 10, which we still use today. The Arabs who had absorbed the Greek and Hindus contributions, used whole numbers, fractions, and irrational numbers, thus introducing new and correct rules for addition, subtraction, multiplication, and division.

   From the 19th century, the tradition of mathematics began to be reexamined and expanded from the boundary where Euclid had started from common notions about space and logical consequences. The non-Euclidean mathematicians chose to study the logical consequences of unconventional actions of space, and used the *coherence* and consistency of these unconventional notions to challenge the mathematical orthodoxy. For examples, applied mathematicians claim that mathematics should be studied so as to be applicable to practical purposes; the intuitionist school has rebelled against the formulistic notion of mathematics as the manipulation of meaningless symbols. The work of Kurt Gödel has shown limitations to such a system of logics. In other words, they advocate that mathematics should have real-world meaning, instead of pure mathematical notions and formulas back to Euclid. They also insist on finite demonstration of all theorems to be proved, instead of the Law of the Excluded Middle that asserts one can prove a proposition by disproving its negation: "Either A or not A."

(1) A proper topic of the passage is A/An _____ of Mathematics. (Subject matter)

   (a) Review   (b) Profile   (c) Origin   (d) Outline   (e) Development

(2.1.) The initial use of mathematics for practical purposes can be found during the _____ era. (2.1. - 2.5. Locating the facts)

   (a) Ancient Greek   (c) Ancient Chinese   (e) Prehistoric

음수로 표현하고, 자산은 양수로 표현하는 음수, 양수를 도입함으로써 수학의 논리적 문제들을 더 증가시켰다. 힌두족의 수학자들이 0의 개념을 창시했고 10을 기본으로 한 현재 우리가 사용하는 십진법을 발달시켰다. 그리스와 힌두족의 공헌을 흡수한 아랍인들이 정수, 분수, 무리수를 사용했으며 이런 식으로 보태기, 빼기, 더하기, 나누기 셈을 도입했다.

19세기부터 수학의 전통이 재검토를 받기 시작했고 유클리드가 공간과 논리적 결론에 관한 일반개념에서 출발했던 경계선으로부터 확장되었다. 비 유클리드 수학자들은 비 전통적인 공간에서 논리적 결과를 연구하기로 선택하였다. 그리고 수학적인 정통성을 공격하기 위하여 비 전통적인 개념의 응집성과 일관성을 사용했다. 예를 들면 응용 수학가들은 수학은 실용적 목적에 쓰여지도록 연구되어야 한다고 주장한다. 직관주의 학파 사람들은 수학의 공식 개념을 무의미한 기호의 조작이라고 반대하여 저항해왔다. Kurt Gödel의 연구는 그런 체계의 논리학이 가지는 한계점을 밝혀왔다. 말을 달리하면 그들은 수학이 유클리드로 거슬러 올라가는 순수한 수학적 개념이나 공식 대신 현실적 의미를 가져야 한다고 주장한다. 그들은 또한 어떤 명제를 증명하는데 그 부정을 반증함으로써, 즉 'A아니면 A아닌 것'으로 증명할 수 있다고 단정하는 '배중율(排中律)' 대신 증명해야 할 모든 공리에는 증명에 한계가 있음을 주장한다.

Note

☐ **penetrate** = enter into, cut into(through) : 침투하다
  • The bullet penetrated his head upwards. (총탄이 머리를 관통하여 위쪽으로 지나갔다.)
☐ **perceive** = notice, understand : 지각하다, 인지하다
  • We perceived that we were unwelcome and left on the spot.
  (환영받지 못한다는 것을 깨닫고 그 자리에서 떠났다.)
☐ **postulate** = accept something (that has not been proved) as true : 인정하다, 가정하다
  Mencius postulated the inherent goodness of man. (맹자는 성선설을 믿었다.)
☐ **woe** = sorrow, grief, distress; cause of trouble : 슬픔, 비탄, 저주
  • Poverty, illness are woes. • a tale of woe (신세타령)
  • Woe be to those who bully the weak. (약자를 괴롭히는 자에게 저주 있으라.)
☐ **decimal system** : 10진법   ☐ **whole number** : 정수(整數)   ☐ **fraction** : 분수
☐ **(ir)rational number** : 유(무)리수
☐ **addition**(+) **subtraction**(−) **multiplication**(×) **division**(÷)
☐ **coherence** : 응집성   ☐ **consistency** : 일관성, 앞뒤가 맞음
☐ **orthodoxy** : 정통, 정설, 정통적 관행   • opp. heterodoxy
☐ **intuition** = immediate understanding without conscious reasoning, or study : 직관, 통찰
☐ **assert** = state an opinion forcefully : 힘있게 주장하다
  • She asserted her belief that he was not guilty. (그 남자가 무죄라는 자기 믿음을 주장했다.)
☐ **disprove** = prove to be wrong or false
☐ **the Law of the Excluded Middle** : 배중율(排中律):형식 논리학에서 'A는 B다'와 'A는 B가 아니다.'와의 두 판단 사이에 중간의 것은 없다는 사유법칙의 하나.

(b) Ancient Egyptian   (d) Babylonian

(2.2) "The phenomena in our universe can be explained by mathematical properties" is believed by the _____.

(a) Arabs   (b) Hindus   (c) Greeks   (d) Egyptians   (e) Chinese

(2.3) The inventions of negative numbers and the decimal system were introduced by the _____.

(a) Greeks   (b) Arabs   (c) Hindus   (d) Egyptians   (e) Chinese

(2.4) The use of whole numbers, irrational numbers, and rules for multiplication and division were introduced by the _____.

(a) Hindus   (b) Arabs   (c) Greeks   (d) Egyptians   (e) Chinese

(2.5) One of the modern mathematicians who challenges the Euclidean system of logics as narrow, imperfect, and limited is _____.

(a) George Boole   (c) North Whitehead   (e) David Hilbert
(b) Bertrand Russell   (d) Kurt Gödel

(3.1) The italicized word, *woes* in the third paragraph refers to _____. (3.1 - 3.2. Words in context)

(a) Problems   (b) Sorrows   (c) Grief   (d) Unhappiness   (e) Misfortunes

(3.2) The antonym of the italicized word, *coherence* in the last paragraph is _____.

(a) Stickiness   (b) Soldering   (c) Adhesion   (d) Separation   (e) Cohesiveness

(4) The writer's attitude toward the formulistic tradition of the Euclidean mathematics seems to be _____. (Tone & attitude)

(a) Paternal   (c) Disapproving   (e) Indifferent
(b) Fascinating   (d) Condescending

(5) Based on the information given, and the assertions, "Either A or not A," it can be concluded that the study of mathematics will be explored more toward the direction of _____. (Conclusion)

(a) Mathematical Orthodoxy   (d) Pure mathematical notions
(b) Mathematical axioms   (e) Applicability for practical purposes
(c) Formulistic principles

Selected proverbs for the study of cross-cultural expressions

영어 격언과 한문 격언과의 만남 (8)

1. **One should not divorce a wife married in poverty.** 糟糠之妻不下堂(조강지처불하당)
   - 조강지처는 쫓아내선 안된다.

2. **Time and tide wait for no man.** 歲月不待人, 歲不我延(세월부대인, 세불아연)
   - 세월은 사람을 기다리지 않는다. 세월이 나를 연장시키지 않는다. · Life is short and time swift.

3. **Old age doesn't protect from folly.** 老賦遲鈍(노부지둔 ; 賦 = give) – 나이 들면 느려지고 둔해진다.
   · The brain doesn't lie in the beard. / · There is no fool like an old fool.

4. **When the sun sets, the moon rises.** 月往卽日來, 日往卽月來(월왕즉일래 일왕즉월래)
   - 달이 지면 해가 뜨고, 해가 지면 달이 뜬다. · When the moon sets, the sun rises.

5. **After a storm comes a calm.** 苦盡甘來, 興盡悲來(고진감래, 흥진비래)
   - 괴로움이 지나면 즐거움이 오고 흥이 끝나면 슬픔이 온다. · The darkest hour is that before the dawn.

6. **A father's goodness is higher than the mountain.** 父母之恩高於山, 深於海(부모지은고어산 심어해)
   - 부모의 은혜는 산보다 높고 바다보다 깊다. · A mother's goodness is deeper than the sea.

7. **Like father, like son.** 父傳子傳(부전자전) – 그 아비에 그 아들(자식은 아비를 닮는다)
   · Parents are patterns. / · Like breeds like. / · Like causes liking.

8. **No man can't serve two masters.** 忠臣不事二君(충신불사이군 ; 事 = serve)
   - 충신은 두 임금을 섬기지 않는다.

9. **An ounce of luck is worth a pound of wisdom.** 智將不如福將(지장불여복장)
   - 꾀 있는 장수가 복 있는 장수만 못하다.

10. **Who will bell the cat?** 猫頭(項)縣鈴(묘두(항)현령 ; 項 = neck) - 고양이 목에 방울 달기 · Easier said than done.

11. **Fortune favors fools.** 人至察卽無徒(인지찰즉무도 ; 徒 = followers)
    - 행운은 어리석은 사람을 사랑한다. · The more knave, the more luck.

12. **When the belly is full, the mind is among maids.** 飽煖思淫慾(포난사음욕)
    - 배부르고 등 따뜻하면 못된 생각을 품는다.

13. **Go up when you choose a friend.** 賢人友勝己者(현인우승기자)
    - 현명한 사람은 자기보다 나은 사람을 벗으로 삼는다.

14. **A good wife makes a good husband.** 賢婦令夫貴 惡婦令夫賤(현부영부귀 악부영부천)
    - 현명한 아내는 남편을 귀하게 만들고 못된 아내는 남편을 천하게 만든다.

15. **Riches adorn the dwelling; virtue adorns the person.** 富潤屋 德潤身(부윤옥 덕윤신)
    - 부는 집을 윤택하게 하고 덕은 몸을 윤택하게 한다.

16. **The mind is the man.** 萬物唯心造(만물유심조) – 모든 것은 오직 마음 먹기에 달렸다.
    · What's a man but his mind? / · A man is well or woe as he thinks himself so.
    · There's nothing either good or bad but thinking makes it so.
    · It's riches of the mind only that make a man rich and happy.

17. **Measure is treasure.** 中庸之道(중용지도) – 어느 쪽으로나 치우침이 없는 것이 바른 길이다.
    · Measure is medicine. / · The half is better than whole. / · Virtue is found in the middle.
    · Safety lies in the middle. / · Love me little, love me long. / · You can have too much of a thing.

18. **Man dies and leaves a name; the tiger a skin.** 人死留名 虎死留皮(인사유명 호사유피)
    - 사람은 죽어서 이름을 남기고 호랑이는 죽어서 가죽을 남긴다.

19. **Nature cures of itself. Nature hates all sudden changes.** 無爲而化, 無爲自然(무위이화, 무위자연)
    - 힘들여 하지 않아도 일이 잘 됨, 인공을 가하지 않고 있는 그대로의 자연 · He that follows nature is never out of his way.

Passage 2 : **The Pythagorean Theorem**

The longest side of a right triangle is opposite the right angle and is called the hypotenuse. The two shorter sides are called legs. Pythagoras provided us a useful fact about right triangles.

The *converse* of the Pythagorean theorem is also true, which can be used to test whether a triangle is a right triangle. The theorem states that "if the sides of a triangle have lengths a, b, and c, such that $c^2 = a^2 + b^2$, then the triangle is a right triangle."

For example : Is a triangle with sides of the given lengths a right triangle?
        (a) 7, 9, 18   (b) 8, 15, 17

Solution : (a) $7^2 = 49$ (b) $8^2 = 64$
              $9^2 = 81$ $15^2 = 225$
            $18^2 = 324$ $17^2 = 289$
            $49 + 81 = 130 \neq 324$ $64 + 225 = 289 = 289$
            $\therefore 7^2 + 9^2 \neq 18^2$ $\therefore 8^2 + 15^2 = 17^2$
            This is not a right triangle   This is a right triangle
            since $49 + 81 \neq 324$ since $64 + 225 = 289$

    (the symbol $\therefore$ stands for "therefore")

(1) A proper title of the passage would be "A/An _____ of Right Triangles." (Subject matter)

    (a) Assumption   (b) Law   (c) Hypothesis   (d) Rule   (e) Theory

(2.1) In a right triangle, the sides have lengths 8, 15, and ___. (2.1 - 2.2. Locating the facts)

    (a) 17   (b) 18   (c) 19   (d) 20   (e) 21

(2.2) The lengths of some triangles are given. Identify the set of lengths that does not make up a right triangle.

    (a) 3, 4, 5   (b) 5, 12, 13   (c) 9, 10, 13   (d) 7, 24, 25   (e) 10, 24, 26

(3) The italicized word, *converse* in the second paragraph refers to _____. (Word in context)

    (a) Same   (b) Similar   (c) Familiar   (d) Opposite   (e) Adjacent

(4) The writer's presentation for the paragraph pattern is based on _____. (Rhetorical techniques)

    (a) Analysis   (c) Comparison & contrast   (e) Definition
    (b) Description   (d) Analogy

(5) It can be concluded that the Pythagorean Theorem has contributed the most to the discipline of _____. (Conclusion)

    (a) Chemistry   (b) Geometry   (c) Algebra   (d) Biology   (e) Astronomy

지문 2 : 피타고라스 정리

직각 삼각형의 가장 긴 변은 직각의 반대편에 있고 사변이라고 불린다. 두개의 짧은 변은 변(밑변과 높이)이라고 불린다. 피타고라스는 직각삼각형에 관하여 유용한 한가지 사실을 우리에게 제공하고 있다.

The Pythagorean Theorem

If the hypotenuse of a right triangle has length c, and the legs have lengths a and b, then

$$c^2 = a^2 + b^2$$

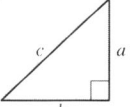
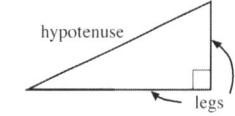

피타고라스 정리

직삼각형의 사변을 c라하고 두변을 각각 a와 b라고 하면, $c^2 = a^2 + b^2$다.

피타고라스 정리의 역도 또한 진이며 어떤 삼각형이 직각삼각형인지 아닌지를 증명하는데 쓰인다. 이 정리는 어느 삼각형의 변의 길이가 a, b, c이고, 다음과 같이 $c^2 = a^2 + b^2$일 때, 그 삼각형은 직각삼각형이라고 명시한다.

Note

- theorem = a statement that can be shown to be true by reasoning : 정리
- right = (of an angle) 90 degrees : 직각
- neither acute : 예각   nor obtuse : 둔각   leg : 변
- hypotenuse = side of a right-angled triangle opposite the right angle : 사변
- converse = opposite to   • I hold the converse opinion. (내 견해는 정반대다.)
- solution = an answer to a problem or difficulty : 해결책, 풀이
  • It's difficult to find a solution to this problem (이 문제의 해답 찾기가 어렵다.)

Passage 3 : Statistical Measures

The range, the mean, the median, and the mode are some statistical measures. To understand these measures, let us use them to analyze two sets of test scores for 2 different classes: Class A and Class B. The test scores are shown in the following table. We can use these measures as a way of concluding or comparing certain sets of data.

	Class A	Class B
The **range** of a set of data is the difference between the greatest and the least numbers.	98	96
	96	95
	94	91
	90	89
	90	83
Range of Class A : 98 - 80 = 18	85	83
Range of Class B : 96 - 76 = 20	83	79
	80	76
	716	692

The **mean** is the sum of the data in a set, divided by the number of items of data in that set. The mean is frequently referred to as the average. For example, in Class A and Class B, both sets have 8 items. The bottom of the chart *depicts* the sum of the individual sets.

Mean of Class A: 716 ÷ 8 = 89.5   Mean of Class B: 692 ÷ 8 = 86.5

When the data is arranged in numerical order, which the above chart is for simplification, the middle number is called the **median**. If the number of items of data is even, the median is the mean of the two middle numbers. We see that Class A and Class B both have 8 items in their sets.

Median of Class A = 90

Median of Class B = 89, 83 = (89 + 83) ÷ 2 = 86

The **mode** is the number in the set of data that occurs the most often. A set of data can have more than one mode or even no mode.

Mode of Class A = 90   Mode of Class B = 83

For Class A, the range is 18, the mean is 89.5, the median is 90, and the

지문 3 : 통계

범위, 평균치, 중앙치, 최빈치는 몇가지 통계 척도들이다. 이들 척도를 이해하기 위하여 다른 A와 B 두 학급의 평가 점수를 분석해보자. 시험 점수는 다음과 같이 나타나 있다. 어떤 묶어진 자료에 대한 결론을 내리거나 비교하는 방법으로 이런 척도를 사용할 수 있다.

자료의 '범위' 란 최대치와 최소치 사이의 차이다.

'평균치' 란 한 집합의 총계를 그 집합의 항목수로 나눈 것이다. 평균치를 흔히 평균이라고 말한다. 예를 들면 A반과 B반은 둘다 항목수가 8이다. 표의 아래 수는 개별 집합의 총계를 표시한다.

자료가 수량 순으로 배열되어 있으면 즉 위표처럼 보기 쉽게 하기 위하여, 중간 숫자를 중앙치라고 부른다. 사례 수가 짝수면 중앙의 2개 숫자의 평균이 중앙치다. A와 B학급 모두 자기 집합의 항목수는 8이다.

'최빈치' 는 자료의 묶음 중에서 가장 많이 나오는 수치다. 한 집합의 자료 속에는 한개 이상의 최빈치도 올 수 있고 전혀 없을 수도 있다.

A학급의 경우, 범위는 18, 평균치는 89.5, 중앙치는 90, 최빈치는 90이다. B반은 범위 20, 평균 86.5, 중앙치 86, 최빈치 83이다. 통계 척도를 총괄해서 볼 때 A반이 B반보다 우수하다고 결론을 내릴 수 있다.

note

- item = single article or unit in a list : 항목, 품목
- depict = describe : 표현하다 • This painting depicts the Battle of Waterloo.
- numerical = showing by a number or numbers : 수리적, 숫자의
    • numerical ability (수리 능력)   • numerical order (번호 = No.)
- even = of numbers that can be divided by 2 with no remainder : 짝수   • opp. odd
- conclude = arrive at a belief or opinion : 결론에 도달하다
- average = the amount found by adding together several quantities and then dividing the number of quantities : 평균

mode is 90. For Class B, the range is 20, the mean is 86.5, the median is 86, and the mode is 83. From a review of the statistical measures, we can conclude that Class A is better than Class B.

(1) The proper title for this passage would be "The ___ of Statistics". (Subject matter)

    (a) Range (b) Mode (c) Measurements (d) Mean (e) Median

(2.1) Given that set T includes the values of (55, 66, 77, 88, 99), the range of set T would be ___. (2.1 - 2.2. Locating the facts)

    (a) 11   (b) 22   (c) 33   (d) 44   (e) 55

(2.2) Which of the following sets of data would have 50 as its mean?

    (a) (100, 55, 66, 40, 44)   (d) (30, 33, 44, 23, 50, 70)
    (b) (45, 46, 79, 79, 80)   (e) (23, 77, 50, 100, 20, 33, 47)
    (c) (50, 51, 48, 50, 46)

(3) The italicized word, *depicts* in the second paragraph refers to _____. (Word in context)

    (a) Represents (b) Rationalizes (c) Returns (d) Restores (e) Revolts

(4) Based on the information given, it can be inferred that the four statistical measures are most likely to be used for the _____. (Making inferences)

    (a) Prediction of weather
    (b) Prediction of winning the lottery
    (c) Control of air traffic
    (d) Taxing purposes
    (e) Comparison of group/individual achievements

(5) It can be concluded that these statistical measures are most likely to be used in/at _____. (Conclusion)

    (a) Schools   (c) Stock markets   (e) Banking institutions
    (d) Census bureaus (b) Trade centers

Selected proverbs for the study of cross-cultural expressions

영어 격언과 한문 격언과의 만남 (9)

1. **He gives twice who gives quickly.** 死後大卓不如生前一盃酒(사후대탁불여생전일배주)
   - 죽은 뒤의 큰 대접보다 살았을 때 한 잔 술이 낫다.
   · Better an egg today than a hen tomorrow. / · Slow help is no help.
   · He that is long in giving knows not how to give. / · Long tarrying takes all the thanks away.
   · Some of these days is none of these days.

2. **Covetousness is the root of all evils.** 務貪卽憂, 憂生於多慾(무탐즉우, 우생어다욕)
   - 탐욕에 힘쓰면 즉시 근심이 생기고 근심은 욕심에서 생긴다.
   All covet, all lose. 禍生於多貪, 保生者寡慾(화생어다탐, 보생자과욕)
   - 화는 탐욕에서 생겨나니 살아남으려면 욕심을 줄여라. · Grasp all, lose all.

3. **Old habits die hard.** 舊習難防(구습난방) – 오래된 습관은 막기 어렵다.
   · Habits are at first cobwebs, at last cables. / · Habit is a second nature.

4. **Laughter makes good blood.** 一笑一少一怒一老(일소일소일노일노)
   - 한 번 웃으면 한 번 젊어지고, 한 번 화내면 한 번 늙는다. · Laugh and grow fat. / · Laughter is the best medicine.

5. **The nearest way is commonly the foulest.** 行不由徑(행불유경 ; 徑 = shortcut)
   - 지름길로 가지 마라(정도로 가라).
   · The longest way round is the shortest way home. / · Slow but sure wins the race.

6. **A constant guest is never welcome.** 久住令人賤(구주영인천 ; 令 = make) – 오래 머물면 천하게 된다.
   · Do not wear out your welcome. / · Long visits bring shortest compliments.

7. **Fish and guests smell in three days.** 看三五日相見不如初(간삼오일상견불여초)
   - 사나흘만 만나도 처음같지 않다.

8. **A hungry man is an angry man.** 貧而無怨難(빈이무원난) – 가난하면서 원망하지 않기는 어렵다.

9. **They must hunger in frost that will not work in heat.**
   春若不耕秋無所望(춘약불경추무소망 ; 若 = if) 봄에 밭을 갈지 않으면 가을에 희망이 없다.

10. **Idleness is the key of beggary.** 懶卽家傾(나즉가경 ; 懶 = idle) – 게으르면 집안이 기운다.
    · An idle youth, a needy age.

11. **Fish begins to stink at the head.** 上濁下不淨(상탁하부정)
    - 윗물이 탁하면 아랫물도 흐리다.(윗물이 맑아야 아랫물이 맑다.)

12. **Neither bribe, nor lose your right.** 賂物亡身(뇌물망신) – 뇌물이 사람 망친다.
    · Gift enters everywhere without a wimble. / · Gift blinds the eye.
    · Show me the man, and I will show you the law. / · Every man has his price.

13. **Every law leaks.** 法網必漏(법망필루) – 법에는 반드시 새는 구멍이 있다.
    · There is no law without exceptions. / · Little thieves are hanged, but great ones escape.

14. **He that practices virtue plans for posterity.** 百年之利莫如種德(백년지리막여종덕)
    - 백년 동안의 이익을 위하여 덕을 쌓는 것만한 것 없다. · Plant goodness for your heirs.

15. **Fortune favors the bold.** 勇者制人(용자제인) – 용감한 자가 사람을 제압한다.
    · A bold heart is half the battle. None but the brave deserve the fair.
    · A man of courage never wants weapons. / · Cowards die many times before their deaths.

16. **Providing is preventing.** 有備無患(유비무환) – 준비가 있으면 걱정이 없다.
    · Ready money is a ready medicine. / · Provide for the worst, the best will save itself.

3.3.6. Physics

Passage 1 : An Introduction to Physics

Physics as the study of nature deals with all natural phenomena not covered by biology and chemistry. To be more specific, it is the study of matter, energy, and their interactions. This includes the studies of (a) force and motion (mechanics); (b) sound (acoustics); (c) heat (thermodynamics); (d) light (optics); (5) electricity and magnetism; and, (6) the study of matter on a submicroscopic scale such as atomic physics, nuclear physics, molecular physics, and solid-state physics.

There is no clear-cut distinction between the fields of physics and chemistry. However, chemistry emphasizes the reactions between various atoms and molecules, whereas physics stresses the properties of the atoms and molecules, the elementary particles (electrons, protons, and neutrons) that make them up, and their interactions with energy. For example, nuclear physics and particle physics deal with nuclei of atoms and their reactions with each other and with elementary particles, and in this respect are similar to chemistry but on a smaller scale of the structure of matter.

Physics can be grouped into two: Classical and Modern. The classical physics deals with the subfields of mechanics, acoustics, thermodynamics, electromagnetism, and optics. These fields were reasonably well understood at the beginning of the 20th century. Classical physics is primarily a foundation of knowledge used in engineering and basic research. Modern physics largely deals with atomic, nuclear, and particle physics which were relatively undeveloped before the advent of the theories of relativity and quantum mechanics. These fields undeveloped before the early 20th century are essential to the understanding of matter and energy at the molecular and atomic level. For example, the relativity that is important when material objects travel at speeds approaching the speed of light, states the *equivalence* of matter and energy through the famous equation, $E = mc^2$.

(Source: Contributed by Dr. George R. Carruthers, September 1993)

(1.1) The main idea of the passage is "_____ physics is." (1.1 - 1.3. Subject matters)

    (a) What   (b) Why   (c) When   (d) Where   (e) How

(1.2) The topic of the second paragraph is " the _____ between physics and chemistry."

    (a) Differences   (c) Common factors   (e) Overlapping & differences
    (b) Similarities   (d) Interactions

(1.3) The topic of the last paragraph is "the _____ of physics."

    (a) Development   (b) Classification   (c) Profile   (d) Outline   (e) Synopsis

3.3.6. 물리학

지문 1 : 물리학 개론

물리학은 자연에 관한 연구로서 생물이나 화학이 다루지 않는 자연 현상을 취급한다. 구체적으로 말하면, 물질, 에너지, 그리고 그들의 상호작용을 연구한다. 물리학 안에는 다음의 학문이 들어 있다. (1) 힘과 운동(역학) (2) 소리(음향학) (3) 열(열역학) (4) 빛(광학) (5) 전기와 자기 (6) 초 현미경적인 크기의 물질 연구로서, 원자 물리학, 핵 물리학, 분자 물리학, 고체 물리학이 있다.

물리학과 화학 분야 사이에 명확한 구분은 없다. 그러나 화학은 다양한 원자와 분자 사이의 반응을 강조하지만 물리학은 원자, 분자 그리고 그들을 구성하는 소립자인 전자, 양성자, 중성자의 특성과 그들이 가지는 에너지와의 상호관계를 중요시한다. 예를 들면 핵물리학과 입자물리학은 원자핵과 그들 상호간의, 그리고 소립자와의 반응을 취급하며 이런 관점에서 화학과 유사하지만 미시 세계의 물질 구조를 다룬다.

물리학은 두 집단으로 묶을 수 있다 : 고전 물리학과 현대 물리학이다. 고전 물리학은 역학, 음향학, 열역학, 전자기(磁氣)학, 그리고 광학의 하부분야를 취급한다. 이 분야들은 20세기 초에 상당히 잘 받아 들여졌었다. 고전 물리학은 일차적으로 공학과 기초연구에 쓰이는 지식의 토대가 된다. 현대 물리학은 주로 상대성 이론과 양자(量子)물리학 출현 이전에 비교적 발달되지 않았던 원자, 핵, 입자 물리학을 다룬다. 20세기 전에는 발달하지

Basic equations

Density
density = $\frac{mass}{volume}$ volume = $\frac{mass}{density}$
mass = volume × density

Velocity
$v = u + at$
where v is the final velocity, u the original velocity, a the acceleration, and t the time taken

Pressure
pressure = $\frac{force}{area}$ $P = \frac{F}{A}$

Energy
potential energy = weight × height above ground
kinetic energy = $1/2\ mv^2$
where m is the mass and v is the velocity

Waves
speed = frequency × wavelength $v = f\lambda$

Electricity
charge = current × time
(coulombs) (amperes) (seconds)
$\frac{resistance}{(ohms)}$ = $\frac{voltage(volts)}{current(amperes)}$ $R = \frac{V}{I}$
$V = I \times R$

Electrical power
power = voltage × current $P = V \times I$
(watts) (volts) (amperes)
$V = \frac{P}{I}$ and $I = \frac{P}{V}$

(2.1) The theories of quantum mechanics were developed in the early ___th century. (2.1 -2.2. Locating the facts)

    (a) 16   (b) 17   (c) 18   (d) 19   (e) 20

(2.2) In physics, the study of heat is called _____.

    (a) Acoustics   (c) Electrostatics   (e) Optics
    (b) Thermodynamics   (d) Quantum mechanics

(3) The italicized word, *equivalence* in the last paragraph refers to _____. (Word in context)

    (a) Similarity   (c) Exchangeability   (e) Independency
    (b) Difference   (d) Dependency

(4.1) It can be inferred that the study related to the engine of the car for the purpose of improving the performance can be categorized in the area of _____. (4.1 - 4.3. Making inferences)

    (a) Acoustics   (c) Thermodynamics   (e) Mechanics
    (b) Optics   (d) Nuclear physics

(4.2) It is inferred that the study related to electric motors can be categorized in the area of _____.

    (a) Acoustics (b) Mechanics (c) Thermodynamics (d) Optics (e) Magnetics

(4.3) It is inferred that the works of _____ greatly contributed to the development of the theory of relativity.

    (a) Christian Doppler   (c) Niels Bohr   (e) Jacques Charles
    (b) Georg Ohm   (d) Albert Einstein

(5.1) It can be concluded that the area in which physicists seem to be least likely to be employed is _____. (5.1 - 5.2. Conclusion)

    (a) Entomology   (d) Free-electron lasers
    (b) Superconductivity   (e) Electronic imaging devices
    (c) Semiconductors

(5.2) It is concluded that the famous equation, "$E = mc^2$" stands for _____.

    (a) Energy = (mass) x (speed of light)^2
    (b) Equivalence = (mass) x (speed)^2
    (c) Energy = (mass x speed of light)^2
    (d) Equation = (mass) x (Celsius)^2
    (e) Efficiency = (mass) x (Celsius)^2

않았던 이 분야들은 분자나 원자 수준에서 물질과 에너지를 이해하는데 필수적이다. 예를 들어 물체가 광속에 가까운 속도로 이동할 때 중요한 상대성 이론은 유명한 방정식 $E = mc^2$을 통하여 물질과 에너지의 등가성을 설명해준다.

> **Note**
> - matter = a material which makes up of the world and everything in space which can be seen or touched : 물질
> - mechanics = the science of the action of forces on object : 역학
> - acoustics = the scientific study of sound : 음향학
> - optics = the scientific study of light : 광학
> - submicroscopic : 현미경으로 보이지 않는, 초 현미경적
> - solid - state physics : 고체 물리학
> - sub = under, below, slightly : 밑에, 아래 • subtitle (부제)
>   • subacid (약간 신랄한) • subordinate (하급의) • subfield (하부분야)
> - suppress : 진압하다
> - advent = the arrival, coming of an important event, period, person : 출현, 강림
> - quantum : 양자(量子) pl. quanta
> - equivalence : (가치, 의의, 힘) 같기, 등가, 동치

Passage 2 : Ohm's Law

A German physicist, Georg Ohm (1787 - 1854), identified a relationship between voltage, current, and resistance. This relationship became a law called Ohm's Law in the field of electricity. The law states that the amount of steady current through a conductor is directly proportional to the voltage across the conductor. The current is also *inversely* proportional to the resistance. This law is most recognized in the following form:

$$I = V \div R$$

"I" represents the current through the conductor which is measured in amps. "V" represents the voltage across the conductor measured in volts. "R" symbolizes the resistance in the conductor measured in ohms.

With the above mathematical relationship, it is possible to determine an unknown value if we only know two of the three values. If the voltage and resistance are known, the above formula can be readily used. If the current and resistance are only known, then the formula can be modified as V = IR. Finally, if only the voltage and current are known, use R = V/I. For example, consider 10 amps flowing through a closed circuit with a resistance measuring 12 ohms. If asked to calculate the voltage of the circuit, then the utilization of the formula, V = IR yields V = (10 amps) x (12 ohms) = 120 volts. It is because the current (I = 10 amps) and the resistance (R = 12 ohms) are given.

(1) The topic of the second paragraph is "the _____ of Ohm's Law. (Subject matter)

    (a) Three forms (b) Voltage (c) Values (d) Current & resistance (e) Derivation

(2) Resistance is measured in ohms. Another way of representing ohms is as _____. (Locating the fact)

    (a) Volts   (c) (Amps) ÷ (volts)   (e) (Volts) ÷ (amps)
    (b) Amps   (d) (Volts) x (amps)

(3) The italicized word, *inversely* in the first paragraph refers to "being _____." (Word in context)

    (a) Inverted (b) Flattered (c) Reversed (d) Commanded (e) Invented

(4) The tone of the second paragraph of the passage is _____. (Tone & attitude)

    (a) Explanatory (b) Self-righteous (c) Pedantic (d) Assertive (e) Persuasive

(5) Based on the information given, it can be concluded that Ohm's Law is most likely to be applicable to the manufacturing of _____. (Conclusion)

    (a) Piano (b) Computer (c) Guns (d) Furniture (e) Cement

지문 2: 옴의 법칙

독일 물리학자 옴은 전압, 전류, 저항 사이의 관계를 밝혔다. 이 관계가 전기 분야에서 옴의 법칙으로 불리게 되었다. 이 법칙은 어느 도체를 흐르는 일정한 전류의 양은 도체를 지나가는 전압과 직접적으로 비례한다고 설명하고 있다. 전류는 또한 저항에 반비례한다. 다음 형식으로 가장 잘 알려진다.

"I"는 암페어로 측정되는 도체를 통과하는 전류다. "V"는 볼트로 도체를 통과하는 전압을 나타낸다. "R"는 옴으로 측정되며 도체 내의 저항이다.

위의 수학적인 관계를 가지고 세가지 값 중 2가지만 알면 미지의 값을 결정하는 것은 가능하다. 만일 전압과 저항만 알면 위 공식을 쉽게 사용할 수 있다. 만일 전류와 저항만 알면 공식은 $V = IR$로 변경할 수 있다. 끝으로 전압과 전류를 알고 있으면 $R=V/I$ 공식을 사용하라.

예를 들면 폐쇄 회로를 흐르는 전류가 10 암페어이고 저항이 12옴인 경우를 생각해 보라. 만일 그 회로의 전압을 계산하라고 하면 공식 $V = IR$을 이용하여 $V=(10암페어) \times (12옴)=120볼트$를 얻는다. 그 까닭은 전류와 저항이 주어졌기 때문이다.

Note

- **identify** = prove or show the identity(정체) : 정체를 밝히다, 확인하다
  - I identified the criminal. (나는 그 범인을 확실히 증명했다.)
- **voltage** = standard measure of electrical force used in causing a flow of electrical current along wires : 전압
- **current** = the flow of electricity past a fixed point : 전류
- **semi-conductor** : 반도체(저온에서는 전류가 거의 전도되지 않고 고온일수록 전기 전도가 높아지는 도체와 절연체와의 중간 성질을 가진 물질, 실리콘, 게루마늄 등) • opp. nonconductor (부도체)
- **be (inversely) proportional to** : (반)비례하다
  - His pay is proportional to the amount of work he does. (그의 보수는 그가 하는 작업의 양에 비례한다.)
- **amp** = ampere : 전류의 실용단위 (from a Frenchman Andrei Marie Ampere)
- **yield** = produce, give
  - His business yields big profits. (그는 그 사업에서 많은 수입을 올린다.)

Passage 3 : Max Planck (1858-1947): A Contributor to Quantum Theory

Max Planck was born in Kiel, Germany, and received from his college education in Munich and Berlin. After serving on the faculties of Munich & Kiev, Planck moved to the University of Berlin, where he remained until he retired. In 1918 Max Planck was awarded the Nobel Prize for the discovery of the quantized nature of energy, which laid the foundation for quantum theory. Quantum theory is important because it helps physicists explain the world on a subatomic level. Modern theories such as Einstein's Theory of Relativity, were derived from the works of Max Planck.

Max Planck (1858~1947)

Quantum theory seeks to explain energy, especially the emission and the absorption of light and heat. The energy carried by a ray of light travels in discrete units called "quanta." Light originates in the rearrangement of atomic electrons. If a molecule changes from a higher to a lower energy state, the difference in the energy between the two states will be released as quanta. The frequency of a light wave is inversely proportional to its length and it thereupon follows that the quanta of long waves, such as radio waves, carry little energy, whereas the quanta of extremely short waves, such as cosmic rays, carry much. This theory has become a major means of understanding of atomic processes, and has revolutionized the method of dealing with such phenomena by discarding 19th-century ideas (i.e. determinism, principles of causality, Newtonian concepts as a basis for fundamental physics).

Planck succeeded in deriving the frequency distribution of blackbody radiation (radiant energy from a perfect radiator), when he realized that an atom can emit radiation only in discrete amounts or quanta. A quantum of radiation has an amount of energy E given by the equation
$E = h\nu$, where "h" is Planck's constant (6.626×10^{-34} Joules-second), and "ν" is the frequency of the radiation. Planck found that the quanta associated with a particular frequency of light must all have the same energy. In 1905, Albert Einstein particularized Planck's theory to the phenomena of photoelectric effect (electrons are emitted by metal when struck by light). He *postulated* that not only is blackbody light quantized, but all absorptions or emissions of radiant energy

지문 3 : 막스 플랑크 — 양자론의 공헌자

플랑크는 독일 키엘에서 태어나 뮌헨과 베를린에서 대학 교육을 받았다. 뮌헨과 키에프에서 교수로 근무하다 베를린 대학으로 옮겨 그곳에서 정년까지 재직하였다. 1918년에 플랑크는 에너지의 양자화 발견으로 노벨상을 수상했다. 그리고 그 발견은 양자론의 토대를 이루었다. 양자론은 물리학자들이 아원자상태(원자 구성 소립자)의 설명을 하는데 도움이 되기 때문에 중요하다. 현대 이론들, 예를 들면 아인슈타인의 상대성 이론 같은 것은 플랑크의 연구에서 도출된 것이다.

양자론은 에너지, 특히 빛과 열의 방출과 흡수를 밝히려고 노력한다. 광선이 나르는 에너지는 '양자(量子)'라고 불리는 개체 단위로 이동한다. 빛은 원자내 전자의 재배열에 의하여 발생한다. 만일 분자가 높은 에너지 상태에서 낮은 상태로 변화하면 두 상태 사이에서 생기는 에너지의 차이가 양자로 방출된다. 광파의 주파수는 그의 파장과 반비례하므로 라디오파와 같은 긴 파장의 양자는 에너지를 적게 내는데 반하여 우주선(宇宙線)과 같은 극히 짧은 파장의 양자는 많은 에너지를 낸다. 이 이론은 원자의 움직임을 이해하는 주요한 수단이 되었으며 19세기의 이론들(예 : 결정론, 인과율, 기초물리학의 토대로서의 뉴톤의 개념들)을 벗어남으로써 그러한 현상을 다루는 방법을 혁신시켰다.

플랑크는 흑체복사(黑體輻射) (완전방사체의 방사 에너지)의 주파수 분포를 끌어내는데 성공하였다. 그리고 그 때 원자는 개체단위 즉 양자로만 복사에너지를 발산할 수 있음을 깨달았다. 한 번의 복사는 다음 방정식에서 말하는 에너지 E의 양을 가진다. $E = h\nu$에서 'h'는 플랑크 상수(常數)이고 'ν'는 복사의 진동수 분포다. 플랑크는 빛의 특정 주파수와 연관된 양자는 모두 같은 에너지를 가지고 있음을 발견했다. 1905년에 아인슈타인은 플랑크의 이론을 광전자 효과(금속에 빛을 조사(照射)했을 때 전자가 방출된다)에 상세하게 적용했다. 그는 흑체광만 양자화되는 것이 아니고 방출 에너지의 방출이나 흡수 모두 동등하게 양자화된다고 주장했다. 1913년에 닐스 보어도 이 이론을 이용하여 한 궤도 위의 전자가 다른 적당한 궤도로 전위할 때 발생하는 원자에너지 변화를 설명하였다.

Note

- **blackbody** : 흑체-모든 파장의 복사를 흡수하는 가상 물체
- **quantum theory** : 양자론(量子論)
- **constant** : 상수(常數)   □ **variable** : 변수   □ **subatomic** : 원자 이하의, 소립자
- **emit = send out, discharge** : 발산하다, 발행하다   □ **orbit = heavenly bodies path**
- **frequency = a rate at which something happens or is repeated** : 빈도, 분포, 주파수
- **inversely = opposite in order or position** : 역으로   □ **thereupon = because of that**
- **cosmic ray** : 우주선(宇宙線):우주의 어느곳에서 발생하여 지구표면에 들어오며 지하 수백미터까지 이르는 방사선의 총칭
- **revolutionize** : 혁신하다   • Peaceful use of atomic energy revolutionized our life.
- **discard = get rid of as useless** : 버리다, 발로 차다
    • Never discard your friends in trouble for any reasons.

are equally quantized. In 1913, Niels Bohr also used the theory to explain energy resulting atomically as an electron on one orbit jumped to another suitable orbit.

(1) The topic of the second paragraph is _____. (Subject matter)

 (a) Theory of relativity   (d) Brownian motion
 (b) Quantum theory   (e) Newtonian concepts
 (c) Bohr's atomic model

(2) Two factors which Quantum theory concentrates on are ____ and _____. (Locating the fact)

 (a) Sound & heat   (d) Pressure & weight
 (b) Heat & light   (e) Time & speed
 (c) Electron & atom

(3) The synonym for the italicize word, *postulated* in the last paragraph is _____. (Word in context)

 (a) Hypothesized   (d) Calculated
 (b) Advocated   (e) Proved
 (c) Supported

(4) Based on the facts given, it can be inferred that one of the theories heavily influenced by Planck's discovery is _____. (Making inferences)

 (a) Newton's 1st law of motion (d) Theory of relativity
 (b) Newton's 2nd law of motion (e) Energy of motion
 (c) Newton's 3rd law of motion

(5) It can be concluded that Quantum theory must have significantly contributed to physics and its related fields, especially the field of _____. (Conclusion)

 (a) Mechanics   (d) Acoustics
 (b) Thermodynamics   (e) Optics
 (c) Atomic physics

Selected proverbs for the study of cross-cultural expressions

영어 격언과 한문 격언과의 만남 (10)

1. **A blunt pencil tells more than wisdom.** 叡智不如鈍筆(예지불여둔필)
   - 예리한 지혜가 뭉툭한 연필만 못하다(기록이 더 낫다).

2. **Nothing ventured, nothing gained.** 不入虎穴不得其子(불입호혈부득기자)
   - 호랑이 새끼를 잡으려면 호랑이 굴에 들어가야 한다.
     · The more danger, the more honor. / · If you don't enter a tiger's den, you can't get his cubs.

3. **All men are mortal.** 無草不枯 莫人不死(무초불고 막인불사) – 시들지 않는 풀이 없고 죽지 않는 사람 없다.
   Death is sure to all. 有生者必有死, 生者必滅(유생자필유사, 생자필멸) – 살아 있는 것은 반드시 죽는다.
     · Nothing is certain but death and taxes. / · As soon as man is born, he begins to die.

4. **Death's day is doom's day.** 蓋棺事始定(개관사시정 ; 棺 = coffin) – 관 뚜껑을 닫아야 모든 일은 결정난다.
     · Praise no man till he is dead. / · The evening crowns the day.
     · Praise a fair day at night. / · He laughs best who laughs last.

5. **Dying man speaks true.** 人之將死其言也善(인지장사기언야선) – 죽어가는 사람의 말은 착하다.
     · When death is on the tongue, repentance is not difficult.

6. **It's no use crying over spilt milk.** 悔之已晚(회지이만 ; 已 = already) – 후회할 때는 이미 늦다.
     · It's too late to mend.

7. **To make the matter worse.** 火上加油(화상가유) – 타는 불에 기름 붓기 · To add fuel on the fire.

8. **Disaster comes out of the mouth.** 禍從口出(화종구출) – 불행은 입에서 나온다.

9. **Time is money.** 一刻千金(일각천금) – 짧은 순간이 천금의 가치가 있다.
   Time works wonders. 一寸光陰不可輕(일촌광음불가경) – 짧은 시간이라도 헛되게 보내지 말라.
     · An inch of gold will not buy an inch of time. / · Time lost cannot be recalled.

10. **Practise what you preach.** 以身作則(이신작칙) – 몸소 실천함으로 법을 가르쳐라.
     · Example is better than precept. / · Precept begins; example accomplishes.
     · Do as you would be done by.

11. **To kill two birds with one stone.** 一石二鳥, 一擧兩得(일석이조, 일거양득)

12. **Nothing is easier.** 易如反掌, 囊中取物(이여반장, 낭중취물)
    – 손바닥 뒤집듯 쉽다. 호주머니 속 물건을 얻듯이 쉽다.
     · As simple as turning one's head.

13. **Walls have ears.** 隔墻有耳(격장유이 ; 墻 = wall) – 벽에도 귀가 있다. · Fields have ears.

14. **Each has special talents.** 各有所長, 角者無齒(각유소장, 각자무치)
    – 각자 한 가지 재주는 있다. 한가지 재주 있으면 다른 재주는 없다.

15. **It takes two to tango.** 孤掌難鳴(고장난명) – 한 손바닥으로는 소리가 나지 않는다.
     · It takes two to make a quarrel.

16. **Dawn will follow darkness.** 苦盡甘來(고진감래) – 고생 끝에 즐거움이 온다.
     · Sweet after bitter. / · Pleasure follows pain. / · No cross, no crown. / · No pains, no gains.

3-4 SOCIAL SCIENCE

This section, "Social science" includes 12 passages related to the target content areas such as (1) Business; (2) Geography; (3) Government; and, (4) World history. These content areas including a variety of sub-areas related to English (i.e. literature, reading, speech, writing) and of foreign language (i.e. Spanish, French, German) are being taught as common curricula for general senior high schools by a number of American school districts across the country.

Social science refers to a variety of academic disciplines that deal with all social phenomena within social context. "All social phenomena" refers to any events, relations, and thoughts that have been with us since the prehistoric time immemorial. These events, relations, and thoughts, with emerging group and social life, have been developed to such specific fields as anthropology, arts, culture, economy, history, language, philosophy, politics, psychology, religion, and other related disciplines based on particular or universal social contexts. Simply put, it can be postulated that social science is interested in studying the relationships between "us and society," whereas natural science is for the relationships between "us and nature."

The progress of social science unlike that of natural science is slow and insignificant. The wisdom, philosophy, and others related to the field of social science between ancient China, India, and Greece, and those of today are not much different. We encourage your significant contributions toward the betterment of society.

3-4 사회 과학

이번 절 '사회과학'에는 목표로 하는 아래와 같은 내용 영역과 관련된 12개의 지문이 들어있다. (1) 실업 (2) 지리 (3) 정부 (4) 세계사. 이런 내용 영역은 영어와 관련된 다양한 하부영역(예: 문학, 읽기, 말하기, 짓기)과 다양한 외국어(예: 스페인어, 불어, 독일어)를 포함하고 있는데 미국 전역의 많은 학교에서 일반계 고교 교육과정으로 가르쳐지고 있다.

사회 과학은 사회적 맥락에서 총체적 사회현상을 취급하는 다양한 학문을 말한다. '총체적 사회적 현상'이란 태고 시대 이래 우리와 함께 존재해 온 모든 사건, 관계, 사상을 가리킨다. 이런 사건, 관계, 사상은 새로운 집단과 사회가 출현함에 따라 인류학, 예술, 문화, 경제, 역사, 언어, 철학, 정치학, 심리학, 종교, 그리고 특정적 혹은 보편적인 사회 배경을 기초로 하여 생긴 다른 관련학과 등과 같이 특정의 분야까지 발달했다. 간단하게 말하면 사회 과학은 '우리와 사회' 사이의 관계를 연구하는데 관심이 있고 반면에 자연 과학은 '우리와 자연'의 관계를 위한 것임을 인정할 수 있다.

사회 과학의 발달은 자연 과학의 발달과 달라 속도가 느리고 보잘 것 없었다. 지혜, 철학, 그리고 사회 과학과 관련된 다른 학과들은 고대의 중국, 인도, 그리스의 사회과학 분야와 오늘날의 그것들 사이에 별로 차이가 없다. 우리는 여러분이 사회 발전을 위해서 중요한 공헌을 하도록 격려하는 바다.

note

- □ curriculum : 교육과정, 이수 과정   • pl. curricula(= course)
- □ from time immemorial : 태고 시절 부터
- □ anthropology = science of man, esp. of the beginnings, development, customs and beliefs of mankind : 인류학
- □ universal = belonging to, done by all, affection all : 전반적인, 보편적인
  • War causes universal miseries. (전쟁은 모두에게 불행을 초래한다.)
- □ insignificant = having little or no value, use, meaning or importance : 하찮은
- □ phenomenon = thing that appears to or in perceived by the senses : 현상
  • pl. phenomena

3.4.1. Business

<u>Passage 1</u> : **Economic Systems**

 The way that a certain group or nation organizes and operates itself for production is called "economic systems." In general, the systems are classified into three: Traditional, Market, Controlled.
 A traditional economic system refers to the settings in which tradition decides what people do for a living and how their work is performed. This traditional system can be found in most villages in developing countries where people are heavily dependent on agricultural products as their necessities of life. A market economic system refers to the settings in which a nation's economic decisions are based on the individual needs between buyers and sellers in the marketplaces. This market system can be found in most industrialized countries where the competition for economic success is very severe. A controlled economic system refers to the settings where government plays a key role for decision-makings regarding the production and sale of products and services. This controlled system can be found in some socialist or communist countries where the leaders believe that this system *benefits* their countries and people.

(1) The topic of this passage is "_____ of economic systems." (Subject matter)

  (a) Definitions (b) Profiles (c) Trends (d) Patterns (e) Types

(2) The system in which economic success is very highly competitive is "_____ system." (Locating the fact)

  (a) Traditional (b) Controlled (c) Market (d) Competitive (e) Demand & supply

(3) The antonym of the italicized word, *benefits* in the last paragraph is _____. (Word in context)

  (a) Harms (b) Enhances (c) Assists (d) Profits (e) Furthers

(4) The country in which the controlled economic system is being implemented is _____. (Making inferences)

  (a) France (b) Spain (c) Cuba (d) Sweden (e) Canada

(5) In 1921, Lenin instituted the New Economic Policy (NEP) in the U.S.S.R. as a way of warding off the threat of famine and rebellion. It can be concluded that the NEP was instituted because of the unsuccessful result of implementing the _____ economic system. (Conclusion)

  (a) Traditional (b) Market (c) Free (d) Competitive (e) Controlled

3.4.1. 실업

지문 1 : 경제 체제

어떤 집단이나 국가가 생산을 위하여 조직하고 일을 하는 방식을 '경제 체제' 라고 부른다. 일반적으로 경제 체제는 '전통, 시장, 계획' 의 세 가지로 분류된다.

전통적 경제 체제는 사람들이 생계를 위하여 무엇을 하며 그들의 경제활동이 어떻게 수행되는가의 문제가 전통에 따라 결정되는 체제를 가리킨다. 전통적 체제는 사람들이 생활 필수품으로서 농업생산품에 주로 의존하는 개발도상국가에서 발견된다. 시장 경제 체제는 한나라의 경제에 관한 결정들이 시장에서 파는 사람과 사는 사람들의 필요에 토대를 두는 체제를 가리킨다. 시장 경제 체제는 경제적 성공을 위한 경쟁이 아주 치열한 산업화가 잘된 나라에서 발견된다. 계획 경제 체제는 생산과 생산품이나 서비스의 판매에 관한 결정을 하는데 정부가 핵심 역할을 한다. 계획 경제 체제는 통치자들이 이 체제가 자기 나라와 국민들에게 이익을 준다고 믿는 몇몇 사회주의 국가나 공산주의 국가에서 발견된다.

Note
- **operate** = cause to work, to be in effect : 가동시키다, 운영하다
  - The company operates three factories and a coal mine. (세개의 공장과 탄광을 하나 운영한다.)
- **competition** = test of ability, skill, strength : 경쟁 • competent (경쟁력이 있는)
- **regarding** = on the subject of, in connection with : …에 관하여
- **socialist** = socialistic : 사회주의적인
- **benefit** = to be useful, profitable : 이익을 끼치다
  - Such a foolish behavior will not benefit your case. (그런 어리석은 짓은 네 경우에 도움이 안될 것이다.)
- **implement** = carry out, put into practice : 이행하다, 가동시키다
  - The committee's suggestions will be implemented immediately. (그 위원회의 제안이 곧 실행될 것이다.)

Passage 2 : Business Education at the Secondary Schools in the United States

Business education in the United States is divided into two major segments: secondary and collegiate. The primary objectives of the secondary school are two-fold: (1) To train students who plan to enter a variety of business and occupational fields; and, (2) To give students competence in the use of business services as citizens and individuals.

Before World War II, business education used to offer typing, bookkeeping, and shorthand as three major subjects. Young women were found to be *adept* in secretarial work, and young men were needed in the field of accountancy. After World War II, and 1950s, electronic data processing has become an integral part of the routine of many office work, and the field of technology and services. For this, both local and federal governments became aware of the need for improved patterns of curriculum and program for business education. With the passage of the Vocational Education Act in 1963, the specific federal and local aid was provided including new equipment, teacher re-education, cooperative work-experience programs of all types. As a result, business education offers a variety of improved curricula and specific programs such as computer operation; technical trade; medical & health services; hotel, restaurant & tourism; construction; auto mechanic; business institute; business & industrial technology; cooperative work-experience which are all geared to meet today's needs.

(1) The topic of the first paragraph is "The ____ of the business education at ____ level." (Subject matter)

    (a) Patterns, secondary   (c) Aims, secondary   (e) Fields, collegiate
    (b) Purposes, collegiate   (d) Segments, secondary

(2) One of the occupations that was commonly produced by the business education before World War II is _____. (Locating the facts)

    (a) Tourist guide   (c) Chef   (e) Auto mechanic
    (b) Computer operator   (d) Stenographer

(3) The italicized word, *adept* in the second paragraph refers to ___. (Word in context)

    (a) Clumsy (b) Awkward (c) Capable (d) Inept (e) Incompetent

(4) The writer did not elaborate one of the objectives (2), "To give students competence in the use of business services as citizens and individuals." It is probably because the topic of the objective is _____ . (Rhetorical techniques)

    (a) Unimportant   (c) Inappropriate   (e) Unrelated to the major contents
    (b) Not objective   (d) Different from (1)

(5) Based on the information given, it can be concluded that the curricula and programs of the business education at secondary school level will be revised so as to meet the needs of the _____. (Conclusion)

    (a) Students' interest   (c) Academic excellence   (e) Business leadership
    (b) Marketability   (d) Technology

지문 2: 미국의 중등학교 실업 교육

미국의 실업교육은 두개의 주요 부분으로 나뉘어진다. 중등학교 실업교육과 대학 실업교육이다. 중등학교의 일차적인 실업교육의 목적은 이중적인데 (1) 다양한 실업 분야나 취업 분야로 가려는 학생들을 훈련시키는 것과 (2) 학생들에게 시민으로서나 개인으로서 비즈니스 서비스를 이용하는 능력을 제공하는 것이다.

세계 2차대전 이전에는 실업 교육은 타자, 부기, 속기를 3대 주요 과목으로 제공했었다. 젊은 여자들은 비서 업무에 탁월한 능력을 인정받았고, 회계분야에서는 젊은 남자들을 필요로 했다. 2차 대전 후와 1950년대에 전자 정보 처리가 많은 일상적 사무직, 기술직, 그리고 서비스업에서 필수적인 것이 되었다. 이것으로, 연방 정부나 지방 정부 다같이 실업 교육의 교육 과정이나 프로그램의 개선된 양식이 필요함을 인식하게 되었다. 1963년에 직업 교육 법안이 통과함에 따라 새로운 설비, 교사 재교육, 모든 형태의 협동적인 작업 체험을 포함하는 구체적인 연방 정부 및 지방 정부의 원조가 제공되었다. 그 결과 실업 교육은 컴퓨터 조작, 기술 관련 직업, 의료 건강 서비스, 호텔, 식당과 관광, 건축, 자동차 기계공, 직업 연구소, 사업 및 산업 기술, 협동적인 작업 체험 등 모두 오늘날의 필요에 맞추어 다양하게 개선된 교육과정과 특수한 프로그램을 제공한다.

Note

- **twofold** : 두 겹의, 이중적인
- **manifold** : 다양한 • a manifold plan (다방면에 걸친 계획)
- **adept = highly skillful** : 숙련된 • cf. adapt (적응시키다) adopt (채택하다)
  • Be careful when you play cards with him. He's very adept in cheating.
- **accountancy = accounting** : 회계업무
- **integral = necessary to complete something** : (전체를 이루는데) 꼭 필요한
  • The arms and legs are integral parts of a human being.
- **be geared to = be fixed in relation to** : …에 맞게 조정되나
  • Education should be geared to the children's needs and abilities.
  (교육은 어린이들의 필요와 능력에 맞게 맞추어져야 한다.)

Passage 3 : **The International Monetary Fund (IMF)**

During the Great Depression in the 1930s, the world economy became *ravaged* and many countries around the world have learned a lesson, "the economic crisis of one country not only affects itself, but also others." The economic system after World War I has become an economic unit of globalization. Some countries during the Depression tried to profit their economies by "competitive devaluation". As a result, the sound trade and the fair currency exchanges between the countries became difficult, undermining the worlds' economy.

To restore and maintain a healthy world economy as a global unit, many economists, political leaders, bankers, and traders advocated to form an international organization "to promote international monetary cooperation by maintaining fixed exchange rates among the currencies of different nations." A British economist and monetary expert, John Maynard Keynes (1883-1946), and Harry Dexter White, Assistant Secretary of the U.S. Department of Treasury were the leading figures for the organization of the IMF, which was established on July 1, 1944 at Bretton Woods, New Hampshire with the delegates of 44 nations.

The IMF was initially established to foster the fixed rate system, but when this failed, the IMF began to expand its role in helping the problem economies of the member countries. It is a lending institution for those member countries which have temporary payment problems. For example, when a member country spends more money than it takes in, or when the country's credit is used up, it faces a loss of buying power. The country can then turn to the IMF for financial support to stabilize its currency and strengthen its trading. Loans granted to only member countries must be paid back to the IMF in between 3 to 5 years (in certain cases, repayment can be extended to 10 years). Two frequently used loan mechanisms are (1) stand-by arrangements, and (2) extended arrangements. Stand-by arrangements are loans which must be repaid in 1 to 2 years, whereas the extended arrangements require repayment within 3 to 4 years.

Contrary to widespread perceptions, the IMF has no effective authority over the domestic economic policies of its members. It is in no position to force a member to spend more money on schools or hospitals or less money for military budget. It often urges members to make the best use of the loan by refraining from senseless spending or maintaining unsound financial sector structuring. In the case of Korea, the IMF advises "restructuring and recapitalizing the troubled financial institutions including the big *conglomerates*." The IMF attempts to promote economic growth and sound policies of each member country, which

지문 3 : 국제 통화 기금

1930년대 대공황 중에 세계경제는 황폐화되었고 전 세계의 많은 국가들은 한 가지 교훈을 얻었으니 "한 국가의 경제 위기는 그 나라뿐만 아니고 다른 국가들에게도 영향을 미친다"는 것이었다. 세계 1차 대전 후의 경제 체계는 세계화의 경제 단위가 되었다. 공황 중에 몇 국가들은 '경쟁적인 평가절하'로 자국의 경제를 이롭게 하려고 했고 그 결과 국가간의 건전한 무역과 공정한 외환거래가 어려워졌고 세계경제를 위태롭게 했다.

전 세계적인 단위로 건실한 세계 경제를 회복하고 유지하려고 많은 경제학자들, 정치지도자들, 은행가들이 "각기 다른 화폐를 가진 국가들

Assistant Secretary, U.S. Treasury, Harry Dexter White(left) and John Maynard Keynes, honorary advisor to the U.K. Treasury at the inaugural meeting of the International Monetary Fund's Board of Governors in Savanah, Georgia, U.S., March 8, 1946.

이 고정 환율을 유지, 국제적인 통화협력을 증진하기 위하여" 국제적인 기구의 조직을 주장했다. 영국의 경제학자이자 통화 전문가인 J. M. 케인즈와 미국 재무부 차관보인 화이트가 IMF조직의 지도적인 인물이었다. 그리하여 1944년 7월 1일에 44국의 대표자가 참석한 가운데 뉴 햄프셔주 브레튼 우즈에서 IMF가 설립되었다.

IMF는 처음 고정 환율 체계를 조성하기 위하여 설립되었지만 이것이 실패했을 때, 문제가 있는 회원국의 경제를 돕는 역할까지 확대하기 시작했다. IMF는 일시적인 지불문제를 가진 회원국가들을 위한 대부기관이다. 예를 들면 회원 국가가 벌어들이는 돈보다 쓰는 돈이 더 많을 때, 그 국가의 신용이 떨어졌을 때, 그 국가는 구매력 상실에 직면한다. 그 때 그 국가는 통화를 안정시키고, 무역을 강화하기 위하여 IMF에 금융지원을 요청할 수 있다. 회원 국가에만 허용되는 대부금은 3~5년 사이에 상환해야 한다 (어떤 경우에는 10년까지 상환을 연장할 수 있다). 자주 쓰이는 두가지 대부 구조는 (1) 대기성 차관 (2) 확장성 차관이 있다. 대기성 차관이란 1~2년 사이에 갚아야하는 것이나, 확장성 차관은 3~4년에 상환해야 한다.

eventually helps the sound economic system of all the member countries as a whole. Currently, the IMF, headquartered in Washington D.C., has now 182 member countries, and its sister institution, the World Bank works exclusively for the economic development of the world's poorest nations.

Headquarters building of the International Monetary Fund, Washington, D.C.

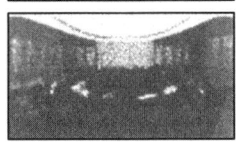

The Executive Board of the International Monetary Fund, Washington, D.C. (Februry 17, 1995)

IMF Managing Director Michel Camdesses the Annual Meetings of the World Bank Group and the International Monetary Fund in Washington, D.C. (1995)

(1.1.) A proper title of the first paragraph is "_____ of founding an international monetary organization." (1.1.-1.3. Subject matters)

    (a) Reasons   (c) Consequences   (e) Introduction
    (b) Ways   (d) Results

(1.2.) A proper title of the second paragraph is "_____ of the IMF."

    (a) Reasons   (c) Contributions   (e) Development
    (b) Introduction   (d) Ways

(1.3.) A proper title of the third paragraph is "_____ of the IMF."

    (a) Roles   (c) Quality   (e) Contributions
    (b) Development   (d) Purposes

(2.1.) One of the initiators of the IMF is _____. (2.1.-2.2. Locating the facts)

    (a) Paul Samuelson   (d) John Keynes
    (b) Adam Smith   (e) Franklin Roosevelt
    (c) Thomas Robert Malthus

널리 인식되어 있는 것과는 반대로 IMF는 회원국가의 국내 경제 정책에 대하여 유효한 권한은 없다. IMF는 어느 회원국가에게 학교나 병원에 더 많은 돈을 쓰고 군사예산에 더 적게 쓰라고 강요할 위치에 있지 않다. IMF는 자주 회원국가들이 무분별한 소비와 잘못된 금융 부문의 구조를 개선함으로써 차관을 최선으로 활용하기를 촉구한다. 한국의 경우, IMF는 대기업들을 포함하여 불건전한 금융기관에 구조조정과 부채비율 감소를 권고한다. IMF는 각 회원국가의 경제 성장과 건전한 정책을 증진시키려고 시도한다. 결국 그것이 전반적으로 모든 회원국가들의 건전한 경제체계를 돕기 때문이다. 오늘날 워싱턴 D.C.에 본부를 둔 IMF는 182개의 회원국가를 가지고 있고, 자매 기관인 세계은행은 오로지 세계의 가장 가난한 국가들의 경제발전을 위하여 일한다.

Note

- **fund** = a sum of money available for a purpose : 기금, 자금
  - reserve fund (적립금) • relief fund (구호자금) • scholarship fund (장학기금)
  - They're raising the relief-fund for the laid - offs. (실업자 구호기금을 모금하고 있다.)
- **the Great Depression** : 미국의 대공황(1929~1930)
  - We are right in the middle of a depression. (우리는 불황의 한 가운데 있다.)
- **ravage** = ruin : 망치다, 파괴하다 • The unexpected storm ravaged the vineyard.
- **affect** = influence : 영향을 끼치다 • Smoking affects health.
- **crisis** = moment of great danger or difficulty : 위기, 중대국면
- **financial crisis** : 재정상의 위기 **globalization** : 세계화
- **devaluation** = reduction in the value of : 평가 절하
  - Will the devaluation of the Chinese currency directly endanger our economy?
    (중국화의 절하가 우리 경제를 직접 위험에 빠트릴까요?)
- **undermine** = weaken gradually, weaken at the base : 밑을 파다, 서서히 위태롭게 하다
  - The president's enemies are spreading rumors of his inappropriate sexual relationship with her to undermine his authority. (대통령의 적대자들이 그의 부적절한 성관계에 대한 소문을 퍼뜨려 대통령의 권위를 위태롭게 하고 있다.)
- **restore** = make well or normal again : 복구하다
  - Public order was quickly restored after the announcement of his resignation.
    (그의 사임 발표에 공공 질서가 빠른 속도로 회복되었다.)
- **monetary** = of money or coins : 화폐의 • monetary unit (화폐단위)
- **exchange rate** : 환율
- **currency** = money that is actually using in a country : 유통 화폐
- **stabilize** = make or become steady or firm : 안정시키다
- **contrary to** = opposite (in nature, tendency) : 반대로
  - What you have done is contrary to the doctor's orders.
- **perception** = 지각, 인식
- **conglomerate** = large business firm producing goods of very different kinds : 대기업
- **exclusively** : 독점적으로, 오직 • This room is exclusively for women. (이 방은 여성 전용이다.)

(2.2.) The headquarters of the IMF is in _____.

    (a) France   (c) Germany   (e) U.S.A.
    (b) Switzerland   (d) Japan

(3.1.) The italicized word, *ravaged* in the first paragraph refers to _____. (3.1.-3.2. Words in context)

    (a) Devastated   (c) Deviated   (e) Protected
    (b) Assisted   (d) Deleted

(3.2.) The italicized word, *conglomerates* in the last paragraph can refer to the following business companies except _____.

    (a) Hyundai   (d) Exxon
    (b) IBM   (e) Sony
    (c) Mass. Institute of Technology (M.I.T.)

(4.1.) The organization of the paragraph patterns is based on _____. (Rhetorical techniques)

    (a) Definition   (d) Cause and effect
    (b) Analysis   (e) Comparison & contrast
    (c) Description

(4.2.) It can be inferred that the country which contributes a larger sum of money than other member countries is _____. This money is called "quota subscription," a sort of membership fee. (Making inferences)

    (a) United States   (d) Germany
    (b) Japan   (e) France
    (c) United Kingdom

(5) Based on the information given, it can be concluded that the member countries of the IMF will _____. (Conclusion)

    (a) Decrease   (d) Increase
    (b) Remain constant   (e) Fluctuate wildly
    (c) Be unpredictable

영어 격언과 한문 격언과의 만남 (11)

Selected proverbs for the study of cross-cultural expressions

1. **Let nature take its course.** 無爲自然, 無爲而化(무위자연, 무위이화) – 자연을 거스르지 말라.
   · Nature is the true law. He that follows nature is never out of his way.

2. **The greatest step is that out of the door.**
   千里之行始於足下(천리지행시어족하) – 천리길도 한 걸음부터

3. **He can who believes he can.** 自信者人亦信之 自疑者人亦疑之(자신자인역신지 자의자인역의지)
   – 자기 자신을 믿으면 남도 믿어주고 자신을 못믿으면 남도 의심한다.

4. **Waiting for a pig to fly.** 百年河淸(백년하청)

5. **Spare the rod and spare the child.** 憐兒多與棒 憎兒多與食(연아다여봉 증아다여식)
   – 예쁜 자식 매 많이 때리고 미운 자식 밥 많이 주어라.
   · The rod break no bones. A pitiful mother makes a scabby daughter.

6. **Birds of a feather flock together.**
   類類相從, 同類相求, 同明相照(유유상종, 동류상구, 동명상조) – 끼리 끼리 모인다.

7. **No work, no pay. No cross, no crown.**
   一日不作一日不食, 無勞動無賃金(일일부작일일불식, 무노동무임금) – 하루 일하지 않으면 하루 먹지 않는다.
   · No bees, no honey. Industry is fortune's right hand; frugality her left.

8. **Human blood is all of a color. No difference of bloods.**
   王侯將相寧有種乎(왕후장상영유종호) – 왕후장상에 씨가 있나?(인간은 평등하게 태어난다.)
   · A cat may look at the king. We are all Adam's children.

9. **When whales fight, shrimps are eaten.** 鯨戰蝦死(경전하사 ; 蝦 = shrimp)
   – 고래 싸움에 새우 등 터진다.

10. **Two to one is odds. No fighting against odds.** 衆寡不敵(중과부적)
    – 작은 수효로 많은 수효를 이기지 못한다.

11. **Experience is slow but sure teacher.** 老馬識途, 耕當問奴(노마식도, 경당문노)
    – 늙은 말은 일을 안다, 밭갈이는 머슴에게 물어야 한다.   · Experience is the best teacher.

12. **Overpoliteness makes no politeness.** 過恭非禮(과공비례) – 지나치게 공손하면 예의가 아니다.

13. **Never hit a man when he is down.** 落井下石(낙정하석)
    – 우물에 돌 던지지 말라.(곤궁에 빠진 사람을 공격하지 말라.)

14. **An able man has many burdens.** 巧者卒之奴, 能者多勞(교자졸지노, 능자다로)
    – 재주 있는 자가 남의 종 노릇한다.

3.4.2. Geography

Passage 1 : Geography

Geography is the interpretative description of the differences between one locality and another on the surface of the earth. All different phenomena of the earth's surface are of *significance* to geography. These phenomena include both natural and cultural features.

Geography as other academic disciplines cannot stand alone; it is interdependent with other fields. For example, a geographer who specializes in climate should have a thorough understanding of meteorology. Divisions of geography can be classified into three with the independency of other related fields: (1) Physical geography (study of geography through the physical sciences); (2) Biogeography (study of geography through the biological sciences); and, (3) Human geography (study of geography through the social sciences).

Subdivisions of Physical geography include (a) Geomorphology (an interpretative description of the land forms or *relief* features of the earth's surface); (b) Climatology (study of the average or general weather conditions of a particular area affected by such phenomena as droughts, storms, floods); (c) Meteorology (study of the physics of the atmosphere, and the origin and prediction of weather); and, (d) Soils geography (study of the distributions of soils, and the characteristic associations of soils with vegetation, drainage, relief, rocks, and climate). Subdivisions of Biogeography include (a) Plant geography (study of plants in relation to their environment, distribution, and control by which the existing distributions have been brought about); and, (b) Zoogeography (the distribution of animals with their adaptations to their environment). Finally, subdivisions of Human geography include (a) Economic geography (the economic activities as manifested in specific localities); (b) Social geography (the areal distribution of distinctive societies or culture groups); and, (c) Historical geography (study of geographical knowledge, factors or historical events, and regional geography of a given area at some specific period in the past).

(1.1.) The title of the first paragraph is "The _____ of geography." (1.1.-1.3. Subject matters)

   (a) History   (b) Description   (c) Phenomena   (d) Definition   (e) Study

(1.2.) The title of the second paragraph is "The_____ of geography."

3.4.2. 지리

지문 1 : 지리

　지리는 지표상의 한 지역과 다른 지역 사이의 차이를 해설적으로 기술하는 것이다. 지표상의 모든 다른 현상들이 지리에서는 의미를 갖는다. 이런 현상들 안에는 자연적인 것과 문화적인 특징들이 들어 있다.

　지리도 다른 학문들처럼 혼자 존재할 수 없다. 즉 상호 의존적이다. 예를 들어 기후를 전공하는 지리학자는 기상학에 대한 철저한 이해가 있어야 한다. 지리를 나누면 다른 관련 분야는 별도로 하고 다음 세가지로 분류될 수 있다 : (1) 자연지리(자연 과학을 통한 지리의 연구) (2) 생물지리(생물학을 통한 지리 연구) (3) 인문지리(사회 과학을 통한 지리 연구).

　자연지리를 세분하면 다음들이 포함된다: (a) 지형학(지형이나 지표면의 고저에 대한 해설적 표현) (b) 기후학(가뭄, 폭풍, 홍수 같은 현상의 영향을 받은 어느 특정 지역의 평균 또는 전반적인 기후 상태의 연구) (c) 기상학(대기권의 물리학, 날씨의 발생 원인과 예언) (d) 토양 지리(토양의 분포와 토양과 식물, 배수유역, 고저, 암석, 기후의 특징적 관련사항의 연구)다. 생물지리를 세분하면 (a) 식물지리(환경, 분포 및 현재의 분포를 초래한 억제 조건과 관련한 식물의 연구) (b) 동물지리(동물의 분포와 그들의 환경 적응 사례). 마지막으로 인문지리를 세분하면 다음이 포함된다. (a) 경제지리(특정 지역의 독특한 경제 활동) (b) 사회지리(독특한 사회나 문화집단의 지역적인 분포) (c) 역사지리(지리적 지식, 중요한 요소나 역사적 사건, 그리고 과거 특정 시기에 주어진 어떤 지방의 지리 연구).

Note

□ interpretative = explanatory : 설명을 하는, 해설적인
□ locality = a place or area esp. in which something happens or has happened : 특정 사건의 장소, 현장, 산지, 소재지
□ significance = importance, meaning, value : 중요성, 의의
□ feature = typical or noticeable part of quality : 특색
　• Wet weather is a feature of life in the country. (시골 생활의 특색은 비가 많은 날씨다.)
□ specialize = limit one's study, business to particular things of subjects. : 전공하다, 전문화하다　• What are you going to specialize in in college?
□ meteorology : 기상학　　□ geomorphology : 지형학　　□ climatology : 기후학, 풍토학
□ physical geography : 자연지리　□ biogeography : 생물지리　□ drainage : 강물의 배수 지역
□ human geography : 인문지리　□ drought = a long period of dry weather : 가뭄
□ manifest = show clearly : 분명히 보여주다
　• The disease manifests itself in the yellowness of the skin and eyes.
　　(그 병은 피부와 눈이 노란색으로 변함으로 확실히 드러난다.)

(a) Structure   (c) Characteristics   (e) Analysis
(b) Classification   (d) Development

(1.3.) The title of the last paragraph is "The _____ of geography."

(a) Patterns   (b) Types   (c) Subjects   (d) Subclasses   (e) Subsidences

(2.1.) A study of the physics of the atmosphere and the prediction of weather is _____. (2.1.-2.2. Locating the facts)

(a) Geomorphology   (c) Soils geography   (e) Meteorology
(b) Climatology   (d) Biogeography

(2.2.) A study of geography through the social sciences is _____ geography.

(a) Economic   (b) Physical   (c) Historical   (d) Social   (e) Human

(3.1.) The italicized word, *significance* in the first paragraph refers to _____. (3.1.-3.2. Words in context)

(a) Meaning   (b) Ambiguousness   (c) Sign   (d) Obscurity   (e) Symbol

(3.2.) The italicized word, *relief* in the last paragraph, stands for _____.

(a) Relaxed   (b) Comfortable   (c) Distinct   (d) Refreshed   (e) Released

(4) The organization of the paragraph pattern of the passage is based on _____. (Rhetorical techniques)

(a) Analysis   (c) Comparison & contrast   (e) Description
(b) Cause & effect   (d) Definition

(5) Based on the information given, especially in the field of Human geography, it can be concluded that the _____ geographers have largely contributed to the development of geographical subjects in India, Burma, Sri Lanka, Malaysia, Australia, and New Zealand. (Conclusion)

(a) French   (c) The U.S.   (e) German
(b) Dutch   (d) British

Selected proverbs for the study of cross-cultural expressions

영어 격언과 한문 격언과의 만남 (12)

1. **Out of use, out of care.** 兎死狗烹, 鳥盡弓臧(토사구팽, 조진궁장) – 쓸모가 없으면, 버림 당한다.

2. **Leave no stone unturned.** 盡人事, 無孔不入(진인사, 무공불입) – 가능한 모든 수단을 강구하다.

3. **Ask and it shall be given.** 有求必應(유구필응) – 구하라, 그러면 반드시 응답이 있다.

4. **To gain the third party's profit.** 漁夫之利, 魚人得利(어부지리, 어인득리)
 – 쌍방이 싸우는 틈을 타서 이익을 얻다.

5. **All are not friends that speak us fair.**
 道吾善者是吾敵 道吾惡者是吾師(도오선자시오적 도오악자시오사)
 – 나를 칭찬하는 사람은 원수고 나쁜 것을 말하는 이가 스승이다.

6. **Virtue has its own reward.**
 積善之家 必有餘慶(적선지가 필유여경) – 덕을 쌓는 집에는 경사가 반드시 온다.
 · Give and spend, and God will send.

7. **He who gives indirectly gains directly.**
 陰德陽報(음덕양보) – 남 몰래 베푸는 덕은 확실하게 보답을 받는다.

8. **Many dishes make many diseases.** 食無求飽(식무구포) – 밥은 배불리 먹어선 안된다.
 · Much meat, much malady. / · Great eaters dig their graves with their teeth.

9. **Much science, much sorrow.**
 人生識字憂患始(인생식자우환시) – 학식이 있는 것이 도리어 근심의 시작이다.
 · Ignorance is a bliss. Ignorance is the peace of life.
 · Ignorance and incuriosity are two very soft pillows.

10. **No land without stones. No rose without thorns.** 萬事不全(만사부전) – 모든 일에 완전이란 없다.
 · No sun without a shadow. No day so clear but has dark clouds.

11. **The initiative is half the battle.** 先卽制人(선즉제인) – 선수를 치는 것이 남을 이긴다.

12. **A little learning is a dangerous thing.** 半識者憂患(반식자우환) – 어중간하게 아는 것이 위험하다.

13. **Though the sword of justice is sharp, it will not slay the innocent.**
 刀刃誰快 斬無罪人(도인수쾌 참무죄인) – 칼날이 아무리 잘 들어도 죄 없는 사람은 베지 못한다.

Passage 2 : **Martha's Vineyard**

The island of Martha's Vineyard, situated 5 miles off the coast of Massachusetts, 20 miles long and 9 miles wide, is rich in codfish, swordfish, and lobsters. The people of this island have always made their living from the sea.

Long ago, whaling and *clipper* ships sailed from the island's harbors. The whaling ships came back loaded with valuable whale oil, and the clippers brought manufactured goods from Europe, and tea and spices from Asia. But then petroleum was discovered in Pennsylvania in 1857. Whale oil became less valuable. Steamships replaced sailing ships. New York and Boston having large harbors, these cities became the center of trade. However, the people of Martha's Vineyard can still make a living by catching fish and lobster.

(1) The title of the passage is "_____ of the island." (Subject matter)

    (a) The center of trade   (d) Whale industry
    (b) Fishing industry   (e) Unchanged means of living
    (c) Import & export business

(2) The industry related to the use of whale oil in the island was unfavorably influenced by _____. (Locating the fact)

    (a) Coal   (d) Electricity
    (b) Oil   (e) Natural gas
    (c) Nuclear energy

(3) The italicized word, *clipper* ship in the second paragraph must mean _____. (Word in context)

    (a) Speedy   (b) Slow   (c) Passenger   (d) Steam   (e) War

(4) The attitude of the writer toward the passage is _____. (Tone & attitude)

    (a) Joyful   (d) Melancholy
    (b) Ambitious   (e) Inspiring
    (c) Romantic

(5) It can be concluded that the island of Martha's Vineyard must have once been a prosperous one largely because of its _____. (Conclusion)

    (a) Sea products   (d) Whaling industry
    (b) Hard working fishermen   (e) Location for fishing & trade
    (c) Beauty of the island

지문 2 : Martha's Vineyard

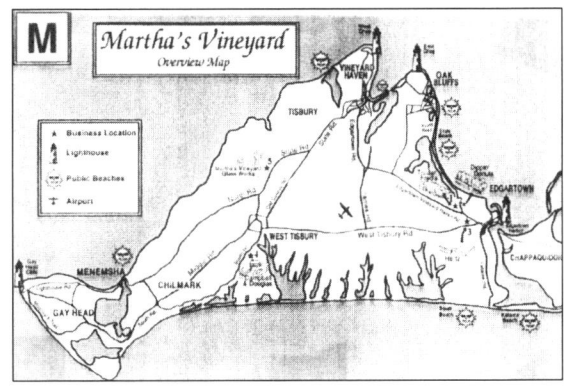

매사추세츠주 해안 5마일 떨어진 곳에 위치하고 있으며 길이가 20마일, 폭이 9마일인 Martha's Vineyard섬은 대구, 황새치, 그리고 바다가재가 풍부하다. 이 섬 사람들은 바다에 의지하여 살아간다.

옛날 포경선과 쾌속 범선들이 이 섬의 항구에서 출항했다. 포경선들은 귀중한 고래 기름을 싣고 돌아왔고 쾌속선들은 유럽에서 공산품을, 아시아에서 차와 향료를 싣고 왔다. 그러나 1857년에 펜실베이니아에서 석유가 발견되었다. 고래 기름의 가치가 떨어졌다. 범선의 자리를 기선이 차지했다. 커다란 항구를 가진 뉴욕과 보스턴이 무역의 중심지가 되었다. 그러나 Martha's Vineyard 사람들은 지금도 고기와 바다가재를 잡아 생활할 수 있다.

Edgartown Map

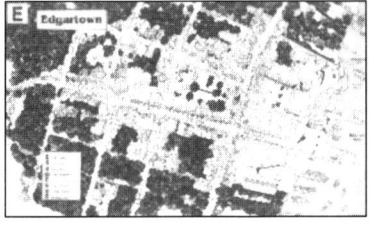

Vineyard Haven Map

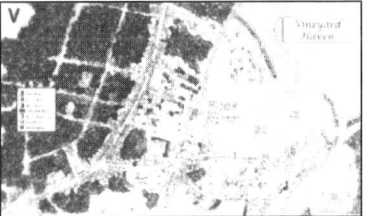

Note

- **codfish** : 대구
- **swordfish** : 황새치
- **clipper** = sailing ship built for speed and used formerly in the tea trade : 쾌속 범선
  - 옛날에는 차 수입에 쓰였음
- **petroleum** : 석유
- **replace** = take the place of : 대체하다
  - Can anything replace a mother's love and care? (그 어느 것이 어머니의 사랑과 보살핌을 대신할 수 있겠소?)

Passage 3 : Reading Maps

Norway, Sweden, and Denmark are the three countries which *make up* the northern European area of Scandinavia. The capital of Norway is Oslo. The capital of Sweden is Stockholm. The capital of Denmark is Copenhagen. All three countries, Norway, Sweden, and Denmark are kingdoms.

Below are two different types of maps of Scandinavia. The first map displays the exports of the Scandinavian countries while the second map shows the types of land located in the region. Study the maps and answer the questions provided.(p. 451)

(1) The best title of the passage is "_____ of the maps." (Subject matter)

    (a) Features (b) Locations (c) Characteristics (d) Profiles (e) Fact findings

(2.1.) Which nation has the most iron mines? (2.1.-2.5. Locating the facts)

    (a) Sweden   (c) Norway & Denmark   (e) Sweden & Norway
    (b) Denmark   (d) Norway

(2.2.) What export do Denmark and Norway have in common?

    (a) Wood   (b) Paper   (c) Copper   (d) Fish   (e) Iron

(2.3.) Which country exports the most farm products?

    (a) Denmark   (d) Sweden   (c) Finland   (b) Norway   (e) None of the above

(2.4.) Which country contains a glacier?

    (a) Denmark   (b) Norway   (c) Finland   (d) Sweden   (e) All of the above

(2.5.) Which two cities are north of the Arctic Circle?

    (a) Stockholm & Narvik   (c) Bergen & Kiruna   (e) Kiruna & Copenhagen
    (b) Narvik & Kiruna   (d) Oslo & Goteborg

(3) The italicized phrase, *make up* in the first paragraph refers to _____. (Phrase in context)

    (a) Repair (b) Compensate (c) Constitute (d) Abolish (e) Repeal

(4) The organization of the second paragraph is structured based on the specific reading skills of _____. (Rhetorical techniques as reading skills)

    (a) Detecting the sequences   (c) Making inferences   (e) Drawing conclusions
    (b) Following the directions   (d) Using the context

(5) Based on the information provided, which country do you conclude imports the most farm and steel products?

    (a) Sweden (b) Denmark (c) Norway (d) Finland (e) None of the above

지문 3: 지도 보기

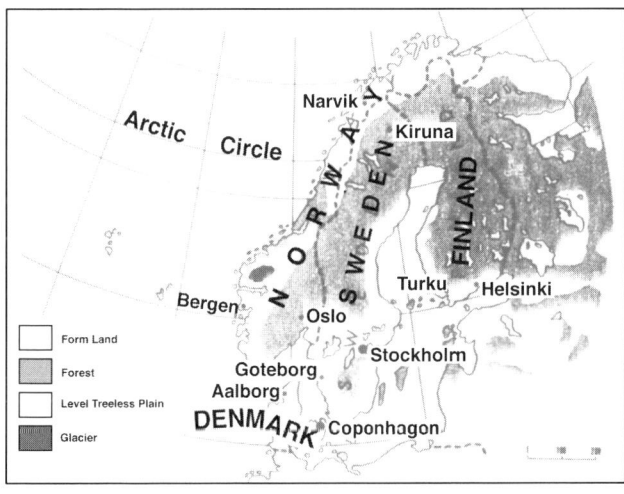

노르웨이, 스웨덴, 덴마크는 북부 유럽 즉 스칸디나비아를 구성하는 3국이다. 노르웨이의 수도는 오슬로, 스웨덴의 수도는 스톡홀름, 덴마크의 수도는 코펜하겐이다. 이 세 나라 모두 왕국이다.

아래 스칸디나비아의 두가지 다른 형태의 지도가 있다. 첫째 지도는 스칸디나비아 국가들의 수출품을 나타내고 둘째 지도는 이 지역 내에 위치한 육지의 형태를 보여준다. 지도를 조사하고 주어진 문제에 대하여 대답하라.

Note
- Arctic Circle : 북극권
- glacier : 빙하 • cf. iceberg (빙산)
- level treeless plains : 평평한 나무가 없는 평원

3.4.3. Government

Passage 1 : **The Purpose of Government**

Several definitions regarding the purpose of government are provided below for your review.

John Locke (1632-1704), author of <u>Two Treaties on Government</u>, held that the chief function of government is to protect the "*natural rights*" of citizens, particularly preservation of their property. Thomas Jefferson, (1743-1826), in the Declaration of Independence, declared that governments are instituted among men in order to make such inalienable rights as "life, liberty, and pursuit of happiness."

The Founding Fathers, in the Preamble of the Federal Constitution (1788), announced that the general aims of the new framework of government were: "We the People of the United States, in order to form a more perfect Union, establish Justice, insure domestic Tranquillity, provide for the common defense, promote the general Welfare, and secure the Blessings of Liberty to ourselves and our *posterity*, do ordain and establish this Constitution for the United States of America."

Abraham Lincoln (1809-1865) explained that the great object of government is "to do for the community of people whatever they need to have done but cannot do at all, or cannot do so well, for themselves in their separate and individual capacities."

(1) The best title of the passage is "The _____ of the aims of government." (Subject matter)

    (a) Purpose   (b) Function   (c) Description   (d) Definition   (e) Illustration

(2.1.) That the purpose of government is "to serve the community in unity" is expressed by _____. (2.1.-2.2. Locating the facts)

    (a) Thomas Jefferson   (c) The Founding Fathers   (e) Abraham Lincoln
    (b) John Locke   (d) Benjamin Franklin

(2.2.) That the aim of government is to protect the absolute and inherent rights of people is expressed by _____.

    (a) Thomas Jefferson   (c) The Founding Fathers   (e) Abraham Lincoln
    (b) John Locke   (d) Benjamin Franklin

(3.1.) The italicized word, *natural rights*, refers to _____. (3.1.-3.2. Words in context)

    (a) General   (b) Common   (c) Habitual   (d) Inalienable   (e) Logical

(3.2.) The antonym of the italicized word, *posterity*, is _____.

    (a) Children   (b) Descendant   (c) Contemporaries   (d) Kinship   (e) Ancestry

3.4.3. 정부

지문 1 : 정부의 목적

여러분의 전반적인 이해를 위해서 정부의 목적에 관한 몇가지 정의를 제공한다.

정부론(정부에 관한 두 논문)의 저자인 존 로크는 정부의 주된 기능은 시민들의 천부적 권리 특히 그들의 재산을 보존해 주는 것이라고 주장했다. '독립 선언'에서 토마스 제퍼슨은 정부는 '생명, 자유, 행복의 추구' 같은 양도할 수 없는 권리를 만들어 내기 위하여 인간들 사이에 조직된다고 선언했다.

미국 건국의 아버지들은 연방 헌법의 서문에서 새로운 체제의 정부가 갖는 일반적인 목표를 다음과 같이 발표했다. '우리 미국 국민은 더욱 완벽한 합중국을 이루기 위하여 정의를 세우고, 국내의 평화를 보장하고, 공동 방어를 마련하고, 전체적인 복지를 증진시키고, 우리 자신과 후손에게 자유의 축복을 확보하기 위하여 미 합중국 헌법을 제정, 확립한다.'

아브라함 링컨은 정부의 위대한 목적은 '공동사회의 인간들이 각각의 개별적인 능력 안에서 자신들을 위하여 할 필요가 있었으나 전혀 할 수 없는, 혹은 조금 밖에 할 수 없는 것을 하기 위한 것'이라고 설명했다.

Note

- Union : 미 합중국
- institute = establish, set up a society, rules etc. for the first time : 최초로 사회, 법률 등을 제정하다
- inalienable = which can't be taken away : 떼 놓을 수 없는, 양도할 수 없는
  - Freedom of speech should be an inalienable right.
    (언론의 자유는 빼앗길 수 없는 권리여야 한다.)
- preamble = foreword, statement at the beginning of a speech or piece of writing : 서문, 머릿글
- insure = ensure, protect against loss of money, life, goods : 보험하다, 보장하다
- tranquil = calm, serene, peaceful : 평온한, 잔잔한
  - a tranquil heart (조용한 마음)   • tranquilizer (신경 안정제)   • tranquility = peace, calmness
- posterity = people who will be born and live after one's own time : 후손
- ordain : (사제) 서품하다, (신, 운명의 힘으로) 정하다
- need to have done : 할 필요가 있었으나 못한 일   • cf. need to do (지금, 앞으로 할 일)
- constitution = the law and principles according to which a country is goverened : 헌법

(4) It can be inferred that Locke's publication, Two Treaties on Government must have influenced the writing of the _____. (Making inferences)

    (a) Communist Manifesto   (c) Magna Charta
    (b) Declaration of Independence   (d) Adam Smith's Wealth of Nations
    (e) Luther's Address to the Christian Nobility of the German Nation

(5) Based on the information given, it can be concluded that the views of John Locke and Thomas Jefferson reflect that government should be instituted for _____. (Conclusion)

    (a) Public administration   (c) Community   (e) Citizens' inherent rights
    (b) Legislation   (d) Collective defense

Passage 2 : **The Rights Enumerated in the Bill of Rights**

The Bill of Rights is in form primarily a bill of "don'ts" for Congress. It's not a theoretical enumeration, but a series of prohibitions of the enactment by Congress of laws infringing certain rights. Aside from the three most discussed: Freedom of Religion, Speech, and Press, the rights include:

  (1) Right to assemble, and to petition Congress.
  (2) Right to bear arms.
  (3) Right not to have soldiers quartered in one's home in peacetime, except as prescribed by law.
  (4) Right to be secure against "unreasonable searches and seizures."
  (5) Right in general not to be held to answer to criminal charges except upon *indictment*.
  (6) Right not to be put twice in jeopardy for the same offense.
  (7) Right not to be compelled to be a witness against oneself.
  (8) Right not to be deprived of life, liberty, or property without due process of law.
  (9) Right to just compensation for private property, taken for public use.
  (10) Right, in criminal prosecution, to trial by a jury — to be notified of the charges, to be confronted with witness, to have compulsory process for calling witness, and to have legal counsel.
  (11) Right to a jury trial in suits at law involving over $20.
  (12) Right, not to have excessive bail required, nor excessive fines imposed, nor cruel and unusual punishments inflicted.

(1) The topic of the passage is "The _____ of certain individual rights" that Congress cannot violate them by making laws. (Subject matter)

    (a) Duty   (b) Protection   (c) Compensation   (d) Prosecution   (e) Jeopardy

(2) The Bill of Rights include 12 Acts. One of the Acts that enumerates the rights for the possession of firearms is found in the Act _____. (Locating the fact)

    (a) 2   (b) 3   (c) 8   (d) 9   (e) 12

(3) The italicized word, *indictment*, refers to _____. (Word in context)

    (a) Acquittal   (b) Prosecution   (c) Acquaintance   (d) Acquittance   (e) Acquisition

지문 2 : 권리장전에 열거된 권리

권리 장전은 형식면에서 기본적으로 의회에 대한 금지의 법안이다. 그건 단지 이론적인 목록이 아니고, 어떤 권리를 침해하는 법이 의회에 의하여 제정되는 것을 금지하는 일련의 조항들이다. 세 가지 자주 논의되는 것: 신앙, 언론, 출판의 자유는 별도로 하고, 다음 권리들이 포함되어 있다.:

(1) 집회와 의회에 청원할 수 있는 권리
(2) 무기를 휴대할 수 있는 권리
(3) 법에 정해진 경우를 제외하고, 평화시에 군인들이 가정에 주둔하는 일을 당하지 않을 권리
(4) 불합리한 수색과 압수를 당하지 않도록 안전할 권리
(5) 일반적으로 고소의 경우를 제외하고 형사 혐의에 응하도록 억류당하지 않을 권리
(6) 똑같은 위법 사항에 두번 유죄의 위험을 당하지 않을 권리
(7) 자신의 의사에 반하여 증인이 되도록 강요 당하지 않을 권리
(8) 적절한 법적 절차 없이 생명, 자유, 재산을 빼앗기지 않을 권리
(9) 공적인 용도로 증발된 사유 재산에 대하여 공정한 보상을 받을 권리
(10) 형사 소추의 경우 배심원의 재판을 받을 권리-혐의 내용에 대한 통고를 받고, 증인을 만날 수 있고, 증인을 부를 필수적인 절차를 받고, 변호사를 세울 권리
(11) 20달러 이상의 소송 사건에 배심원의 재판을 받을 권리
(12) 과도한 보석금을 요구당하지 않고, 과도한 벌금을 부과당하지 않으며, 잔인하고 비정상적인 처벌을 당하지 않을 권리

Note

- don'ts : (구어) 금지 사항집
- enumerate : 열거하다, 늘어 놓다
  • He enumerated the necessary qualities of a good teacher.(훌륭한 선생이 되기 위해서 필요한 사질을 열거했다.)
- enactment : 법의 제정   enforcement : 법의 시행
- infringe = break a rule, transgress, trespass, violate : 어기다, 침범하다
  • infringe a copyright (patent) (저작권(특허권)을 침해하다)
- aside from = apart from = without considering, except for : …은 제외하고, 별도로 하고
  • It's a good work aside from a few slight faults. (몇 개의 하찮은 흠을 제외하면 잘한 일이다.)
- assemble = gather, collect together : 모으(이)다, 조립하다
  • If we can assemble everyone, then we can leave. (모두 모이면 출발한다.)
- prescribe = say with authority : 규정을 정하다, 지시하다, 처방하다
  • He always prescribes us to do what we ought to do.
- seizure = taking possession of by force or authority of the law : 압수
- indict = accuse someone for a charge : 고소하다   • n. indictment
- charge : 형사상의 혐의   • a false charge (무고)   • retract a charge (고소를 취하하다)
- compensation = something given to make a suitable payment for some loss : 보상
- jury = a group usu. of 12 people chosen to decide questions of fact in a court of law : 배심원

(4) Based on the information given, it can be inferred that the first Bill of Rights in the Western society must have been proclaimed in _____. (Making inferences)

    (a) Germany   (b) Italy   (c) Denmark   (d) England   (e) Spain

(5) It can be concluded that the Bill of Rights is largely related to _____ Law. (Conclusion)

    (a) Common   (b) Civil   (c) Commercial   (d) Administrative   (e) Public

Passage 3 : Democracy

Democracy is a form of government in which the management of public affairs remain in the hands of the people themselves, so that they can make laws, *levy* taxes, decide questions of war and peace, and determine all other matters of public business of such nature as to require personal and continuous attention. To this end, the following basic principles are stressed.

    (1) The state exists for the good of the greatest number of individual citizens.
    (2) Reliance upon a body of established legal principles and political customs that are freely accepted by a majority of the citizens should be honored as the basis for their government.
    (3) Subordination of all government officials to those legal principles and customs, and to the will of the majority of the citizen as expressed in free elections held at stated intervals should be honored.
    (4) All qualified adult citizens regardless of rank, wealth, race, creed or sex, should exercise their right to vote.
    (5) Acceptance of the doctrine that the decision of the majority of the voters binds the entire group, and that any change in this decision may be brought about only through legal and orderly processes.

(1) The best title of the passage is "_____ of Democracy." (Subject matter)

    (a) Decisions   (b) Patterns   (c) Characteristics   (d) Purposes   (e) Management

(2) Democracy is a form of government for the _____. (Locating the fact)

    (a) Legal principles & customs   (c) Public affairs   (e) Ethnic groups
    (b) Government officials   (d) Majority of people

(3) The italicized word, *levy*, refers to _____. (Word in context)

    (a) Distribute   (b) Charge   (c) Allocate   (d) Allot   (e) Alienate

(4) The writer's style in this passage can best be described as ____. (Tone & attitude)

    (a) Informal   (b) Pedantic   (c) Factual   (d) Cynical   (e) Abiding

(5) It can be concluded that this form of rule, democracy, seems to be one of the least oppressive ones ever _____. (Conclusion)

    (a) Cultivated   (b) Discovered   (c) Instituted   (d) Nurtured   (e) Manufactured

- prosecution = bring a criminal charge against someone in a court of law : 기소, 고발, 소추
- legal = allowed or made by law, lawful : 합법적인, 법적인
  - legal defence (정당방위)   • legal wife (호적상으로만 아내)   • legal action (법적 조치)
- counsel : 충고, 상담, 고문 변호사, 변호인단
- suit = lawsuit = a noncriminal case in a court of law : 민사상의 소송
- bail = money left with a court of law so that a prisoner may help set free : 보석금
- impose = lay or place a tax, duty : (세금) 부과하다
  - New duties were imposed on beer. (맥주에 새로운 세금이 부과되었다.)
- inflict = impose, give a blow, cause to suffer : 부과하다, 괴롭히다
  - The judge inflicted the death penalty upon the murderer. (살인자에게 사형을 내렸다.)

지문 3 : 민주주의

민주주의는 공무의 수행이 국민 자신들의 수중에 있는 정부 형태고, 그 결과 국민은 법을 제정하고, 세금을 부과하며, 전쟁과 평화의 문제를 결정하며, 사적이고 계속적인 주의를 요구하는 그런 성질의 공적인 모든 일을 결정할 수 있다. 이 목적을 위해서 다음의 기본적인 원칙들이 강조된다.

(1) 국가는 최대 다수의 개별적인 시민들의 이익을 위하여 존재한다.
(2) 다수의 시민들이 자유의사로 인정하여 확립된 합법적 원칙과 정치적 관행의 체제를 믿고 따르는 일은 그들 정부의 토대로서 존중되어야 한다.
(3) 이 법적 원칙과 관행 및 정해진 간격으로 실시된 자유 선거에서 표현된 다수 시민의 의사를 모든 공무원들은 복종해야 한다.
(4) 모든 자격이 있는 성인은 지위, 재산, 인종, 신조, 성별에 상관없이 그들의 투표권을 행사해야 한다.
(5) 다수의 투표자의 결정이 집단 전체에 구속력을 가지며 이 결정을 변경하려면 오직 합법적이며 질서있는 절차를 통해서만 가능하다는 원칙을 수락할 것.

Note

- levy = impose, collect by authority or force : (세금) 부과하다, 징수하다
  - The new government plans to levy new kinds of taxes to fill up the defict.
  (신 정부는 그 손실을 메우기 위하여 신종 세금을 부과할 계획이다.)
- reliance = trust, confidence : 의지
  - Do you place much reliance upon your doctor? (의사 말을 믿고 따르느냐?)
- subordination : 하위에 서기, 복종하기
- interval = time between two events : 간격
  - The buses run at 10 - minute interval. (버스는 10분 간격으로 운행한다.)
- bind = cause to obey, esp. by a law : 구속력을 갖다, 묶다

3.4.4. World History

Passage 1 : Ancient Greece

The ancient Greek civilization flourished over 2000 years ago. The Greeks are known for many things, but one of the most popular is their worshipping of many different gods. Some of these gods were Apollo, the god of light and youth; Zeus, the ruler of all other gods and goddesses; Athena, the goddess of war and wisdom; Poseidon, the god of the seas; and, Aphrodite, the goddess of love and beauty. To worship their gods, the Greeks built many temples. One of the most famous temples that has survived today is the Parthenon which stands on top of the <u>Acropolis</u> *overlooking* Athens.

Ancient Greece was made up of two main cities, Athens and Sparta. The Spartans trained in physical activities since their childhood, grew up to be strong soldiers, athletes, and citizens. But, they did not respect literature, writing, mathematics, philosophy, music, and arts too much. Whereas the Athenians were trained to develop not only their bodies, but also their minds. They studied a variety of academic disciplines which were not respected by the Spartans. They also developed their individual talents. As a result, Athens became the center of Greek culture and civilization.

(1) The best title of the second paragraph is "The _____ between two cities." (Subject matter)

   (a) Similarities   (c) Academic disciplines   (e) Individual talents
   (b) Differences   (d) Physical activities

(2.1) During wars with other nations, which god do you think the Greeks worshipped to bring them victory? (2.1 - 2.3. Locating the facts)

   (a) Apollo   (b) Aphrodite   (c) Athena   (d) Zeus   (e) Poseidon

(2.2) The Spartans were best known for their _____.

   (a) Love of music and dance   (d) Interest in mathematics and philosophy
   (b) Physical strength and discipline (e) Physical strength and god worship
   (c) Illiteracy and dance

(2.3) The word "Aphrodisiac" means something that helps arouse love, and the word originated from the Greek goddess, Aphrodite. Suppose you want to name an ocean liner, based on a safety and strength, which Greek god/goddess would you use?

   (a) Poseidon   (b) Apollo   (c) Athena   (d) Zeus   (e) Aphrodite

3.4.4. 세계사

지문 1 : 고대 그리스

고대 그리스 문명은 2000여년 전에 번창했다. 그리스인들은 여러가지로 유명하지만, 가장 널리 알려진 것 중의 하나는 그들이 많은 신들을 숭배했다는 것이다. 이 신 중의 몇몇은 빛과 젊음의 신인 아폴로, 다른 신과 여신들의 지배자인 제우스, 전쟁과 지혜의 여신 아테나, 바다의 신 포세이돈, 사랑과 미의 여신 아프로디테 등이다. 그들의 신을 경배하기 위하여 그리스인들은 많은 신전을 지었다. 오늘까지 남아있는 가장 유명한 신전 중의 하나는 아테네가 내려다 보이는 아크로폴리스 성채 꼭대기에 있는 파르테논 신전이다.

고대 그리스는 주요한 두 도시 아테네와 스파르타로 구성되어 있었다. 스파르타인들은 어린시절 이후 신체적인 활동을 훈련했고, 자라서 강력한 병사, 체육인, 시민이 되었다. 그러나 그들은 문학, 글 쓰기, 수학, 철학, 음악, 그리고 예술을 그다지 존중하지 않았다. 반면에 아테네인들은 신체 뿐 아니라 정신을 개발시키기 위하여 훈련을 받았다. 그들은 스파르타인들이 존중하지 않는 다양한 학문을 연구했다. 또한 그들 개인의 재능을 개발했다. 그 결과 아테네는 그리스 문화와 문명의 중심이 되었다.

Note

- **flourish** = grow in a healthy manner, be well and active, prosper : 번창하다
  - His business is flourishing.
- **overlook** = have a view from above : 내려다 보다
  - From my apartment window, I overlook the Han River.
- **be made up of** = consist of, be composed of : …로 만들어지다
  - What is this dish made up of? (이 요리는 무엇으로 만들어지나?)
- **philosophy** = the search for knowledge, esp. the nature and meaning of existence : 철학

(3) The italicized word, *overlooking* in the first paragraph refers to _____.
 (Word in context)

  (a) Acknowledging   (b) Blaming   (c) Heeding   (d) Serving   (e) Overseeing

(4) The style of the second paragraph is structure based on the paragraph pattern of _____. (Rhetorical techniques)

  (a) Narration   (b) Description   (c) Definition   (d) Sequences   (e) Analysis

(5) Based on the information given, the underlined word, <u>Acropolis</u> can be concluded from the context as a _____. (Conclusion)

  (a) House   (b) Forest   (c) Island   (d) Fortress/citadel   (e) Lake

Passage 2 : Genghis Khan: The Great Conqueror

Genghis Khan (1162 - 1227) who became one of the greatest military and political leaders of the world, was born near the Onon River in Mongolia. His father, Yesugei named him Temujin. During his childhood, he experienced a great deal of hardship due to tribal conflicts, which he overcame wisely. He united *fragmented* Mongol tribes into one in the early 1200s. With great mobility and striking force armed with armor-piercing arrows, his cavalry could encircle, compress, and *eliminate* the enemy. His aggressive and well-trained military force assisted him to conquer Mongolia and northern China. His grandson, Kublai Khan, conquered Central Asia, Persia, Korea, Russia, and even most eastern European countries.

The impact of the Mongol Empire is very enormous. First, during the period of Mongol rule, Russia adopted the practice of isolating upper-class women in separate quarters. The absolute power of the Mongols served as a good model for Russian rulers who had a strong desire to rule that country without interference from nobles, clergy, or wealthy merchants. Second, the huge Mongol Empire brought the cultural, political, and commercial exchanges between East and West by reopening the Silk Road. It was during this era when the Venetian merchants came to the Mongolian Empire to initiate trade between East and West.

In 1271, Maffeo and Niccolo Polo together with Marco started a journey to China, and they came to Kublai Khan's court. The following story illustrates Marco Polo's first audience with the Khan.

"Highness, I would like to ask you one question. Why are you interested in the beliefs of people who live far away from here?" asked Marco Polo.
"Excellent question, Marco. You see, I am very curious. I must know about everything that exists in this world of ours. Before I die, I must be sure that there are no puzzles left to solve, no secrets that are unknown to me," said the Khan.

지문 2: 위대한 정복자 징기스칸

세계의 가장 위대한 군사 및 정치 지도자의 한 사람이었던 징기스칸은 몽고 오논강 가까운 곳에서 태어났다. 그의 아버지 Yesugei는 그에게 테무진이라는 이름을 지어주었다. 어린 시절에 종족간의 갈등으로 인한 많은 고난을 경험했지만 그는 그것을 현명하게 극복했다. 그는 1200년대 초기에 분열된 몽고족들을 하나로 통일했다. 대단한 기동력과 갑옷을 꿰뚫는 화살로 무장한 공격력으로 그의 기병대는 적을 포위하고, 포위망을 좁히고, 제거할 수 있었다. 그의 공격적이고 훈련이 잘 된 군병력은 그가 몽고와 북중국을 정복하는데 도왔다. 그의 손자인 쿠빌라이 칸은 중앙 아시아, 페르시아, 고려, 러시아, 그리고 동부 유럽 국가들까지 정복했다.

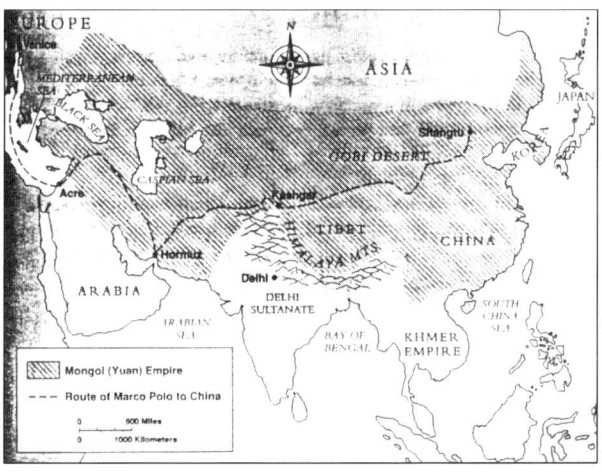

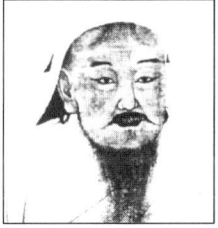

Genghis Khan ruled an empire strectching from Korean to the Black Sea, and was attacking China when he died in 1227.

몽고제국의 충격은 엄청나다. 첫째, 몽고통치기간동안 러시아는 상류사회 여성들을 별도의 지역에 소외시키는 관례를 채택했다. 몽고인들의 절대권력은 귀족이나 승려, 부호상인들의 간섭없이 나라를 통치하기를 간절히 바랬던 러시아 통치자들에겐 훌륭한 선례로서 역할했다. 둘째, 거대한 몽고제

Kublai Khan (left) greets Marco Polo and his father on their arrival in China.

(1) A suitable title for the passage is "_____ of/about Genghis Khan." (Subject matter)

    (a) Contributions   (b) Conquests   (c) Ambition   (d) Growth   (e) Facts

(2.1) One of the major hurdles in uniting the Mongolian tribes during the Genghis Khan's time is _____. (2.1 - 2.3. Locating the facts)

    (a) Geographic conditions   (c) Group disputes   (e) Lack of nationalism
    (b) Climate conditions   (d) Shortage of food

(2.2) One of the factors that enabled the Mongolian cavalry to defeat the well-armored European soldiers is _____.

    (a) Strong weapons   (d) Stabilized defense
    (b) Quick adaptability   (e) Fixed strategies
    (c) Mobility & strength of arms

(2.3) One of the most important impacts of the Mongol Empire to other countries is _____.

    (a) Domination of the Mongol Empire   (d) Spread of religion
    (b) Spread of science   (e) Exchange between East & West
    (c) Introduction of the Western language

(3.1) The italicized word, *fragmented* in the first paragraph refers to _____.

    (3.1 - 3.2. Word in context)

    (a) Separated   (c) Whole   (e) Inseparable
    (b) United   (d) Total

(3.2) The antonym of the italicized word, *eliminate* in the first paragraph is _____.

    (a) Annihilate   (c) Terminate   (e) Expel
    (b) Defeat   (d) Accept

(4) The Mongols conquered China in 1279, and founded one of the most powerful dynasties: Yuan. But this powerful dynasty did not last long; it collapsed in 1368 in less than a century. It can be inferred that the following reasons except one led to this collapse. (Making inferences)

    (a) Loss of fearless spirit   (d) Ability as horsemen & archers
    (b) The death of Kublai Khan   (e) Corruption of the ruling class
    (c) Inactivity of the cavalry & training

(5) Base on the information given including that of question (4), it can be concluded that the Mongol regime in China Proper did not have _____. (Conclusion)

    (a) Political power   (d) Religious support
    (b) Military power   (e) Popular support
    (c) Economic power

국은 실크로드를 재개함으로써 동서양의 문화, 정치, 상업의 교류를 가져다 주었다. 베니스의 상인들이 동서양의 교역을 개시하기 위하여 몽고 제국에 온 것은 바로 이 시기였다.

 1271년에 마페오와 니콜로 폴로가 마르코 폴로와 함께 중국을 여행했고, 쿠빌라이 칸의 왕궁에 왔다, 다음은 마르코 폴로가 최초로 칸을 알현하는 것을 보여준다.

 "각하, 제가 한 가지 여쭙고 싶습니다. 각하께서는 어찌 여기서 먼 곳에 사는 사람들이 믿고 있는 것에 관심을 가지십니까?"라고 마르코 폴로가 물었다.

 "훌륭한 질문이다, 마르코. 나는 호기심이 강하다네. 나는 이 세계에 존재하는 것은 모두 알아야 하네. 죽기 전에 해결 못한 어려운 문제, 내가 모르는 비밀은 없도록 확인해야겠네."라고 칸이 대답했다.

> **Note**
>
> ☐ **tribal** : 종족의 • tribal conflicts (종족간의 충돌)
> ☐ **fragment** : 파편, 단편 • fragmented parts (분열된 지방들)
>   • I could remember only the fragments of the story. (그 이야기의 단편들만 생각난다.)
> ☐ **mobility** : 기동성 ☐ **striking force** : 공격력 ☐ **cavalry** : 기병대
> ☐ **aggressive** = always ready to quarrel or attack : 공격적인
> ☐ **impact** = the force of one object hitting another : 충격, 영향
>   • His new idea made a great impact in the office.
> ☐ **clergy** = persons ordained as priests or ministers : 성직자

Passage 3 : Japan Justifies Its Attack on Manchuria

(Situation : The invasion of Manchuria by Japan in 1931 provoked worldwide protest.
Below is a Japanese official's justification for his government's action.)

We have already said that there are only three ways left for Japan to escape from the pressure of surplus population. We are like a great crowd of people packed into a small and narrow room, and there are only three doors through which we might escape, namely emigration, advance into world markets, and expansion of territory. The first door, emigration, has been barred to us by the anti-Japanese immigration policies of other countries. The second door, advance into world markets, is being shut by tariff barriers and the *abrogation* of commercial treaties. What should Japan do when two of the three doors have been closed against her?

It is quite natural that Japan should rush upon the last remaining door···. What moral right do the world powers who have themselves closed to us the two doors of emigration and advance into world markets have to criticize Japan's attempt to rush out of the third and last door? If they do not approve of this, they should open the doors which they have closed against us and permit the free movement overseas of Japanese emigrants and merchandise···. At the time of the Manchurian incident, the entire world joined in criticism of Japan. They said that Japan was an untrustworthy nation. They said that she had recklessly brought cannon and machine guns into Manchuria, which was the territory of another country, flown airplanes over it, and finally occupied it···.

And if it is still protested that our actions in Manchuria were excessively violent, we may wish to ask the white race just which country it was that sent warships and troops to India, South Africa, and Australia and slaughtered innocent natives, *bound their hands and feet with iron chains*, lashed their backs with iron whips, proclaimed these territories as their own, and still continues to hold them to this very day? They will invariably reply, these were all lands inhabited by untamed savages. These people did not know how to develop the abundant resources of their land for the benefit of mankind. Therefore it was the wish of God, who created heaven and earth for mankind, for us to develop these underdeveloped lands and to promote the happiness of mankind in their stead. This is quite a convenient argument for them.

(Source: World History, Voices From the Past, Teacher's Annotated Edition, 1994.)

(1) An appropriate parable for the passage would be "_____." (Subject matter)

    (a) My side of the story   (d) Birds of a feather flock together
    (b) The brave get the fair   (e) Where there is a will, there is a way
    (c) Strike the iron while it's hot

(2.1) What excuse did the writer make regarding the prevention of Japan from advancing into world markets? (2.1 - 2.3. Locating the facts)

    (a) Surplus population   (c) Tariff barriers   (e) World powers
    (b) Anti-Japanese immigration policy   (d) Moral right

(2.2) What was the third excuse given regarding the reduction of the Japanese surplus population?

    (a) Emigration   (c) Commercial treaties   (e) World market

지문 3 : 일본이 만주 침략을 정당화하다.

(1931년의 일본의 만주 침공은 전 세계의 항의를 불러 일으켰다. 아래 글은 어느 일본 관리가 일본 정부의 행동을 정당화한 내용이다.)

우리는 이미 일본이 잉여 인구의 압력으로부터 벗어나는 길은 세가지 밖에 남지 않았다고 말한 적이 있다. 우리는 작고 좁은 한 개의 방안에 차곡차곡 틀어 박힌 커다란 한무리의 사람들과 같고 우리가 빠져나갈 문은 세 개밖에 없으니 다시 말하면 이민, 세계시장으로 진출, 그리고 영토 확장이다. 첫째 문인 이민가는 것은 다른 국가들의 반일본 이민 정책으로 차단되어 있다. 둘째 문인 세계시장 진출은 관세 장벽과 무역 협정의 파기로 우리에게 닫혀지고 있다. 일본은 세 문 중 두 문이 일본에 불리하게 닫혀질 때 어떻게 해야 되는가?

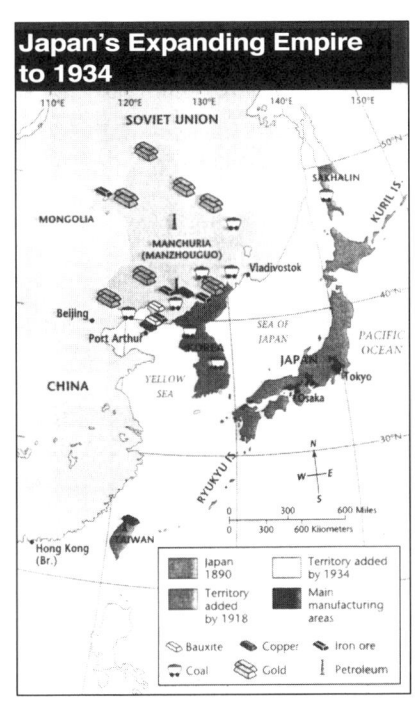

일본이 마지막 문으로 몰려가는 것은 당연하다. 스스로 우리에게 이민과 세계시장 진출을 닫아버린 세계 강대국들은 일본의 마지막 셋째 문으로 급히 빠져 나가려는 시도를 비평할 무슨 도덕적 권리를 가지고 있는가? 그들이 만일 이것을 인정하지 않는다면, 그들이 우리에게 폐쇄한 문을 열고 해외에서의 일본 이민과 상품을 허락해야 한다. 만주사변 때, 전세계가 합세하여 일본을 비난했었다. 그들은 일본은 '믿을 수 없는 나라'라고 했다. 일본이 무분별하게 대포와 기관총을 다른 나라 영토인 만주에 가지고 들어 왔고 만주 상공에 비행기를 날리고 마침내 만주를 점령했다고 말했다.

Militarists Rule Japan Japan's military steadily increased their power over the government during the 1930s. The army used propaganda, like this poster, to win public support. **Art and Literature**

만주에서의 행동이 지나치게 난폭했다고 아직도 항의한다면 우리는 다음을 백인들에게 묻고 싶다: 인도와 남아프리카, 그리고 오스트렐리아에 군함과 군부대를 보냈고, 죄없는 원주민을 학살했으

(b) Territory proclamation   (d) Territory expansion

(2.3) What excuse as a self-defense did the writer make against the European powers for the justification of invading Manchuria? It can be summarized, "You (white race) have done _____ things than us in Asia, Africa, and Australia treating the native people as slaves or savages."

    (a) Better   (c) Worse   (e) More constructive
    (b) More fruitful   (d) More sophisticated

(3.1) The italicized word, *abrogation* in the first paragraph refers to ____. (3.1 - 3.2. Word & phrase in context)

    (a) Repeal (b) Enforcement (c) Placement (d) Acceptance (e) Addition

(3.2) The italicized phrase, "*bound their hands and feet with iron chains*," in the last paragraph refers to _____.

    (a) Aided (b) Boosted (c) Overthrew (d) Oppressed (e) Dispirited

(4.1) First, the writer justified the invasion of Manchuria by using the _____ as an excuse for self-defense. (4.1 - 4.4. Rhetorical techniques)

    (a) Territory expansion   (c) Surplus population   (e) Advance into world market
    (b) Emigration   (d) Commercial treaties

(4.2) Second, the writer justified the invasion by _____ the wrongdoing of other Imperialist European Powers.

    (a) Absorbing (b) Accusing (c) Absolving (d) Accepting (e) Acclaiming

(4.3) The underlined sentence, "We have already said that there are only three ways left for Japan…" in the first paragraph is used for _____.

    (a) Bandwagon appeal   (c) Plain folks appeal   (e) Proposition & justification
    (b) Testimonial appeal   (d) Flattery appeal

(4.4) The underlineed sentence, "This is quite a convenient argument for them," in the last paragraph serves as a very _____ conclusion.

    (a) Neat (b) Bitter (c) Sarcastic (d) Humorous (e) Complimentary

(5.1) Based on the context of the information given, it can be concluded that the country referenced in the last paragraph is _____. (5.1 - 5.2. Conclusions)

    (a) Germany (b) Britain (c) Spain (d) United States (e) France

(5.2) It can be concluded that the article used for the justification of invasion in 1931 against worldwide protest, can be summarized as follows: "_____."

    (a) We have to do this to reduce our surplus population
    (b) We have to do this to maintain and enhance peace and prosperity in Asia
    (c) We have to do this to eliminate anti-Japanese immigration polices from other nations
    (d) What we are doing is to protect the interest and security of Manchuria
    (e) After all, what we are doing is no worse than what you have already done

며, 쇠사슬로 손발을 묶고 쇠 채찍으로 등을 매질했고, 이들 영토들을 자기들 것이라고 선포하고 바로 오늘까지 계속 영토를 차지하고 있는 게 어느 국가였는가? 그들은 한결같이 이 땅은 훈련되지 않은 야만족이 살았던 땅이라고 대꾸할 것이다. 이 사람들은 인류를 위해서 그 풍부한 자원들을 개발할 방법을 몰랐다고. 따라서 우리가 그들 대신 이들 저개발 국가들을 개발하고 인류행복을 증진시키는 것은 인간을 위해서 하늘과 땅을 창조하신 하느님의 소원이었다고 대답할 것이다.

이는 자신들을 위한 편리한 주장이다.

> **Note**
>
> ☐ **merchandise** = things for sale, goods for trade : 상품 • general merchandise (잡화)
> ☐ **incident** = happening, e. g. rebellion, bomb explosion, war : 사건
> ☐ **untrustworthy** = unreliable : 믿을 수 없는
> ☐ **recklessly** = without thinking of the consequences : 무분별한, 난폭한
>   • He was fined $20 for the reckless driving. (난폭 운전으로 20달러 벌금 물었다.)
> ☐ **lash** = strike violently : 매질하다 • He lashed the horse across the back with his whip.
> ☐ **untamed** = wild : 길 들여지지 않은, 말괄량이의, 미개한
> ☐ **provoke** = irritate, make angry = vex : 약 올리다, 화나게하다
>   • He was provoked beyond endurance. (참을 수 없을 만큼 화가 나 있었다.)
>   • If you provoke the dog, it will attack you.
> ☐ **surplus** = amount that remains after needs have been supplied = excess of receipts over expenditure : 잉여, 과잉 • opp. deficit
> ☐ **namely** = that is to say • Only one boy is absent, namely Harry. (한 사람, 즉 해리만 불참이다.)
> ☐ **bar** = to block : 방해하다, 금지하다 • They have barred smoking at work. (근무시간에 흡연금지 시켰다.)
> ☐ **anti-** = against : 반대, 항거의 접두사
>   • anticlimax (용두사미) • anticlockwise (시계방향의 반대로) • antitank (대전차 포)
> ☐ **tariff** = list of taxes on goods imported or exported : 수출입 관세
> ☐ **barrier** : 장벽 • language barrier (언어 장벽) • tariff barrier (관세 장벽)
> ☐ **abrogate** = repeal, annul : 무효화, 취소하다 • abrogate a contract (계약을 무효화하다)
> ☐ **annotate** = add notes to explaining difficulties : 주석을 붙이다
>   • This is an elaborately annotated text, I'm sure. (자세한 주석을 단 교재다.)

CHAPTER 4

제4장

언어 교과목을 통한 독해

READING THROUGH LANGUAGE ARTS

CHAPTER 4

This Chapter, "Reading Through Language Arts" is designed for the readers to develop comprehensive reading skills through language arts. The language arts refers to the use of language in its various forms including listening, speaking, reading, writing, and thinking skills for a variety of audiences, purposes, topics and situations. The primary purpose of the language arts is for human growth and development, because it is through language arts that makes us become human beings. It offers a basis for hope that human life can indeed become human, and human societies become worthy of man's promise. The centrality of language in human life and culture should not be underestimated.

To meet the goals of this publication, Comprehensive Reading Skills, the language arts in this chapter are categorized, for convenience sake, to the following sections: (1) Literature; (2) Discourse Analysis; and, (3) Public Speech. Specific skills directly related to the areas of the language arts, Listening, Speaking, and Writing are not heavily dealt with here, since the primary goal of this publication is for the development of reading skills. However, those interrelated areas to reading are indirectly dealt with, since they are all related to one another.

Literature section includes (1) Drama; (2) Fiction; and, (3) Poetry as sub-sections. Each sub-section includes 3 passages or models for study and review. Discourse analysis includes speech samples from (1) Sociolinguistic implications; (2) Negotiation; and, (3) Interpersonal relationship. Each sub-section includes 1 speech sample for speech and context analyses. Finally, Public Speech section includes the speeches for (1) Informative; (2) Persuasive; and, (3) Special Occasional purposes. Each sub-section includes 1 speech sample for study and review.

In the previous chapter, we have seen the framework in which five questions to answer are provided at the end of each passage. Those questions are (1) Subject matter/Main idea; (2) Locating the facts; (3) Using the context; (4) Making inferences, Tone and attitude, or Rhetorical techniques; and, (5) Drawing conclusions. In this chapter, however, the questions to answer will not be confined within a certain fixed framework. It is largely due to the complexity some literary passages or speech samples create. The questions will be constructed based on flexibility or adaptability the passage/model presents.

제4장 언어 교과목을 통한 독해

제4장

'언어 교과목을 통한 독해'는 독자들이 여러 언어 기술을 통하여 종합적인 독서 기능을 발달시키도록 계획되었다. 언어 기술이란 다양한 청중과 다양한 목적, 다양한 주제, 상황을 위하여 듣기, 말하기, 읽기, 쓰기, 그리고 사고하는 기술들을 포함하는 다양한 형태로 언어를 사용하는 것을 의미한다. 언어 기술들의 일차적인 목적은 인간의 성장과 발달이다. 왜냐하면 우리를 인간이 되게 만드는 것은 언어 기술이기 때문이다. 언어는 인간의 삶이 진정 사람다워지고 인간 사회가 인간이 바라는 가치를 갖게 만들 수 있다는 희망의 토대를 제공한다. 인간의 생활과 문화 속에서 언어가 차지하는 중심성은 과소평가 되어서는 안된다.

'종합 독해 기술'의 함양이라는 출판 목적을 충족시키기 위하여 이번 장의 언어기술은 다음 절로 분류되어있다: (1)문학 (2)대화 분석 (3)대중 연설. 듣기, 말하기, 쓰기 영역과 직접 관련된 구체적인 기술은 여기서 많이 취급하지 않았다. 왜냐하면 이 책의 일차적인 목표가 독서 기술의 개발이기 때문이다. 그러나 읽기와 연관된 분야는 그들 모두가 관련되기 때문에 간접적으로 다루어져 있다.

문학을 다룬 절에는 (1)연극 (2)소설 (3)시 등이 하부절로서 포함되어있다. 각각의 하부절에는 연구와 복습을 위하여 세개의 지문이나 모델이 들어 있다. 대화 분석은 (1)사회 언어학적 함축 (2)협상 (3)대인관계에서 발생하는 담화 표본이 들어있다. 각 하부절에서는 담화와 문맥 분석을 위한 하나의 담화 표본이 들어있다. 끝으로 대중 연설은 (1)내용 전달적인 것 (2)설득적인 것 (3)특수한 경우를 목적으로 하는 대화가 들어 있다. 각각의 하부절에는 연구와 복습용으로 하나의 담화 표본을 넣었다.

앞장에서 각 지문 끝에 대답할 5개의 질문이 마련된 구조를 살펴보았다. 그 질문들은 (1)주제/요지 (2)사실의 위치 찾기 (3)문맥 이용 (4)추론, 어조와 태도, 수사학상 기법 (5)결론 추출 등이었다. 그러나 이 장에서는 답해야 할 질문들이 어떤 고정된 구조안에서 한정되어 있지 않다. 그 이유는 대체로 어떤 문학적인 혹은 담화 표본이 만들어 내는 복합성 때문이다. 질문들은 지문이나 모델들이 제시하는 융통성, 적응성을 토대로 구성될 것이다.

Note

- □ confine=enclose within limits, keep in a small space : 국한, 감금시키다
  - John was confined to bed for a week with his cold. (존은 감기로 일주일 간 누워서 꼼짝 못했다.)
- □ impersonate=act the part of in a play, etc pretend to be a person by copying his appearance, behavior : …의 역을 하다, 분장하다 • He impersonates all the well-known politicians. (그는 모든 유명 정치인들의 역할을 (흉내를) 한다.)
- □ flaw=a small sign of damage that makes an object not perfect : 하자, 결함
  - Make sure that there is not a flaw in the contract. (그 계약에 단 하나의 하자도 없도록 확실히 하라.)
- □ satire=a work of literature intended to show the foolishness of something in an amusing way : 풍자(극, 물)
  - The play is a satire on the Government's defense policy. (그 연극은 정부의 국방 정책을 희화한 풍자물이다.)
- □ exaggerate=make something seem larger, better or worse than in reality:과장하다
  - We can't exaggerate the importance of good health. (건강의 중요성은 아무리 강조해도 지나치지 않는다.)
- □ unfold = open from a folded position : 접었던 것을 펴다, 공개하다
  - She opened the envelope, took out the letter and unfolded it carefully.
- □ revenge = punishment given to someone in return for harm done to oneself:복수하다
  - The village was bombed in revenge for protecting enemy soldiers.(그 마을은 적군들을 보호해 준 데 대한 복수로 폭격당했다.)
- □ trap = catch in a trap or buy a trick : 함정에 빠트리다, 꼼짝 못하게 하다 • The poachers trap wild animals for quick money against the law.(밀렵자들은 법을 어기면서 손쉽게 돈을 벌려고 야생동물들을 올가미로 잡는다.)
- □ tantalizing = making you feel a strong desire to have something that you cannot have : 감질나게하는, 애태우는
  - -Tantalus의 신화에서 유래 :Tantalus는 Zeus의 아들로서 신들의 비밀을 누설한 벌로 지옥의 호수 속에서 턱까지 잠기어져, 목이 말라 물을 마시려면 물이 빠지고, 배가 고파 머리 위의 나무 열매를 따먹으려면 가지가 물러가서 괴로움을 당했다는 신화의 주인공 -tantalizing은 될 것 같으면서도 번번히 실패하여 애태우는 뜻의 형용사. • A tantalizing smell of food reached the hungry prisoners.

4-1 LITERATURE

This section, Literature, includes (1) Drama; (2) Fiction; and, (3) Poetry as sub-sections. As previously mentioned, each sub-section has 3 passages/models for study and review.

4.1.1. Drama

Drama is a form of art in which actors impersonate characters to communicate a story by means of dialogue and movement, usually in a theater before an audience. Major forms of drama include (1) tragedy (a play in which a hero/heroine is destroyed by some flaw central to their character); (2) comedy (humorous or satiric, and ending happily based on real-life situations in a light-hearted way); (3) Melodrama (a play in which a lot of exciting, tragic, or romantic things in real-life situations happen and in which people's emotions are often exaggerated); and, (4) tragicomedy (a play or other written forms that is both sad and funny).

Passage 1 : **Hamlet (circa 1600) by William Shakespeare (1564 - 1616)**

Background :
   Hamlet is considered as one of the greatest plays in the English language. Written about 1600, this play unfolds a story of murder and revenge. Prince Hamlet of Denmark, called upon by his father's ghost to avenge his murder, is trapped between tantalizing agony and action; ultimately his delay leads to a far bloodier outcome than would have resulted from quick revenge.

Dramatis Personae : Hamlet, only son of the late King Hamlet.
   Claudius, King of Denmark, brother of the former King, Hamlet's uncle. Gertrude, widow of the former King, new wife of Claudius, Hamlet's mother. Horatio, loyal friend to Prince Hamlet. Marcellas & Bernardo, sentinels.

4-1 문학

이 절 문학에는 (1)연극 (2)소설 (3)시 등이 하부절로서 포함된다. 앞에서도 말했듯이 각 하부절에는 연구와 복습을 위하여 3개의 지문과 모델이 들어 있다.

4.1.1. 연극

연극은 배우들이 대체로 극장 관중 앞에서 대화와 동작을 수단으로 어떤 이야기를 전달하기 위하여 극중 인물의 역할을 하는 예술의 한 형태다. 연극의 주요 형식에는 다음과 같은 것들이 포함된다. (1)비극 (남녀 주인공들이 그들 성격상 어떤 주요 결함 때문에 망해가는 극) (2)희극 (실생활 상황을 토대로 명랑, 해학적이고 풍자적이며 결말이 행복하게 끝나는 극) (3) 멜로 드라마 (실제 상황에서 매우 자극적이고, 비극적이며 낭만적인 사건이 일어나고 사람들의 감정이 과장되는 극) (4) 희비극 (슬프면서도 우스운 극).

지문 1 : 햄릿 (약 1600년경) 세익스피어 작

배경 : 햄릿은 영국 문학에서 가장 위대한 희곡으로 여겨진다. 1600년 경에 씌어진 이 희곡은 살인과 복수의 이야기를 전개하고 있다. 덴마크의 왕자 햄릿은 살해당한 아버지 혼령의 복수 요청을 받고 애타는 고민과 실행 사이에서 이러지도 저러지도 못하는 함정에 빠진다. 결국 그의 지연은 신속한 복수를 했더라면 일어났을 결과 보다 훨씬 더 피비린내 나는 결과를 초래한다.

등장 인물 : 햄릿 – 고 햄릿 왕의 외아들
　　　　　　 클로디어스 – 덴마크 왕, 선왕의 동생, 햄릿의 숙부
　　　　　　 거트루드 – 선왕의 미망인, 클로디어스의 새 아내, 햄릿의 어머니
　　　　　　 호레이쇼 – 햄릿 왕자의 충직한 친구
　　　　　　 마셀러스 & 바나아도 – 보초병들

Horatio : My lord, I think I saw him yesternight.
Hamlet : Saw? Who?
Horatio : My lord, the King, your father.
Hamlet : The King my father!
Horatio : *Season your admiration for a while*. With an attent ear, till I may deliver. Upon the witness of these gentlemen, this marvels to you.
Hamlet : For God's love, let me hear!
Horatio : Two nights together had these gentlemen, Marcellus and Bernardo, on their watch in the dead waste and middle of the night been thus encountered. A figure like your father at all points from head to foot appear before them, and with solemn march goes slowly and stately by them…
Hamlet : But where was this?
Marcellus : My lord, upon the platform where we watched.
Hamlet : Did you not speak to it?
Horatio : My lord, I did; but answer made it none. Yet once methought it lifted up its head and did address itself to motion like as it would speak; but even then the morning cock crew loud, and at the sound it shrunk in haste away and vanished from our sight.
Hamlet : It's very strange…

(1) What is the conversation about? (Main idea)

    (a) Identifying the time they met the ghost
    (b) Verification of the King's ghost
    (c) Identifying the place they met the ghost
    (d) What they talked with the ghost

(2) Who saw the ghost of King Hamlet? (Locating the facts)

    (a) Hamlet & Horatio   (c) Marcellus & Bernardo
    (b) Horatio & Bernardo   (d) Bernardo, Marcellus, Horatio

(3) The italicized sentence, *Season your admiration for a while*, refers to _____. (Phrase/sentence in context)

    (a) Moderate your astonishment   (c) Hold your tongue
    (b) Calm down your anger   (d) Keep it secret

(4.1) The tone of the conversation seems to be _____. (Tone & attitude)

    (a) Secretive but assertive   (c) Sad but vindictive
    (b) Delightful but vindictive   (d) Interested but doubtful

호레이쇼 : 왕자님, 어제 밤에 그 분을 뵈었다고 생각하는데요.

햄릿 : 뵈었다니? 누구를?

호레이쇼 : 왕자님, 선왕이셨습니다. 선친 말씀입니다.

햄릿 : 선왕, 나의 아버님이셨다고?

호레이쇼 : 잠시 놀라움을 진정하십시요. 제가 말씀드릴 때까지 귀를 기울여 주십시요. 이 사람들의 증언을 토대로 이 괴상한 일을 말씀드리겠습니다.

햄릿 : 제발, 들려주게.

호레이쇼 : 이 사람들, 마셀러스와 바나아도가 이틀 밤을 함께 쥐죽은 듯이 황량함 속에서 한밤중에 망을 보던 중 당한 일이었습니다. 머리에서 발 끝까지 어느 모로 보나 선친 같으신 모습이 그들에게 나타나시어 엄숙한 걸음걸이로 천천히 그리고 당당하게 그들 옆을 지나가시더군요.

햄릿 : 그런데 그게 어디였나?

마셀러스 : 왕자님, 저희가 망보던 망대 위였습니다.

햄릿 : 말을 걸어 보지 않았느냐?

호레이쇼 : 왕자님, 제가 말을 걸었습니다만 응답이 없었습니다. 그러나 한 번 고개를 들고 마치 말을 시작하려는 듯이 보였습니다. 그러나 바로 그때 아침 수탉이 큰소리로 울었습니다. 그 소리에 급히 움츠리더니 우리 눈에서 사라져 버렸습니다.

햄릿 : 해괴하구나.

William Shakespeare

A motion picture crew at Kronborg Castle, Elsinore, the setting of Shakespeare's play.

(4.2) Why do you think the ghost of King Hamlet appears to them during the night? It is probably because the ghost _____. (Making inferences)

   (a) Misses his son
   (b) Wants to regain his stolen throne
   (c) Wants justice to be done
   (d) Wants to train Hamlet to be a good King

(5) It can be concluded that this drama is a _____ .(Conclusion)

   (a) Comedy   (b) Tragedy   (c) Melodrama   (d) Tragicomedy

Passage 2 : **Match-Making Agency**

Setting = Time: One morning in 1973, during the era the Korean economy is beginning to boom due to industrialization.
         Place: At the office of "Match-Making Agency" in Seoul
         Situation: Mr. Lee lost his wife and asked the service of the agency for the introduction of his future wife. The business of the agency was slow, and they needed customers desperately.

Dramatis Personae : Mr. Kim, 40 years old, Director of the Match-Making Agency. Ms Chung, 28, employee of the agency.
         Mr. Lee, 38, customer, Managing Director of a company.

Mr. Kim : (With a big, flattering smile) <u>Is it seonsangneem</u> (Sir) who called me just a few minutes ago?
Mr. Lee : (Giving him a business card) Yes, I am.
Mr. Kim : (After reading the card) Oh, <u>jeonmooneem</u> (Managing director)! Is it so? It's my honor to serve you.
Ms Chung : How come you look so handsome and gentle? Ho ho.
Mr. Lee : As a matter of fact, I lost my wife and am looking for a good companion.
Ms Chung : The lady we are going to introduce to you will *make a nice bride* for you, sir, no, Managing director Lee.
Mr. Kim : Yes, yes. She is staying at a hotel nearby… We need a deposit of 100,000 Won for taking an *initial* step.
Mr. Lee : Oh, is that so? I thought I should pay after our matching is over.
Ms Chung : Director Lee, how can we trust anyone in this tricky world these

Note

- □ be worthy of = deserve : …을 받을 자격이 있다
  - His behavior is well worthy of acclamation. (그의 행위는 갈채를 받기에 충분하다.)
- □ underestimate = have too low an opinion of : 과소 평가하다   opp. overestimate
  - I underestimated the cost of journey, and now I have no money left.
  (여행 경비를 과소 평가했기에 지금은 남은 돈이 없다.)
- □ categorize : 분류하다   □ for convenience sake : 편의상, 편의를 위하여
- □ discourse = serious conversation of speech, lecture, sermon : 담화, 강연, 담론
- □ sociolinguistic : 사회언어학적   □ attent = attentive : 주의 깊은
- □ even = (고어) just at that time when : 바로, 정확히
  - Even as I gave the warning, the car skidded. (막 경고를 하는데 차가 옆으로 미끄러 졌다.)
- □ encounter = find oneself faced by danger, difficulties: meet unexpectedly : 뜻밖에 마주치다
  - To my embarrassment, I encountered the creditor in the subway train.
  (지하철에서 채권자를 마주쳤을때 어쩔줄을 몰랐다.)
- □ dramatis personae = characters : (극의) 등장 인물
- □ loyal = true to one's friends, group, country etc. : 충성스런, 성실한
  - He has remained loyal to the party even though they lost the election.
  (자기 정당이 선거에 졌어도 당에 충실해 왔다.)
- □ sentinel = guard : 보초   □ admiration(고어) = wonder : 놀라움
- □ deliver = give forth in words : 말로 표현하다, 연설, 설교를 하다.
  - He delivers a course of lectures on the subject of reading comprehension.
  (그는 독해에 관하여 한 과정의 강의를 한다.)
- □ stately = formerly and grandly : 당당하게,
- □ Answer made it none. = It made no answer. : 도치구문
- □ haste = quick movement or action : 서두름, 급속   • Haste makes waste. (욕속반졸-欲速反拙)
  - in haste = in a hurry (서둘러서)   • The more haste, the less speed. (바쁘면 돌아가라.)
- □ methought(고어) = it seems to me, I think : 내 생각에는
- □ address oneself to = put oneself to work : 착수하다
  - He addressed himself to the main difficulty. (가장 어려운 부분의 일을 착수했다.)
- □ shrink=cause someone to become smaller, be afraid of; move back and away : 두려워
  움츠리다, 겁을 먹어 회피하다   • Never shrink from your responsbility.

지문 2 : 결혼 중매업

배경 – 시기 : 1973년의 어느날 오전, 이 시기에 한국경제는 공업화로 인하여
부흥하기 시작함.

장소 : 서울 소재 결혼 상담소

상황 : 이씨는 상처하고, 미래의 아내를 소개해 달라고 중매를 부탁했다.
중매업은 불황이어서 손님을 몹시 기다림.

등장인물 : 김씨 - 40세, 결혼 상담소 소장

days? Sir, no, Director Lee, if everybody can be trusted like you, how happy we are!

(Source: Translated and adapted from "Match-Making Agency (1973)" by Kyungchang Park)

(1) What is the main issue of the conversation? (Subject matter)

    (a) Mr. Lee lost his wife
    (b) Introduction of a woman for Mr. Lee
    (c) Deposit money
    (d) Mr. Lee is handsome and gentle

(2.1.) The italicized phrase, *make a nice bride*, refers to _____. (2.1. - 2.2. Phrase and Word in context)

    (a) Produce a nice bride   (c) Become a nice bride
    (b) Obtain a nice bride   (d) Build a nice bride

(2.2.) The antonym of the italicized word, *initial*, is _____.

    (a) Primary   (c) Antecedent
    (b) Elementary   (d) Final

(3.1) Mr. Kim said, "Is it so? It's my honor to serve you." Why did he give such a complimentary remark to Mr. Lee? It is probably because Mr. Lee is _____. (3.1 - 3.2. Making inferences)

    (a) A teacher   (c) A Managing director
    (b) Rich   (d) Handsome and gentle

(3.2) Why did Ms Chung twice correct her using form of address from Sir to Managing Director? It can be inferred that the form of address, Managing Director is _____ more respected than Sir during the time of Korean industrialization of 1970s in which the value of economic power is highly respected. And the agency needs the customers who pay the match-making fees.

    (a) Socially   (c) Professionally
    (b) Financially   (d) Culturally

(4) It can be concluded that this drama can be considered as a _____. (Conclusion)

    (a) Comedy   (c) Melodrama
    (b) Tragedy   (d) Tragicomedy

정 여인 - 28세, 상담소 직원

이씨 - 38세, 손님, 회사 전무

김씨 : (비위를 맞추듯 활짝 웃으며) 몇분 전에 전화 주신 분이 선생님이셨습니까?

이씨 : (명함을 건네면서) 그렇습니다.

김씨 : (명함을 읽고 나서) 전무님, 아, 그렇습니까? 모시게 되어 영광입니다.

정 여인 : 어쩌면 그렇게 미남이시고 점잖으세요? 호,호.

이씨 : 사실은 제가 상처를 해서 좋은 반려자를 구하고 있습니다.

정 여인 : 저희가 소개해 드리려는 여자분이 선생님께 좋은 신부감이 될 것입니다. 선생님, 아니 이 전무님.

김씨 : 예, 예, 그렇습니다. 그분이 지금 근처 호텔에 묵고 계십니다…. 착수조로 십만원의 보증금이 필요한데요.

이씨 : 아, 그렇습니까? 저는 중매 후에 지불해야 되는 걸로 알았습니다.

정 여인 : 이 전문님, 요사이 이 속임수 많은 세상에 누구를 믿을 수 있겠습니까? 선생님, 아니 이 전무님. 만일 선생님 같이 모든 사람을 믿을 수 있다면 우리가 얼마나 행복하겠습니까!

Note

- **match-maker**=a person who encourages people who are thought suitable to marry each other : 결혼 중매자
  - They decided to make a match of it between the two persons.
    (그들 두 사람을 결혼 시키기로 작정했다.)
- **agency**=the business of a person who acts for, or who manages the business affairs of another or others : 대행업
- **boom**=a sudden increase in trade activity, esp. a time when money is being made quickly : 호경기, 활황   opp. slump
  John is booming as a novelist. (소설가로 잘 나간다.)
- **desperately** : 절망적으로, 필사적으로
  I'm desperately in love with you.
- **flatter**=praise too much, praise insincerely : 아첨하다, 비위 맞추다
  This photograph flatters you. (사진이 잘 나왔다.)
- **business card** : 영업용 명함   □ **deposit** : 공탁금, 보증금

Passage 3 : **Three Kingdoms**

Background : From the fall of the Han Dynasty (206 B.C. - 220 A.D.), three smaller states emerged and began warring for sovereignty. La Kwanjung's Three Kingdoms as an epic drama depicts this fatal moment in Chinese history. Three Kingdoms, one of the greatest Chinese literary masterpieces, is a semifictional history crowded with stories and peopled with kings and courtiers, peasants, soldiers, and scholars, presenting power, loyalty, and obligation as themes. Among the young men who respond to the call for the people are YuBee, KwanYoo, and ChangBee, they become friends and swear brotherhood, promising to live and die as one in the service of their country and its people. This is the well-known Peach Garden Oath, from which the long story begins.

ChangBee : My surname is Chang, my given name, Bee. We've been in this country for generations and farm a bit of land, sell wine, and slaughter pigs. I was looking for men of adventure and, coming upon you reading the recruitment call, took the liberty of addressing you.

YuBee : Actually, I am an imperial relation, and I want to raise troops to destroy the Yellow Scarves for the protection of people.

ChangBee : I have resources that could be used to outfit some local youths. What if you were to join with me in serving this great cause? (YuBee was delighted, and together they went to a nearby inn. As they drank, they noticed a striking fellow stopped at the inn's entrance to rest. YuBee invited him to share their table and asked who he was).

KwanYoo : My surname is Kwan and Yoo is my given name. One of the notables in our district was using his position to *exploit* people. I killed him and had to flee⋯ When I heard of the mobilization, I came to answer the call. (YuBee then told of his ambitions and together they went to ChangBee's farm to talk further).

ChangBee : Behind the farm is a peach garden. The flowers are at their fullest. Tomorrow we must make offerings there to Heaven and Earth,

지문 3 : 삼국지

배경 – 한나라가 멸망한 뒤 세 개의 작은 나라들이 나타나서 통치권을 얻기 위하여 싸움을 시작했다. 나관중의 삼국지는 서사극으로서 중국 역사에서 운명적인 시기를 묘사하고 있다. 중국 문학 작품의 걸작 중의 하나인 삼국지는 많은 이야기가 들어있고 주제로서 권력, 충성, 그리고 책임들을 표현하면서, 왕과 조정 신하들, 소작농, 병사, 학자들 다수가 등장하는 반(半) 소설적 역사서다. 백성을 위한 부름에 응답하는 젊은이들 중 유비, 관우, 장비는 친구가 되고, 의형제를 맹세하고, 나라와 국민을 섬기는 일에 한 형제로서 살고 죽기를 맹세한다. 이것이 그 유명한 도원결의이고, 그로부터 긴 이야기가 시작된다.

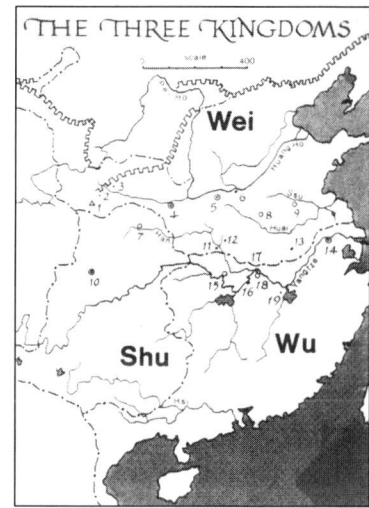

Peach Garden Oath

장비 – 내 성은 장이요, 이름은 비입니다. 우리는 이 나라에서 여러 세대 동안 살면서 약간의 땅을 경작하고, 술을 팔며, 돼지를 도살해 왔습니다. 나는 모험심이 강한 남자들을 찾고 있었는데, 신병 모집 공고를 읽고 있는 당신을 우연히 보고 결례를 무릅쓰고 이렇게 인사를 드리오.

유비 – 사실 나는 황족이오. 그리고 백성을 보호하기 위하여 황건족을 무찌를 군대를 모집하고 싶소.

장비 – 나에게는 지방 젊은이들의 장비를 갖추는데 쓰일 수 있는 재원이 있오. 만일 당신께서 이 위대한 대의에 이바지하기 위하여 저와 힘을 합하면 어떻겠소?

(유비는 기뻐서 함께 근처의 술집으로 갔다. 술을 마실 때 주막 입구에 멈춰서 쉬고 있는 눈에 띄는 한 사람을 눈여겨 본다. 유비는 그를 불러 술상을 함께 하고 누구냐고 묻는다.)

declaring that we three join together as brothers combining strength and purpose. (The next day, they prepared their offerings, which included a black bull and a white horse. Amid burning incense, the three men performed obeisance and spoke their vow).

(Source: Translated and adapted from Three Kingdoms (1981), translated from Chinese into Korean by Chonghwa Park. Ue Moon Kak Publishing Co., Seoul)

(1) What is the conversation about? (Subject matter)

    (a) Existing social crisis
    (b) To make an oath at Peach Garden
    (c) To destroy the Yellow Scarves
    (d) To fight for their country as brothers

(2.1.) Who proposed to make an oath as brothers for common purpose at the Peach Garden? (2.1. - 2.2. Locating the facts)

    (a) YuBee   (c) KwanYoo
    (b) ChangBee   (d) Three of them

(2.2.) Who came to answer the recruitment call after murdering one of the corrupt local officers?

    (a) YuBee   (c) KwanYoo
    (b) ChangBee   (d) Three of them

(3) The italicized word, *exploit*, refers to _____. (Word in context)

    (a) Explore   (c) Explode
    (b) Explicate   (d) Take advantage of

(4) The tone of the conversation seems to be _____. (Tone and attitude)

    (a) Sincere & honest   (c) Friendly & curious
    (b) Serious but treacherous   (d) Speculative but sincere

(5) It can be concluded that the theme of the conversation in the drama, especially the vow at the Peach Garden seems to require the unbreakable bondage of _____ as brothers among them. (Conclusion)

    (a) Power   (c) Obligation
    (b) Loyalty   (d) Morality

관우 – 나는 성이 관이고 이름은 우요. 우리 지방의 유지 중 하나가 지위를 이용하여 백성들을 착취하고 있었오. 나는 그를 죽이고 도망쳤소. 동원 소식을 듣고 모병에 응하려 왔오. (그때 유비는 자기 꿈을 이야기하고 그들은 함께 장비의 농장으로 가서 더 자세한 이야기를 한다.)

장비 – 농장 뒤에 복숭아 밭이 있오. 꽃이 만발했지요. 내일 그곳에서 하늘과 땅에 제사를 올리고 한 형제로서 힘과 뜻을 함께하기로 맹세합시다.

(그 다음 날, 그들은 제물을 마련했고 제물 중에는 검은 수소와 흰 말이 들어 있었다. 향이 피어있는 가운데 예를 올리고 구두로 맹세를 했다.)

Note

- **rise and fall** : 흥망 성쇠 • The government has fallen. (정부가 실각했다.)
  • Berlin fell to the Allies. (베를린이 연합군 손에 떨어졌다.)
- **sovereignty** : 주권, 통치권, 독립국
- **epic**=(of stories, events) full of brave action and excitment : 영웅의 모험 등의 호쾌한 서사시
  • an epic journey to the South Pole (웅장한 남극 탐험 이야기)
  • The Odyssey is an epic of an ancient Greece.
- **depict**=represent by a picture, describe : 그리다, 묘사하다
  • This painting depicts the peaceful life of the farming village.
- **fatal**=causing or resulting death : 운명을 갈라 놓는, 치명적인, 중요한
  • a fatal (mistake, wound) accident (치명적 사고 (실수, 부상))
- **masterpiece**=a piece of work, esp. art which is the best of its type : 최고 걸작
  • Man, they say, is the masterpiece of God.
- **courtier** : 조정 신하, 아첨꾼
- **peasant**=a countryman working on the land, esp. one who owns and lives on a small piece of land : 소작농, 영세농
  • cf. pheasant (꿩)   • pageant (야외극)
- **call**=summons, invitation : 부르심, 초대
  • Many young men answered the call of their country and volunteered for the military service. (많은 젊은이들이 조국의 부름에 응하여 자원 입대했다.)
- **swear**=take an oath : 서약하다 • He swore that he would tell the truth, only the truth.
- **in the service of** : …을 (섬기기) 위하여
  • I will gladly devote myself in the service of my country. (내 나라를 섬기는 일에 기꺼이 몸 바치겠다.)
- **oath**=a solemn promise=vow : 맹세, 서약 • a false oath=perjury (위증)
- **slaughter**=kill animals, people in large numbers : 살륙하다, 도살하다
- **make obeisance to** : …에게 경의를 표하다
- **exploit**=take advantage of, use unfairly for one's own profit : 이용하다, 착취하다
  • It's against the law to exploit the minors. (미성년자를 착취하는 것은 위법이다.)
- **flee**=escape by hurrying away : 서둘러 도망가다
- **amid**=in the middle of
- **mobilize**=gather together for a particular service of use, esp. for war : 동원하다

4.1.2. Fiction

Fiction is a literary genre usually defined as a consecutive and fictional narration in prose. In present-day term, "fiction" primarily refers to prose narratives (the novel and the short story), and it is sometimes used simply as a synonym for the novel.

Passage 1 : The Pearl (1947) by John Steinbeck (1902 - 1968)

Characters : Kino, protagonist, a fisherman at La Paz.
　　　　　　Juana, Kino's wife.
　　　　　　Coyotito, Kino and Juana's baby.
　　　　　　Juan Tomas, Kino's brother-in-law.

Plot : Kino finds a pearl beyond price, the Pearl of the World, with which he hopes to buy peace and happiness for himself and his family. Instead of peace and happiness, he finds a variety of disasters (murder, arson, vandalism of his canoe, panic flight, nightmare, fear of being slain) fallen upon them not only in his village but also on the way to the capital city. Kino does not sell the pearl, instead he gets rid of the pearl: the source of all types of disaster, by throwing it to the sea where it came from.

Excerpt from the story:
"Kino drew back his arm and flung the pearl with all his might. Kino and Juana watched it go, winking and glimmering under the setting sun. They saw a little splash in the distance, and they stood side by side watching the place for a long time. And the pearl settled into the lovely green water and dropped toward the bottom⋯ It settled down to the sandy bottom among the fern-like plants⋯ A crab *scampering* over the bottom raised a little cloud of sand, and when it settled the pearl was gone. And the music of the pearl *drifted to a whisper* and disappeared."

(1) The story is largely structured based on _____ conflicts caused by the pearl. (Subject matter)

　　(a) Social　　(b) Economic　　(c) Cultural　　(d) Psychological

(2.1.) The italicized word, *scampering*, refers to _____. (2.1. - 2.2. Word/Phrase in context)

　　(a) Dashing　　(b) Scanning　　(c) Penetrating　　(d) Peeling

4.1.2. 픽션 : 소설

픽션은 산문체로 쓰여지는, 일관되고(필연적) 허구적인 이야기로 정의 되는 하나의 문학 범주다. 오늘날의 용어에서 픽션은 주로 산문체 이야기(소설, 단편)를 가리키며 때때로 소설과 동의어로 쓰여지고 있다.

John Steinbeek

지문 1 : 존 스타인벡의 진주

등장 인물 : 키노 - 주인공, 라파즈의 어부
주아나 - 키노의 아내
코요티토 - 키노와 쥬아나의 애기
주안 토마스 - 키노의 처남

Steinbeek was awarded the Nobel Prize for Literature in 1962.

구성 : 키노는 값을 매길 수 없을 만큼의 엄청난 세계 최고의 진주를 발견하고, 그것으로 자신과 가족의 평화와 행복을 사려고 희망한다. 그러나 평화와 행복 대신 자기 마을에서 뿐아니라 수도로 가는 도중에도 가족에게 내리는 여러 종류의 재난(살인, 방화, 자기 카누의 파괴, 공포의 도주, 악몽, 살해 위협)을 당한다. 키노는 온갖 형태의 재난 원인인 그 진주를 팔지 않고, 그것을 발견했던 그 바다로 던져 없애 버린다.

소설의 일부 발췌 : "키노는 팔을 당겨 전력을 다해 그 진주를 던졌다. 키노와 주아나는 진주가 황혼 빛에 깜빡이고 희미하게 빛을 내며 사라지는 것을 지켜보았다. 그들은 멀리서 물이 튀는 것을 쳐다보고 오랫동안 나란히 서서 진주가 떨어진 장소를 바라보았다. 진주는 아름다운 푸른 물 속으로 내려 앉아 바닥으로 떨어졌다. 그리고 고사리 같은 식물들 사이의 모래바닥에 가라 앉았다. 바닥 위로 급히 도망가던 게 한마리가 약간의 모래 구름을 일으켰다. 게가 제자리를 잡았을 때 그 진주는 보이지 않았다. 그리고 진주의 음악 소리 (진주를 팔아 행복과 자식의 교육을 이룩하려던 희망의 소리)는 물결에 흘러 점점 작아지더니 사라져 버렸다."

(2.2.) The italicized phrase, *drifted to a whisper*, refers to _____.

    (a) Become almost inaudible   (c) Echoed
    (b) Silenced   (d) Suspended

(3.1.) The symbolic implications of the pearl can be _____. (3.1. - 3.2. Making inferences)

    (a) Happiness & peace   (c) Wealth & fame
    (b) Prosperity & peace   (d) Integrity & power

(3.2) The symbolic implication of Kino can be a/an _____ person.

    (a) Common   (b) Industrious   (c) Gifted   (d) Honest

(4) One of the following statements which can serve as the best theme of this fiction is _____. (Conclusion)

    (a) At the door of the rich are many friends. (Hebrew proverb)
    (b) He who knows his proper place is wise.
    (c) Solitude is the best nurse of wisdom.
    (d) The love of money and the love of learning seldom meet.

Passage 2 : Moby Dick (1851) by Herman Melville (1819 - 1891)

Characters : Ahab, the Captain of the Pequod
               The Officers: Starbuck, 1st mate
                           Stubb, 2nd mate
                           Flask, 3rd mate
          Harpooners: Tashtego, Indian
                     Daggoo, Negro with gigantic size and strength
                     Queequeg, Native of Kokovoko Island
          Ishmael, a young sailor who narrates the story

Herman Melville

Plot : Moby Dick is the story of the fateful voyage of the Pequod, a whaling ship commanded by the compelling yet tantalizing figure, Captain Ahab. Throughout the story, Ahab relentlessly pursues the white whale that has years before taken off his leg. Ahab, the stubborn and persistent captain, stirs up the crew to be on alert for his enemy, and chases the formidable enemy, Moby Dick. At the final battle with the whale, Captain Ahab including his officers and ship are destroyed by the whale. This tragic but somewhat heroic or mad story is told by a young, survived sailor Ishmael whose name symbolizes the "wanderer."

Note

- **get rid of** = throw, give away or destroy, free oneself of : 없애다, 제거하다
  - How can I get rid of the flies in the kitchen? (어떻게 주방 파리를 없애나?)
- **excerpt** = a piece taken from a book, speech, or musical work : 발췌문, 인용구
- **consecutive** = following in regular order, coming one after the other in regular order : 질서 있게 계속하는 : (픽션의 정의에서 우연적인 사건은 배제하고 필연적 인과로 계속되는)
- **prose** = language not in verse form : 산문   **verse** : 운문
- **genre** = kind, style, category esp. of literary form, e.g. poetry, drama, the novel : 범주, 종류, 장르
- **protagonist** = chief person in a drama, by extension a chief person in a factual event : 주인공, 주창자
- **disaster** = great or sudden misfortune, a terrible accident : 재난, 천재
  - The election results will bring political disaster. (그 선거 결과는 정치에 불행을 초래할 것이다.)
- **arson** = the crime of setting fire to property in order to cause destruction : 방화
- **vandalism** = intentional, needless, and usu. widespread damage and destruction, esp. of public property : 의도적인 문화, 예술의 파괴, 고의적 파괴
  - Vandal (반달인, 5세기경 로마를 침략하여 예술, 문화를 파괴한 게르만의 한 민족)
- **canoe** : 통나무 배, 카누
- **panic** = a state of sudden uncontrollable fear or terror : 공포   • panic flight (공포의 도주)
- **slay : slew : slain** = kill, murder violently : 살해하다
  - The armed deserter slew the innocent shopkeeper. (무장 탈영병이 무고한 가게 주인을 살해했다.)
- **fling** = throw violently or with force : 던지다, 내동댕이 치다
  - Boy, don't fling your clothes on the floor; hang them up. (애야, 옷을 방바닥에 내던지지 말고 잘 걸어라.)
- **glimmer** = give a very faint unsteady light : 희미하게 빛나다
- **scamper** = (esp. of small animals) run quickly : 허겁지겁 달아나다
  - The mice scampered away when the cat came.
- **drift** = flow or be driven away by wind and waves : 표류하다, 흘러가다
  - The snow was drifting in great piles against the house. (눈이 바람에 밀려 집안에 쌓이고 있었다.)

지문 2 : 허먼 멜빌의 모비 딕

등장 인물 : 에이허브 – 피쿼드호 선장
　　　　　고급 선원들 : 스타버그-1등 항해사, 스텁-2등 항해사, 플라스크-3등 항해사
　　　　　작살 잡이들 : 태슈테고 – 인디언
　　　　　　　　　　　대구 – 놈집과 힘이 엄청난 흑인
　　　　　　　　　　　퀴이퀘그 – 코코보코 섬의 원주민
　　　　　　　　　　　이스마엘 – 이 이야기를 하는 젊은 선원

구성 : 모비 딕은 사람을 꼼짝 못하게 하면서도 조바심나게 하는 에이허브 선장 지휘의 포경선, 피쿼드호의 운명적인 항해 이야기다. 이야기 전체를 통해서 에이허브 선장은 수년 전에 그의 다리를 잘라간 그 흰고래를 냉혹하게 쫓는다. 완고하고 집념이 강한

Excerpts from the story : (Ahab encourages his crew to chase the whale.)

"I'll chase him round Good Hope, and round the Horn, and round the Norway Maelstrom, and round *perdition's flames* before I give him up. And this is what you have shipped for, men! Chase that white whale on both sides of land, and over all sides of earth, till he *spouts* black blood and rolls fin out!" shouted Ahab.

(After the battle with Moby Dick, three harpooners in their small boat see their ship sink.)

Now great circles began to form on the water about the ship, moving round and round with ever increasing speed··· Soon not a piece of wood or anything connected with the ship was left anywhere on the surface. All had fallen; all lay deep under the water, covered now by the great sea which rolled on and on again fast as it had done five thousand years ago.

(1) Moby Dick can be considered as a fiction related to _____. (Subject matter)

    (a) Challenge   (b) Romance   (c) Morality   (d) Mystery

(2) The places such as Good Hope, the Horn, and the Norway Maelstrom refer to the off-shore parts of _____. (Locating the facts)

    (a) S. Africa, E. Africa, N. Europe   (c) S. Africa, S. America, N. Europe
    (b) S. Africa, Asia, N. Europe   (d) S. Africa, N. America, N. Europe

(3.1.) The italicized word, *spouts*, refers to _____. (3.1. - 3.2. Word & Phrase in context)

    (a) Drains   (b) Pours   (c) Boasts   (d) Evaporates

(3.2.) The italicized phrase, *perdition's flames*, refers to _____.

    (a) Glory in Paradise   (c) Happiness in Nirvana
    (b) Burning hell   (d) Realities in abyss

(4.1.) The symbolic figure of Moby Dick can be regarded as _____. (4.1. - 4.2. Making inferences)

    (a) Unlimited power/Omnipotence   (c) Mammoth animal
    (b) Evil monster   (d) Enemy of humans

(4.2.) The symbolic figure of Captain Ahab can be regarded as a/an _____.

    (a) Sick man   (c) Evil man
    (b) Ambitious challenger   (d) Well-prepared pioneer

(5) One of the following statements which can serve as the best theme of this fiction is _____. (Conclusion)

    (a) Slow and steady wins the race. (Aesop)
    (b) Fortune favors the brave.
    (c) In great attempts, it's glorious even to fail. (Cassius Longinces)
    (d) Better a good enemy than a bad friend. (Yiddish proverb)

선장인 에이허브는 승무원들에게 자기의 원수를 찾는데 경계를 늦추지 말라고 부추기며 가공할 적인 모비딕을 추적한다. 그 고래와의 마지막 싸움에서 항해사들, 배와 함께 에이허브 선장은 고래에게 죽음을 당한다. 비극적이면서 약간 영웅적이고 미친듯한 이 이야기는 방랑자라는 상징적인 이름의 살아 남은 젊은 선원, 이스마엘에 의하여 들려진다.

소설의 일부 발췌 : (에이허브는 승무원들에게 그 고래를 쫓으라고 용기를 준다.)

"나는 희망봉, 케이프 혼, 노르웨이의 마엘스트롬을 돌고 지옥의 불길을 돌아 그놈을 계속 추격할 것이오. 이것이 이 배에 승선한 여러분의 목적이오. 그 놈이 검은 피를 뿜고 지느러미를 뻗을 때까지 대륙의 양 끝에서, 지구의 구석

Melville particularly admired this 1834 French aquatint : "A nimble Sperm Whale," wrote Moby-Dick's author, "is depicted in full majesty of might."

구석에서, 백경을 추격하시오." 에이허브는 소리쳤다. (모비딕과의 싸움이 끝난 후 작은 보트에 탄 작살잡이들에게 그들의 배가 침몰하는 것이 보인다.)

이제 커다란 원들이 배 주위에 생겨나기 시작하더니 계속 더 빠른 속도로 움직이고 있다. 얼마 안되어 배의 나무 조각이나 배와 관련된 것은 어느 것도, 어느 곳에도, 수면 위에 남아 있지 않았다. 모든 것이 무너졌고 모든 것이 물 밑 깊숙이 가라 앉았다. 지금 오천년 전에 그랬던 것처럼 다시 빠른 속도로 휘도는 바다물에 덮인 채로.

> **Note**
> □ mate=ship's officer below the rank of captain : 선장 밑 고급 항해사
> □ gigantic=of immense size : 엄청 큰, 어마어마한
>   • He has a gigantic appetite and eats gigantic meals. (엄청난 식욕으로 엄청나게 먹는다.)
> □ tantalizing : 애를 닳게 하는, 조바심나게 하는, 속 마음을 털어 놓지 않는
> □ relentlessly : 무자비하게, 인정사정 없이 • He beat his students relentlessly. (학생들을 무자비하게 때렸다.)
> □ persistent=continuing in a habit or course of action in spite of opposition or warning :
>   집요한, 떨어지지 않는 • I'm weary of this persistent cold. (감기가 떨어지지 않아 질린다.)
> □ formidable=requiring great effort to deal with or overcome : 가공할, 무서운
> □ Good Hope=Cape of Good Hope : 아프리카 남단의 곶
> □ Horn=Cape Horn : 남미 남단의 갑
> □ fin=winglike part that a fish uses in swimming : 지느러미

Passage 3 : **The Good Earth (1931) by Pearl Sydenstricker Buck (1892 - 1973)**

Background : <u>The Good Earth</u> has been one of the most popular fictions of this century since its publication in 1931. The fiction won the Pulitzer Prize and the William Dean Howells Medal for fiction, serving as a major role in shaping Western attitude toward China.

Characters : Wang Lung, protagonist, a humble Chinese farmer.
O-lan, Wang Lung's wife.
Lotus and Pear Blossom, Wang Lung's concubines.
Wang Lung's three sons.

Plot : Wang Lung, a simple and poor Chinese farmer, after many years of hard work and by a fortune during his refuge in the South, becomes a wealthy landowner and enjoys his new socioeconomic power and prestige in his village. He regards this type of traditional sociocultural privilege above his family, even above his gods. But his happiness does not last long. A series of uncontrollable disasters such as flood, drought, pestilence, starvation affect him and his family, from which he learns an invaluable lesson. He comes to firmly believe that land is the source of all blessings and life supports. When the land is destroyed, a variety of disasters as previously mentioned will fall on us. Therefore, we cannot live without the support of the land; selling the land is like selling ourselves. Through the surviving tales of Wang Lung and his family, our understanding regarding the interdependency between men and the land, or the universal destiny of men to it is to be explored more intensively.

Excerpt from the story :

But one day he saw clearly for a little while. It was a day on which his two sons had come and after they had greeted him courteously··· Now Wang Lung followed them silently, and they stood··· and Wang Lung heard his second son say in his *mincing* voice.

"This field we will sell and this one, and we will divide the money between us evenly. Your share I'll borrow at good interest, for now with the railroad straight through I can ship rice to the sea and I ···" But the old man heard only these words, "sell the land," and he cried out and he could not keep his voice from breaking and trembling with his anger.

"Now, evil, idle sons! Sell the land?" He choked and would have fallen, and

지문 3 : 펄벅의 대지

배경 : 1931년 출판 이래 대지는 금세기에 가장 인기 있는 소설 중의 하나였다. 이 소설은 소설 부문의 플리처상과 W.D. Howells메달을 수상했고 중국에 대한 서양의 태도를 형성하는데 중요한 역할을 했다.

등장 인물 : 왕룽 - 주인공, 소박한 중국인 농부
오란 - 왕룽의 처
렌화와 리화 - 왕룽의 소실
왕룽의 세 아들

구성 : 단순하고 가난한 중국인 농부, 왕룽은 수년간 힘든 고생 후 남부에서 피난하던 중에 큰 재산을 얻어 부유한 지주가 되고 그의 마을에서 사회경제적인 힘과 위세를 누린다. 그는 이런 전통적인 사회문화의 특권을 자기 가족 보다, 심지어 자기가 믿는 신보다 더 귀중한 것으로 생각한다. 그러나 그의 행복은 오래 가지 못한다. 계속되는 어쩔 수 없는 재난, 예를 들면 홍수, 가뭄, 역병, 기아 등이 그의 가족에게 영향을 미친다. 그리고 그는 그것으로부터 귀한 교훈을 얻는다. 그는 땅이 모든 복과 생명

Pearl S. Buck

부지의 근원임을 확고하게 믿게 된다. 땅이 파괴될 때 앞에서 말한 여러가지 재난이 우리에게 닥친다. 그러므로 우리는 땅의 후원 없이는 살 수 없고 땅을 판다는 것은 우리 자신을 파는 것과 같다. 왕룽과 그의 일가가 살아가는 이야기를 통해서 인간과 땅 사이의 상호의존성과 인간의 모든 운명이 토지에 직결되어 있다는 것이 좀 더 집중적으로 탐구되어져야 할 것이다.

소설내용의 일부 발췌 :
그러나 어느날 그는 잠시 동안 머리가 (눈이) 명료해졌다. 그 날은 두 아들이 와서 그에게 공손히 인사하고… 왕룽은 그들 뒤를 말없이 따라갔다. 그들이 발걸음을 멈추었고… 왕룽은 둘째 아들이 으스대며 말하는 소리를 들었다.
"우리 이 밭과 저 밭을 팝시다. 그리고 그 돈을 우리 둘이 공평하게 나눕시다. 형 몫은

they caught him and held him up, and he began to weep. Then they *soothed* him and they said, soothing him, "No, no, we'll never sell the land." "It is the end of a family, when they begin to sell the land," he said brokenly. "<u>Out of land we came and into it we must go</u>, and if you will hold your land you can live, no one can rob you of land." And the old man let his scanty tears dry upon his cheek and they made salty stains there. And he stooped and took up a handful of the soil and he held it and he muttered, "If you sell the land, it is the end." And his two sons held him, one on either side, each holding his arm, and he held tight in his hand the warm loose earth… "Rest assured, our father, rest assured. The land is not to be sold." <u>But over the old man's head they looked at each other and smiled.</u>

(1) This fiction seems to depict human struggles for _____ based on the land as a socioeconomic unit. (Subject matter)

    (a) True love   (b) Adventure   (c) Survival   (d) Power

(2.1.) The italicized word, *mincing*, refers to _____. (2.1. - 2.2. Words in context)

    (a) Extroverted   (b) Unaffected   (c) Unpretentious   (d) Artificial

(2.2.) The antonym of the italicized word, *soothed,* is _____.

    (a) Agitated   (b) Alleviated   (c) Appeased   (d) Pacified

(3.1.) The underlined sentence, <u>"Out of land we came and into it we must go"</u> can be interpreted that the land is the basic source of _____. (3.1. - 3.2. Making inferences)

    (a) Income   (b) Life & death   (c) Prosperity   (d) Power

(3.2.) The underlined sentence, "<u>But over the old man's head they looked at each other and smiled</u>" can be inferred that Wang Lung's children _____.

    (a) Agreed with him   (c) Respected his point
    (b) Despised his point   (d) Had different ideas

(4) One of the following statements that can serve as the best theme of this fiction is _____. (Conclusion)

    (a) Earth has no sorrow that Heaven cannot heal.
    (b) Those who really thirst for knowledge always get it.
    (c) The way of this world is to praise dead saints and persecute the living ones.
    (d) He who forgets his own roots wanders.

내가 높은 이자로 빌리겠어요. 왜냐하면 철도가 똑바로 뚫려서 쌀을 바다로 수송하면 내가…" 그러나 노인의 귀에는 '땅을 판다' 는 말만 들렸다. 그는 소리를 질렀다. 그는 화가 나서 목소리가 갈라지고 떨리는 것을 어쩔 수가 없었다.

"아니, 이 못 된 게으른 자식들 같으니! 땅을 판다고?" 그는 숨이 막히고 넘어질 뻔했다. 아들들이 붙잡고 부축하여 일으켰다. 그는 울기 시작했다. 그들은 아버지를 달래며 말했다. "아닙니다, 아니예요. 절대 땅을 팔지 않겠습니다." "땅을 팔기 시작하면 그 집안은 끝나는 법이니라." 그는 또박또박 말했다. "사람은 땅에서 태어나 땅으로 돌아가는 게 운명이니라. 그러니 너희들이 살 수 있는 땅이 있다면, 어느 누구도 너희들에게서 삶의 터전을 빼앗아 갈 수 없다." 노인은 뺨에 묻은 눈물을 닦지 않아 그대로 말라 소금 얼룩이 되었다. 그는 허리를 굽혀 한 줌의 흙을 집어 올려든 채 중얼거렸다. "땅을 팔면 끝장이다." 두 아들이 그를 양 쪽에서 부축하고 그의 팔을 잡았다. 그 노인은 손 안에 부드럽고 따뜻한 그 흙을 꼭 쥐고 있었다. "안심하십시요, 아버지, 믿고 안심하세요. 땅을 팔지 않겠어요." 그러나 그들은 노인의 머리 위에서 서로 쳐다보며 미소를 지었다.

Note

- concubine=woman who lives with a man as if she were his wife, without being lawfully married to him. (in some countries, where polygamy is legal) lesser wife : 첩, 소실
- fortune=a large amount of money : 거금, 큰 재산
  - This car must have cost you a fortune. (이차에 거금을 지불했겠구나.)
- drought=a long period of dry weather : 가뭄 • The crops died during the drought.
- pestilence=a disease that causes death and spreads quickly to large number of people : 역병, 괴질
- invaluable=too valuable for the worth to be measured : 귀중한
- interdependency : 상호의존
- mince : 잘게 썰다, 조심스레 말하다 • Not mince matters (words) (까놓고 말하면)
- interest=money paid for the use of money : 이자 cf. principal : 원금
  - He lent me the money at 12% interest.
- choke=struggle to breathe, cause to stop breathing : 목이 막히다, 질식시키다
  - Water went down his throat and he started to choke.(물이 목구멍 (인후)으로 넘어가 목이 막히기 시작했다.)
- soothe=make less angry or anxious, comfort, calm : 위로하다, 달래다
  - Have a drink to soothe your nerves. (불안을 가라 앉히도록 한잔 하여라.)
- brokenly : 또박또박, 띄엄띄엄   □ stain : 얼룩, 오점
- stoop=bend the head and shoulders forwards and down : 허리를 구부리다, 머리 숙이다
- mutter=speak angry or complaining words in a low voice, not easily heard : 작은 소리로 투덜거리다 • He muttered a threat. (그가 남이 안듣게 작은 소리로 위협했다.)

4.1.3. Poetry

Poetry is a form of literature that formulates a concentrated imaginative awareness of experience in language chosen and arranged to create a specific emotional response through its meaning, sound, and rhythm. It is usually concerned with feelings of greater complexity and intensity. To sustain, emphasize, and shape these feelings, poets employ such resources as rhyme, meter, stanza forms, and lines of a limited length, thus creating distinction between prose and poetry. Prose is for the communication of specific information, whereas poetry is for the expression of emotions and ideas by exploring or rendering ordinary thoughts fresh and vivid through the imaginative use of language. Consequently, poetry can carry a further range of meaning than prose, because it as a form of verbal art capable of eliciting an emotional response from the reader, often suggests a value judgment.

Poetry can be classified into three major categories, (1) Lyric; (2) Narrative; and, (3) Dramatic. The Lyric poetry includes (a) Lyrics; (b) Ode; (c) Elegy; (d) Sonnet; and, (e) Haiku. The Lyrics are usually direct spontaneous expressions of strong personal emotion, and they are generally short and well unified. Today, lyric poetry stands for any short poem that has marked rhythms and musical effects, vigorous comparisons, and words that have been carefully chosen for their effectiveness. The Ode, which is a longer and more complex lyric on a particular theme, is a serious and elaborate lyric full of high praise and noble feeling. The Elegy is usually a poem of mourning in the form of a long and serious lyric. The Sonnet is a 14-line lyric with a certain pattern of rhyme and rhythm many of which are love poems. The Haiku, a Japanese form, is one of the shortest types of lyrics. The first line has 5 syllables, the second 7, and the third 5.

The Narrative poetry which tells stories includes (a) Epics, and (b) Ballads. The Epic is a long narrative poem composed in an elevated style dealing with the deeds of heroes in battle or conflicts between human beings and natural and divine forces. The theme of an Epic is usually the origin or destiny of a national or religious groups. A ballad is a story poem intended to be sung, which deals with a particular person (e.g. Robin Hood).

Dramatic poetry is often used as a medium for play. In this poetry, the poet lets one or more of the story's characters act out the story as shown by most of Shakespeare's plays.

4.1.3. 시

시는 의미, 음향, 운율을 통해 특별한 감정적 반응을 창조하기 위하여 언어를 배열, 선택함으로써 집약된 상상의 경험을 하게 하는 문학의 형태이다. 시는 훨씬 복합적이고 강한 감정과 관련되어 있다. 이러한 감정을 지속하고, 강조하고 구체화하기 위하여 운율, 보격, 절의 형식, 일정한 길이를 가진 행(시구) 같은 그런 수단을 동원하다. 그리하여 산문과 시의 차별을 만들어 낸다. 산문은 특정 정보를 전달하기 위하여 쓰이나 시는 언어의 창의적 사용을 통해서 평범한 생각들을 신선하고 생생하게 만들거나, 탐구함으로써 감정과 사상을 표현한다. 따라서 시는 산문보다 더 광범위한 의미를 전달한다. 왜냐하면 시는 독자로부터 감정적인 반응을 끌어낼 수 있는 언어 예술의 한 형태로써 하나의 가치 판단을 시사하기 때문이다.

시는 다음 세가지 주요한 범주로 분류될 수 있다. (1)서정시 (2)서사시 (3)극시. 서정시에는 (a)서정시(敍情詩) (b)송가(頌歌) (c)비가(悲歌) (d)소네트(14행시)와 (e)하이쿠(俳句)가 포함된다. 서정시는 보통 강력한 개인적인 느낌의 직접적이고 자연발생적 표현이며 대체로 길이가 짧고 통일 되어있다. 오늘날에는 서정시가 뚜렷한 리듬과 음악적 효과, 활발한 비유, 효과를 위하여 주의 깊게 선택된 어휘를 가진 모든 짧은 시를 대표한다. 송가는 어떤 주제에 대하여 좀 더 길고 보다 복잡한 서정시로서 진지하고 높은 찬미와 고귀한 감정이 가득한, 정교한 시다. 비가는 대개 길고 진지한 서정시의 형태로 애도의 시다. 소네트는 특정 양식의 음운과 운율을 가진 14행시이며 사랑의 시가 많다. 하이쿠는 일본시로서 서정시 중에서 가장 짧은 형태다. 제 1행은 5음절, 제 2행은 7음절, 제 3행은 5음절이다.

서사시는 이야기를 말하는 시로서 (a)서사시(敍事詩) (b)담시(譚詩)가 들어간다. 서사시는 격조높은 형태로 전투나 인간과 자연 및 신 사이에서 투쟁하는 영웅들의 행위로 구성되는 긴 시다. 서사시의 제목은 대개 국민적 혹은 종교적 집단의 기원이나 운명이다. 담시는 노래로 불리어지도록 의도된 이야기 시로 어떤 특정 인물을 다룬다(예: 로빈 훗).

극시는 연극을 위한 수단으로 자주 쓰여진다. 이 시에서 시인은 이야기 속의 등장 인물 중 하나 혹은 그 이상의 사람이 대부분의 세익스피어 희곡에서처럼 이야기를 실연하도록 한다.

Note

- formulate=express in a short clear form : 간단히 명쾌하게 표현하다
- concentrated=increased in strength by the removal of liquid : 농축된, 밀집된
- awareness=knowledge or understanding of a particular subject or situation : 각성, 깨달음, 자각, 인식
- be concerned with=be interested in, take part in : 관심이 있다, 관련되다
- rhyme=ending with the same sound of words or lines of poetry : 음운
  - 'House' rhymes with 'mouse'. (두 단어는 모음 / au / 로 운이 잡혀있다.)
- rhythm=regular, repeated pattern of sounds or movements in speech, music etc. : 운율, 리듬, 박자, 율동
- meter=arranged of notes into strong and weak beats : 보격, 격조
- stanza=a group of lines forming a division of a poem : 시의 연-보통 4행
- elicit=draw out, extract : 끌어내다
- mourn=show sorrow or regret : 애도하다
- ballad=simple song or poem that tells an old story : 속요, 민요, 담시
- divine=of, from or like God : 신의, 신성한, 신이 내려 준
  - divine rights of kings (왕의 신권)   • Divine Comedy (신곡)

Passage 1 : "I Wandered Lonely as a Cloud (1807)" by William Wordsworth (1770-1850)

        I wandered lonely as a cloud
        That floats on high o'er vales and hills,
        When all at once I saw a crowd
        A host, of golden daffodils;
(5)   Beside the lake, beneath the trees,
        Fluttering and dancing in the breeze.

        Continuous as the stars that shine
        And twinkle on the milky way,
        They stretched in never-ending line
(10)   Along the margin of a bay;
        Ten thousand saw I at a glance,
        Tossing their heads in sprightly dance.

        The waves beside them danced; but they
        Outdid the sparkling waves in glee;
(15)   A poet could not but gay,
        In such a *jocund* company;
        I gazed - and gazed - but little thought
        What wealth the show to me had brought.

        For oft, when on my couch I lie
(20)   In vacant or in pensive mood,
        They flash upon *that inward eye*
        Which's the bliss of solitude;
        And then my heart with pleasure fills,
        And dances with the daffodils.

(1) The highlighted point of this poem is the _____. (Subject matter)

   (a) Cloud   (b) Crowd   (c) Daffodil   (d) Star

(2.1) The synonym of the italicized word, *jocund* in line 16 is _____. (2.1 - 2.2. Word & Phrase in context)

   (a) Depressed   (b) Cheerful   (c) Reliable   (d) Sincere

(2.2) The italicized phrase, "*that inward eye*" refers to the writer's _____.

   (a) Insight   (b) Wisdom   (c) Memory   (d) Enlightenment

지문 1 : 윌리엄 워즈워스의 '나는 구름처럼 떠돌았네'

산과 골짜기 위로 높이 떠가는 구름처럼
나 혼자 쓸쓸히 떠돌아 다녔네,
그 때 문득 나는 보았네
한무리의 수많은 노란 수선화들을
호숫가 나무 밑으로
산들바람에 몸을 흔들며 춤추고 있었네.

밝게 반짝이는 은하수의 별들처럼,
끝 없는 줄을 이루어
연달아 뻗어 있었네
호수의 가장자리를 따라
한 눈에 만 송이나 보였네
머리를 흔들어 대며 즐겁게 춤추고 있는.

옆에 있는 물결들도 춤추었지만
기뻐서 반짝이는 그 파도가 꽃만은 못했네
시인이라면 기쁘지 않을 수 없겠지,
이렇게 즐거운 친구들과 함께 있으면
나는 보고 또 보았네 그러나 생각 못했네
이 장관이 얼마나 많은 보배를 가져다 주었는지.

자주 허전하고 구슬픈 마음으로
자리에 누워있을 때면,
고독의 축복인 마음의 눈에
그들이 빛나기 때문이라네.
그러면 내 마음은 기쁨이 넘치고
내 마음은 수선화와 함께 춤을 춘다네.

References

□ **시형** : 약강 4보격의 리듬
□ **운** : 행의 어미의 모음을 맞추는 여성운의 각운 : 8개의 모음(au, i, iː, ai, ei, u, uː, æ)으로 압운
□ **시의 이해** : 외형적 이해 : 리듬, 라임, 미터의 분석, 시형 등 외부적인 요소를 분석하고 이해한다.
　　　　　　　운율상 문법적 구문형식을 초월하는 경우가 허다하므로 입체적으로 전체를 조망하는 자세가 필요함.
□ **내용의 이해, 감상** : 담겨있는 사상과 미를 주체적인 명상을 통하여 꿰뚫어 보고, 느끼고 작가와의 공감대를
　　　　　　　　　　　이루도록 상상력을 발휘하여 음미한다.

(3.1) The symbolic implication of "the cloud" can be _____. (3.1 - 3.2. Making inferences)

    (a) Peace   (b) Vagabondage   (c) Tranquillity   (d) Attachment

(3.2) The symbolic meaning of "the daffodil" can be _____.

    (a) Settled/attached   (c) Vagrant/contented
    (b) Aimless/detached   (d) Vain/delusive

(4.1.) This poem can be classified as a/an _____. (4.1. - 4.2. Conclusions)

    (a) Lyric   (b) Elegy   (c) Ode   (d) Epic

(4.2.) One of the following statements that can serve as the best theme of the poem is _____.

    (a) Heaven is not reached at a single bound.
    (b) When a man grows angry, his reason rides out.
    (c) Amusement is the happiness of those who cannot think.
    (d) Home is where the heart is.

Passage 2 : Gitanjali (Song offerings) by Rabindranath Tagore (1861 - 1941)

Background : Gitanjali, like Song of Jayadeva used for religious purposes, was first published in 1913 as a collection of prose and poetic translations made by Tagore from the original Bengali poems. Gitanjali is a long poem consisting of 103 verses sung for the Hindu Gods. Rabindranath Tagore is a world-renowned poet, India's only Nobel laureate accepted in 1913, one of modern India's greatest poets and the composer of independent India's national anthem.

Verse XIV : My desires are many and my cry is pitiful,
            but ever didst thou save me by hard refusal;
            And this strong mercy has been wrought
            into my life through and through.

    (5) Day by day thou art making me worthy
        of *the simple, great gifts* that thou gavest
        To me unasked - this sky and the light,
        this body and the life and the mind -
        Saving me from *perils* of overmuch desire.

Note

- **vale**=a broad low valley : 넓고 낮은 골짜기
- **daffodil** : 수선화
- **flutter**=move the wings quickly and lightly without flying : 파닥거리다
  - I could hear a little bird fluttering caught on the spider's web.
    (작은 새가 거미줄에 걸려 파닥이는 소리가 들렸다.)
- **stretch**=spread out : 뻗치다, 뻗쳐 있다
- **stretching** : 기지개 켜기
  - The corn fields stretched out as far as we could see. (옥수수밭이 시선이 미치는 한 멀리 뻗어 있었다.)
- **toss**=throw, move about rapidly : 던지다, 퉁기다, 이리저리 움직이다
  - He tossed the keys to Ann.
  - Unable to sleep, he tossed and turned all night. (잠 못들고 밤새껏 전전반측(轉轉反側)했다.)
- **sprightly**=cheerfully, lively : 쾌활하게, 명랑하게
- **outdo**=do or be better than : …보다 잘하다, 능가하다
  - He outdid his wife in cooking. (아내보다 요리를 잘 했다.)
- **glee**=feeling of joyful satisfaction : 흡족한 기쁨
  - The child danced with glee when she heard the good news.
- **jocund**=merry, cheerful : 즐거운
- **pensive**=deeply thoughtful : 깊은 생각에 잠긴, 구슬픈
  - The woman in this painting has a pensive smile. (그림 속의 여인이 구슬픈 미소를 짓는다.)
- **flash**=shine for a moment : 순간 빛나다
- **inward**=on or towards the inside : 내면의
- **bliss**=complete happiness : 지복, 행복
  - Ignorance is a bliss. (무지는 축복이다.)

지문 2: 타고르의 '기탄잘리'

배경 : 기탄잘리(신에게 바치는 송가(頌歌))는, 종교적 목적에 쓰이는 Jayadeva의 노래처럼, 뱅골의 원주민 시를 타고르가 번역하고 산문들을 수집하여 1913년에 최초로 출판되었다. 기탄잘리는 힌두의 신들을 위하여 불리어지는 103절로 구성된 한 편의 장시이다. 타고르는 세계적으로 유명한 시인이며, 1913년에 노벨상을 수상한 인도에 하나 밖에 없는 영광의 시인이고, 인도의 가장 위대한 시인 중의 한 사람이고, 독립한 인도의 애국가를 지은 사람이다.

Rabindranath Tagore(1861~1941)
Nobel laureate for literature(1913)

(10) There are times when I languidly linger
and times when I awaken and hurry
In search of my *goal*; but cruelly thou hidest
thyself from before me.

Day by day thou art making me worthy
(15) of thy full acceptance by refusing me
Ever and anon, saving me *from perils*
of weak, uncertain desire.

(1.1.) The highlighted point of this poem is _____. (1.1. - 1.2. Main idea)

    (a) Desire   (b) Refusal   (c) Acceptance   (d) Cry

(1.2.) For whom are these song offerings? They are for _____.

    (a) India   (b) Bangladesh   (c) God   (d) Bengali people

(2.1.) The antonym of the italicized word, *perils*, in line 9 is _____. (2.1. - 2.4. Word, phrase in context)

    (a) Danger   (b) Safety   (c) Risk   (d) Destruction

(2.2.) The italicized word, "In search of my *goal*" in line 12 implies my _____.

    (a) Objective   (b) Inspiration   (c) Desire   (d) Life style

(2.3.) The italicized phrase, "*the simple, great gifts*" in line 6 refers to _____.

    (a) Desire, mercy, passion   (c) Body, mind, light
    (b) Sky, light, life   (d) Goal, body, mind

(2.4.) The italicized phrase, "*from perils of weak, and uncertain desire*" in lines 16-17 can be interpreted "from my _____ desire."

    (a) Worthless   (b) Dangerous   (c) Timid   (d) Vigorous

(3.1.) This poem, Gitanjali, consisting of 103 verses, can be classified as a narrative _____. (3.1. - 3.2. Conclusions)

    (a) Lyric   (b) Ballad   (c) Epic   (d) Sonnet

(3.2.) One of the following statements that can serve as the best theme of this verse in Gitanjali is _____.

    (a) Our desires always increase with our possessions.
    (b) The gifts God gives to us are the best; it is His will; it is ours.
    (c) He who is firm and resolute in will molds the world himself. (Goethe)
    (d) He who does not appreciate the gifts from God tortures himself with worthless desires.

14절 : 나의 욕심은 많고 내 외침은 가련하지만,
당신께선 완강하게 거절하시어 나를 구하셨습니다.
그리하여 이 강력한 자비하심이
내 삶 속에 깊이 새겨졌나이다.

날마다 당신께선 나로 하여금
내가 요구하지 않았어도 나에게 주시는
간단하지만 위대한 선물-하늘과 빛, 몸과 생명과 마음-
이것들을 받을 자격이 있는 자로 만드시고
과욕의 위험에서 저를 구하십니다.

때로는 나른하여 흐느적거리고
때로는 정신차려 내 목표를 서둘러 찾지만
당신은 잔인하게
저에게서 모습을 감추십니다.

날마다 당신은 제 부탁을 거절하시어
당신께서 저를 완전히 받아드릴 수 있는 자로 만드십니다.
때때로 부질 없고 불확실한 욕망의 위험으로부터
저를 구하여 주시나이다.

Note

- **thou** : 고대 영어 및 시에서 2인칭 단수 주격
- **thee** : 목적격 　　　　　**thine** : 소유격 　• cf. ye (복수 주격, 목적격)
- **-st** : (고대 영어) thou를 받는 동사의 현재, 과거의 어미에 쓰임
- **world-renowned**=world - famous
- **laureate** : 월계관; 영국 왕실에서 위대한 시인에게 내리는 계관 시인, 명예로운 사람.(인도가 영국령이었기에 타고르도 laureate칭호가 따라다님)
- **wrought** : (work의 과거분사)공들여 만들어진, 노력으로 이룩한
- **overmuch**=too much
- **languid**=lacking strength or will, slow and weak : 나른한, 노곤한
  • After the exams I felt languid body and mind. (시험 후 심신이 녹초가 되었다.)
- **linger**=wait for a time instead of going, delay going : 머뭇거리다, 꾸물거리다

Passage 3 : Haiku

Background : Haiku is a traditional Japanese poetry form of 17 syllables, divided into three lines of 5 - 7 - 5 syllables each. Associated with Zen Buddhism, the haiku reflects fleeting images of the impermanence of life amidst the magnitude of nature. The haiku experience is made from three elements: where (place), what (object), and when (time), which are bound in and with emotion to create an entity as a unified whole. The haiku poets use very concise words and phrases while concentrating deep spiritual understanding into the poems. They often take up the changes of nature which have impressed them in order to express the intangible world of mind, while striving for the absolute that may not be easily attainable.

Spring
In the rains of spring (5 syllables, place)
An umbrella and raincoat (7 syllables, object)
Pass by, conversing. (5 syllables, time)
By Yosa Buson

Summer
In the cicada's cry
There is no sign that can foretell
How soon it must die.
By Basho

Autumn
In the twilight gloom
Of the redwood and the pine
Some wisterias bloom.
By Shihota

Winter
See the river flow
In a long unbroken line
On the field of snow.
By Boncho

(1) The highlighted time(s) of these short poems is/are _____. (Topic)

    (a) Death of cicada   (c) Blooming of wisteria
    (b) Changes of nature   (d) "Pass by" of umbrella & raincoat

(2.1.) The symbolic object of the spring season used in this poem is _____. (2.1. - 2.2. Locating the facts)

    (a) Cicada (b) Umbrella & raincoat (c) Wisteria (d) Broken line of river flow

(2.2.) The symbolic object of summer is _____.

    (a) Wisteria   (b) Rain   (c) Redwood & pine   (d) Cicada

지문 3: 하이쿠(俳句)

배경: 하이쿠는 일본의 전통 시로서 17음절로 구성되어 있고 각각 5-7-5음절로 된 3행 시로 나뉘어져 있다. 선종과 관련되어 있기에 하이쿠는 거대한 자연 속에서 잠깐 지나가는 인생의 일시성을 반영한다. 하이쿠의 (의식된) 체험은 세 가지 요소에서 오는데 장소, 대상, 시간이며 이것들은 하나의 통일된 전체로서의 실체를 창조하려는 정서와 연관된다. 하이쿠 시인들은 매우 간결한 단어나 어구를 사용하여 심오한 정신적 오성을 시 속에 압축시킨다. 그들은 자주 미묘한 마음의 세계를 표현하기 위하여 그들에게 감명을 주었던 자연의 변화들을 이용한다. 한편으로 도저히 달성할 수 없는 절대적인 것을 얻으려고 노력한다.

봄

봄비 속에 (장소)
우산과 비옷이 (대상)
지나간다, 소근 거리며. (시간)

여름

매미 울음 속에는
그가 곧 죽어야 한다는
아무런 낌새도 없구려.

가을

어스름 황혼의
삼나무 소나무 그늘에
몇몇 등나무가 꽃을 피우네.

겨울

눈 덮인 벌판에서
끊기지 않고 긴 선으로
강이 흐르는 걸 보시오.

(3.1.) The poet, Yosa Buson, uses "Umbrella and raincoat related to the spring rains." The spring rains can be inferred as a symbolic meaning of _____.
(3.1. - 3.4. Making inferences)

    (a) Growth   (b) Maturity   (c) Dynamic events   (d) Silence

(3.2.) The poet, Basho, uses "Cicada's cry" for the symbolic implication of summer. The life span of the cicada is estimated to be 17 days. The life and death of the cicada as symbolic meanings can be inferred as _____.

    (a) Growth   (b) Silence   (c) Dynamic events   (d) Power of nature

(3.3.) The poet, Shihota, uses "Blooming of wisteria" as a symbolic meaning of autumn. The blooming of wisteria can be inferred as an inevitable _____.

    (a) Transition   (b) Silence   (c) Growth   (d) Dynamic event

(3.4.) The poet, Boncho, uses "The river flow…" for winter. The symbolic implication of "The river flow…" can be inferred as _____.

    (a) Dynamic event   (b) Power of nature   (c) Growth   (d) Maturity

(4) One of the followings that can serve as the best theme of these poems is _____. (Conclusion)

    (a) The changes of nature are the art of the Absolute.
    (b) Old foxes want no tutors.
    (c) I wept when I was born, and every day shows why.
    (d) I love to lose myself in other men's minds.(Charles Lamb, 1775 - 1834)

Extra Passage : Diamond Poem

To those who are interested in reading or writing poems, the author introduces the Diamond Poem as an introductory attempt to be written in English. The Diamond Poem is very interesting and easy for you to construct. The poem builds and diminishes the number of words and phrases in each line forming the shape of a diamond.

    1st line : 1 word, usually Noun
    2nd line : 2 words, can be Adjective or Participles
    3rd line : 3 words, can be Prepositional phrase(s)
    4th line : 4 words, can be Predicative phrase(s)
    5th line : 5 words, a complete simple sentence
    6th line : 4 words, can be Predicative phrase(s)
    7th line : 3 words, can be Prepositional phrase(s)
    8th line : 2 words, can be Adjective or Participles
    9th line : 1 word, Repeat the first line.

Note

- **Zen Buddhism**=form of Buddhism asserting that enlightenment comes from meditation and intuition with less dependence upon the scripture : (불교)선종:경전이나 설법보다 개인의 참선과 직관으로 깨달음을 얻는다는 불교의 한 종파
- **fleeting**=passing quickly : 덧없는　　• Life is fleeting. (인생은 일장 춘몽)
- **impermanence** : 비영속성, 일시성
- **be bound with**=be connected with, depend on : 연결되어 있는, 묶여있는
  • Our welfare is directly bound with that of the country. (우리의 행복은 국가의 그것과 직접 관련되어 있다.)
- **entity**=something that has separate and independent existence : 독립된 실체
- **intangible**=which can't be touched or grasped : 만져서 알 수 없는, 무형의
- **strive for**=struggle for, make great efforts : 얻으려고 노력, 투쟁하다
- **absolute** : 절대적인　　□ **cicada** : 매미　　□ **wisteria** : 등나무
- **converse**=talk informally : 대화하다
- **reflect**=think carefully : 깊이 생각하다, 반성적으로 사고하다

특별 지문: 다이아몬드 시

시를 읽고 짓는 일에 관심이 있는 분들께 영어로 씌여지는 다이아몬드형 시를 소개한다. 이 시는 짓기에 용이하고 재미 있다. 이 시는 각 행의 단어와 어구를 불리고 줄여서 다이아몬드 형을 이룬다.

제 1행 : 1 단어, 대개 명사

제 2행 : 2 단어, 형용사나 분사

제 3행 : 3 단어, 전치사구

제 4행 : 4 단어, 술어

제 5행 : 5 단어, 완전한 단문

제 6행 : 4 단어, 술어

제 7행 : 3 단어, 전치사구

제 8행 : 2단어, 형용사나 분사

제 9행 : 1단어, 제 1행의 반복

The poem is used as an exercise in the use of words and phrases to create images and feelings of people, things, and ideas. The following poems constructed by the author's 11th grade students in 1985, are provided below.

<table>
<tr><td>

Snow
Crystalline ice
On the ground
Falling from the sky
The snow blankets the earth
Making the ground white
Upon the trees
Frozen light
Snow

Deborah Gibson (201)

</td><td>

Rainbow
Infinite beauty
From the heavens
Appearing after a rain
Rainbows are spectrums of color
Higher than mountain ranges
Across the sky
Radiant light
Rainbow

Andrea Singleton (202)

</td></tr>
<tr><td>

Friendship
Nice, trusting
Always being there
Helping me in need
My best friend loves me
And I love him
Needing each other
Caring, sharing
Friendshi

Yolanda Smith (201)

</td><td>

Space
Unknown mysteries
Universal and unlimited
Man's last frontier beyond
Children dream of its wonders
Wonder throughout the year
Planets are born
God's home
Space

Andrea Singleton (202)

</td></tr>
</table>

Good News for the readers who have composed good poems! Please send your poems for "New Poetry Contest" now.

New Poetry Contest — $48,000.00 in Prizes
The National Library of Poetry to award 250 total prizes to amateur poets in coming months

Owings Mills, Maryland — The National Library of Poetry has just announced that $48,000.00 in prizes will be awarded over the next 12 months in the brand new North American Open Amateur Poetry Contest. The contest is open to everyone and entry is free.

"We're especially looking for poems from new or unpublished poets," indicated Howard Ely, spokesperson for The National Library of Poetry. "We have a ten year history of awarding large prizes to talented poets who have never before won any type of writing competition."

Possible Publication
Many submitted poems will also be considered for inclusion in one of The National Library of Poetry's forthcoming hardbound anthologies. Previous anthologies published by the organization have included *On the Threshold of a Dream*, *Days of Future's Past*, *Of Diamonds and Rust*, and *Moments More to Go*, among others.

"Our anthologies routinely sell out because they are truly enjoyable reading, and they are also a sought-after sourcebook for poetic talent," added Mr. Ely.

How To Enter
Anyone may enter the competition simply by sending in ONLY ONE original poem, any subject, any style, to:

The National Library of Poetry
Suite 6963
1 Poetry Plaza
Owings Mills, MD 21117-6282

Or enter online at www.poetry.com

The poem should be no more than 20 lines, and the poet's name and address must appear on the top of the page. "All poets who enter will receive a response concerning their artistry, usually within seven weeks," indicated Mr. Ely.

이 시는 어떤 이미지, 사람들의 감정, 사물들, 사상 등을 창조하는 단어나 어구의 사용을 연습하는 데 쓰인다. 저자의 학교 11학년 학생들이 1985년에 지은 다음 시들을 소개한다.

눈
얼음의 결정
온 대지 위에
하늘에서 내리는
그 눈이 대지를 덮는다
마당을 하얗게 만들고
나무들 위에도
차가운 빛
눈

무지개
무한한 미
하늘로 부터
비 뒤에 나타나는
무지개는 색의 스펙트럼
산맥 보다 더 높이
하늘을 가로질러
환하게 빛나는
무지개

우정
상냥하고 믿어주는
언제나 거기 존재하여
어려울 때의 나를 도와주는
내 가장 좋은 친구는 나를 좋아한다.
그리고 나도 그를 사랑한다
서로를 필요로 하며
돌봐주고, 함께하는
우정

우주
미지의 신비
우주 전체의 끝이 없는
저 너머 인간의 최후 변경
어린이들이 그 신비를 꿈꾼다
일년 내내 불가사의
혹성들이 태어나고
하느님의 집
우주

Note

- **diminish**=become smaller, lessen : 줄어들다, 삭감하다
  - His illness diminished his strength. (그는 앓고 나서 기력이 떨어졌다.)
- **crystalline** : 수정같은, 결정체의
- **blanket** : 담요(로 덮다) • The valley was covered with a blanket of snow.

4-2 DISCOURSE ANALYSIS

Language contains a variety of meanings; one of them is literal meaning, and the other is underlying meaning. Let us see the following speech samples.

Literal

1. <u>Let's have lunch</u> at Lotte Hotel at 1:00 today.
2. <u>Thank you very much</u> for the coffee.
3. Look at that <u>gorgeous dress</u> hanging on the rack.

Underlying

<u>Let's have lunch</u> together sometimes.

Let's not discuss it any more.
<u>Thank you</u>.

Your <u>dress is very gorgeous</u> today.

As we know, there are differences in meaning between the literal and the underlying statements. The speech sample 1 in the Underlying Meaning Category, "Let's have lunch together sometimes," can refer to "politeness, greeting, or just social linguistic gesture." It does not necessarily mean that "We have to have lunch together." The speech sample 2 in the same category, "Thank you" can serve as a "topic termination, confirmation, cooperation, or request." The speech sample 3 in the same category, "Your dress is very gorgeous today" simply serves as a compliment. These types of underlying social meaning often create a lot of confusion, embarrassment, or understanding difficulty for non-native speakers of English who are not familiar with the sociocultural contexts of the English speaking societies.

To investigate the underlying social meanings attached to the linguistic utterances, a "micro-approach" is to be used for this publication. This approach examines the linguistic utterances and accompanying nonlinguistic ones collected from actual conversation. Once data are obtained, they are transcribed with utmost care and every utterance (e.g. "uh"), overlapping, unusual stress, sigh, laugh, and pause is accurately shown in the transcript. It is because each may have a special underlying meaning or function in accomplishing the speaker's practical goals.

"Macro-approach" is used to seek the coherency of discourse pattern as a whole. This approach is designed to find out "global coherence" which helps us to see the characteristic of a sequence of coherence pattern such as (a) initiation, (b) response, (c) feedback, (d) issue-event structure, taken as a unit or whole.

4-2 담화 분석

언어는 다양한 의미를 내포하고 있다. 그 중 하나는 문자 그대로의 의미고 다른 하나는 함축적 의미. 다음 담화 표본을 살펴 보자.

1. 오늘 한 시에 롯데 호텔에서 <u>점심을 먹읍시다.</u>   <u>때때로 점심이나 함께 합시다.</u>
2. 커피를 사주셔서 <u>감사합니다.</u>   더 이상 그 이야기 하지 맙시다. <u>감사합니다.</u>
3. 저 옷걸이에 걸려있는 <u>멋진 드레스를 보세요.</u>   당신의 드레스가 <u>아주 멋지네요.</u>

우리가 아는대로 문자 그대로의 진술과 함축적인 진술 사이에는 커다란 차이가 있다. 함축적 의미 범주 〈표본 1〉의 '때때로 함께 점심이나 합시다.' 는 '예절, 인사, 단지 사회언어적 표현'을 가리킬 수 있다. 그게 반드시 '함께 점심을 해야한다.' 를 의미하지는 않는다. 같은 범주의 〈표본 2〉 '감사합니다.' 는 '주제 종결, 확인, 협조, 혹은 청탁' 의미의 구실을 할 수 있다.

〈표본 3〉의 '드레스가 아주 멋져요.' 가 단순히 찬사로 쓰일 수 있다. 이런 형태의 사회적으로 함축된 의미가 영어를 사용하는 사회의 사회문화적 환경에 익숙하지 않은 비영어권의 사람들에게는 자주 많은 혼동, 당황, 이해의 곤란을 일으킨다.

언어 표현과 관련한 사회적으로 함축된 의미를 조사하기 위하여 이 책에서는 '미시적-접근' 법을 사용할 것이다. 이 접근법은 실제 대화로부터 수집된 언어 표현과 거기 수반하는 비언어적 표현들을 조사한다. 일단 자료들이 얻어지면 최대한 주의하여 옮겨쓰고 모든 표현 (예를 들어 '으음' 까지), 겹치는 말, 특이한 강세, 한숨소리, 웃음소리, 말의 잠시 멈춤 등이 정밀하게 그 옮겨쓴 것에 표시 된다. 그 이유는 그 각각이 말하는 사람의 실질적인 목적을 달성하는 데 어떤 특별하게 함축적인 의미나 기능을 가지고 있을 수 있기 때문이다.

(주) : '거시적 접근' 은 전체적으로 담화유형의 응집성을 찾는데 쓰인다. 이 접근 방법은 전체적 응집성을 찾아내기 위하여 마련된 것으로 우리가 한 단어나 전체로 취급하는 (a)발단, (b)응답, (c)확인, (d)사건 / (e)현안 구성 같은 일련의 응집성 유형의 특징을 알아내는데 도움이 된다.

Note

- □ discourse=speech, lecture, conversation : 담화, 대화, 강의
- □ analysis : 분석 • opp. synthesis (종합)
- □ underlie : be or lie under, not explicitly seen : 밑에 존재하다, 깔리다
  • Did you catch the underlying meaning of his praise? (그가 칭찬하는 속 뜻을 알아차렸니?)
- □ gorgeous=richly coloured, magnificent : 화려한, 멋진
  • That's gorgeous (terrific, wonderful, great)! (그것 멋지다.)
- □ termination=ending : 끝내기 • termination of pregnance (임신 중절, 낙태)
- □ confirmation=something that shows other things to be ture : 확인, 다짐
- □ compliment=expression of admiration, approval, praise : 찬사
- □ utterance=something said, spoken word or words : 입밖에 낸 말, 발화
- □ transcribe=copy in writing : 옮겨쓰다 • transcribe shorthand notes (속기를 보통글자로 쓰다)

4.2.1. Sociolinguistic Implications

Symbols : ( ) = interruption or cannot be transcribed
[ ] = overlapping. (0.5) = half second. Capitalized letters = strong vocal emphasis

Speech Sample.

1. **Setting** = Time: Around 4:00 p.m. Place: In a building.
   Situation : Two friends, John and Dave, happened to meet by chance.

2. **Participants** = John, mid-20s, CKU employee.
   Dave, mid-20s, an office clerk

3. **Purpose** = (1) Small talk, (2) Face-saving proposal & acceptance

01 J : Dave!
02 D : Hey, John! How are ya?
03 J : Not too bad and yourself?
04 D : Oh, I'm doing really great. Long time, no see.
05 J : Yeah, it's been awhile, hasn't it?
06 D : Yeah, I guess so. Um (0.2), hey, are you still working for, um (0.1), CKU?
07 J : Yeah, yeah (in a low voice).
08 D : Hey, did you see anything of Gary?
09 J : No. I haven't seen him in, oh, two years probably.
10 D : Well, it's been almost that long for me, but I've heard, like, that he lost almost all his hair now.
11 J : (Chuckles)
12 D : Too much, eh? (Chuckling)
13 J : That poor guy, I don't know.
14 D : So (0.4), hey, we should go out sometimes.
15 J : Yeah, we should. We should get together for a beer. Maybe, go see a game or something.
16 D : Yeah.
17 J : Um (0.2). What are you driving?
18 D : Oh, I got my Audi.
19 J : Oh, great. Um (0.2), gee, you know, I don't even have my keys. (Searches through pockets) I got. I, uh (0.4). You give me a call.
20 D : I will.
21 J : Or drop in.
22 D : Will do.
23 J : OKAY?
24 D : [Okay] (Very shortly in a low voice).
25 J : Well, see ya later. (John starts to walk away)
26 D : Yeah, see ya later.

4.2.1. 사회언어학적 함축

기호 : ( ) = 말의 중단, 글로 기록할 수 없는 것
　　　　[ ] = 대화가 겹치는 부분　　　(0.5) = 1/2초　　　대문자 = 힘찬 목소리

대화 표본
1. 배　경 : 시간 : 오후 4시 무렵　장소: 어느 건물 안
　　　　　상황 : 두 친구, 존과 데이브, 우연히 만났다.
2. 참가자 : 존. 20대 중반 CKU직원　데이브, 20대 중반, 사무직원
3. 목　적 : (1) 잡담 (2) 체면치레의 제안과 수락

01. 존 : 데이브!
02. 데 : 안녕, 존! 어떻게 지내니?
03. 존 : 그저 그래. 너는?
04. 데 : 아, 아주 잘 지내. 오랜만이구나!
05. 존 : 그래, 꽤 오래 되었지?
06. 데 : 그래, 내 생각에도 그렇구나. 음, 그런데 아직도 CKU에 근무하니?
07. 존 : (힘없는 목소리로) 그렇지 뭐.
08. 데 : 그런데, 게리 좀 만나니?
09. 존 : 아니, 아마, 아-2년 간은 못 만났어.
10. 데 : 글쎄 나에게도 그렇게 오래된 것 같네.
　　　　그러나 그가 지금 머리가 거의 다 빠졌다는 그런 비슷한 말을 들었네.
11. 존 : (쿡쿡 웃는다.)
12. 데 : 너무했지, 그렇잖아? (쿡쿡거리며)
13. 존 : 가엾은 친구군, 모르겠다.
14. 데 : 그래서, 여보게, 우리 때로 외출하세.
15. 존 : 그래, 그래야 되겠어. 만나서 맥주도하고.
　　　　어쩌면 시합 같은 것 구경도 좋겠지.
16. 데 : 좋지.

(1) What is the conversation about? (Subject matter)

    (a) Gary lost his hair   (c) Seeing a game or something
    (b) Getting together for a beer   (d) Small talk

(2.1.) "So, hey, we should go out sometimes" in line 14 can be inferred as a _____ proposal. (2.1. - 2.7. Making inferences)

    (a) Face-saving   (b) Sincere   (c) Serious   (d) Cordial

(2.2.) "Yeah, we should" in line 15 can be interpreted as a _____ acceptance.

    (a) Sincere   (b) Face-saving   (c) Serious   (d) Reluctant

(2.3.) "Oh, great" in line 19 can imply a/an _____.

    (a) Agreement   (b) Compliment   (c) Encouragement   (d) Positive feedback

(2.4.) "Um (0.2), gee, you know" in line 19 can be regarded as a linguistic utterance for topic _____.

    (a) Change   (b) Termination   (c) Confirmation   (d) Feedback

(2.5.) "OKAY?" in line 23 is used as a _____.

    (a) Compliment   (b) Confirmation   (c) Agreement   (d) Response

(2.6.) " Okay " in line 24 can be inferred as a/an _____ agreement.

    (a) Positive   (b) Face-saving   (c) Sincere   (d) Serious

(2.7.) "Well, see ya later" in line 25 can imply a topic _____.

    (a) Termination   (b) Opening   (c) Change   (d) Confirmation

4.2.2. Negotiation

Speech Sample

1. **Setting** = Time : Around 5:00 p.m.
                Place : At a car dealership.
                Situation : B attempts to know the price of a car he wants while negotiating.

2. **Participants** = A (male, mid-30s), car salesman
                      B (male, mid-40s), teacher

3. **Purpose** = Proposing vs. avoiding in negotiation.

    01 A : Good afternoon! I'm John O'Brien. Call me John.
    02   : What can I do for you today, sir?

17. 존 : 음, 자넨 무슨 차를 모는가?

18. 데 : 에, 아우디를 샀네.

19. 존 : 야, 대단하구나. 음, 제길헐, 난 내 열쇠도 없는 걸. (호주머니를 뒤져 열쇠를 찾는다) 여기 있구나. 나는, 에. 전화해라.

20. 데 : 그러지.

21. 존 : 들르게나.

22. 데 : 그럴께.

23. 존 : 알았지?

24. 데 : [좋아.] (작은 소리로 퉁명스럽게)

25. 존 : 그럼, 다음에 또 만나자. (걸어서 떠나기 시작한다.)

26. 데 : 그래, 다음에 만나자.

> **Note**
> □ overlap=partly cover by extending beyond one edge : 일부 겹치다
>   • Tiles are laid overlapping each other. (기와는 서로 겹쳐 놓여진다.)
> □ by chance=by accident=not by design, not on purpose : 우연히
>   • If by any chance I should fall into poverty, I won't be servile.
>   (혹시 내가 가난해 지더라도 나는 비굴하지 않겠다.)
> □ save one's face=evade shaming oneself, avoid losing one's dignity, : 체면을 세우다
>   • The move was just a face - saving, not a serious one. (그 조치는 단지 체면용이지 진심이 아니다.)
> □ small talk=talk about everyday and unimportant=chitchat : 잡담, 세상 사는 이야기
> □ Long time, no see= It's a long time since we saw last time. : 오랜만이다.
> □ chuckle=low, quiet laugh with closed mouth, indicating satisfaction or amusement :
>   (흐뭇하여) 낄낄 웃다, 쿡쿡 웃다
>   • He was chuckling to himself over what he was reading. (읽고 있는 것에 혼자 쿡쿡 웃고 있었다.)

4.2.2. 협상

대화 표본 : 1. 배 경 - 시간 : 오후 5시 무렵, 장소 : 자동차 판매소

장면 : B는 협상을 하면서 자기가 원하는 차의 가격을 알려고 한다.

2. 참가자 - A(남, 30대 중반) - 자동차 판매원

03 B : John. I'd like to know something about this sedan.
04 A : This is a very popular model. (0.4) What are you
05   : looking for in a car?
06 B : I want something that I can enjoy driving, while having
07   : enough room for my FAMILY.
08 A : (Nodding his head in agreement) Yes! THIS is a very
09   : good car for your family. But (0.3), the BLUE ONE over
10   : there has the same amount of room with a better feel for
11   : the road. An⋯
12 B :   [THE] BLUE one looks like the same car.
13   : What's the DIFFERENCE, Mr. O'Brien?
14 A : The blue model has a bigger engine with a tighter
15   : suspension that really lets you feel the car's
16   : handling. Another nice thing about the car is that
17   : it has more leg room.
18 B : (Looking at the sticker price of the blue car (0.8))
19   : (In a very low voice) I don't think the gas mileage is
20   : as good as I would like it to be.
21 A :   [This car] gets on average 9
22   : miles per gallon, and it comes with a 3 year or 36,000
23   : mile warranty. WHY don't you come over to my desk and
24   : we can talk about it?
25 B :   [I think] the price is a little more
26   : than I was looking to spend.
27 A: Well, give me a chance to see what I can do for you.
28 : Let's go to my desk and let you drive that car home
29 : TONIGHT.
30 B: [I'm] very interested in the car, but before I
31 : buy anything, I have to talk it over with my wife.
32 A: DON'T you WANT to know exactly what kind of DEAL I can
33 : come up with for you, sir?
34 B: (In a low voice) Thanks for your help today, John. I'll
35 : contact you soon.

(1) What is the conversation about? (Subject matter)

    (a) Car price   (c) Choice of car to be transacted
    (b) Features of the car   (d) The blue car is better than first choice

(2.1.) "Yes!" in line 8 is a/an _____. (2.1. - 2.6. Making inferences)

    (a) Agreement   (b) Compliment   (c) Avoidance   (d) Greeting

(2.2.) "But (0.3), the BLUE ONE over there has the same amount of room⋯
      An⋯" in lines 9 - 11 can be inferred as a/an _____.

B(남, 40대 중반) - 선생

3. 목 적 - 협상에서 제안하기와 거절하기

01. A: 안녕하십니까! 존 오브라이언입니다. 존이라 합니다. 무슨 일로 오셨습니까, 선생님?

03. B: 존. 이 세단에 대하여 알고 싶은데.
04. A: 이 형이 아주 인기인데요. 차 내부에 무엇을 원하십니까?

06. B: 운전 중에 즐길 수 있는 무언가를 원하며 또한 우리 식구들이 탈 충분한 공간이 있으면 합니다.

08. A: (좋다고 고개를 끄덕이며) 알았습니다. 이 차야 말로 선생님 가족에 맞춤입니다. 그러나 저기 파란 모델은 보다 좋은 승차감을 가진 같은 공간의 크기를 가진 차입니다. 그리고…

12. B: 저 파란 차도 같은 차 같은데요. 어떻게 다르지요?

14. A: 그 파란 모델은 더 튼튼한 차대 받이 장치를 가지고 있어 정말로 차를 조종하는 느낌이 나게 합니다. 또 하나 좋은 점은 다리 뻗을 공간이 더 넓습니다.

18. B:(파란 차의 가격 스티커를 보면서) (아주 작은 소리로) 총 마일수가 내가 바라는 것보다 많군요.

21. A:이 차는 갤론당 평균 9마일을 달립니다. 그리고 연 3,600마일의 보증이 붙어 출시됩니다. 제 책상으로 오셔서 말씀하시지요.

25. B: 내 생각에는 내가 지불하려고 예상했던 것보다 가격이 좀 비싸군요.

27. A: 제가 도와드릴 수 없나 알아볼 기회를 좀 주십시요. 제 책상으로 가시면 오늘 밤에 댁까지 저 차를 운전하고 가시게 해드리겠습니다.

30. B: 저 차에 관심이 가지만 나는 무엇이든 사기 전에 아내와 상의를 해야합니다.

32. A: 제가 선생님을 위해서 어떤 거래 조건을 제시하는지 정확하게 알고 싶지 않으십니까?

34. B: (작은 소리로) 존씨, 오늘 도와주셔서 고맙소. 곧 연락 드리지요.

(a) Compliment (b) Command (c) Agreement (d) Recommendation

(2.3.) "What's the DIFFERENCE, Mr. O'Brien?" in line 13 seems to have been used as a/an _____ question.

(a) Sincere (b) Protesting (c) Curious (d) Interrogative

(2.4.) "I don't think the gas mileage…" in lines 19 - 20 can imply a/an _____.

(a) Complaint (b) Disagreement (c) Protest (d) Refusal

(2.5.) "WHY don't you come over…?" in lines 23 - 24 can be interpreted as a strong _____.

(a) Avoidance (b) Complaint (c) Proposal (d) Feedback

(2.6.) "I am very interested in the car, but before I buy anything…" in lines 30 - 31 can be a/an _____.

(a) Refusal (b) Negotiation (c) Confirmation (d) Avoidance

(3) The negotiation between the customer and the salesman has failed. It is largely due to the fact that the customer began to distrust the salesman. From which line do you conclude that the customer begins to distrust him? From line _____. (Conclusion)

(a) "But, the BLUE…" in line 09   (c) "THE BLUE…" in line 12
(b) "What's the difference?" in line 13   (d) "I don't think…" in line 19

4.2.3. Interpersonal Relationship

Speech Sample

1. **Setting** = Time : Around 1:00 p.m.
   Place : In a classroom.
   Situation : B, an English teacher, was asking one of her foreign students regarding the class retreat to Fellowship Farm.

2. **Participants** = B, a female teacher, mid-40s.
   P, a female student, 17 years old.

3. **Purpose** = Clarification vs. assertion

   01 B : ( ) We're planning a trip to Fellowship Farm.
   02   : And we wanted you to go with us. What HAPPened?
   03 P : No, I don't know. (In a very low voice)
   04 B : Did you ask your, your, your mother, your father if you could go?

> **Note**
> ☐ negotiate=discuss, confer in order to come to an agreement : 협상하다, 교섭하다
>   • We've decided to negotiate with my employers about our wage claims.
>   (임금 요구에 대하여 회사측과 협상키로 결정했다.)
> ☐ nod=bow slightly as a sign of agreement or as a familiar greeting : 고개를 끄덕이다
>   • Homer sometimes nods. (호머도 때로는 고개를 끄덕인다. (실수를 자인한다.) =원숭이도 나무에서 떨어진다.)

4.2.3. 개인간의 대화

대화 표본 : **1. 배 경** - 시간 : 오후 1시 무렵,   장소 : 교실
                장면 : 영어 교사인 B가 자기반 외국인 학생에게 학급 휴양지인
                       협동농장에 관하여 참가를 요청하고 있다.
   2. 참가자 - B : 40대 중반의 여교사   P : 17세의 여학생
   3. 목 적 - 설명 VS. 주장

01. B: 우리 반이 협동 농장에 갈 계획이다. 우린 네가 함께 가기를 바랬는데 무슨 일이 있었니?

03. P: 아니요. 없어요. (아주 작은 소리로)

04. B: 혹시 가도 좋으냐고 어머니나 아버지께 여쭈어 보았니?

05. P: 예, 어머니는요, 어머니께 물어 보았는데요, 안된데요.

06. B: 허락할 수 없다고, 너는 자고 오면 안되니?

07. P: 예.

08. B: 만일 당일치기로 주간에만 갈 계획을 하면 갈 수 있을까? 자고 오지 말고

10. P: [안돼요.] (아주 작은 소리로)

11. B: 당일치기라도 갈 수 없을 거라고?

12. P: [못가요.] 왜냐하면요, 아시겠지만 캄보디아에서 처녀는 집에서 멀리 못나가요.

```
05 P : Yeah. My mother say, I asked her about, she say "No."
06 B : She can't, You can't stay overnight?
07 P : Yeah.
08 B : If we plan a trip during the daytime, for just the day, would you
09    : be able to go, and not stay overnight?
10 P :                          [No] (In a very low voice)
11 B : Wouldn't be able to go for just the day.
12 P :                    [CAN'T go]
13    : Because (0.3), you know, (0.5) in Cambodia, the girl may be going
14    : away from the house.
15 B : Oh, I see.
16 P :         [Then, that's] why my mother don't let me go.
17 B : I see. Uh-huh (0.4).
18    : O.K. What do you do when you're home?
```

(1) The topic of the conversation is about _____. (Subject matter)

    (a) Trip   (b) Overnight stay   (c) Fellowship Farm   (d) Mother's permission

(2.1.) "( ) We're planning a trip to Fellowship Farm" in line 1, can be interpreted as a/an _____. (2.1. - 2.7. Making inferences)

    (a) Channel opening   (b) Feedback   (c) Response   (d) Confirmation

(2.2.) "And we wanted you… What HAPPened?" in line 2, can be inferred as a/an _____.

    (a) Initiation   (b) Request   (c) Clarification   (d) Assertion

(2.3.) "No, I don't know" in line 3, can imply a/an _____.

    (a) Counter-attack   (b) Justification   (c) Avoidance   (d) Topic termination

(2.4.) The overlapping [No] in line 10, can imply a mild _____.

    (a) Acceptance   (b) Disinterest   (c) Consideration   (d) Rejection

(2.5.) The overlapping [CAN'T go] in line 12, can imply a strong _____.

    (a) Negotiation   (b) Assertion   (c) Request   (d) Response

(2.6.) The "Uh-huh" in line 17, can imply a/an _____.

    (a) Request   (b) Agreement   (c) Assertion   (d) Consideration

(2.7.) The "O.K." in line 18, seems to have been used as a/an _____.

    (a) Agreement   (b) Topic change   (c) Negotiation   (d) Positive response

15. B: 아, 알겠다.

16. P: [그래서, 그것이] 어머니가 못가게 하는 이유입니다.

17. B: 알겠다. 아, 음. 집에 있을 땐 무얼 하니?

Note
- retreat=a place into whice one can go for peace and safety : 피난처, 은신처, 심신을 쉬는 곳
  - summer retreat (피서지)   • mountain retreat (산장)
- interpersonal=between persons : 대인간의
- clarification : 확실히 밝히기
  - Your explanation has clarified the difficult sentence. (설명이 어려운 문장을 확실하게 밝혀주었다.)
- assert=state or declare forcefully : 단언하다, 주장하다   • Truth asserts itself. 사필귀정(事必歸正)
  - He asserted that he was not guilty of the embezzlement of the fund.
    (그는 그 기금을 유용하지 않았다고 강력 주장했다.)
- vs(=versus) = (in law and sport) against : 상대로
- overnight=for, during the night : 밤새워
  - We discussed the issue overnight. (그 현안을 밤새워 토론했다.)
- channel opening : 대화 개시   □ topic termination : 주제 종결

4-3 PUBLIC SPEECH

Public speech is a form of speech for public purposes in public situations. Unlike conversation, it needs a variety of specific features such as (1) the time limitation of presentation; (2) choice of language (slang, jargon, grammatical mistakes have little place in public speech); and, (3) different method of delivery.

Public speech includes (1) Informative; (2) Persuasive; and, (3) Speeches for special occasions (e.g. Speeches of information, presentation, acceptance, apology, eulogy, commemoration, entertainment, and after-dinner). The Informative Speech is to inform specific topic to the audience based on certain categories such as (a) Objects (e.g. whales, Taj Mahal, the Great Wall), (b) Processes (e.g. How perfume is made. What makes an airplane fly? How to stop smoking?), (c) Events (e.g. assassination of John F. Kennedy, San Francisco earthquake, the fall of Saigon in 1975); and, (d) Concepts (e.g. theories, ideas, beliefs). For example, when a professor lectures theories of evolution in a classroom, or a business manager explains next year's budget, it is a type of Informative speech. But remember that there are few speeches which exclusively include information or persuasion only. Every good speech is a merger of information and persuasion; it is just a matter of degree.

The Persuasive Speech is to influence the audience by modifying their beliefs, values, and attitudes. Beliefs refer to judgments about what is true or probable (e.g. belief system in religion); value are abstract judgments about such matters as what is desirable, moral, important, or beautiful; attitudes refer to judgments about how to act. To modify the audience's beliefs, values, and attitudes, an effective speaker employs a variety of methods for persuasion such as (1) building credibility; (2) using evidence; (3) reasoning; and, (4) motivational appeals. (Note: Please refer to the sub-section, 2.11.3.2.5, Persuasion.)

Building credibility refers to professional knowledge, experience, and skills of a specific person (e.g. a medical doctor has credibility for health problems, so does a lawyer for legal problems). Using evidence refers to supporting materials (i.e. examples, statistics, testimony) used to prove or disprove some generalizations or statements. Reasoning is the process of drawing a conclusion

4-3 대중연설

대중연설은 공적인 상황에서 공적인 목적으로 하는 연설의 한 형태다. 대화와는 달라서 다음과 같이 다양한 구체적인 특색을 가진다 : (1)설명 시간 제한 (2)언어 선택 (속어, 특수 용어, 문법적인 잘못은 대중연설에서는 용납되지 않는다) (3)다른 전달 방법.

대중연설에는 (1)정보 제공적인 것, (2)설득을 위한 것 (3)특별한 경우를 위한 연설 (정보, 제시, 수락, 사과, 찬사, 기념, 여흥, 만찬 후 연설 등)이 있다. 정보 전달 연설은 다음과 같은 부류를 토대로 특별한 주제를 알리기 위한 것이다. (a) 사물 (예 : 고래, 타지 마할, 만리장성 등) (b) 과정 (예 : 향수 제조법, 비행기는 어떻게 나는가? 금연법) (c) 사건 (예 : 케네디의 암살, 샌프란시스코의 지진, 1975년 사이공의 함락) 그리고 (d) 개념 (예 : 학설, 사상, 신앙). 예를 들어 어느 교수가 강의실에서 진화론을 강의할 때나 기업체 과장이 다음해의 예산을 설명할 때 그것은 정보 제공적 연설이다. 그렇지만 오직 정보만, 설득만을 포함하는 연설은 별로 없다는 사실을 기억하라. 모든 훌륭한 연설은 정보나 권유가 함께 들어 있다. 단지 정도의 문제일 뿐이다.

설득형 연설은 청중들이 가지고 있는 신념, 가치관, 태도를 수정해서 그들에게 영향을 끼치는 것이다. 신앙이란 진실한 것, 있을 수 있는 것(종교에서의 신앙체계)에 대한 판단을 가리킨다. 가치관은 바람직한 것, 도덕적인 것, 중요한 것, 아름다운 것 같은 문제에 관한 추상적 판단이다. 태도란 행동하는 법에 대한 판단을 가리킨다. 청중들이 가지고 있는 신앙, 가치관, 태도를 수정하기 위해서 말하는 사람은 설득을 위한 여러가지 방법, 즉 (1) 신뢰성 쌓기 (2) 증거를 사용하기 (3) 추론하기 (4) 동기 유발적 요소 등을 사용한다.

신뢰성 구축은 특수한 사람의 전문적인 지식, 경험, 기술과 관련된다. (예 : 건강 문제는 의사, 법률 문제는 변호사). 증거 사용이란 어떤 일반화된 사실이나 발표 내용을 증명하거나 반증하는데 쓰여지는 보충자료를 가리킨다. (예 : 보기, 통계, 증명). 추론이란 증거에 입각한 결론 도출을 가리킨다. 때로 우리는 바르게 추리한다. (모든 인간은 죽는다. 소크라테스는 인간이다. 그러므로 소크라테스도 죽는다.) 그리고 때로 잘못 추론한다. (예 : 건물의 4층에 사는 사람들은 운이 나쁘다. 김씨와 그 가족은 4층에 살았다. 그러므로 그들은 불행을 당했다.) 대중연설에서 추론은 삶의 다른 측면에서 추론을 연장하는 것이다. 그러므로 말하는 사람은 자기의 추론이 첫째 건실한가를 확인해야 하고 청중으로 하여금 자기와 동의하도록 노력해야한다. 동기를 끌어내기 위한 호소는 듣는 이로 하여금 슬퍼하고, 분노하고, 죄의식을

based on evidence. Sometimes we reason well (e.g. All men are mortal. Socrates is a man. Therefore, Socrates is mortal), and other times we reason poorly (e.g. People who live on the fourth floor of a building usually face misfortunes. Mr. Kim and his family lived on the fourth floor. Therefore, they met a misfortune). Reasoning in public speech is an extension of reasoning in other aspects of life. Therefore, the speaker must make sure that his/her reasoning is sound first; and, he/she must try to get the audience to agree with the speaker. Motivational appeals are intended to make listeners feel sad, angry, guilty, afraid, happy, proud, sympathetic, or nostalgic. People feel fearful when they are informed of nuclear war; they feel compassionate for the starving children; they feel proud in one's country; and they feel angry at the actions of political terrorists.

This section, public speech, includes (1) Informative; (2) Persuasive; and, (3) Speech of special occasion: Apology. Each sub-section contains one speech sample, abridged or unabridged, for the purpose of understanding basic elements of public speech.

4.3.1. Informative Speech

Passage 1 : Topic, "Black History" by Rufus L. Billips

Background : Rufus Billips, Major General in the U.S. Air Force, delivered this speech at a Black History Week Banquet at Chatnute Air Force Base, Illinois, on February 10, 1979. The speech is introduced here to study an informative speech, since it serves as a role model in terms of speech organization, and the quality of information related to "Black Heritage," merging information and persuasion together.

Abridged Speech :

<u>I am delighted to be here, and I am grateful for your invitation</u> to meet and talk with each of you about Black Americans····. Our National theme is "Black History, Torch for the Future." This popular observance, which has become a feature of American life, was the design and plan of Dr. Carter G. Woodson, a native of New Canton, Virginia, who is revered as the "Father of Black History" in America. In 1915, he founded the Association for the Afro-American Life and History. Later, in 1926, he launched the celebration of Black History Week. Dr. Woodson wanted more than anything for Black persons to appreciate their heritage. He wanted them to know about Black contributions to the development of America. He wanted <u>all Americans</u> to appreciate the Blacks of our great nation····.

느끼고, 두려워하고, 행복해하고, 긍지를 느끼고, 동정하며, 혹 향수를 느끼게 하려고 의도하는 것이다. 핵전쟁 이야기를 듣고 두려워 하고 굶주리는 어린이들을 불쌍히 여기며, 자기 나라를 자랑스럽게 여기고 정치 테러범들에게 분노를 느낀다.

이 절 대중연설에는 다음이 포함된다. (1) 정보 전달형 연설 (2) 설득형 연설 (3) 특수한 경우의 연설 : 사과. 각 하부절은 요약이든, 전문이든 대중 연설의 기본 요소를 이해할 목적으로 하나의 대화 표본을 갖는다.

> **Note**
> ☐ slang=words, phrases commonly used in talk but not suitable for good writing, or formal occasions : 속어, 은어,   • 'Cop' is a slang for policeman.
> ☐ jargon=language difficult to understand because it's a bad form or spoken badly, language full of technical or special words : 뜻을 알 수 없는 말, 특수 분야의 전문 용어
>   • Only mother can undersatand her baby's jargon.
> ☐ apology=statement of regret for doing wrong, being impolite, hurting one's feelings : 사과
>   • Please accept my apology for not being able to keep the appointment. (약속을 못 지킨데 대하여 사과하네.)
> ☐ eulogy=speech or writing full of high praise : 찬사
> ☐ compassionate : 동정심이 많은
> ☐ commemoration : 기념, 축하   • A stone mounment was erected in commemoration of his merits. (그의 공을 기념하기 위하여 비석을 건립했다.)
> ☐ assassinate=kill, esp. an important person violently treacherously for political reasons : 암살하다
> ☐ merger=combining of estates, business companies : 합병
> ☐ M&A=Merger and Acquisition : 인수합병
> ☐ modify=change something slightly : 수정하다
>   • Since the IMF, the whole structure has been modified.
> ☐ abstract : 추상적인   • opp. concrete   ☐ abridge=make shorter : 요약, 단축하다   • opp. lengthen

4.3.1. 정보 전달형 연설

지문 1 :

주제 : "흑인의 역사"

배경 : 미 공군 소장인 Rufus Billips는 1979년 2월 10일 일리노이주 Chatnute 공군 기지에서 있었던 흑인역사 주간 기념연회에서 다음과 같은 연설을 했다. 그 연설을 여기 소개하는 것은 정보전달형 연설을 공부하기 위해서다. 왜냐하면 이 연설이 정보와 설득을 섞어가는 '흑인 유산' 과 관련된 연설구조와 정보의 질이라는 관점에서 역할 모델이 될 수 있기 때문이다.

Our great Blacks, past and present, have a history that truly is fascinating and phenomenal. Out of the mists of time has come evidence that the Blacks were prevalent in all of old world culture, and sailed the Indian Ocean from Africa to Japan. From prehistoric to medieval times, and even later, Black Africans left their mark in India and Melanesia. Nor was the Black race a stranger to Europe. Their blood flowed in the veins of Frenchmen; in King Alexander de Medici of Italy; in professor John Latino of Spain; in Saint Benedict the Moor of Italy; and in painters, sculptors, and authors like Alexander Dumas; and in composers like Samuel Coleridge-Taylor of England···.

African contributions to the Americas from Canada to Argentina have been relatively recent though some go back beyond 400 years. In the light of these realities, we must view Black people as a powerful influence in world exploration and settlement. On our own American soil, the first recorded instances of Black settlement in the 1500s were connected with early Spanish explorers, the travels of D'Allyon and DeSoto, and in the old world settlement that became Alabama, and in the deep south···. For the next 200 years, Blacks in America displayed remarkable talents. From the signing of American Independence to the Bicentennial celebration in 1976, and forward, American Black men and women explored, invented, and contributed immensely to the growth and development of this great land of ours···. Later, the "Golden Voice of Abolition," and one of the greatest spokesmen for the Black people in the 1800s, was Frederick A. Douglass. Then came Harriet Tubman, "The Black Moses of her Race." ···.Within a span of some 116 years, an impressive 327 Black American inventors gained patents for their original ideas···. The list goes on and on, and is truly fascinating.

America is a nation of some 25 million Blacks, the third largest number of Blacks within a nation anywhere in the world. We are also the most highly developed Black people in the world with approximately 7,500 physicians, some 2,700 dentists, over 4,000 attorneys, and thousands of public school teachers. We are an academic, learned, scholarly people, today, in 1979, and we are a family-loving, nation-loving race, a happy people. Black Americans are the 9th wealthiest race in the noncommunist world. In the early 1970s, for example, Blacks earned $51.8 billion dollars, spent some $46 billion, and generated more than $900 million in advertising and public relations. These figures are growing each year, and could be staggering by the 1980s.

···I say to you, hold your head high, be proud and confident of your future, try to attain higher educational goals, and make use of your opportunities on behalf of yourselves, your forefathers, and those who will follow you in times to come. And, I say to you, above all, have <u>pride in your heritage, pride in your country, pride in yourself, and pride in your United States Air Force</u>. Thank you.

(Source: Adapted from <u>Vital Speeches of the Day 45</u>. (Sept. 15, 1979)

요약된 연설 :

　이곳에 오게되어 기쁩니다. 여러분들을 만나서 흑인 미국인에 대하여 여러분들과 서로 대화할 수 있도록 초대해 주셔서 감사합니다. 우리의 국가적 주제는 '흑인 역사, 미래의 횃불' 입니다. 미국 생활의 특징이 되어버린 이 대중적 행사는 버지니아주 뉴 캔턴의 토착민이신 카터 우드선 박사의 의도와 계획이었습니다. 그분은 미국에서 '흑인 역사의 아버지'로 존경받고 계십니다. 1915년에 흑인의 생활과 역사를 위한 협회를 설립하셨습니다. 그 후 1926년에 '흑인역사 주간'의 기념행사를 시작하셨습니다. 우드선 박사께서는 그 어느 것보다도 흑인들이 그들의 유산을 가치있게 생각하기를 원했습니다. 그 분께서는 흑인들이 미국의 발전에 끼친 공로를 알기를 원했습니다. 그분은 모든 미국인들이 우리 위대한 나라의 흑인들의 가치를 깨닫기 원했습니다.

　우리의 위대한 흑인들은 예나 지금이나 진정 매력적이고 경이로운 역사를 지니고 있습니다. 희미한 먼 과거로부터 흑인들이 고대 세계문명 속에 널리 퍼져 있었고 인도양을 건너 일본까지 항해한 증거가 있습니다. 선사시대부터 중세까지, 그리고 훨씬 후까지 아프리카계 흑인들은 인도와 멜라네시아에 자취를 남겼습니다. 유럽에도 흑인종이 안 살았던 건 아닙니다. 흑인들의 피가 프랑스인의 혈관에도 흐르며, 이탈리아 알렉산더 드 메디치 왕의 혈관에도, 스페인 존 라띠노 교수의 혈관에도, 이탈리아의 무어인 성 베네딕트에게도, 그리고 화가, 조각가, 알렉산더 뒤마같은 작가, 영국의 사뮤엘 컬러리지 테일러 같은 작곡가의 혈관에도 흐르고 있습니다.

　아메리카에 끼친 공로는 카나다에서 아르헨티나에 이르기까지 비록 더러는 400년 전 이상이기도 하지만 비교적 근대의 일입니다. 이런 현실에 비추어 볼 때 흑인들을 세계의 개척과 정착에 강력한 영향력을 가진 존재로 간주해야 합니다. 우리 자신의 땅인 미국에 최초로 기록된 1500년대 흑인 정착의 경우는 초기 스페인의 개척민들, D'Allyon과 DeSoto의 여행, 구세계 정착지인 알라바마 및 남부 깊은 곳 등과 관련을 갖습니다. 그 다음 200년 간 아메리카의 흑인들은 놀라운 재능을 발휘하였습니다. 미국 독립의 조인으로부터 1976년의 200주년 기념식까지, 그리고 다음에도 미국 흑인 남녀들은 우리의 위대한 나라를 성장 발전시키는데 탐험하고, 발명하며, 지대하게 공헌하였습니다. '노예 폐지에 대한 황금 목소리'는 1800년대 흑인의 위대한 대변자인 프레드릭 더글러스였습니다. 그 후 '흑인의 모세' 해리엇 터브만이 나타났지요. 약 116년의 세월 동안 327명의 당당한 흑인 발명가들이 독창적인 아이디어로 특허를 얻었습니다. 그 수는 계속 증가하고 있으며 놀랄만 합니다.

　미국은 약 2천 5백만의 흑인으로 구성되어 있고 이는 전 세계 단일 국가 내의 흑인 숫

(1.1) The first paragraph serves as a/an _____ and _____ of the speech. (1.1 - 1.5. Organizational patterns)

    (a) Introduction & credibility
    (b) Introduction & reinforcement
    (c) Introduction & attention getting
    (d) Introduction & purpose

(1.2) The second paragraph introduces a brief history of the Blacks from the _____ to _____ eras of the world.

    (a) Ancient, medieval
    (b) Medieval, modern
    (c) Modern, present
    (d) Prehistoric, medieval

(1.3) The third paragraph illustrated the past contributions of the Blacks in _____ and _____ Americas.

    (a) North, Central   (b) North, South   (c) Central, South   (d) Canadian, Argentine

(1.4) The fourth paragraph briefly exemplifies facts about the Blacks in _____.

    (a) Canada   (b) North America   (c) U.S.A.   (d) The World

(1.5) The final paragraph concludes the speech by restating the speaker's major _____ and attempts to _____ the audience to act on what the speaker has said.

    (a) Premises, motivate
    (b) Examples, motivate
    (c) Thesis, motivate
    (d) Supporting details, impose

(2.1) The fact that the speaker is a Major General and black can create considerable _____ of the topic to the audience. (2.1 - 2.5. Rhetorical techniques)

    (a) Credibility   (b) Evidence   (c) Reasoning   (d) Motivational appeal

(2.2) The underlined sentences, "I am delighted…" and "I am grateful…" in the first paragraph, are used for _____.

    (a) Building credibility
    (b) Getting attention
    (c) Building common ground
    (d) Expressing gratitude

(2.3) The underlined phrase, "…all Americans…" in the first paragraph, stresses the _____ of the audience.

    (a) Creativity   (b) Uniqueness   (c) Solidarity   (d) Value system

(2.4) The underlined structure "…pride in your heritage, pride in your country, pride in yourself, and pride in your U.S. Air Force," in the final paragraph, unifies a sequence of ideas by stating the main idea more than once, and helps create a strong emotional effect. This type of structure can be called _____.

    (a) Antithesis   (b) Parallelism   (c) Inversion   (d) Repetition

(2.5) The speech illustrates the contributions of the Blacks based on a _____ pattern.

    (a) Spatial   (b) Chronological   (c) Problem - solution   (d) Topical

자로는 세번째입니다. 우리는 세계에서 가장 고도로 발달된 국민으로 대략 7,500명의 의사, 2,700명의 치과의사, 4,000명의 변호사, 수천명의 공립학교 교사를 가지고 있습니다. 우리는 1979년 현재 학구적이며, 박식하고, 학문을 즐기며, 가족을 사랑하고 국민을 사랑하는 행복한 국민입니다. 미국 흑인은 비공산국가들 중에서 9번째로 부유합니다. 예를 들어 1970년대에 흑인들은 518억 달러를 벌었고 460억 달러를 소비하였으며 광고나 홍보에서 9억 달러를 생산했지요. 이들 숫자는 매년 상승하고 있으며 1980년대에는 깜짝 놀랄 숫자가 될 것입니다.

저는 여러분들에게 말씀드립니다. 고개를 높이 들고, 긍지를 가지고, 미래에 대하여 자신감을 가지고, 보다 높은 교육 목표를 달성하도록 노력하며, 자신과 선조들과 미래에 태어날 후손들의 이익을 위하여 기회를 이용하십시오. 또한 무엇보다도 여러분의 유산, 여러분의 나라, 여러분 자신, 그리고 여러분의 미공군을 자랑스럽게 생각하십시오. 감사합니다.

Note

- observance=act performed as part of a ceremony, or as a sign of respect or worship : 관습, 행사
- revere=have respect for, regard as sacred, venerate : 존경하다
  - She revered her father all her life.
- heritage=something passed down over many years within a family or nation : 유산
  - Much of country's cultural heritage was destroyed during the foreign invasions. (외침 때 많은 문화 유산이 파괴되었다.)
- prevalent=existing commonly, generally or widely in some place : 널리 퍼진, 유행하는
  - Eye diseases are prevalent in some tropical countries. (열대 지방의 몇몇 국가에서 눈병이 창궐하고 있다.)
- medieval=of the period in European history between about A.D. 1100 and A.D. 1500, Middle Ages : 중세의
- bicentennial=the day or year exactly 200years after a particular event : 200년 째의
  - They celebrated the bicentennial of the opening of the diplomatic relations.
- immensely=very much   □ patent : 특허(권, 증)
- abolition (of slavery)=bringing to an end : 철폐
- span : 기간   • the span of life (수명)   • eye-span (한번에 읽는 길이)
- staggering=shocking deeply : 깜짝 놀랄만한
- in behalf of=in the interest of : …의 이익을 위하여
  - cf. on behalf of acting for someone : (대신하여)

4.3.2. Persuasive Speech

Passage 1 : Topic, "Mussolini Applies the Torch of Civilization to Ethiopia," delivered by Mussolini on October 2, 1935.

Background : Mussolini (1883-1945) was born in Dovia in northeastern Italy. He founded Fascism in 1919, and the Black Shirts who had supported him staged a march in Rome in 1922, forcing King Victor Emanuel III to appoint Mussolini Prime Minister. Mussolini ruled Italy for almost 21 years with torture, murder, exile as essential instruments of maintaining his dictatorial regime. The Italian people grew more dubious of the blessings of Fascism. Under such circumstances, a large-scale diversion of attention is always the dictator's solution: a war with a country of hostility. The fact that Ethiopia had defeated Italy in 1896 served a good excuse for revenge, building a colonial empire for Italy, and implantation of so-called "Western civilization" to Ethiopia. Mussolini delivered the following persuasive speech from his customary balcony in Rome on the day that Italian planes began to drop bombs on Ethiopia.

Unabridged Speech :

　　Black shirts of the Revolution! Men and women of all Italy! Italians all over the world -beyond the mountains, beyond the seas! Listen!
　　A solemn hour is about to strike in the history of the country. Twenty million Italians are at this moment gathered in the squares of all Italy. It is the greatest demonstration that human history records. Twenty millions!

05　One heart alone! One will alone! One decision! This manifestation signifies that the tie between Italy and Fascism is perfect, absolute, unalterable. Only brains softened by puerile illusions, by sheer ignorance, can think differently because they do not hear what exactly is the Fascist Italy of 1935.

10　For many months, the wheels of destiny under the impulse of our calm determination move toward the goal. In these last hours the rhythm has increased and nothing can stop it now. It is not only an army marching toward its goal, but it is 44,000,000 Italians marching in unity behind this army because the blackest of injustices is being attempted against them, that of taking from them their place in the sun.

15　When in 1915, Italy threw in her fate with that of the Allies, how many cries of admiration, how many promises! But after the common victory, which cost Italy 600,000 dead, 400,000 lost, one million wounded, when peace was being discussed around the table, only the crumbs of rich colonial booty were left for us to pick up. For thirteen years we have been patient while the circle tightened

4.3.2. 설득형 연설

지문 1 :

제목 : '무솔리니는 문명의 횃불을 이디오피아에 적용시키다' -1935년 10월 2일 무솔리니가 행한 연설.

배경 : 무솔리니는 이탈리아 북부 도비아에서 출생했다. 그는 1919년에 파시즘을 일으켰고 그를 지지했던 블랙셔츠 단원들이 1922년에 로마 진군을 감행하여 빅토르 임마뉴엘 3세 왕에게 무솔리니를 수상에 임명하도록 강요했다. 무솔리니는 그의 독재 정권을 유지하기 위한 기본적인 수단인 고문과 추방으로 거의 21년간 이탈리아를 통치했다. 이탈리아 국민들은 파시즘이 내건 축복을 의심하기 시작했다. 그런 상황 하에서는 대규모로 국민의 관심을 딴데로 돌리는 것 — 적대 국가와의 전쟁같은 것 — 이 항상 그 독재자의 해결 방법이었다. 1896년에 이디오피아가 이탈리아를 격파시켰던 사실은 이디오피아에게 복수하고 그 나라를 이탈리아의 식민지로 만들고 소위 서양문명을 이디오피아에 심는다는 좋은 구실로 작용하였다. 무솔리니는 이탈리아 비행기들이 이디오피아에 폭격을 개시하는 날 로마에서 그가 으레 사용하던 발코니에서 다음과 같은 설득을 위한 연설을 했다.

Hitler och Mussolini

Benito Mussolini used dramatic poses. Clenched fist, jutting jaw, and theatrical actions were all part of this fiery speeches. He gained the support of millions of Italians.

연설 전문 :

혁명의 블랙셔츠 단원 여러분! 전국에 계시는 남녀 여러분! 그리고 산과 바다를 건너 전세계에 계시는 이탈리아인들이여, 제 말을 들어주십시오!

우리 나라의 역사상 엄숙한 시간이 닥치고 있습니다. 지금 이 순간에 2천만 이탈리아인들이 전국의 모든 광장에 집결해 있습니다. 이는 기록된 역사상 가장 위대한 궐기입니다. 2천만이 한 마음, 한 의지, 하나의 결정으로 궐기하였습니다. 이 의지 표명은 이탈리아와 파시즘의 결합은 완전하고 절대적이며 바꿀수 없는 것임을 의미하는 것입니다. 철부지같은 환상과 완전 무지에 의하여 나약해진 인간들만이 생각을 달리할 것입니다. 왜냐하면 그들은 1935년의 파시즘 이탈리아가 정확하게 무엇을 의미하는지 들은 바가 없기 때문입니다.

수개월간 운명의 수레바퀴는 우리의 침착한 결정에서 이룬 추진력으로 목표를 향하여

around us at the hands of those who wish to suffocate us. We have been patient
20   with Ethiopia for forty years - it is enough now. Instead of recognizing the rights of Italy, the League of Nations dares to talk of sanctions. But until there is proof to the contrary, I refuse to believe that the authentic people of France will join in supporting sanctions against Italy.

25   The six thousand dead at the action of Boligny - whose devotion was so heroic that the enemy commander was forced to admire them - those fallen would now turn in their graves. And until there is proof to the contrary, I refuse to believe that the authentic people of Britain will want to spill blood and send Europe to its catastrophe for the sake of a
30   barbarian country unworthy of ranking among civilized nations.

Just the same, we cannot afford to overlook the possible developments of tomorrow. To economic sanctions we shall answer with our discipline, our spirit of sacrifice, our obedience. To military sanctions we shall answer with militarism. To acts of war, we shall answer with acts of war.

35   A people worthy of their past and their name cannot and never will take a different stand. Let me repeat, in the most categorical manner, the sacred pledge I make at this moment before all the Italians gathered together today, that I should do everything in my power to prevent a colonial conflict from taking on the aspect and weight of a European war. This conflict may be attractive to certain minds which hope to avenge their disintegrated
40   temples through this new catastrophe. Never, as at this historical hour, have the people of Italy revealed such force of character, and it is against this people, to which mankind owes its greatest conquest, this people of heroes, of poets, of saints, of navigators, of colonizers, that the world dares threaten sanctions.

Italy! Italy! Entirely and universally <u>Fascist! The Italy of the Black Shirt Revolution</u>, rise to your feet, let the cry of your determination rise to the
45   skies and reach our soldiers in East Africa. <u>Let it be a comfort to those who are about to fight</u>. <u>Let it be an encouragement to our friends and a warning to our enemies</u>. It is the cry of Italy, which goes beyond the mountains and the seas out into the great big world. It is the cry of justice and victory.

(Source: "Mussolini Applies the Torch of Civilization to Ethiopia," In <u>A Treasury of the World's Great Speeches</u>, (1954)).

(1) The lines 1 and 2, "Black shirts of the Revolution!⋯" can be considered as a/an _____. (1 - 10. Rhetorical techniques)

   (a) Attention getting   (b) Case building   (c) Using evidence   (d) Reasoning

(2) The lines from 3 to 6, "A solemn hour is about to strike⋯" are used as a/an _____.

   (a) Exigency   (b) Reasoning   (c) Building credibility   (d) Using evidence

움직이고 있습니다. 이 최후의 시간에 그 고동은 더욱 강력해져서 이제는 어느 것도 멈추게 할 수 없습니다. 그 힘은 단지 목표를 향하여 진군하고 있는 군대뿐 아니라 군의 배후에서 단결하여 전진하고 있는 4,400만명의 이탈리아인들입니다. 왜냐하면 가장 사악한 불의가 그들을 해치려고, 그들을 양지에서 몰아내려고 음모를 꾸미고 있기 때문입니다.

1915년에 이탈리아가 연합군과 운명을 같이 하고 참전했을 때 얼마나 많은 아우성과 얼마나 많은 약속들이 있었습니까? 그러나 우리에게 60만의 전사자와 40만의 행방 불명자와 100만의 부상자라는 희생을 요구했던 공동의 승리 후에 평화를 이야기하는 회의에서 단지 귀중한 식민지 전리품 중에서 부스러기만 남겨져 우리에게 주으라고 합니다.

13년간 우리는 우리의 목을 조르는 손아귀에서 꼼짝 못하면서 인내하여 왔습니다. 우리는 40년 간 이디오피아를 참아주었습니다. 이제는 더 참을 수가 없습니다.

이탈리아의 권리를 인정하기는커녕 국제 연합은 감히 제재 이야기를 합니다. 그러나 그 반대의 증거가 나타날 때까지 나는 신뢰할 수 있는 프랑스인들이 이탈리아를 해치는 제재를 지지하리라고 믿고 싶지 않습니다. Boligny 전투에서 6천명의 전사자들 ─ 그들의 헌신성이 하도 영웅적이어서 적의 사령관도 칭찬하지 않을 수 없었던 ─ 그들 쓰러진 자들도 무덤 속에서 꿈틀거릴 것입니다. 그 반대의 증거가 나올 때까지 영국의 믿음직한 국민이 문명국가 대열에 낄 수 없는 저 야만적인 국가를 위하여 피를 흘리고 유럽을 재난으로 빠뜨리고 싶어한다고 믿고 싶지 않습니다.

마찬가지로 우리는 앞으로 일어날 지도 모르는 사태의 진전을 간과할 여유도 없습니다. 경제적 제재에는 단련과, 희생정신과 순응으로 해결해야 할 것입니다. 군사적 제재는 군사적으로 대응해야 할 것입니다. 전투행위는 전투로 맞대응해야 할 것입니다.

과거와 명성에 걸맞는 국민은 다른 입장을 취할 수도, 결코 취하지도 않을 것입니다. 다시 한번 오늘 모이신 모든 이탈리아인들께 가장 단호하게 되풀이 하겠습니다. 나는 이 순간에 어떤 식민지 충돌이 유럽전쟁의 모습이나 무게를 띠지 않도록 나의 역량을 다하여 모든 일을 하겠다는 신성한 서약을 하는 바입니다. 이 싸움이 이런 새로운 재난 중에 파괴된 사원에 대한 복수를 원하는 사람들에게 매력적일 수도 있습니다. 이와같은 역사적인 시간에 이탈리아인들이 이만한 국민성의 위력을 발휘한 적은 한번도 없었으며 인류가 가장 위대한 정복의 혜택을 입고 있는 이 국민, 영웅, 시인, 성인, 항해자, 식민지 개척자의 이 국민에게 감히 제재를 하려는 것은 그들에게 거슬리는 일입니다.

이탈리아여! 이탈리아여! 완전한 그리고 전체적인 파시스트여! 블랙셔츠 혁명의 이탈리아여, 일어나시오, 결의의 함성이 하늘까지 오르도록 하시오, 그리고 동부 아프리카의 우리 병사들에게 들리도록 하시오. 싸우려는 그들에게 위로가 되도록 해주시오. 우리 우방에게는 격려가 되고 우리 적에게는 경고가 되게 하시오. 그 함성이야말로 산과 바다를 건너 커다란 세계로 나가 깊이 파고드는 이탈리아의 함성입니다. 그것은 바로 정의와 승리의 함성입니다.

(3) The underlined, "One heart alone! One will alone! One decision!" in lines 5, can be considered as _____.

    (a) Inversion   (b) Antithesis   (c) Parallelism   (d) Repetition

(4) The underlined, "This manifestation … the tie between Italy and Fascism is perfect, absolute, unalterable" in lines 5 and 6, is a/an _____.

    (a) Prestige suggestion   (c) Appeal to ignorance
    (b) Faulty analogy   (d) Post-hoc fallacy

(5) The lines from 15 to 20, "When in 1915,…of the Allies,… - it is enough now," are used as a/an _____.

    (a) Identification of possible solutions   (c) Definition of the problems
    (b) Evaluation of the solutions   (d) Identification of the problems

(6) The underlined, "Entirely and universally Fascist! The Italy of the Black Shirt Revolution…" in line 44 and 45, can be considered here as _____.

    (a) Name calling   (c) Bandwagon appeal
    (b) Glittering generality   (d) Plain-folks appeal

(7) The underlined, "colonial booty" in line 18, is used as a/an _____.

    (a) Name calling   (c) Bandwagon appeal
    (b) Glittering generality   (d) Plain-folks appeal

(8) The final paragraph (lines from 44 to 48) is used as emotional appeals for the audience to _____.

    (a) Agree with the speaker   (c) Be motivated
    (b) Support the speaker   (d) Take actions

(9) The underlined, "Let it be a comfort… and a warning to our enemies" in lines 45 and 47, are used here as a/an _____.

    (a) Post-hoc fallacy   (c) False dichotomy
    (b) Prestige suggestion   (d) Appeal to ignorance

(10) Persuasive speeches often include such steps as, especially for the declaration of war, (1) Identification of the immediate or significant problems; (2) Identification of possible solutions; (3) Justification for the cause of hostility or fight; (4) Internal solidarity; and, (5) Action taking. In your opinion, what is one of the most important objectives of the speaker, Mussolini at that time and situation?

    (a) Action taking   (c) Identification of solutions
    (b) Internal solidarity   (d) Justification for the cause

Note

- **Black Shirt** : 블랙 셔츠 당원: 검은 셔츠를 입었던 이탈리아 파시스트 당원
- **unalterable** = that can't be changed
  - Promise to God, once made, is unalterable. (신에게 한번 한 약속은 바꿀 수 없다.)
- **puerile** = suitable only to a child, childish : 어린애 같은, 유치한
- **crumb** = very small piece of dry food, esp. from bread or cake : 빵 부스러기
  - Sweep up the crumbs from under the table. crumbs of information (하찮은 정보)
- **sheer** = pure, unmixed with anything else • He won by sheer luck. (순전히 운으로 이겼다.)
- **booty** = goods stolen by thieves, taken by a victorious army : 전리품
- **suffocate** = cause to die because of lack of air : 질식시키다, 목조르다
  - She was suffocated with grief. (슬픔으로 목이 메었다.)
- **regime** = a particular government : 정부, 체제
  - The country has been under a military regime as long as 27 years.(그 나라는 27년이나 군정하에 있었다.)
- **dubious** = feeling doubt : 의심하는 • I'm still dubious of his honesty.
- **diversion** = something that turns someone's attention away from something else that one does not wish to be noticed : 상대방의 주의를 딴 데로 돌리는 수작
  - cf. distraction (기분 전환을 위한 취미, 오락)
- **hostility** = the state of being unfriendly : 적개심, 적의
  - I bear no hostility toward those who backbite me, for they do not deserve my concern. (나는 등뒤에서 나를 헐뜯는 사람들에게 적의를 품지 않는다. 왜냐하면 그들은 나의 관심을 받을 자격도 없으니까.)
- **implant** = fix in deeply, usu. into the body or mind : 깊이 심다, 주입시키다
  - He implanted the necessity of sound consumption in the minds of the housewives. (그는 가정 주부들에게 건전 소비의 필요성을 심어주었다.)
- **manifestation** = act of showing, making clear : 표명, 표시
- **sanction** = an action taken against person or esp. a country that has broken a law or rule : 제재조치
- **take (lift) a sanction against** : …에게 제재조치를 취하다(풀다)
- **authentic** = reliable, trustworthy : 진실한, 믿을 만한
- **catastrophe** = sudden happening that causes great suffering and destruction : 재난
- **overlook** = fail to see or notice, pay no attention to : 간과하다
  - I will overlook your lateness this time, but don't be late again.
- **stand** = a clear, publicly - stated position : 입장, 주장 • take a stand (입장을 취하다)
  - If he wants my vote, he'll have to take a firm stand on the issue. (그가 내 표를 바란다면 그 문제에 대해서 확고한 입장을 취해야 한다.)
- **in the categorical manner** : 절대적으로, 확실하게 **opp. hypothetical** : 가정적인
- **disintegrated** : 붕괴된 **exigency** = emergency : 위기, 위급상황
- **post - hoc fallacy** : 시간의 전후가 바뀐 오류
- **Fascism** = philosophy, principles and organization of the aggressive nationalist and anti-communist governmental system started in Italy in 1922 and dissolved in 1943 : 제 1차 세계 대전 후 무솔리니를 중심으로 일어난 주의, 정치적으로는 독재주의를, 경제적으로는 노사 협조주의를, 대외적으로는 반 공산주의적 민주주의, 조국 지상주의를 고집함

4.3.3. A Speech for Special Occasion: Apology

Passage 1 : Topic, "Clinton's Address to the Nation," delivered by President Clinton on August 17, 1998.

Background : For several months leading up to the grand jury testimony, President Clinton adamantly denied that he had any physical relationship with Ms Monica Lewinsky, a former White House intern. Clinton testified in front of the grand jury on August 17, 1998 to answer questions brought forth by Special Independent Counsel, Kenneth Starr, on allegations of improper relations Clinton had with Lewinsky. The issue is related to possible perjury done by Clinton. That same evening, Clinton admitted his relationship with Lewinsky, saying that "… that was not appropriate. In fact it was wrong. It constituted a critical lapse in judgment and a personal failure on my part for which I am solely and completely responsible." His "apology" to the nation casts doubt by some people who feel that his address is not a sincere apology.

Unabridged Speech :

Good evening. <u>This afternoon in this room, from this chair</u>, I testified before the Office of Independent Counsel and the grand jury. I answered their questions truthfully, including questions about my private life, questions no American citizen would ever want to answer. Still, I must take complete responsibility for all my actions, both public and private.

05   And that is why I am speaking to you tonight.
As you know, in a deposition in January, I was asked questions about my relationship with Monica Lewinsky. While my answers were legally accurate, I did not volunteer information. Indeed, I did have a relationship with Ms Lewinsky that was not appropriate. In fact, it was wrong. It constituted a critical lapse in judgment and a personal failure on my part for which I am solely and completely responsible.

10   But I told the grand jury today and I say to you now that at no time did I ask anyone to lie, to hide, or destroy evidence or to take any other unlawful action. I know that my public comments and my silence about this matter gave a false impression. I misled people, including even my wife. I deeply regret that.

15   I can only tell you I was motivated by many factors. First, by a desire to protect myself from the embarrassment of my own conduct. I was also very concerned about protecting my family. The fact that these questions were being asked in a politically inspired lawsuit, which has since been dismissed, was a consideration, too.

4.3.3. 특수한 경우를 위한 연설 : 사과문

지문 1 :

주제 : 클린턴 대통령의 '국민에게 드리는 담화'-1998년 8월 17일

배경 : 대배심 증언까지 이르는 서너 달 동안 클린턴 대통령은 전 백악관 인턴이었던 모니카 르윈스키양과 어떤 육체적 관계를 가졌다는 사실을 완강히 부인했다. 1998년 8월 17일에 클린턴은 특별 검사 케니스 스타가 제출한 르윈스키양과 가졌던 부적절한 관계의 혐의에 대한 질의에 대답하기 위하여 대배심원들 앞에서 증언했다. 현안 문제는 클린턴이 저질렀을 법한 위증과 관계가 있다. 같은 날 저녁 클린턴은 르윈스키와의 관계를 다음과 같은 말로 시인했다. "그것(그 관계)은 적절하지 못했습니다. 사실 그건 잘못된 일이었습니다. 그것은 판단의 결정적인 착오와 제가 혼자 그리고 전적으로 책임져야 할 저의 개인적인 실수가 되었습니다." 그의 국민에 대한 '사죄'는 그의 담화가 성실한 사과가 아니라고 느끼는 사람들에 의하여 의심을 낳고 있다.

Bill Clinton

연설 전문(全文) :

안녕하십니까. 저는 오늘 오후 이 방, 이 의자에 앉아 특별 검사와 대배심 앞에서 증언했습니다. 저는 제 사생활에 대한 질문, 어느 미국인도 대답하기 원치 않

A small loop: *Because of Starr's subpoena power, the president can safely speak to just two people: his lawyer, David Kendall, and Hillary*

을 질문을 포함하는 그분들의 질의에 진실하게 대답하였습니다. 그러나 제가 취한 모든 행동에 대하여 공적이든 사적이든 완전한 책임을 져야 합니다. 이것이 오늘밤 여러분들에게 말씀드리는 이유입니다.

여러분께서 아시는 바와 같이 1월에 어느 선서증언에서 모니카 르윈스키양과의 관계에 대하여 질문을 받았습니다. 제 대답은 법적으로 정확했지만 스스로 내용을 말씀드리고 싶지는 않았습니다. 정말로 저는 르윈스키양과 적절치 못한 관계를 틀림없이 가졌습니다. 실제로 그건 잘못이었습니다. 그것은 결정적인 판단의 잘못과 제가 혼자 그리고 전적으로 제 쪽에서 책임져야 할 개인적인 실수로 이뤄졌습니다.

In addition, I had real and serious concerns about an independent counsel investigation that began with private business dealings 20 years ago, 20 dealings, I might add, about which an independent federal agency found no evidence of any wrongdoing by me or my wife over two years ago. The independent counsel investigation moved on to my staff and friends, then into my private life. And now the investigation itself is under investigation. This has gone on too long, cost too much and hurt too many innocent 25 people.

Now, this matter is between me, the two people I love most - my wife and our daughter -and our God. I must put it right, and I am prepared to do whatever it takes to do so. Nothing is more important to me personally. It is time to stop the pursuit of personal destruction and the prying into private lives and get on with our national life.

30 Our country has been distracted by this matter for too long, and I take my responsibility for my part in all of this. That is all I can do. Now it is time - in fact, it is past time - to move on. We have important work to do - real opportunities to seize, real problems to solve, real security matters to face.

And so tonight, I ask you to turn away from the spectacle of the past seven months, to repair the fabric of our national discourse, and to return our 35 attention to all the challenges and all the promise of the next American century. Thank you for watching. And good night.

(Source: The Philadelphia Inquirer, Tuesday, August 18, 1998)

(1) Why did Clinton have to make the speech to the nation? It was to ask the people to _____. (1 - 10. Rhetorical techniques)

    (a) Understand & forgive him   (c) Forget the past & forgive him
    (b) Forgive his mistake & start anew   (d) Listen to his case & start anew

(2) The underlined, "This afternoon in this room, from this chair,⋯." in lines 1 and 2, as an indication of specific time and place, can be considered as _____.

    (a) Building credibility   (c) Using evidence
    (b) Reasoning   (d) Motivational appeals

(3) The lines from 2 to 4, "I answered their questions truthfully,⋯" can be considered as a justification for being _____.

    (a) Thoughtful   (b) Honest   (c) Serious   (d) Meditative

(4) The lines from 4 to 5, "Still, I must take⋯. And that is why I am speaking to you tonight," can be considered as implications for his being _____ and

그러나 오늘 대배심원들에게 말씀드렸고 지금 여러분들께 말씀드립니다. 저는 한번도 누구에게든지 거짓말을 하거나, 숨기거나, 증거를 파괴하거나 다른 어떤 불법적인 행동을 하라고 요구한 적은 없습니다. 저는 이 문제에 대하여 제가 공적으로 언급한 것이나 제가 침묵을 지킨 것이 잘못된 인상을 주었다고 알고 있습니다. 저는 사람들에게 심지어 제 처까지 오해하게 만들었습니다. 여러가지 요인들이 동기였다고 말씀드릴 수밖에 없음을 대단히 유감으로 생각합니다. 첫째, 제가 저지른 행동때문에 당황하는 제 자신을 보호해야겠다는 욕구에 의한 것이었습니다. 저는 가족을 보호하는 일을 매우 걱정했습니다. 이러한 질문들이 정치적으로 부추겨진 소송 중에, 그 후 기각되었지만, 일어나고 있다는 사실도 한가지 고려사항이었습니다.

그 외에도, 20년 전에 있었던 개인적인 사업상 거래, 부연 설명을 드리자면 2년 이상 전에 연방 특별 검사가 나나 내 처의 불법 증거를 발견하지 못한 그 거래와 관련하여 시작한 특별검사의 수사에 대해서도 실로 심각한 우려를 하였습니다. 그 특별 검사 수사는 계속하여 나의 직원들, 나의 친구들 그리고 나의 사생활 내부까지 확대되었습니다. 그런데 지금 그 수사 자체가 수사를 받고 있습니다. 이 사건은 너무 오래 계속되었고 너무 많은 경비가 들었으며 너무 많은 죄없는 사람들에게 상처를 입혔습니다.

이제 이 문제는 저와 제가 가장 사랑하는 두 사람 제 딸과 처, 그리고 하느님 사이에 존재하고 있습니다. 저는 이 문제를 바로 잡아야 하고 그렇게 하기 위하여 어떠한 대가도 치를 각오가 되어 있습니다. 저에게 개인적으로 이보다 더 중요한 일은 없습니다. 이제는 개인을 파괴하기 위한 추구나 사생활을 파고드는 일을 중단하고 국민의 생활을 위하여 앞으로 나아갈 때입니다.

우리 나라는 이 일로 너무 오래 주의를 빼앗겼으며 제가 이 모든 일에서 제몫의 책임을 집니다. 이것이 제가 할 수 있는 모든 일입니다. 이제는 — 사실은 늦었지만 — 앞으로 전진해야 할 시간입니다. 우리는 해야 할 중요한 일을 가지고 있습니다. 붙잡아야 할 좋은 기회들이 있고, 해결해야 할 현실 문제들이 있으며, 외면할 수 없는 중요한 안전상의 문제들이 있습니다.

그러므로 오늘 밤, 저는 여러분에게 지난 7개월의 볼썽 사나운 구경거리에서 눈을 돌리고, 국민적 대화의 구조를 개선하며, 우리의 주의를 모든 도전과 다음 세기 미국의 전망에 되돌릴 것을 부탁드리는 바입니다. 지켜봐주셔서 감사합니다. 안녕히 계십시오.

_____.

    (a) Responsible, determined   (c) Sincere, adventurous
    (b) Responsible, blameless   (d) Humble, courteous

(5) The lines from 7 to 8, "While my answers were legally accurate, I did not volunteer information," can be considered _____ for his withholding information.

    (a) Down-play   (b) Justification   (c) Avoidance   (d) Refusal

(6) The lines from 8 to 10, "Indeed, I did have a relationship…," can be regarded as a/an _____ of his error, and _____ of responsibility.

    (a) Denial, refusal   (c) Initiation, termination
    (b) Acceptance, avoidance   (d) Admission, acceptance

(7) The lines from 13 to 14, "I know that my public comments…. I misled people,…. I deeply regret that," can be regarded as a/an _____.

    (a) Apology   (b) Assertion   (c) Justification   (d) Diversion

(8) The lines from 22 to 25, "The independent counsel investigation… and hurt too many innocent people," can be considered as Clinton's _____ the independent counsel.

    (a) Warning to   (b) Attack on   (c) Support for   (d) Petition to

(9) The lines from 30 to 36, "Our country has been distracted…, the next American century," can be considered as a request to _____.

    (a) Forget the past   (c) Forgive the President
    (b) Terminate the gossip   (d) Turn our attention to more important issues

(10) Based on the information in the speech presented, what do you think is the central message that the speaker wants to achieve?

    (a) I am sorry for my error. Please forgive me.
    (b) All human beings can make mistakes. I made a mistake. Let's stop gossiping.
    (c) I'm sorry for my error. Let's concentrate on more important issues facing us.
    (d) The independent counsel went too far, hurting too many innocent American people.

Note

- **lead up to** : ~문제로까지 이르는, 커지는
  - The investigation led up to the traffic in weapon. (그 수사는 무기 거래까지 확대되었다.)
- **constitute=make up, form** : 구성하다
  - Comprehensiveness is not enough to constitute wisdom. (이해력만으로 지혜를 구성하기는 부족하다.)
- **adamant=hard, immovable and unyielding** : 단호한, 의지가 굳은
  - I've tried to persuade him to change his mind but he was adamant.
- **lapse=a small fault, mistake or failure in behavior, slip of the tongue/ memory or pen** : (기억, 말, 글)작은 실수
- **grand jury** : 대배심. 23명 이하의 특별 선임된 배심원으로 구성되며 고소장의 예심을 하고 12인 이상이 증거가 충분하다고 인정하면 정식 기소함. • cf. petty jury (소배심 12~3명으로 구성)
- **Special Independent Counsel** : 특별 검사   **independent** : 무소속의
- **Perjury** : 위증, 거짓 맹세
- **allegation=statement esp. made without proof** : 증거 없는 진술, 혐의
  - You have made serious allegations, but can you substantiate them?
  - (자네 심각한 혐의 내용을 말했는데 실증할 수 있는가?)
- **deposition=statement made on oath** : 선서 증언, 녹취
- **comment=an opinion, explanation or judgement written or spoken** : 논평, 언급
  - No comment=I have nothing to say.
- **mislead=cause someone to form a mistaken idea or to act wrongly or mistakenly** : 오해를 불러 일으키다, 현혹시키다
  - Don't let his sweet talk mislead you; he is a playboy. (그 남자의 감언이설에 현혹되지 말라. 그 남자 제비야.)
- **embarrassment=state of being ashamed, uncomfortable, anxious** : 당황(스런 일)
  - I could not hide my embarrassment at his pointing out of my mistake in public.
  - (그가 여러사람 앞에서 내 실수를 지적하는데 당혹감을 감출 수가 없었다.)
- **be concerned about=worry about** : 걱정하다
  - Every worker is concerned about job security. (모두 직장의 안정성을 우려하고 있다.)
- **inspire=put uplifting thoughts, feelings** : 고무하다, 격려하다
  - A good leader inspires his men with hope, enthusiasm and confidence.
  - (훌륭한 지도자는 자기 부하들에게 희망, 열성과 자신감을 불어 넣는다.)
- **lawsuit=noncriminal case in a court of law** : 민사 소송
- **dismiss=reject** : 취하하다, 기각하다   • dismiss an appeal (공소를 기각하다)
- **wrongdoing=illegal behavior** : 비행
- **move on=make progress, go forward** : 발전하다, 전진하다
  - Things were not moving on as rapidly as we had hoped.
- **pry into=inquire too curiously** : 꼬치꼬치 캐다

CHAPTER 5

제5장

일반지식을 통한 독해

한국 수능시험(학업적성검사) 대비

READING THROUGH GENERAL KNOWLEDGE FOR THE KOREAN SCHOLASTIC APTITUDE TEST

CHAPTER 5

This Chapter, The final chapter of this publication, "Reading Through General Knowledge for the Korean Scholastic Aptitude Test," is designed for the readers with three-fold:

(1) To review a variety of specific reading skills covered in Chapter 2;
(2) To strengthen reading skills acquired from a number of subject matters both in Content Areas, and Language Arts, which we studied in Chapters 3 and 4; and,
(3) To provide the readers with opportunities to be able to read a variety of passages related to General Knowledge, which serves as another comprehensive preparation for the Korean Scholastic Aptitude Test (Hereafter it will be called "KSAT").

The "General Knowledge" refers to any information and understanding about a topic/subject that we can share with others in everyday life without heavy dependency of using complicated and technical terminologies. The topic can be "broadly" related to any subject matter from any field, but very specialized, theoretically difficult information about the topic is avoided as much as possible. The selection of the topic is carefully chosen so as to be both informative and interesting.

The questions asked for the English Section of the KSAT for the past five years (94 - 98) were published in March, 1998 by Kyuchangkhak Book Publishing Company, Seoul with the editing support from English Town. Based on those questions published, a general tendency for the questions presented has been analyzed and concluded according to the areas of the specific reading skills. As displayed in the following table, the rank order of the questions asked from 1994 to 1998 includes: (1) Subject matter (28%); (2) Word/Phrase/Sentence in Context (21%); (3) Structure: (Grammatical Usages) (15%); (4) Making Inferences (12%); (5) Drawing Conclusions (12%); (6) Idioms / Expressions / Sequences (8%); (7) Analogy (2%); and, (8) Figures/Charts (2%). This information related to the tendency of the questions being asked for the English Section can provide us with clear direction and concentration for the specific reading skills concerned. As such, this chapter includes 25 passages of various lengths; short, medium, and long. The questions to be asked at the end of each passage are: (1) Subject matter; (2) Word/Phrase/Sentence in context; (3) Structure; (4) Making Inferences; and, (5) Drawing Conclusions, which is geared for the preparation of the KSAT. In the previous chapters, we have intensively and extensively dealt with the above reading skills except Structure. The questions related to the Structure are given "to measure your ability to recognize grammatical rules and uses of language that are appropriate and acceptable for Standard Written English."

As we have seen, the array of the above construction is for the readers who are preparing for the KSAT; however, the contents included in this chapter are meant to be very informative as well as instructive so as to serve as an invaluable reference section for general readers. Enjoy reading them, while acquiring new knowledge and experience.

제5장

이 책의 마지막 장인 '일반적 지식을 통한 독해'는 세가지 목적을 가지고 수능시험 독자들을 위해서 계획되었다 :

(1) 제 2장에서 다룬 다양한 구체적인 독서 기법의 복습
(2) 제 3,4장에서 공부한 내용영역과 언어교과목의 수 많은 주제문에서 습득한 독서기법의 강화
(3) 독자들에게 일반적 지식과 관련된 다양한 지문을 읽을 수 있는 기회 제공. 이는 한국의 수능시험을 위한 또 다른 종합적인 준비에 도움을 줌

'일반적 지식' 이란 일상생활에서 복잡하고 전문적인 용어를 힘들여 사용하지 않고 타인들과 나눌 수 있는 모든 정보와 이해를 가리킨다. 주제는 어떤 분야의 어떤 제재와 광범위하게 관련될 수 있으나 어느 주제에 관한 매우 전문적이고 이론적으로 어려운 정보는 가능한 한 피했다. 주제 선정은 정보 제공적이며 또한 흥미롭도록 하려고 주의깊게 선택했다.

지난 5년간 (94~98)의 수능시험 영어영역 출제문항들이 '영어마을'의 편집 후원으로 서울의 '규장각 서적 출판사'에 의하여 출판되었다. 출판된 이 문항들을 토대로 특수한 독서기법 영역에 의거하여 제시된 문제들의 일반적 경향을 분석하고 결론을 내렸다. 다음 표에 밝힌 바와 같이 (1) 주제문제 (28%) (2) 문맥 내의 단어, 어구, 문장 (21%) (3) 구문 (문법상의 용법) (15%) (4) 추론 (12%) (5) 결론 도출 (12%) (6) 관용어구, 표현, 글의 전후관계 (8%) (7) 유추 (2%) (8) 도형, 도표(2%).

영어영역에 출제되는 문항의 경향과 관련된 정보는 관련된 독서기술을 연마하기 위한 명확한 방향과 집중적인 노력을 제공해 준다. 이와 같은 것으로서 이 장에는 단문, 중문, 장문 25개 예문을 넣는다. 각 지문 끝에 출제되는 문제는 (1) 내용 (2) 문맥 속의 어휘, 문장 (3) 구문 (4) 추론 (5) 결론 내리기며 이들은 한국의 대입 수능 시험 준비를 목표로 하고 있다. 앞선 여러 장에서 구문을 제외하고 위에서 말한 독서기술을 집중적으로 광범위하게 취급해 왔다. 구문 관련 문제는 표준 문어체 영어를 위해서 적절하고 올바른 문법 규칙과 언어사용을 이해하는 능력을 측정하기 위하여 출제된다.

지금까지 살펴본 바와 같이 위의 구성 배열은 수능시험을 준비하는 독자들을 위한 것이지만 이 장에 들어있는 내용들은 일반 독자들을 위하여 귀중한 참고자료로서 도움이 되도록 정보제공적이며 교훈적인 것으로 의도되었다. 새로운 지식과 경험을 얻으면서 한편으로 읽는 재미를 느끼기 바란다.

KOREAN SCHOLASTIC APTITUDE TEST (1994 - 1998)

Year	94	95	96	97	98	Total # (216)	%
Subject Matter (Main Idea, Topic)	8	9	10	11	23	61	28
Word/Phrase/ Sentence in Context	8	9	8	6	14	45	21
Structure: (Grammatical Usages)	4	2	6	8	12	32	15
Making Inferences	5	4	3	4	9	25	12
Drawing Conclusions	6	6	3	4	7	26	12
Idioms, Expressions, Sequences	3	1	4	3	7	18	8
Analogy	0	0	1	1	3	5	2
Figures/Charts	1	1	1	1	0	4	2

Passage 1 : "On the Origin of Inequality" by Rousseau, Jean-Jacques (1712-1778)

Background : Rousseau, Swiss philosopher, came from a poor and unhappy family. When he came to Paris, he always felt out of place among the sophisticated intellectuals who gathered there. Yet his political and social ideals were an important part of Enlightenment thought. He believed that human nature was basically good, but society corrupted people. He argued that all people should be equal and that all titles of rank and nobility be abolished. "Man is born free," he wrote, "and everywhere is in chains." In The Social Contract, he described an ideal society in which people would form a community and make a contract with one another, not with a ruler. His beliefs in equality and in the will of majority made him a spokesman for the common people. Revolutionaries in many countries would later adopt his ideas. The following paragraph is excerpted from his publication, On the Origin of Inequality published in 1755.

    I conceive of two sorts of inequality in the human species; one, which I call natural or physical, because it is established by nature and consists in the difference of ages, health, bodily strengths, and qualities of mind or soul; the other, which may be called moral or political inequality, because it depends upon a sort of *convention* and is established, or at least authorized, by the consent of men. The latter consists in the different privileges that some men enjoy to the prejudice of others, such as to be richer, honored more, more powerful than they, or even to make themselves obeyed by them.

(Source: Rousseau, Jean-Jaques (1755). On the Origin of Inequality. Translated by Roger D. & Judith R. Masters in The First and Second Discourses (1964), ed. Roger D. Masters.

Note

- **related to (with)**=connected with, of the same family or kind : 관련된, 친척의
  - painting and related arts (회화와 관련 예술)
- **aptitude**=natural ability or skill in learning : 적성 • He showed great aptitude for music.
- **comprehensive**=inclusive, broad : 종합적인 • comprehensive school (종합학교)
- **terminology**=술어(학) • technical terminology (전문용어)
- **sequence**=the order in which things or events follow one another : 앞 뒤의 순서
  - Please keep the cards in sequence. Don't mix them up.
- **be geared for**=be adjusted to, make dependent upon : …에 맞게 조정하다
  - Education should be geared for the children's needs and abilities.
    (교육은 어린이의 능력과 필요에 맞추어야 한다.-눈높이 교육)
- **acceptable**=good enough, established : 옳다고 인정되는, 마음에 드는
  - Your work is not acceptable. Do it again.
- **array**=arrangement : 배열, 배치
  - in battle array (전투대형으로) • an array of umbrellas (죽 늘어선 우산들)
- **appropriate**=suited to : 적절 • Write in a style appropriate to your subject. (주제에 적합한 문체로 써라)

지문 1 : '인간 불평등의 근원에 관하여'-루소

배경 : 스위스 철학자인 루소는 가난하고 불행한 가정 출신이었다. 그가 파리에 왔을 때, 그는 언제나 그곳에 모이는 세련된 지식인들 사이에서 자신이 어울리지 않는다고 느꼈다. 그러나 그의 정치적, 사회적 이상은 계몽주의 사상에 중요한 일부를 이루었다. 그는 인간은 근본적으로 선하나 사회가 사람들을 타락시킨다고 믿었다. 그는 모든 사람들은 평등해야 하며 모든 계급이나 귀족의 칭호는 철폐되어야 한다고 주장했다. 그는 글에서 '인간은 평등하게 태어나지만 도처에서 구속당한다'고 썼다. '사회계약론'에서 사람들이 공동사회를 구성하고 통치자가 아니라 상호간에 계약을 맺는 이상적인 사회를 그렸다. 그의 평등과 다수의 의지에 대한

Rousseau, Jean-Jacques

신념이 그를 평민들의 대변자로 만들었다. 여러 나라들의 혁명가들이 후에 그의 사상을 채택했다. 다음 글은 1755년에 출판된 그의 저서 '불평등의 근원에 관하여'에서 발췌한 것이다.

(1) The topic of the passage is "Inequality as a _____ problem." (Subject matter)

    (a) Social & natural   (c) Cultural & technological   (e) Educational & natural
    (b) Economic & political   (d) Industrial & natural

(2) The italicized word, *convention*, refers to _____. (Word in context)

    (a) Condition   (b) Congregation   (c) Corporation   (d) Precept   (e) Tradition

(3) The underlined phrase, "honored more" should be restructured as_____.(Structure)

    (a) Most honored   (c) The most honored   (e) Much more honored
    (b) More honored   (d) Better honored

(4) Based on the information given, it can be inferred that Rousseau was clearly against _____. (Making inferences)

    (a) Imperialism (b) Colonialism (c) Communism (d) Socialism (e) Social evils

(5) Based on the information presented, it can be concluded that the impact of Rousseau's opinions including those of other philosophers and scholars during the Age of Enlightenment (1715-1815) helped the _____ develop in America and France. (Conclusion)

    (a) Social unrest (b) Anarchy (c) Absolute monarchism (d) Revolutions (e) Civil wars

Passage 2 : Language as a Political Issue.

    Literature on nationalism, ethnicity, and related topics has for more than <u>a half century</u> reflected a deep awareness of the political sensitivity of language *preference*, *imposition*, and promotion. It is clear why blood is drawn over language in certain situations; language is the key, or the set of keys, needed to unlock the gates to access to survival kits - employment, advancement, social security, and physical security.

(Source: Bretton, Henry (1976). "Political Science, Language, and Politics." In Language and Politics. ed. by William M. & Jean F. O'Barr. Mouton)

(1) The topic of the passage is "The _____ of language." (Subject matter)

    (a) Political role (b) Aspect (c) Importance (d) Survival (e) Imposition

(2.1) The italicized word, *imposition*, refers to _____ . (2.1 - 2.2. Words in context)

    (a) Inheritance (b) Implication (c) Enforcement (d) Explication (e) Ingenuity

(2.2) The antonym of the italicized word, *preference*, can be _____.

    (a) Avoidance (b) Inclination (c) Coherence (d) Inclusion (e) Landslide

(3) The underlined phrase "<u>a half century</u>" should be restructured as "_____." (Structure)

    (a) The half century   (c) Half the century   (e) Half century
    (b) The century of the half   (d) Half a century

나는 인류에는 두 종류의 불평등이 있다고 생각합니다: 하나는 내가 선천적 또는 육체적인 불평등이라고 부르는 것으로, 선천적으로 결정되고 연령, 건강, 신체적 강점, 정신, 영혼적 특질의 차이로 나타납니다. 다른 하나는 도덕적, 혹은 정치적 불평등으로 불릴 수 있는 것으로 인간의 동의에 의하여 설정되거나 공인되어지는 일종의 인습에 따라 좌우되는 것입니다. 후자는 어떤 사람들이 다른 사람들에게 해를 끼치면서 향유하는 다른 특권 -타인들 보다 더 부자가 되려는, 더 존경을 받으려는, 더 많은 권세를 가지려는, 심지어 그들을 복종하게 만들려는- 에 존재합니다.

Note

- **out of place**=not in the right or proper place, unsuitable : 어울리지 않는, 부적절한
  - Your remarks were rather out of place. (자네가 한 말은 그 장면에 어울리지 않는 것이었네.)
- **sophisticated**=having lost the natural simplicity : 닳아빠진, 세련된, 기교적인
- **precept**=moral instruction : 교훈 • Example is better than precept. (모범이 낫다.)
- **abolish**=put an end to, do away with : 폐기하다, 철폐하다
  - Slavery was abolished in the US in the 19th century.
- **spokesman**=a person chosen to speak for a group officially : 대변인 • cf. speaker (국회의장)
- **conceive**=think of, imagine : 생각을 품다
  - Scientists conceived the idea of the atomic bomb in the 1930's.
- **consist in**=lie in, have as the chief element : …에 존재한다, 주요소로 갖는다
  - In what does happiness consist? (행복은 어디에 있는가?)
- **privilege**=right or advantage available to a particular person, group : 특권
- **anarchy**=absence of government or control, disorder : 무정부 상태, 혼란

지문 2: 정치적 문제로서의 언어

민족주의, 종족의 특성 및 이와 관련된 주제에 대한 문학은 반세기 이상 언어의 선호, 강요, 그리고 장려함에 있어 정치적 민감성에 대한 깊은 인식을 반영해 왔다. 어떤 상황에서 언어문제 때문에 왜 피흘려 투쟁했는가는 분명하다 : 언어란 고용, 승진, 사회적 안전, 신체적 안전 등 살아남기 위한 구명도구를 얻을 수 있는 문을 여는데 필요한 하나의 혹은 한벌의 열쇠이기 때문이다.

(4.1) The statement, "It is clear why blood is drawn over language in certain situations" can infer that "There have been bloody _____ for the problems related to language preference, imposition, and promotion." (4.1 - 4.4. Making inferences)

    (a) Arguments   (b) Debates   (c) Efforts   (d) Struggles   (e) Wars

(4.2) During the Japanese colonial rule in Korea, Japan imposed the use of the Japanese language on the Korean people. It can be inferred that one of the primary objectives of this language imposition was "to secure _____ for the Japanese."

    (a) Employment   (c) Economic & political gains   (e) Educational benefits
    (b) Advancement   (d) Cultural superiority

(4.3) Henry Bretton (1976) advocates, "Language is the key needed to unlock the gates to access to survival kits - employment, advancement, social security, and physical security," which can be inferred as an implication of the following statements.

    (a) Your socioeconomic success depends on your ability of commanding language, whether it is native, foreign, or dialectal.
    (b) If you command an international language, your success is promising.
    (c) If you command language, your employment and advancement are guaranteed.
    (d) If you maintain your native language, you have the key for your cultural heritage.
    (e) Your employment, advancement, and social and physical security depend on your ability of commanding language, whether it is native, foreign, or dialectal.

(4.4) If North and South Koreas are united under the strong leadership of the South Korean government and economy, then it is likely that the "_____ Language or Dialect" will be imposed on the North Korean people.

    (a) Standard   (b) Cultured   (c) Kyungsang   (d) Jeolla   (e) Hamkyung

Note ("The Standard Language" is used as an official language in most authorized publications and through mass media in the South; whereas, "the Cultured Language" is used as an official one in the North.)

(5.1) Most Korean students regardless of their regional background of dialect can speak and use "Standard Language" which is taught at school as an official language. If the students studying in Chejoo Island do not command the Standard Language, then it can be concluded that they are deprived of the access to "_____" in their society. (5.1 - 5.2. Conclusions)

    (a) Political control   (c) Being educated   (e) Economic power
    (b) Survival   (d) Cultural heritage

(5.2) It can be concluded that the majority of the high school and college students who study English in Korea are preparing for _____. (5.1 - 5.2. Conclusions)

    (a) Exams, employment   (d) Academic inquiries, pleasure
    (b) Cultural exchange, travel abroad   (e) Social prestige, intellectual inquiries
    (c) Study abroad, conversation with foreigners

Note

- **ethnicity**=the character of a race of the mankind : 인종적 특성, 민족성
  - ethnic group (인종집단)   • ethnic psychology (민족심리학)
- **preference**=the act of preferring, favoring : 선호, 편애, 우선권
  - I have a preference for French films.
- **impose**=lay or place tax, duty on : 부과하다, 강요하다
- **language imposition** : 언어강요, 일본이 일본말을 쓰도록 강요한 것이 좋은 예
  - New duties were imposed on wines and spirits.(포도주와 독한 술 (위스키류)에 새로운 세금이 부과되었다.)
- **access**=right or opportunity of means of reaching, using or approaching : 접근, 도달, 사용권 및 기회, 수단   • gain(get, have)access to (…에 도달하다)
  - Students must have access to good books. (학생들은 쉽게 양서를 구할 수 있어야 한다.)
- **survival**=state of continuing to live or exist : 생존, 살아남기
  - the survival of the fittest (適者生存)   • a survival kit (구명장비)
- **kit**=tools, equipment : (집합적)도구, 설비   • a plumber's kit (배관공의 장비)
- **advocate**=speak publicly in support of : 옹호하다
  - Do you advocate keeping all the students at school till late night?
- **inheritance** : 유산, 상속   □ **enforcement** : 강요, 시행
- **ingenuity**=cleverness and skill, originality in design : 창의성, 독창성
- **explication**=explanation : 해설   □ **implication** : 포함, 함축
- **coherence**=stick together, consistent : 통일성, 응집성

Passage 3 :

A powerful tide is surging across much of the world today, <u>creating a new, often *bizarre*, environment ( ) which to work, play, marry, raise children, or retire</u>. In this bewildering context, businessmen swim against highly erratic economic currents; politicians see their ratings bob wildly up and down; universities, hospitals, and other institutions battle desperately against inflation. Value systems splinter and crash, while *the lifeboats of family, church, and state are hurled madly about⋯*. Many of today's changes are not independent of one another. Nor are they random⋯. They are, in fact, parts of a much larger phenomenon: the death of industrialism and the rise of a new civilization.

(Source : Toffler, Alvin (1980). <u>The Third Wave</u>.)

(1) The most appropriate topic of the passage is "_____." (Subject matter)

    (a) Erratic economic currents (c) The rise of a new civilization (e) A new environment
    (b) Battle against inflation   (d) A powerful tide

(2.1) The italicized word, *bizarre*, refers to _____. (2.1. - 2.2. Word & sentence in context)

    (a) Afflictive (b) Normal (c) Poignant (d) Rigorous (e) Odd

(2.2) The italicized sentence, "*the lifeboats of family, church, and state are hurled madly about⋯*" means "the_____⋯."

    (a) Systems of family, church, and state are destroyed.
    (b) Structures of family, religion, and government are broken.
    (c) Functions of family, church, and government are not working any more.
    (d) Family, church, and state do not cooperate with one another.
    (e) Value and support of family, religion, and government are in crisis.

(3) The underlined structure, "<u>creating a new, often bizarre, environment ( ) which to work, play, marry, raise children, or retire</u>," needs a proper preposition to best fit in the parenthesis. (Structure).

    (a) For (b) To (c) In (d) On (e) With

(4.1) It can be inferred that the writer's remark, "the death of industrialism" can refer to "the _____ of our current socioeconomic structure." (4.1. - 4.3. Making inferences)

    (a) Fall (b) Corruption (c) Malice (d) Drastic change (e) Destruction

(4.2) "The rise of a new civilization" can be inferred as "the ____ Age of ____ Industry."

    (a) Different, Economic   (d) Emerging, Agricultural
    (b) Another, Technology   (e) Emerging, Information
    (c) Forthcoming, Computer science

(4.3) It can be inferred that the writer of the passage, Alvin Toffler is a _____.

    (a) Sociologist (b) Anthropologist (c) Prophet (d) Futurist (e) Philosopher

(5.1) It can be concluded that one of the primary reasons for the development of a new

지문 3 :

오늘날 하나의 강력한 물결이 세상의 많은 부분을 가로질러 밀려와서 우리가 일하고, 놀고, 결혼하고, 자녀를 기르고, 은퇴 후 살아야 할 새로운 — 기괴하다고 해야 할 때가 자주 있지만 — 환경을 만들어 가고 있다. 이 당황스런 상황 속에서 사업가들은 극히 예측불가능한 경제적 조류와 맞서 헤엄치며, 정치인들은 그들의 평가가 심하게 오르내리는 것을 보며, 대학, 병원 그리고 다른 기관들은 인플레이션에 맞서 필사적으로 싸운다. 가치 체계가

Toffler, Alvin

박살나서 무너지며 그런 와중에서 가족, 교회 그리고 국가라는 구명정들이 격렬하게 이리 저리 내던져진다. 오늘날의 많은 변화들이 서로 별도로 떨어져 있지 않으며 제멋대로도 아니다. 사실 그것들은 산업주의의 종말이며 새로운 문명의 출현이라는 훨씬 커다란 현상의 부분들이다.

Note

- **surge**=move forward, roll on, in like waves : 밀려오다, 솟구치다
- **a surge of anger (envy)** : 분노 (부러움)의 치밈
  - A great wave was surging over the swimmer. (커다란 파도가 수영하는 사람의 머리 위로 덮쳤다.)
- **bizzare**=grotesque, odd, strange, peculiar : 기묘한, 기괴한
- **bewilder**=puzzle, confuse : 어리둥절하게 하다
  - The woman from the country was bewildered by the crowds and traffic in the big city. (시골에서 온 그 여자는 그 대도시의 인파와 교통량에 어리둥절했다.)
- **context**=circumstance in which an event occurs : 주변 정황
- **erratic**=eccentric, queer, irregular, likely to do unusual things : 별난, 괴상한
  - He was an erratic sort of painter. (그는 괴짜 화가였다.)
- **bob**=move up and down : 오르내리다
  - The cork on his fishing line was bobbing on the water. (그의 낚시찌가 수면에서 위아래로 움직였다.)
- **splinter**=break into small needle - like pieces : 찢어지다, 쪼개지다, (N) 가시
  - I get a splinter in my finger. (손가락에 가시가 들었다.)
- **hurl**=throw violenlty : 내던지다
  - They hurled themselves and attacked the enemy. (그들은 몸을 던져 적을 공격했다.)
- **afflictive** : 괴로움을 주는, 쓰라린   □ **poignant** : 매서운, 신랄한
- **malice**=the wish to hurt other people : 악의
- **bear malice to** : …에게 악의를 품다
- **drastic**=having a strong or violent effect : 철저한, 과감한   • a drastic measure
- **anthropologist** : 인류학자   □ **futurist** : 미래학자   □ **prophet** : 예언자

civilization is largely due to the collapse of _____ value systems. (5.1 - 5.2. Conclusions)

    (a) Political   (b) Economic   (c) Religious   (e) Socioeconomic   (d) Traditional

(5.2) According to the content of the passage, our current socioeconomic structure, industrialism, is criticized as an unsuitable environment in which to work, to play, marry, raise children, or retire. One of the primary reasons leading to this type of conclusion can be drawn from the value systems developed and established based on severe _____.

    (a) Political ideology   (d) Socialistic philosophy
    (b) Socioeconomic competition   (e) Religious doctrine
    (c) Economic exploitation

Passage 4 : Big Trouble Loom for Korea's New Leader, Daejung Kim

    Washington : South Korea's new leader, Daejung Kim, defiled prison and exile, kidnappers, and killers on his way to his storybook triumph in last week's presidential elections. And now, he's learning, the first prize for his efforts is a pocketful of troubles.

    Kim, whose bravery *in the face of* persecution won him repeated nominations for the Nobel Peace Prize, inherits South Korea's deepest crisis in a generation. He faces the challenge of uniting a worried country behind unpopular austerity programs, as financial markets judge his every move. And Kim must do it as an economic *novice* and a political outsider.

    "He's an incredible character," said Don Oberdorfer, who published a book on South Korea this year. "<u>His time in prison greatly deepened his self-knowledge and his feelings for the country. ( ), he's like Gandhi, Ho Chi Minh and Nelson Mandela.</u> But he comes to office under the most trying circumstances you can think of."…

(Source : The Philadelphia Inquirer, Dec. 21, 1997)

(1) The topic of the article is "The _____ that South Korea's New Leader has to deal with." (Subject matter)

    (a) Triumphs   (b) Efforts   (c) Prizes   (d) Hurdles   (e) Circumstances

(2.1) The italicized phrase, *in the face of*, refers to _____. (2.1 - 2.2. Word & phrase in context)

    (a) Despite   (b) Toward   (c) Although   (d) Confronted with   (e) In front of

(2.2) The antonym of the italicized word, *novice*, is _____.

    (a) Amateur   (b) Probationer   (c) Expert   (d) Connoisseur   (e) Apprentice

(3) The underlined structure, "His time in prison… for the country. ( ), he is like Gandhi, Ho Chi Minh…." One of the most suitable word or phrase that fits in the parenthesis is _____. (Structure)

    (a) With that   (b) In that   (c) But that   (d) At that   (e) So that

(4.1) Based on the information given, it is predicted that the new leader will face

지문 4 : 한국의 새 지도자 김대중에게 큰 곤란이 어렴풋이 나타나다

워싱턴발 : 남한의 새 지도자 김대중은 투옥과 망명, 납치범들, 살인자들을 극복하고 지난주 대통령 선거에서 소설같고 행복한 승리를 거두었다. 그러나 그는 지금 자기 노력에 대한 최초의 전리품이 상당히 많은 어려운 문제들로 가득찼음을 깨닫고 있다.

박해를 무릅쓴 용기 때문에 노벨 평화상 후보로 여러 번 지명 받았던 김은 한 세대 중에 있었던 위기 중 가장 깊은 위기를 물려받는다. 그는 그의 모든 조치 심판받는 가운데 인기 없는 금융시장 긴축정책을 앞세워가며 위태한 나라를 단결시켜야하는 도전에 직면한다. 그는 경제적 초보자로 정치적 문외한으로서 그런 일을 해내야 한다.

금년에 남한 관련 책을 펴낸 Don Oberdorfer는 "그는 믿을 수 없을 만큼 놀라운 인물이다. 감옥안에 있던 시간이 그의 자기이해와 나라를 위한 연민의 정에 깊이를 크게 더해 주었다. 그런 점에서 그는 간디, 호치민 그리고 넬슨 만델라와 흡사하다. 그러나 그는 우리가 생각할 수 있는 가장 힘든 주변환경에서 취임하는 것이다."

Note

- **loom**=appear indistinctly and in threatening way : 어렴풋이 무섭게 나타나다
- **defile**=make dirty or impure : 불결하게 하다, 모독하다
- **in the face of**=in the presence of; in spite of : 면전에서, …를 무릅쓰고
  - What could he do in the face of all these difficulties?
- **nominate**=put forward for election : 후보로 지명하다
  - How many persons have been nominated for governorship so far?
  - (지금까지 몇 명이 지사 후보로 지명 받았소?)
- **austere**=lacking comfort, hard : 내핍의, 간소한, 엄격한   • austere life (내핍생활)
- **novice**=beginner : 초심자   **connoisseur** : (미술품등) 감정가

problems. One of the primary reasons for this prediction is based on that "He was
_____." (4.1 - 4.2. Making inferences)

(a) A political prisoner
(b) Exiled abroad
(c) Not an economic expert & political insider
(d) A political outsider
(e) Kidnapped

(4.2) It can be inferred that the underlined structure, "His time in prison greatly deepened his self-knowledge and his feelings for the country." refers to his strong

(a) Wish for democracy restoration
(b) Support for unification
(c) Wish for political stability
(d) Patriotism/nationalism
(e) Plan for economic recovery

(5.1) The underlined structure, "In that, he's like Gandhi…" can be concluded to be a/an _____. (5.1 - 5.3. Conclusions)

(a) Simile   (b) Comparison   (c) Connotation   (d) Metaphor   (e) Contrast

(5.2) Don Oberdorfer's statements, "He's an incredible character," and "He comes to office under the most trying circumstance…" can be concluded to be a/an _____.

(a) Truth   (b) Opinion   (c) Syllogism   (d) Fact   (e) Enthymeme

(5.3) The first paragraph, "South Korea's new leader, …. And now, he's learning, the first prize for his efforts is a pocketful of troubles." The tone of the writer implied in this paragraph can be concluded to be a/an _____.

(a) Opinion   (b) Fact   (c) Irony   (d) Exaggeration   (e) Satire

Passage 5 : "When I First Came to This Land": Traditional German American Folk Poem

Background : As we know, the United States of America is a "nation of immigrants." Except for Native American Indians, everyone's family has come to the United States from another country some time during the last three or four hundred years.

Two distinctive waves of immigration arrived in the United States during the 1800s. The first phase of immigration, lasting until about 1800, is called the "Old Immigrants." The bulk of these settlers were Protestants from northern and western Europe-from Germany, England, Ireland, and Sweden. Most were farmers leaving behind poverty and famine. Attracted by the availabilities of land, they settled in the Midwest and Great Plains working at farming.

Beginning in the 1880s came another wave of immigration, known as the "New Immigrants." These settlers were mostly Catholic and Jewish, and came from southern and eastern Europe - from Italy, Greece, Poland, Hungary, and Russia. Like the "Old Immigrants," these people came to escape poverty, hunger, or unjust governments. Many new immigrants worked in the factories and mines.

Immigration continues in the United States today. Every year, thousands of new

지문 5: '내가 처음 이 나라에 왔을 때': 전통적인 독일계 미국인의 민속시

배경: 우리가 아는 바와 같이 미합중국은 이주민들의 나라다. 토착 아메리카 인디안들을 제외하고 모든 가족은 지난 300 ~ 400년 동안 어느 땐가 외국에서 미국으로 왔다.

1800년대 중에 두번의 두드러진 이민의 물결이 미국에 몰아쳤다. 약 1800년까지 계속되었던 첫번째 이민 단계를 Old Immigrants라 부르며 이들 정착민들의 태반은 유럽의 북부와 서부 -독일, 영국, 아일랜드, 스웨덴- 에서 온 청교도들이다. 대부분은 가난과 기근을 뒤에 두고 떠나 온 농부들이었다. 토지를 취득, 이용할 수 있는 가능성에 이끌려서 중서부와 대평원에서 농사에 종사하며 정착했다.

1880년대부터 시작하여 New Immigrants로 알려진 또 하나의 이민 물결이 밀려왔다. 이 정착민들은 대부분 캐톨릭 신자나 유대인이었고 남부나 동부 유럽-이탈리아, 그리스, 폴란드, 헝가리, 러시아-에서 왔다. 많은 새 이주민들은 공장이나 광산에서 일했다.

이민은 지금도 미국에서 계속된다. 해마다 수천명의 새로운 미국 이주민들이 여러 다른 지방에 정착한다. 그들은 전쟁, 굶주림, 그리고 종교적, 정치적 자유 때문에 온다. 이 새 정착민들의 대부분은 남아시아 국가들 (베트남, 캄보디아, 라오스)과 중남미의 스페인어를 사용하는 국가들 (멕시코, 베네수엘라, 페루, 아르헨티나)로부터 온다. 약 20,000명의 한국인들이 1969년 이래 매년 미국으로 이민을 떠났다.

다음은 1880년대 이전의 독일 이민들의 생활 방식을 보여주는 전통적인 독일계 미국인의 민속시다.

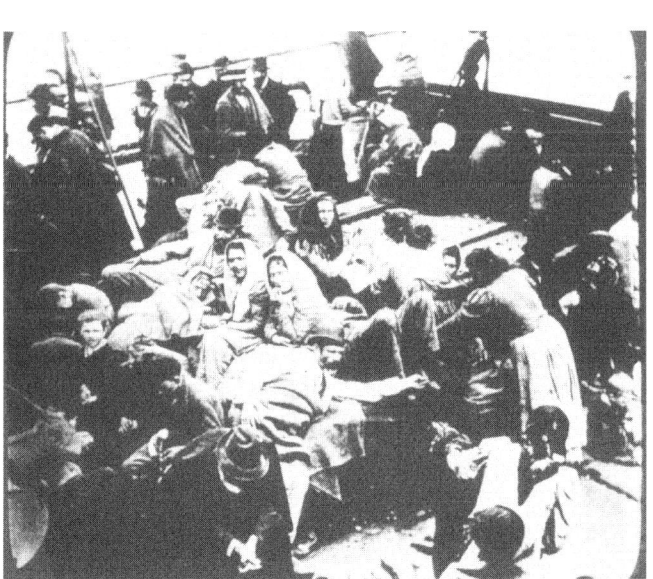

This photograph from 1890 shows immigrants on the deck of the ocean liner, S.S. Westernland.

Americans settle in different parts of the country. They come because of war, hunger, and religious or political freedom. The bulk of these new settlers are from South Asian countries (Vietnam, Cambodia, Laos) and from Spanish- speaking countries in Central and South Americas (Mexico, Venezuela, Peru, Argentina). About 20,000 Koreans have emigrated to the States every year since 1969. The following is a traditional German American poem which reflects one of the lifestyles of the German immigrants before the 1880s.

When I first came to this land, I was not a wealthy man.
I got myself a *shack*. And I called that shack "Break My Back,"
And the land was sweet and good, And I did what I could.

When I first came to this land, I was not a wealthy man.
I got myself a farm. And I called my farm "Muscle in My Arm,"
And I called my shack "Break My Back," And the land was sweet and good,
And I did what I could.

When I first came to this land, I was not a wealthy man.
I got myself a wife. And I called my wife "Love of My Life,"
And I called my farm "Muscle in My Arm," And I called my shack "Break My Back,"
And the land was sweet and good, And I did what I could.

When I first came to this land, I was not a wealthy man.
I got myself a cow. And I called that cow *No Milk Now*,"
And I called my wife "Love of My Life," And I called my farm "Muscle in My Arm,"
And I called my shack "Break My Back," And the land was sweet and good,
And I did what I could.

When I first came to this land, I was not a wealthy man.
I got myself a son. And I called that son "Lots of Fun,"
And I called that cow "No Milk Now," And I called my wife "Love of My Life,"
And I called my farm "Muscle in My Arm," And I called my shack "Break My Back,"
And the land was sweet and good, And I did what I could.

When I first came to this land, I was not a wealthy man.
I got myself a tree. And I called that tree "Family Tree,"
And I called that son "Lots of Fun," And I called that cow "No Milk Now,"
And I called my wife "Love of My Life," And I called my farm "Muscle in My Arm,"
And I called my shack "Break My Back," And the land was sweet and good,
And I did what I could.

(1) The most appropriate topic of the poem is "_____." (Subject matter)

    (a) My country, America   (d) My life of immigration in American
    (b) The culture shock I got in America (e) My family tree in America
    (c) My life in America

(2.1) The italicized word, *shack*, refers to "a small, old, _____." (2.1 - 2.2. Word & phrase in context)

    (a) Comfortable house   (c) Clean mansion   (e) Duplex house
    (b) Rough cabin   (d) Single house

내가 처음 이 땅에 왔을 때, 나는 부자가 아니었네.
나는 오두막을 하나 마련했지. 그리고 그것을 '노력의 결과'라고 불렀지.
땅은 향기로우며 친절했고 내가 할 수 있는 일은 다했지.

내가 처음 이 땅에 왔을 때, 나는 부자가 아니었네.
나는 농장을 하나 마련했지. 그리고 그것을 '노동의 대가'라 불렀지.
오두막은 '노력의 결과'로 불렀고 땅은 향기롭고 친절했지.
그리고 내가 할 수 있는 일은 다했지.

내가 처음 이 땅에 왔을 때, 나는 부자가 아니었네.
나는 아내를 얻었지. 그리고 그녀를 '내 생명의 사랑'이라 불렀지.
농장은 '노동의 대가'라 부르고, 오두막을 '노력의 결과'로 불렀네.
땅은 향기롭고 친절했지.
그리고 내가 할 수 있는 일은 다했지.

내가 처음 이 땅에 왔을 때, 나는 부자가 아니었네.
나는 암소 한마리를 구했지. 그리고 그 암소를 '미래의 보장'으로 불렀지.
아내를 '내 생명의 사랑'이라 부르고, 농장은 '노동의 대가'라 부르고
오두막은 '노력의 결과'로 불렀네. 땅은 향기롭고 친절했지.
나는 내가 할 수 있는 모든 일을 다했지.

내가 처음 이 땅에 왔을 때, 나는 부자가 아니었네.
나는 아들을 하나 얻었네. 그리고 그애를 '기쁨 덩어리'라 불렀지.
암소는 '미래의 보장'으로 부르고 아내는 '내 생명의 사랑'이라 불렀네.
농장은 '노동의 대가'라 부르고 오두막은 '노력의 결과'로 불렀네.
땅은 향기롭고 친절했고 나는 내가 할 수 있는 모든 일을 다했지.

내가 처음 이 땅에 왔을 때, 나는 부자가 아니었네.
나는 나무 한 그루를 얻었지. 그리고 그 나무를 '가족나무 (가계도)'라 불렀지.
아들은 '기쁨 덩어리'라 부르고, 암소는 '미래의 보장'으로 불렀지.
아내는 '내 생명의 사랑', 내 농장은 '노동의 대가'라 부르고
내 오두막은 '노력의 결과'로 불렀다네. 땅은 향기롭고 친절했지.
그리고 나는 내가 할 수 있는 모든 일을 다했지.

(2.2) The italicized phrase, "*No Milk Now*," implies _____.

  (a) Cash   (b) Insurance   (c) Auction   (d) Pawn   (e) Investment

(3) The underlined structure, "I was not a wealthy man," can be restructured as "I was not a man of _____."

  (a) Worth   (b) Poverty   (c) Resources   (d) Luxury   (e) Fame

(4.1) "I got myself a cow" can be inferred as an implication, "I could save some money for a _____ business." (4.1 - 4.2. Making inferences)

  (a) Farming   (b) Construction   (c) Dairy products   (d) Trading   (e) Mining

(4.2) The sentences, "I got myself a tree. And I called that tree 'Family Tree,'" can be inferred that the age of the farmer, "I" in the poem is probably in his _____.

  (a) Late 20s   (b) Early 30s   (c) Mid 30s   (d) Late 30s   (e) Late 50s

(5) Based on the information given, it can be concluded that the poem reflects the lifestyle of an immigrant from an agricultural area about _____ years ago. (Conclusion)

  (a) 50   (b) 75   (c) 100   (d) 200   (e) 500

Passage 6 : Language and Thought by Edward Sapir (1884 - 1939)

Background : Edward Sapir, one of the well-known pioneers of American ethnology, was born in Pomerania, Germany, and came to the United States at the age of five. He made his reputation as an expert on languages of American Indian. He, like Benjamin Lee Whorf who grasped the relationship between human language and thinking, was one of the first to explore the relations between language studies and anthropology. His publication, Language published in 1921, is his only full-length book for a general audience. He published a great number of articles and some verses in periodicals. The following is excerpted from "Introductory: Language Defined" in Language : An Introduction to the Study of Speech.

   Most people, asked if they can think without speech, would probably answer, "Yes, but it is not easy for me to do so. Still I know it can be done."··· No one believes that even the most difficult mathematical proposition is inherently dependent on an *arbitrary* set of symbols, but it is impossible to suppose that the human mind is capable of arriving at or holding such a proposition without the symbolism. The writer, for one, is strongly of the opinion that the feeling entertained by so many that they can think, or even reason, without language is an illusion. The illusion seems to be due to a number of factors. The simplest of these is the failure to distinguish between imagery and thought. As a matter of fact, no sooner do we try to put an image into conscious relation with another (_____) we find ourselves slipping into a silent flow of words. Thought may be a natural domain *apart from* the artificial one of speech, but speech would seem to be the only road we know that leads to it.

(Source: Edward Sapir (1921). Language: An Introduction to the Study of Speech. Harvest/HBJ Book, New York.)

Note

□ **distinctive**=serving to mark a difference or make distinct : 차별지우는, 특색있는
　• Scouts wear a distinctive uniform. (소년단원들은 특이한 제복을 입습니다.)
□ **phase**=stage of development : 발달 단계, 국면
　• The whole world has entered upon a totally new phase of history.
　　(세계는 전혀 새로운 역사의 국면에 접어 들었다.)
□ **bulk**=mass, the greater part or number of : 태반, 대부분
　• He left the bulk of his property to his brother. (그는 재산의 대부분을 동생에게 남겨 주었다.)
　• The ocean forms the bulk of the earth's surface.
□ **famine**=extreme scarcity esp. of food : 식량 부족, 기근
　• A lot of children in some Asian countries are reported to be suffering from famine.
　　(보도에 의하면 아시아 몇몇 나라 어린이들이 굶주림으로 고통받고 있다한다.)
□ **shack**=small, roughly built hut or house = hut : 오두막
□ **duplex** : 2중의, 양면 이용의 　• duplex hammer (양면 이용 망치)
　• duplex apartment (복식 아파트 : 실내 계단을 이용하는 아래 윗층 통합 아파트)
□ **pawn** : 저당 　• put sth in pawn (저당 잡히다)
□ **auction**=a public meeting to sell goods to the person who offers the most money : 경매
□ **dairy**=a place on the farm where milk is kept and butter and cheese are made : 낙농장
　• dairy cattle (젖소) 　• dairy products (낙농 제품)

지문 6 : 언어와 사고

배경 : 유명한 미국 민족학의 선구자의 한 사람인 에드워드 사피르는 독일 Pomerania 태생으로 5세 때 미국에 왔다. 그는 미국 인디안 언어들에 관한 전문가로서 명성을 얻었다. 그는 인간의 언어와 사고작용간의 관계를 파악한 벤자민 리 워프처럼 언어 연구와 인류학사이의 관계를 탐구한 최초의 사람들 중 한 사람이다. 1921년에 출간된 그의 저서 「언어 : 담화 연구 개론」에 실린 '서론 : 언어 연구'에서 발췌한 글이다.

Edward Sapir

　대부분의 사람들은 혹시 언어 없이 사고할 수 있느냐는 질문을 받으면 "그렇소, 그러나 쉽지는 않지요. 그래도 가능하지요…"라고 십중팔구는 대답할 것이다. 가장 난해한 수학의 명제도 원래부터 임의적인 기호들로 이뤄졌다고 믿는 사람은 아무도 없다. 그러나 인간의 마음이 기호사용 없이 그런 명제에 도달하거나 그것을 지닐 수 있다고 가정하는 것은 불가능하다. 나는 개인적으로 아주 많은 사람들이 갖고 있는, 언어 없이 사고할 수 있고 심지어 논리적으로 추리할 수 있다는 느낌은 하나의 망상이

(1) The topic of the passage is "Relations between _____." (Subject matter)

    (a) Language & symbols   (d) Thought & mathematical proposition
    (b) Language & imagery   (e) Thought & arbitrary set of symbols
    (c) Language & arbitrary set of symbols

(2.1) The antonym of the italicized word, *arbitrary*, is _____. (2.1. - 2.2. Word & phrase in context)

    (a) Absolute   (b) Dictatorial   (c) Autocratic   (d) Democratic   (e) Whimsical

(2.2) The italicized phrase, *apart from*, refers to _____.

    (a) Adjoining   (b) Surrounded   (c) Special   (d) Separated   (e) Apathetic

(3) The underlined structure, "no sooner… (_____) we find ourselves…." One of the following that fits well in the parenthesis is _____. (Structure)

    (a) Than   (b) Then   (c) That   (d) But   (e) As

(4.1) Based on the information given, it can be inferred that the relation between language and thought is _____. (4.1. - 4.2. Making inferences)

    (a) Logical   (b) Distinguished   (c) Independent   (d) Interdependent   (e) Symbolic

(4.2) It can be inferred that _____ is a vehicle through or with which we formulate and develop our _____.

    (a) Thought, language   (d) Language, thought
    (b) Thought, ideas   (e) Language, arbitrary set of symbols
    (c) Language, mathematical proposition

(5) Based on the information given, although language and thought are complementary to each other, language seems to serve as "the road" leading to thought. Therefore, it can be concluded that _____ controls a primary domain over _____. (Conclusion)

    (a) Language, thought   (c) Language, speech   (e) Thought, cognition
    (b) Thought, language   (d) Thought, illusion

Passage 7 : Dr. Philip Jaisohn (Jaepil Suh, 1866-1951): A Man of Reform, Science, and Publication

    Philip Jaisohn was born at Bosung in 1866. At the age of seven, he was adopted by a clansman who did not have a male heir. His adoptive parents sent him to Seoul to study Confucian classics to pass the governmental exam. He passed the exam with the highest honors at the age of thirteen.

    At the end of the 19th century, Korea(Yi Dynasty) was in turmoil. The government had severe power conflicts between the conservative and the reformative. The former attempted to maintain traditional sociopolitical stability under the influence of Chinese political power; whereas the latter tried to create a modern and independent state based on new western ideals

다 라는 의견을 강하게 가지고 있다. 그 망상은 여러가지 요인들 때문이다. 요인들 중 가장 단순한 것이 심상과 사고의 차이를 구분할 수 없다는 것이다. 실제로 우리가 하나의 심상을 다른 그것과 의식적으로 관계를 지으려고 하자마자 우리는 단어들의 흐름 속에 급히 빠져드는 자신을 발견한다. 사고란 언어가 만들어 내는 인위적인 사고와는 별개의 자연스런 영역일 수 있으나 언어는 그런 사고의 영역으로 우리를 인도하는 우리가 알고 있는 것 중 유일한 길인 것 같다.

Note

- ethnology : 민족학
- grasp=understand with the mind : 파악하다
  - Now I can grasp the true meaning of the maxim. (이제 그 경구의 참 뜻을 알겠다.)
- inherently : 원래부터, 타고 날 때 부터
- anthropology : 인류학
- arbitrary=based on impulse only, not on reason : 제 멋대로의
  - in arbitrary order (무순으로)
  - My choice of the candidate was just arbitrary. (아무렇게나 골라 찍었다.)
- illusion=seeing of something that does not really exist : 망상
- slip into : 미끄러져 빠지다, 급히 입다
- apart from=leaving on one side=independently of : …은 별도로 하고
- autocratic=dictatorial : 독재적인
- apathetic : 냉담한 • cf. sympathetic (동조적인)
- antipathetic : 반감을 가진

지문 7 : 서재필 박사—개혁, 과학, 출판의 인물

PHILIP JAISOHN, M.D.
(1866~1951)

필립 제이슨은 1866년 보성에서 태어났다. 7세 때 남자 상속인이 없는 어느 문중에 양자로 들어갔다. 그의 양부모는 그를 유학 공부를 해서 국가고시에 합격하도록 서울로 보냈다. 13세 때 최고의 성적으로 그 시험에 합격했다.

19세기 말에 조선(이 왕조)은 혼란에 빠져 있었다. 조정에서는 수구파와 개혁파 사이에 심각한 권력 싸움이 있었다. 전자는 중국 정치적 힘의 영향하에서 전통적인 사회정치적 안정을 유지하려고 했고 반면에 후자는 새로운 서양의 이상과 제도의 토대 위에 현대적이며 독립된 국가를 건설하려고 노력했다. 중국 군대의 개입으로 개혁파들의 조선 현대화 노력이 실패한 직후 필립과 관련 인사들은 일본으로 도피했다. 도쿄에서 그

and systems. Soon after the reformatists' attempts to modernize Korea failed by the intervention from the Chinese army, Philip and his associates escaped to Japan. In Tokyo, he stayed with American missionaries to whom he taught Korean, and they taught him about America. In April 1885, he left for San Francisco.

In the United States, Jaisohn took a Civil Service exam, and was appointed to the Surgeon General's library. He began medical studies at Corcoran Scientific School, an evening division of Columbia University. He met Dr. Walter Reed with whom he conducted experiments in microphotography and biochemistry. In 1891, he received his medical degree from Columbia Medical College. He moved to Philadelphia and did research at the Wister Institute of *Anatomy* and Biology at the University of Pennsylvania.

In late 1895, he returned to Korea with his wife, Muriel, at the request of his old friend, Younghyo Park. He became an advisor to the Korean Government Privy Council. As a way of *disseminating* information and news widely to the Korean people, which would eventually help his people to be more informed, he began publishing "The Independent," the first Korean-language newspaper on April 7, 1876. This date has been observed as the birthday of modern journalism in Korea.

Philip and Muriel had two daughters, Muriel and Stephanie. On June 19, 1888, he became the first naturalized citizen of the United States by Congressional Act, and the first Korean to become an American educated physician in 1891. On January 5, 1951, during the midst of the Korean War, Philip Jaisohn died of cancer of the bladder with a remarkable devotion of his life for the down-trodden people in two countries on two continents. Rose Tree Park in Media has a monument honoring his humanitarian devotion and his active commitment for those people he loved very much.

(Source: Supplemented and adapted from Press Focus, May 16, 1990. Drexel Hill, Haverford, & Springfield Press.)

(1.1) The main idea of the second paragraph is _____. (1.1. - 1.2. Subject matters)

  (a) How he escaped to Japan
  (b) The Yi Dynasty at the end of the 19th Century
  (c) The conflicts between the conservative and the reformative.
  (d) When he left for San Francisco.
  (e) The sociopolitical realities of the Yi Dynasty when he was young

(1.2) The main idea of the fourth paragraph is _____.

  (a) How and why he published the newspaper.
  (b) When he published the newspaper.
  (c) An introduction of modern Korean journalism.
  (d) The published date of the first Korean-language newspaper.
  (e) When he and his wife returned to Korea.

(2.1) The italicized word, *disseminating*, in the fourth paragraph refers to _____.
   (2.1. - 2.2. Words in context)

   (a) Analyzing   (b) Collecting   (c) Synthesizing   (d) Concealing   (e) Spreading

(2.2) The italicized word, *anatomy*, in the third paragraph refers to the study of the _____ of animals and plants.

가 한국말을 가르쳐 준 선교사들과 함께 지냈고 그들은 그에게 미국에 관하여 가르쳐 주었다. 1885년 4월에 그는 샌프란시스코로 떠났다.

미국에서 제이슨은 공무원 시험에 응시했고 공중 위생국의 도서관원으로 임명되었다. 컬럼비아 의대의 야간부인 Concoran 과학부에서 의학을 공부했다. 그는 월터 리드 박사를 만나 함께 축소 사진과 생화학 실험을 했다. 1891년에 컬럼비아 의대에서 의학 박사학위를 받았다. 필라델피아로 이사를 하여 펜실베이니아 대학의 Wister 해부학과 생물학 연구소에서 연구했다.

1895년에 옛 친구인 박영효의 요청으로 아내 뮤리엘과 함께 귀국했다. 그는 조선정부 추밀원의 자문이 되었다. 조선 백성들에게 널리 정보와 뉴스를 전파함으로써 결과적으로 그들에게 더 많은 정보를 알려 주는데 도움이 되도록 하려고 1876년 4월 7일, 한국 최초의 한글신문인 독립신문을 발행했다. 이 날짜는 한국 현대 언론의 창시일로 기념되어 오고 있다.

필립과 뮤리엘에게는 딸이 둘이 있었는데 뮤리엘과 스테파니였다.

This monument to Jaisohn was erected in 1975 in the country's Rose Tree Park in Upper Providence, near the 4-H building.

Photo by Paula Williams

1888년 6월 19일에 그는 미 의회법에 의하여 최초의 미국 귀화시민이 되었으며, 1891년에 미국 의사교육을 받은 최초의 한국인이 되었다.

1951년 1월 5일, 한국 전쟁 중에 필립 제이슨은 2개 대륙에 있는 2개 국가의 억압받는 사람들을 위해 평생토록 열성적으로 헌신한 후 방광암으로 세상을 떠났다. Rose Tree Park에는 그가 사랑했던 사람들에게 행한 인도주의적 헌신과 적극적인 열성을 기리는 기념비가 하나 있다.

Museum Sought For Jaisohn Home

Though Dr. Philip Jaisohn passed away in 1951, his memory is being honored by the Philip Jaisohn Memorial Foundation, Inc., which was started in 1975. The year it was established, a memorial was erected to Jaisohn in the county's Rose Tree Park in Upper Providence, and the Philip Jaisohn Medical Center opened in Philadelphia. In 1980, the foundation established a social service for immigrants, a cultural activities department and a education and research department.

In 1987, the Jaisohn foundation bought the Jaisohn house at 100 E. Lincoln St., Upper Providence. On March 29 of this year the foundation was granted a special exception for the home to become a museum from the Upper Providence Zoning Board.

"Whatever he (Jaisohn) touched would be considered sacred," Media architect Dongkyu Bak, a Korean born American and former member of the Rose Tree-Media School Board, said.

Dr. Bong Sik Lee president of the Jaisohn foundation says when they open the museum it will house Korean antiques, some of Jaisohn's original furniture, and copies of historical documents with which Jaisohn was involved.

Dr. Philip Jaisohn lived most of his last 25 year in this house at 100 E. Lincoln St., Upper Providence. There are plans to turn it into a museum.

Photo by Paula Williams

(a) Function of major organs   (c) Structure of bodies   (e) Structure of bones
(b) Structure of cells   (d) Structure of chemicals

(3) The underlined word, <u>whereas</u>, in the second paragraph can be substituted as "_____." (Structure)

    (a) While   (b) Because   (c) Since   (d) As   (e) Although

(4.1) During the period of turmoil in Korea, it can be inferred that Philip was one of the members of the _____. (4.1. - 4.2. Making inferences)

    (a) Conservative   (b) Traditional   (c) Anarchistic   (d) Communist   (e) Reformative

(4.2) "April 7" has been observed as the birthday of modern Korean journalism. One of the significant reasons can be inferred as "He _____."

    (a) Published "The Independent" newspaper.
    (b) Disseminated information and news.
    (c) Helped his people to be more informed.
    (d) Helped his people to be more democratic.
    (e) Published the first Korean-language newspaper with patriotism.

(5.1) This type of article can be concluded as a style of _____. (5.1. - 5.3. Conclusions)

    (a) Drama   (b) Autobiography   (c) Biography   (d) Entertainment   (e) Fiction

(5.2) The whole paragraph patterns of this article can be concluded as an organization of _____.

    (a) Analysis   (c) Description   (e) Comparison and Contrast
    (b) Analogy   (d) Definition

(5.3) One of the most significant reasons Philip Jaisohn is still remembered with respect by Koreans and Americans can be concluded that he _____.

    (a) Became the first physician.
    (b) Became the first naturalized Korean.
    (c) Published the first Korean-language newspaper.
    (d) Was an active reformist.
    (e) Devoted himself to the destitute people in two countries based on humanitarianism.

Passage 8 : Queen Liliuokalani (1838 - 1917) : The Last Monarch of Hawaii

Queen Liliuokalani was the last of the Hawaiian monarchs. She became queen in 1891 at a time when the native population had been *decimated* by introduced diseases from the outside world, and when the influence of the missionary and the U.S. on the local economy was extremely tremendous. Many ambitious foreigners saw the Queen as an obstacle to their grandiose dreams of profit and power. Led by Sanford B. Dole, the Missionary Party asked for her abdication in January 1893, and, declaring the Queen deposed, announced the establishment of a provisional government pending annexation by the U.S. To avoid

Note

- **reform**=improve, make or become right : 개혁하다
  - Harry has completely reformed his character; now he has stopped taking drugs.
  (해리는 완전히 품성을 고쳤다 ; 그는 마약 흡입을 끊었다.)
- **clansman** : 같은 씨족의 사람, 문중 사람
- **turmoil**=trouble, agitation, disturbance : 소란, 동요, 소요
  - The town was in turmoil during the elections. (선거 중 떠들썩했다.)
- **conservative**=opposed to great or sudden change : 보수적, 수구적
  - Old people are usually more conservative than young people.
- **Surgeon General** : 의무감, 공중 위생국 장관
- **intervention**=interference, interruption : 개입, 방해
  - They made an armed intervention in the affairs of our country. (우리 국내 문제에 무력 개입을 했다.)
- **biochemistry** : 생화학   □ **anatomy** : 해부학
- **Privy Council** : 추밀원   □ **cancer of bladder** : 방광암
- **disseminate**=spread, distribute news, ideas, doctrines widely : 유포하다, 퍼뜨리다
- **observe**=celebrate festivals, birthdays, anniversaries : 기념하다
- **downtrodden**=oppressed, kept down and treated badly : 유린당한, 학대받는
- **monument**=a building, pillar, statue that preserves the memory of a person or event : 기념비
  - This pillar is a monument to all those who died in the war. (이 柱石은 모든 전사자들을 위한 기념비다.)
- **humanitarian** : 인도주의자 (적)   □ **antique** : 골동품   □ **anarchistic** : 무정부 상태인
- **synthesize**=make up or produce by combining parts : 종합, 합성하다 • opp. analyze (분석하다)

지문 8: 하와이의 마지막 군주 Liliuokalani 여왕

Lili. 여왕은 하와이의 마지막 군주였다. 그녀는 외부 세계에서 들어온 전염병으로 토착 주민들이 많이 죽고 선교사와 미국이 그 지역 경제에 엄청난 영향력을 끼치던 때인 1891년에 여왕이 되었다. 야심에 찼던 많은 외국인들은 여왕을 이익과 권력을 잡으려는 그들의 웅대한 꿈에 대한 방해자로 생각했다. Sanford B. Dole의 지휘로 선교단들은 1893년에 1월에 그녀의 퇴위를 요구했고, 여왕의 하야를 선언하고, 미국에 의한 합병시까지 임시정부의 수립을 발표했다. 유혈 참극을 피하기 위하여 여왕은 항복했지만 미 대통령 그로버 클리블랜드에게 그녀와 그의 국민들에게 끼친 불법 침해를 돌이켜 달라고 애원했다. 미 대통령은 외국 정부를 전복시키는데

Queen Liliuokalani
By courtesy of the Bernice P. Bishop Museum

bloodshed, the Queen surrendered, but she appealed to the U.S. President, Grover Cleveland for the reversal of the injustice done to her and her people. The President was outraged at the American role in the overthrow of a foreign government, and he ordered the Queen to be restored. But Dole and other American business leaders *defied* the order, claiming that Cleveland had not the authority to interfere. Dole became President of the Hawaiian Republic; whereas the Queen was placed under house arrest in 1895 and forced to swear allegiance to the new republic. Before Cleveland could right this terrible wrong, he was voted out of office and replaced with President McKinley who signed the annexation bill on July 7, 1898. The Hawaiian Islands became part of the U.S.

Queen Liliuokalani loved her country and wanted ( ) to stay independent, but she failed in protecting Hawaii's independence. She was loved and respected by her people until her death. She wrote her memoirs, Hawaii's Story By Hawaii's Queen in 1898. Today millions of people visit the royal palace where Queen Liliuokalani, the Last Monarch of Hawaii, once lived.

(1) One of the most appropriate topics of the passage is _____. (Subject matter)

    (a) A sad story about the Queen   (d) The injustice done to the Queen
    (b) The provisional Hawaiian government   (e) Facts about the Queen & her country
    (c) The annexation of Hawaii

(2.1) The italicized word, *decimated*, in the first paragraph refers to _____. (2.1 - 2.2. Words in context)

    (a) Destroyed   (b) Murdered   (c) Captured   (d) Dissected   (e) Dispersed

(2.2) The antonym of the italicized word, *defied*, refers to _____.

    (a) Challenged   (b) Thwarted   (c) Confronted   (d) Disregarded   (e) Yielded

(3) The underlined structure, "Queen Liliuokalani loved her country and wanted ( ) to stay independent," includes a parenthesis to be filled in. The proper word that best fits in the parenthesis is ____. (Structure)

    (a) Herself   (b) It   (c) Them   (d) Her country   (e) The island

(4.1) It can be inferred that the governmental form of Hawaii before the annexation in 1898 was a _____. (4.1 - 4.5. Making inferences)

    (a) Republic   (b) Democracy   (c) Totalitarian rule   (d) Kingdom   (e) Imperialistic rule

(4.2) The U.S. government annexed Hawaii in 1898. Primary reasons for this annexation can be inferred from the conclusion that the Hawaiian Islands could serve as important bases for _____ and _____ purposes.

    (a) Agricultural, commercial   (d) Recreational, tourism
    (b) Military, commercial   (e) Territorial expansion, fishing
    (c) Industrial, agricultural

(4.3) Based on the information given, it can be inferred that most native Hawaiians _____ the establishment of a provisional government led by the Missionary Party.

미국이 한 역할에 격분하고 여왕의 복위를 지시했다. 그러나 Dole과 다른 사업 지도자들은 이 명령을 무시하고 클리블랜드는 간섭할 권한이 없다고 주장했다. Dole은 하와이 공화국의 대통령이 되었고 반면에 여왕은 1895년에 가택 연금에 처해지고 신공화국에 충성을 맹세하도록 강요 당했다. 클리블랜드대통령이 이 끔찍한 부당행위를 바로 잡기 전에 투표에서 패배하여 대통령직에서 물러나고 매킨리로 대치되었으며 그는 1898년 7월 7일에 합병법안에 서명했다. 하와이 군도가 미국의 일부가 되었다.

Lili. 여왕은 자기 나라를 사랑했고 그 나라가 독립된 상태로 유지되기를 원했지만 하와이의 독립을 지키는 데 실패했다. 그녀는 죽을 때까지 국민의 사랑을 받았다. 그녀는 1898년에 회고록 '하와이 여왕의 하와이 이야기'를 썼다. 오늘날 수많은 사람들이 하와이 최후의 군주 Lili 여왕이 한 때 살았던 궁전을 찾아온다.

Note

- **decimate**=destroy a large part of : 10명 중 한 사람이 죽다, 많이 죽다
  - The plague of cholera decimated the population of Europe.
- **introduced disease** : 풍토병이 아닌 외부에서 들어온 질병
- **obstacle**=something in the way that stops progress or make it difficult : 방해물
  - Their nuclear tests are serious obstacles to world peace.
- **grandiose**=planned on a large scale, imposing : 웅대한, 숭고한, 위압적인
  - He made a grandiose speech in front of the complaining workers. (거드름 피는 연설)
- **abdicate**=give up, renounce a high office, authority : 퇴위하다, 하야하다
  - King Edward VIII abdicated in 1937, and was created Duke of Windsor.
    (에드워드 8세는 1937년에 퇴위하고 윈저공이 되었다.)
- **depose**=remove, esp. a ruler such as a king=dethrone : 고위직에서 면직시키다, 퇴위시키다
  - The premier was deposed by the revolution. (혁명에 의하여 총리가 쫓겨났다.)
- **pending**=until
  - I will wait pending his acceptance of the offer. (그가 그 제안을 수락할 때까지 기다리겠다.)
- **annexation**=action of joining something as a subordinate : 합병
  - The U.S. annexed Texas in 1845.
- **reversal** . 전환하기, 바꾸기 • Our positions have been reversed. (입장이 역전 됐다.)
- **outrage**=offend greatly : 분개하게 하다
  - The closing of the hospital has outraged public opinion. (그 병원을 문닫는 일은 여론을 들끓게 했다.)
- **overthrow**=defeat, remove from official power : 전복시키다, 타도하다
  - The angry farmers roused themselves to overthrow the evil government.
    (화난 농부들이 악질 정부를 타도하려고 궐기했다.)
- **restore**=give or bring back : 복위시키다, 회복시키다
  - The employees were restored to their old post. (피고용인들이 옛날 직위로 복직되었다.)
- **defy**=resist openly, refuse to obey : 공공연히 반항하다, 무시하다
  - He has a constitution that defies any climate. (그는 어떤 기후에도 끄떡하지 않는 체질을 가졌다.)
- **interfere**=break in without invitation : 멋대로 방해하다
  - Please don't interfere in my business. (제발 내일을 방해하지 마시오.)

(a) Were strongly for (c) Were indifferent to (e) Mildly disliked
(b) Were strongly against (d) Lightly supported

(4.4) After the annexation, the average socioeconomic status of the native Hawaiians compared to that of other ethnic groups in Hawaii is inferred to be in the _____ class.

(a) Upper upper (c) Low upper (e) Below middle
(b) Middle upper (d) Above middle

(The class (a) refers to the people who don't have to work to live; their wealth is usually inherited. The class (b) refers to the very rich people who have worked and amassed their fortune as most celebrities. The class (c) means white-collar professionals such as doctors, lawyers, etc. The word, "middle" in classes (d) & (e) refer to the middle-class people.)

(4.5) It can be inferred that most native Hawaiians are able to speak and write their native language _____ today.

(a) Very fluently (b) Fluently (c) Fairly (d) Moderately (e) Very poorly

(5) One of the following statements/proverbs that best reflects the theme of the passage can be _____. (Conclusion)

(a) Life is in labor. (Russian proverb)
(b) Paddle your own canoe.
(c) Hope is the poor man's income. (Danish proverb)
(d) Happiness is made to be shared. (French proverb)
(e) History repeats itself.

Passage 9 : Harry Truman (1884-1972) Writes Home from His New Office in The White House

<u>Background</u> :President Franklin D. Roosevelt died on April 12, 1945 in the midst of World War II. Vice President Harry S.Truman became the new president. Germany agreed to surrender on May 7. Truman, Winston Churchill, and Joseph Stalin met at Potsdam in Germany to discuss the fate of Germany and how to end the war with Japan. On his way home from Potsdam, Truman made one of the most difficult decisions, and ordered American fliers to drop an atomic bomb on Hiroshima, and later on Nagasaki as a way of ending the war quickly.

Truman, 33rd President of the United States (1945-1953), was the son of a mule trader and farmer in Missouri. Below is a letter that Truman wrote to his mother, Martha Ellen Young (92 years old), and his sister, Mary Jane, on his 61st birthday, after Germany surrendered.

> ☐ house arrest : 가택연금
> • They placed the dissident under house arrest. (그들은 그 반대자를 가택연금 시켰다.)
> ☐ allegiance=loyalty, faith and dutiful support to a leader, country, idea : 충성
> ☐ thwart=oppose successfully : 방해하다
> • My plan was thwarted by the bad weather. (계획이 악천후로 실행되지 못했다.)
> ☐ confront=face boldly or threateningly : 당당히 맞서다, 대항하다
> • You will confront lots of difficulties in the course of your life. (살아가자면 많은 난관에 부딪치게 된다.)

지문 9 : 해리 트루만 백악관 집무실에서 집에 편지 쓰다

배경 : 프랭클린 루즈벨트 대통령은 세계 2차 대전 중인 1945년 4월 12일에 사망했다. 부통령이었던 해리 트루만이 새 대통령이 되었다. 독일이 7일에 항복하기로 동의했다. 트루만, 처칠, 스탈린은 독일의 포츠담에서 만나 독일의 운명과 일본과의 전쟁을 끝내는 방법을 토의했다. 투르만은 포츠담으로부터 귀국길에 가장 어려운 결정을 하고 미 비행사들에게 전쟁을 속히 끝내는 한 방법으로 히로시마에 그리고 그 후에 나가사키에 원자폭탄 투하를 명령했다.

Truman, 1945

미국 33대 대통령인 트루만은 미조리의 노새 상인이자 농부의 아들이었다. 다음은 그가 독일 항복 후 61세 생일에 92세의 노모인 마르타 엘렌 영과 여동생 마리 제인에게 써 보낸 편지다.

사랑하는 어머니와 누이에게

오늘 아침이 저의 61세 생일입니다. 어젯밤은 백악관 대통령 집무실에서 잤습니다. 페인트칠도 끝내고 가구도 제자리에 놓았습니다. 모든 것이 금요일에 어머님과 누이를 맞이할 수 있게 준비되고 있습니다. 제 비싼 금만년필이 제대로 글씨를 쓰지 못하네요.

오늘은 역사적인 날이 될 것입니다. 오늘 오전 9시 전국에 독일의 항복을 발표

Harry Truman greets his 92-year-old mother, Martha Truman. It was her first visit since he became president in 1945.

Dear Mama & Mary :   May 8, 1945

    I am sixty-one this morning, and I slept in the President's room in the White House last night. They have finished the painting and have some of the furniture in place. I'm hoping it will all be ready for you by Friday. My expensive gold pen doesn't work as well as it should.

    This will be a historical day. At 9:00 o'clock this morning I must make a broadcast to the country, announcing the German surrender. The papers were signed yesterday morning and *hostilities* will cease on all fronts at midnight tonight. Isn't that some birthday present?

    Have had *one heck of a time* with the Prime Minister of Great Britain. He, Stalin, and the U.S. President made an agreement to release the news all at once from the three capitals at an hour that would fit us all. We agreed on 9 a.m. Washington time which is 3 p.m. London and 4 p.m. Moscow time.

    Mr. Churchill began calling me at daylight to know if we shouldn't make an immediate release without considering the Russians. He was refused and then he kept pushing me to talk to Stalin. He finally had to stick to the agreed plan - but he was *mad as a wet hen*.

    Things have moved at a terrific rate here since April 12. <u>Never a day has gone by that some momentous decision didn't have to be made</u>. So far luck has been with me. I hope it keeps up. It can't stay with me forever however and I hope when the mistake comes it won't be too great to remedy. We are looking forward to a grand visit with you. I may not be able to come for you as planned but I'm sending the safest, finest airplane and all kinds of help so please don't disappoint me.

                                            Lots & lots of love to you both.
                                                      Harry

(Source: Lang, Jack (1982). Letters in American History.)

(1) The message of the letter can be briefly summarized as "_____." (Subject matter)

    (a) Churchill and Stalin do not get along well
    (b) I will make a broadcast, announcing the German surrender
    (c) Since I am sending the safest and finest airplane to you, please come to see me
    (d) Please come to see your son and brother who serves his new job with pride
    (e) Please come to see your son and brother who misses both of you

(2.1) The opposite word of the italicized word, *hostilities*, refers to _____. (2.1. - 2.3. Word & phrases in context)

    (a) Hospitality (b) Antagonism (c) Abhorrence (d) Animosity (e) Antipathy

(2.2) The italicized colloquial phrase, *one heck of a time*, refers to "a _____ time."

    (a) Plenty   (b) Boring   (c) Difficult   (d) Great   (e) Disgusting

 ("One heck of a time" is often used by the people from the South; whereas "One hell of a time" is often used by the Northerners.)

(2.3) The italicized phrase, "*Mad as a wet hen*," can be substituted as "Angry as a/an ____."

하는 방송을 해야합니다. 문서들은 어제 아침에 조인됐고 오늘밤 자정을 기하여 모든 전선에서 전쟁행위는 종식될 것입니다. 이 사실이 생일 선물이지 않겠습니까?

영국 수상과 한바탕 승강이를 했지요. 그와 스탈린 그리고 나는 그 뉴스를 우리 모두에게 적당한 시간에 세 수도에서 동시 발표하기로 합의했습니다. 워싱턴 시간으로 오전 9시, 런던은 오후 3시, 모스크바 시간은 오후 4시로 동의했지요.

처칠씨가 혹시 소련 사람들 생각은 않고 즉시 발표를 하면 안되겠는가를 알아보려고 새벽에 전화를 걸어왔어요. 제가 거절했더니 저더러 스탈린에게 이야기하라고 계속 조르네요. 그는 원안을 지켜야 했지만 비맞은 닭처럼 화를 냈어요. 4월 12일 이후 상황이 빠른 속도로 진행되어 왔습니다. 하루도 어떤 중대한 결정을 하지 않아도 될 날은 없었습니다. 지금까지는 운이 좋았습니다. 계속 운이 따랐으면 좋겠습니다. 그러나 행운이 영원히 저와 함께 있을 수는 없겠지요. 그래서 어떤 잘못이 생긴다면 그것이 손을 쓸 수 없을 만큼 중요한 것이 아니기를 바랍니다. 저는 어머님과 누이와의 멋진 대화를 학수고대하고 있습니다. 제가 계획대로 모시러 갈 수 없을지도 모르지만 가장 안전하고 훌륭한 비행기와 모든 것에서 도와드릴 사람들을 보내겠습니다. 그러니 꼭 오셔야 합니다.

　　　　　　　　　　　　　　　1945년 5월 8일　　　　두 분을 몹시 사랑하는 해리 올림

Note

- □ hostilities=acts of war : 전쟁행위　　• open(suspend) hostilities (전쟁을 시작하다(끝내다))
- □ cease=come or bring to an end : 끝나(내)다
  - The factory has ceased making bicycles. (그 공장은 자전거 생산을 그만 두었다.)
- □ heck=hell : used in exclamation : 지옥, 감탄에 쓰임
  - Heck! (빌어먹을! 제기랄!)　　• I had a heck of time. (아주 험한 꼴을 당했다.)
- □ release=allow to be known or published : 공표하다, 개봉하다
  - The scientist agreed to release his article for publication.
    (그 과학자는 자기 논문을 발표해도 좋다고 합의했다.)
- □ momentous=important, serious : 중요한
  - We listened on the radio to the momentous news that war had begun.
    (라디오로 전쟁이 시작되었다는 중대한 뉴스를 들었다.)
- □ hospitality=friendly and generous reception and entertainment of guests esp. in ones' own home : 환대, 후하게 대접하기
- □ disappoint=fail to do or be equal to what is hoped for or expected : 실망시키다
  - I hope this book will not disappoint you.
- □ animosity=hatred : 증오, 원한　　□ antagonism=active opposition : 적대감
- □ abhorrence : 혐오
- □ never... without : …하면 꼭 …한다　• It never rains without pouring. (불행은 겹쳐 온다.= 禍不單行)
- □ hornet : 말벌　　□ jaded=tired out, worn out : 몹시 지친, 넌더리 나는

(a) Hornet (b) Bull (c) Lion (d) Tiger (e) Cheetah

(3) The underlined structure, "Never a day has gone by that some momentous decision didn't have to be made," can be restructured as "Never a day has gone by without some momentous decisions _____ made." (Structure)

(a) Are (b) Are being (c) Being (d) Having been (e) Were

(4) The tone of the passage seems to be _____. (Making inference)

(a) Mildly cynical (b) Jaded (c) Sarcastic (d) Respectful (e) Optimistic

(5) Based on the information given from the section of the "Background" and the "letter," it can be concluded that Truman was a/an _____ leader. (Conclusion)

(a) Timid (b) Popular (c) Determined (d) Aggressive (e) Conservative

Passage 10 : El Niño and La Niño

About a hundred years ago, inhabitants along the northwest coast of Peru had long noticed the periodic appearance of warm seawater. They called it "El Niño," meaning literally "the boy." Today, "El Niño" refers more broadly to the appearance of warm sea surface water in the central and eastern equatorial Pacific Ocean; whereas, La Niño (means "the girl") that of cold sea surface water.

(1) How often does El Niño occur? Every two to ten years.

(2) How does it work? In normal, non-El Niño conditions, the trade winds blow toward the west across the tropical Pacific. These winds pile up warm surface in the west Pacific, so that the sea surface is about $\frac{1}{2}$ meter higher at Indonesia than at Ecuador. During El Niño event, the trade winds relax in the central and western Pacific leading to a depression of the *thermocline* in the eastern Pacific, and an elevation of the thermocline in the west. The result is a rise in sea surface temperature, and rainfall follows the warm water eastward with associated flooding in Peru and drought in Indonesia and Australia.

(3) Does El Niño represent unusual behavior of the global climate?
No. During an El Niño event, the sea surface temperatures in the eastern and central Pacific rise above the long-term average. But the change is really just a normal part of the global climate system. El Niño has been around for thousands of years, and 'to go through a *decade* or two without El Niño would be unusual.'

(4) Is El Niño part of a cycle?
Yes. El Niño is the media darling, so few people have heard of its *counterpart*, La Niña. El Niño and La Niña are the two faces: warm and cold, of a cycle. During La Niña, sea surface temperatures in the eastern and central Pacific are lower than usual. And the impacts of La Niña events are thought to be the opposite of those related to El Niño.

(5) Will global warming make El Niño bigger and meaner?
Don't know. There has been plenty of *speculation* about how global warming will affect El Niño. Will El Niño appear more frequently, be more intense, last longer? At this point, the

□ sarcastic=intended to hurt feelings, sneering : 비꼬는, 빈정거리는
□ timid=easily frightened, shy : 소심한, 수줍은   • The fellow is as timid as a rabbit.
□ aggressive=disposed to attack, quarrelsome, offensive : 공격적인, 걸핏하면 싸우려 드는

지문 10 : 엘니뇨와 라니냐

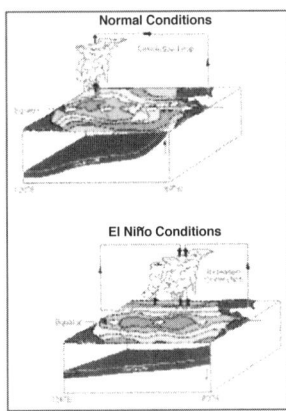
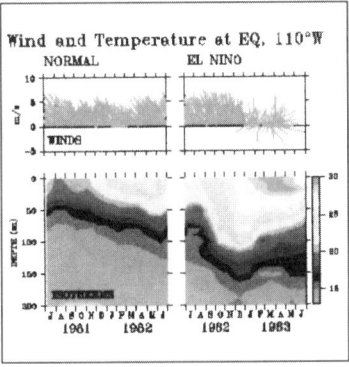

약 100년 전에 페루의 북서 해안에 살던 주민들이 정기적으로 따뜻한 해수가 나타나는 것을 목격했다. 그들은 소년을 의미하는 뜻을 가진 엘니뇨라고 불렀다. 오늘날 엘니뇨는 더 광범위하게 중앙 및 동부 적도 태평양에서 따뜻한 해수면의 출현을 가리킨다. 반면에 소녀를 의미하는 라니냐는 찬 해수면의 출현을 의미한다.

(1) 얼마나 자주 엘니뇨는 발생하는가?

2년에서 10년마다 일어난다.

(2) 어떻게 작용하는가?

정상적인 非엘리뇨 상태에서는 무역풍이 열대 태평양을 가로질러 서쪽으로 분다. 이 바람들이 서태평양에 따뜻한 수면을 모아 올리고, 그리하여 해수면이 에콰도르에서보다 인도네시아에서 약 50cm가량 높다. 엘니뇨가 발생하면 그 무역풍이 중앙 및 서부 태평양에서의 변온층 상승을 낳는다. 그 결과 수면 온도가 올라가고 동쪽으로 따뜻한 해수를 따라 비가 내려 페루에는 부수적인 홍수가, 인도네시아와 오스트렐리아에서는 가뭄이 온다.

(3) 엘니뇨는 지구 기상의 異常 움직임을 대표하는가?

그렇지 않다. 엘니뇨 발생 중에는 동, 中央 태평양의 수면 온도가 장기간의 평균 온

likely impacts are not predictable with any degree of certainty.

(Source: Adapted from "El Niño Information of 1997-1998" (1998). U.S. Department of Commerce. Glantz, Michael (1997). "Seven Things People Ought To Know About El Niño." <u>Fragilecologies</u>, Dec. 12, 1997.)

(1) The main idea of the passage is _____ (Subject matter)

    (a) How often do El Niño and La Niña occur?
    (b) How do El Niño and La Niña work?
    (c) Do El Niño and La Niña represent unusual behavior of the global climate?
    (d) Are El Niño and La Niña parts of a cycle?
    (e) What are El Niño and La Niña?

(2.1) The italicized word, *thermocline*, refers to the sharp change of _____. (2.1 - 2.4. Words & phrase in context)

    (a) Temperature   (b) Weather   (c) Climate   (d) Trade winds   (e) Rainfall

(2.2) The italicized word, *decade*, refers to _____ years.

    (a) 5   (b) 10   (c) 15   (d) 20   (e) 25

(2.3) The antonym of the italicized word, *counterpart*, is _____.

    (a) Partner   (b) Associate   (c) Equivalent   (d) Mate   (e) Opposite

(2.4) The italicized word, *speculation*, most closely refers to a/an _____.

    (a) Wild guess   (b) Opinion/view   (c) Proven theory   (d) Rule   (e) Law

(3) The underlined structure, "There has been plenty of speculation…," can be substituted as "There has been _____." (Structure)

    (a) A plenty of speculation…   (d) A great deal of speculation…
    (b) The great number of speculation…   (e) The great deal of speculation…
    (c) Lots of speculation…

(4.1) "El Niño is the media darling," can be interpreted as "For higher ratings, the media _____ El Niño." (4.1 - 4.2. Making inferences)

    (a) Loves the name of   (c) Downplays   (e) Sensationalizes
    (b) Likes to use the name of   (d) Has created

(4.2) Based on the information given, it can be inferred that the cycle of El Niño and La Niño could be controlled by science within _____ decades.

    (a) 2   (b) 4   (c) 6   (d) 8   (e) Undeterminable

(5.1) It can be concluded that El Niño is often created by the global climate system with an interval from _____ to _____ years. (5.1 - 5.2. Conclusions)

    (a) 2, 4   (b) 5, 7   (c) 2, 10   (d) 6, 9   (e) 7, 12

(5.2) The creation of El Niño and its counterpart can be concluded as a/an _____ phenomenon of global climate system.

    (a) Unusual   (b) Normal   (c) Unexpected   (d) Weird   (e) Unpredictable

도 이상으로 상승한다. 그러나 그 변화는 사실 지구 기후체계의 정상적인 일부일 뿐이다. 엘니뇨는 수천년간 찾아 왔었고 만일 10~20년간 엘니뇨가 일어나지 않고 계속된다면 그게 이상(異常)일 것이다.

(4) 엘니뇨는 한 순환주기의 일부인가?

그렇다. 엘니뇨는 매스컴의 총아다. 그래서 그의 다른 한 쪽인 라니냐에 대해서 들어 본 사람이 별로 없다. 엘니뇨와 라니냐는 한 주기의 차고 따뜻한 두 얼굴들이다. 라니냐 중에는 동(東) 및 중앙(中央) 태평양의 수면 온도가 평소보다 낮다. 그래서 라니냐 발생의 영향은 엘니뇨와 관련된 영향의 반대라고 생각된다.

(5) 지구 온난화가 엘니뇨를 더욱 키우고 심술궂게 만들 것인가?

모른다. 지구 온난화가 어떻게 엘니뇨에 영향을 미칠 것인가에 대하여 많이 생각해 왔다. 엘니뇨가 더 자주 나타날 것인가, 더 강렬하고 오래 지속될 것인가? 등이다. 지금 시점에서 있을 수 있는 영향에 대한 예언은 전혀 확실성이 없다.

Note

□ **thermocline** : 변온층, 호수와 늪의 수온이 갑자기 바뀌는 수온층   □ **elevation** : 상승

□ **counterpart**=a person or thing exactly like or closely corresponding to another : 쌍을 이루는 한 쪽
 • The counterpart of man is woman.

□ **mean**=bad-tempered, liking to hurt : 심술 궂은, 비열한
 • That's a mean dog. Be careful. It may bite you.

□ **speculation**=thinking about a matter without facts that would lead to a firm result : 추측, 생각, 투기

□ **intense**=high in degree : 강렬한   • an intense heat (폭서)

□ **sensationalize** : 떠들썩하게 만들다   □ **downplay** : 얕다

□ **literally**=word by word, exactly : 문자 그대로, 정확하게
 • I took what he said literally, but afterward it became clear that he really meant something else.
 (그가 한 말을 그대로 받아들였으나 그게 아니라는 것이 밝혀졌다.)

□ **trade winds**=strong winds blowing always towards the equtor from the SE and NS :
무역풍·적도를 중심으로 북위 30°, 남위 30° 사이에서 일어나는 일정한 방향의 강풍. 북반구에서는 북동풍, 남반구에서는 남동풍

Passage 11 : **A Stroke: Controllable?**

    When a person suffers a stroke, reduced blood flow damages part of the brain. Then a powerful chain of chemical reactions occurs. Called the glutamate cascade, it rains terrible destruction down on brain cells in the initial days after a stroke, causing further damage. As glutamate levels build, excess calcium and toxic form of oxygen destroy brain cells. Today, doctors can only stand by and watch-hoping that the cascade will end before massive damage occurs. But there is hope. Pharmaceutical company researchers are currently developing 19 new drugs that could help reduce the terrible damage to the brain that occurs after a stroke. Simply put, new medicines currently being tested may be able to stop destruction of brain cells in the *crucial* hours after a stroke.

    Anyone can have a stroke. But age, gender, race, and *medical history* play a key role. Some people also experience the following warning signs: temporary weakness or *numbness* on one side of the body, blurry or dimmed vision in one eye, a sudden, severe headache, or speech difficulty. To prevent a possible stroke, seek immediate medical help if you have any of these symptoms. Fortunately, there are things that you can do to reduce your risk of a stroke: Quit smoking, Exercise regularly, Maintain a low cholesterol diet, and Limit alcohol.

(Source: Health Guide Third in a Series: What You Need to Know About Strokes (1998). Presented by America's Pharmaceutical Research Companies.)

(1) The topic of the passage is "The _____ strokes." (Subject matter)

    (a) Treatment for   (c) Prevention of   (e) New medications for
    (b) Symptoms of   (d) Damage caused by

(2.1) The italicized word, *crucial*, refers to ____. (2.1 - 2.3. Words & phrase in context)

    (a) Unimportant (b) Trivial (c) Critical (d) Senseless (e) Insecure

(2.2) The italicized phrase, *medical history*, means "medical _____".

    (a) Education (b) Practice (c) Prescription (d) Coverage (e) Records

(2.3) The opposite of the italicized word, *numbness*, is _____.

    (a) Heartless (b) Powerless (c) Unfeeling (d) Emotionless (e) Sensation

(3) The underlined structure, "new medicines currently being tested may be…" can be expanded as "new medicines _____ may be…" (Structure)

    (a) That were tested   (c) That are being tested   (e) That were being tested
    (b) That are tested   (d) That have been tested

(4.1) One of the following signs which does not constitute a symptom of stroke is _____. (4.1 - 4.2. Making inferences)

    (a) Speech difficulty   (d) Severe sore throat
    (b) Blurring in one eye   (e) Numbness of one side of the body
    (c) Sudden, severe headache

지문 11 : 뇌일혈. 억제할 수 있는가?

어떤 사람이 뇌일혈을 당하면, 줄어든 혈류량으로 뇌의 일부가 손상된다. 그때 강력한 연쇄 화학 반응이 발생한다. 글루탄산염 캐스케이드라고 불리어지는 이것이 뇌일혈 발작 후 초기 며칠 사이에 흘러서 뇌세포에 무서운 괴사를 일으키며 더욱 심한 파손을 야기시킨다. 글루탄산염 정도가 커짐에 따라 과잉 칼슘과 유해한 형태의 산소가 뇌세포를 파괴한다. 오늘날, 의사들은 단지 옆에 서서 지켜볼 수밖에 없다. 막대한 파손이 일어나기 전에 그 출혈이 멎기를 기다리며. 그러나 희망은 있다. 제약회사 연구원들이 지금 뇌일혈 후 발생하는 뇌에 대한 끔찍한 피해를 줄이는데 도움이 될 19가지 신약을 개발하고 있다. 간단히 말하면 지금 시험 중인 신약들이 뇌일혈 후 고비가 되는 몇시간 안에 일어나는 뇌세포의 파괴를 정지 시킬 수 있을 것이다.

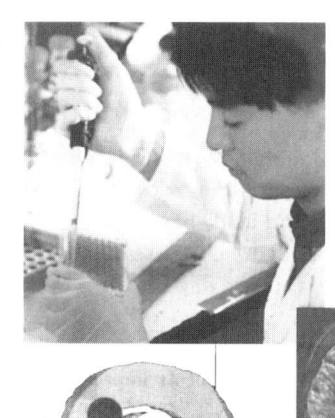
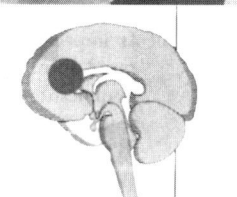
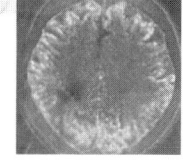

누구나 뇌일혈을 당할 수 있다. 그러나 연령, 성별, 인종, 그리고 병력(病歷)이 결정적인 역할을 한다. 어떤 사람들은 다음과 같은 사전 징후를 갖는다 : 일시적인 나른함, 신체의 한쪽에 오는 마비, 한쪽 눈이 흐려지거나 희미한 시각, 갑작스럽고 심한 두통, 언어곤란 등이다. 있을지도 모르는 뇌일혈을 예방하기 위하여 위와 같은 징후가 나타나면 즉시 의사의 도움을 받아라. 다행히 뇌일혈의 위험을 줄이기 위하여 할 수 있는 몇가지 사항들이 있다: 금연하라, 규칙적으로 운동하라, 저콜레스테롤 식사를 유지하라, 그리고 술을 삼가하라.

Note
- stroke=sudden attack of illness in the brain with loss of feeling, power to move : 뇌일(출)혈
- cascade : 작은 폭포, 원폭포에서 갈라져 나온 소폭포, 뇌혈관에서 흘러나온 혈행=stenosis(협착)에 의한 출혈
- toxic=poisonous : 중독성의, 유해한
- glutamate : 글루탄산염
- pharmaceutical company : 제약회사
- Simply put=If it is simply put : 간단히 말하면
- crucial=decisive, critical : 고비의, 위급한
- at the crucial moment : 결정적인 순간에
- gender : 문법적인 성, 구어체에서(sex)
- medical history : 병력
- blur=make a dirty mark or smear : 흐릿하게 하다 • Tears blurred her sight.
- symptom=change in the body's condition that indicates illness : 징후, 증상
  • a subjective symptom (자각증세)   • cf. syndrome (전체적 증세(症候群))

(4.2) Based on the information given, it can be inferred that a stroke _____.

    (a) Is controllable
    (b) Is easily controllable
    (c) Is seldom controllable
    (d) Is easily curable
    (e) May eventually be controllable

(5.1) It can be concluded that one of the initial causes for stroke is _____. (5.1 - 5.2. Conclusions)

    (a) Chain of chemical reactions   (c) Glutamate cascade   (e) Toxic form of oxygen
    (b) Reduced blood flow   (d) Excess calcium

(5.2) One of the following proverbs that best reflects the theme of the passage is _____.

    (a) Gratefulness is the poor man's payment. (English)
    (b) No peacock envies another peacock's tail. (Latin)
    (c) A bird in the hand is worth two in a bush. (English)
    (d) Silence was never written down. (Italian)
    (e) An apple a day keeps the doctor away. (English)

Passage 12 : The Aspect of Woman

    Throughout the world, women are culture bearers. They transmit the history and the tradition of the people from generation to generation. They are the heart of the home and the *matrix* of the family. According to the Vedas, "the wife is the home." Indeed, they are in the pivotal position of culture bearer and home maker. Over the span of their lives, whether as princesses or beggars, women learn and grow.

    Women are Child, Maiden, Lover, Mother, and Crone. The *archetypical* goddesses reappear within our own personal life spans. The Child greets the world with inquisitiveness, certainty, and all the clear-eyed freshness of youth. The Maiden senses the changes in herself and in the world around her and begins to assume her role in the circle of women. The Lover combines the knowledge of sensuality and coquetry with the quiet, wistful knowledge of loves lost. The Mother nurtures and empowers all humankind and gazes on the world with tolerant benevolence. The Crone, from her pedestal of wisdom, regards it all with affectionate amusement and offers *sage* lessons to those who know how to listen.

    Wherever you are on the circle of the ages of woman, share with those around you in other places on the circle. Help and teach the ways of women to the Maiden. Share the joy with the Lover. Nurture and empower as the Mother. Listen, learn from, and share knowledge with the Crone. Which age is best? The one you are enjoying now. Be sure to get the best from it; that's where true beauty and contentment ( ).

(Source: Adapted from Harris, Jessica B. (1995). The World Beauty Book.)

(1) The best topic of the passage is "The _____ of a Woman." (Subject matter)

    (a) Responsibility   (c) Developmental features   (e) Life span
    (b) Characters   (d) Contributions

지문 12 : 여인의 모습

전 세계적으로 여인은 문화의 전달자다. 그들은 그 국민의 역사와 전통을 대대로 전달한다. 그들은 가정의 심장이며 가족의 모태다. 베다에 의하면 '아내는 가정이다'. 실로 그들은 문화 전달자와 주부라는 중심축에 존재한다. 전생애를 통해서 황태자비든 거지든 간에 배우면서 성숙한다.

여인은 어린이, 처녀, 애인, 어머니 그리고 노파다. 원형적인 여신들이 우리 자신의 생애에 다시 나타난다. 어린이는 호기심과 확신과 맑은 눈의 젊음으로 이 세상을 맞이한다. 처녀는 자신과 주변 세계에서 일어나는 변화를 느끼며 여자로서의 자기 역할을 담당하기 시작한다. 애인은 관능과 교태에 대하여 알고 있으며 잃어버린 사랑에 대하여 은밀하게 더 알고 싶어한다. 어머니는 모든 인간을 양육하며 능력을 길러주고 관대한 자비심으로 이 세상을 응시한다. 노파는 그녀가 가진 지혜의 토대로부터 애정어린 즐거움으로 지켜보며 들을 줄 아는 이들에게 현명한 교훈을 제공한다.

당신이 어느 연령권의 여인이든 간에 다른 분야의 여인들과 함께 하시오. 처녀들에게 여자의 길을 도와 가르치시오. 사랑에 빠진 여인과 그 기쁨을 함께 하시오. 어머니로서 기르고 능력을 길러주시오. 노파들의 말을 경청하고 배우고 지식을 나누시오. 어느 나이 때가 제일 좋으냐고요? 지금 당신이 누리는 그 나이지요. 부디 현재의 나이에서 최선을 얻으시오. 그곳이 바로 진정한 미와 만족이 있는 자리니까요.

Note

- **transmit**=pass, hand on : 전달한다, 옮기다
  - Parents transmit their characteristics to their children. (부모는 자식에게 특징들을 유전시킨다.)
- **matrix**=mould into which hot metal or material in a soft or liquid condition is poured to shape : 모체, 발생지
- **pivot**=a fixed central point on which something turns : 회전 축, 중심적
- **pivotal**=of great importance because other things depend on : 중추적인
- **crone**=withered old woman : 노파, 쪼그랑 할멈
- **archetypical** : 원형적인, 모범적인   • atypical (무정형의)
- **inquisitive**=inquiring into other people's affairs : 꼬치꼬치 캐묻는
  - Don't be so inquisitive. I'm not telling you what I did last night.
  (그렇게 캐묻지 마세요. 어제 밤에 있던 일은 말 안할래요.)
- **sensuality** : 관능, 육욕   **coquetry** : 교태, 아양, 추파   **Veda** : 베다(바라문교의 성전)
- **wistful**=having a rather unsatisfied desire : 탐내는 듯한, 더 갖고 싶어하는
- **nurture**=give care and food, training, education : 양육하다, 훈련, 교육
  - Which is more important, nurture or nature. (소질과 교육, 어느 것이 더 중요한가?)
- **benevolence**=wish to do good, good will : 자비심, 자선
- **pedestal**=base of a column, statue, or other work of art : 받침대, 대좌, 기초
- **sage**=wise, having the wisdom of experience : 현명한

(2.1) The italicized word, *matrix*, refers to a/an _____. (2.1 - 2.3. Words in context)

   (a) Nucleus   (b) Circle   (c) Age   (d) Time   (e) Part

(2.2) The antonym of the italicized word, *archetypical*, is _____.

   (a) Paradigmatic   (b) Ideal   (c) Original   (d) Classical   (e) Atypical

(2.3) The synonym of the italicized word, *sage*, is _____.

   (a) Wise   (b) Helpful   (c) Supportive   (d) Spiritual   (e) Inspiring

(3) The underlined structure, "that's where true beauty and contentment ( )," needs a proper word. One of the best candidates for the word needed in the parenthesis is _____. (Structure)

   (a) Lie   (b) Lay   (c) Lying   (d) Lies   (e) Is

(4.1) Based on the information given, it can be inferred that "The Female Child" is portrayed by the writer as "_____." (4.1 - 4.5. Making inferences)

   (a) Gentle   (b) Intelligent   (c) Childish   (d) Curious   (e) Wise

(4.2) "The Maiden," is portrayed as "_____."

   (a) Giving   (b) Maturing   (c) Caring   (d) Loving   (e) Devoting

(4.3) "The Lover," is portrayed as "_____."

   (a) Gentle & nurturing   (c) Coquettish & cooperative   (e) Attractive & romantic
   (b) Passionate & caring   (d) Attractive & realistic

(4.4) "The Mother," is portrayed as "_____."

   (a) Nurturing   (b) Respecting   (c) Protecting   (d) Instructing   (e) Supporting

(4.5) "The Crone," is portrayed as a "_____."

   (a) Protector   (b) Jester   (c) Saint   (d) Scholar   (e) Person of wisdom

(5) Based on the information given, "The aspects of woman" can be concluded to be "_____." (Conclusion)

   (a) Unique & traditional   (d) Conservative & dependent
   (b) Specific & responsible   (e) Particular & affectionate
   (c) Dedicating & emotional

Selected proverbs for the study of cross-cultural expressions

영어 격언과 한문 격언과의 만남 (13)

1. **Ignorance is the night of the mind.** 人生不學如冥夜行(인생불학여명야행)
   - 사람은 배우지 않으면 어두운 밤길을 가는 것과 같다. · There's no blindness like ignorance.

2. **You can't get blood out of a stone.** 乾木水生, 緣木求魚(건목수생, 연목구어)
   - 마른 나무 물짜기, 나무에 올라가 물고기 구하기. · Money doesn't grow on trees.

3. **A small leak will sink a great ship.** 千丈之堤潰自蟻穴(천장지제궤자의혈 ; 潰 = collapse)
   - 긴 제방도 개미구멍으로부터 무너진다.

4. **A miss is as good as a mile.** 五十步笑百步(오십보소백보) – 오십보 도망간 사람이 백보 도망간 자를 비웃는다.

5. **Many a little makes a mickle.** 塵合泰山, 集少成大(진합태산, 집소성대)
   - 티끌 모아 태산, 작은 것이 모여 큰 것을 이룬다. · Many drops make a shower. / · Many sands will sink a ship.

6. **The tongue is not steel, but it cuts.** 口是傷人斧, 言卽割舌刀(구시상인부, 언즉할설도)
   - 입은 사람을 다치게 하는 도끼고, 혀는 사람을 베는 칼과 같다.
   · Under the tongue men are crushed to death. / · The tongue breaks bone, and herself has none.
   · The tongue stings. / · The tongue is more venomous than serpents's sting.
   · There is no venom to that of the tongue. / · Words cut more than swords.

7. **A penny saved is a penny earned.** 以約失之者鮮,(이약실지자선 ; 鮮 = rare)
   - 절약으로 잃은 사람은 드물다.
   Of saving comes having. 成家之道儉與勤(성가지도검여근 ; 與 = and) – 검약과 근면이 집안을 이룬다.
   · Sparing is the first gaining.
   · Better spare at brim than at bottom. (at brim: 넘칠 때, at bottom: 바닥 났을 때)
   · Take care of the pence, and the pounds will take care of themselves.
   · For age and want, save while you may; no morning sun lasts a whole day. / · Waste not, want not.
   · Waste makes want.

8. **First try and then trust.** 疑人莫用 用人莫疑(의인막용 용인막의 ; 莫 = don't)
   - 의심스런 사람들은 쓰지말고, 사람을 쓴다면 의심을 말라. · Prove your friend before you have need.

9. **Truth will assert itself.** 事必歸正, 邪不犯正(사필귀정, 사불범정)
   - 일이란 반드시 옳은 길로 돌아가고, 거짓이 참을 침범하지 못한다. · Truth will out. / · Truth will come to light.

10. **The absent will get farther off every day.** 去者益疎, 見物生心(거자익소, 견물생심)
    - 없는 사람은 점점 멀어진다. 보면 생각난다. · Far from eye, far from heart. / · Out of sight, out of mind.
    · Present to the eye, present to the mind. / · Unseen, unrued. / · Seldom seen, soon forgotten.

11. **When the cat's away, the mice will play.** 無虎洞中狸作虎(무호동중이작호 ; 作 = become)
    - 호랑이 없는 곳에는 살쾡이가 범노릇한다.

12. **Misery loves company.** 同病相憐(동병상련) – 처지가 어려운 사람끼리 서로 동정한다.
    · Adversity makes strange bedfellows. / · Woes unite foes.

Passage 13 : The Republic of Uzbekistan

    Uzbekistan is a country of desert landscapes, fertile oases, and high mountain ranges. The republic lies in the heart of Central Asia largely between the Amu Darya and Syrdarya Rivers. Uzbekistan has a climate that is very dry and *distinctly* continental. The summer is long and warm, and the winter is short with occasional severe frosts; mean temperatures in the winter are as low as 10 degrees F (-12 degrees C).

    Modern Uzbekistan is the descendent of a series of Islamic Kingdoms dating back to the empire of Genghis Khan. Russian armies easily moved into the weakened kingdoms, capturing the capital city, Tashkent, in 1865. The effects of the Soviet Revolution in 1917 were of *seismic* proportions. Lenin pushed Uzbekistan's small farmers into big collective farms that grew cotton for export, after which the country became the world's third-largest source of cotton.

    Uzbekistan is a famous region for the raising of Karakul sheep, cattle, and silkworms, including the farming of orchards and fur. The republic has unusually large resources of natural gas, petroleum, coal, and a variety of metallic ores. However, <u>most of the profits were sent to Moscow ( ) social and agricultural problems stayed at home, causing Uzbekistan to be *impoverished*</u>. When the government of the U.S.S.R. collapsed in 1991, Uzbekistan declared its independence.

    Facts = Area: 172,587 sq. mi. (448,726 km^2)
                          Population: 22.8 million
                          Population density: 132.1 per sq. mi. (51.0 per km^2)
                          Life expectancy: Female, 74. Male, 66.
                          Infant mortality: 43 per 1,000 births
                          Annual inflation rate since independence: More than 80%
                          Rank of affluences among the 183 U.N. members: 113

(Source: <u>Material World</u> (1996). Pomegranate Calendars & Books, Rohnert Park, California)

(1) The topic of the passage is "_____ the Republic of Uzbekistan." (Subject matter)

    (a) Geographical features of   (c) Natural resources of   (e) Facts about
    (b) Climate patterns of   (d) Agricultural products of

(2.1) The italicized word, *distinctly*, in the first paragraph refers to _____ (2.1. - 2.3. Words in context)

    (a) Ambiguously (b) Obviously (c) Idiosyncratically (d) Insignificantly (e) Vaguely

(2.2) The italicized word, *seismic*, in the second paragraph can be substituted as _____.

    (a) Unusual (b) Titanic (c) Inconsequential (d) Trivial (e) Commonplace

(2.3) The antonym of the italicized word, *impoverished*, in the last paragraph refers to _____.

    (a) Affluent (b) Exhausted (c) Depleted (d) Destitute (e) Barren

(3) The underlined structure, "<u>most of the profits were sent to Moscow (_____) social</u>

지문 13 : 우즈베키스탄 공화국

우즈베키스탄은 사막이 있는 풍경, 비옥한 오아시스, 그리고 높은 산맥들이 있는 나라다. 이 공화국은 Amu Darya강과 Syrdarya강의 대략 중간에 있는 중앙 아시아의 한복판에 있다. 우즈베키스탄은 매우 건조하고 뚜렷한 대륙성 기후를 가지고 있다. 여름은 길고 덥고 겨울은 짧고 가끔씩 혹독한 서리가 내린다. 겨울의 평균 기온은 화씨 10도 (섭씨 -12도)까지 내려간다.

현대 우즈베키스탄은 징기스칸 제국까지 거슬러 올라가는 일련의 이슬람 왕국들의 후예국가다. 러시아군들이 1895년에 쇠약해진 왕국들에 쉽게 이동해 들어와서 수도인 타쉬겐트를 빼앗았다. 1917년의 소비에트 혁명의 영향은 엄청났다. 레닌은 우즈베키스탄의 영세농들을 수출용 목화를 재배하는 커다란 집단 농장으로 몰아 넣었다. 그리고 그 후 이 나라는 세계 3대 목화 공급원이 되었다.

우즈베키스탄은 과수원과 모피 농사를 포함하여 카라쿨 양과, 소, 누에의 유명한 재배지이다. 그 공화국은 보기 드물게 많은 천연가스, 석유, 석탄 그리고 다양한 금광석의 자원을 가지고 있다. 그러나 이익의 대부분은 사회적, 농업적인 문제들이 온존하고 있는 모스크바로 보내졌으며 이로 인하여 우즈베키스탄을 가난하게 만들었다. 1991년에 소련 정부가 붕괴되었을 때 우즈베키스탄은 독립을 선언했다.

실상 — 면적 : 172,587평방 마일
　　　　인구 : 2천 2백 80만
　　　　인구밀도 : 1평방 마일 당 132.1명
　　　　평균 수명 : 여-74, 남-66
　　　　유아 사망률 : 1000명당 43
　　　　연간 통화팽창률 (독립 이후) : 80%이상
　　　　풍요의 서열 (UN 183 국가 중) : 113

and agricultural problems…." One of the appropriate conjunctions that fits in the parenthesis is _____. (Structure)

(a) Yet   (b) If   (c) While   (d) Since   (e) Unless

(4.1) Based on the information given, the Republic of Uzebekistan is inferred as a/an _____ unstabilized country now. (4.1. - 4.3. Making inferences)

(a) Culturally   (b) Politically   (c) Religiously   (d) Ideologically   (e) Economically

(4.2) One of the potentially strong economic assets of the Republic seems to be _____.

(a) Tourism   (b) Fruits   (c) Cattle   (d) Natural gas   (e) Silkworms

(4.3) One of the major religions in the Republic seems to be _____.

(a) Hinduism   (b) Catholic   (c) Moslem   (d) Protestant   (e) Judaism

(5) Based on the information given, it can be concluded that the Republic will economically prosper in the near future when the country begins to sell/export a potentially huge amount of _____. (Conclusion)

(a) Silk   (b) Meat   (c) Coal   (d) Cotton   (e) Natural gas

Passage 14 : **The Anthem of Imperialism.**

Background : Rudyard Kipling (1865-1936), a British poet and novelist, winner of England's first Nobel Prize for Literature in 1907, wrote a number of poems and fictions. He is best known for two "Jungle Books (1894-95)," "Captain Courageous (1894)," "Kim (1901)," and the poem, "White Man's Burden (1899)." The poem interprets an attitude of white man's superiority shared by many in the West at that time in which the British imperialism during the Victorian Age was at its peak. The following poem consists of six verses, but for this publication only the first four verses are introduced. In the poem, there are some vocabularies used during the Victorian age.

The White Man's Burden

Take up the White Man's burden -
Send forth the best ye breed -
Go bind your sons to exile
To serve your captives' need;
To wait in heavy *harness*
On *fluttered* folk and wild -
Your new-caught, sullen peoples,
Half devil and half child.

Take up the White Man's burden -
In patience ( ) abide,
To veil the threat of terror

Note

□ **fertile**=able to produce or grow many young, fruits or seeds : 비옥한, 다산의
  • a fertile mind (창의력이 풍부한 마음) • a fertile hen (알을 많이 낳는 닭)
  • This district is fertile of potatoes. (이 지역은 감자가 잘 된다.)
  • opp. infertile, barren (메마른, 새끼를 못낳는)

□ **mean**=average : 평균 • The mean yearly rainfall is 20 inches. (연 평균 강우량)

□ **seismic** : 지진의, 엄청난 • seismic proportion (엄청난 크기)

□ **impoverish**=make poor, weaken : 가난하게하다, 메마르게 하다
  • Many a family has been impoverished by the unemployment. (실직으로 많은 가족이 몰락했다.)

□ **collapse**=cause to fall down or inwards : 붕괴하다
  • The bridge collapsed with cars and commuters' buses on it.
  (그 다리가 승용차들과 통학 버스들이 위에 있는 채 무너졌다.)

□ **mortality**=the rate of the number of the deaths : 사망률
  • If this disease spreads, the doctors fear that there'll be a high mortality.
  (이 병이 퍼지면 사망률이 높을 거라고 두려워 있다.)

□ **idiosyncratically** : 특이하게 • idiosyncrasy (특이성, 개인적 성벽, 특이체질)

□ **destitute**=without food, clothes and other thigs necessary for life : 극빈의, 궁핍한
  • He is utterly destitute of shame. (전혀 염치가 없다.)

□ **affluence**=wealth, abundance : 부유, 풍요 • rise to affluence=become wealthy

지문 14 : 제국주의 송가

배경 : 키플링 (영국의 시인, 소설가 영국 최초의 노벨 문학상 수상자(1907)) 은 많은 시와 소설을 썼다. 그는 2편의 '정글북(Jungle Book)'과 '용기있는 지휘자(Captain Courageous)', '킴(Kim)' 그리고 '백인의 책임(White Man's Burden)'으로 가장 유명하다. 이 시(White Man's Burden)는 빅토리아 여왕 재위 중 영국의 제국주의가 절정에 달했던 당시 서양의 많은 사람들이 공유하고 있었던 백인의 우월주의 태도를 말해주고 있다. 다음 시는 6연으로 구성되어 있지만 이 책에는 처음 4연만 소개한다. 이 시 안에는 빅토리아 시대에 쓰였던 어휘들이 있다.

Rudyard Kipling

백인의 책임

백인의 책임을 다 하시오.
당신이 기르는 가장 소중한 것을 내주고

And check the show of pride;
By open speech and simple,
An hundred times made plain,
To seek another's profit,
And work another's gain.

Take up the White Man's burden -
The savage wars of peace -
Fill full the mouth of Famine
And bid the sickness cease;
And when your goal is nearest
The end for others sought,
Watch Sloth and heathen Folly
Bring all your hope to nought.

Take up the White Man's burden -
And reap his old reward:
The blame of those ye better,
The hate of those ye guard -
The cry of hosts ye humour
(Ah, slowly!) toward the light:-
Why brought ye us from bondage,
Our loved Egyptian night?'

(1) The most appropriate topic of the poem is "_____ non-Europeans." (Subject Matter)

(a) Expensive medical care for unhealthy
(b) Economic development for unworthy
(c) Introduction of civilization to ungrateful
(d) Distribution of adequate food to starving
(e) Imposition of imperialism on sullen

(2.1) The italicized word, *harness*, in the first verse refers to _____. (2.1. - 2.5. Words, phrases, sentence in context)

(a) Freedom   (b) Leash   (c) Delivery   (d) Dispensation   (e) Liberty

(2.2) The antonym of the italicized word, *fluttered*, is _____.

(a) Agitated   (b) Fluctuated   (c) Drifted   (d) Peaceful   (e) Oscillated

(2.3) "On fluttered folk and wild" in the first verse refers to _____.

(a) Asian Indians (b) Africans (c) Non-Europeans (d) American Indians (e) Asians

(2.4) "Your new-caught, sullen peoples, Half devil and half child" in the first verse refers to _____.

(a) Europeans   (b) Arabs   (c) Asians   (d) Non-Europeans   (e) Africans

(2.5) "Watch Sloth and heathen Folly" in the third verse refers to "Watch _____."

아들들은 묶어 먼 곳으로 보내고
그리하여 포로들의 요구를 들어주시오.
반은 악마같고 반은 어린애 같은
겁을 먹고 서성대며 난폭한 사람들,
새로 붙들어 온 화난 사람들,
충분히 준비하고 그들의 시중을 드시오.

백인의 책임을 다하시오.
인내 속에서 생활하고,
테러에 대한 공포를 숨기며,
자만심은 억제하시오.
말은 아주 쉽게 풀어 쓴 분명한 말로,
그들의 이익을 찾아주고,
그들의 이익이 되는 일을 하시오.

백인의 책임을 다하시오.
평화를 위한 야만과의 싸움이오.
굶주린 입은 채워주고,
질병은 끝내주시오.
그들을 위하여 추구한 목표가
거의 달성되었으면,
그들의 나태함과 이교도의 어리석음으로
그것이 물거품이 되지 않도록 감시하시오.

백인의 책임을 다하시오.
그리고 오랜 보답을 거두시오.
당신이 개화시켜 주려는 자들의 원망,
당신이 지켜주는 자들의 증오,
당신이 달래어 빛으로 인도하려는(이렇게 시간이 걸릴 줄이야!)
많은 자들의 아우성 소리.
"왜 우리를 속박에서,
우리가 사랑하는 이집트의 암흑에서 데려왔오?"

(a) Treacherous people   (c) Atheistic people   (e) Uneducated people
(b) Lazy barbarians   (d) Uncivilized people

(3) The underlined structure in the second verse, "In patience ( ) abide," can be restructured as "In patience _____ abide."

    (a) With   (b) Of   (c) For   (d) At   (e) To

(4) Kipling describes benefits to non-Europeans as shown in the second verse, "To seek another's profit, And work for another's gain." His reference to benefits can be inferred as "_____." (Making inference)

    (a) Imposition of imperialism   (d) Economic development
    (b) Educational development   (e) Imposition of English
    (c) Agricultural development

(5) Kipling praises the achievement of the British imperialism while suggesting that the British Empire should pay her share to maintain the imperialistic prosperity as implied in the phrase, "The White Man's Burden." One of the following maxims/proverbs that can represent the theme of the poem is to be concluded "_____." (Conclusion)

    (a) Two captains will sink the ship (Turkish)
    (b) Pour gold on him, and he'll never thrive (Latin)
    (c) It is better to be born a beggar than a fool (Spanish)
    (d) A bird in the hand is worth two in a bush (English)
    (e) There are no free rides in this world

Passage 15 : Du Fu (*"Doo Bo," 712 - 770): A Poet of the Poets

Background : Du Fu was born into a scholarly family, received a traditional Confucius education, but failed in the Imperial Examination of 736. As a result, he spent much of his youth traveling, during which he won renown as a poet and met the other poets of the period including the great Li Bo (*"Yee Baek," 701 - 762). After a brief *flirtation* with Taoism while traveling with Li Bo, Du Fu returned to the capital, ChangAn (now Xian), and the conventional Confucianism of his youth.

    Du Fu's early poetry celebrated the beauties of the natural world and *bemoaned* the passage of time. He soon began to write bitingly of war, and with hidden satire, of the conspicuous luxury of the court. As he matured, and especially during the years of extreme personal and national turmoil of 755 - 759: An Lu-shan (*"Ahn Rok San") Rebellion, his verse began to sound a note of profound compassion for humanity *caught in the toils of senseless war*. <u>Du Fu's paramount position in the history of Chinese literature rests, finally, ( ) his superb classicism and his complete ease in handling the rules of prosody</u>. He was an expert in all poetic genres current his day, but his mastery was at its height in the regulated verse, which he refined to a point of glowing intensity.

    Among many, two of his poems are introduced here along with the original ones written during the Tang Dynasty (618 - 904). Du Fu composed memorial remarks in

Note

□ 영시의 이해를 위하여: 영시는 라임과 리듬을 살리기 위하여 행의 길이를 결정하기 때문에 시의 내용을 이해하기 위해서는 **line by line**이 아니고 한 **stanza**를 전체로 보아야한다. 각행 끝의 문장 부호에 주의를 기울이는 것이 도움이 된다.

□ **anthem=song of praise** : 송가 • national anthem (애국가)
□ **interpret=explain** : 해설, 통역하다
□ **burden=something difficult to bear** : 힘든 일, 부담 • the burden of taxation (과세부담)
□ **breed=give birth to, bring up, keep** : 낳아 기르다, 사육하다
  • He was born and bred a soldier. (그는 군인으로 낳아서 자랐다.)
□ **harness=the bands which are used to control horses, routine work** : 마구, 고삐, 일
  • die in harness (집무 중에 죽다)
□ **flutter** : 깃털, 깃발을 나부끼다, 흥분시키다, 안절부절 못하다
  • She was fluttering anxiously in the room. (방안에서 이리저리 초조하게 서성거렸다.)
□ **sullen=silently showing dislike and lack of cheefulness** : 시무룩함, 뚱함
□ **abide=stay, live**   □ **veil** : 덮어감추다, 가리다
□ **sloth=laziness**   □ **heathen** : 비기독교도, 이교도   □ **folly** : 어리석음
□ **bondage** : 굴레, 예속 • Human bondage. (인간의 굴레 (모음의 대표작))
□ **imperialism** : 제국주의, 영토확장주의, 침략주의
□ **leash=leather strap for controlling an animal esp. a hound** : 개가죽 끈
□ **dispensation** : 분배, 신의 섭리
□ **fluctuate=rise and fall, change from time to time** : 심하게 변동하다
  • The prices fluctuate according to the seasons. (철에 따라 가격이 변동한다.)
□ **treacherous=disloyal** : 배반하는 • a treacherous branch (튼튼해 보이나 약한 가지)
□ **oscillate** : 진동하다 • He always oscillates between ideas. (생각이 갈팡질팡한다.)

지문 15 :. 杜甫 — 시인 중의 시인

배경 : 두보는 학자 가문에 태어났고, 전통적인 유교 교육을 받았으나, 736년 황실고시에서 낙방했다. 그 결과 그는 생애의 대부분을 여행을 하면서 보냈으며 그 여행 중에 시인으로서 명성을 얻었고 위대한 이백(李白)을 비롯한 당시의 많은 시인들을 만났다. 이 백과 여행하는 동안 잠시 도교(道敎)에 관심을 가졌으나 수도인 장안으로 돌아와서 젊은 시절의 전통 유교로 복귀했다.

두보의 초기 시는 자연의 아름다움을 찬양했고 시간이 흐르는 것을 탄식했다. 곧 그는 전쟁에 관하여 통렬하게 글을 썼으며 은밀한 풍자로 황실

Du Fu, stone rubbing, Ch'ing dynasty (1644~1911/12)

praise of Zhuge Liang (*"Jae Kal Yang"), his lifelong dedication, and accomplishments for his country and Emperors.

 The symbol, *, refers to the Korean pronunciation of the Chinese characters.

The Temple of the Prime Minister of Shu[1]

Where to find the deceased Prime Minister's temple?
Outside Chengdu, under the cypress arch ample.
The grass round the steps reflects the color of spring;
The oriole amid the leaves vainly sings its strain.
Thrice the Emperor to him came for the plan to rule;
Two reigns the noble statesman served heart and soul.
Before seeing victory, he died in the camp ground,
It oft makes later heroes weep with sighs profound!

蜀相　　　杜甫
丞相祠堂何處尋？錦官城外柏森森。映階碧草自春色，
隔葉黃鸝空好音。三顧頻煩天下計，兩朝開濟老臣心。
出師未捷身先死，長使英雄淚滿襟！

1. The Prime Minister of Shu is Zhuge Liang (181 - 234), the famous statesman and strategist in the period of the Three Kingdoms (220 - 265).
2. Zhuge Liang had served Emperor Liu Bei (161 - 223) and his son Liu Chan (207 - 271).

The Eight-Battle-Formations

None of the Three Kingdoms had done greater deeds;
Your Eight-Battle-Formations are famous feats.
The running river couldn't make the stones roll;
To annex Wu had led to a regretful fall!

八陣圖　　　杜甫
功蓋三分國，名成八陣圖。江流石不轉，遺恨失吞吳。

1. The Eight-Battle-Formations, separately named Heaven, Earth, Wind, Cloud, Dragon, Tiger, Bird and Snake Formations, were designed by Zhuge Liang. So the story goes that he made the formations with huge stones, and these relics have remained in three or four places.

(Source: <u>300 Tang Poems</u> (1987). Bureau of Chinese Translation Publishing Company, Hong Kong Branch)

의 눈에 띄는 사치에 대하여 비판하는 시를 썼다.

그가 원숙해감에 따라 특히 몇 년 간 극도의 개인적인 그리고 국가적인 소란기에(안 녹산의 반란), 그의 시는 무의미한 전쟁의 함정에 빠진 인간에 대한 연민을 표현하기 시작했다. 중국 문학사에서 두 보의 최고 위치는 뛰어난 고전적 어법과 운율법을 완벽하리 만큼 용이하게 다루는 데 있다. 그는 그당시 유행하던 모든 시적 쟝르에 숙달했으며 특히, 그가 열렬한 감정 표현 단계까지 세련시킨 정형시에서 그의 숙련은 정상에 있었다.

많은 그의 시 중에서 당나라 때 쓰여진 두 편을 원문과 함께 소개한다. 두 보는 제갈 량과 그의 평생의 충성, 나라와 황제를 위한 업적을 칭송하는 추모의 글을 썼다.

(*표는 한자의 한글 발음을 가리킨다.)

촉나라 재상의 사당 (蜀相)

고인이 되신 승상의 사당을 어디메서 찾을까?
금관성 밖 넓은 잣나무 숲이련다.
계단 둘레의 풀은 봄빛을 띠고;
나뭇잎 사이에서 꾀꼬리는 헛되이 지저귀는구나.
세 번씩이나 황제가 정치를 물으려 왔다 갔으니
고매하신 이 정객은 양조(兩朝)에 걸쳐 성심껏 섬기셨구나.
승리도 못보고 싸움터에서 먼저 돌아가시다니
장차 영웅들이 깊은 한숨을 쉬게하는구나.

- Shu : 蜀, Zhuge Liang – 제갈량 : 유비와 유선 2대를 섬겼다. Wu : 魏
- 丞相(승상) : 우리나라 정승에 해당하는 옛 중국의 벼슬 이름
- 祠堂(사당) : temple
- 柏 森森(백 삼삼) : 잣나무 숲
- 階 碧草(계 벽초) : 계단에 난 푸른 풀
- 隔葉(격엽) : amid the leaves
- 好音 : like to sing
- 頻煩 = 頻數(빈번 = 빈삭) : 도수가 잦음
- 濟老臣心(제노신심) : 늙은 신의 마음을 구해주다
- 捷(첩) = victory
- 使(사) = cuaseto, make
- 何處(하처) : where
- 映(영) : reflect : 빛날 영
- 自(자) : 저절로
- 黃鸝 : 노란 꾀꼬리
- 三顧(三顧草廬) : 초가 집을 세번 방문함
- 兩朝(양조) : 유 비와 그의 아들 유 선의 두 대
- 長(장) = long : 오랜 동안
- 淚(누) = make sb weep
- 尋(심) : seek, find
- 春色 : 봄 빛깔
- 空 : vainly
- 襟(금) : 옷깃
- 안녹산의 난 : 당나라 중기 현종 때 무신인 안녹산이 현종이 양귀비를 총애하여 정사를 문란시킨다는 구실로 일으킨 난. 현종은 당으로 난을 피하고, 양귀비는 자살하고, 안녹산은 후에 내분으로 아들에게 피살 됨.

(1) The topic of the passage in the section of "Background" is "Du Fu's _____."
(Subject matter)

    (a) Personal sad experiences   (d) Excellence in all poetic genres
    (b) Rules of prosody   (e) Background that helped create his poems
    (c) Flirtation with Taoism

(2.1) The italicized word, *flirtation*, in the first paragraph refers to _____. (2.1 - 2.3. Words & phrase in context)

    (a) Courtesy   (b) Modesty   (c) Interest   (d) Drought   (e) Detachment

(2.2) The antonym of the italicized word, *bemoaned*, in the second paragraph is _____.

    (a) Lamented   (b) Celebrated   (c) Bewailed   (d) Deplored   (e) Mourned

(2.3) The italicized phrase, *caught in the toils of*, in the second paragraph refers to _____.

    (a) Fallen into a trap   (c) Captured by a trap   (e) Seized by a trap
    (b) Caught by a trap   (d) Caught with a trap

(3) The underline structure, "Du Fu's paramount position in the history of Chinese literature rests, finally, ( ) his superb classicism and his complete ease in handling the rules of prosody," needs a suitable preposition to fill in the parenthesis. (Structure)

    (a) By   (b) On   (e) Of   (d) At   (c) In

(4.1) Du Fu composed memorial remarks for Zhuge Liang, one of the protagonists of Three Kingdoms: the well-known Chinese semifictional epic drama. In the poem, "The Temple of the Prime Minister of Shu", the "Emperor" must be _____. (4.1 - 4.5. Making inferences)

    (a) Liu Pei (*Yoo Bee)   (c) Ssuma Yi (*Sah Ma Uhee)   (e) Tsao Tsao (*Jo Jo)
    (b) Liu Chan (*Yoo Sun)   (d) Tsao Pei (*Jo Bee)

(4.2) The tone of the line, "The oriole amid the leaves vainly sings its strain," seems to be _____.

    (a) Cheerful   (b) Bitter   (c) Arrogant   (d) Melancholy   (e) Cynical

(4.3) "Two reigns the noble statesman served heart and soul," can be inferred as an expression in praise of Zhuge Liang's _____.

    (a) Courage   (b) Wisdom   (c) Honesty   (d) Loyalty   (e) Tactics

(4.4) The topic of the second poem, "The Eight-Battle-Formations," was a separate formation of Heaven, Earth, Wind, Cloud, Dragon, Tiger, Bird and Snake as described in "note 1". This type of "mysterious concept" can be drawn from the mystics of _____.

    (a) Confucianism   (b) Buddhism   (c) Hinduism   (d) Shintoism   (e) Taoism

(4.5) The tone of the line, "To annex Wu had led to a regretful fall!" seems to be _____.

    (a) Regretful   (b) Speculative   (c) Self-righteous   (d) Treacherous   (e) Argumentative

팔진도

삼국 중 어느 나라도 더 위대한 공을 세우지 못했고;
팔진도는 유명한 위업이지만
흐르는 강물이 바위를 굴리지 못했으니
위나라 합병은 한 많은 실패로 끝났구나!

- 三分國 = Three kingdoms
- 江流 = running river
- 恨 = regret
- 名成 = 成名 : get renowned
- 石不轉 = 不轉石 : don't make the stones roll
- 呑(탄) : 삼키다 : annex
- 각각 하늘, 땅, 구름, 용, 호랑이, 새, 그리고 뱀의 대형을 호칭하는 팔진도는 제갈량이 고안했다. 그리하여 들리는 이야기에 의하면 이 유적들이 3, 4곳에 남아 있다고 한다.

Note

- **flirt with** : 장난 삼아 손대다, 희롱하다
  - I've been flirting with idea of changing my job. (장난으로 직업을 바꿀까 생각해봤다.)
- **Taoism** : 도교
- **Confucianism** : 유교
- **stone rubbing** : 탁본
- **bemoan=feel very sorry** : 한탄하다 • He bemoaned his fate. (팔자를 한탄하다.)
- **satire=form of writing holding up a person or society to ridicule or showing the foolishness of wickedness of an idea, customs** : 풍자
- **conspicuous=easily seen** : 눈에 잘 띄는 • Traffic signs should be conspicuous.
- **mature=come or bring to full developed** : 원숙해지다
  - These years matured his performance. (몇 년 사이에 그의 연기가 원숙해졌다.)
- **compassion=pity, feeling for the suffering of others** : 연민, 동정
  - She gave some coins to the child out of compassion.
  - Compassion begets compassion. (연민은 연민을 낳는다.)
- **paramount=supreme, superior in power** : 정상의, 최고의
  - Regular attendance is a duty paramount to all others. (모든 의무 중에서 규칙적인 출석이 최고의 의무다.)
- **superb=first class, magnificent** : 가장 우수한
- **prosody=science of verse rhythms** : 작시법, 운율학
- **oriole** : 꾀꼬리의 일종
- **caught in the toils of=caught in the trap (snare) of** : 함정에 빠지다
  - They were caught in the toils of the law. (법망에 빠져들었다.)
- **strain** : (시어) song, music
- **feat=a clever action** : 위업, 공적
- **relic=something old that reminds us of the past** : 유물, 유적

(5) For many centuries, Du Fu's poems have been popular not only with the Chinese people, but also with East Asian intellectuals. The primary reasons for his everlasting popularity besides his literary talents can be drawn from his deep insight and background related to _____. (Conclusion)

  (a) Confucianism & Buddhism
  (b) Confucianism & Taoism
  (c) Buddhism & Taoism
  (d) Animism & Buddhism
  (e) Animism & Confucianism

Passage 16 : Confucius (552 - 479 B.C.)

Background: Confucius, as a great teacher and philosopher, initiated the development of Confucian doctrines the significance of which have been powerfully influential all through East Asia. His social and moral ideas developed by the authorities of Chinese tradition (e.g. *maxims*, examples drawn from history or classical literature) are found primarily in the Analects. The book includes stories about Confucius and his comment upon life situations, and also tells of his proposals for the good of his countrymen. The Analects comprising 20 chapters and 497 verses include the sayings and anecdotes compiled by Confucius' disciples after his death.

Both Confucius and Lao Tzu were concerned with the social and moral weaknesses of their generation. Lao Tzu met the challenge of life that the social institutions and customs of his days were so unnatural that they should be avoided; ( ), Confucius believed that the best from the past should be kept and properly improved. It is because the past is the key to the present and the future. Confucius did not seek to start either a new religion or a new system of ethics.

Confucius faced such basic questions as, "What is life all about? How can I get along best in the world? How can I live a happy life?" He concluded that a man should follow the ways of nature and harmony. If a man would do the best thing based on "harmony," he could do well in the world. Confucius believed that a man's entire responsibility should be "social," - not only for the individual well-being, but also for the social welfare and betterment, since a man could not be apart from his fellows, and his society. Therefore, a man should cooperate with others and perform the duties society expected of him. When a man developed his capacity for harmony with his fellow human beings, then he could understand *universal* harmony for individuals and society in which peace and social order could prevail. Consequently, Confucianism developed based on this type of concept: "proper social rules and harmonious relations," for the "individual and social well-being." The observance of social rules and relations serves as the key leading to the individual and social peace and prosperity.

The following verses interpret the concept of harmony as a means for maintaining and improving interpersonal and social relationships. A few verses are excerpted from the Analects.

Verse 1.

"… in the usages of ritual it is harmony that is prized; the Ways

지문 16 : 공자

배경 : 위대한 스승이자 철학가인 공자는 동아시아 전체에 강력하게 영향력을 행사해 온 유교를 창시했다. 중국 전통의 권위자들에 의하여 발달된 그의 도덕적, 사회적 사상 (예: 역사나 고전 문학에서 뽑아 온 예문들인 경구)은 주로 논어에서 발견된다. 이 책에는 공자에 관한 이야기, 일상 생활에 대한 그의 논평, 백성의 행복을 위한 제언이 있다. 20장과 497의 시문으로 구성된 논어는 그의 사후 그의 제자들이 편찬한 격언과 일화들이 들어 있다.

IMAGE OF CONFUCIUS This image of Confucius was painted by Prince Ho-shuo-kuo in the year 1735 A.D. On the top are Chinese characters of an ancient script which, roughly translated, read : "Confucius, the Sage and the Teacher." The small characters on the right read : "Respectfully painted by Prince Hoshuo-kuo on the day of the full moon, in the ninth lunar month of the year of Chia-yin, during the reign of Emperor Yung-cheng." Below these characters are the prince's official seal which shows hie name in Manchu on the left and Chinese on the right.

공자도 노자도 그들이 살던 세대의 도덕적인 문제들에 관심을 가지고 있었다. 노자는 그가 살던 시대의 사회적 제도나 풍습이 너무 부자연스러우니 없애야 한다는 삶의 문제에 직면했고 반면에 공자는 과거의 가장 훌륭했던 것을 보존하고 적절히 개선해야 한다고 믿었다. 왜냐하면 과거야 말로 현재와 미래를 여는 열쇠이기 때문이다. 공자는 새로운 종교나 새로운 윤리체계를 창시하려 하지는 않았다.

공자는 '산다는 게 무언가? 어떻게 하면 이 세상에서 가장 사이좋게 사는 것인가? 어떻게 하면 행복하게 사는가? 등의 문제에 마주쳤다. 그는 자연과 조화의 길을 따라야 한다고 결론을 내렸다. 만일 '조화'를 토대로 가장 좋은 일을 하면 이 세상에서 성공할 수 있을 것이다. 공자는 사람의 전적인 책임은-개인의 행복을 위해서 뿐만 아니라 사회적 행복과 개선을 위해서-사회적인 것이어야 한다고 믿었다. 그 까닭은 사람이란 그의 동료나 사회로부터 분리될 수 없기 때문이다. 그러므로 타인들과 협동하고 사회가 기대하는 의무를 수행해야 한다. 동료와의 조화할 수 있는 능력을 기를 때, 개인과 평화와 사회적 질서가 우선하는 사회를 위한 보편적인 조화를 알 수 있기 때문이다. 결과적으로 '개인 및 사회적 복지를 위하여 적절한 사회적 규칙과 조화로운 관계'라는 생각에 입각한 유교를 발전시켰다. 사회적 규칙과 관계의 준수는 개인과 사회의 평화와 번영으로 나아가는 열쇠의 역할을 하는 것이다.

다음 시문들은 대인 및 사회적 관계의 유지와 개선을 위한 수단으로써 조화의 사상을 설명한다.

of the Former Kings from this got its beauty. Both small matters and great depend upon it. If things go amiss, he who knows the harmony will be able to attune them. But if harmony itself is not modulated by ritual, things will still go amiss." (I, 12).

Verse 2.

TzuKung asked: "Is there any one word that can serve as a principle for the conduct of life?"   Confucius said: "Perhaps the word '*reciprocity*'…." (XV, 23).

Verse 3.

Confucius said, "Perfect indeed is the virtue which is according to *the Mean*. For long people have seldom had the capacity for it." (VI, 27).

(Source: Waley, Arthur (1938). The Analects of Confucius. translated. and annotated by Arthur Waley, Vintage Books, New York)

(1) The main idea of the passage in the "Background" is "_____?" (Subject matter)

   (a) How to solve social and moral problems
   (b) How can I get along best in the world
   (c) What is life all about
   (d) How can we develop and maintain harmonious relationships
   (e) What should we do for individual and social well-being

(2.1) The italicized word, *maxims*, in the first paragraph of "Background" refers to _____. (2.1. - 2.4. Words in context)

   (a) Axioms/sayings   (b) Maximums   (c) Absurdity   (d) Ambiguity   (e) Paradox

(2.2) The antonym of the italicized word, *universal*, in the third paragraph refers to _____.

   (a) Entire   (b) All-inclusive   (c) Global   (d) Particular   (e) All-embracing

(2.3) The italicized word, *reciprocity*, in Verse 2 includes a similar concept and meaning to _____.

   (a) Independency   (b) Unilaterality   (c) One-way   (d) Uniqueness   (e) Harmony

(2.4) The italicized word, *the Mean*, in Verse 3 includes a different concept and meaning from the _____.

   (a) Average   (b) Common   (c) Humble   (d) Extreme   (e) Insignificant

(3) The underlined structure, "Lao Tzu met… be avoided; ( ), Confucius believed…." One of the suitable conjunctions that best fits in the parenthesis is _____. (Structure)

   (a) Because   (b) If   (c) Whereas   (d) Since   (e) Before

(4.1) Based on the information given, it can be claimed that Confucius attempted to solve social problems for _____. (4.1. - 4.4. Making inferences)

시문 1.

"예(禮)를 행할 때 중요한 것은 조화이다. 여기에서 비롯한 선왕들의 방식이 최상이었다. 작은 일이나 큰 일이나 이것이 기준이다. 만일 일이 잘못되면 조화를 아는 사람이 조절할 수 있을 것이다. 그러나 만일 조화 자체가 예에 따라 조절되지 않으면, 일은 역시 그르쳐질 것이다."

시문 2

자공이 물었다. '살아가는데 원칙으로 쓰일 한마디가 있습니까?'
공자 왈, "아마 '호혜' 라는 말이겠지".

시문 3.

공자 왈. "진실로 중용을 따르는 덕이 완전하다. 오랫동안 사람들은 중용을 지킬 능력을 갖지 못했느니라."

Note

- **initiate** = start something working, a new method : 창시하다
  - Do you know who initiated the digital phone? (디지털 전화는 누가 먼저 사용했는지 아니?)
- **doctrine** = a principle or sets of principles : 원리, 주의
  - Monroe Doctrine : (몬로주의)   • the Buddhist doctrine (불교교의)
- **maxim** = a rule for good and sensible behavior : 처세훈, 격언
- **a golden maxim** : 금언   □ **Analect** : 논어   cf. analect (어록)
- **comprise** = consist of, include, be made up of : 구성하다, 포함하다
  - North America comprises the U.S. Canade, and Mexico.
    (북아메리카에는 미국, 카나다, 멕시코가 있다.)
- **verse** = written language in the form of poetry : 시문, 시가, 운문
- **saying** = a well-known wise statement, proverb : 격언, 속담
  - As the saying goes, "There is no smoke without fire."
    (속담에 이르기를 '突不煙 不生煙 : 無風不起浪 : 불안 땐 굴뚝에 연기 날까.')
- **anecdote** = a short interesting or amusing story about a particular person or an event : 일화
- **compile** = make an article or a book etc. from facts and information found in many places : 편찬하다, 편집하다
- **disciple** = follower of any great teacher esp. one of the first followers of Christ : 제자, 도제
- **Lao Tzu(e)** : 노자(老子)
- **be concerned with** = have a relation to : 관심을 가지다, 관계하다
  - authorities concerned (관계당국)
- **To whom it may concern** : 담당자 귀하
- **well-being** = welfare, health, happiness and prosperity
  - That department is working for the well-being of the nation. (그 부서는 국민 복지를 위하여 일한다.)
- **universal** = belonging, done by, affecting all : 전반적인, 보편적인
  - War causes universal miseries. (전쟁은 총체적인 불행을 일으킨다.)
- **prevail** = gain victory over, fight successfully : 이기다, 득세하다
  - We prevailed over the enemy. (우리가 적을 압도했다.)

(a) Social prosperity   (d) National security
(b) Social & individual well-being   (e) Social order & peace
(c) Harmonious interpersonal relations

(4.2) To Confucius, "_____" serves as a means for developing and maintaining social relations and order.

    (a) Ritual   (b) Responsibility   (c) The Mean   (d) Conduct   (e) Harmony

(4.3) Confucianism values "prescriptive rules" for individual and social well-being. The prescriptive rules refer to the directions/rituals of "Do" or "Don't" in interpersonal relations. For example, under the tradition of Confucianism, a junior is supposed to respect a senior while the junior is protected or taken care of by the senior, which is a reciprocal principle. This type of relationship can be hardly seen _____.

    (a) In the levels of speech style   (c) Between teachers & students   (e) At war
    (b) In family bond   (d) In greeting

Note: (The level of speech style refers to a variety of levels (e.g. Honorific, Common, Vulgar) used in verbal interactions.)

(4.4) One of the following concepts/movements/rituals that is considered to have hardly been influenced by the tradition of Confucianism is _____.

    (a) Different sex roles   (d) Gender equal rights
    (b) Loyalty to superiors   (e) Memorial services for ancestors
    (c) Reciprocal interpersonal relations

(5.1) Confucius social and moral ideas were developed by the authorities of Chinese tradition as a way of solving social and ethical problems at the time. What historical or sociopolitical events do you conclude prompted Confucius to develop his social and moral concerns? (5.1. - 5.2. Conclusions)

    (a) Fall of Zhou Dynasty (256 B.C.)
    (b) Unification of China (221 B.C.)
    (c) Decentralized political power of Zhou Dynasty (1122 - 249 B.C.)
    (d) Spring and Autumn Warring Period (771 - 476 B.C.)
    (e) Work begun on the "Great Wall of China" (214 B.C.)

(5.2) It can be concluded that Confucianism is likely to prevail in a/an _____ community where people have to collectively support one another for their survival.

    (a) Academic (b) Technological (c) Agricultural (d) Entertaining (e) Commercial

Passage 17 : Siddhartha Gautama (563-483? B.C.)

The story about Siddhartha's birth and childhood is legend. But he actually lived on

> ☐ observance=behavior in accordance with a law, ceremony or custom : 준수
>   • observance of the speed limit (제한속도의 준수)
> ☐ ritual=all the rites, one or more ceremonies of customary acts : 의식, 제례, 전례
> ☐ amiss=wrong   • Is something amiss? (뭐가 잘 못 됐니?)
> ☐ attune=causes to become used to : 조율하다, 조정하다
> ☐ modulate=change the strength, nature of a sound : 변조하다, 조정하다
> ☐ reciprocity : 상호성, 호혜주의 = 己所不欲勿施於人
> ☐ the mean=a state or way of behavior which is not too strong or weak : 중용
>   • Perfect indeed is the virtue which is according to the mean. (도치구문)
>   • The virtue which is according to the mean is indeed great. (중용을 지키는 덕이 실로 중요하다.)
> ☐ annotate=add notes to a book to explain : 주석을 달다
> ☐ ambiguity=being able to be understood in more than two ways : 애매모호, 불분명
>   • Her reply was full of ambiguities. (그녀의 대답이 온통 모호했다.)
> ☐ unilaterality : 일방성   ☐ prescriptive : 지시적, 규범적   ☐ honorific : 경칭의, 존대를 나타내는
> ☐ vulgar=ill-mannered, in bad taste : 비천한, 야비한, • vulgar language (비어(卑語))

지문 17 : 싯다르타 석가모니

싯다르타 (정반왕의 태자였을 때의 이름)의 출생과 어린시절의 이야기는 전설이다. 그러나 그는 실제로 아대륙(亞大陸) 인도에서 살았고 살아가는데 의지할 수 있는 사상을 추구했다. 수년간 방황하며 힌두교의 학자와 성인(聖人)들에게서 해답을 찾으려 했지만 허사

Buddhism, founded in India, eventually spread across Asia. In many places, Buddha came to be worshipped as a god. Here, he is shown surrounded by four minor deities.

the Indian subcontinent, seeking new ideas to live by. He wandered for many years, *vainly* seeking answers from Hindu scholars and holy men. Eventually, he sat down to meditate under a bo or pipal tree for 48 days, and he understood the cause and cure for suffering and sorrow, which helped him be the "Enlightened One," or "Buddha."

After reaching enlightenment, Buddha spent the rest of his life teaching others what he had learned. He explained the Four Noble Truths that ( ) at the heart of Buddhism:

(1) Human life is full of suffering and sorrow.
(2) Suffering and sorrow are caused by people's greedy desires for power, pleasure, and possessions.
(3) Suffering and sorrow will end when people overcome their greed.
(4) The way to overcome desire is to follow the Eightfold Path.

Buddha asked his followers to try to live all eight steps at once, not one after the other, when observing the Eightfold Path:

(1) Right View: Believing in the Four Noble Truths and the Eightfold Path.
(2) Right Resolve: Making a firm decision to live according to the Eightfold Path.
(3) Right Speech: Speaking in a manner that does not harm others; not gossiping, lying, or using angry words.
(4) Right Conduct: Acting in a way that does not harm others; not killing, not stealing, and also not acting selfishly.
(5) Right Livelihood: Earning a living in a way that does not harm others.
(6) Right Effort: Striving *to get rid of* any evil within oneself.
(7) Right Mindfulness: Paying attention to responsibilities.
(8) Right Meditation: Thinking deeply for answers to problems.

(Source: Adapted from Beers, Burton (1991). World History. Ellis, G. Elizabeth & et al. (1977). World History: Connections to Today. Holt, Sol & et al. (1990). Exploring World History.)

(1) The topic of the passage is "_____." (Subject matter)

   (a) Gautama's life   (d) Gautama's teachings
   (b) Gautama's Enlightenment   (e) Facts related to Gautama
   (c) Development of Buddhism

(2.1) The italicized word, *vainly*, in the first paragraph refers to _____. (2.1 - 2.2. Word & phrase in context)

   (a) Fruitfully   (b) Arrogantly   (c) Uselessly   (d) Beneficially   (e) Effectively

(2.2) The italicized phrase, *to get rid of*, in the third paragraph refers to _____.

   (a) Accept   (b) Ratify   (c) Sanction   (d) Eliminate   (e) Disregard

(3) The underlined structure, "He explained the Four Noble Truths that ( ) at the heart of Buddhism," needs a suitable verb that fits best in the parenthesis. (Structure)

   (a) Rest   (b) Refer   (c) Stand   (d) Signify   (e) Account

였다. 결국 48일간 인도 보리수 아래 앉아 명상을 한 끝에 고통과 슬픔의 원인과 치유법을 깨달았고 그것이 그를 '깨달음을 얻은자' 즉 '부처'가 되는데 도움이 되었다. 깨달음에 도달한 후 여생을 자기가 깨달은 것을 다른 사람들에게 가르치는 데 바쳤다. 그는 불교의 정수인 사성제(四聖諦)를 설법했다.

(1) 인생은 고통과 슬픔으로 가득하다. (苦諦)
(2) 고통과 슬픔은 인간의 권력, 쾌락, 재산에 대한 탐욕으로 말미암는다. (集諦)
(3) 고통과 슬픔은 이 탐욕을 끊을 때 끝난다. (滅諦)
(4) 탐욕을 극복하는 길은 八正道를 따르는 것이다. (道諦)

부처는 자기 제자들에게 팔정도를 지킬 때는 하나씩이 아니라 한꺼번에 전체 여덟가지 길을 지키면서 살 것을 요구했다.

(1) 바른 견해(正見) : 四聖諦와 八正道를 신봉
(2) 바른 사유(正思惟) : 팔정도를 따라 살 굳은 결심
(3) 바른 말(正語) : 타인을 해치지 않는 말씨, 험담, 거짓말, 성낸 말을 않기
(4) 바른 행동(正業) : 타인을 해치지 않는 길로 행동하기, 살인하지 않기, 도둑질하지 않기, 이기적으로 행동하지 않기
(5) 바른 생활(正命) : 타인을 해치지 않는 생계활동
(6) 바른 노력(正精進) : 내부의 악을 없애려는 노력
(7) 바른 새김(正念) : 맡은 일에 대하여 주의를 기울이기
(8) 바른 정신통일(正定) : 문제의 해답을 얻기 위한 명상

Note

- legend=an old story about ancient times, which is probably not true
- subcontinent : 亞大陸 (인도나 그린랜드 같은 대륙)
- words to live by : 기준을 삼아 살아갈 말씀
- meditate=think deeply, give oneself up to serious thoughts : 명(묵)상
  - cf. mediate=act as go between or peacemaker (중재하다, 화해시키다)
- Enlightened one : 깨달은 사람 : 覺者
- greed=strong desire for more food, wealth : 탐욕
  - He eats because of greed, not of hunger. (시장해서가 아니라 식탐 때문에 먹는다.)
- Eightfold Path : 八正道=八聖道 : 불교 수행에서의 여덟가지 명목 : 正見, 正思惟, 正語, 正業, 正命, 正精進, 正念, 正定.
- Four Noble Truths : 四聖諦 – 불교의 영원한 진리(苦諦, 集諦, 滅諦, 道諦,)
- metaphysical : 형이상학 (아리스토텔레스가 물리학 후에 온다고 한 말에서)   meta=after
- respectively=each, separately in the order mentioned : 앞에서 말한 순서대로 각각
  - The nurses and miners received pay increase of 85% and 12% respectively.

(4.1) Buddhism founded in India developed into two: Mahayana and Theravada. The former spread to northeastern countries of Asia; whereas the latter to the southeastern regions. Of the following lists, which one contains two countries from the northeastern and the southeastern regions respectively? (4.1 - 4.6. Making inferences)

    (a) Thailand, Japan; China, Laos   (d) Korea, Vietnam; Cambodia, Laos
    (b) China, Japan; Burma, Thailand   (e) Sri Lanka, Japan; Burma, Laos
    (c) China, Sri Lanka; Burma, Laos

(4.2) Although Buddhism was founded and once flourished in India, it is not the dominant religion today. The reason for this decline can be largely due to the influence of _____.

    (a) Islam   (b) Jainism   (c) Christianity   (d) Sikhism   (e) Hinduism

(4.3) The following country which has the largest number of Buddhist followers can be inferred to be _____.

    (a) China   (b) Korea   (c) Japan   (d) Malaysia   (e) Thailand

(4.4) According to the Four Noble Truths, life is full of suffering and sorrow which are caused by _____ motivation.

    (a) Religious   (b) Spiritual   (c) Social   (d) Psychological   (e) Metaphysical

(4.5) Siddhartha suggested The Eightfold Path as a way of _____.

    (a) Reaching enlightenment   (c) Overcoming desire   (e) Living accordingly
    (b) Being a Buddhist   (d) Being responsible

(4.6) We can infer that Buddhism owes to _____ for the development of its philosophy and precept.

    (a) Hinduism   (b) Islam   (c) Jainism   (d) Sikhism   (e) Taoism

(5) It can be concluded that Buddhism as a salvation from the burden of human suffering stresses _____ and _____ concerns of how to live in this world. (Conclusion)

    (a) Spiritual, materialistic   (c) Metaphysical, moral   (e) Theological, social
    (b) Psychological, humanistic   (d) Psychological, ethical

영어 격언과 한문 격언과의 만남 (14)

Selected proverbs for the study of cross-cultural expressions

1. Dead men will tell no tales. 死者無言(사자무언) – 죽은 자는 말이 없다.

2. A word and a stone let go can't be called back. 駟不及舌(사불급설 ; 駟 = horse)
   – 빠른 말이 혀를 따라 잡지 못하다.

3. No reply and soft pillow. 笑而不言心自閑(소이불언심자한) – 웃기만 하고 말을 안하니 마음이 저절로 한가하다.

4. Great things are done more through tenacity than through wisdom.
   愚公移山(우공이산) – 어리석은 사람이 산을 옮긴다.(위대한 일을 해낸다.)

5. All must be as God will. 萬事分已定(만사분이정 ; 分 = lot) – 모든 일의 운명은 이미 정해져 있다.
   · No flying from fate. / · Every bullet has its billet. / · What will be will be.

6. Diligence is the mother of good fortune. 勤卽家起(근즉가기) – 부지런함이 집안을 일으킨다.

7. Knowing oneself and the enemy is the surest way to victory.
   知彼知己百戰不殆(지피지기백전불태) – 나를 알고 상대를 알면 백번 싸워도 위태롭지 않다.

   Knowing oneself but not the enemy is half defeat.
   知己不知彼一勝一敗(지기부지피일승일패) – 나는 알고 상대를 모르면 일승 일패다.

   Not knowing oneself or the enemy is the surest way to defeat.
   不知己不知彼百戰必敗(부지기부지피백전필패) – 자신도 모르고 상대도 모르면 반드시 패한다.

8. Do to others as you would be done by.
   己所不欲勿施於人, 推己及人(기소불욕물시어인, 추기급인)
   – 내가 하기 싫은 것은 남에게 시키지 말라, 나를 미루어 보아 남에게도 그대로 하라.

9. One man's good deed serves many thereafter.
   前人種樹後人乘凉(전인종수후인승량 ; 乘 = sit on) – 앞사람이 심은 나무가 뒷사람에게 시원함을 준다.

10. Never utilize public means to satisfy private ends. 憑公營私, 假公爲私(빙공영사, 가공위사)
    – 공을 빙자하여 사적인 일을 하다.

11. Willing in mind, unable in body. 心有力而力不足(심유력이역부족)
    – 마음으로는 할 것 같은데 몸이 말을 안 듣는다.

12. An ass in a lion's skin. 狐爲虎威, 狐假虎威(호위호위, 호가호위) – 여우가 호랑이 위세를 부리다.

13. Seeing is believing. 百聞不如一見(백문불여일견) · The proof of pudding is in the eating.

14. One swallow does not make a summer. 單絲不成綿(단사불성면)
    – 한 오라기의 실이 솜을 만들지 못한다.

Passage 18 : Lao Tzu (604-531? B.C.) and Tao Te Ching

<u>Background</u>: Lao Tzu (*"No Ja"), a presumably mythical Chinese philosopher and the author of Tao Te Ching (*"Doh Deok Kyung"), is considered as a founder of Taoism. He, an older contemporary of Confucius, was keeper of the imperial *archives* at Loyang in the province of Honan. According to ancient legend, as he was riding off into the desert to die - sick at heart at the ways of men - he was persuaded by a gatekeeper in northwestern China to write down his teaching for *posterity*. The essence of Taoism is contained in the 81 verses of the book, Tao Te Ching, with roughly 5,000 words which have for 2,500 years provided one of the major underlying influences in Chinese culture and thought. <u>Whereas Confucianism is concerned ( ) practical day-to-day social rules of conduct,</u> Taoism highlights a more spiritual level of being. Two verses, I and VIII, excerpted from Tao Te Ching are introduced here.

Verse I

The Tao that can be told is not the eternal Tao.
The name that can be named is not the eternal name.
The nameless is the beginning of heaven and earth.
The named is the mother of ten thousand things.
Ever desireless, one can see the mystery.
Ever desiring, one sees the manifestations.
These two spring from the same source but differ in name;
this appears as darkness.
Darkness within darkness.
The gate to all mystery.

Verse VIII

The highest good is like water.
Water gives life to the ten thousand things and does not strive.
It flows in places men reject and so is like the Tao.
In dwelling, be close to the land.
In meditation, go deep in the heart.
In dealing with others, be gentle and kind.
In speech, be true.
In ruling, be just.
In daily life, be competent.
In action, be aware of the time and the season.
No fight : No blame.

(Source : <u>Tao Te Ching</u>. Translated by Gia-Fu Feng & Jane English (1989).

(1.1) The best topic of Verse I can be "The _____ of Tao." (1.1 - 1.2. Subject matters)

    (a) Essence   (b) Mystery   (c) Manifestations   (d) Definition   (e) Role

지문 18 : 노자와 도덕경

Lao Tzu

배경 : 추측하기로 신화적인 중국의 철학가이자 도덕경의 저자인 노자는 도교의 창시자로 여겨지고 있다. 공자보다 나이가 많은 동시대 인물인 노자는 하남성 낙양에 있는 황실 문서보관소 관리인이었다. 고대 전설에 의하면 인간들의 생활방식에 구역질이 나서 죽으려고 사막으로 말을 타고 떠날때 중국 북서쪽에 있는 성문(함곡관)의 수문장(윤희)이 후손들을 위하여 가르침을 써달라고 권하였다 한다. 도교의 본질은 도덕경의 81개의 시문에 약 5,000단어 속에 들어 있고 2,500년간 중국의 사상과 문화의 바탕에 주요한 영향을 끼쳐오고 있다. 유교가 실제적인 일상 사회적 행동 규범을 다루고 있는데 반해 도교는 인간존재의 좀더 정신적인 수준을 강조한다. 도덕경에서 뽑은 두개의 시문 1편과 8편을 다음에 소개한다.

Lao-tzu(centre), detail from a Taoist temple fresco, southern Shansi, China, Yüan dynasty(1206~1368); in the Royal Ontario Museum, Toronto
by courtesy of the Royal Ontario Museum, Toronto

1편
도라고 말할 수 있는 것은 영원한 도가 아니다. - 道可道 非常道
이름 붙일 수 있는 이름은 영원한 이름이 아니다. - 名可名 非常名
이름 없는 것이 천지의 시초다. - 無, 名天地之始
이름 가진 것이 만물의 어머니다. - 有, 名萬物之母
고로 욕심이 없어야 신비가 눈에 보이고 - 故常無, 欲以觀其妙
항상 욕심이 있으면 만물이 눈에 보인다 - 常有, 欲以觀其徵
이 두가지는 같은 근원에서 나오지만 이름은 다르다 - 此兩者, 同出而異名
이것은 현묘함으로 나타난다. 현묘함에서 현묘함으로 - 同謂之玄, 玄之又玄
모든 신비의 문이다. - 衆妙之門

(1.2) The best topic of Verse VIII is "The _____ of the Highest Good."

    (a) Alliteration   (b) Metaphor   (c) Characteristic   (d) Denotation   (e) Simile

(2.1) The italicized word, *archives*, in the section of "Background" is similar to our modern _____. (2.1 - 2.2. Words in context)

    (a) Museums   (b) Depositories   (c) Laboratories   (d) Repository   (e) Courts

(2.2) The antonym of the italicized word, *posterity*, is _____.

    (a) Children   (b) Lineage   (c) Descendants   (d) Ancestry   (d) Offspring

(3) The underlined structure, "Whereas Confucianism is concerned ( ) practical day-to-day social rules of conduct," needs a suitable preposition for the parenthesis. The best choice is _____. (Structure)

    (a) Of   (b) By   (c) For   (d) To   (e) With

(4.1) Based on the interpretations of Verse I, it can be inferred that the essence of Tao is _____. (4.1. - 4.5. Making inferences)

    (a) Manifestation   (d) The unexplainable
    (b) Darkness within darkness   (e) The mysterious work of nature
    (c) The undefinable

(4.2) "The Tao" can be better understood if we _____.

    (a) Analyze the factors   (d) Tell the truth
    (b) Study the manifestations   (e) Knock at the door of mystery
    (c) Empty our desires

(4.3) According to Verse VIII, the Tao is compared with the role of water, "The highest… like water… Water gives life… It flows… like the Tao." The function of "water" can be inferred as the work of _____.

    (a) Acculturation   (c) Nature   (e) Social institutions
    (b) Socialization   (d) Religious organizations

(4.4) "In dwelling, be close to the land… In action, be aware of the time and season" in Verse VIII, can be interpreted as a piece of advice for _____.

    (a) Social upgrade   (c) Being desireless   (e) Being respected
    (b) Leadership   (d) Being humble

(4.5) "No fight: No blame," can be interpreted as "_____."

    (a) No pain, no gain   (c) No desire, no manifestations   (e) No water, no life
    (b) No love, no hatred (d) No fight, no victory

(5.1) Based on the interpretations of Verses I and VIII, it can be concluded that Lao Tzu stressed the _____ as a way of living. (5.1. - 5.2. Conclusions)

    (a) Law of nature   (c) Religious rituals   (e) Moral obligations
    (b) Social rules   (d) Ethical standards

8편

최고의 선은 물과 같다. - 上善若水

물은 만물에 생명을 주지만 다투지 않는다. - 水善利萬物而不爭

물은 인간이 꺼리는 곳을 흐르고 도 또한 이와 같다 - 處衆人之所惡, 故幾於道

거처는 땅에 가까이 하고 - 居善地

생각은 마음 깊이하여라 - 心善淵

타인은 온유와 친절로 상대하고 - 與善仁

말은 진실로 하고 - 言善信

정치는 바르게 하라 - 正善治

일은 능력있게 하라 - 事善能

행동은 시간과 철을 알아라 - 動善時

다투지 않으면 원망이 없다 - 夫唯不爭 故無尤

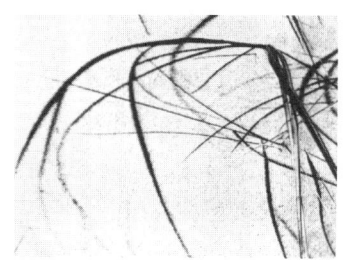

Note

- 若=like 而=but 惡=dislike, reject 故=therefore 尤(우)=blame, resentment
- presumably=probably, it may be reasonably supposed that : 아마
  - Presumably there is a good reason for her absence. (아마 그가 못 오는 충분한 이유가 있을 것이다.)
- mythical=not real, imagined or invented : 사실이 아닌, 상상적인
- contemporary=a person living at the same time : 동시대인
- archives=a place for storing old papers for historical interest : 문서 보관소
- posterity=people who will be born and live after one's own time : 후손
- highlight=pick out something as an important part, throw attention to : 강조하다
- being=existence, life : 존재   • human being (인간)
  - When did the club come into being? (그 클럽이 언제 생겼나?)
- competent=having ability or skill to do what is needed : 유능한, 경쟁력이 있는
- alliteration : 두운(頭韻)   □ denotation : 단어의 뜻   □ depository : 저장소
- repository : 매장지   □ lineage : 가계, 혈통   □ acculturation : 문화변용
- social upgrade : 신분상승   □ pragmatism : 실용주의

(5.2) For many centuries, the influences of Buddhism, Confucianism, and Taoism have contributed to the development of the Chinese tradition and to the character building of the people. One of the following concluded to have been influenced by Taoism is _____.

(a) Protest against injustice
(b) Tolerance of hardship
(c) Pragmatism
(d) Opportunism
(e) Diligence

Passage 19 : "Love" described by St. Paul

Background: The city of Corinth was situated in a very profitable geographical position between east and west, building with its prosperity from the trade routes - sea and land - which had to pass through the territory. But the city was never famous for its culture and teaching. Instead it became notorious for all its types of vice and licentiousness (e.g. idolaters, sexual perverts, thieves, drunkards, robbers). To "Corinthianize" became a polite way of saying "Go to the devil."

A delegation from the Church in Corinth wrote a letter of complaints to St. Paul concerning general quarrels and problems (i.e. marriage, spiritual gifts, disorders in public worship, meat sacrificed to idols, The Resurrection Doctrine) at the Church. Paul visited the Corinthian Church three times and instructed them on the two issues: (1) Division; and, (2) Love. For the first issue, Paul said, "Division, disunity, schism are sins to be avoided. This kind of behavior is typical of Christian immaturity and that such people should learn to grow up! This leads to pride, arrogance, and an air of superiority in the Church." For the second issue, he said, "Love must be a leading principle… The matter of pure love is fundamental to any proposed change in behavior. Crucial to a Church wishing to resolve its division, its weaknesses, its doctrinal failures and relationship is love. Not the kind of love that the Corinthians were used to in their sexually perverted culture." This concept of love based on the meaning of agape was quite new for those people. St. Paul, one of the writers of Epistles in the New Testament, and the greatest Apostle was martyred in Rome A.D. 64 or 65. The following is excerpted from 1 Corinthians 13.

(Source: Lee, Richard L. (1996). "Biblical Studies in 1 Corinthians." East Midlands School of Christian Ministry).

If I speak in the tongues of men and of angels, but have not love, I am only a *resounding* gong or a clanging cymbal. If I have the gift of prophecy and can *fathom* all mysteries and all knowledge, and I have a faith that can move mountains, but have not love, I am nothing. If I give all I possess to the poor and surrender my body to the flames, but have not love, I gain nothing.

Love is patient, love is kind. It does not envy, it does not boast, it is not proud. It is not rude, it is not self-seeking, it is not easily angered, it keeps no record of wrongs. Love does not delight in evil but rejoices with the truth. It always protects, always trusts, always hopes, always perseveres.

…. And now these three remain: faith, hope and love. But the greatest of these is love.

(Source: "1 Corinthians 13" The Old and New Testament (1987). Korean Bible Society, Seoul.)

지문 19 : 성 바울이 말하는 '사랑'

배경 : 고린도시는 지리적으로 매우 유리한 동·서간의 사이에 위치하고 있으며 그 영토를 통과해야하는 육로 및 수상의 무역로가 번창함에 따라 확대되고 있었다. 그러나 이 도시는 결코 문화나 예수의 가르침으로는 유명하지 못했다. 그대신 온갖 형태의 악과 방종(예 : 우상숭배, 성적 도착자들, 도둑, 술주정뱅이, 강도)으로 악명이 높았다. '고린도화하다' 는 단어는 '지옥에 떨어진다' 는 말의 점잖은 표현이 되었다.

고린도 교회에서 보낸 한 사람이 교회 내의 전체적인 언쟁과 문제들 (환언하면, 결혼, 영적 선물, 공중 예배 때의 무질서, 우상에게 바치는 고기, 부활의 교리)에 대하여 호소하는 편지를 바울에게 보냈다. 바울은 고린도 교회를 세 차례 방문하여 (1)분란, (2) 사랑의 두 쟁점에 대하여 가르쳤다. 첫째 문제에 대하여 바울은 "분열, 내분, 분파는 피해야할 죄입니다. 이런 형태의 행동은 기독교적으로 대표적인 미숙이며 그런 사람들은 성숙해져야 합니다. 그런 행동은 교회 내에서 교만과 불손과 잘난 체하는 태도를 낳습니다." 두번째 문제인 사랑에 대하여, "사랑을 제 1의 원칙으로 삼아야 합니다. 순수한 사랑의 문제는 모든 행동이 요구되는 변화의 기본입니다. 사랑이란 교회의 분열, 약점들, 교리의 불이행, 관계를 해결하는데 필수적입니다. 내가 말하는 사랑은 고린도 사람들이 과거 도착된 성문화와 같은 형태의 것이 아닙니다." 아가페적 의미에 바탕을 둔 이런 의미의 사랑이 그 사람들에겐 전혀 새로운 것이었다. 신약성서의 서간문의 작자이자 가장 위대한 사도였던 바울은 기원 64년이나 65년에 순교당했다. 다음은 고린도 전서 13장 1절로부터 13절까지를 발췌한 것이다.

내가 인간의 여러 언어를 말하고 천사의 말까지 하더라도 사랑이 없으면 나는 울리는 징과 요란한 꽹과리와 다를 것이 없습니다. 내가 하느님의 말씀을 받아 전할 수 있다 하더라도 온갖 신비를 환히 꿰뚫어 보고 모든 지식을 가졌다 하더라도 산을 옮길 만한 완전한 믿음을 가졌다 하더라도, 사랑이 없으면 나는 아무 것도 아닙니다. 내가 비록 모든 재산을 남에게 나누어 준다 하더라도 또 내가 남을 위하여 불 속에 뛰어 든다 하더라도 사랑이 없으면 나는 아무 소용이 없

1st Corinthians

(1.1) The topic of the passage is "The _____ of love." (1.1. - 1.2. Subject matter)

    (a) Definition   (b) Characteristic   (c) Purpose   (d) Effect   (e) Truth

(1.2) Paul offered love as the greatest _____ for solving human problems existing at the church and in society, and for serving God.

    (a) Means   (b) Doctrine   (c) Goal   (d) Faith   (e) Hope

(2.1) The italicized word, *resounding*, in the first paragraph refers to _____. (2.1 - 2.2. Words in context)

    (a) Resisting   (b) Resting   (c) Resolving   (d) Repugnant   (e) Resonating

(2.2) The antonym of the italicized word, *fathom*, in the first paragraph is _____.

    (a) Sharpen   (b) Misunderstand   (c) Recognize   (d) Discern   (e) Apprehend

(3) The underlined structures, "<u>but have not love</u>", can be restructured as "_____" in today's English. (Structure)

    (a) Only love   (b) Without love   (c) Except love   (d) But love   (e) Having not love

(4.1) Paul's description of love is basically "gracious, determined, and active interest in the true welfare of others based solely on the nature of God without being deterred by hatred and abuse." This type of love can be classified as _____. (4.1. - 4.2. Making inferences)

    (a) Eros   (b) Philia   (c) Agape   (d) Logos   (e) Ethos

(4.2) Based on the information given, it can be inferred that the Corinthians were influenced by _____ as part of their culture.

    (a) Eros   (b) Philia   (c) Agape   (d) Ethos   (e) Pathos

(5) It can be concluded that the central theme of Paul's love can be the most similar to one of the following sayings or statements. (Conclusion)

    (a) Every man is of importance to himself.
    (b) Friendship is love without his wings (Lord Byron)
    (c) He who can give love has many a good neighbors.
    (d) Love is the only universal tongue.
    (e) Love conquers all.

습니다.

　사랑은 오래 참습니다. 사랑은 친절합니다. 사랑은 시기하지 않습니다. 사랑은 자랑하지 않습니다. 사랑은 교만하지 않습니다. 사랑은 무례하지 않습니다. 사랑은 사욕을 품지 않습니다. 사랑은 성내지 않습니다. 사랑은 앙심을 품지 않습니다. 사랑은 불의를 보고 기뻐하지 아니하고 진리를 보고 기뻐합니다. 사랑은 모든 것을 덮어 주고 모든 것을 믿고 모든 것을 바라고 모든 것을 견디어 냅니다. 믿음, 소망, 사랑 중 제일은 사랑입니다.

References

- 당시의 고린도 교회 : 성적 부도덕(근친상간), 성도간의 고발 고소, 부활에 대한 오해, 우상 숭배에 대한 문제로 내분이 있어 분열함 : 이런 문제로 바울에게 편지를 보내어 도움을 청함.

Note

- notorious=famous for something bad, unfavorably known : 악명 높은
  - He is notorious for his goings-on. (그는 못된 행동으로 악명이 나있다.)
- licentiousness : 방종, 음탕　　□ idolater=the worship of idols : 우상 숭배, 맹목적 신앙
- pervert=turn to a wrong use, cause someone to tun away from right behavior : 타락시키다, 도착시키다
  - Do pornographic books pervert those who read them? (포르노 잡지는 읽는 사람을 성적으로 도착시키는가?)
- idol=an image worshiped as a god : 우상, 존경의 대상
  - The soccer player is the idol among the girls of the early teens. (그 축구 선수는 10대 초반 소녀들의 우상이다.)
- Resurrection : 예수의 부활　　□ division : 분열　　□ disunity : 내분
- schism : 교회의 분파　　□ agape : 인간 상호간의 사랑, 기독교적 사랑
- eros : 이성간의 성애적 사랑　　• opp. logos (理性)
- ethos : 윤리성　　□ pathos : 비애감, 애절감
- epistle=a long and important letter　　• Epistle (使徒의 서한)
- Apostle : 12사도 중의 한사람
- martyr=put to death, cause to suffer for a belief : (신앙 때문에) 죽이다, 순교하다
- resound=be loudly and clearly heard : 울려 퍼지다
  - Their laughter resounded through the hall. (그들 웃음 소리가 실내에 울렸다.)
- clang=make a loud ringing sound : 요란하게 울리다
  - The metal tool clanged when it hit the wall. (그 금속 연장이 벽에 닿자 쨍소리가 났다.)
- prophecy=foreseeing and foretelling of future events : 예언
- fathom=measure, get at the true meaning of : 수심을 재다, 사람 마음을 통찰하다
  - I can hardly fathom what you mean. (도저히 무슨 뜻인지 모르겠다.)
- self-seeking : 자기 이익만 챙기기, 이기적 행동
- persevere=continue firmly in spite of difficulties : 난관을 무릅쓰고 인내하다
  - To achieve something in life, you must persevere in what you're doing. (인생에서 뭔가 성취하려면 하는 일을 참고 계속해야 한다.)
- apprehend=fear; understand : 두려워하다; 이해하다
  - A guilty man apprehends a danger in every sound. (죄인은 어떤 소리에도 겁을 낸다.)

Passage 20 : Billy Graham (1918 -): A Great Evangelist

Background : Billy Graham was born to William Franklin and Morrow Coffey Graham near Charlotte, North Carolina. He was the first of four children and his parents were both Christians. But it wasn't until 1934 through a series of revival meetings led by an evangelist, Mordecai Fowler, that Billy personally dedicated his life to Christ. In 1940, he graduated from Florida Bible Institute (now Trinity College) with a Th.B, and in 1943 from Wheaton College with a B.A. in anthropology. He became the pastor of the United Gospel Tabernacle while attending Wheaton where he met his future wife, Ruth Bell. Ruth and Billy got married in 1943 after graduation.

While pastoring a baptist church in Chicago, Graham took over a religious radio program, *Songs in the Night*, and began preaching every Sunday evening. Eventually, he began holding evangelistic rallies of his own, traveling the country and became well-known within evangelist communities. In the decades to come, Billy held evangelistic campaigns in all the major U.S. cities as well as around the world. The Billy Graham Evangelistic Association (B.G.E.A.) was born in the late 1950s, and he generally held three to five crusades a year after 1957.

Billy has been listed by the Gallop organization as one of the "10 Most Admired Men in the World" and unparalleled 37 times. Since his career began over 50 years ago, he has preached the Gospel to more people in live audience than anyone in history - over 210 million people. Hundreds of millions more have been reached through the channels of mass media. Billy and Ruth Graham live in the mountains of North Carolina. The following is excerpted from Graham's message from the "Mission Follow-Up" published in August 1997.

Question: How to be sure that you have a personal relationship with Christ?

Answer: The central theme of the Bible is God's love for you and for all people. This love was *revealed* when Jesus Christ, the son of God, came into the world as a human being, lived a sinless life, died on the cross, and rose from the dead. Because Christ died, your sins can be forgiven, and because he conquered death you can have eternal life. You can know for sure what will become of you after you die. You have probably heard the story of God's love referred to as the "Gospel." The word Gospel simply means "Good News." The Gospel is the Good News that, because of what Christ has done, we can be forgiven and can live forever. But this gift of forgiveness and eternal life cannot be yours unless you willingly accept it. God requires an individual response from you.

The following verses from the Bible show God's part and yours in this process: "For God so loved the world that He gave His one and only son, that whoever believes in him should not perish but have eternal life" (John 3:16)…

Throughout all of human history, people have sinned in their separation from God. They have tried *to bridge* the gap in many ways… without success… There is only one remedy for this problem of separation: <u>Jesus Christ who died on the cross, and paid the penalty for our sins, and bridged the gap between God and us</u>. The Bible says… "There is

지문 20 : 빌리 그레이엄—위대한 복음 전도사

배경 : 빌리 그레이엄은 노스 캐롤라이나의 샬럿에서 윌리암과 모로우 코피 그레이엄 사이에서 태어났다. 4형제 중의 맏이었으며 양친이 기독교 신자였다. 그러나 그가 개인적으로 그리스도에게 생애를 바친 것은 1934년 모디카이 파울러라는 복음 전도사가 지도하는 일련의 부흥회를 통해서였다. 1940년에 그는 플로리다 성경학교(현재 트리니티 대학)를 졸업하고 신학 석사를 취득  했고, 1943년에는 휘튼 대학을 인류학 석사로 졸업했다. 그는 그의 아내인 루스 벨을 만난 휘튼 대학을 다니면서 미국 복음교회의 목사가 되었다. 루스와 빌은 1943년 졸업 후 결혼했다.

시카고의 어느 침례교회의 목사로 재직하면서 'Songs in the Night'라는 라디오 프로그램을 맡았고 주일마다 설교를 시작했다. 마침내 자신의 복음집회를 개최하기 시작했고 전국을 순회하며 복음 전도사 교단 내에서 유명해 졌다. 그후 수십 년 간 미국의 주요 도시에서 뿐만아니라 전 세계적으로 복음 선교 운동을 했다. 빌리 그레이엄 복음 협회가 1950년대에 탄생하고 1957년 후 연 3~5회 일반적인 신앙 개혁 운동을 개최했다.

빌리는 여론 조사기관에 의해 '세계에서 가장 존경받은 인물 10인'의 한 사람으로 올랐는데 37차례나 오른 것은 그 예가 없었다. 50년 전에 그가 목사직을 가진 이래 역사상 누구보다 더 많은 청중—2억 천만명 이상—에게 직접 복음을 설교했다. 대중 매체를 통하여 수억 이상의 사람들에게 그의 복음설교가 전달됐다. 지금 빌리 부부는 노스 캐롤라이나의 산악지대에서 살고 있다. 다음은 1997년 8월에 발행된 '복음의 속보'의 메시지에서 발췌한 것이다.

질의 : 당신은 어떻게 그리스도와 직접 관계를 갖는다고 확신할 수 있는가?

대답 : 성서의 중심 주제는 당신과 모든 사람을 위한 하나님의 사랑입니다. 이 사랑은 하나님의 아들인 예수 그리스도께서 사람으로 이 세상에 태어나 죄없이 사시다가 십자가에서 돌아가시

one God and one mediator between God and men, the man Jesus Christ (1 Timothy 2:5). Jesus answered, 'I am the way and the truth and the life. No one comes to the Father except through me'" (John 14:6).

(1) The main idea of Billy Graham's message is _____. (Subject matter)

    (a) What is God's love?   (c) Why should we read the Bible?   (e) Who is Jesus?
    (b) Why does God love us?   (d) Why should we receive Jesus?

(2.1) The italicized word, *bridge*, in the second paragraph refers to _____. (2.1. - 2.2. Words in context)

    (a) Support   (b) Detach   (c) Explore   (d) Explicate   (e) Connect

(2.2) The antonym of the italicized word, *revealed*, in the first paragraph is _____.

    (a) Disclosed   (b) Represented   (c) Concealed   (d) Displayed   (e) Manifested

(3) The underlined words of the following model in the final paragraph includes an unnecessary word in terms of grammatical usage. Which one should be deleted? (Structure)

"Jesus Christ who died <u>on</u> the cross, <u>and</u> paid the penalty for our <u>sins,</u> <u>and</u> bridged
                         (1)   (2)   (3) (4)

the gap between God and <u>us</u>."
                       (5)

    (a) (1)   (b) (2)   (c) (3)   (d) (4)   (e) (5)

(4.1) The question in the passage, "Does God really love us?" can be answered by inferring the fact that God sent His only son to us, and he _____. (4.1. - 4.2. Making inferences)

    (a) Lived a sinless life   (d) Died for us
    (b) Preached us   (e) Came into the world as a human being
    (c) Rose from the dead

(4.2) In John 14:6, Jesus says, "I am the way and the truth and the life. No one comes to the Father except through me," can be inferred as a possible implication leading to the salvation through _____.

    (a) Only Hindu Gods (b) Only Allah (c) Only Jesus (d) Polytheism (e) Only Jehovah

(5) Based on the message given by Billy Graham, it can be concluded that he sincerely wants us to _____ Jesus Christ for _____. (Conclusion)

    (a) Believe in, eternal life   (d) Glorify, sinless life
    (b) Follow, the conquest of death   (e) Trust, our sins to be forgiven
    (c) Accept, eternal life

고 죽은자들 가운데서 부활하셨을때 나타났습니다. 그리스도께서 죽으셨기 때문에 여러분의 죄가 용서함을 받고 그분이 죽음을 이기셨기 때문에 여러분이 영생을 할 수 있습니다. 여러분들은 죽은 후에 어떻게 될까를 확실히 알고 있습니다. 여러분은 하나님의 사랑 이야기를 복음이라고 말하는 걸 들은 적이 있겠지요. 복음이라는 단어는 단지 좋은 소식을 의미합니다. 복음은 그리스도께서 하신 일 때문에 우리가 용서받고 영원히 살 수 있다 라는 희소식입니다. 그러나 이 용서와 영생의 선물이 그것을 기꺼이 받아들이지 않으면 여러분의 소식이 아닙니다. 하나님은 여러분의 개인적인 응답을 요구하십니다.

다음 성경 말씀은 이 과정에서 하나님의 역할과 여러분의 역할을 밝혀 줍니다.
"하나님이 여러분을 사랑하사 독생자를 주셨으니 그를 믿는 자는 누구나 멸망하지 않고 영생을 얻으리라."(요한복음 3장 16절)

인간의 전체 역사를 통하여 인간은 하나님으로부터 멀어지면서 죄를 지었습니다. 그들은 여러가지 방법으로 그 갈라진 틈을 메우려고 노력했지만 허사였습니다. 이 분리의 문제를 치료할 방법이 오직 한가지 있습니다 : 십자가에서 돌아가시고 우리 죄를 대신하여 벌을 받으시고 하나님과 우리 사이를 이어주신 예수 그리스도이십니다. 성서에 말씀이 있습니다 : "하나님은 한 분 뿐이시고 하나님과 사람 사이의 중재자도 한 분 뿐이신데 그 분이 바로 사람으로 오셨던 그리스도 예수이십니다." 예수께서 대답하셨습니다 : '나는 길이요 진리요 생명이다. 나를 거치지 않고는 누구도 하느님께 갈 수 없다.' (요한 복음 14장 6절)

Note

- evangel=gospel : 복음(서)
- evangelist : 복음 전도사
- revival meeting : 부흥성회
- anthropology : 인류학
- pastor=a Christian leader in charge of a church and its members : 담당 목사
- baptism : 세례, 침례, 영세
- rally=a large public meeting, gathering : 집회, 농성, 시위
  - A large political rally, they say, will be held in front of the Cathedral.
  (성당 앞에서 대대적인 정치 시위가 열린다는데.)
- crusade : (교황이 인정한) 성전(聖戰), 십자군, 사회 개혁운동
- follow-up : 속보(續報), 추적
- reveal=make known, display : 폭로하다, 시현하다
  - Research has revealed him a monster of iniquity. (조사해보니 그는 나쁜 놈이었다.)
- perish=be destroyed, come to an end, die
  - Hundreds of people perished in the earthquake. (그 지진으로 수백명이 죽었다.)
- bridge=join : 메우다 • bridge the gap of difference (차이점의 간격을 메우다)
- remedy=cure • It's a good remedy for unhappiness.
- mediator : 중재자, 신과 인간의 중재자=예수 그리스도

Passage 21 : The Colorful Carp: Koi

"Koi" are essentially the same species of fish as carp. They grow to be over three feet long, weigh over 30 pounds, and can live more than 50 years. They eat almost anything that is of animal or vegetable origin small enough to be swallowed as they have no teeth. The finest quality of Koi are bred in Japan where raising Koi is a $100 million a year business, and the hobby of keeping Koi has attracted thousands of persons in scores of countries.

Koi are bred specifically for the color and patterns on their backs because their backs are the most visible part of their bodies as they swim in their ponds. The fish are normally bottom feeders, but by feeding them floating foods you can teach them to feed at the surface where they are easier to see and appreciate. They become extremely tame very quickly and will happily feed from their owner's hand.

The cultivation of carp for food and later for pleasure goes back in recorded history over 2,000 years. In China written instructions on the raising of carp date back to the year 500 B.C. The carp was chosen to *cultivate* because it's fast growing, extremely hardy, and can live and thrive in most of the climate zone where human beings inhabit.

When the carp was introduced into China and then Japan, it created great interest. As time passed, *mutations* with different colors were sometimes found in the spawnings, and these were then selectively bred to improve their color and subsequently their patterns. Thus, from the homely carp slowly emerged the magnificent Nishiki Koi (Brocaded Carp). Over the years, the carp also became a Japanese symbol of strength, courage, and other positive character traits. In Japan each year on Son's Day in May, parents ( ) one flag in the shape of a carp outside their homes for each of their sons.

Koi are classified into color, pattern, scale types, and body shape. Body shape, pattern, and color are the three general judgment areas with each attribute being allotted a numerical value. The patterned varieties of Koi do not produce young with *identical* patterns, and only a small number of quality Koi are produced in each breeding; the rest must be disposed of. Choosing the 50 to 75 quality Koi out of about 300,000 young is a difficult and time-consuming undertaking. Each patterned Koi is like a work of art; each is different, but as with art very few are considered masterpieces. Those few Koi which are judged champions at the large shows in Japan are considered masterpieces and have been known to sell for more than $20,000 a piece.

(Source : Contributed by Joe Zuritsky (Spring 1991) from The Japanese House and Garden. Fairmount Park, Philadelphia, Pennsylvania)

(1) The topic of the passage is "_____." (Subject matter)

    (a) The cultivation of Koi   (c) Raising Koi for business   (e) Facts about Koi
    (b) The life span of Koi   (d) Selection of Koi as an art

(2.1) The italicized word, *cultivate*, in the third paragraph refers to _____. (2.1. - 2.3. Words in context)

    (a) Neglect   (b) Raise   (c) Educate   (d) Develop   (e) Discipline

(2.2) The italicized word, *mutations*, in the fourth paragraph refers to _____.

    (a) Alterations   (b) Inactions   (c) Stagnation   (d) Measures   (e) Prejudice

지문 21 : 비단 잉어

　　비단 잉어 (고이 : 일본어)는 본질적으로 잉어와 같은 어종이다. 그들은 길이가 3피트 이상 자라고 무게는 30파운드 이상 나가며 50년 이상 산다. 그들은 이빨이 없기 때문에 크기가 삼킬 만큼 작은 것이면 동물성이든 식물성이든 거의 모든 것을 먹는다. 가장 고품질의 고이는 일본에서 양식되며 그곳에서는 고이 양식이 연 1억 달러의 사업이며 고이양식 취미는 20여 국가에서 수천명을 매료시켰다.

　　고이는 특히 등의 색깔과 무늬를 위해서 양식되는데 그 까닭은 등이 그들이 물 속에서 수영할 때 가장 눈에 띄는 부분이기 때문이다. 고이는 밑바닥의 먹이를 먹는 게 정상이지만 뜨는 먹이를 줌으

Koi Images

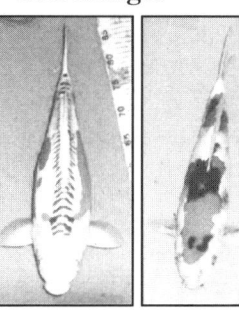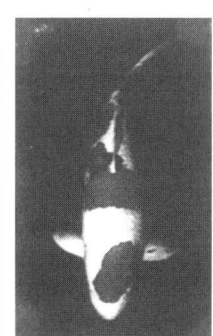

로써 사람들이 보고 감상하기 쉬운 수면에서 먹도록 훈련시킬 수 있다. 그들은 아주 빠르게 아주 잘 길들여지고 즐거이 주인 손에서 먹이를 먹게 될 것이다.

　　식용 잉어 양식과 그 후의 관상용 양식은 기록된 역사로 2000년 이상 거슬러 올라간다. 중국에서는 잉어양식에 대한 기록된 지식들이 기원 전 500년 전부터 내려 온다. 잉어를 양식용으로 선택한 이유는 성장 속도가 빠르고 내구력이 강하며 사람이 사는 곳이면 어떤 기후대에서도 살 수 있고 번창하기 때문이다.

　　잉어가 중국에, 그리고 나서 일본에 도입되었을 때 굉장한 흥미를 자아냈다. 세월이 흐르면서 산란 때 색깔이 다른 변종들이 때때로 발견되었고, 이들은 색깔과 그 후에 무늬를 개량하기 위하여 선택적으로 양식되었다. 이렇게하여 예쁘지 않은 일반 잉어로부터 서서히 기막힌 비단잉어가 출현했다. 여러 해가 지나는 동안 잉어는 또한 힘과 용기와 적극적인 성격을 나타내는 일본의 상징이 되었다. 일본에서는 매년 5월 아들의 날에 부모들이 각각의 아들 몫으로 하나씩 잉어 모양의 깃발을 집 밖에 게양한다.

　　고이는 색깔, 무늬, 비늘의 형태, 그리고 몸의 형체로 분류된다. 체형, 무늬, 색깔은 절대치의 가치를 배당받는 속성을 가진 일반적인 세가지 평가 영역이다. 무늬가 있는 고이의 변종들은 동일한 무늬를 가진 새끼를 생산하지 않고, 일회의 배양에서 고품질의 고이는 소수 뿐이며, 그 나머지는 없애야 한다. 30만 마리의 치어에서 50에서 70마리의 고품

(2.3) The antonym of the italicized word, *identical*, is _____.

    (a) Different (b) Indistinguishable (c) Equal (d) Corresponding (e) Equivalent

(3) The underlined structure, "… <u>parents ( ) one flag in the shape of a carp</u> …," needs a suitable verb to best fit in the parenthesis. (Structure)

    (a) Wave   (b) Operate   (c) Drive   (d) Fly   (e) Lower

(4.1) Based on the information given, it can be inferred that Koi are cultivated for _____. (4.1. - 4.3. Making inferences)

    (a) Food & hobby   (c) Business & food   (e) Business & pleasure
    (b) Pleasure & hobby (d) Pleasure & food

(4.2) Only a small number of carefully selected Koi can be candidates for the large shows or as expensive commercial products. What factor(s) do you infer contribute to the production of quality Koi?

    (a) Quality of food   (c) Mutations in the eggs   (e) Effort devoted
    (b) Quality of water   (d) Time devoted

(4.3) On Son's Day, a flag in the shape of a carp is flown by the parents in Japan. What are the symbolic implications of a carp? It can be inferred that sons should be "_____" like carps.

    (a) Faithful & diligent   (c) Intelligent & healthy   (e) Responsible & generous
    (b) Strong & courageous (d) Brave & ambitious

(5) For many centuries, Koi have been popular with the Japanese as a symbol of "courage and strength," and as an artistic "pleasure and appreciation." Based on this hypothesis, it can be postulated that the Japanese are likely to show their interest both in "_____ and _____." (Conclusion)

    (a) Buddha, lotus   (c) Cards, cherry blossom   (e) God, gold
    (b) Sword, chrysanthemum (d) Pen, rose

Passage 22 : **Apollo Exploration**

On July 16, 1969, the first of six manned missions to the moon was successfully launched. The prime mission objective of Apollo XI, crewed by Neil A. Armstrong, Michael Collins, and Edwin "Buzz" Aldrin, simply stated, "Perform a manned lunar landing and return." On July 20, 1969, Armstrong and Aldrin landed their lunar module, named Eagle, touched down on the moon's surface. Collins had stayed in the command service module, named Columbia. Here is a transcript of the final minute of their breathtaking flight:

Houston: Sixty seconds.

Eagle : Lights on. Down two and a half. Forward, forward 40 feet. Down two and a half.

질 잉어를 선택하는 일은 어렵고 시간이 소모되는 일이다. 무늬가 각기 다른 고이는 하나의 예술품과 같다. 각자가 다르고 이는 마치 예술의 경우처럼 걸작품으로 간주된다. 일본의 대규모 품평회에서 우승품으로 평가되는 소수의 고이는 걸작으로 여겨져 한 마리당 2만 달러 이상의 가격으로 팔린다고 알려져있다.

Note

- □ colorful=full of color : 형형 색색의, 다채로운
  - a colorful event (다채로운 행사)   • a colorful narrative (생생한 이야기)
- □ carp : 잉어   □ silver carp : 붕어
- □ swallow=move food or drink down the throat from the mouth : 삼키다
  - cf. swallow (제비)   • Chew your food well before you swallow it. (음식을 삼키기 전에 잘 씹어라.)
- □ cultivate=raise a crop by preparing the soil, providing with water : 양식, 배양하다
- □ bottom feeder : 붕어나 잉어 처럼 강 바닥에서 먹이를 찾는 어류
- □ tame=(animals) brought up under control, accustomed to living with human beings,
- □ not wild or fierce : 길들여진   • opp. untamed (말괄량이의)
- □ thrive=prosper, grow strong and healthy : 번창하다, 무성해지다, 성공하다
  - A business can't thrive with good management. (사업이란 경영을 잘못하면 번성할 수 없다.)
- □ mutation=alteration : 변형, (생)돌연변이
  - Are mutations in plants caused by cosmic rays? (식물 돌연변이는 우주광선에 의해서 일어나요?)
- □ spawn=eggs of fish and a certain water animals : 물고기 알, 알을 낳다
- □ trait=distinguishing quality or characteristic : 특징, 특색
  - Two traits in American character are generosity and energy. (미국 문화의 두가지 특색은 아량과 힘이다.)
- □ scale : 고기 비늘   □ varieties : 변종들
- □ attribute=quality looked upon as naturally or necessarily belonging to somebody or something : 속성, 특질
- □ identical=exactly alike, agreeing in every way : 똑같은, 일란성의
  - The finger prints of no two persons are identical. (지문은 다 다르다.)
- □ dispose of=finish with, get rid of : 처분하다, 제거하다
  - The old man doesn't want dispose of the land. (노인은 그 토지 팔기를 원치않는다.)
- □ masterpiece=something made or done with very great skill : 걸작, 명작, 대작
- □ equivalent=equal in value, amount, meaning : 동등한, 같은 의미의
  - Giving no refusal is equivalent to acceptance. (거절않는 것은 승락과 같다.)
- □ contribute to=help, bring about : 공헌하다   • Drink contributed to his ruin.

지문 22 : 아폴로 탐험

1969년 7월 16일 6번의 유인 달 탐색 임무 중 최초의 임무가 시작되었다. 닐 암스트롱과 마이클 콜린즈 그리고 에드윈 버즈 올드린이 승선한 아폴로 11호의 일차적인 목적은 단순히 '유인 달 착륙을 수행하고 귀환하는 것'으로 진술되었다. 1969년 7월 20일 암스트

Things look good. Picking up some dust. 30 feet. Two and a half down. Faint shadow. Four forward, four forward, drifting to the right a little. Contact light! O.K., engine stop. Modes control, both auto, descent engine command override off. Engine arm off. Houston, Tranquillity Base here. The Eagle has landed.

When Neil Armstrong stepped onto the moon, much of the world was watching him on television. They heard Armstrong say, *"That was one small step for a man, one giant leap for mankind."* For two and a quarter hours, Armstrong and Aldrin collected 20 kilograms of lunar surface materials and **deployed** various lunar observation equipment. An American flag and plaque were left when they reentered the Eagle for return to Columbia. The plaque read, "HERE MEN FROM THE PLANET EARTH FIRST SET FOOT UPON THE MOON JULY 1969 A.D. WE CAME IN PEACE FOR ALL MANKIND."

Apollo XII followed the Apollo XI mission by four months. It was the first lunar landing that planned detailed scientific lunar exploration. The following ( ) a list of the top ten scientific discoveries ( ) during the Apollo Exploration of the moon.

- ☐ The Moon is not a *primordial* object; it is an evolved *terrestrial* planet with internal zoning similar to that of Earth.
- ☐ The Moon is ancient and still preserves an early history (the first billion years) that must be common to all terrestrial planets.
- ☐ The youngest Moon rocks are *virtually* as old as the oldest Earth rocks. The earliest processes and events that probably affected both planetary bodies can now only be found on the Moon.
- ☐ The Moon and Earth are genetically related and formed from different proportions of a common reservoir of materials.
- ☐ The Moon is lifeless; it contains no living organisms, fossils, or native organic compounds.
- ☐ All Moon rocks originated through high-temperature processes with little or no involvement with water. They are roughly divisible into three types: basalts, anorthosites, and breccias.
- ☐ Early in its history, the Moon was melted to great depths to form a "magma ocean." The lunar highlands contain the remnants of early, low density rocks that floated to the surface of the magma ocean.
- ☐ The lunar magma ocean was followed by a series of huge asteroid impacts that created basins which were later filled by lava flows.
- ☐ The Moon is slightly *asymmetrical* in bulk form, possibly as a consequence of its evolution under Earth's gravitational influence. Its crust is thicker on the far side, while most volcanic basins - unusual mass concentration - occur on the near side.
- ☐ The surface of the Moon is covered by a rubble pile of rock fragments and dust, called the lunar regolith, that contains a unique radiation history of the Sun which is important to understanding climate changes on Earth.

This magnificent view of earth-from the Mediterranean Sea area to the Antarctic polar ice cap-was photographed from space by the Apollo 17 team during the final manned lunar landing mission. Almost the entire coastline of the continent of Africa is clearly delineated, with the Arabian Peninsula at the northeastern edge of Africa.

(Source: Adapted from Suter, Joanne (1994). United States History. Globe Fearon Educational Publishers, Paramus, NJ; Berkin, Carol & et al (1983). Land of Promise: A History of the U.S. from 1865. Scott, Foresman & Co., Glenview, IL; History of Our Country (1997). Steck-Vaughn Co.; Webpage created by the National Air and Space Museum: http://www.nasm.edu:80/APOLLO/LunarTop10.html)

롱과 올드린은 '독수리'라고 불리는 그들의 달 착륙선을 착륙시키고 달 표면에 닿았다. 콜린즈는 컬럼비아로 명명된 사령선에 남아 있었다. 다음에 그들의 숨막히는 비행의 최후 순간 기록을 소개한다.

휴스턴 : 60초

착륙선 : 불이 켜졌다. 아래로 2.5피트, 전방으로 40피트. 아래로 2.5피트 모든 것이 순조로와 보인다. 약간의 먼지가 일고 있다. 30피트. 2.5피트 하강. 희미한 그림자가 보인다. 전방 4피트, 전방 4피트.

약간 우측으로 밀려가고 있다. 접촉등이 켜졌다! 성공이다. 엔진이 꺼졌다. 모드가 제어한다, 자동, 하강 엔진이 수동장치로 떨어져 나왔다. 엔진 팔이 꺼졌다. 휴스턴, 여기는 고요의 바다지다. 독수리호가 착륙 완료했다.

An American astronaut during the Apollo 11 mission, the first mission to land astronauts on the moon.

닐 암스트롱이 달 표면에 발걸음을 내딛었을 때, 세계의 많은 사람들이 그를 텔레비전으로 지켜보고 있었다. 그들은 암스트롱이 '그것은 한 사람에게는 작은 한걸음이었지만 인류에게는 거대한 도약이었다'고 말하는 소리를 들었다. 2시간 15분 간 암스트롱과 올드린은 달표면 물질 20킬로그램을 수집하고 다양한 달 관찰 설비를 배치했다. 그들이 컬럼비아로 되돌아 오기 위하여 독수리호로 다시 들어 왔을 때, 성조기와 금속판이 달표면에 남아 있었다. 그 금속판에는 다음과 같이 쓰여 있었다: "이 곳에 지구행성에서 온 인간들이 1969년 7월에 발을 딛었다. 우리는 모든 인류의 평화에 대한 기대속에 왔다."

아폴로 11호가 임무를 끝낸 4개월 후에 아폴로 12호가 뒤따랐다. 12호는 최

Mirrored in his teammate's helmet visor, an Apollo astronaut sets out experiments on the lunar floor. (Courtesy Space Division, Roockwell International)

(1) The topic of the passage is "_____." (Subject matter)

    (a) The historic event of man's first lunar landing & return with scientific discoveries
    (b) Apollo Exportation, man's first lunar landing & return
    (c) Man's first lunar landing & return
    (d) Apollo Exploration and scientific discoveries
    (e) Apollo Exploration to the Moon and scientific discoveries

(2.1) The italicized word, *deployed*, in the third paragraph refers to _____. (2.1 - 2.5. Words in context)

    (a) Set up (b) Manufactured (c) Packed (d) Disassembled (e) Deplored

(2.2) The italicized word, *primordial*, in the fourth paragraph refers to _____.

    (a) Modern (b) Original (c) Sophisticated (d) Dominant (e) New

(2.3) The italicized word, *terrestrial*, in the fourth paragraph refers to _____.

    (a) Aquatic (b) Heavenly (c) Earthly (d) Cosmic (e) Celestial

(2.4) The antonym of the italicized word, *virtually*, in the fourth paragraph is _____.

    (a) Nominally (b) Potentially (c) Tacitly (d) Basically (e) Essentially

(2.5) The antonym of the italicized word, *asymmetrical*, in the fourth paragraph is _____.

    (a) Irregular (b) Disproportional (c) Swollen (d) Uneven (e) Proportional

(3) The italicized structure, "The following ( ) a list of the top ten scientific discoveries ( ) during the Apollo Exploration of the moon." The suitable verbs that best fit in the parentheses are "( ), ( )."

    (a) Is, discovered (b) Are, discovered (c) Is, investigated (d) Is, made (e) Are, made

(4.1) Based on the information given, it can be claimed that the Moon has _____ on its surface. (4.1 - 4.5. Making inferences)

    (a) Oceans (b) Rocks (c) Water (d) Living organisms (e) Native organic compounds

(4.2) The situation and the tone of the communication between the Eagle and Houston seem to be _____.

    (a) Amusing (b) Pitying (c) Respectful (d) Breathtaking (e) Sentimental

(4.3) The underlined phrase, *"That was one small step for a man, one giant leap for mankind,"* can be interpreted as a "Great_____ for human beings."

    (a) Acquisition (b) Achievement (c) Commitment (d) Performance (e) Adventure

(4.4) The underlined phrase, "HERE … WE CAME IN PEACE FOR ALL MANKIND," can be inferred as a/an "_____ gesture."

    (a) Gleeful (b) Triumphant (c) Sympathetic (d) Friendly (e) Beneficial

(4.5) Based on the information given, it can be inferred that the Moon was a mass of _____ during its initial stage of development.

초로 상세한 과학적 달 탐색을 계획한 달 착륙이었다. 다음은 12호의 달 탐색 동안에 이룩된 10가지 과학적 발견을 수록한 목록이다.

- 달은 태초의 물체 그대로가 아니고 지구와 유사한 내부 층준이 일어나고 있는, 진화된 지구형 행성이다.
- 달은 아주 오래된 것으로 모든 지구형 행성(수성, 금성, 지구, 화성)과 공통되는 초기의 역사(최초 10억년)를 아직도 보존하고 있다.
- 가장 최근의 달 암석은 실제로 오래된 지구 암석만큼 오래된 것이다. 아마 두 행성에 영향을 미쳤을 최초의 과정과 사건들이 달에서 발견될 수 있을 것이다.
- 달과 지구는 발생학적으로 관계가 있고 공통적으로 매장된 물질이 다른 비율로 형성되어 있다.
- 달에는 생명체가 없다; 살아있는 유기체나 화석이 없고 유기 화합물이 없다.
- 모든 달 암석은 물의 개입이 거의 또는 전혀 없는 고온의 과정을 통하여 생겨났다.
  암석들은 대체로 세가지 형태로 나누어 질 수 있는데 현무암, 사장암, 각력암들이다.
- 달은 먼 역사 속에서 이 깊은 곳으로 녹아 들어가서 '마그마' 바다를 형성했다. 달의 고지대는 마그마 바다 표면에서 떠다니던 초기 저밀도 암석의 나머지를 가지고 있다.
- 달의 마그마 바다가 생긴 후에 용암유동으로 메워진 분지를 만들었던 일련의 소행성 충돌이 뒤따라 있었다.
- 달은 전체적으로 약간 비대칭이다. 아마 지구인력의 영향을 받은 진화의 결과일 것이다. 달의 표층은 먼 곳에서 (지구로부터) 두껍고, 반대로 대부분의 화산 분지-보기드문 선광 덩어리-는 가까운 곳에서 발생한다.
- 달 표면은 표토(表土)라고 부르는 암석 파편과 먼지의 바스러진 층으로 덮여있고 이는 지구 기후 변화를 이해하는데 중요하고 독특한 태양 복사의 역사를 함유하고 있다.

Note

- manned landing : 유인 착륙   □ crew=all the people working in a ship, plane : 승무원
- launch=send a rocket into the sky : 발사하다   • opp. land (착륙하다)
- module=a part of a space vehicle that can be used independently of other parts : 착륙선
  • command service module (사령선)   • lunar excursion module (달 착륙선)
- breathtaking=very exciting : 숨막힐 듯한,   □ faint=weak, indistinct, not clear : 희미한
- override : 우주선이 지상으로부터의 명령을 받지 않는 수동장치
- tranquility : 고요, 평온   • The Path to Tranquility : Diel(고요의 바다)
- deploy=to arrange for esp. military action : (군) 배치하다
- plaque=a flat metal or stone plate with writing on it : 금속판, 석판, 상패, (치과) 프라그
- primordial=in existence at or from the beginning, primeval : 태초의, 본원의
- evolve=develop gradually : 진화하다, 발전하다
- terrestrial=of or related to the earth : 지구의   • terrestrial globe (지구본)
- terrestrial planets : 지구형 행성-수, 금, 지, 화, 목, 토, 천, 해, 명   • opp. celestial (천상의)
- zoning : 띠 모양의 구획, 地帶설정, 層準
  • zone the world into climatic provinces. (지구를 氣候帶로 구분하다)

(a) Gas & basin (b) Water & rock (c) Soil & rock (d) Dust & rock (e) Gas & magma

(5) One of the most significant contributions of the Apollo Exploration can be concluded as "_____." (Conclusion)

   (a) Scientific discoveries of the Moon
   (b) Man's first exploration of space
   (c) One giant step towards the advancement of space exploration
   (d) Man's first exploration of the Moon
   (e) Space exploration for peaceful purposes

Passage 23 : William H. Gates III (1955 -) : King of Personal Computer Software

Background : William H. Gates was born to William H. Gates II, Seattle attorney, and Mary Gates, school teacher. At the age of 13 at the Lakeside School in North Seattle, Gates began his career in personal computer software and programming computers. In 1973, Gates entered Harvard University, and developed a version of the programming language BASIC for the first microcomputer - the MITS Altair. In his junior year, Gates dropped out of Harvard to devote his energies full-time to Microsoft, a company he had started in 1975 with his friend, Paul Allen. Guided by a belief that the personal computer would be a valuable tool on every office desktop and in every home, they began developing software for personal computers. Gates' foresight and vision regarding personal computing have been central to the success of Microsoft and the software industry.

In 1995 Gates wrote The Road Ahead, his vision of where information technology will take society. In 1996, while strategically redeploying Microsoft to *take advantage of* the emerging opportunities created by the Internet, Gates thoroughly revised The Road Ahead to reflect his view that interactive networks are a major milestone in human communication.

The following is excerpted from the Bill Gates' 26 pages of Keynote Speech at Microsoft's Second Annual CEO (Chief Executive Officer) Summit, Seattle, May 29, 1998.

Well, good morning. I'm going to talk about two things this morning, digital nervous system and Web lifestyle.

··· The term "digital nervous system" is kind of an interesting one. The analogy, of course, is to the biological nervous system where you always have the information you need. You always are alert to the most important things, and you *block out* the information that's not important. And companies really need to have that same kind of thing: the information that's valuable getting to the people who need to know about it ···.

The Internet is fundamental, partly because it's a critical mass. The innovation, the tools, the communicating companies coming in to provide *bandwidth, (*Tech. term: Time period between two peaks)···, the hardware companies doing the equipment that will move that information at really unbelievable speeds, software companies like Microsoft

□ virtually : 사실상, 실제로   • opp. nominally=in name (이름으로만, 명목상으로)
□ genetically : 유전적으로, 발생학적으로
□ reservoir=a place where water is stored, supply of facts, knowledge : 저수지, 저장고
□ proportion=relation of one thing to another in quantity, size etc. : 비례, 비율
□ compound : 화합물, 복합체   • compound interest (복리)
□ basalt : 현무암   □ anorthosite : 사장암   □ breccia : 각력암
□ remnant=a part that remains : 나머지, 자취   □ asteroid : 소행성
□ basin : 분지   □ lava : 용암   □ asymmetrical : 비대칭의, 부조화의
□ rubble : 바스러진 암석 조각   □ regolith : 표토(表土)

지문 23. 윌리암 게이츠 3세 – PC 소프트웨어의 왕

배경 : 게이츠는 시애틀의 변호사인 윌리암 게이츠 2세와 학교 교사인 메리 게이츠 사이에서 태어났다. North Seattle의 Lakeside학교를 다니던 13세 때, 게이츠는 PC 소프트웨어와 컴퓨터 프로그래밍의 경력을 쌓기 시작했다. 1973년에 하버드대학에 입학하여 MITS Altair라는 최초의 마이크로컴퓨터용 프로그래밍 베이직 언어를 개발했다. 대학 3학년 때 하버드를 자퇴하고 1975년에 친구인 폴 알렌과 공동으로 설립한 회사인 마이크로소프트사에 전심전력을 다해 헌신했다. PC가 모든 사무실과 가정의 탁상용으로 귀중한 도구가 되리라는 확신에 이끌려 PC용 소프트웨어 개발을 시작했다. PC에 대한 게이츠의 통찰과 선견지명이 마이크로소프트사와 소프트산업의 성공에 중추적 역할을 해왔다.

**William H. Gates
Chairman and Chief
Executive Officer
Microsoft Corporation**

1995년에 게이츠는 정보기술이 어느 방향에서 사회를 점령할 것인가에 대한 그의 전망인 The Road Ahead를 썼다. 1996년에 인터넷으로 말미암아 새로 떠오르는 기회를 이용하기 위하여 전략적으로 마이크로소프트사의 인원을 재배치하면서 쌍방향 네트워크가 인

building these things, the pace of investment is *mind-blowing*…. And so, the Internet continues to evolve. If you used the Internet a year ago, or someone gave you a demo, don't think that it stayed the same. <u>The breadth of material and the quality of material change quite rapidly there (   ) that investment and competition.</u>

(Source: Bill Gates' Keynote Speech at Microsoft's Second Annual CEO Summit, Seattle, May 28, 1998)

(1) The topic of the Gates' speech is "The _____." (Subject matter)

    (a) Investment & competition of digital nervous system & Web lifestyle
    (b) Information of digital nervous system & Web lifestyle
    (c) Operation of Web lifestyle & digital nervous system
    (d) Investment & competition of Microsoft Corporation
    (e) Investment & production of digital nervous system & Web lifestyle

(2.1) The italicized phrase, *take advantage of*, in the section of "Background" refers to _____. (2.1 - 2.3. Phrases & word in context)

    (a) Influence   (b) Sanction   (c) Protect   (d) Benefit   (e) Empower

(2.2) The italicized phrase, *block out*, in the "speech" refers to _____.

    (a) Arrest   (b) Enlarge   (c) Obstruct   (d) Deflate   (e) Tighten

(2.3) The italicized colloquial compound word, *mind-blowing*, in the "speech" refers to ___.

    (a) Ambitious   (b) Amazing   (c) Boring   (d) Composed   (e) Expected

(3) The underlined structure, "<u>The breadth of material and the quality of material change quite rapidly there ( ) that investment and competition</u>," needs a suitable prepositional phrase that best fits in the parenthesis. (Structure)

    (a) Instead of   (b) On behalf of   (c) Because of   (d) On top of   (e) Away from

(4.1) Based on the information given from the section of "Background," one of the most important factors that helped Gates be successful in business can be inferred as "_____." (4.1 - 4.3. Making inferences)

    (a) Investment   (b) Competition   (c) Proper time   (d) Technology   (e) Vision

(4.2) Based on the information given from his speech, the Internet will _____.

    (a) Continue to evolve steadily
    (b) Develop quickly for better quality and scope
    (c) Dominate over other businesses because of investment and competition
    (d) Be innovated for better quality and scope because of investment
    (e) Develop quickly with better quality and diversity on account of investment and competition

(4.3) Based on the information given, one of the major milestones of human communication can be claimed as "The _____."

    (a) Letter   (b) Telegram   (c) Television   (d) Radio   (e) Interactive networks

간의 통신의 중요한 이정표라는 자신의 견해를 나타내기 위하여 The Road Ahead를 완전히 고쳐썼다.

다음은 빌 게이츠가 1998년 5월 29일에 시애틀의 제 2차 연례 마이크로소프트사 경영 최고책임자 수석회의에서 행한 26페이지의 기조연설에서 발췌한 것이다.

안녕하십니까. 나는 오늘 아침 두가지 문제, 디지털 신경망과 웹라이프 스타일에 대하여 말씀드리고자 합니다.

'디지털 신경망(DNS)' 이라는 용어는 약간 흥미로운 용어지요. 그와 유사한 것은 물론 우리가 필요할 때면 언제나 정보를 얻는 생물학적 신경 조직이지요. 우리는 아주 중요한 것에 민감하게 반응하지만 불필요한 정보는 막아버리지요. 회사들도 마찬가지로 같은 것이 필요하지요. 즉 중요한 것에 대하여 알고 싶어하는 사람들에게 도달하는 그 귀중한 정보 말입니다.

인터넷이 바탕입니다. 그 이유 중 하나는 인터넷이 결정적인 매체이기 때문입니다. 기술혁신, 도구, 통신회사들이 나타나 특수 주파수 대역폭을 공급하고, 하드웨어 회사들이 정말 믿기지 않는 속도로 그 정보를 전달하는 설비를 하고 있으며, 마이크로소프트같은 소프트회사들은 이러한 것들을 제작하고 있으며, 투자 속도는 정말 놀랄만합니다…. 그래서 인터넷은 계속 진화합니다. 만일 우리가 1년전에 인터넷을 사용했다면, 누군가가 견본을 주었다면, 그것이 지금도 같은 상태일거라고 생각하지 마십시오. 재료의 범위와 품질이 그런 투자와 경쟁 때문에 아주 빠르게 변화하는 것입니다.

Note

- **bandwidth** : (전자 공학): 송신 전파 또는 증폭기가 유효하게 작용하는 주파수 대역폭
- **analogy=likeness** : 유추, 유사   • be analogous to (서로 비슷하다)
  • Pity is analogous to love. (연민과 사랑은 비슷하다)
- **mind-blowing** : 환각제 사용으로 황홀한, 놀랄만한
- **redeploy** : 인원등을 재배치하다
- **guided by the belief** : …라는 확신에 이끌려
- **version** : 번역, 변형, 판, 형, 버전
- **microcomputer** : microprocessor를 내장한 소형 컴퓨터
- **desktop computer** : 탁상용 컴퓨터
- **keynote=note on which a key is based** : (음)주음   • keynote speech (기조연설)
  • The keynote of the Minister's speech was the need for higher productivity.
  (그 장관 연설의 골자는 생산성의 제고였다.)
- **foresight=ability to see future needs** : 선견지명, 통찰력
  • If you had had more foresight, you'd have saved yourself a lot of trouble.
  (앞을 보는 눈이 있었더라면 많은 고생을 덜수 있었을 텐데.)
- **strategically** : 전략적으로, 작전상
- **revise=reconsider in order to correct and improve** : 수정하다, 변경하다
  • I can't help revising my opinion of him. (그 남자에 대하여 생각을 다시 하지 않을 수 없다.)
- **interactive** : 상호작용하는
- **milestone=an important event in a person's life or in history** : 획기적 사건, 이정표
- **block out=prevent** : 차단하다   • My nose is all blocked out. (코가 꽉 막혔다.)
- **innovation** : 개혁, 혁신
- **the innovation of school education** : 학교교육 개혁

(5) It is a well-known fact that the Microsoft business of Gates has been successful, which should be credited to his vision and excellent management. It can be concluded that the following proverb that best reflects this success story is _____. (Conclusion)

    (a) God comes to see without ringing the bell (Spanish)
    (b) To endure what is unendurable is true endurance (Japanese)
    (c) Money lent, is an enemy made (Portuguese)
    (d) Who sows thorns should not go barefoot (Italian)
    (e) To open a shop is easy, to keep it open is an art (Chinese)

Passage 24 : **Harvard University**

Background : Harvard College was established in 1636 by vote of the Great and General Court of Massachusetts Bay Colony, and was named for its first benefactor, John Harvard of Charlestown, a young minister who upon his death in 1638, left his library and half his estate to the new institution. The University has grown from 9 students with a single master to an enrollment of more than 18,000 degree candidates, including undergraduates, and students in 10 graduate and professional schools. Over 14,000 people work at Harvard, including more than 2,000 faculty. There are more than 7,000 faculty appointments in *affiliated* teaching hospitals.

    Six presidents of the United States - John Adams, John Quincy Adams, Theodore and Franklin Delano Roosevelt, Rutherford B. Hayes, and John Fitzgerald Kennedy - were graduates of Harvard. Its faculty have produced 34 Nobel Laureates.

    During its early years, the College offered a classic academic course based on the English University model but consistent with the prevailing Puritan philosophy of the first colonists. Although many of its early graduates became ministers in Puritan congregations throughout New England, the college never formally affiliated with a specific religious denomination. An early brochure, published in 1643, justified the College's existence: "To advance Learning and *perpetuate* it to Posterity; dreading to leave an illiterate Ministry to the Churches."

    The election in 1708 of John Leverett, the first president who was not also a clergyman, marked a turning of the College toward intellectual independence from Puritanism. As the College grew in the 18th and 19th centuries, the curriculum was broadened, particularly in the sciences, and the College produced or attracted a long list of famous scholars, including Henry Wadsworth Longfellow, James Russell Lowell, William James, the elder Oliver Wendell Holmes, and Louis Agassiz.

    Charles W. Eliot, who served as president from 1869 to 1909, transformed the relatively small provincial college into a modern college. During his tenure, the Law and Medical Schools were *revitalized*, and the Graduate schools of Business, Dental Medicine, and Arts and Sciences were established. Enrollment grew from 1,000 to 3,000 students, the faculty grew from 49 to 278, and the endowment increased from $2.3 million to $22.5 million

    Neil L. Rudenstine took office as Harvard's 26th president in 1991. As part of an

지문 24 : 하버드 대학교

배경 : 하버드 대학은 1636년에 매사추세츠 영국 식민지 주의 입법의회의 투표에 의하여 설립되었으며 최초의 후원자인 찰스타운의 존 하버드의 이름을 따서 명명되었다. 존 하버드는 젊은 목사로서 1638년에 사망했을 때 자기 도서관과 부동산의 반을 대학에 남겼다. 이 대학은 학생 9명에 선생 단 한 사람으로부터 시작해서, 재학생을 포함하여 18,000의 학위후보생이 등록된, 10개의 대학원과 전문직업 학교의 학생과 학교로 성장했다. 2,000 이상의 교수직원을 포함하여 14,000 이상의 사람들이 하버드에서 근무하고 있다. 관련 대학 병원들에는 7,000이상의 교수 관직이 있다.

미국의 대통령 중 여섯 사람이 하버드 출신이다: 존 아담스, 존 퀴시 아담스, 테오도르 루즈벨트, 프랭클린 델라노 루즈벨트, 러더퍼드 B. 헤이스, 존 피츠제럴드 케네디 등이다. 교수중에는 34명의 노벨 수상자가 있다.

The statue of John Harvard in Harvard Yard is the most popular photographic subject for visitors to the Cambridge campus.

초창기에 이 대학은 영국 대학을 모델로 하되 최초의 식민지 정착민들을 지배했던, 청교도 철학에 일치하는 고전적 인문과정을 제공했다. 비록 초기의 졸업생의 많은 사람들이 뉴 잉글랜드 전역 청교도 회중의 목사가 되었지만 대학은 공식적으로 어느 특정 종교 교파와 관련된 적은 한번도 없었다. 1643년에 출판된 초기 학교 소개 책자에 대학의 존재이유를 '교회에 무식한 목사를 보내는 것이 두려워 학문을 발달시키며 그것을 후손들에게 영원히 전하기 위함이다.' 고 정당화하였다.

Below, classic Ivy League "gold domes"

역시 성직자가 아니었던 존 레버레트를 1708년에 초대 총장으로 선출한 것은 대학을 청교도로부터 지적으로 독립시키려는 의도를 보여주었다. 18~19세기에 대학이 성장해 감에 따라, 교육과정이 특히 과학에서 폭이 넓어지고 대학은 다수의 많은 유명한 학자를 배출했고 영입했다. 그들 중에는 다음들이 있다 : 헨리 오디워스 롱펠로우, 제임스 러셀 로웰, 윌리엄 제임스, 윌리엄 웬델 홈스, 루이스 아가시.

overall effort to achieve greater coordination among the University's schools and faculties, Rudenstine set in motion an intensive process of University-wide academic planning, intended to identify some of Harvard's main intellectual and programmatic priorities. Those have become an integral part of the current five-year capital campaign. In addition, Rudenstine has stressed the University's commitment to excellence in undergraduate education, <u>the importance of ( ) Harvard's doors open to students from across the *economic spectrum*</u>, the task of adapting the research university to an era of both rapid information growth and serious financial constraints, and the challenge of living together in a diverse community committed to freedom of expression.

Application Checklist :

Immediately

- Return both the Common Application and the Harvard Supplement with a check or money order for $60 made payable to Harvard University. Please be sure the applicant's name appears on the check or money order. If you need a fee waiver, have your guidance counselor write a request and attach it to the front of your Common Application.

- Give the School Report and Mid-year School Report to your school counselor or college advisor and ask him/her to return the completed School Report form to our office as soon as possible. If you have attended more than one high school, give a second copy of the School Report to your former counselor. The Mid-year School Report should be returned in February, 1999 with your latest grades.

- Give the two Teacher Evaluation forms to teachers in different academic subjects who know you well.

- If you have not already done so, register to take the required SAT I or ACT (American College Test) and three SAT II Subject Tests and have official reports of your scores sent to us. The last testing date for Regular Action applicants is January 23, 1999.

After four weeks

- Telephone the Admissions Office if you have not received acknowledgment of your Common Application and Harvard Supplement. This is very important, because applications can get lost in the mail.

As early as possible and before January 1, 1999

Send the Personal Statement on a separate sheet of paper if you have not already sent it with the Common Application.

January 1, 1999 is the final postmark deadline for all materials.

If you wish to have music tapes, slides of artwork, or selected samples of academic work evaluated as part of your application, send them directly to our office. We are not able to return these materials. (Please see the notes about supplementary materials in the Harvard Supplement.)

By February 1, 1999

If you have not been contacted by an alumna/us for an interview, please notify the Admissions Office.

1869년에서 1909년까지 총장으로 근무했던 찰스 W. 엘리어트는 하버드를 비교적 작은 지방대학에서 현대적인 대학으로 변모시켰다. 그의 재임 기간에 법대와 의대를 활성화시켰고 경영, 치과, 예술, 과학 대학원을 설립했다. 학생수도 1,000명에서 3,000명으로 불었고 교수진도 49명에서 278명으로 커지고 대학 기금도 2백 30만 달러에서 2천 2백 50만 달러로 불어났다.

The Harvard College Yard, center of the original college, still keeps much of its Old World charm and dignity today. This picture comes from an engraving made in the 1770's by Paul Revere, the colonial patriot and silver-smith. The small Holden Chapel, far left, was built in 1744. The other four buildings, built in the Georgian Colonial style of architecture, are, left to right, Hollis Hall, and Massachusetts Hall.

1991년에 루덴스틴이 하버드의 26대 총장으로 취임했다. 단과대와 교수단 간의 보다 강력한 조화를 이루기 위한 종합적인 노력의 일환으로, 루덴스틴은 하버드의 지적, 학과 프로그램 우위를 지속시키기 위하여 대학 전체 교육계획의 강도높은 한 가지 과정을 시행했다. 그런 것들이 최근의 5개년 계획의 중요 부분이 되고 있다. 그외에 루덴스틴은 재학생 교육의 우수성이라는 대학의 임무를 강조하고 경제적인 처지에 상관없이 하버드의 문호를 계속 개방해야 한다는 중요성, 연구전문 대학을 빠른 정보 성장과 심각한 경제적 제약이 많은 시대에 적응시키는 일, 표현의 자유를 가진 다양한 공동사회 안에서 함께 살아가는 문제를 강조해 왔다.

Harvard Houses stand along the Charles River. Leverett House Towers are the left, and the cupola of Dunster House at right center.

입학 지원 절차 검색 항목

즉시 해야할 일 :

공통원서와 하버드대 보충원서와 60달러에 해당하는 수표나 우편환을 하버드대 수취인으로 하여 하버드 대학교로 제출하시오. 반드시 지원자의 성명이 수표나 우편환 앞면에 나타나도록 하시오. 수수료 포기증서가 필요하면 가이던스 상담역에게 써달라고 부탁하여 공통원서 전면에 부치시오.

If you will need financial assistance, file the 1999-2000 PROFILE with the College Scholarship Service (CSS) and the Free Application for Federal Student Aid (FAFSA) with the appropriate federal processor. The CSS code is 3434; FAFSA code is E00468. All financial aid applicants who are not citizens or permanent residents of the United States must submit Harvard's Financial Statement for Students from Foreign Countries instead of the PROFILE and FAFSA. For more information, refer to pages 35-37 in the application booklet.

The Committee's decisions will be mailed in early April.

(Source: Adapted from webpages maintained by Harvard University: http://www.news.harvard.edu/hno.subpages/intro_harvard/index.html & http://adm-is.fas.harvard.edu/Time.htm)

(1.1) The topic of the "Background" is "A ____ of the school." (1.1. - 1.2. Subject matters)

    (a) Brief history   (b) Silhouette   (c) Description   (d) Review   (e) Survey

(1.2) The topic of the "Application Checklist" is _____.

    (a) The committee's decisions   (d) American College Test
    (b) College Scholarship Service   (e) Interview for admission
    (c) Application procedures

(2.1) The italicized word, *affiliated*, in the first paragraph of the Background refers to _____. (2.1. - 2.4. Words & phrase in context)

    (a) Asserted   (b) Attested   (c) Ratified   (d) Associated   (e) Separated

(2.2) The antonym of the italicized word, *perpetuate*, in the third paragraph of the Background is _____.

    (a) Conserve   (b) Cease   (c) Maintain   (d) Preserve   (e) Sustain

(2.3) The italicized word, *revitalized*, in the fifth paragraph of the Background refers to _____.

    (a) Reclaim   (b) Realize   (c) Rebut   (d) Re-energize   (e) Recapture

(2.4) The italicized phrase, *economic spectrum*, in the last paragraph of the Background means "_____ economic _____."

    (a) Commensurable, background   (c) Identical, capacity   (e) Collateral, background
    (b) Diverse, background   (d) Similar, capacity

생활기록부 사본과 학년 중간 기록표를 학교 상담교사나 대학 상담자에게 보내서 그 분이 완전한 학교생활기록을 가능한 한 빨리 본대학 사무처로 보내달라 부탁하시오. 고등학교를 두 곳 이상 다녔으면 그 학교의 기록 사본을 한 통 더 만들어 이전 상담자에게 보내시오. 학년 중간 기록표는 최종 성적을 기록하여 1999년 2월에 제출해야 합니다. 담임 교사 작성 평가서를 두 통, 당신을 잘 아는 다른 교과 담임 교사에게 보내시오.

President Neil L. Rudenstine congratulates a graduate at Commencement.

만일 이미 그렇게 하지 않았으면 필수의 SAT I 시험이나 ACT시험과 세 과목의 SAT II 시험에 응시하도록 등록하고 득점의 공식 보고서를 우리에게 보내도록 부탁하시오. Regular Action 응시자의 최종 시험 일자는 1999년 1월 23일입니다.

OLDEST BUILDING at Harvard, built in 1720, is Massachusetts Hall, used both for offices of the president and as a student residence hall.

4주 후에 할 일 :

만일 공통원서와 하버드대 원서를 접수했다는 수령 통지를 안받았으면 입시관리처에 전화하시오. 이것은 대단히 중요합니다. 왜냐하면 원서가 우편물 속에서 분실될 수도 있기 때문입니다.

가능한대로 빨리 그리고 1999년 1월 1일 이전에 할 일 :

만일 공통원서와 함께 보내지 않았으면 본인 작성 소개서를 별지에 작성하여 보내시오. 1999년 1월 1일은 모든 자료의 최종 우편 소인 날짜입니다.

만일 음악 테이프, 예술활동의 슬라이드, 교과활동의 선택된 표본 등을 응시의 일부로 평가받고 싶으면 직접 우리 사무처로 보내시오. 이런 자료는 반송할 수 없습니다 (보충적인 사항은 하버드 보충 원서의 유의란을 보시오).

1999년 2월 1일까지 할 일 :

만일 면접을 위해서 졸업생이나 우리와 연락이 안됐으면 입시관리처에 통지하여 주시오. 만일 재정 지원이 필요하면 대학학자금 서비스(CSS)나 적절한 연방 프로세서를 첨부하여 연방학생원조 무상신청 (FAFSA)으로 1999-2000 프로필을 제출하시오. CSS코드는 3434이고 FAFSA코드는 E00468입니다. 미국 시민이나 영주권자가 아니면 프로필과 FAFSA대신 외국인 학생을 위한 하버드대의 진술서를 제출해야 합니다. 좀더 자세한 안내가 필요하면 지원 소책자의 35-37페이지를 참조하시오.

<u>위원회의 결정은 4월 초에 우송됩니다.</u>

Memorial Church in the Yard, oldest part of Harvard

(3) The underlined structure, "the importance of ( ) Harvard's doors open to students from across the economic spectrum," needs a suitable gerund that best fits in the parenthesis. (Structure)

    (a) Manipulating   (b) Imposing   (c) Developing   (d) Making   (e) Keeping

(4.1) It can be inferred that the oldest institution of higher education in the United States is _____. (4.1. - 4.5. Making inferences)

    (a) Brown   (c) University of Pennsylvania   (e) Yale
    (b) Harvard   (d) Princeton

(4.2) Based on the information given, we can infer that John Harvard (1607 - 1638), graduate of Cambridge University and benefactor of Harvard College might have been a _____ and _____.

    (a) Minister, philanthropist   (d) Social reformer, politician
    (b) Businessman, philanthropist   (e) Engineer, philanthropist
    (c) Scholar, anthropologist

(4.3) "The Personal Statement" in the Application Checklist can be inferred as a section which requires excellent _____ skills to comply with.

    (a) Listening   (b) Organizational   (c) Reading   (d) Speaking   (e) Writing

(4.4) Based on the information given, it is suggested that the students from foreign countries fill out the _____ for financial assistance.

    (a) College Scholarship Service   (d) Harvard's Financial Statement
    (b) 1999-2000 Profile   (e) Free Application for Federal
    (c) Federal Student Aid Student Aid

(4.5) The following group which does not include any Ivy League schools can be inferred as _____.

    (a) Harvard, Cornell, Princeton, Yale
    (b) Brown, Columbia, Princeton, University of Pennsylvania (UP)
    (c) Brown, Columbia, Cornell, Yale, Dartmouth
    (d) Columbia, Harvard, Princeton, Yale
    (e) Stanford, Berkeley, William & Mary, Amherst

Note: (The Ivy League refers to the most prestigious and oldest institutions of higher education located in the northeastern part of the U.S. They are Brown, Columbia, Cornell, Dartmouth, Harvard, Princeton, University of Pennsylvania, Yale)

(5) Admission to Harvard is considered one of the most competitive in the United States. One of the major reasons for this serious competition can be concluded as a factor of "_____." (Conclusion)

    (a) Too many applicants   (c) Reasonable tuition   (e) Academic programs
    (b) Academic excellence   (d) Name value

Note

☐ **Great and General Court** : 식민지 시대 매사추세츠주, 뉴햄프셔주 양주의 입법, 사법권을 가졌던 입법의회
☐ **benefactor=a person who does good or who gives money for a good purpose** : 은인, 후원자, 독지가
☐ **enroll=make oneself an official member of a society or a school** : 등록하다, 회원이 되다
  • enrollment (등록자 수, 입학자 수)
☐ **affiliate=enter into association** : 지부, 자회사, 부속이 되다
  • The hospital is affiliated to Seoul National University. (저 병원은 서울대 부속 병원이다.)
☐ **teaching hospital** : 의대 부속 병원   ☐ **Nobel Laureate** : 노벨상 수상자
☐ **congregation** : 교회 회중, 청교도회 • How large is your congregation? (당신 교회의 신도수는 몇입니까?)
☐ **denomination=a division of a religious body** : 교파
☐ **The baptist** : 침례교   ☐ **The presbyterian** : 장로교
☐ **perpetuate=preserve, cause to be continued or remembered** : 영원한 것으로 만들다
  • This monument was build to perpetuate the memory of the heroes.
    (이 기념비는 국민적 영웅들을 영원히 기념하려고 세워졌다.)
☐ **dread to=fear greatly** : 몹시 두려워하다
  • I dread to think what will happen if she comes. (그녀가 오면 무슨 일이 일어날까 생각하니 겁이 난다.)
☐ **illiterate=unable to read or write** : 문맹의, • computer illiterate (컴맹)
☐ **transform=change completely in form, appearance, nature** : 변형, 변모시키다
  • The engine is designed to transform heat into energy. (그 엔진을 열을 동력으로 전환하도록 고안되었다.)
☐ **tenure=the length of time one holds office** : 재직기간, 대학교수의 종신 재직권
☐ **revitalize=put new life into, restore vitality** : 다시 활력을 넣다, 활성화하다
☐ **endow=give money, property to provide a regular income** : 기부하다
  • endowment (기본 재산)
  • They are looking for the benefactors to endow their hospital.
    (그들은 자기들 병원에 기부금을 낼 독지가를 찾고 있다.)
☐ **identify=prove who or what is** : 신분, 정체를 밝히다 • Let me identify myself. (저를 소개하겠습니다.)
☐ **integral=necessary to complete something** : (전체를 이루는데) 꼭 필요한
☐ **spectrum=a range of any various kinds** : 범위
  • across economic spectrum (빈부 격차를 뛰어 넘어)
  • the wide spectrum of opinions on this question (이 문제에 대한 광범위한 의견)
☐ **adapt=change so as to make suitable for new needs** : 맞게 조종하다, 적응시키다
  • He adapted an old car motor to his boat. (자동차 모터를 배에 쓰게 고쳤다.)
☐ **constraint=something that limits one's freedom of action** : 제약
  • I felt constraint in his presence. (그가 있어 부자유스러웠다.)
☐ **diverse=different, various** : 다양한
  • Diverse people have diverse interests. (사람마다 흥미도 다 각각이다.)
☐ **money order=postal order** : 우편환
☐ **waiver** : 권리 포기증서
☐ **postmark deadline** : 우표 소인에 따른 접수 마감시간
☐ **comply with=act in accordance with** : 준수하다, 따르다
  • People who refuse to comply with the law will be punished. (법을 따르지 않는 자는 처벌 받는다.)
☐ **profile=a short description, esp. of a person's life and character** : 간단한 소개
☐ **SAT=Scholastic Aptitude Test** : 학력 적성 검사
☐ **ACT=American College Test** : 미국 대학 입학 학력 고사

Passage 25 : Marriage

The family cycle begins with the decision to marry. But before we study the important decision to marry, let us look at why people marry and some important considerations leading up to marriage. In this country, there is great social pressure to marry. At least 90% of all Americans marry at some time in their lives. However, before people make such a major life decision, they must clearly identify their motives for marrying if they expect to be successful.

Reasons for Getting Married

If a person is getting married because of social pressure, it might be wise to reconsider. If a person is considering marriage to escape from problems at home or because a girl is pregnant or *to prove a point*, he or she is starting out on very *shaky* ground. With current statistics indicating that over one-half of all marriages end in divorce, such a start is potential for real concern.

Most people say they are marrying because they are "in love," and on the surface level that may be true. Often, however, these other motives, as mentioned above, may be hidden deep inside. Without close self-examination, a person may not even be aware of them. Other people may be aware of these motives, but may not be willing to admit them. If a person has any doubt or questions about the personal reasons for getting married or about the person that he or she is marrying, the best time to reconsider is before the marriage.

"But we are in love." The idea of romantic love is very glamorized in our society today. Countless movies and books portray the Romeo and Juliet type of romance. These stories are full of passion and excitement and usually end "happily ever after." Unfortunately, they present an inaccurate picture of relationships. Almost all relationships do begin with romantic love, physical attraction, an aura of excitement and energy in the two individuals. Many couples are successful in maintaining this romantic side of their relationship. However, all relationships go through various stages. When this first stage - the newness and excitement - settles, the couple must look closely to determine whether their oneness of mind extends to other aspects of their lives.

Marriage and Maturity.

Unfortunately, many young couples make decisions about marriage based only on the romantic phase of their relationship. To be successful, marriage requires social and *emotional maturity*. Maturity can be difficult to define, yet it can be described:

A mature person has the ability to establish and maintain relationships.
A mature person has the ability to give as well as receive.
A mature person can perceive others' feelings.
A mature person is personally stable. Mature people have established values by which they live. They know their interests and though open to new experiences, have goals and plans for achieving those goals.

지문 25 : 결혼

가족은 결혼의 결정부터 시작된다. 그러나 우리가 그 중요한 결혼 결정을 연구하기 전에 왜 사람들이 결혼을 하며, 결혼에 이르기까지 중요한 고려 사항들을 살펴보자. 미국에서는 결혼을 해야하는 커다란 사회적 압력이 있다. 최소한 90%의 모든 미국인들이 일생의 어느 시점에 결혼을 한다. 그러나 사람들이 그렇게 중요한 인생결정을 하기 전에 성공하기를 기대한다면 결혼의 동기를 분명히 확인해야한다.

NEWLYWEDS pose after their wedding in Melbourne, Australia. The rites that accompany marrige vary greatly around the world.

결혼을 하는 이유

만일 어떤 사람이 사회적인 압력 때문에 결혼을 한다면 재고해 보는 것이 현명하다. 만일 가정문제에서 도피하기 위해, 어떤 여자가 임신했기 때문에, 또는 어떤 주장을 증명해 보이기 위하여 결혼을 고려하고 있다면 그는 희박한 이유에서 출발하는 것이다. 반 이상의 결혼이 이혼으로 끝난 것을 보여주는 최근의 통계를 보면 그러한 출발은 진짜 우려할 만 하다.

대부분의 사람들은 사랑하고 있기 때문에 결혼을 하겠다고 말하는데 표면상으로는 맞는 말이다. 그러나 위에서 말한 그런 다른 동기들이 내부에 깊이 숨어 있을 수 있다. 자신을 잘 살펴보지 않으면 그런 동기를 모를 수도 있다. 다른 사람들은 그런 동기를 알고 있지만 그걸 스스로 인정하려고 하지 않을 것이다. 만일 어떤 사람이 결혼하는데 대하여, 또는 자기가 결혼하려는 사람에 대하여 의심이나 의문이 있다면 다시 생각해 볼 최선의 시간은 결혼 전이다.

A bride and groom exchange marriage vows at a wedding ceremony. Couples traditionally include a best man and a maid of honor in the ceremony to serve as official witnesses.

"그러나 우리는 사랑하고 있다." 낭만적인 사랑에 대한 생각이 오늘 우리 사회에서 매우 미화되어 있다. 수많은 영화와 책들이 로미오와 줄리엣 형의 낭만을 그리고 있다. 이런 이야기늘은 정열과 흥분이 가능하고 대개 끝이 '영원한 행복' 으로 끝난다. 불행히도 그런 이야기들은 부정확한 모습을 제공한다. 거의 모든 관계는 두 개인간의 낭만적인 사랑, 신체적 매력, 흥분과 원기의 분위기에서 분명히 시작된다. 많은 부부들이 그들 관계의 낭만적인 측면을 유지하는데 성공한다. 그러나 모든 관계는 다양한 단계를 겪는다. 최초의 단계-새로움과 흥분-이 가라앉을 때면 부부는 그들의 마음의 일치가 생활의 다른 면으로 확대되고 있는지의 여부를 결정하기 위하여 자세히 살펴보아야 한다.

The Most Important Factor.

Perhaps the most important factor is that a mature person is aware of his or her emotional needs and how to meet them in healthy ways. How does this affect the success of a marriage? The marriage has a better chance of being successful if both individuals have found healthy ways to meet their emotional needs. They have friends, belong to a group, and are in some way making a contribution; that is, they feel worthwhile. Both individuals will not go into a marriage depending only on the marriage or the spouse to meet these needs.

As you can see, a person must consider many complex areas before getting married. Knowing your spouse is, of course, very important to the success of a marriage. However, knowing yourself - your *innermost* thoughts, feelings, fears, and dreams - is perhaps the most critical element for ( ) a marriage ( ).

(Source: Merki, M. Bronson & et al. (1989). Health: A Guide to Wellness.)

(1) The topic of the passage is "_____." (Subject matter)

   (a) Reasons for getting married
   (b) Marriage "in love"
   (c) Marriage & maturity
   (d) Considerations before getting married
   (e) Requirements for a successful marriage

(2.1) The antonym of the italicized word, *shaky*, in the second paragraph refers to _____. (2.1 - 2.4. Words & phrases in context)

   (a) Indecisive   (b) Firm   (c) Unreliable   (d) Shabby   (e) Kempt

(2.2) The italicized phrase, *to prove a point*, in the second paragraph means "to _____."

   (a) Demonstrate one's stubbornness
   (b) Show off one's wisdom
   (c) Negotiate one's demands
   (d) Show one's decision is right
   (e) Solve complex problems

(2.3) The italicized phrase, *emotional maturity*, in the fourth paragraph refers to "_____ maturity."

   (a) Psychological & mental
   (b) Mental & temperamental
   (c) Impulsive & sensitive
   (d) Temperamental & spontaneous
   (e) Cognitive & enthusiastic

(2.4) The italicized word, *innermost*, in the last paragraph refers to "the _____."

   (a) Broadest
   (b) Most inquisitive
   (c) Most personal
   (d) Most obvious
   (e) Most subconscious

(3) The underlined structure, "However, knowing yourself - your innermost thoughts, feelings, fears, and dreams - is perhaps the most critical element for (____) a marriage (____)," needs a gerund and a verb that best fit in the parentheses. (Structure)

   (a) Creating, perform
   (b) Making, work
   (c) Creating, act
   (d) Making, operate
   (e) Making, produce

결혼과 성숙

불행하게도 많은 젊은 부부들이 그들의 낭만적인 관계만을 토대로 결혼에 대한 결정을 한다. 성공하려면 결혼은 사회적, 정서적 성숙을 필요로 한다. 성숙은 정의하기 어렵지만 다음과 같이 말할 수 있다.

- 성숙한 사람은 관계를 수립하고 유지할 수 있는 능력을 가진다.
- 성숙한 사람은 받을 수 있는 능력뿐 아니라 줄 수 있는 능력을 가진다.
- 성숙한 사람은 다른 사람들의 감정을 안다.
- 성숙한 사람은 개인적으로 안정되어 있다. 성숙한 사람은 그들이 살아가는데 의지할 가치관을 확립하고 있다. 그들은 자기들의 관심사들을 알고 비록 새로운 경험을 해나가야 하지만 그러한 목적들을 달성하기 위한 목표와 계획을 가진다.

가장 중요한 요소

아마 가장 중요한 요소는 성숙한 사람은 자기의 정서적 욕구와 그것들을 건강한 방법으로 충족시키는 방법을 알고 있다는 것이다. 이것이 결혼의 성공에 어떻게 영향을 미치는가? 만일 두사람 다 정서적 욕구를 충족시킬 건강한 방법을 찾았으면 성공할 가능성이 더 높다. 그들에게는 친구가 있고 어느 집단에 소속되고 어떤 방식으로 공헌하고 있다. 다시 말하면 자신이 가치있는 인간이라는 느낌을 갖는다. 두 사람이 모두 이런 욕구를 충족시키기 위하여 결혼하고 배우자에게 의지하는 마음으로 결혼하는 것은 아니다.

아는 바와 같이 사람은 결혼 전에 여러 복합적인 부분을 고려해야한다. 배우자를 아는 것은 성공적인 결혼에 매우 중요하다. 그러나 당신 자신을 아는것-당신의 가장 은밀한 생각, 감정, 꿈-이 아마 결혼이 기능을 잘 발휘하도록 만드는 가장 결정적인 요소일 것이다.

J. M. Bertrand, Shostal

Some societies permit polygamy, the practice of having more than one wife or husband. This photograph shows an African prince with five of his wives.

WORLD BOOK photo

Raising a family is one of the many rewards of marriage, but it is also a serious responsibility for the parents. The family shown above are enjoying a meal together at home.

(4.1) Based on the information given, it can be inferred that many young people in the U.S. tend to get married mainly because of _____. (4.1 - 4.4. Making inferences)

   (a) Emotional needs   (c) Financial needs   (e) Romantic phase of their relationship
   (b) Physical attraction   (d) Social pressure

(4.2) It can be inferred that many young people around the world get married because of _____.

   (a) Emotional needs   (c) Financial needs   (e) Romantic phase of their relationship
   (b) Physical attraction   (d) Social pressure

(4.3) Based on the information presented, the best time to get married is "When both parties are _____ mature."

   (a) Mentally & financially   (d) Socially & professionally
   (b) Emotionally & socially   (e) Physically & financially
   (c) Socially & psychologically

(4.4) Based on the information given, more than one-half of all marriages in the U.S. end in divorce. It can be inferred that the reason for this is _____.

   (a) Romantic view of love   (d) An inaccurate picture of marriage
   (b) Emotional & social immaturity   (e) Alcoholic & drug problems
   (c) Unfaithful spouses

(5.1) Based on the information given, it can be concluded that the most important factor leading to a successful marriage is "Knowing _____." (5.1 - 5.2. Conclusions)

   (a) Your spouse   (c) Your dreams & feelings   (e) Your spouse's wealth & profession
   (b) Yourself   (d) Your spouse's maturity

(5.2) The following proverb which best reflects the theme of the passage can be concluded as "_____."

   (a) He that marries for wealth sells his liberty (English)
   (b) Better fortune in a wife than with a wife (German)
   (c) He who marries a widow with four children marries four thieves (Italian)
   (d) The most fascinating women never make the best marriages (French)
   (e) Pray one hour before going to war, Two hours before going to sea, And three hours before getting married (Indian)

Note

- **shaky**=weak, unreliable : 허약한, 기대할 수 없는 • My English is rather shaky. (내 영어는 취약하다.)
- **ground**=reason for saying, doing or believing something : 근거, 이유, 동기
  • On what ground do you suspect him? (무슨 근거로 그를 의심하는가?)
- **statistics** : 통계(학)   □ **self-examination** : 자성, 자기 성찰
- **divorce**=legal ending of marriage so that husband and wife are free to marry again :
  이혼 • He is suing for divorce. (그는 이혼 소송 중이다.)
- **potential**=possibility for developing or being developed : 발전 가능성, 발발 가능성
  • There still exists a war potential in the Korean Peninsula. (한반도에는 아직도 전쟁 가능성이 있다.)
- **glamorize**=make something appear better, more attractive than in reality : 미화하다, 돋보이게 하다   • Newspapers glamorize the lives of film stars.
- **portray**=describe vividly in words : 그리다, 표현하다
  • The author portrays the campus life as a very romantic place. (작가는 대학을 매우 낭만적인 장소로 그리고 있다.)
- **aura**=an effect or feeling that seems to surround and come from a person or place :
  영기, 분위기, 그런 효과 • The village had an aura of decay. (그 마을은 쇠퇴해가는 느낌을 풍겼다.)
- **perceive**=become aware of : 지각하다, 알아차리다
  • On entering the house, we perceived that he was a man of taste.
  (그 집에 들어서자마자 그분이 고상한 취미를 가진 분임을 알았다.)

부록

해답편

해답

Page No.	Sect No.	Chpt, tpc	S-sect No.	Pasg No.	Mod Ans (모범 정답)	Reason(s) for the answer (비고)
30	2-1	Speed Reading	EXERCISE. 1		속독발음에 중점을 두었음.	
32	2-1	Speed Reading	EXERCISE. 2		미국 국민학생 저학년(1~3학년)발음 및 의성화 연습에 중점.	
32	2-1	Speed Reading	EXERCISE. 3		저학년 발음 연습 및 수업 분위기 고취에 중점.	
34	2-1	Speed Reading	EXERCISE. 4		발음 및 구 띄어 읽기에 중점.	
36	2-1	Speed Reading	EXERCISE. 5	5.1	속독을 위한 구 및 문장 띄어 읽기 연습.	
36	2-1	Speed Reading	EXERCISE. 5	5.2	위와 같음. 읽는데 필요한 시간(예, 30초, 1분 등)	
40	2-2	Detecting the Sequences	EXERCISE. 1	1.1	(2, 1, 4, 3)	
40	2-2	Detecting the Sequences	EXERCISE. 1	1.2	(2, 4, 1, 3)	
40	2-2	Detecting the Sequences	EXERCISE. 1	1.3	(2, 3, 1)	
42	2-2	Detecting the Sequences	EXERCISE. 2		(1, 2, 3, 4, 5, 7, 6, 8)	
42	2-2	Detecting the Sequences	EXERCISE. 3	3.1	(3, 2, 1)	
42	2-2	Detecting the Sequences	EXERCISE. 3	3.2	(3, 2, 4, 1)	
44	2-2	Detecting the Sequences	EXERCISE. 3	3.3	(4, 2, 3, 1)	
44	2-2	Detecting the Sequences	EXERCISE. 3	3.4	(2, 4, 1, 3, 5)	
44	2-2	Detecting the Sequences	EXERCISE. 3	3.5	(1, 3, 5, 4, 2)	
46	2-2	Detecting the Sequences	EXERCISE. 3	3.6	(5, 1, 4, 3, 2)	
46	2-2	Detecting the Sequences	EXERCISE. 3	3.7	(5, 4, 2, 1, 3)	
48	2-2	Detecting the Sequences	EXERCISE. 3	3.8	(1, 3, 6, 7, 2, 8, 5, 4, 9)	
50	2-3	Following the Directions	Direction 1		1(3) ; 2(4) ; 3(5) ; 4(3) ; 5(2)	
52	2-3	Following the Directions	Direction 2		1(4) ; 2(5) ; 3(4) ; 4(1) ; 5(2)	
52	2-3	Following the Directions	Direction 3		1(5) ; 2(4) ; 3(5) ; 4(2) ; 5(5)	
56	2-3	Following the Directions	Direction 4		1(5) ; 2(2) ; 3(1) ; 4(2) ; 5(3)	
56	2-3	Following the Directions	Direction 5		1(4) ; 2(2) ; 3(3) ; 4(2) ; 5(3)	
58	2-3	Following the Directions	Direction 6		1(1) ; 2(1) ; 3(3) ; 4(4) ; 5(1)	
60	2-3	Following the Directions	Direction 7		1(4) ; 2(3) ; 3(3) ; 4(5) ; 5(5)	
62	2-3	Following the Directions	Direction 8		1(1) ; 2(2) ; 3(3) ; 4(1) ; 5(4)	
64	2-3	Following the Directions	Direction 9		1(4) ; 2(4) ; 3(2) ; 4(2) ; 5(4)	
68	2-3	Following the Directions	Direction 10		1(3) ; 2(1) ; 3(2) ; 4(5) ; 5(3)	
70	2-4	Using the context	EXERCISE.	1	(1)(b) ; (2)(a)	
70	2-4	Using the context	EXERCISE.	2	(1)(d) ; (2)(d)	
72	2-4	Using the context	EXERCISE.	3	(1)(b) ; (2)(a)	
72	2-4	Using the context	EXERCISE.	4	(1)(b) ; (2)(a)	
72	2-4	Using the context	EXERCISE.	5	(1)(b) ; (2)(d)	
72	2-4	Using the context	EXERCISE.	6	(1)(c) ; (2)(a)	
72	2-4	Using the context	EXERCISE.	7	(1)(a) ; (2)(c)	
74	2-4	Using the context	EXERCISE.	8	(1)(c) ; (2)(a)	

(Chpt = Chapter ; Sect = Section ; S-sect = Sub-section ; Pasg = Passage ; Mod = Model ; tpc = topic ; Ans = Answer)

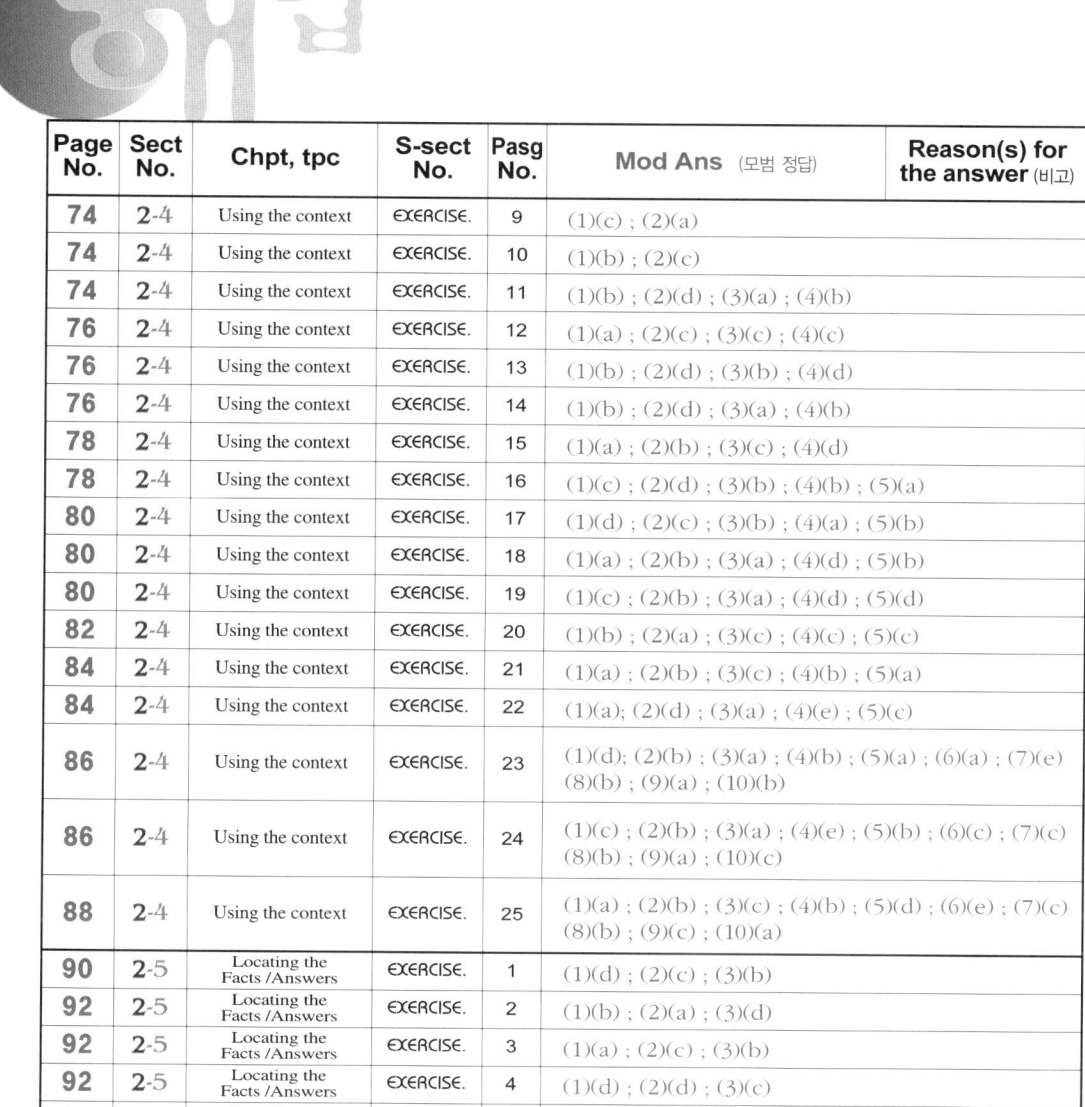

Page No.	Sect No.	Chpt, tpc	S-sect No.	Pasg No.	Mod Ans (모범 정답)	Reason(s) for the answer (비고)
74	2-4	Using the context	EXERCISE.	9	(1)(c) ; (2)(a)	
74	2-4	Using the context	EXERCISE.	10	(1)(b) ; (2)(c)	
74	2-4	Using the context	EXERCISE.	11	(1)(b) ; (2)(d) ; (3)(a) ; (4)(b)	
76	2-4	Using the context	EXERCISE.	12	(1)(a) ; (2)(c) ; (3)(c) ; (4)(c)	
76	2-4	Using the context	EXERCISE.	13	(1)(b) ; (2)(d) ; (3)(b) ; (4)(d)	
76	2-4	Using the context	EXERCISE.	14	(1)(b) ; (2)(d) ; (3)(a) ; (4)(b)	
78	2-4	Using the context	EXERCISE.	15	(1)(a) ; (2)(b) ; (3)(c) ; (4)(d)	
78	2-4	Using the context	EXERCISE.	16	(1)(c) ; (2)(d) ; (3)(b) ; (4)(b) ; (5)(a)	
80	2-4	Using the context	EXERCISE.	17	(1)(d) ; (2)(c) ; (3)(b) ; (4)(a) ; (5)(b)	
80	2-4	Using the context	EXERCISE.	18	(1)(a) ; (2)(b) ; (3)(a) ; (4)(d) ; (5)(b)	
80	2-4	Using the context	EXERCISE.	19	(1)(c) ; (2)(b) ; (3)(a) ; (4)(d) ; (5)(d)	
82	2-4	Using the context	EXERCISE.	20	(1)(b) ; (2)(a) ; (3)(c) ; (4)(c) ; (5)(c)	
84	2-4	Using the context	EXERCISE.	21	(1)(a) ; (2)(b) ; (3)(c) ; (4)(b) ; (5)(a)	
84	2-4	Using the context	EXERCISE.	22	(1)(a); (2)(d) ; (3)(a) ; (4)(e) ; (5)(c)	
86	2-4	Using the context	EXERCISE.	23	(1)(d); (2)(b) ; (3)(a) ; (4)(b) ; (5)(a) ; (6)(a) ; (7)(e) ; (8)(b) ; (9)(a) ; (10)(b)	
86	2-4	Using the context	EXERCISE.	24	(1)(c) ; (2)(b) ; (3)(a) ; (4)(e) ; (5)(b) ; (6)(c) ; (7)(c) ; (8)(b) ; (9)(a) ; (10)(c)	
88	2-4	Using the context	EXERCISE.	25	(1)(a) ; (2)(b) ; (3)(c) ; (4)(b) ; (5)(d) ; (6)(e) ; (7)(c) ; (8)(b) ; (9)(c) ; (10)(a)	
90	2-5	Locating the Facts /Answers	EXERCISE.	1	(1)(d) ; (2)(c) ; (3)(b)	
92	2-5	Locating the Facts /Answers	EXERCISE.	2	(1)(b) ; (2)(a) ; (3)(d)	
92	2-5	Locating the Facts /Answers	EXERCISE.	3	(1)(a) ; (2)(c) ; (3)(b)	
92	2-5	Locating the Facts /Answers	EXERCISE.	4	(1)(d) ; (2)(d) ; (3)(c)	
94	2-5	Locating the Facts /Answers	EXERCISE.	5	(1)(b) ; (2)(a) ; (3)(a) ; (4)(a) ; (5)(d) ; (6)(c)	
96	2-5	Locating the Facts /Answers	EXERCISE.	6	(1)(b) ; (2)(c) ; (3)(c) ; (4)(a) ; (5)(d) ; (6)(d) ; (7)(c) ; (8)(a)	
98	2-5	Locating the Facts /Answers	EXERCISE.	7	(1)(b) ; (2)(c) ; (3)(d) ; (4)(d) ; (5)(b) ; (6)(a) ; (7)(d)	
100	2-5	Locating the Facts /Answers	EXERCISE.	8	(1)(b) ; (2)(a) ; (3)(a) ; (4)(c) ; (5)(d) ; (6)(a) ; (7)(b) ; (8)(a) ; (9)(c) ; (10)(a)	
102	2-5	Locating the Facts /Answers	EXERCISE.	9	(1)(b) ; (2)(c) ; (3)(a) ; (4)(b) ; (5)(a) ; (6)(a) ; (7)(b) ; (8)(d) ; (9)(a)	
104	2-5	Locating the Facts /Answers	EXERCISE.	10	(1)(b) ; (2)(d) ; (3)(c) ; (4)(d) ; (5)(b) ; (6)(b) ; (7)(c) ; (8)(d)	
106	2-5	Locating the Facts /Answers	EXERCISE.	11	(1)(b) ; (2)(b) ; (3)(c) ; (4)(d) ; (5)(a) ; (6)(c) ; (7)(b) ; (8)(b)	
108	2-5	Locating the Facts /Answers	EXERCISE.	12	(1)(b) ; (2)(a) ; (3)(b) ; (4)(c) ; (5)(b)	

(Chpt = Chapter ; Sect = Section ; S-sect = Sub-section ; Pasg = Passage ; Mod = Model ; tpc = topic ; Ans = Answer)

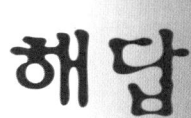

Page No.	Sect No.	Chpt, tpc	S-sect No.	Pasg No.	Mod Ans (모범 정답)	Reason(s) for the answer (비고)
108	2-5	Locating the Facts /Answers	EXERCISE.	13	(1)(d) ; (2)(c) ; (3)(b) ; (4)(b) ; (5)(a) ; (6)(a) ; (7)(c) ; (8)(b) ; (9)(c) ; (10)(a) ; (11)(a) ; (12)(c)	
110	2-5	Locating the Facts /Answers	EXERCISE.	14	(1)(b) ; (2)(e) ; (3)(c) ; (4)(d) ; (5)(a) ; (6)(b) ; (7)(a) ; (8)(e) ; (9)(a) ; (10)(b) ; (11)(e) ; (12)(a)	
114	2-5	Locating the Facts /Answers	EXERCISE.	15	(1)(e) ; (2)(a) ; (3)(c) ; (4)(c) ; (5)(a) ; (6)(b) ; (7)(b) ; (8)(a) ; (9)(b) ; (10)(c)	
120	2-6	Subject matter	EXERCISE.	1	(1)(a) ; (2)(c)	
120	2-6	Subject matter	EXERCISE.	2	(1)(b) ; (2)(d)	
120	2-6	Subject matter	EXERCISE.	3	(1)(e) ; (2)(d)	
122	2-6	Subject matter	EXERCISE.	4	(1)(c) ; (2)(a)	
122	2-6	Subject matter	EXERCISE.	5	(1)(b) ; (2)(e)	
124	2-6	Subject matter	EXERCISE.	6	(1)(d) ; (2)(c)	
126	2-6	Subject matter	EXERCISE.	7	(1)(c) ; (2)(b)	
126	2-6	Subject matter	EXERCISE.	8	(1)(c) ; (2)(e)	
128	2-6	Subject matter	EXERCISE.	9	(1)(e) ; (2)(c)	
128	2-6	Subject matter	EXERCISE.	10	(1)(c) ; (2)(b)	
130	2-6	Subject matter	EXERCISE.	11	(1)(b) ; (2)(d)	
132	2-6	Subject matter	EXERCISE.	12	(1)(b) ; (2)(d)	
132	2-6	Subject matter	EXERCISE.	13	(1)(a) ; (2)(b)	
134	2-6	Subject matter	EXERCISE.	14	(1)(a) ; (2)(a)	
134	2-6	Subject matter	EXERCISE.	15	(1)(d) ; (2)(d)	
		pp 140~156에 나오는 The Topic Sentence and the Supporting Details은 교재에 설명되어 있음.				
158	2-8	Making inferences	EXERCISE.	1	(1)(b)	
158	2-8	Making inferences	EXERCISE.	2	(1)(d)	
158	2-8	Making inferences	EXERCISE.	3	(1)(b)	
160	2-8	Making inferences	EXERCISE.	4	(1)(e)	
160	2-8	Making inferences	EXERCISE.	5	(1)(d)	
160	2-8	Making inferences	EXERCISE.	6	(1)(e)	
162	2-8	Making inferences	EXERCISE.	7	(1)(a)	
162	2-8	Making inferences	EXERCISE.	8.1	Done as an example	
162	2-8	Making inferences	EXERCISE.	8.2	(1)I ; (2)I ; (3)F ; (4)I ; (5)T	
164	2-8	Making inferences	EXERCISE.	8.3	(1)I ; (2)F ; (3)T ; (4)T ; (5)F	
164	2-8	Making inferences	EXERCISE.	8.4	(1)(a)F ; (b)F ; (c)T ; (d)I ; (e)F (2)(a)T ; (b)T ; (c)I (d)F ; (e)T	
166	2-8	Making inferences	EXERCISE.	8.5	(1)I ; (2)T ; (3)I ; (4)F ; (5)I	
166	2-8	Making inferences	EXERCISE.	8.6	(a)F ; (b)I ; (c)F ; (d)T ; (e)F	

(Chpt = Chapter ; Sect = Section ; S-sect = Sub-section ; Pasg = Passage ; Mod = Model ; tpc = topic ; Ans = Answer)

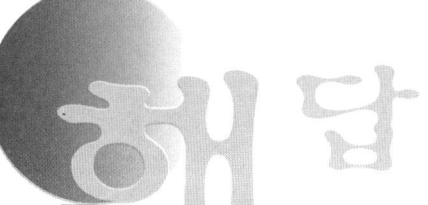

해답편 **647**

Page No.	Sect No.	Chpt, tpc	S-sect No.	Pasg No.	Mod Ans (모범 정답)	Reason(s) for the answer (비고)
168	2-8	Making inferences	EXERCISE.	8.7	(a)T ; (b)F ; (c)I ; (d)I ; (e)F	
168	2-8	Making inferences	EXERCISE.	8.8	(a)I ; (b)T ; (c)T ; (d)F ; (e)F	
170	2-8	Making inferences	EXERCISE.	8.9	(a)I ; (b)F ; (c)T ; (d)F ; (e)I	
172	2-8	Making inferences	EXERCISE.	8.10	(1)T ; (2)F ; (3)I ; (4)F ; (5)I	
176	2-9	Drawing conclusion	EXERCISE.	1	(1)(d) ; (2)(c) 비고:Romeo&Juliet은 소설, The Arabian Nights은 우리나라의 "흥부와 놀부 또는 심청전" 같이 folktale로 간주됨	
176	2-9	Drawing conclusion	EXERCISE.	2	(1)(b) ; (2)(a)	
178	2-9	Drawing conclusion	EXERCISE.	3	(1)(d) ; (2)(c)	
178	2-9	Drawing conclusion	EXERCISE.	4	(1)(e) ; (2)(d)	
178	2-9	Drawing conclusion	EXERCISE.	5	(1)(e) ; (2)(b)	
180	2-9	Drawing conclusion	EXERCISE.	6	(1)(c) ; (2)(a)	
180	2-9	Drawing conclusion	EXERCISE.	7	(1)(c) ; (2)(a)	
182	2-9	Drawing conclusion	EXERCISE.	8	(1)(a) ; (2)(e)	
182	2-9	Drawing conclusion	EXERCISE.	9	(1)(e) ; (2)(a)	
184	2-9	Drawing conclusion	EXERCISE.	10	(1)(e) ; (2)(b)	
186	2-9	Drawing conclusion	EXERCISE.	11	(1)(a) ; (2)(b)	
188	2-9	Drawing conclusion	EXERCISE.	12	(1)(b) ; (2)(c)	
188	2-9	Drawing conclusion	EXERCISE.	13	(1)(e) ; (2)(a)	
190	2-9	Drawing conclusion	EXERCISE.	14	(1)(b) ; (2)(c)	
192	2-9	Drawing conclusion	EXERCISE.	15	(1)(e) ; (2)(e)	
194	2-9	Drawing conclusion	EXERCISE.	16	(1)(c) ; (2)(c)	
196	2-9	Drawing conclusion	EXERCISE.	17	(1)(e) ; (2)(a)	
202	2-10	Tone & Attitude	EXERCISE.	1	(1)(d) ; (2)(a)	
202	2-10	Tone & Attitude	EXERCISE.	2	(1)(a) ; (2)(c) ; (3)(a)	
204	2-10	Tone & Attitude	EXERCISE.	3	(1)(d) ; (2)(b)	
206	2-10	Tone & Attitude	EXERCISE.	4	(1)(d) ; (2)(a)	
206	2-10	Tone & Attitude	EXERCISE.	5	(1)(b) ; (2)(e)	
208	2-10	Tone & Attitude	EXERCISE.	6	(1)(a) ; (2)(e) 대부분의 공용문은 "formal" style이며 내용은 "reasonable" (감정에 호소보다는) 하여야 됨	
210	2-10	Tone & Attitude	EXERCISE.	7	(1)(a) (Academic & professional writing은 분명한 증거를 위주로 하기 때문에, 객관적 설득력을 갖음) (2)(b)	

(Chpt = Chapter ; Sect = Section ; S-sect = Sub-section ; Pasg = Passage ; Mod = Model ; tpc = topic ; Ans = Answer)

해답

Page No.	Sect No.	Chpt, tpc	S-sect No.	Pasg No.	Mod Ans (모범 정답)	Reason(s) for the answer (비고)
210	2-10	Tone & Attitude	EXERCISE.	8	(1)(a) (2)(b)	
214	2-10	Tone & Attitude	EXERCISE.	9	(1)(a) (2)(a)	
214	2-10	Tone & Attitude	EXERCISE.	10	(1)(b) ; (2)(a)	
216	2-10	Tone & Attitude	EXERCISE.	11	(1)(c) Eulogy의 특성과 같이 "슬픔을 나누고, 그리고 슬픔을 이기고 가신 그 분의 뜻을 받들어 내일을 위하여 희망을 가지고 더 열심히 일하자는 inspiration을 줌"에 있음 (2)(a)	
220	2-10	Tone & Attitude	EXERCISE.	12	(1)(a) ; (2)(a)	
222	2-10	Tone & Attitude	EXERCISE.	13	(1)(d) 자유세계의 한 기자가 Saigon의 멸망하는 마지막날을 회상하여 기록한 슬픈 사연 (2)(e)	
222	2-10	Tone & Attitude	EXERCISE.	14	(1)(d) ; (2)(b)	
226	2-10	Tone & Attitude	EXERCISE.	15	(1)(a) ; (2)(b)	
240	2-11	Rhectorical techniques	EXERCISE.	1	Definition	
240	2-11	Rhectorical techniques	EXERCISE.	2	Analysis	
242	2-11	Rhectorical techniques	EXERCISE.	3	Cause and Effect	
242	2-11	Rhectorical techniques	EXERCISE.	4	Description	
242	2-11	Rhectorical techniques	EXERCISE.	5	Comparison and Contrast	
258	2-11	Word Choice	Simile questions		(1)(d) ; (2)(b) ; (3)(a) ; (4)(d) ; (5)(b) ; (6)(c) ; (7)(b) (8)(c) ; (9)(d) ; (10)(a)	
258	2-11	Word Choice	Analogy questions		(1)(d) ; (2)(c) ; (3)(c) ; (4)(c) ; (5)(d) ; (6)(d) ; (7)(d) (8)(c) ; (9)(b) ; (10)(a)	
260	2-11	Word Choice	Confused Words		(1)(a) ; (2)(a) ; (3)(c) ; (4)(a) ; (5)(d) ; (6)(a) ; (7)(a) A number of 복수사용(명사 및 본동사) The number of 단수사용(명사 및 본동사) (8)(c) ; (9)(c) ; (10)(b)	
280	3-1	Arts	3.1.1 Dance	1	(1)(e) ; (2)(d) ; (3)(b) ; (4)(c) ; (5)(a)	
282	3-1	Arts	3.1.1 Dance	2	(1)(d) ; (2)(e) ; (3)(a) ; (4)(e) ; (5)(a)	
284	3-1	Arts	3.1.1 Dance	3	(1)(c) ; (2)(c) ; (3)(d) ; (4)(c) ; (5)(c)	
286	3-1	Arts	3.1.2 Painting	1	(1)(c) ; (2)(d) ; (3)(e) ; (4)(b) (Painting에 대한 객관적 서술이지, Definition이 아님) (5)(c)	
290	3-1	Arts	3.1.2 Painting	2	(1)(c) (2)(c) ; (3)(d) ; (4)(d) (5)(d)	

(Chpt = Chapter ; Sect = Section ; S-sect = Sub-section ; Pasg = Passage ; Mod = Model ; tpc = topic ; Ans = Answer)

Page No.	Sect No.	Chpt, tpc	S-sect No.	Pasg No.	Mod Ans (모범 정답)	Reason(s) for the answer (비고)
294	3-1	Arts	3.1.2 Painting	3	(1)(a) ; (2)(a) ; (3)(b) ; (4)(e) ; (5)(c)	
298	3-1	Arts	3.1.3 Music	1	(1)(d) ; (2)(d) ; (3)(d) ; (4)(a) ; (5)(d)	
300	3-1	Arts	3.1.3 Music	2	(1)(a) ; (2)(a) ; (3)(a) ; (4)(a) ; (5)(d)	
302	3-1	Arts	3.1.3 Music	3	(1)(e) ; (2)(e) ; (3)(a) ; (4)(c) ; (5)(c)	
306	3-2	Popular Culture	3.2.1 Celebrity	1	(1)(d) ; (2)(b) ; (3)(a) ; (4)(b) ; (5)(e)	
310	3-2	Popular Culture	3.2.1 Celebrity	2	(1)(a) ; (2)(b) ; (3)(b) ; (4)(A)(d) ; (B)(b) ; (C)(d) ; (5)(e)	
316	3-2	Popular Culture	3.2.1 Celebrity	3	(1)(a) ; (2)(c) ; (3)(b) ; (4)(c) ; (5)(b)	
320	3-2	Popular Culture	3.2.2 Fashion	1	(1)(a) ; (2)(b) ; (3)(c) ; (4)(c) ; (5)(b)	
324	3-2	Popular Culture	3.2.2 Fashion	2	(1)(c) ; (2)(d) ; (3)(c) ; (4)(c) ; (5)(b)	
330	3-2	Popular Culture	3.2.2 Fashion	3	(1)(e) ; (2)(d) ; (3)(a) ; (4)(b) ; (5)(c)	
332	3-2	Popular Culture	3.2.3 Film	1	(1)(a) ; (2)(d) ; (3)(b) ; (4)(c) ; (5)(a)	
336	3-2	Popular Culture	3.2.3 Film	2	(1)(b) ; (2.1)(a) ; (2.2)(d) ; (2.3)(b) ; (3)(b) ; (4)(b) (biography:남이 자기인생을 저술, autobiography:자기가 자신의 인생을 저술) ; (5)(c)	
344	3-2	Popular Culture	3.2.3 Film	3	(1)(e) ; (2.1)(c) ; (2.2)(b) ; (2.3)(d) ; (2.4)(c) ; (2.5)(d) (3.1)(c) ; (3.2)(d) ; (4.1)(a) (종교의 경전들은 대부분 parable로 쓰여졌음) ; (4.2)(b) ; (4.3)(e) ; (5.1)(c) ; (5.2)(e)	
352	3-2	Popular Culture	3.2.4 Sports	1	(1)(a) ; (2.1)(e) ; (2.2)(c) ; (2.3)(c) ; (3)(c) ; (4)(b) ; (5)(e)	
358	3-2	Popular Culture	3.2.4 Sports	2	(1.1)(b) ; (1.2)(c) ; (2)(d) ; (3.1)(d) ; (3.2)(c) ; (4)(a) ; (5)(c)	
364	3-2	Popular Culture	3.2.4 Sports	,3	(1)(a) ; (2.1)(c) ; (2.2)(a) ; (2.3)(e) ; (2.4)(d) ; (2.5)(b) (3.1)(d) ; (3.2)(e) ; (4)(b) ; (5)(a)	
370	3-3	Natural science	3.3.1 Biology	1	(1)(c) ; (2)(d) ; (3.1)(d) ; (3.2)(e) ; (3.3)(c) ; (3.4)(a) (3.5)(a) ; (4)(a) ; (5)(c)	
374	3-3	Natural science	3.3.1 Biology	2	(1)(c) ; (2.1)(b) ; (2.2)(d) ; (2.3)(a) ; (3)(a) ; (4)(d) (5)(e)	
376	3-3	Natural science	3.3.1 Biology	3	(1)(e) ; (2.1)(b) ; (2.2)(a) ; (2.3)(d) ; (2.4)(b) (2.5)(e) ; (3)(a) ; (4)(a) ; (5)(e)	

(Chpt = Chapter ; Sect = Section ; S-sect = Sub-section ; Pasg = Passage ; Mod = Model ; tpc = topic ; Ans = Answer)

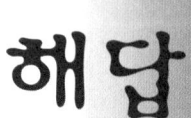

Page No.	Sect No.	Chpt, tpc	S-sect No.	Pasg No.	Mod Ans (모범 정답)	Reason(s) for the answer (비고)
380	3-3	Natural science	3.3.2 Chemistry	1	(1)(e) ; (2)(e) ; (3.1)(c) ; (3.2)(a) ; (4)(a) ; (5)(b)	
384	3-3	Natural science	3.3.2 Chemistry	2	(1)(b) ; (2.1)(a) ; (2.2)(b) ; (2.3)(c) ; (2.4)(d) ; (3)(e) (4)(a) ; (5)(d)	
388	3-3	Natural science	3.3.2 Chemistry	3	(1.1)(c) ; (1.2)(a) ; (2)(c) ; (3)(b) ; (4)(c) ; (5)(e)	
392	3-3	Natural science	3.3.3 Computer	1	(1)(a) ; (2.1)(e) ; (2.2)(d) ; (2.3)(a) ; (2.4)(b) (2.5)(e) ; (3)(a) ; (4)(a) ; (5)(b)	
376	3-3	Natural science	3.3.3 Computer	2	(1)(b) ; (2.1)(e) ; (2.2)(c) ; (3)(b) ; (4)(e) ; (5)(d)	
398	3-3	Natural science	3.3.3 Computer	3	(1.1)(b) ; (1.2)(c) ; (2.1)(b) ; (2.2)(e) ; (3.1)(b) (3.2)(a) ; (4)(b) ; (5)(c)	
402	3-3	Natural science	3.3.4 Health	1	(1.1)(a) ; (1.2)(d) ; (2.1)(e) ; (2.2)(a) ; (3.1)(b) (3.2)(a) ; (4)(d) ; (5)(c)	
406	3-3	Natural science	3.3.4 Health	2	(1)(d) ; (2)(e) ; (3)(a) ; (4)(b) ; (5)(c)	
408	3-3	Natural science	3.3.4 Health	3	(1)(b);(2.1)(d);(2.2)(e);(3.1)(a);(3.2)(b);(4)(c);(5)(e)	
412	3-3	Natural science	3.3.5 Math	1	(1)(e) ; (2.1)(e) ; (2.2)(c) ; (2.3)(c) ; (2.4)(b) (2.5)(d) ; (3.1)(a) ; (3.2)(d) ; (4)(c) ; (5)(e)	
416	3-3	Natural science	3.3.5 Math	2	(1)(e) ; (2.1)(a) ; (2.2)(c) ; (3)(d) ; (4)(e) ; (5)(b)	
420	3-3	Natural science	3.3.5 Math	3	(1)(c) ; (2.1)(d) ; (2.2)(e) ; (3)(a) ; (4)(e) ; (5)(a)	
422	3-3	Natural science	3.3.6 Physics	1	(1.1)(a) ; (1.2)(e) ; (1.3)(b) ; (2.1)(e) ; (2.2)(e) ; (3)(c) (4.1)(e) (이유 "engine" is heat source, where as "mechanics" deals with "forces of motion.") (4.2)(e) (이유: "electricity" and "magnetics" are closely related because one can produce the other.) (4.3)(e) ; (5.1)(a) ; (5.2)(a)	
426	3-3	Natural science	3.3.6 Physics	2	(1)(a) ; (2)(e) ; (3)(a) ; (4)(a) ; (5)(b)	
430	3-3	Natural science	3.3.6 Physics	3	(1)(b) ; (2)(b) ; (3)(a) ; (4)(d) ; (5)(c)	
434	3-4	Social science	3.4.1 Business	1	(1)(e) ; (2)(c) ; (3)(a) ; (4)(c) ; (5)(e)	
436	3-4	Social science	3.4.1 Business	2	(1)(d) ; (2)(d) ; (3)(c) ; (4)(e) ; (5)(b)	
440	3-4	Social science	3.4.1 Business	3	(1.1)(a) ; (1.2)(e) ; (1.3)(a) ; (2.1)(d) ; (2.2)(e) (3.1)(a) ; (3.2)(c) ; (4.1)(c) ; (4.2)(a) ; (5)(d)	
444	3-4	Social science	3.4.2 Geography	1	(1.1)(d) ; (1.2)(b) ; (1.3)(d) ; (2.1)(e) ; (2.2)(e) (3.1)(a) ; (3.2)(c) ; (4)(d) ; (5)(d)	
448	3-4	Social science	3.4.2 Geography	2	(1)(e) ; (2)(b) ; (3)(a) ; (4)(e) ; (5)(e)	
450	3-4	Social science	3.4.2 Geography	3	(1)(e) ; (2.1)(a) ; (2.2)(d) ; (2.3)(a) ; (2.4)(b) (2.5)(b) ; (3)(c) ; (4)(b) ; (5)(d)	
452	3-4	Social science	3.4.3 Government	1	(1)(d);(2.1)(e);(2.2)(b);(3.1)(d);(3.2)(e);(4)(b);(5)(e)	
454	3-4	Social science	3.4.3 Government	2	(1)(b) ; (2)(a) ; (3)(b) ; (4)(d) ; (5)(b)	
456	3-4	Social science	3.4.3 Government	3	(1)(c) ; (2)(d) ; (3)(b) ; (4)(e) ; (5)(c)	
458	3-4	Social science	3.4.4 World history	1	(1)(b) ; (2.1)(c) ; (2.2)(b) ; (2.3)(a) ; (3)(e) ; (4)(b) (5)(d)	

(Chpt = Chapter ; Sect = Section ; S-sect = Sub-section ; Pasg = Passage ; Mod = Model ; tpc = topic ; Ans = Answer)

해답편 651

Page No.	Sect No.	Chpt, tpc	S-sect No.	Pasg No.	Mod Ans (모범 정답)	Reason(s) for the answer (비고)
462	3-4	Social science	3.4.4 World history	2	(1)(e) ; (2.1)(c) ; (2.2)(c) ; (2.3)(e) ; (3.1)(a) (3.2)(d) ; (4)(d) ; (5)(e)	
464	3-4	Social science	3.4.4 World history	3	(1)(a) ; (2.1)(c) ; (2.2)(d) ; (2.3)(c) ; (3.1)(a) ; (3.2)(d) (4.1)(c) ; (4.2)(b) ; (4.3)(e) ; (4.4)(c) ; (5.1)(b) ; (5.2)(e)	
474	4-1	Literature	4.1.1 Drama	1	(1)(b) ; (2)(d) ; (3)(a) ; (4.1)(a) ; (4.2)(c) ; (5)(b)	
478	4-1	Literature	4.1.1 Drama	2	(1)(c) ; (2.1)(c) ; (2.2)(c) ; (3.1)(c) ; (3.2)(b) ; (4)(c)	
482	4-1	Literature	4.1.1 Drama	3	(1)(d) ; (2.1)(b) ; (2.2)(c) ; (3)(d) ; (4)(a) ; (5)(c)	
484	4-1	Literature	4.1.2 Fiction	1	(1)(d) ; (2.1)(a) ; (2.2)(a) ; (3.1)(c) ; (3.2)(a) ; (4)(b)	
488	4-1	Literature	4.1.2 Fiction	2	(1)(a) ; (2)(c) ; (3.1)(b) ; (3.2)(b) ; (4.1)(a) ; (4.2)(b) ; (5)(c)	
492	4-1	Literature	4.1.2 Fiction	3	(1)(c) ; (2.1)(d) ; (2.2)(a) ; (3.1)(b) ; (3.2)(d) ; (4)(d)	
496	4-1	Literature	4.1.3 Poetry	1	(1)(c) ; (2.1)(b) ; (2.2)(c) ; (3.1)(b) ; (3.2)(a) (4.1)(a) ; (4.2)(d)	
500	4-1	Literature	4.1.3 Poetry	2	(1.1)(a) ; (1.2)(c) ; (2.1)(b) ; (2.2)(c) ; (2.3)(b) (2.4)(a) ; (3.1)(b) ; (3.2)(d)	
502	4-1	Literature	4.1.3 Poetry	3	(1)(b) ; (2.1)(b) ; (2.2)(d) ; (3.1)(a) ; (3.2.)(c) (3.3)(a) ; (3.4)(b) ; (4)(a)	
512	4-2	Discourse Analysis	4.2.1 Soc. Imp.	1	(1)(d) ; (2.1)(a) ; (2.2)(b) ; (2.3)(b) ; (2.4.)(a) (2.5)(b) ; (2.6)(b) ; (2.7)(a)	
514	4-2	Discourse Analysis	4.2.2 Negotiation	1	(1)(a) ; (2.1)(a) ; (2.2)(d) ; (2.3)(b) ; (2.4.)(a) (2.5)(c) ; (2.6)(d) ; (3)(a)	
518	4-2	Discourse Analysis	4.2.3 Int. R	1	(1)(a) ; (2.1)(a) ; (2.2)(c) ; (2.3)(c) ; (2.4)(d) (2.5)(b) ; (2.6)(b) ; (2.7)(b)	
526	4-3	Public speech	4.3.1 Inf. Sp	1	(1.1)(c) ; (1.2)(d) ; (1.3)(b) ; (1.4)(c) ; (1.5)(c) (2.1)(a) ; (2.2)(b) ; (2.3)(c) ; (2.4)(d) ; (2.5)(b)	
530	4-3	Public speech	4.3.2 Pus. Sp.	1	(1)(a) ; (2)(a) ; (3)(d) ; (4)(b) ; (5)(d) ; (6)(b) (7)(a) ; (8)(d) ; (9)(c) ; (10)(b)	
536	4-3	Public speech	4.3.3 Pus. Sp.	1	(1)(b) ; (2)(c) ; (3)(b) ; (4)(a) ; (5)(b) ; (6)(d) (7)(a) ; (8)(b) ; (9)(d) ; (10)(c)	
546	5		Passage	1	(1)(a) ; (2)(e) ; (3)(b) ; (4)(e) ; (5)(d)	
546	5		Passage	2	(1)(b) ; (2.1)(c) ; (2.2)(a) ; (3)(d) ; (4.1)(d) ; (4.2)(c) (4.3)(e) ; (4.4)(a) ; (5.1)(b) ; (5.2)(a)	
550	5		Passage	3	(1)(c) ; (2.1)(e) ; (2.2)(e) ; (3)(c) ; (4.1)(a) ; (4.2)(e) (4.3)(d) ; (5.1)(e) ; (5.2)(b)	
552	5		Passage	4	(1)(d) ; (2.1)(a) ; (2.2)(c) ; (3)(b) ; (4.1)(c) ; (4.2)(d) (5.1)(a) ; (5.2)(b) ; (5.3)(c)	
556	5		Passage	5	(1)(d) ; (2.1)(b) ; (2.2)(e) ; (3)(c) ; (4.1)(c) ; (4.2)(e) ; (5)(d)	

(Chpt = Chapter ; Sect = Section ; S-sect = Sub-section ; Pasg = Passage ; Mod = Model ; tpc = topic ; Ans = Answer)

Page No.	Sect No.	Chpt, tpc	S-sect No.	Pasg No.	Mod Ans (모범 정답)	Reason(s) for the answer (비고)
560	5		Passage	6	(1)(e) ; (2.1)(d) ; (2.2)(d) ; (3)(a) ; (4.1)(e) ; (4.2)(e) ; (5)(b)	
562	5		Passage	7	(1.1)(e) ; (1.2)(a) ; (2.1)(e) ; (2.2)(c) ; (3)(a) ; (4.1)(e) ; (4.2)(e) ; (5.1)(c) ; (5.2)(c) ; (5.3)(e)	
566	5		Passage	8	(1)(e) ; (2.1)(a) ; (2.2)(e) ; (3)(b) ; (4.1)(d) ; (4.2)(b) ; (4.3)(b) ; (4.4)(e) ; (4.5)(e) ; (5)(b)	
570	5		Passage	9	(1)(d) ;(2.1)(a) ;(2.2)(c) ;(2.3)(a) ;(3)(c) ;(4)(e) ;(5)(c)	
574	5		Passage	10	(1)(e) ; (2.1)(a) ; (2.2)(b) ; (2.3)(e) ; (2.4)(b) ; (3)(d) ; (4.1)(e) ; (4.2)(e) ; (5.1)(c) ; (5.2)(b)	
576	5		Passage	11	(1)(e) ; (2.1)(c) ; (2.2)(e) ; (2.3)(e) ; (3)(c) ; (4.1)(d) ; (4.2)(e) ; (5.1)(b) ; (5.2)(e)	
578	5		Passage	12	(1)(c) ; (2.1)(a) ; (2.2)(e) ; (2.3)(a) ; (3)(a) ; (4.1)(b) ; (4.2)(b) ; (4.3)(d) ; (4.4)(a) ; (4.5)(e) (5)(a)	
582	5		Passage	13	(1)(e) ; (2.1)(b) ; (2.2)(b) ; (2.3)(a) ; (3)(c) ; (4.1)(e) ; (4.2)(d) ; (4.3)(c) ; (5)(e)	
586	5		Passage	14	(1)(c) ; (2.1)(b) ; (2.2)(d) ; (2.3)(c) ; (2.4)(d) ; (2.5)(b) ; (3)(e) ; (4)(d) ; (5)(e)	
592	5		Passage	15	(1)(e) ; (2.1)(c) ; (2.2)(e) ; (2.3)(a) ; (3)(b) ; (4.1)(a) ; (4.2)(e) ; (4.3)(d) ; (4.4)(e) ; (4.5)(a) ; (5)(b)	
596	5		Passage	16	(1)(e) ; (2.1)(a) ; (2.2)(d) ; (2.3)(e) ; (2.4)(e) ; (3)(c) ; (4.1)(b) ; (4.2)(e) ; (4.3)(e) ; (4.4)(d) ; (5.1)(d) ; (5.2)(c)	
600	5		Passage	17	(1)(e) ; (2.1)(c) ; (2.2)(d) ; (3)(a) ; (4.1)(e) ; (4.2)(e) ; (4.3)(c) ; (4.4)(d) ; (4.5)(c) ; (4.6)(a) ; (5)(b)	
604	5		Passage	18	(1.1)(a) ; (1.2)(e) ; (2.1)(d) ; (2.2)(d) ; (3)(e) ; (4.1)(e) ; (4.2)(c) ; (4.3)(c) ; (4.4)(c) ; (4.5)(c) ; (5.1)(a) ; (5.2)(b)	
610	5		Passage	19	(1.1)(b) ; (1.2)(a) ; (2.1)(e) ; (2.2)(b) ; (3)(b) ; (4.1)(c) ; (4.2)(a) ; (5)(e)	
614	5		Passage	20	(1)(d) ;(2.1)(e) ;(2.2)(c) ;(3)(d) ;(4.1)(d) ;(4.2)(c) ;(5)(c)	
616	5		Passage	21	(1)(e) ; (2.1)(b) ; (2.2)(a) ; (2.3)(a) ; (3)(d) ; (4.1)(e) ; (4.2)(c) ; (4.3)(b) ; (5)(b)	
622	5		Passage	22	(1)(c) ;(2.1)(e) ;(2.2)(b) ;(2.3)(e) ;(2.4)(a) ;(2.5)(e) ;(3)(d) ; (4.1)(b) ;(4.2)(e) ;(4.3)(b) ;(4.4)(d) ;(4.5)(e) ;(5)(c)	
626	5		Passage	23	(1)(a) ; (2.1)(d) ; (2.2)(c) ; (2.3)(b) ; (3)(c) ; (4.1)(e) ; (4.2)(e) ; (4.3)(e) ; (5)(e)	
632	5		Passage	24	(1.1)(a) ;(1.2)(c) ;(2.1)(d) ;(2.2)(b) ;(2.3)(d) ;(2.4)(b) ;(3)(e) ; (4.1)(b) ;(4.2)(a) ;(4.3)(e) ;(4.4)(d) ;(4.5)(e) ;(5)(d)	
638	5		Passage	25	(1)(d) ;(2.1)(b) ;(2.2)(d) ;(2.3)(a) ;(2.4)(c) ;(3)(b) ;(4.1)(e) ; (4.2)(d) ;(4.3)(b) ;(4.4)(b) ;(5.1)(b) ;(5.2)(e)	

(Chpt = Chapter ; Sect = Section ; S-sect = Sub-section ; Pasg = Passage ; Mod = Model ; tpc = topic ; Ans = Answer)

English for Business communications

미국에서 가르치는 **Dr. Yang**

Business English
비즈니스 영어

for Executives & CEO
for Employment
for MBA

친절한 '의사소통'은 긍정적인 관계를,
불쾌한 '의사소통'은 부정적인 관계를,
진실한 '의사소통'은 진정한 관계를,
믿을 수 없는 '의사소통'은 불신의 대인관계를
갖게 되기 마련이다.

의사소통의 중요성은 부부, 가족, 친척, 친구, 동료, 직장, 사업, 공무, 넓게는 국제 사회 관계면에서 '성공과 실패'를 좌우하는 열쇠가 된다. 이러한 열쇠는 개인 뿐만 아니라 국내 및 국제 사회인을 대상으로 하는 기업이 운영에 있어서 더욱 중요하다. 그래서 이 책은 저자가 미국에서 오랫동안 강의한 과목 〈Business Communications〉을 골자로, 고국의 '광범위한 독자층'의 편의를 위해 내용을 집약하여 쉽고 재미있게 엮어 놓았다.

양규철 박사 지음 / 에디터 펴냄 / 값 20,000원